160201

Racism, Eh?

A Critical
Inter-Disciplinary
Anthology of Race
and Racism
in Canada

DATE DUE

Edited by
Camille A. Nelson
Charmaine A. Nelson

Captus Press

RACISM, EH?: A Critical Inter-Disciplinary Anthology of Race and Racism in Canada

© 2004 by Camille A. Nelson and Charmaine A. Nelson
and Captus Press Inc.

National Library of Canada Cataloguing in Publication

Racism, Eh? : a critical inter-disciplinary anthology of race and racism in Canada / Camille A. Nelson, Charmaine A. Nelson, editors.

Includes bibliographical references.
ISBN 1-55322-061-7

1. Racism — Canada.   2. Ethnology — Canada.   I. Nelson, Camille A. (Camille Antoinette), 1968-   II. Nelson, Charmaine

FC104.R358 2004   305.8'00971   C2004-901301-7

Cover painting by:
Tod, Joanne Canadian 1953
Research & Development 1986 (Detail)
Oil on canvas.
175.7 × 241.6 cm
ART GALLERY OF ONTARIO, TORONTO
Gift of Alison and Alan Schwartz, 1997
Photo Credit: Peter MacCallum

Captus Press Inc.
Mail: Units 14–15
          1600 Steeles Avenue West
          Concord, Ontario
          L4K 4M2
Telephone: (416) 736–5537
Fax: (416) 736–5793
Email: info@captus.com
Internet: www.captus.com

Canada ▪▪ We acknowledge the financial support of the Government of Canada through the Book Publishing Industry Development Program (BPIDP) for our publishing activities.

0 9 8 7 6 5 4 3 2 1
Printed in Canada

To Mom and Dad
Barbara E. Nelson and Maxwell B. Nelson

Contents

Contents

Contents

Contents

Foreword

Joan Acland
Art History Department
Concordia University
Montreal

Canada as a nation-state was largely defined within the idealism prevalent in a settler colony during the mid-nineteenth century. Initially understood as a geopolitical site wherein old-world dreams could be literally mapped onto the surface of the land and its body politic, Canadian national identity was forged through a profound belief in a better life devoid of racial, economic, and class restrictions — an expectation that is still prevalent today. Yet from the beginning, various categories of subcitizenry existed in the new Canada. Among these were Aboriginal people. Formerly partners in trade, warfare, and exploration, First Peoples were relegated to the periphery of the nation — a process fixed in a series of laws commonly known as the Indian Act. While absorbing minority immigrant and indigenous communities within the ideal of the "imaginary" national community, even acknowledging their integral and important contributions, the seamless construct of Canada denied many Canadians full participation and inclusion.

The essays in *Racism, Eh?* address the mismatch between the dream of Canada and the actual histories of various communities of people within Canada. In this compendium, emerging scholars, in typical Canadian fashion, and with great affection for their country, are dialoguing across these differences, difficulties, and discrepancies. Relinquishing the safety of a bystander position, these writers are addressing head-on the impediments to the ideal of a fully democratic nation-state that respects a diversity of people. These compelling essays are well grounded in facts of law, multicultural policy, social structures, economic realities, cultural production, and personal experience. As a body of ideas, the writings give evidence of a cleansing process. The authors avoid a blind patriotism in favour of rearticulating ways in which to think the nation and its state apparatus, bringing us closer to the ideal of a just society.

What is clearly evident here is that the process of rethinking Canada can be painful; it entails accepting responsibility for the history of the nation-state as well as active participation in reshaping the nation. This book marks a celebratory moment signalled by the integrity and commitment of these scholars, who have taken the steps necessary to "get us a little further on down the road" by "wrestling with the angels" [Stuart Hall]. It is with a sense of hope that I read these essays, knowing my beloved Canada is in good hands.

Acknowledgements

Acknowledgements

Although the idea for this anthology had been brewing within us for quite some time, it is interesting to note that it began in earnest in 1999 when we were both living outside Canada — one in the United States and the other in the United Kingdom. In retrospect, our absence from our national homeland likely provided much of the emotional and intellectual impetus to commence such a project. It is a cliché to note that absence makes the heart grow fonder but, perhaps more important for our purposes and concerns, absence provided the cultural and social distance from which to assess Canada, and our interim homes provided the foils against which significant and often dramatic comparisons were discussed.

Teaming up was a non-question. As sisters who are scholars, it seems that we can recall a lifetime of being each other's intellectual partner and touchstone. Our positions in differently situated fields, Law and Art History, simply made our proposed interdisciplinary project all the more natural. This anthology has absolutely been a team effort, and we have acted as true intellectual partners throughout, collaborating in every aspect of the decision-making process and the writing and editing of the text. It is a testament to the power of partnership and the dedication of sisters.

This project has been realized because of the hard work, dedication and generosity of many individuals and the support of two key universities. We would like to thank all of our contributors for their commitment to this project and their patience over the course of this publication process. Both of our home institutions, the University of Western Ontario and the School of Law at Saint Louis University, provided the stellar research assistants without whose essential research and editorial and administrative support this project would not have been possible. These hard-working, dedicated and exceptionally bright students included: Shannon Proudfoot and Leanne Carroll (University of Western Ontario, London, Canada) and Leslie Butler, Robin Hill and Michael Bernard (Saint Louis University, School of Law, St. Louis, Missouri, USA). Both Lori Owens and Vicki Boeckelmann, at Saint Louis University School of Law, provided invaluable administrative assistance, as the School of Law became the administrative hub. In this regard, we wish to thank Dean Jeffrey Lewis of the Saint Louis University School of Law for his unwavering support.

The striking and politically resonant painting that graces the cover of the anthology is the labour of a tremendous Canadian artist, Joanne Tod, who also happens to be a contributor to this collection. We thank Joanne for the use of this poignant and exemplary painting. Professor Joan Acland has contributed the foreword, which provides a considered social and historical context for our work. We greatly appreciate the endorsement of such a remarkable human being, professor and scholar. To the staff of Captus Press Inc., and especially to Ania Czyznielewski, who has been our constant contact, support and guide through the maze of scholarly publishing, we thank you for your unwavering commitment to us and to this project and for your stalwart support throughout this entire process. We have both learned so much from you.

Finally, as human beings, as women, and as scholars, we have been deeply influenced by our parents, Barbara E. Nelson and Maxwell B. Nelson, who provided a politically, culturally, and intellectually stimulating and supportive environment for our young minds and hearts to grow, who supported our every physical and intellectual endeavour and aspiration, and who loved us well and always. Thank you. This is for you both.

Introduction

Camille A. Nelson

Charmaine A. Nelson

1

A "mythology of racelessness" and "stupefying innocence" — these would appear to be the twin pillars of the Canadian history of race.

Constance Backhouse[1]

Sacrifice your freedom, / Sacrifice your prayer, / Take away your language, / Cut off all your hair. / Sacrifice the loved ones, / Who always Stood by me, / Stranded in the wasteland, / Set my spirit free.

Robbie Robertson, *Sacrifice*[2]

The words "silencing," "absence," "invisibility," "exclusion," and "non-representation" have come to be considered, in Canadian mainstream feminism, as clichés or the rhetoric of "women of colour" and black feminist politics. But their importance remains undiminished for anyone who has searched for a developed critical voice of non-white women in Canada, and/or tried to put together a course on gender, race and class with Canadian content.

Himani Bannerji[3]

Racism, Eh? addresses issues of race and racism in Canada, focussing fundamentally on two key aspects of identity or identification — race and nationality — and the complex ways in which they intersect. The urgency of this book emerged for us out of a growing concern that experiences of racism and issues of race were not being comprehensively addressed or documented within popular cultural discourse or academic practice in Canada in an inclusive interdisciplinary manner. The racism that many people of colour and First Nations often face, whether institutional or informal, is often met with the denial of white Canadians, who insist that these experiences are not representative of **their** Canada:

> 72% of Canadians believe that different ethnic and racial groups should try to adapt to Canadian society; the majority of Canadians believe there is less or "a lot less" racism in Canada than in the United States; 68% of Canadians agree or strongly agree that "one of the best things about Canada is our acceptance of people from all races and backgrounds."[4]

> Racism, among other things, is a contest over meanings. Canada's cherished image as a tolerant society leads even progressive Canadians to the view that racism means only *overt* acts by some nasty individuals against other individuals. I do not see it that way. **No** Aboriginal person in Canada sees it that way. What we see, experience, and understand on a daily basis, is racism interwoven in the very fabric of the social system in Canada.[5]

---

[1] Backhouse, 1999, p. 14.

[2] Robertson, 1998.

[3] Bannerji, 1993, p. x.

[4] 1993 CCCJ Survey Highlights Decima Research (1,200 Canadians, 18 years of age or older). Retrieved July 11, 2002, from http://www.interlog.com/~cccj/survey/1993/highlights.html

[5] Fontaine, 1998. *See also* Grayson, 1996.

This disavowal is often mediated through a dichotomization of Canada with the United States, which is made to bear the full burden of the collective racial sins of North America. Operating under a national myth of racial tolerance and inclusivity, Canada has been constructed as a victim of racism that originates elsewhere. As Eva Mackey has noted, this type of

> "...strategic essentialism" based upon particular images of Canada as victim also plays another ambiguous and problematic role. The construction of Canada as a genedered body, victimised by external and more powerful others, creates a fiction of a homogenous and unified body, an image that elides the way the Canadian nation can victimise internal "others" on the basis of race, culture, gender or class.[6]

To be fair, vilifying the United States as a place of extreme racial (dis)ease is all too easy with its histories of explicit racial violence, segregation, oppression and, significantly, American frankness and honesty about its racial past and contemporary racial issues. However, this characterization of the United States as "that country to our south with its awful racism" can only be achieved if Canada's colonial histories are ignored, minimized, or denied, and if contemporary issues of race and racism are ignored within its borders. Much Euro-Canadian complacency on issues of race is based on ignorance — a literal obliviousness to our complex colonial legacies; our diverse racial, ethnic, linguistic and religious populations; and how these factors have affected the regulation and meanings of racial identity in this country. But it is also grounded within the privilege of whiteness as the unquestioned normative Western and Canadian identity, which, until recently, has not been fully understood or scrutinized as a racialized position. In what has been called "Critical Whiteness Studies", Whiteness is addressed as a historically-specific construct. By locating bodies and cultures within a dominantly visual register, this construct affords cultural, social and political privilege largely through its normativity, which is only possible when compared with the "other" bodies/cultures of non-whites.[7] (As Mackey has argued, this normative racial identity is an "...unmarked, non-ethnic, and usually white, 'Canadian-Canadian' identity."[8] Through this colonial logic, while white people **are** just people, everybody else is raced. But when the historical interconnectedness of national identity and race is revealed (in this case, whiteness as the dominant sign of Canadianness), the selective acknowledgement of the racial positions and investments of white Canadians becomes increasingly problematic. The privilege of whiteness often allows Euro-Canadians to assume that their experience of race, or supposed racelessness, in Canada is everybody's experience — or at least that those victimized by racism are not sufficiently credible, reasonable, or dispassionate enough to interpret their experiences in an objective and disinterested manner.

Within Canadian Studies, it is unfortunate that Canada's colonial legacy has been either underexplored or disavowed. Like many of the different branches of studies that have emerged within academia over the past few decades (Women's Studies, Black Studies, etc.), Canadian Studies does not denote a

---

6 Mackey, 2002, p. 12.

7 *See* Fine, 1997; *See also* Frankenberg, 1993; Thompson, 1996; Delgado & Stefanic, 1997; Roediger, 2002; Alba, 1990.

8 MacKay, 2002, p. 20.

discipline-specific practice. Rather, its unifying element is a shared focus on Canada as a topic of scholarly inquiry. A fundamental part of the nation-building process in Canada was the management of racial populations by competing British and French colonial interests.[9] This management entailed the active "othering" of specific **undesirable** racial groups and the strict control of definitions of citizenship that produced immigration policies and assimilation strategies and affected the ability of different racial and ethnic groups to build communities and experience an unfettered sense of belonging. The practice of various disciplines that engage in the study of Canada has often commenced with Europeans' purported discovery of the New World, utterly dismissing pre-contact histories and the obvious colonial impact and burden of contact. Instead, scholars of Canadian Studies must contend with the specificity of Canada's history as a nation forged through the violence of European imperialism and the multiple and complex histories of various racial groups who lay claim to Canada as home, whether through pre- or post-contact heritage and voluntary or forced migrations.

Disputing the Canons

Although we are active in quite distinct fields, Law and Art History respectively, we have shared the perception that there is a need for greater dialogue and scholarship of a critical post-colonial nature on issues of race and racism in Canada. We have been challenged in our attempts to find acceptable collections of post-colonial scholarly writings on race in and from Canada that include the voices of traditionally marginalized groups. In particular, we are concerned about the lack of racial, ethnic, gender and sexual inclusivity among scholars, as well as the lack of recognition of the interconnectedness of systems of oppression. From the inception of the anthology, we have been particularly mindful of the desire to recruit a diverse group of scholars and to support a range of ideas. Our call for participation was extremely broad. It was sent to all faculties and departments at universities across Canada, as well as to Canadian Studies Departments in the United States and Britain. Interestingly, some institutions may not even have posted our call, as affirmed by one school of pharmacy in western Canada that returned our call for papers and letter of invitation with the following notation on a Post-it-Note: "What makes you think this would be relevant here?" It is noteworthy that the administrator in the pharmacy department to which this package was sent went beyond what might have been expected of one disinterested in this project — namely, throwing the entire package into the garbage — and actually took it upon herself to attach the above notation and return the package, in its entirety, to the editors. Of course, when we brought this matter to the attention of the deans of this department, they were most embarrassed and concerned that someone in their department had behaved in this way, and acknowledged the obvious utility of our endeavour in light of this incident.

---

[9] Ibid., p. 23.

Additionally, we invited the participation of academics who have made recognized contributions to scholarship on race and racism in Canada. While some of these scholars could not participate due to prior commitments, the final selection of essays for the anthology is informed by our commitment to showcase a range of disciplines, approaches, and theoretical concerns across issues of historical and contemporary relevance and to remove the hierarchical disciplinary limitations of tenure and the idea that one voice should be heard above another's. In this way, we have sought out people from diverse walks of life: male and female, junior and senior, within the academy and without.

As academicians, we acknowledge that we are only one part of the discursive equation that has perpetuated this void. Other key elements in this equation include our places of employment (the universities and their various faculty, the departmental, disciplinary and curricular politics and policies they wield) and our resources (the books, articles, journals, and videos at our disposal; the libraries and archives we use; and, ultimately, the publishers who decide what is publication worthy). Discursive structures vary from discipline to discipline but ultimately achieves the same effect. As Michel Foucault has demonstrated, the power of discourse is not only its ability to reproduce itself and to disguise itself, but also its ability to produce **effects of truth**, which are neither true nor false.[10]

To question academic discursiveness is to question the structure, boundaries and function of a discipline and what it deems acceptable objects of inquiry and valid issues of intellectual contemplation. In significant ways, this questioning directs us to the issue of the identity and location of the scholar-academic as well as the specific discursive structures within which the scholar operates. With the advent of critical theories and the questioning of disciplinarity, the ideal of the "objective" and disinterested scholar is increasingly the domain of the exclusive structure of traditional patriarchal academic practice. For many academics, our disciplines rely, to differing extents, upon a canon of accepted texts or objects of inquiry that also imply predetermined methodological positions. Much of the humanities are so inclined, and Art History, with its canons of "master" works and "master" artists, is a case in point. As the art historian Griselda Pollock has argued, "[t]he canon is fundamentally a mode for the worship of the artist, which is in turn a form of masculine narcissism."[11] Pollock continues, "[t]here are, however, productive and transgressive ways to re-read the canon ... ways to question our own texts for the desires they inscribe, for the investments which feign through telling the stories of our ideal egos."[12]

The canonical texts of legal practice are not master works; rather, they are jurisprudence — cases, statutes, regulations and constitutions that are the foundation of the legal system and subject to the partial interpretation of lawyers and judges alike.

> Theoretical "legal understanding" is characterized, in Anglo-American jurisprudence, by at least three features of thought and rhetoric:

---

[10] Foucault, 1980, p. 118.

[11] Pollock, 1999, p. 13.

[12] Ibid., p. x.

1. The hypostatization of exclusive categories and definitional polarities, the drawing of bright lines and clear taxonomies that purport to make life simpler in the face of life's complication: rights/needs, moral/immoral, public/private, white/black.
2. The existence of transcendent, a contextual, universal legal truths or pure procedures....
3. The existence of objective, "unmediated" voices by which those transcendent, universal truths find their expression.[13]

Inherent in Western "intellectual" tradition is the disavowal of subjective concerns, investments and desires within scholarly practice — the consistent historical deployment of white, male, heterosexual values, interests, and ideas as universal and objective.[14] The exclusive canons of the West have functioned through the abjection of the female, the non-white and the homosexual body. This scholarly purging of self-identification and subjectivity is part of academic regulation, which refuses inclusivity and plurality. That being the case, we have consciously included contributions that unmask the political and social investments of scholarship on race. Our attempt at a canonical (de)regulation also includes a focus on diversity of region, discipline, methodology, and identity and an attempt to subvert hierarchy.

The epithet "revisionist" is frequently hurled at any critical approach that challenges traditional patriarchal and colonial disciplinarity. This is a ploy that functions to re-entrench traditions of white male heterosexual-dominated scholarship as objective and universal sites of Knowledge and Truth. Historically, these traditions have constituted sex/gender and race/colour "others" as objects of knowledge and rarely as producers or practitioners. Michel Foucault and, years before him, Aimé Césaire drew similar conclusions about knowledge systems and their function and result. For Foucault, power not only implies knowledge (and vice vera) but is also activated by the ability to turn bodies into **objects of knowledge**.[15] For Aimé Césaire, "...colonization = 'thing-ification'."[16] The violent transformation of bodies into objects for Césaire was a concern not only for the colonized subject but also for the dehumanizing colonizer. In terms of race in the West — and Canada is no exception — we must address not only the state of racial politics past and present, but also the processes and implied power dynamics through which race has been, and is continuously being, produced.

Race and nationality are equally complex markers of identity that have come under intense critical scrutiny. Recent scholarship has problematized the notion of identity as fixed and stable, and rather conceives of identity as fluid, shifting and constantly under negotiation.[17] As Stuart Hall has noted:

Identification is, then, a process of articulation, a suturing, an over-determination not a subsumption. There is always "too much" or "too little" — an over-determination or

---

[13] Williams, 1991, pp. 8–9.

[14] "Desire" is being used in the psychoanalytical sense of unconscious or conscious motivating forces or drives that propel a subject towards choices and actions that provide an often narcissistic pleasure that is connected to the subject's idea and experience of self and "other".

[15] Foucault, 1977, pp. 27–28.

[16] Césaire, 1972, p. 21.

[17] Jackson, Peter & Penrose, 1993; Gerstle, 2002; Backhouse, 2001; Marx, 1996.

a lack, but never a proper fit, a totality.... It requires what is left outside, its constitutive outside, to consolidate the process.[18]

Identity, its organization, logic and function have been at the forefront of critical theory for decades. Most notably, feminist scholarship has intervened powerfully within the traditionally patriarchal exclusivity of Western thought to excavate histories of women and to introduce questions of gender and sex into all realms of academic inquiry. However, white feminists have come under increasing criticism for their deployment of the essentializing category of Woman that replicates Western patriarchy by disavowing issues of race, colour and colonialism, which effectively privileges the experiences, thoughts, issues and investments of white women over those of women of colour.[19]

Recent post-colonial and post-colonial feminist scholarship have addressed this absence of voice through strategic critical practices that have often focussed upon race and racial identity as products of colonial discourse. It is not surprising that the force of this practice is driven predominantly by aboriginal, indigenous and people of colour scholars with intimate connections to colonial or post-colonial histories and those sharing experiences of racial marginalization.[20] Like feminists, post-colonial practitioners are often scholars and/or activists who are invested in the problematization of race and other aspects of colonial identity, location and organization that were effects of European imperial agendas. Although "post-colonialism" is a much contested term that is the subject of ongoing debate, it is, to date, the most useful label to indicate an investment in a critical consideration of colonialism and its disparate effects.[21] As Ania Loomba has argued:

> It has been suggested that it is more helpful to think of post-colonialism not just as coming literally after colonialism and signifying its demise, but more flexibly as the contestation of colonial domination and the legacies of colonialism.[22]

As such, post-colonialism does not indicate an actual state of being **after** or **beyond** the colonial in the sense of a political or social reality; instead, it functions dominantly as a theoretical and conceptual description of a set of practices or means of engagement that are consciously politicized and antagonistic to the colonial. The impact of post-colonialism has, perhaps, been most widely felt within the humanities, where the relatively new discipline of Cultural Studies has fundamentally challenged the exclusive and, often, territorial structures of traditional Western disciplinarity.[23] To be a feminist in the scholarly sense is not merely to do one's research "on women." Similarly, a post-colonial perspective or methodology does not merely indicate one's desire to speak or write

---

[18] Hall, 1996, p. 3.

[19] Mohanty, 1991; hooks, 1997; Day, 2000; Williams Crenshaw, 1995; Truth, 1851.

[20] The terms "aboriginal" and "indigenous" are more suitable here than "First Nations" or "Native" since within the context of Western global colonization, many diverse populations with the experience of colonization (i.e., Africans) cannot be encompassed by the latter terms.
[21] Loomba, 1998, p. 7.

[22] Ibid., p. 12.

[23] Bhabha, 1994; Goldberg & Solomos, 2002; Warren & Vavrus, 2002; Lewis, 2002; Hall, 1996; Hall & Gieben, 1992; Hall & du Gay, 1996.

about racial "others." Rather, post-colonialism describes a type of critical intervention and location that focuses on issues of racial identity and is engaged in the scrutiny and understanding of colonialism as the governing structure of racial marginalization and oppression.

This anthology is a post-colonial intervention because we have set and upheld a standard that examines race and racism within a critical academic and social framework seeking to address the Western histories of colonialism and to create a space for discussion of, and by, traditionally marginalized racial subjects. That is not to say that whiteness and Europeanness are not a part of this discussion.[24] To leave whites and whiteness out of the equation would be to cancel one of the crucial axes around which the colonial dichotomy has revolved and operated for centuries and to ignore the social construction of whiteness. A post-colonial methodology discusses whiteness not as an unquestioned paradigm of racial superiority but as one of many possible racialized positions that has historically been a site of great cultural, social and political privilege.

It is important for us that these post-colonial discussions not be externalized or segregated from the dominant disciplinary structures of academic practice. We are conscious and aware of the danger posed by an academic marginalization of post-colonial scholarship into programs and departments that deal exclusively with race issues, leaving the dominant university structure and its white majorities free to deal with the supposed "real research".[25] We are concerned for what Pollock has named the potential ghettoization of the scholars whose focus on race does not declare their allegiance to the traditional status quo of their fields.[26] Although we are not antagonistic to the possibilities and strengths of such new academic configurations (i.e., Women's Studies, African-American Studies, African-Canadian Studies, Natives Studies, Cultural Studies, etc.), we are conscious of a need to integrate post-colonial concerns into the current departmental structures of academic practice.[27] Such an acceptance will necessarily provoke the (re)examination of many disciplines whose foundational structures presupposed the exclusion of race.

Signifiers of Identity

Race and nationality have been deemed problematic markers of identity in part because they have historically been based upon exclusive criteria that separated, segregated and valued bodies through systems of supposed scientific classification. They are also problematic because although the classification of bodies by race or nationality is often supposedly based upon material data and physical

---

[24] A more recent development in post-colonial studies is Critical Whiteness Studies, wherein whiteness is situated as a racialized identity that has historically been a site of great social, economic and cultural privilege and possibility (Frankenberg, 1993. *See also* Bell, 1995; Hill, 1997; Nakayama & Martin, 1999; Foster, 1999).

[25] Boynton, 2002.

[26] Pollock, 1999, pp. xiv, 12.

[27] Du Bois, 1994, p. 90; Seltzer et al., 1995; Hillis, 1995.

knowledge, both categories have increasingly been exposed as equally psychic or imaginary constructs.[28] Another similarity between these two forms of identification is their historical organization through hierarchy and binaries within Western thought. Race and nationality also intersect powerfully since colonialism constituted national belonging as embodied in the ideal citizen — a product of racial identity. In the New Worlds, as in the European seats of empire, citizenship was largely a matter of preferable racial types, or standards of whiteness, and a subject's proximity to such standards. Such distinctions were obviously deeply invested in ethnocentric and racist ideals of difference. In Canada, Europeans, especially those of British and French origin, have been constituted as the normative national population. This designation is a grave irony given that contemporary white Canadians are largely the descendants of European colonialists whose establishment of settler colonies was significantly based upon the ideology of *terra nullius,* which defined new territories as "empty land," effectively erasing Native presence in order to facilitate resource extraction and, eventually, settlement.[29] For many of these early settlers, the process of becoming Canadian involved centuries of struggle over the contested definition of whiteness and the limits of its ethnic inclusivity. As Mackey has argued, "[w]hiteness sustains its dominance by refusing categorisation as other than just 'normal' and 'human'."[30]

The visibility of corporeal signs is a crucial aspect of identity and identification. Our contemporary idea of race is an inheritance of eighteenth- and nineteenth-century Western human sciences[31] and, as such, was largely concerned with vision and visual signs, which were used to differentiate bodies.

This is not to dismiss the importance of the other ways and senses through which we process and assign race. For instance, race is often determined, and racial ideals applied, by the simple sound of someone's voice. It is not uncommon for people of colour to experience racist discrimination enacted by an invisible party on the other end of a telephone who decides whether or not a job interview or housing appointment will be granted on the basis of an accent or vocal quality that is perceived as non-white and, therefore, threatening or inferior.[32] However, the importance of vision and visual determinations of race is paramount since racism is often inflicted, and prejudicial determinations and decisions are made, solely on the basis of what somebody looks like, long before any real contact is ever established.

The issue of vision is also crucial in a world of increasingly aggressive visual stimuli. Popular culture is often dependent upon visual representations of bodies, whether in fine art, television, film, advertising, music videos, or on the World Wide Web. When considering the power of representation as an active generative force of racial identity and an historically colonial cultural activity in

---

[28] Anderson, 1991; Bhabha, 1990a; Ore, 2001; Freeman, 2002; Holt, 1995; Harrison, 1995; Malik, 1996.

[29] Mackey, 2002, pp. 14, 25, 26.

[30] Ibid., p. 22.

[31] The following works offer summaries of the human science's colonial investment in racial differentiation: Gould, 1996; Gilman, 1985b. For unabridged discussion of the human science's colonial investment in racial differentiation: Knox, 1862; Blyth, 1840; Prichard, 1851.

[32] Matsuda, 1991.

the West, we must consider not only the image itself, but also the active engagement of the image by a viewing audience whose ability to read and interpret an image is informed by their own identity, racial and otherwise.

A recent study of two groups of basketball-loving Canadian male teenagers proved the importance of the viewer's race in the interpretation of representations. Asked to examine various athletic apparel commercials from 1994 featuring black athletes, responses emerged from the all-black group decidedly different than from the mixed-race group, which did not include black youth. While the black youth sometimes identified with the ads, they were also much more likely to be critical of the ads' deployment of stereotypes of black community and black masculinity and far more aware of the intersection between media representations of black men and the racism they experienced in their own lives. In contrast, the mixed-race, non-black group was far more willing to accept the commercials as authentic representations of black males, although they admitted to having little or no personal experience or contact with blacks. This second group was also less mindful of how blacks were portrayed in the media overall, and their ideas about race were less comprehensive and developed than the black group's. (Wilson & Sparks, 1999)

The history of race in the West is indeed the history of a normative white male body and a systematic, multidisciplinary process of "othering" the bodies brought into violent contact with Europe through the processes of global colonization. When we speak of race in the West, should not simply discuss an *a priori* body that is objectively analyzed and read by non-biased parties; instead, we must address the very processes and practices through which race was produced and deployed — the institutions, disciplines and parties which racialize bodies and their function, effect and investments as a part of colonial discourse. As Cameron McCarthy and Warren Crichlow have argued:

> What we are saying is that racial difference is the product of human interests, needs, desires, strategies, capacities, forms of organization, and forms of mobilization. And that these dynamic variables which articulate themselves in the form of grounded social constructs such as identity, inequality, and so forth, are subject to change, contradiction, variability, and revision within historically specific and determinate contexts. We maintain that "race" is a social, historical, and variable category.[33]

However, to expose the social and constructed nature of race is not in any way to diminish its historical and contemporary relevance and potency as a dominant mode of identification that has had. and continues to produce, very real material, social and psychic effects. In other words, race is as real as our collective belief in its existence and "truth".

Colonial discourse produced race by hierarchizing anatomical and physiognomical traits as signs of fixed racial positions. Since the unquestioned moral, intellectual, and physical Western ideal was the white male body, all other bodies were identified according to their difference and their implied inferiority to this ideal. The corporeal signs of race that inhabit our contemporary visual archives are an inheritance of this colonial discourse of the body. Kobena Mercer has argued that second only to skin colour, hair texture is the primary site

---

[33] McCarthy & Crichlow, 1993, p. xv.

of racial difference and identification.[34] Countless eighteenth- and nineteenth-century human science studies, largely targeting the bodies of white female prostitutes and black women, confirm a parallel obsession with other anatomical and physiognomical traits such as nose width, lip shape and thickness, skull shape and size, etc.[35] These questionable "scientific" inquiries reveal a prolific and invasive social obsession with the regulation of "other" bodies, a regulation that was itself a part of the very process through which racial difference was constituted and deployed.

Western academic practice has a deep and largely unchallenged colonial legacy. Disciplines such as medicine, law, anthropology, ethnography, archaeology, geography, museology, and history and their institutional organizations (hospitals, court houses, museums, universities, etc.) were constituted in and through colonial discourse and the need for new ways of organizing physical and material knowledge **produced** by Europeans through colonization. The very types of inquiry; the structures within which they were organized and performed; their agents, investments and motivations; and the effects of the individual discourses are products of a Eurocentric bias that must be addressed at the most basic structural level of the conception, function and purpose of each discipline.

National identity is equally slippery. In his influential anthology *Nation and Narration,* Homi K. Bhabha has written of nations as "...a powerful historical idea in the west. An idea whose cultural compulsion lies in the impossible unity of the nation as a symbolic force."[36] In Canada, when we commonly speak of the 49th parallel, the boundary between us (Canada) and them (the United States of America), we are, indeed, referring to an imaginary marker and not a precise geographical or natural dividing line. As many of us who have taken a road trip to the States can attest, the two sets of Customs and Immigration Officials who police the border between Canada and America are a political effect of national organizations that have nothing to do with the natural or geographical specificity of a particular site. Rather, they are political products of a **man**-made boundary and, very recently, products of a spectacular and complex network of legal obstacles.

In the wake of the tragedy of September 11, 2001, the issue of national security has been paramount and complex, complicated by discussions of anti-terrorism strategies that have increasingly defined potential threats along racial, ethnic and religious lines. The popular cultural and academic debates have increasingly focussed upon the effectiveness and ethics of racial profiling, which has predominantly targeted Arab and Muslim males as potential terrorist threats. Although the Oklahoma City bombing demonstrated the extent of domestic terrorism in the form of white Christian males, and while the best evidence indicates that those behind the anthrax assaults were equally homegrown, it still appears that racial profiling in the West is reserved only for the scrutiny and surveillance of non-white populations. The Anti-Terrorism Act: Bill C-36 is the means by which the Government of Canada has taken steps to combat ter-

---

[34] Mercer, 1990; De Cille, 1996, p. 8; Caldwell, 1997; Jones, 1994; Lee & Jones, 1988.

[35] Gilman, 1985a; Levy, 1991.

[36] Bhabha, 1990a, p. 1.

rorism and terrorist activities at home and abroad through tough new anti-terrorism measures.[37]

Among others, the Canadian Association of University Teachers (CAUT) has expressed concern for this bill in an official statement from the president of the CAUT as follows:

> Sadly, this legislation is fundamentally misguided. The hope it provides is not to Canadians, but rather to the perpetrators of the attacks on the Pentagon and the World Trade Center. Bill C-36, like the events of Sept. 11, represents an assault on security and freedom. One goal of those who planned and executed the violence of Sept. 11 is certainly to cause panic. In this regard they are succeeding. Bill C-36 is a hastily written and ill-conceived response arising not from wise council, but rather from the fear sown by the Sept. 11 perpetrators and, potentially, from those eager to advance their own political agendas on the events of that day.[38]

Consequences of Racial/National Demarcation

The purpose of these obstacles and checks and balances is to determine belonging. Who is Canadian, who has a right to enter Canada, and who is a threat to Canada? The expulsion of alien bodies from within our national borders or the refusal of admittance is a process of mapping self/other, citizen/alien. But if the constitution of the self is always also the active constitution and deployment of an "other," then national identity and nationhood have as large a stake in creating the legitimate citizen as they do in creating the abject body of the alien "other." Most Canadians who have struggled to define who we are without recourse to defining who we are not (mainly American) will know the reality of this part of national identification. To what extent is a nation defined not only by who **is** a citizen and who **does** belong, but by who is **not** and who **does not**? And what is the significance of race within this discussion of national identity and belonging?

With each boundary constituting national identity, certain bodies are included and accorded the status of citizen, while others are excluded, marginalized and expelled. To complicate matters, what of the persons granted citizenship or residency yet not fully accepted, protected or empowered as Canadians? This anthology's stated parameters of race and racism within the Canadian context create a post-colonial intervention capable of examining the specificity of a discreet national location. As Loomba has argued, although

> ...the word "postcolonial" is useful in indicating a general process with some shared features across the globe ... if it is uprooted from specific locations, "postcoloniality" cannot be meaningfully investigated, and instead, the term begins to obscure the very relations of domination that it seeks to uncover.[39]

---

[37] *See* http://canada.justice.gc.ca/en/news/nr/2001/doc_28217.html

[38] *See* http://www.caut.ca/english/bulletin/2001_nov/president.asp

[39] Loomba, 1998, p. 19.

Canada's record of exclusions and inclusions, like many nations constructed through European imperial expansionism and colonialism, reveals histories of explicitly racist immigration policy and the racial limits of citizenship and nationality. The reservation system and treaty exploitation of First Nations lands and culture, the Indian Act, the Chinese Immigration Act, the Canada First Movement, the selective ethnic and racial internment of Canadians in World Wars I and II, the selective racial enlistment and assignment of Canadian men in World Wars I and II, the legacy of transatlantic slavery, the underground railroad, abolitionism and the Separate School Act of 1850 are all significant aspects of our racial histories that demonstrate the inextricability of national and racial identities within the social construction of Canadianness.[40]

Although it should go without saying that the geographical space of Canada was first occupied by First Nations peoples, Western and, indeed, Canadian histories and academic practices have functioned to erase/(e)race and suppress that very legacy. Indigenous claims must be distinguished from other claims of colonized populations because of their geographical primacy, which is often challenged by both colonizers and other racially marginalized groups. Furthermore, indigeneity calls forth questions of competing definitions of nationhood. Audra Simpson has argued that "[t]he very notion of an **indigenous** nationhood, which demarcates identity and seizes tradition in ways that may be antagonistic to the encompassing frame of the state, may be simply unintelligible to the [We]stern and/or imperial ear."[41] We must view the historical, philosophical and scholarly exclusion and erasure of Native presence and sovereignty within the colonial boundaries of Canada as connected with the physical and material practices of colonization and Western systems of knowledge and research. Writing from an indigenous perspective, Linda Tuhiwai Smith has argued that Western research

> ...brings to bear, on any study of indigenous peoples, a cultural orientation, a set of values, a different conceptualization of such things as time, space and subjectivity, different and competing theories of knowledge, highly specialized forms of language, and structures of power.[42]

Indigenous populations were positioned as objects of knowledge within various Western disciplines — bodies to be represented, documented, measured, poked, prodded, tested, exploited, experimented upon and regulated. The systematic objectification of Native populations was a deliberate means of social, material and psychic domination and control that facilitated the simultaneous European encroachment upon Native land. To speak of Canada as a nation with specific geographical limits and governance requires an understanding of how those boundaries usurped the original First Nations organization of the continent and superimposed a colonial structure, utterly ignorant of and aggressively defiant towards those original societies. The effect of this colonial strategy upon the First Peoples cannot be underestimated, for the colonial logic that

---

[40] Morrison & Wilson, 1995; Harring, 1998; Milloy, 1999; Ciaccia, 2000; Sansgster, 2001; Smith, 1999; Yee, 1996; Li, 1998; Jakubowski, 1997; Beckow, Stephen 1974; Koenig, 1991; Mackey, 2002; Nakano, 1980; Iacovetta et al., 2002; Boswell, 2001; Ruck, 1987; Winks, 1997; Backhouse, 1999.

[41] Simpson, 2000, p. 114.

[42] Smith, 1999, p. 42.

allowed European nations to lay claim to the land of the Natives was the same logic that allowed them to lay claim to their bodies based upon a fundamental belief in their racial inferiority.[43]

Western notions of identity have long been and are now, still, a matter of the body.[44] By "matter" we do not simply indicate a consequence of, but "matter" as the very materiality of a subject's presence. Although this matter of bodies or its corporeality has many markers or categories that divide and prioritize its being, in the West, the dominant mode of processing or reading these markers has been vision. The overwhelming patriarchal and colonial logic of the West has made gender/sex and race/colour two of the most historically dominant and significant categories of physical identification. The academically diverse group of scholars who have contributed to a consideration of racial and national identity have, through their contributions to our anthology, demonstrated the complexity and scope of intersectionality by also addressing issues like sexuality, language, ethnicity and class. Increasingly, these various aspects of identity have been explored not in isolation, but as complex intersecting, inextricable, and simultaneous attributes that together constitute a subject's identity and inform their experience of the world. To understand racial identity, one must come to grips with not only the visible signs of a body but also what those signs have historically signified and the actual process of interpretation through which such signs are read. To what extent does the process of reading race on a body have more to do with the subjective lens of the viewer, their identity and location, than with the subject they are seeing? To what extent are ideals of race, especially colonial stereotypes, products of the fear/desire of the viewing subject, projections onto bodies that are a fundamental part of the "othering" process?

In the frank essay "Confessions of a Nice Negro, Or Why I Shaved My Head", Robin Kelley reminisces about running into a movie theatre to escape a blustery winter evening.[45] Rushing to buy a ticket in order to meet his wife and daughter, the verbal and physical response from the young white woman behind the counter was one of obvious fear. To her, Kelley was a criminal there to rob the cinema, not a devoted husband, father and professional about to meet his family. The pressing question raised by this tale is, what were the corporeal or material signs of criminality this black male professor exuded that allowed this white woman to judge him a threat? At what point and through which

---

[43] The specificity of Native issues has given rise to Native Studies departments and programs that focus, in part, on an critical examination of Native experiences of colonization and colonialism and the recuperation of Native language, culture, social structures and spirituality. Native Studies can be seen as having strong scholarly, social and political affiliations to post-colonial agendas. Due to the specificity of Native experiences of colonization, issues of sovereignty, self-determination and land claims often take precedence in contemporary political discourse. That other racially marginalized populations locate other issues as urgent for their own communities is understandable given their specific experiences of colonialism. For example, black Canadians, especially African-Canadians and Caribbean-Canadians, who share an experience of diaspora, have been divested of their sense of an "original" or "authentic" homeland due to the fragmentation and dispersal of African populations through slavery. Colonization has, therefore, impacted various communities' and peoples' prioritization and articulation of issues for redress differently.

[44] Butler, 1993.

[45] Kelley, 1998.

signs did Kelley cease to be a respectable member of society, a university professor, and morph into a black thug? What allowed the white clerk to see him as a stereotype? Although Kelley's clothing was casual and his manner was brusque, clearly the deciding factor in the clerk's mischaracterization of the academic was his brown skin. Though some would suggest that this was an isolated and rare incident, similar tales have been memorialized.[46]

Raising Race in Canada

For many First Nations and people of colour, to speak of race is to speak of racism and the frequency of their experiences as someone else's stereotype. Race issues have been constant throughout Canadian history, and the following list indicates that there is no shortage of incidents of explicit racism within contemporary Canadian society. For instance:

* The increasing electronic dissemination of hate mail:
  * A Toronto-based white supremacist website posted information designed to incite physical violence against Muslims. Members of the Sikh, Muslim and Jewish communities responded by filing a complaint with police.[47]
  * A series of anti-Semitic fax transmissions espousing Jewish conspiracy propaganda was sent to various Toronto recipients. One transmission was received by a Holocaust survivor who compared the message to the assaults experienced in World War II Poland.[48]

* Labatt's stereotypical ad campaign for the 2001 Montreal Jazz Festival. The Black Coalition of Québec (ABCQ) accused Labatt Brewery of racism when they ran an advertisement created by BBDO Montreal featuring a caricature of a black man with arguably stereotypical physiognomical features for the Montreal Jazz Festival. While Dan Philip, the president of the ABCQ, characterized the promotion as irresponsible and degrading, Paul Wilson, the vice-president of public affairs for Labatt, refused to apologize, describing the ad as a work of good taste that was compatible with the spirit of the festival. After meeting with Labatt, Philip eventually concluded that Labatt's (mis)representation of blackness was more a product of ignorance than malice.[49]

* The deadly abuse of Native men by Saskatoon police. Charges surfaced in February 2000 that two Native men, Lawrence Wegner and Rodney Naistus, had been deliberately endangered by police in a penal tactic in which they were driven to remote areas and stranded in sub-zero temperatures. Wegner's and Naistus's frozen corpses (Wegner's only partially clothed) were recovered from a field near a power plant. The allegations surfaced after a third man, Darrell Night of the Saulteaux Reserve, experienced a similar assault at the

---

[46] Armour, 1997.
[47] Moller, 2002.
[48] Lungen, 2001.
[49] Kucharsky, 2001.

hands of two uniformed officers in early February. The public allegations sparked an outpouring of concern, many from civilians who made similar claims of racially motivated mistreatment and abuse at the hands of the police department. In the wake of calls for an independent review, Saskatoon Police Chief Dave Scott ceded control of the investigation to a RCMP task force, which determined there was no basis for criminal charges in either death. However, in the case of Darrell Night, officers Dan Hatchen and Ken Munson were convicted of unlawful confinement and sentenced to eight months in jail.[50]

- Racial profiling. The head of Canada's biggest municipal police service ordered an independent inquiry into the way the police force deals with the black community after the *Toronto Star* published a series of stories in October 2002, concluding that the city's police force treats white people better than blacks. The reports were based partly on the police department's own data, including statistics about arrests and charges. Toronto Police Chief Julian Fantino has asked retired Ontario Chief Justice Charles Dubbin to conduct a review of race relations on the police force.[51]

- Over-policing and racist brutalization of black populations. Although racist policing in Canada is more closely associated with cities with large black populations such as Toronto and Montreal, a number of incidents focussed attention on the Ottawa-Carelton Regional Police Services in the mid-1990s. Three cases, close in proximity, ignited concern in the area's black populations: (1) the 1991 police shooting of Vincent Gardner, (2) the aggressive arrest and detention of Ralph Kirkland, the president of the National Council of Jamaicans and Supportive Organizations, for failing to provide identification and, (3) Wayne Johnson's drowning death in the Rideau River, the result of police response to a domestic dispute. In Johnson's, case further questions were raised when the police failed to recover his corpse, a task instead performed by his family and friends.[52]

- Toronto Mayor Mel Lastman's Olympic racial blunderings. During the 2008 Olympic bid process, Toronto Mayor Mel Lastman jeopardized the city's chances to host the Olympics when he disparaged Mombasa, Kenya,[53] as a place of snakes and cannibals. "What the hell do I want to go to a place like Mombasa? Snakes just scare the hell out of me. I'm sort of scared about going there, but the wife is really nervous." "I just see myself in a pot of boiling water with all these natives dancing around me."

    In a written apology, Lastman described his comments as jocular. However, they prompted great international outrage and local calls for his resignation. Lastman's comments raised questions about his sensitivity to other

---

[50] *See* Tebbutt & Coolican, 2001; "No Charges", 2001; "Native Leaders", 2001; Zakreski, 2000; McNairn, 2000; Herald News Services, 2000.

[51] "Toronto police", 2002. *See also* "Allegations of profiling", 2002.

[52] "Black and Blue", 1995.

[53] Mombasa was the scheduled location for a meeting of the Association of National Olympic Committees of Africa, and a place where Lastman was meant to lobby for votes.

cultures and races, and Canada's and Toronto's ability to host the world during the Olympics.[54]

- The Head Tax class-action lawsuit of Chinese Canadians. In 1988, under then Prime Minister Brian Mulroney, Japanese Canadians negotiated an approximately $300 million compensation package for internments suffered during World War II. The successful result galvanized seven other racial or ethnic groups who had suffered discrimination at the hands of the Canadian government into action. The Chinese-Canadian National Council has similarly petitioned the Canadian government since 1984 for compensation for the $23 million collected through the racialized imposition of a Head Tax on approximately 81,000 Chinese immigrants between 1885 and 1923. In 1904, the $500 tax was an exorbitant debt, equivalent to the price of two new houses that would have taken most people years to pay off. The geographical unification of Canada, conceived by Prime Minister John A. Macdonald in 1871, was made possible through the building of the Canadian Pacific Railway, an engineering feat that was primarily realized because of the imported foreign labour of Chinese immigrants. A class-action lawsuit was filed at the Ontario Superior Court of Justice in December 2000. In November 2001, Justice Peter Cumming threw out what had become a $1.2 billion class-action suit, holding that Canada's federal government cannot be compelled to compensate victims of past discrimination. The ruling appeared to absolve the federal government from the consequences of past discriminatory practices or policies enacted prior to the Charter of Rights and Freedoms, despite the obvious and painful moral and ethical debts.[55]

- The residential school class-action lawsuits of Native Canadians. Thousands of aboriginal children, taken from their families and forced to attend religious residential schools from the mid-nineteenth century into the 1970s, suffered horrific physical and sexual abuses through this government-sponsored kidnapping. Compulsory by 1920, this educational policy was a colonial program of forced racial and cultural assimilation designed to "civilize" the Native populations by prohibiting the practice of religious and cultural traditions and rituals, confiscating sacred cultural objects, enforcing Christianity, forbidding communication in Native languages, and implementing bodily regulation through tactics such as haircutting and uniforms. Class-action suits involved demands for compensation from the Canadian government as well as individual Church denominations. In October 2000, the Anglican Church of Canada was faced with over 350 lawsuits. The Organization of United Reborn Survivors was forged to lobby the federal government and churches in the wake of the residential school disclosures. While lengthy delays in federal negotiations prompted many Natives to settle out of court, Prime Minister Jean Chrétien instituted a new Office of Indian Residential Schools Resolution of Canada on June 7, 2001. Yet, while the Law Commission of Canada recommended

---

[54] *See* Wallace, 2001; Elder, 2001; "Outrage over Lastman", 2001; Ewing, 2001; "ATO Mayor Lastman", 2001.
[55] *See* Vincent, 2001; "Policies: Judge", 2001; Thomas, 2000; "Chinese Canadian Files", 2000; Wilkey, 1998; "Chinese Canadian Group", 1995; "Big Cash", 1994.

that victims of residential schools be compensated in the range of $100,000 to $600,000, many of the awards failed to approach that target. And further, upholding a 30-year statute of limitations, judges utterly dismissed many claims, citing that too much time had passed since the victims' childhood abuse. After months of unsuccessful negotiations with the churches, on October 29, 2001, the federal government announced that they would pay 70 percent of proven out-of-court damage settlements related to Native residential schools while not limiting churches' liability in potential lawsuits.[56]

• The lethal racism of several Canadian soldiers in Africa, the Somalia Inquiry, and the subsequent disbanding of the Royal Canadian Airborne Regiment. While on duty overseas, several Canadian troops shot Somali civilians on March 4, 1993. Later that March, Canadian soldiers tortured and killed Shidane Arone, a Somali teenager, capturing the ritualized and brutal murder in photographs. A government-appointed commission, headed by two judges and the dean of Journalism from the University of Western Ontario, was abruptly disassembled in the wake of accusations that the military and government orchestrated elaborate cover-ups and deliberately hindered prosecutorial progress through political and physical threats.[57]

After having situated the colonial histories of Canada, we raise these contemporary examples of racism to locate race as a pressing contemporary social concern with urgent consequences for Natives and people of colour.

Theorizing Race

Throughout the process of completing this anthology, we have been keenly aware of the need to balance both theoretical and pragmatic issues and concerns. This is a difficult and yet necessary juggling act since race, as we have detailed above, is not only a physical or material consideration, but also a political, emotional and psychic one. The theories that have been employed in the service of post-colonialism are as disparate as the end goals that they have been harnessed to achieve. Accordingly, different types of theory, having distinct investments and foci, are better equipped to serve some intellectual or scholarly objectives than others. Furthermore, the post-colonial theorization of race has been an important means of understanding the pragmatism of racism.

When Frantz Fanon stated the purpose of his seminal *Black Skin, White Masks* as an attempt to "...help the black man to free himself of the arsenal of complexes that has been developed by the colonial environment,"[58] he established the link between racism and mental and psychic health and alluded to the trap of racism as a social matrix that had the ability to imprison those it defined. Fanon still stands as a compelling template for the theorization of race

---

[56] *See* De Santis, 2001; Landry, 2001; Culhane, 2001; Petten, 2001; "Former Residential School", 2000; "Lawsuits Force", 2000; "Law Group Wants", 2000; "Our Secret Past", 1996.
[57] *See* Rose, 1996. *See also* Razack, 1998.
[58] Fanon, 1968, p. 30.

through psychoanalysis. Although concerned with the binary of black and white, Fanon poignantly demonstrated the burden of any racial marginalization. Indeed, Fanon recognized the stigma of visible difference as a peculiarly "racial epidermal schema".[59] It was from inside his tortured black body, split into three to bare personal, racial and ancestral sins, that Fanon articulated a racial objectification that was active not only from the outside in, but also from the inside out. Fractured by the incessant punitive gaze of the chanting white child, "Look, a Negro! . . . I'm frightened!" Fanon recalls a dislocation from self that reduced him to an object: "What else could it be for me but an amputation, an excision, a hemorrhage that spattered my whole body with black blood?"[60] Racism affects self-perception. It enforces an abject sense of self upon its victims until recourse to other ideas of selfhood is painfully inaccessible.

Within this psychoanalytical tradition, Bhabha has acknowledged the importance of the act of repetition in colonial stereotypes and the ambivalence of Western colonial authority as a significant function of discriminatory power structures. According to Bhabha:

> It is the force of ambivalence that gives the colonial stereotype its currency; ensures its repeatability in changing historical and discursive conjunctures; informs its strategies of individuation and marginalization; produces that effect of probabilistic truth and predictability which, for the stereotype, must always be in **excess** of what can be empirically proved or logically construed.[61]

One way to problematize the colonial stereotype is to scrutinize the myth of its supposed fixity and stability, its *a priori* quality that is belied by the frequency in which supposedly secure racial types become illegible. The destabilization of race as a secure signifier of the body and social status is triggered by the performative nature of identity that often, particularly in a multicultural and multiracial, increasingly global context, like Canada, appropriates and weaves elements from other cultures and races. Add to this the historical fact of miscegenation, a definite by-product of colonial contact, and the reliability of racial types and our ability to identify race become destabilized.[62]

Twining with the idea of race's performative nature, Judith Butler's concept of the ritualized repetition of norms as a mechanism for the construction of an ideal subject is useful in understanding how racial identity is **practised** into being. This performativity, as Butler names it, is precisely the reiterative power of discourse to produce the phenomenon that it regulates and constrains, but is also the ability to conceal the conventions of which it is a repetition.[63] Simply put, colonial discourse have the power not only to produce race but also to

---

[59] Ibid., p. 112.

[60] Ibid., p. 112.

[61] Bhabha, 1990b, p. 71.

[62] *See* documentary film, *Speakers for the Dead*, 2000, directed by Jennifer Holness and David Sutherland. The film examines a small town in rural Ontario and its quest to restore the history and dignity of its black descendants. The story traces the journey of discovery begun in the 1980s by descendants of Priceville's black and white settlers. As they delve into the story of blacks in the Priceville area, new truths are revealed and the townspeople are divided. (*See* National Film Board, http://www.onf.ca/speakers/)

[63] Butler, 1993, p. 12.

normalize it as a supposedly natural aspect of human categorization. If indeed race is not a biological certainty, as histories of Western thought would have us believe, but an inherently biased social regulation of the body, racial identity is not merely a **matter** of the body, but also includes the symbolic meanings attached to that body.

If, for example, we address race as a symbolic position — as in the Lacanian sense of sex as a symbolic position — then signs that are taken as biological marks of race (kinky hair texture, brown skin colour, wide nose, etc.) serve to activate the subsequent colonial meanings of race with the symbolic order (blackness equals unintellectual, immoral, sexually degenerate and inferior, etc.). The trick of the symbolic is that the regulatory apparatus that **precedes** the symbolic marking comes to be seen as a later condition or application of an essential racial marking (if it is seen at all). These two types of marks, symbolic and biological, are not of necessity predetermined in their definitions or correlations. Race, then, is **of** the body, but not essential to it. Race is assigned to the body when biological marks are given symbolic meanings within language through the process of differentiation from other marks. Quite simply, the word "white" only has meaning as a racial identity in relation to words such as "black" and "Asian".

Race is relational. The process of identification is itself a process of differentiation wherein the self-ness and "otherness" of bodies are constituted and object relations can be established. Since the reference point for the image of the "other" body is the image of the body of the self, the process of bodily materialization is inherently narcissistic. But the ability to project an image of the body and have it confirmed, outside of oneself, bespeaks a social mobility, access, authority and power that have historically been relatable to specific sex, class and racial positions. Hence the ability to be narcissistic is not equally available to all. Acknowledging the inherent phallocentrism and Eurocentrism of bodily identification in the West is to recognize that not all bodies have the same opportunity or power to generate and register the self as the point from which differentiation begins. The marginalization of the subject disrupts the subject's ability to think its body outside of the organizing structure that effected the marginalization in the first instance — Fanon's inability to escape the gaze of the jeering child. How and to what extent can any of us, then, escape the legacy of colonialism and our assigned racial positions within this discourse? A subject's performance of an assigned racial identification is not an indication of an essential nature of a specific symbolic position, but instead points to the power of regimes of identification and their material and psychic efficacy.

The burden of race is multiple and complex. Race precedes us and determines, to a large extent, our possibilities, access, mobility and social value. On the simplest of levels, our race determines how other people engage us and, indeed, whether they will choose to engage us at all. Our race, or how an observer perceives our race, allows them to **know** us, or to feel as though they do, before they have truly engaged us. As something visible yet possessed decided mental implications, race needs to be scrutinized not only as a material phenomenon — how subjects embody a racialized position — but as a psychic one — how subjects are indoctrinated into ideologies of race, and how the discursive effects of this indoctrination determine their mental experience of their own and other bodies on a conscious and unconscious level.

Racism, Eh?

Canadians are the inheritors of this colonial legacy. Although we often proudly discuss and glorify our national origins as the history of two European forces — British and French — we rarely address or confront the inherent racism of their imperial projects, nor the colonial logic that allowed them to disavow the legitimate presence of First Nations peoples, enslave and import black Africans, and selectively manage immigration for "desirable" racial populations. The language of race is carefully policed in Canada. By this we mean the specificity of various scholarly discourses discussed above, but also the language of everyday social engagement and popular culture that only authorizes and rewards racial dialogue that celebrates Canada as an anti-racist, multicultural state. This myth of a racism-free Canada is, of course, not substantiated by the thoughts, fears, feelings, histories and experiences of most First Nations- and people of colour-Canadians.

The organization of the anthology is our attempt to contribute to a dialogue on race and allow previously suppressed voices to be heard; to broaden the possible topics of research and debate; to challenge traditionally Eurocentric methodological approaches; and to encourage interdisciplinary cooperation. We have deliberately sought and included contributions from a diverse group of scholars within a wide range of disciplines. The disciplinary breadth of the anthology poses certain obvious methodological challenges. Although post-colonialism has impacted all the fields represented in the anthology, precisely how the disciplines have been impacted, and through which theoretical and conceptual frames, is unique to each. We should also note that each discipline is governed by normative standards of writing, research and methodology that result in different styles of writing, objects of inquiry and areas of concern. The anthology's organization resists an easy discipline-specific structure. Instead, we have deliberately grouped essays into different parts, eight in total, that address specific types of issues and topics of inquiry regarding the intersection of racial and national identity in Canada. It is our hope that the process of reading across disciplines will render the issues at stake in each part more relevant, clear and accessible.

Part 1 tackles the subject of Institutional Racism in three distinct yet relatable contexts. Anthony Stewart bravely elaborates on his personal trials and tribulations as a graduate student and, now, a professor within Canadian academia. His recollections and experiences will be painfully familiar and relevant to many both inside and outside his specific field and career. Johanna Mizgala penetrates the traditional sacredness and stoicism of the Western museum to question its traditional racial inaccessibility through the politicized cultural interventions of the contemporary Native Canadian artist Lance Belanger. Colin McFarquhar's exhaustive archival research has culminated in a contribution that illuminates the historical patterns of racial segregation and exclusion of blacks within nineteenth-century labour practices in Ontario.

In Part 2, Crime and Justice, three essays explore the racial limits of Canadian legal and judicial discourse. Mapping histories of a racialized and inequitable justice system in Canada, George Elliot Clarke recognizes and challenges a Canadian resistance to engage in a discussion of the racial implications of capital punishment. He analyzes and "unearths" the history of Angélique in an effort to commence a national race-conscious creative literature on crime and punishment. Faizal Mirza articulates an equality rights crisis in the Canadian criminal justice system and explores a provocative role for the Canadian Charter of Rights and Freedoms, while Wendy Chan problematizes and suggests a new framework for the conceptualization of "race" as it has been used in research on race and crime in Canada.

Part 3, First Nations — Of Land, Law and Power, is devoted to the exploration of Native issues and the specificity of race within the social, political and economic contexts of Canada's First Peoples. Sarah de Leeuw tracks and summarizes the racial implications of the white media coverage and popular response to the Nisga'a land claims treaty. Gina Cosentino examines the benefits of viewing Canadian federalism through the lens of treaty federalism in order to broaden the agenda and include marginalized perspectives and narratives about the meaning and place of the First Nations within the federation. Wendy Hoglund calls for critical redress of the traditional methodological paradigms for the social investigation of child poverty that have proven incapable of incorporating the specificity of Native economic issues and social challenges.

Race, Place and Nation, Part 4, examines the significance of location — geographical, social, spiritual and psychic — in racial identifications within Canada. Camille Nelson explores questions of longing and belonging within the context of the Caribbean diaspora and the impact of unscrupulous immigration incentives and policies on the impoverishment of Jamaica, while Melanie Fogell scrutinizes the logic and consequences of migration within the Jewish-Israeli context. Karen Dubinsky's contribution examines the strategic importance of Natives as racial "others," commodities exchanged for their spectacular value within the exoticized domain of Canadian tourism.

In Part 5, The Complexity of Intersectionality and the Performance of Racial Identity, three scholars deal with the challenge of examining race as only one part of complex identities. How do various facets or markers of our identity intersect, and what are the ramifications of their simultaneity and inextricability? While Josée Makropoulos questions the combination of whiteness and Frenchness, Bruce Retallack examines the historical gendering of Chinese males. Awad Ibrahim's essay tackles the contemporary evolution of blackness as a type of vital cultural capital among black immigrant youths today.

Our Popular Culture contributions in Part 6 combine scholarly research in the area of Canadian television, radio and film. While Michele Byers assesses the racial dynamics of Canada's popular teen show *Degrassi (Junior) High,* Ryan Edwardson plots the racial implications of the evolution of ethnic broadcasting in Canada, and Sheila Petty examines the deployment of racial identities within early Prairie cinema.

Part 7, Production and Representation, tackles issues of production and representation within Canadian culture. Lynda Hall scrutinizes the literature of contemporary black female author Dionne Brand, challenging the ways that white critics use race to exclude her from the Canadian literary canon. Alice Jim's discussion of contemporary black female Canadian visual artists situates the racial, sex and gender specificity of their production within various recent exhibitions, while challenging the rationale of their continuing exclusion from the white mainstream of Canadian visual art. Charmaine Nelson challenges the dominance of traditional art history discourse and its inability to accommodate issues of race, while exposing the racialization of female sexuality as a product of colonial cultural practice. Artist Joanne Tod, whose paintings have for years exemplified a commitment to, and consciousness of, race issues, sheds light on the evolution of her oeuvre and the personal and social details that inform her production.

In Part 8, Multiculturalism, our contributors assess the evolution and ramifications of this official Canadian policy. Melanie Ash scrutinizes the ignorance of assuming, and ascribing to Canadians of colour, a foreign "otherness". She examines the ironic perspective of Canada as a "white" country, given official Canadian policies that espouse multiculturalism within a bilingual framework. While Anver Saloojee explores the extent to which the official policy of multiculturalism has allowed for the proliferation of multiple identities and has detracted from the creation of national social cohesion, Augie Fleras links the policy of multiculturalism with a "pretend pluralism" that simultaneously includes and excludes and, thus, creates a system where multicultural racism has superseded race-based racism as the preferred exclusionary discourse. Last but not least, Jakeet Singh weighs in and acknowledges some of the problematic consequences of multiculturalism but ultimately endorses the policy and makes suggestions for its revision.

References

Alba, Richard. (1990). *Ethnic identity: The transformation of white America*. New Haven: Yale University Press.

Allegations of profiling rock Toronto police. (2002, October 21). CBC News. Retrieved October 17, 2003, from http://www.cbc.ca/storyview/CBC/2002/10/21/toronto_cops021021.

Anderson, Benedict. (1991). *Imagined communities: Reflections on the origins and spread of nationalism*. London, UK: Verso.

Armour, Jody David. (1997). *Negrophobia and reasonable racism: The hidden costs of being black in America*. London, UK: New York University Press.

ATO Mayor Lastman offers apology for Africa comment during 2008 bid business. (2001, June 21). *Canadian Press Newswire*.

Backhouse, Constance. (1999). *Colour coded: A legal history of racism in Canada, 1900–1950.* Toronto, ON: Published for the Osgoode Society by University of Toronto Press.

Backhouse, Constance. (2001). *Canadian mythologies about race.* Ottawa, ON: University of Ottawa Press.

Bannerji, Himani. (Ed.). (1993). Returning the gaze: An introduction. In *Returning the gaze: Essays on racism, feminism and politics.* Toronto, ON: Sister Vision Black Women and Women of Colour Press.

Beckow, Stephen M. (1974). *Keeping British Columbia white: Anti-orientalism in the West, 1858–1949* [Motion picture]. Montreal, PQ: National Film Board of Canada.

Bell, Derrick. (1995). Property rights in whiteness — their legal legacy, their economic costs. In Richard Delgado (Ed.), *Critical race theory: The cutting edge.* Philadelphia, PA: Temple University Press.

Bhabha, Homi K. (1990a). Introduction: Narrating the nation. In Nation and narration. London, UK: Routledge.

Bhabha, Homi K. (1990b). The other question: Difference, discrimination and the discourse of colonialism. In Russell Ferguson et al. (Eds.), *Out there: Marginalization and contemporary culture.* New York, NY: The New Museum of Contemporary Art and the Massachusetts Institute of Technology.

Bhbha, Homi K. (1994). *The location of culture.* London, UK: Routledge.

Big cash for historic slights: Seven ethnic groups want redress for perceived past wrongs. (1994, August 29). *Western Report, 9*(31): 9.

Black and Blue. (1995, June). *Ottawa Magazine*, 16–25.

Blyth, Edward. (1840). *Cuvier's animal kingdom, arranged according to its organization; forming the basis for a natural history of animals and an introduction to comparative anatomy.* London, UK: Wm. S. Orr.

Boswell, Randy. (2001, April 24). PM faces flip-flop accusation over Ukranian internment bill. *Ottawa Citizen,* p. A6.

Boynton, Robert S. (2002). Black studies today: Out of Africa, and back [Education life supplement]. *The New York Times,* April 14, 2002. Sunday Late Edition, Section 41, p. 36.

Butler, Judith. (1993). Bodies that matter: On the discursive limits of "Sex". New York, NY: Routledge.

Caldwell, Paulette M. (1997). A hair piece: Perspectives on the intersection of race and gender. In Adrien Katherine Wing (Ed.), Critical Race Feminism (pp. 297–305). New York, NY: New York University Press.

Césaire, Aimé (1972). *Discourse on colonialism* (Joan Pinkham, Trans.). New York, NY: Monthly Review Press.

Chinese Canadian files 1.2 b Suit to reclaim head tax from Ottawa. (2000, December 19). *Canadian Press Newswire.*

Chinese Canadian group wants compensation. (1995, March 21). *Canadian Press Newswire.*

Ciaccia, John. (2000). *The Oka crisis: A mirror of the soul.* Dorval, PQ: Maren Publications.

Culhane, Erin. (2001, September). Canada's actions speak louder than words. *Windspeaker, 19*(5), 5.

Day, Shelagh. (2000). Toward women's equality: Canada's failed commitment. Retrieved June 3, 2002, from Canadian Feminists Alliance for International Action website: http://www.fafia.org/Bplus5/altrepf4_e.htm

De Cille, Ann. (1996). Toy theory: Black barbie and the deep play of difference. In Skin Trade. Cambridge, UK: Harvard University Press.

Delgado, Richard & Stefanic, Jean. (Eds.). (1997). *Critical white studies: Looking behind the mirror*. Philadelphia, PA: Temple University Press.

De Santis, Solange. (2001, December). Ottawa makes unilateral offer. *Anglican Journal, 127*(10), 1, 3.

Du Bois, David G. (1994). Racism in academia. *The Journal of Blacks in Higher Education, 2,* 90.

Early, Gerald. (2002) The invisible intellectual: A place of our own [Education life supplement]. In *The New York Times* April 14, 2002. Sunday Late Edition, Section 4A, p. 34.

Elder, Jules. (2001, June 25). Outrage over Mel's remarks. *Toronto Sun*, p. 16.

Elgersman, Maureen G. (1999). *Unyielding spirits: Black women and slavery in early Canada and Jamaica*. New York, NY: Garland Publishing.

Ewing, Lori. (2001, June 21). Toronto Olympic bid group in damage control over Toronto mayor's gaffe. *Canadian Press Newswire*.

Fanon, Frantz. (1968). Black skin, white masks (Charles Lam Markmann. Trans.). New York, NY: Grove Press.

Fine, Michelle. (1997). *Off white: Readings on race, power and society*. New York, NY: Routledge.

Former residential school students get together to lobby for compensation. (2000, December 25). *Canadian Press Newswire*.

Fontaine, Phil. (1998). Modern Racism in Canada. Donal Gow Lecture, School of Policy Studies, Queen's University, Kingston ON at Holiday Inn Waterfront Hotel, Kingston, April 24.

Foster, Gwendolyn Audrey. (1999). *Captive bodies: postcolonial subjectivity in cinema*. Albany, NY: State University of New York Press.

Foucault, Michel. (1977). *Discipline and punish: The birth of the prison* (Alan Sheridan, Trans.). New York, NY: Vintage Books.

Foucault, Michel. (1980). Truth and power. In Gordon Colin et al. (Eds.), *Power/knowledge: Selected interviews and other writings 1972–1977*. New York, NY: Pantheon Books.

Frankenberg, Ruth. (1993). *White women, race matters: The social construction of whiteness*. Minneapolis, MN: University of Minnesota Press.

Freeman, Harold P. (2002). *The meaning of race in science and society*. New York, NY: Columbia University Press.

Gerstle, Gary. (2002). *American crucible: Race and nation in the twentieth century*. Princeton, NJ: Princeton University Press.

Gilman, Sander L. (1985a). Black bodies, white bodies: Toward an iconography of female sexuality in late nineteenth-century art, medicine and literature. Critical Inquiry, 12, 204–242.

Gilman, Sander L. (1985b). *Difference and pathology: Stereotypes of sexuality, race, and madness*. Ithaca, NY: Cornell University Press.

Goldberg, David Theo, & Solomos, John. (Eds.). (2002). *A Companion to racial and ethnic studies*. Malden, MA: Blackwell Publishing.

Gould, Stephen Jay. (1996). *The mismeasure of man.* New York, NY: W.W. Norton and Company.

Grayson, J. Paul. 1996. *White racism in Toronto?* New York, NY: New York University Press.

Hall, Stuart. (1996). Introduction: Who needs identity? In *Questions of cultural identity.* London, UK: Sage Publications.

Hall, Stuart, & du Gay, Paul. (Eds.). (1996). *Questions of cultural identity.* London & California: Sage.

Hall, Stuart, & Gieben, Bram (Eds.). (1992). *Formations of modernity.* Cambridge, UK: Polity Press & Open University Press.

Hall, Stuart, et al. (Eds.). (1992). *Culture, media, language: Working papers in cultural studies, 1972–79.* London & New York: Routledge & the Centre for Contemporary Cultural Studies: University of Birmingham. (Original work published 1980)

Herald News Services. (2000, 17 February). RCMP take over Native death probe. *Calgary Herald,* p. A5.

Harring, Sidney L. (1998). *White man's law: Native people in nineteenth-century Canadian jurisprudence.* Toronto, ON: Published for the Osgoode Society for Canadian Legal History by the University of Toronto Press.

Harrison, Faye V. (1995). The persistent power of race in the cultural and political economy of racism. *Annual Review of Anthropology, 24,* 47–74.

Hill, Mike. (Ed.) (1997). *Whiteness: A critical reader.* New York, NY: New York University Press.

Hillis, Michael R. (1995). Allison Davis and the study of race, social class, and schooling. *Journal of Negro Education, 64,* 33–41.

Holt, Thomas C. (1995). Marking: Race, race-making, and the writing of history. *The American Historical Review, 100,* 1–20.

hooks, bell. (1997). Sisterhood: Political solidarity between women. In *Dangerous liaisons: Gender, nation, and postcolonial perspectives.* Minneapolis, MN: University of Minnesota Press.

Iacovetta, Franca, Perin, Roberto, & Principe, Angelo. (Eds.). (2000). *Enemies within: Italian and other internees in Canada and abroad.* Toronto: University of Toronto Press.

Jackson, Peter, & Penrose, Jan (Eds.). (1993). *Constructions of race, place, and nation. Minneapolis,* MN: University of Minnesota Press.

Jakubowski, Lisa Marie. (1997). *Immigration and the legalization of racism.* Halifax, NS: Fernwood.

Jones, Lisa M. (1994). The Hair Trade. In *Bulletproof diva: Tales of tace, sex, and hair.* New York, NY: Dell.

Kelley, Robin D.G. (1998). Confessions of a nice negro, or why I shaved my head. In *Race, class, gender and sexuality: The big questions.* Malden, MA: Blackwell Publishing.

Knox, Robert. (1862). *The races of men: A philosophical enquiry into the influence of race over the destinies of nations* (2nd ed.). London, UK: Henry Renshaw.

Koenig, Wolf. (1991). *Enemy alien* [Motion picture]. Montreal, PQ: National Film Board of Canada.

Kucharsky, Danny. (2001, August 13). Black and bleue: Labatt refuses to bend in the face of allegations that its Montreal Jazz Fest posters are racist. *Marketing Magazine, 106*(32), 7.

Landry, Frank. (2001, September 27). Manitoba court tells residential school complainants their suits are too old. *Canadian Press Newswire.*

Law group wants a stop to preying on residential school victims. (2000, August 20). *Canadian Press Newswire.*

Lawsuits force Anglican church to cut staff and programs. (2000, October 20). *Presbyterian Record, 124*(9): 34.

Lee, Spike, & Jones, Lisa. (1988). Straight and nappy: Good and bad hair. In *Uplift the race: The construction of school daze* (pp. 143–164). New York, NY: Simon & Schuster.

Levy, Anita. (1991). *Other women: The writing of class, race and gender, 1832–1898.* Princeton, NJ: Princeton University Press.

Lewis, Jeff. (2002). *Cultural studies — the basics.* London, UK: Sage.

Li, Peter S. (1998). *The Chinese in Canada.* Toronto, ON: Oxford University Press.

Loomba, Ania. (1998). *Colonialism/postcolonialism.* London, UK: Routledge.

Lungen, Paul. (2001, August 2). Fax campaign promotes anti-Semitic stereotypes. *Canadian Jewish News, 31,* 32.

Mackey, Eva. (2002). *The house of difference: Cultural politics and National identity in Canada.* Toronto, ON: University of Toronto Press.

Malik, Kenan. (1996). *The meaning of race.* New York, NY: New York University Press.

Marx, Anthony W. (1996). Race-making and the nation-state. *World Politics, 48,* 180–208.

Matsuda, Mari. (1991). Voices of America: Accent, antidiscrimination law and a jurisprudence for the last reconstruction. *Yale Law Journal, 100*(5), 1329–1407.

McCarthy, Cameron, & Crichlow, Warren (1993). Introduction: Theories of identity, theories of representation, theories of race. In *Race, identity and representation in education.* New York, NY: Routledge.

McNairn, Kim. (2000, February 18). Natives claim police abandon drunks, rowdies at city's edge. *National Post*, p. A4.

Mercer, Kobena. (1990). Black hair/style politics. In Russell Ferguson et al. (Eds.), *Out there: Marginalization and contemporary cultures.* New York, NY: The New Museum of Contemporary Art.

Milloy, John Sheridan. (1999). *A national crime: The Canadian government and the residential school system, 1879–1986.* Winnipeg, MB: University of Manitoba Press.

Mohanty, Chandra Talpade. (1991). Under Western eyes: Feminist scholarship and colonial discourse. In Chandra Talpade Mohanty, Anne Russo, & Lourdes Torres (Eds.), *Third world women and the politics of feminism.* Bloomington, IN: Indiana University Press.

Moller, Jonathan Bjerg. (2002, February 13). Hate images on Web site. *Toronto Star*, p. 3.

Morrison, R. Bruce, & Wilson, C. Roderick (Eds.). (1995). *Native peoples: The Canadian experience.* Toronto, ON: Oxford University Press.

Nakano, Takeo. (1980). *Within the barbed wire fence: A Japanese man's account of internment in Canada*. Toronto, ON: University of Toronto Press.

Nakayama, Thomas K., & Martin, Judith N. (Eds.). (1999). *Whiteness: The communication of social identity*. Thousand Oaks: Sage Publications.

Native leaders blame police for blocking probes into deaths. (2001, July 29). *The Whitehorse Daily Star*, p. 18.

No charges to be laid in Native man's death. (2001, July 27). *The Times Colonist* (Victoria), p. A10.

Ore, Tracy E. (2001). *The social construction of difference and inequality race, class, gender, and sexuality*. Columbus, OH: McGraw-Hill.

Our secret past: Canada's history. (1996, April). *Canada and the World Backgrounder, 61*(6), 16–17.

Outrage over Lastman's comments mounts as he refuses to resign. (2001, June 23). *Canadian Press Newswire*.

Petten, Cheryl. (2001, July). Chief optimistic about new office. *Windspeaker, 19*(3), 1.

Policies: Judge. (2001, July 11). *The Whitehorse Daily Star*, p. 12.

Pollock, Griselda. (1999). *Differencing the canon: Feminist desire and the writing of art's histories*. London, UK: Routledge.

Prichard, James Cowles. (1851). *Researches into the physical history of mankind* (4th ed., 3 vols.). London, UK: Houlston & Stoneman.

Razack, Sherene. (1998). *Looking white people in the eye: Gender, race, and culture in courtrooms and classrooms*. Toronto, ON: University of Toronto Press.

Robertson, Robbie. (1998). Sacrfice. *Contact from the underworld of red boy*. Los Angeles, CA: Capitol.

Roediger, David R. (2002). *Colored white: Transcending the racial past*. Berkely, CA: University of California Press.

Rose, George. (1996, February 19). Canada generals quit as abuses exposed. *The Militant, 60*(7), 1–4.

Ruck, Calvin W. (1987). *The Black Battalion 1916–1920: Canada's best kept military secret*. Halifax, NS: Nimbus Publishing Limited.

Ruck, Calvin W. (1986). *Canada's Black Battalion: No. 2 construction 1916–1920*. Halifax, NS: The Society for the Protection and Preservation of Black Culture in Nova Scotia.

Sansgster, Joan. (2001). Native women, sexuality and the law. In *Regulating girls and women: sexuality, family, and the law in Ontario*. Don Mills, ON: Oxford University Press.

Seltzer, Richard et al. (1995). Multiculturalism, race, and education. *Journal of Negro Education, 64*, 124–140.

Simpson, Audra. (2000). Paths towards a Mohawk Nation: Narratives and citizenship and nationhood in Kahnawake. In Duncan Ivison et al. (Eds.), *Political theory and the rights of Indigenous people*. Cambridge, UK: Cambridge University Press.

Smith, Linda Tuhiwai. (1999). *Decolonizing methodologies: Research and Indigenous peoples*. London, UK: Zed Books.

Tebbutt, Charlene & Coolican, Lori. (2001, 8 December). Punishments fit crime of ex-cops, Native groups say. *The Leader-Post* (Regina), p. B3.

Thomas, Don A. (2000, December 20). Seeking refund of infamous head tax. *Edmonton Journal*, p. A3.

Thompson, Lowell. (1996). *Whitefolks*. Chicago, IL: Author.

Toronto police to probe racism allegations. (2002, October 25). CBC News. Retrieved October 17, 2003, from http://www.cbc.ca/storyview/CBC/2002/10/25/fantino_021025

Truth, Sojourner. (1851). Ain't I a woman? Speech delivered in Akron, OH at the 1851 Women's Rights Convention.

Tulloch, Headley (1996). Our secret past: Canada's history. *Canada and the World Backgrounder, 61*(6), 16–17.

Tulloch, Headley. (1975). *Black Canadians: A long line of fighters*. Toronto: NC Press.

Vincent, Donovan. (2001, July 11). Head-tax lawsuit struck down. *The Toronto Star*, p. B04.

Wallace, James (2001, August 31). Magazine quotes mayor's scrum verbatim. *National Post*, p. A17.

Warren, Catherine A., & Vavrus, Mary Douglas. (Eds.). (2002). *American cultural Studies*. Urbana, IL: University of Illinois Press.

Wilkey, Craig D. (1998, Spring). British Columbia's error regarding the Chinese Immigrant. *British Columbia Historical News, 31*(2), 14–17

Williams, Patricia J. (1991). *The alchemy of race and rights*. Cambridge, MA: Harvard University Press.

Williams Crenshaw, Kimberle. (1995). Mapping the margins: intersectionality, identity politics, and violence against women of color. In *Critical race theory: The key writings that formed the movement*. New York, NY: New Press.

Wilson, Brian & Sparks, Robert E. (1999). Impacts of black athlete media portrayals on Canadian youth. *Canadian Journal of Communication 24*(4): 589–627.

Winks, Robin W. (1997). *Blacks in Canada: A history* (2nd ed.). Montreal, PQ: McGill-Queen's University Press.

Yee, Paul. (1996). *Struggle and hope: The story of Chinese Canadians*. Toronto, ON: Umbrella Press.

Zakreski, Dan. (2000, February 27). Victims froze to death, helped spark the investigation. *Calgary Herald*, p. A8.

Part 1

1

Institutional Racism

While face-to-face, explicit racism still exists, more covert and, often, more virulent forms of racism predominate. The systemic and structural racism prevalent in institutions such as government departments, educational institutions, corporate boardrooms, hospital wings, religious organizations, media outlets and family networks is often so entrenched that it becomes part of the normative culture of an organization.

Racism in any institution or organization operates to exclude and force conformity or to enforce silence. Each essay in Part 1 examines a specific context and explores the operation and ramifications of racism in an institutional setting.

The first essay, "Penn and Teller Magic: Self, Racial Devaluation and the Canadian Academy", outlines the racialized structure of Canadian academia. The essay explores the common struggle many people of colour face in their work lives — the constant battle between one's consciousness as a person of colour and the norm of racial conformity that is rewarded and prized in the working world.

The second essay, "Lance Belanger's Tango Lessons: Infiltrating the Museum", highlights institutional racism in the realm of the museum. Art is a prolific mechanism of cultural creation and the perpetuation of a cultural legacy. Accordingly, art is a particularly important venue of forced conformity and assimilation. In Canada, there has been a reluctance to accept certain forms of art by First Nations people — that which is seen as out of step with stereotypical notions of the Native "other" is not highly valued. Additionally, First Nations art has traditionally been segregated from other mainly Euro-Canadian art, thereby creating a distinct separation, both mental and physical, from the canonical ideal of Canadian art.

The third essay, "The Black Occupational Structure in Late-Nineteenth-Century Ontario: Evidence from the Census", discusses the racialized forces that encouraged and prevented occupational representation in nineteenth-century Canada. The essay establishes that it was no accident that the majority of black workers were confined to blue-collar labour. The lower-status jobs occupied by blacks were carefully controlled and encouraged. Accordingly, there was, and still is, a relative absence of blacks from high-paying jobs in Canadian society. Traditionally, blacks have been limited to manual-labour jobs, or occupations that pay the least. Overall, blacks were much more likely to be represented in lower-skill jobs than whites and were virtually non-existent in white-collar jobs. This trend was found in each Canadian city examined and has lasted for at least 30 years.

1

Penn and Teller Magic

Self, Racial Devaluation and the Canadian Academy

Anthony Stewart
English Department
Dalhousie University
Halifax

Anthony Stewart

Penn and Teller are an American comedy-magic act who have made themselves unpopular with many of their fellow magicians by first performing their magic tricks the conventional way and then performing the tricks again with the panels up: that is, exposing the sleights-of-hand that create illusions. A willingness to expose the secrets that confer membership within a club will invariably be resented by some of the members of that club. But the maintenance of exclusivity has long been a strategy for keeping out people who look like me, so I don't have much of a vested interest in keeping the secrets, even at the cost of the resentment of some who might prefer that the secrets be maintained. As a black Canadian who teaches and studies literature for a living, it has often felt to me as if part of being in this particular club has meant keeping its secrets, sometimes at the expense of feeling like a hypocrite. My experiences as a graduate student and, now, as a faculty member have enabled me to formulate perspectives on the particular challenges faced by black Canadian academics — challenges rarely expressed inside, let alone outside, the academy — as well as to speculate on why there aren't more black Canadian academics in the first place.

While racism is, of course, more than a question of black versus white, this is the venue to which I'm restricting myself, not in the interest of exclusion, but because I do not want to create the illusion that I know what it's like to be Japanese or Cree in Canada. In many ways, even claiming expertise about what it's like to be black in Canada is seriously problematic considering the multifariousness of the black Canadian population — Africans, Americans, Caribbeans, not to mention African-Canadians with a centuries-old history live in this country. But being black in Canada has taught me the central lesson of racism: It rarely has anything to do with the individual. In all the times I've had things yelled at me from a passing car or have received a hostile look, not once was it the result of someone thinking, "There's Anthony Stewart." Rather, each incident was, simply, the depersonalised observation of skin colour.

But while "racism" carries its myriad costs and is the term usually employed when considering interracial discord, it is comparatively rare in Canada to experience explicit displays of racist sentiment, as many blacks living in Canada will tell you. In the April 1992 issue of *The Atlantic* magazine, Claude Steele wrote about what he calls "racial devaluation." His description of how devaluation works illuminates what many refer to as the "subtlety" of Canadian racism. Steele relates the story of a small African-American boy named Jerome whose obvious artistic talents are ignored by his grade three teacher. In fact, Jerome's reputation from one grade to the next includes "only the slightest mention of his talent."[1] Steele speculates that if Jerome had had a reading problem, this fact would have featured prominently in his file because it would

---

[1] Steele, 1992.

34

have fit the prevailing stereotypes about a small African-American boy. Steele's point about racial devaluation is this:

> Terms like "prejudice" and "racism" often miss the full scope of racial devaluation in our society, implying as they do that racial devaluation comes primarily from the strongly prejudiced, not from "good people" like Jerome's teacher. But the prevalence of racists — deplorable though racism is — misses the full extent of Jerome's burden, perhaps even the most profound part.[2]

The society Steele is talking about is the United States. Nevertheless, I have found myself coming back again and again to this idea of racial devaluation because it strikes a chord with me about living in Canada that I am only now starting to grasp fully.[3] It is one thing to be called a name from a passing car or to have your car spat on as you sit in the driver's seat (both of which happened to me as a Ph.D. student in Kingston, Ontario); such events are obviously enraging and can lead to unthinking reactions (as when, after the spitting incident, I engaged in a police-style car chase for several blocks before thinking better of the enterprise, since there were four young white men in the other car). But it is something else altogether when the offence is subtler. When, for instance, a professor whom I did not know compared me to Ben Johnson as I stood in a hallway during the year of my Master's degree in 1988 — it was, after all, an Olympic year — he wasn't calling me a nigger outright or saying that we all look alike, or was he?

Instances such as these cause serious crises to one's sense of self. On the one hand, it was I alone who worked for 12 years to earn three university degrees, each rarer than the one before it. It's my name on the degree and, for that matter, my office door. On the other hand, at any unthinking moment I can be demoted from the August personage, "Anthony Stewart, Ph.D." to "that nigger" or just any dark-skinned person easily confused with any other dark-skinned person.

So, when at a conference I was introduced to a senior scholar from another Canadian university who promptly confused me with another black graduate student (I'm 6'6" tall; the other student is about 5'9" and more lightly complected than I am, but, hey, we're both black), I found myself conducting the rest of the conversation with that senior scholar while thinking about how, or if, I should say something about her insulting mistaken identification. As with the Ben Johnson remark or the car-spitting, I had instantly and unthinkingly been rendered interchangeable and anonymous. The experience of double consciousness that DuBois talked about has taken different forms over the hundred years since he first coined the expression, but it certainly hasn't gone away. The surreal sensation of "always looking at one's self through the eyes of others, of measuring one's soul by the tape of a world that looks on in amused contempt and pity,"[4] as he so memorably put it, has meant for me a sense of double consciousness that sometimes actively but always, at least, passively

---

[2] Ibid.

[3] I have also discussed racial devaluation in an article that appeared in *Dalhousie Review* (Stewart, 1996).

[4] DuBois, 1903/1999, p. 11.

inflects every part of my life within this profession. One can only imagine what Harvard must have been like for DuBois.

After the spitting incident and the ensuing car chase, I went home to complete a seminar presentation I had to deliver in a class the following day. The class was on post-coloniality, and the seminar was supposed to be on Chinua Achebe's landmark novel *Things Fall Apart* (1958); but after just having my car spat on, I no longer wanted to talk about Achebe. Instead, I decided to talk about how having my car spat on made questions of post-coloniality purely theoretical and, for the time being anyway, irrelevant to me. In effect, how having my car spat on made me less me. After I finished my presentation, the stunned, awkward silence was finally broken by a classmate who wanted to know how my remarks related to *Things Fall Apart*. For this, I didn't have an answer, although I attempted to mumble something in an effort to answer the question and distract myself from my rage and the intense desire to scream at him, "WE'RE NOT TALKING ABOUT THAT NOW!"

That day in class taught me something that wasn't on the syllabus. It taught me that the academic space was a different space for me than it was for most of my classmates. I now recognize that will probably always be the case. It would have been all right for me to talk about Achebe in the expected way — academically, dispassionately, according to the frame of reference we'd agreed upon in advance — but to incorporate into the seminar room the personal experience of the only person in the room who had actually encountered the effects of racial devaluation in the post-colonial world was to breach the rules of the club and, as I felt at the time and on numerous occasions since, to risk my membership in the club altogether.

I also learned that while everyone within the academy talks about equity, diversity, and representation within the classroom and the profession as a matter of course, some have the privilege to choose when they are going to struggle with such questions while "others" don't. Privilege is nothing if not the ability to take things — and oneself — for granted. What if I had yelled at my classmate on that day or in another class when, as we left the room for a break, a classmate informed me that I resembled Michael Jordan? Would I be confirming an already-existing stereotype, never stated but never far from the surface, of the potential threat of the black man? For some, probably. And this is a group of highly educated people who "should know better." These are the lessons of racial devaluation: that, even among people who should know better, one isn't safe from the unintentional or unthinking slights and insults that remind you that you don't necessarily, or at least unproblematically, belong in a particular space.

The car-spitting episode also provides another example of how racial devaluation makes the space in which I make my living different from that in which most of my colleagues work. Sure, someone thought so little of me (and again, not even of **me** as an individual, but as an anonymous member of a hated group) that he decided to make his point by spitting on my car as I waited for a traffic light to change colour. But to me, the crucial additional information is that the young man in question was of university age. While some would like to harbour the belief that a university-educated person wouldn't do such a thing, my experience says different. And so I can't help but wonder if, out there somewhere, a male student had a great laugh at my expense by spitting on my car one night and then walking past me unrecognized in the hall, even the following day. Every time a young person says something bigoted in my hearing, I can't help but wonder what some of my students really think of me and people who look like me. And I'm here to tell you that sometimes, in class even, you can see it in their faces.

The various costs of membership extend far beyond merely the ability to be counted among the elite who teach at the nation's universities. It also includes the ability to call oneself "Canadian." To be a Canadian, it would appear, is to be more open-minded, less nationalistic, and, perhaps most of all, less bigoted than an American. But as someone who has experienced all of the slights, insults, and injuries of racial devaluation while growing up in Canada, I have often wondered where that national self-image came from. If anything, to live in Canada is to pretend that race is not a problem. Again, privilege is nothing if not the ability to take things for granted. This is a luxury to which Americans simply do not have access. By contrast, in Canada we live in a state of dishonesty that is at times offensive when it comes up against the reality, obvious to some who live here, that Canada has not transcended questions of race, nationalist proclamations notwithstanding. But once again, to say such things is to risk one's acceptance, one's membership, as a Canadian — if we don't have the image as a just, fair, and, most important, colour-blind society, then what do we have?

I should say at this point that I am not trying to make the case that Canadian racism is "better" or "worse" than American racism. Such a comparison would be stupid, as well as beside the point. I am saying that they are different and complex in their own ways. But it's crucial to say that Canada should not be let off the hook when it comes to questions of race even if saying this means breaking rank with the national myth. To continue such pretense also actively increases the frustration of people like me.

The notion of breaking rank adds a further level of complexity to the question of race and my position in the academy in Canada. After all, I have the privilege of expressing in print what many black Canadians already know and have experienced in private, or at least in silence. If I'm right, and most blacks living in Canada know already what I'm talking about here, then am I writing in order to inform those white Canadians who otherwise would continue to insist that Canada does not have a race problem? More important, does my writing these words actually allow me to be co-opted by the interest I am trying to resist — the illusion of racial tranquillity in Canada? After all, I am "allowed" to make these statements in print, which suggests enough space, peace, and leisure to contemplate such problems. In fact, to think and write about such things is a substantial part of my job.

But if most blacks in Canada know as much as I do about the effects of racial devaluation, and most whites in Canada do not know — or do not have to know — what I and other blacks in Canada already know, and if very few blacks in Canada work in the academy, as is obviously the case, then who am I writing for? bell hooks says that "every black writer knows that the people you may most want to hear your words may never read them...."[5] If this is true anywhere, it is true in the academy, where we write mostly for the consumption of other academics.

What all this means is that who I am in this job necessitates looking outside the profession and requires that I periodically break rank, reminding me that my membership does not come with the same privileges that most of my colleagues enjoy. But maybe it's best that it doesn't. Bonnie TuSmith's comments about the hierarchical relationship between the "Big-T" Theory, which has as its basis the Western Enlightenment tradition, and the "small-t" theory which attempts to make space for historically marginalized perspectives, helps to explain the dynamics of the insider and the outsider in relation to the academic profession as a whole:

> If Theory requires ironic distance, as the thinking goes, then active — or "subjective" in a negative sense — engagement with a work of literature could not be Theory. In the need for hierarchical division, Theorists retain the high ground of pure thought while everyone else — especially those who do not maintain the mandatory distance from the creative text, the writer, or the reader — is relegated to the inferior realm of practice.[6]

In the present context, only if I restrict my gaze to the inner sanctum of the academy — with the ironic distance that does not take into account questions of, for instance, why there are so few black students in my classes — do I stand a chance of approximating membership in the academy on the terms as they appear to me at present. But such membership would come at the high cost of no longer being who I really am.

···

Three university degrees and six years of experience teaching at a university behind me, and yet I still do not feel like I "belong" in the academy. Moreover, I am not convinced I will ever completely feel that I do. If this is the case, then it is no wonder that there aren't more blacks in my classes, or in the English program at my university, or, for that matter, at other Canadian universities in general. This deficit is interesting when you remember that there is more discussion of the work of non-white writers in classrooms than ever before. But discussions of post-coloniality, which are dominated by the discourse of the Big-T, do not make black students feel any more comfortable in the university setting than they would feel if they were reading Shakespeare, Dickens, and Eliot. Post-colonialism sets out an array of theoretical problems that are of little help when someone is called a nigger, has his car spat on, or feels out of place in the university environment. The awkward silence in the classroom or at the conference when such an observation is raised by the only black person in the room does not help either. Such everyday conditions, compounded by implicit and explicit suspicions that persist about blacks, make the university environment not only uncomfortable but, for some, downright hostile. It's no wonder that our classrooms still look as they do. If the student popula-

---

[5] hooks, 1990, p. 11.

[6] TuSmith, 1996, p. 63.

tion is changing slowly in the United States, it is changing at a positiv
pace in Canadian universities.

This said, the extreme minority position occupied in the university by someone like me actually brings with it opportunities and glimpses of progress. I see
the positive potential every year in the expressions of some of my students on
the first day of class as they realize: "**He's** the professor?" Since I don't look
like what they expect, I don't have any model, in their eyes, to restrict me.
This is liberating. I will usually, at some point in a course, address this question of expectations, irrespective of whether the class is "African-American Literature" or "Modern British Literature." While some of my students resent my
suggestion that I don't "look like a university professor" to some of them —
they resent this assertion because Canada doesn't have a race problem, after all
— my relative uniqueness in this profession and in their time at university gives
me the opportunity to draw to their attention to details and experiences that
might otherwise continue to be overlooked.

One such detail I like to stress is the "pale, well dressed Negro"[7] in Fitzgerald's *The Great Gatsby* (1925). He is the only character who can identify
Gatsby's yellow car after it kills Myrtle Wilson; he and Nick Carraway are the
only people who hear Tom Buchanan tell the distraught Mr. Wilson, Myrtle's
husband, that he had not seen the yellow car all afternoon, thus securing in
Wilson's mind, erroneously, that it must have been Gatsby who ran Myrtle
down. In a great irony in the book, the "pale, well dressed Negro's" identification of Gatsby's car helps out Tom Buchanan because Wilson subsequently
murders Gatsby as a result of this identification, even though Daisy was actually driving the car. Since Tom Buchanan is the most explicitly bigoted character in the novel, citing at one point the warning in *The Rise of the Coloured
Empires*[8] that "if we don't look out the white race will be — will be utterly sub-
merged,"[9] the "pale, well dressed Negro's" appearance at this precise moment
in the novel is a clever commentary on the nature of America, in which peoples of different races and opposing interests can routinely share space at the
most crucial of moments.[10] As Ralph Ellison writes in his essay "The Little
Man at Chehaw Station":

> How ironic it was that in the world of *The Great Gatsby* the witness who could have
> identified the driver of the death car that led to Gatsby's murder was a black man
> whose ability to communicate (and communication implies moral judgment) was of no
> more consequence to the action than that of an ox that might have observed Icarus's
> sad plunge into the sea.[11]

---

[7] Fitzgerald, 1925/1995.

[8] As Matthew J. Bruccoli (1991) tells us, the title *The Rise of the Coloured Empires* is an allusion
to *The Rising Tide of Color* by Lothrop Stoddard, "but it seems clear that Fitzgerald did not want
to provide the correct title and author" (p. 208).

[9] Fitzgerald, 1925/1999, p. 17.

[10] As I completed an early draft of this essay, the world was still in shock from the attacks on the
World Trade Center and the Pentagon. One cannot help but lament that the solidarity of "one nation under God" seems only possible in the United States in such moments of crisis. Even now, as
the first anniversary of the tragedy recedes into memory, things appear to be returning, unfortunately, to normal.

[11] Ellison, 1986, p. 14.

Ellison finishes his observation tellingly, pointing out that it is not "intended as a criticism of Fitzgerald, only to suggest some of the problems and possibilities of artistic communication in the U.S.A."[12] In other words, this unnamed and, usually, unnoticed character is racially devalued by the text and, more important, by most readings of it. In order to counteract this insidious effect, this character must be acknowledged consciously. This is not how *Gatsby* was ever taught to me as an undergraduate or in graduate school but, because of my experience with and sensitivity to questions of race, I can now present such observations to my students. It strikes me that this is progress.

My reliance upon American sources in this paper is, finally, illustrative of the point I've been making about the inevitability of breaking rank as a black academic in Canada and, maybe, as a black Canadian generally. For all of the problems of race that form the history of the United States, that is the national culture that has provided me with the most consistently sustaining, consoling, and inspiring stories. Since Canada's national story pretends that race is not a Canadian problem, such stories have, generally, not tended to emerge from here. As I look outside the country for sustenance, though, I can still bring back to the classroom what I've found elsewhere. Such a position is never easy, but in the ways it illuminates the profession and momentarily relieves the pressures of maintaining one's membership, it's a relief to perform with the panels up from time to time.

References

Bruccoli, Matthew J. (1991). Notes and Preface. *The Great Gatsby: The authorized text* (pp. vii–xvi). New York: Scribner. (Original work published in 1925.)

DuBois, W.E.B. (1999). *The souls of black folk* (Henry Louis Gates, Jr. & Terri Hume Oliver, Eds.) (Norton Critical Edition). New York: Norton. (Original work published 1903)

Ellison, Ralph. (1986). The little man at Chehaw station. In *Going to the Territory*. New York: Vintage.

Fitzgerald, F. Scott. (1995). *The great gatsby*. New York: Simon & Schuster. (Original work published in 1925)

hooks, bell. (1990). *Yearning: Race, gender, and cultural politics*. Toronto: Between the Lines.

Steele, Claude. (1992, April). Race and the schooling of black Americans. *The Atlantic*, 72.

Stewart, Anthony. (1996, Autumn). The professional sports shell game: A black Canadian's reflections on twentieth-century American sports history. *Dalhousie Review, 76*(3), 371–388.

TuSmith, Bonnie. (1996, Fall). Opening up theory. *Colorizing Literary Theory, Modern Language Studies, 26*(4), 59–70.

---

[12] Ibid.

2

Lance Belanger's Tango Lessons
Infiltrating the Museum

Johanna K. Mizgala
Curator — Exhibitions
Strategic Initiatives and Exhibitions
Portrait Gallery of Canada
Library and Archives Canada
Ottawa

I am grateful to Charmaine Nelson and to Camille Nelson for the opportunity to participate in this project. This essay draws from my continuing research on the nature of museums and their collection policies and practices and, in particular, from my Master's thesis, entitled *The Museum in the Work of Lance Bélanger and Richard Purdy*, completed at Concordia University in 1996. My sincere appreciation to both artists for their active collaboration as well as to my professors and mentors for their encouragement and support: the late Jacqueline Fry, Philip Fry, Francine Périnet, Viviane Gray, Olivier Asselin and David Thomas at the University of Ottawa; and Joan Acland, Brian Foss, Catherine Mackenzie, Yolande Racine and Janice Helland at Concordia University. I would also like to thank Jill Delaney and Eva Major-Marothy, my colleagues at the National Archives of Canada, for thoughtful discussion related to this topic. This essay profited from the insightful criticism and commentary of my husband, Jeff Pappone, and to him I extend my heartfelt appreciation.

Johanna K. Mizgala

At first glance, the museum is a space in which objects are displayed in an historical context. This activity is designed to appear neutral, yet further consideration of the museum's societal functions reveals its highly charged political nature. The discourse of the museum is revealed through the selection and exhibition of key objects that typify a dominant cultural ideology. Objects are the punctuation marks that give credence to the creation of "history". As Donald Preziosi has argued:

> All history is perforce a production — a deliberate selection, ordering, and an evaluation of past events, experiences, and processes. Any museum, in incorporating selections and silences, is an ideological apparatus. In addition, every museum generates ways of not seeing and inhibits the capacity of visitors to imagine alternate histories or social orders, past or future.[1]

The exhibition label serves as a metaphor for an exchange occurring within the museum, as it is the site for dialogue between three positions — the maker/creator of the object; the maker/creator of the exhibition; and the viewer. Once inside the museum, an object adopts an explicit context. It is severed from its origins and recontextualized by its relationship to this new space. Its meaning is thus relational — one that cannot be separated from its place in the museum's collection. The object functions as a passage that may be quoted for proof of the validity of a canon, thereby giving credence to the notion of culture as evidence. This form of history, however, is always a meta-narrative. As this kind of exhibition must appear complete, where is the space for alternate and/or contradictory voices?

Museum collections are subjective interpretations of cultural beliefs and values. Moreover, the fact that an exhibition is a construction from a particular point of view is subverted by its design, which seduces the viewer into believing that the objects have either effortlessly come together on their own, or that they represent some kind of accurate whole. The silences, those objects that do not fit into this structure, are rendered invisible within the exhibition. Likewise, in order to preserve the seamless quality of the exhibition, the objects must be frozen in time. According to Robert Harbison:

> The result museums seek is an end to change, a perfect stasis or stillness; they are the final buildings on the earth. We point to the denial embodied in museums by our difficulty imagining the inclusion in them of objects now outside. In order to enter, an object must die, and a non-museum object chosen for a museum is enviable like a maiden elected for sacrifice.[2]

---

[1] Preziosi, 1989, p. 70.

[2] Harbison, 1977, p. 147.

The gaps in a collection are sometimes more revealing about the ideology of the museum than those objects that are on display, as they signify those things that do not conform. Seeing is believing. If something is not present in the museum, it has been deemed unworthy of collection and display. Adherence to the supremacy of the visible, as opposed to acceptance of a necessary absence, conforms to Praises's assertion that the silences within exhibitions inhibit the viewer's ability to question the accepted version of history.[3]

Museums collect objects in order to name them, study them and, ultimately, exhibit them in a means that produces and validates knowledge of them. Collecting is the sustenance that keeps museums alive. Stockpiling material for emphasis implies a need to accumulate the "best" things available. This requirement is increased exponentially when the material in question is chosen from another culture. When objects signify cultures, the selection process follows a predetermined criterion — they must be **beautiful**, **unique**, and **authentic**. It is essential to "rescue" culture through object collecting in order to avoid the effects of change, or the disappearance of culture in its pristine condition. Provided that objects are preserved in climate-controlled cases, the work of the museum is done.

This debate extends to the **art gallery** as well. Commercial galleries have their own history of selection, rarefaction and exclusion, but here I speak of the gallery as a space that houses art for exhibition in a canonical representation. Both the gallery and the museum subscribe to what James Clifford characterizes as the "salvage paradigm":

> The salvage paradigm, reflecting a desire to rescue "authenticity" out of destructive, historical change is alive and well. It is found not only in ethnographic writing but also in the connoisseurships and collections of the art world and in a range of familiar nostalgias. In short, the term names a geopolitical, historical paradigm that has organized western practices of "art-and-culture-collecting".[4]

The museum functions both as a system of administration and instruction. Museums, those treasure troves of the past, promote national or regional identities. This activity is by no means unique to the Canadian context, but the fact that "identity" is mentioned so forcefully in its museums' mandates merits further consideration.[5] We must ask ourselves whose identity is promoted, by whom and for whom. Is it possible to represent identity at all? What happens when identity is spoken for you, as borrowed pieces are utilized to paint a larger picture for the dominant culture? This is the situation of First Nations peoples in Canada, as notions of plurality, diversity and difference historically were erased in favour of the myths explored by Daniel Francis in his book *The Imaginary Indian: The Image of the Indian in Canadian Culture*. Francis traces

---

[3] Preziosi, 1989, p. 70.

[4] Clifford, 1987, p. 121.

[5] The mandate of the Department of Canadian Heritage, the governmental body that stewards Canadian museums, is to "promote Canada's distinctive identity and its cultural and natural heritage." One of the programs the department operates is entitled the "Canadian Identity Program", and Canada's cultural institutions are outlined as one of the main activities of this program. For more information, please consult the department's website: http://www.pch.gc.ca

the effigy of the Imaginary Indian through the work of artists and writers who believed they had captured the essence of a "vanishing" people:

> When they drew the Indians or took their photographs, artists like Kane, Curtis and the rest were taking possession of the Indian image. It was now theirs to manipulate and display in any way they wanted. The image-makers returned from Indian Country with their images and displayed them as actual representations of the way Indians really were. Fanciful as they were in so many respects, these images nevertheless became Indian for most non-Native Canadians who knew no other.[6]

The Imaginary Indian is a construction that extends to all aspects of cultural production, with profound implications for issues around museum practice. The "fixity" of an image is what gives rise to its power.[7] Alternative voices are silenced through the destruction of instances of difference. As Francis points out, while the museum was greedily walling up Native objects, the Canadian government was ensuring that the images stayed "fixed":

> Government attempts to eradicate displays of traditional Native culture were part of a larger policy aimed at stamping out all practices which the Indian department believed stood in the way of the assimilation of Native people. Chief among these were the potlatch on the West Coast, and the sun dance among Plains Natives.[8]

The Imaginary Indian must be addressed not only in light of accepted doctrines of history, but also in relation to the canon of art history, which likewise eradicated dissension from its hierarchies through erasures and omissions.

The 1990s witnessed unprecedented interest in Contemporary First Nations Art in Canada. The decade was marked by a media frenzy surrounding the Oka Crisis, debate and legal action around abuses committed in residential schools, growing civil unrest over land claim issues, and the call to self-government and self-determination.[9] Indigenous artists responded socially and politically through their practice, which was both activist and introspective. In 1992, two Canadian federal cultural institutions presented large-scale special exhibitions of First Nations work — *Land, Spirit, Power* at the National Gallery of Canada, and *Indigena: Contemporary Native Perspectives* at the Canadian Museum of Civilization. The year marked the 500th anniversary of the arrival of Columbus in the Americas, and the call for sombre reflection greatly outweighed plans for celebration. Following these high-profile exhibitions, both institutions made a number of significant acquisitions for their collections. It appeared that First Nations artists' work would hold a place of rightful honour within Canadian art institutions. A little more than a decade later, however, the earlier fervour has merely inched museums towards more inclusionary exhibition strategies, and the work of indigenous artists is still, for the most part, dis-

---

[6] Francis, 1992, p. 43.

[7] Please refer to the discussion of colonial stereotypes in Bhabha, 1990.

[8] Francis, 1992, pp. 98–99.

[9] To review news coverage of the Oka Crisis, please consult the following National Film Board videos: *CBC News in Review: Charlottetown Accord Pre-Referendum Developments*: first segment, October 1992; *Kanehsatake: 270 Years of Resistance*, NFB 1993; *Acts of Defiance:* NFB 1992; *CBC News in Review: Oka Crisis*, second segment, September 1990; as well as the following website: http://www.newsworld.cbc.ca/flashback/1990/index.html

played only in relation to that of other indigenous artists — approximating the equivalent of a reserve inside the museum.

In efforts to combat the museum's exclusions and silences, Maliseet artist Lance Belanger employs a position of resistance as a strategy to infiltrate its walls. He categorically situates himself in the margins and, by doing so, hopes to turn the tables by embracing the perimeter as a position of strength:

> A margin has been created for us, a place on the sidelines for our enjoyment. We are allowed to play with appropriate toys given to us to occupy our time and make little accomplishments. The margin is necessary as a way to explain our existence. It is necessary as a way to understand why we are here. It is a lifeboat to cling to in a sea of historical ambiguity. It is a place on the sidelines to scream from as the game is played on the field. It is the place between the edge of the page and the content of dialogue and opinion. I take no pleasure in being a fleeting image from the margin, nor is it my ambition to find fame there among my peers. It is simply the excitement of the thrill of the chase and the need to continue to think as a free man with opinions about the world. There is no margin in the ballroom of the Tango.[10]

From this space of contemplation and production, Belanger critiques the museum's collection and exhibition practices. His works pay homage to the monuments and to the moments of the past, and though they are generated from his lived experience, they do not define the extent of his expression. As Claudette Fortin has commented:

> Born a New Brunswick Maliseet Indian, [Bélanger] rejects being cast as a spokesperson on behalf of the Native Indian people. He has chosen instead to make manifest his personal experience as an individual, and as an artist to communicate a visual record of the realities and the particulars of his own existence.[11]

Thus, while Belanger's racial/tribal affiliations are inseparable from who he is, they do not represent **all** he is. This is a very subtle distinction within the context of the art world, as it can prove difficult to discern between analysis of a work and analysis of an artist. The danger in too much focus on an artist's origins is that it leads to a neglect of the work itself — who it can speak to, and who it speaks about. To be "traditional" as a First Nations artist is to risk becoming stuck in the museum's ethnographic margins. To reject tradition, however, is to deny the opportunity to reclaim, to redefine, and to rediscover the past. Belanger's works are rooted in traditions that he does not deny, but he is conscious that they exist and were created in a larger context.

In 1988, Belanger began to explore the boundaries of painting, prompting him to question its envelope — the frame. Using enclosures made from found objects, Belanger marked out terrain for observation, referring to the gilded frames as "icons of European art."[12] In this way, the frame was a determining factor that enabled Belanger to direct the viewer's eye away from a straightforward appreciation of the painted surface or assemblage, shifting the focus to the act of looking at art. The frame is an undeniable reference to the spaces within the museum. It signifies that the object has been deemed worthy to be

---

[10] Belanger, 1995, p. 14.

[11] Fortin, 1988, p. 10.

[12] Belanger, 1990, p. 3.

beheld, as it is "the usual sign of art as precious object."[13] Using this condition as a key, Belanger works under the assumption that he has a captive audience. He is thus at liberty not only to examine whatever object he desires, but also to deconstruct some assumptions about aesthetic values. In effect, the frame transforms the paintings into sculptures, as they must be read in terms of the sum of their parts. Belanger states:

> [The] frames form a consistent envelope, a border or boundary for the Indigenous aesthetic inherent in the fur. The paintings or assemblages speak of an issue in contemporary Indigenous art that addresses the relationship of Contemporary Indigenous expression to contemporary western art. A bitter peel for a sweet fruit.[14]

Belanger expanded upon the frame series by incorporating an icon of modern technology — the computer chip. There is a simple beauty to the microchips he uses, with their colours and arrangement suggestive of an aerial view of the urban landscape. The unifying component in these works is undeniably the human hand, as the found objects have been used, and thus valued. Belanger's juxtaposition of fur pelts with computer chips acts as a metaphor for the complexity of contemporary existence by incorporating aspects of the traditional and the historical significance of the fur trade in Canada and aspects of technology, which are simultaneously a help and a hindrance to traditional ways of life. For Belanger, an additional layer of reference personalizes the works:

> [I realized] the similarity they had with Indian political organizational charts, that depicted diagrams and flow charts of what forms Indian self-government might take. While I had been employed with the National Indian Brotherhood[15] in the late 70s and early 80s, I saw literally hundreds of those organizational charts that projected Indian political systems of government and how they might be associated with provincial and federal governments.[16]

For Belanger, the circuitry is emblematic of his community and of himself. This coupling returns Belanger to the tango metaphor — contemporary existence firmly rooted in, and acknowledging, the traditional.

Belanger created the work entitled *Canadian Summer Colours* (1991) during the aftermath of the Oka Crisis (Figure 2–1). In the spring of 1990, a group of Mohawk people blocked a road going through the Kanehsatake reserve leading to the town of Oka, Québec, in protest over the proposed extension of a golf course over the Mohawks' ancestral burial ground.[17] This crisis escalated into a media event, and Belanger's work explores this scrutiny through the use of a television screen filled with camouflage fabric mounted on an olive-drab background. The screen appears to be held on the canvas by pins, much in the same way that insects are displayed. The most striking component of this work is the gold frame around the television screen — it is broken. Breaking the

---

[13] Greenberg, 1982, p. 30.

[14] Belanger, 1990, p. 3.

[15] Now called the Assembly of First Nations.

[16] Belanger, 1990, p. 4.

[17] For further information, please consult Alanis Obomsawin's film *Kanehsatake: 270 Years of Resistance* (1993).

Figure 2–1

Lance Belanger, Canadian Summer Colours, 1991. Mixed media, 16 × 20 inches. Collection of the Indian Art Centre, Indian and Northern Affairs Canada.

frame implies a physical display of anger as well as a rejection of the privileging of Western aesthetic values.

In his installations such as *Taino Memorial* (1989), Belanger ventures away from the exploration of the European versus the Indigenous aesthetic towards the recovery of memories and peoples that have been lost to "history". The installation is a testament to the first peoples encountered by Columbus in the "New World." The Taino were annihilated as a result of this encounter. Bélanger unites painting and assemblage in this work, creating a space in which the viewer can reflect upon the people's absence. The central aspect of the work is the black cross, which divides the field of vision. Around the neck of the cross is a rosary made of alternating rows of beer caps and beads, alluding to the devastating effects of alcoholism and the legacy of the Catholic Church on First Nations communities. An opened chest below the cross contains spices — the much-sought-after riches of the land. Behind the black cross is a grey canvas. This piece possesses a quiet, sombre beauty. Like any memorial, it requires a moment of silence.

Belanger's subsequent installation, *Lithic Spheres* (1991), is deliberately ambiguous. The work is a scattered mound of round "stones," painted in metallic colours, creating an air of "pricelessness". There are, in fact, 500 spheres — one for each year after Columbus, and while this information lends a certain poignancy to the work, it isn't crucial to count them. The sheer volume presented emphasizes the element of time in the work, as the placement of the spheres is measured and deliberate. Confronted with this work, the desire to reach out and pick up one of the spheres is overwhelming. At the same time, there is the distinct sensation that this pile is important, and that the integrity of its placement should be respected. Whether or not the viewer is aware of the fact that the spheres recall Taino monuments unearthed in South and Central America,[18] there is no question that they are significant in some way.

Both *Taino Memorial* and *Lithic Spheres* pose questions about loss — the loss of tradition itself, and the loss of objects that enable a community to maintain tradition. For Indigenous peoples in North America, the power of the keepers of tradition has been eroded by the power of the museum and its creation — the "Imaginary Indian".

The legitimacy of oral traditions is jeopardized by the devious authority of the museum. Belanger's installations speak out against the silences present within the walls of the museum. Likewise, the works from his *Fur Series* share this desire to overcome silence, as the meaning of the objects encompassed within the frames has been altered by virtue of this position. Belanger merges influences from the past and the present in order to create a body of work that exemplifies what it means for him to navigate through Canadian society as a First Nations person. His works offer no easy answers; instead, they open up paths upon which one can begin a journey.

Any practice, including art history, that fixes a given culture, class, gender or race is a mechanism for the dominant group's ideological position. Changing the way art is collected, exhibited, and discussed becomes a conscious effort to do away with the practice that Griselda Pollock terms the "**and** syndrome":

> Society is a historical process; it is not a static entity. History cannot be reduced to a manageable block of information; it has to be grasped itself as a complex of processes and relationships. I suggest that we have to abandon all the formulations such as "art **and** society" or "art **and** its social context," "art **and** its historical background," "art **and** its formation," "art **and** gender relations." All the real difficulty which is not being confronted resides in those "**ands**".[19]

That tradition or convention keeps art separate from the rest of experience by an "and" is at the root of the museum question. First Nations art has been kept and exhibited separately from the rest of Canadian art. In spite of the fact that museums are inherently resistant to change, there are signs of encouragement. Plans are under way at the National Gallery of Canada and at the Art Gallery of Ontario to reinstall their galleries of Canadian art, in a manner that would be more inclusive of First Nations works. Moreover, the Art Gallery of Ontario has implemented shifts in its hiring practices with the inauguration of the position of First Nations Curator. The new hangings at both institutions will integrate historical and contemporary First Nations art within the chronological spaces that traditionally display works by the dominant Canadian culture, and will be carried out in consultation with a panel of First Nations curators, artists

---

[18] Author's conversation with the artist, February 24, 1994.

[19] Pollock, 1988, p. 30.

and community leaders. These are bold steps for institutions, as the resulting exhibition spaces will force them to examine their own relationship to the legacy of erasure. Meaningful dialogue where once there was silence and immovability will lead the way to measurable changes.

Referennces

Belanger, Lance (1990, April). New fur for the old frame. Unpublished lecture notes.

Belanger, Lance. (1995). Title essay. *Tango*. Ottawa: The Ottawa Art Gallery.

Bhabha, Homi K. (1990). The other question: Difference, discrimination and the discourse of colonialism. In Russell Ferguson et al. (Eds.), *Out There: Marginalization and Contemporary Culture*. Cambridge: The M.I.T. Press.

Clifford, James. (1987). Transcript of discussion section from "Of Other Peoples: Beyond the 'Salvage Paradigm'". In Hal Foster (Ed.), *DIA Art Foundation Discussions in Contemporary Culture*. Seattle: Bay Press.

Fortin, Claudette (1988). *Lance Bélanger* Santo Domingo: Paiewonsky Gallery.

Francis, Daniel. (1992). *The Imaginary Indian: The Image of the Indian in Canadian Culture*. Vancouver: Arsenal Pulp Press.

Greenberg, Reesa. (1982, March–May). MOMA and Modernism: The frame game. *Parachute*, 42, 30.

Harbison, Robert. (1977). *Eccentric Spaces*. Boston: David R. Godine.

Obomsawin, Alanis. (1993). *Kanehsatake: 270 Years of Resistance* [Motion picture]. Montreal, PQ: National Film Board of Canada.

Pollock, Griselda. (1988). *Vision and Difference: Femininity, Feminism and the Histories of Art*. New York: Routledge.

Praises, Donald. (1989). *Rethinking Art History: Meditations on a Coy Science*. New Haven: Yale University Press.

3

The Black Occupational Structure in Late-Nineteenth-Century Ontario
Evidence from the Census

Colin McFarquhar
Researcher
Leclair Historical Research
Toronto

In the years prior to the American Civil War, what is now the province of Ontario became the home for thousands of American blacks. This period, the era of the Underground Railroad, has received considerable attention from historians.[1] The period after 1865, however, has received less attention. Indeed, Ontario's black population was relatively small in the late nineteenth century and steadily decreased in size from the end of the Civil War until the turn of the century. Census figures reveal that there were 13,435 people of African origin in the province in 1871, but by 1901 this number had shrunk to 8,935.[2] The decline can be attributed to the fact that relatively few blacks arrived in Ontario during these years, and others moved back to the United States. With the end of the Civil War, blacks no longer needed to come to Canada to escape slavery. Nor did they need to worry about being captured by their former slaveowners while they lived as freemen in the northern states. Consequently, few blacks entered Ontario after 1865. Most movement was in the other direction, as an unknown number of blacks returned to the United States after the Civil War, often to return to their former homes or to be with family members who remained in the United States.

Although blacks were scattered throughout the province (most Ontario towns had at least a few) they were more prevalent in some places than in others. Demographic patterns that had been established prior to the American Civil War continued in the years after 1865. Blacks were most heavily concentrated in southwestern Ontario, in Essex and Kent counties, while others gathered in the Niagara region.[3] Cities and towns such as Toronto, Hamilton, and London also had sizeable populations. Few blacks lived in other parts of the province, places that had little connection with or proximity to Underground Railroad entry points.

For the blacks who lived in Ontario, what were conditions like? How were they adapting to Ontario in the late nineteenth century? One clue is to examine the occupational histories of blacks. This paper uses three Ontario censuses, those of 1871, 1881, and 1901, to reveal the black occupational structure.[4] Three central questions will be considered. One is the extent to which the types of occupations blacks performed differed from the surrounding white population. (Blacks, of course, were not the only visible minorities in Ontario at this time. There were large numbers of Native people as well, but during the examined time periods they were not common in the places discussed in this paper

---

[1] See, for example, Murray, 1960; Silverman, 1985; Simpson, 1971; Stouffer, 1992.

[2] *Census of Canada,* 1873, p. 280 and *Report of the Fourth Census,* 1902, p. 313.

[3] Blacks initially concentrated in these places because of their proximity to Windsor, Amherstburg, and St. Catharines, major terminuses for the Underground Railroad.

[4] The 1891 census has not been used because this census did not record people by ethnic origin, and the number of blacks in the province therefore cannot be identified.

and are, therefore, not discussed). A second question is the extent to which the black occupational pattern varied over different parts of the province. A third question is the degree to which the black occupational structure changed over the years in question.

Census data is highly useful for this task because census takers recorded the occupation of each person while they were conducting the enumeration. This paper will focus on five different towns or cities in Ontario. The five places studied were Toronto, Hamilton, St. Catharines, Windsor and Amherstburg. Each place was somewhat special. Toronto was the largest city in the province and had a significant black population. There were 551 blacks in Toronto in 1871, and 592 in 1901.[5] However, as can be seen in Table 3–1, blacks formed only a small percentage of the city's total population, never more than 1 percent. Toronto had a history as a centre of abolitionist activity during the 1850s, and the Anti-Slavery Society of Canada, an organization that opposed slavery and assisted fugitive slaves arriving in Canada, had been based there. Toronto was also unique among Ontario towns with significant black populations in that it had never had separate schools for blacks. Hamilton also had a sizeable black population although, like Toronto, it was a relatively small percentage of the total city population. St. Catharines was a smaller city, close to the American border, and many blacks had fled there during the pre-Civil War period. In fact, St. Catharines had served as the chief terminal for the anti-slavery activities of noted black American Harriet Tubman.[6] The presence of blacks was more evident in this community than in Toronto or Hamilton, at least as evidenced through the press. The unsuccessful attempt of blacks in the 1870s to gain access to the common schools, for example, was given consider-able attention in the community's newspapers.[7] The black presence, however, was especially pronounced in Windsor and Amherstburg, both located in Essex county, in the southwestern part of the province. These places had served as major terminuses of the Underground Railroad. Like St. Catharines, both places had separate black schools. Blacks were a significant and much more vis-ible part of the population in these places. As can be seen in Table 3–1, blacks made up a much greater percentage of the total population in these communi-ties. Blacks in Windsor, for example, made up more than 20 percent of the town's population in 1871, while in Amherstburg they accounted for more than 15 percent of the population.

How did the black occupational structure compare with that of the white population? And how did the black occupational structure vary over different parts of the province? Census data shows that blacks were consistently under-represented, in comparison with the population of the province as a whole, in white collar occupations, and were consistently over-represented in low-skill blue-collar occupations. This pattern was evident throughout the province. It existed in places where blacks formed a comparatively large proportion of the

---

[5] *Census of Canada,* 1873, p. 266 and *Report on the Fourth Census,* 1902, p. 345.

[6] Hill, 1981, p. 39.

[7] The *Evening Journal* and the *Daily Times* gave considerable attention to the controversy over sep-arate schools in the early 1870s.

Table 3–1   Blacks as a Percentage of the Total Population of
             Amherstburg, St. Catharines, Hamilton, Toronto,
             and Windsor in 1871 and 1901

City/Town	Blacks as % of population in 1871	Blacks as % of population in 1901
Amherstburg	15.5	12.4
Windsor	20.6	7.7
St. Catharines	6.1	1.8
Hamilton	1.3	0.9
Toronto	1.0	0.4

Source: *Census of Canada*, 1873 and *Report of the Fourth Census*, 1901.

population, such as Essex county, and in places where they made up a much smaller percentage of the population, such as Hamilton and Toronto.

Tables 3–2, 3–3 and 3–4 are based on the 1881 census returns for Toronto, Hamilton, and Essex county. The 1881 census is especially valuable for determining how the black population compared with the surrounding population in terms of occupations performed. The tables illustrate the extent to which the occupational structure of blacks differed from the remainder of the population in these three places. An examination of the tables suggests that a much higher percentage of black workers were employed as common labourers than was the case for the population as a whole. In Essex county, blacks were twice as common as labourers than the population as a whole. In the cities of Hamilton and Toronto, black overrepresentation as common labourers was almost as pronounced, as can be seen by Tables 3–2 and 3–3. Other low-skill occupations tended to have black overrepresentation as well. As can be seen in Table 3–2, blacks in Toronto dominated the whitewashing profession. Throughout the province, blacks were much more prevalent as laundresses than were whites. Since this was a profession dominated by women, it seems reasonable to conclude that black women as well as men tended to occupy low-skill jobs.

These tables also make clear that blacks tended to be somewhat under-represented in more skilled blue-collar occupations. They were, for example, less common as carpenters and joiners. It is, however, important to note that many blacks performed certain semi-skilled occupations. There were significant numbers of black dressmakers and milliners, and tailors and clothiers. Blacks were certainly not restricted to low-skill labouring jobs, but they tended to be more pronounced in this area, and less common in more skilled work.

What is most striking about the tables, however, is the almost complete absence of blacks in white-collar occupations throughout the province. Blacks were almost non-existent as commercial clerks in all three of the places represented in the tables. Of the 259 commercial clerks in Essex county, only two were black. There were, in 1881, 2,363 commercial clerks in Toronto, but only

Table 3–2 **Percentage of Employed Blacks and Percentage of Employed Persons in Various Occupations in Toronto in 1881**

Occupation	% of employed blacks in this occupation	% of all workers in this occupation
Labourers	13.1	7.9
Barbers and Hairdressers	13.5	0.4
Laundresses	9.1	0.6
Commercial Clerks	0.4	7.4
Accountants and Bookkeepers	0.0	1.8
Engineers and Machinists	0.4	2.5

Table 3–3 **Percentage of Employed Blacks and Percentage of Employed Persons in Various Occupations in Hamilton in 1881**

Occupation	% of employed blacks in this occupation	% of all workers in this occupation
Labourers	18.2	9.9
Barbers and Hairdressers	9.5	0.5
Laundresses	5.9	0.4
Commercial Clerks	1.4	6.7
Accountants and Bookkeepers	0.0	1.4
Engineers and Mechanics	0.0	4.9

Table 3–4 **Percentage of Employed Blacks and Percentage of Employed Persons in Various Occupations in Essex County in 1881**

Occupation	% of employed blacks in this occupation	% of all workers in this occupation
Labourers	28.0	14.7
Barbers and Hairdressers	2.7	0.3
Laundresses	2.4	0.2
Commercial Clerks	0.1	1.7
Accountants and Bookkeepers	0.0	0.3
Engineers and Mechanics	0.5	1.1

one was black.[8] Blacks were almost non-existent as agents, accountants, and bookkeepers. There were also few black printers or publishers, and almost no black doctors or physicians. There were also other professions with disproportionately few blacks. Blacks tended to be significantly under-represented as merchants in all three places, although there were more black merchants than clerks. Such staggering results can indicate that such professions were virtually off-limits to blacks throughout the province at this time.

Whites appear to have been uncomfortable or sometimes hostile about having blacks as co-workers. For instance, when Albert Jackson, a black man who lived in Toronto, was appointed a letter carrier in that city in 1882, his white co-workers refused to train him. Only after the prime minister, John A. Macdonald, intervened was Jackson finally allowed to assume his new job.[9] Evidence of white opposition to black co-workers can also be seen by examining the response in the Hamilton press in 1889 to a request by a deputation of black gentlemen for a separate black fire brigade. Blacks in Ontario received few government appointments, and they often protested this state of affairs.[10] The deputation argued that "positions of public trust ... have not hitherto been awarded and distributed with regard to the colored people ... who ... are entitled to a fair share of the public trusts of the city."[11] The *Hamilton Herald*, in an editorial, supported the idea of a separate black fire brigade and acknowledged that "colored citizens are as much entitled to receive public positions which they are competent to fill as are white men," but also noted "that his color is a bar to his getting a position among his white fellow citizens." A separate fire brigade seemed a fair solution to the problem, as in this way "the white people can do justice to the colored class without creating discontent among themselves."[12] In other words, there seemed to be an assumption that a "separate but equal" philosophy was most appropriate in late-nineteenth-century Ontario, since whites did not want blacks as co-workers. This philosophy worked to the disadvantage of blacks, however, as they did not have the numbers or economic clout to form separate institutions such as businesses and banks. In fact, the proposed separate fire brigade never materialized.

Besides low-skill work, there was one other area where blacks were consistently over-represented throughout the province. Many black men were barbers, and a significant number of black women were hairdressers. More than one-half of the barbers and hairdressers in Essex county in 1881 were black, while such was the case for more than one-third in Hamilton, and almost one-quarter in Toronto.[13] It was in this profession, more than anywhere else, where blacks were over-represented. The barbers in these cities must have had a significant

---

[8] *Report of the Census of 1881*, 1884, pp. 294, 305.

[9] *Daily Telegram*, May 20, 1882; *The Evening Telegram*, May 31, 1882, and *The Globe*, June 3, 1882.

[10] Blacks in Hamilton, for example, protested in 1890 that there were no black letter carriers in that city. See *Hamilton Spectator,* July 17, 1890.

[11] *The Globe*, December 26, 1889.

[12] *Hamilton Herald*, December 26, 1889. The idea of a separate brigade seems to imply the racial segregation of the city itself.

[13] *Report of the Census of 1881*, pp. 292, 304 and Microfilm of 1881 Census Rolls, Hamilton, Toronto, and Essex County.

white clientele since the black population could not have supported the number of barbers.

What is clearest from the tables is that the black occupational pattern was similar throughout the province. Blacks were consistently almost non-existent in white-collar occupations. It does not appear to have mattered whether they lived in large or small cities, or in areas that had significant or less significant black populations. The black occupational pattern remained more or less the same. Blacks appear to have faced the same discrimination and opposition to their performance of certain jobs, even in places where they were only a very minor part of the population, such as Hamilton and Toronto. This finding is especially significant in the case of Toronto. Contemporaries of the era often argued that Toronto was different from other cities, and historians have echoed these sentiments.[14] Anderson Ruffin Abbott, a Toronto-born black doctor who lived in southwestern Ontario for a number of years but returned to Toronto in 1890, exuded some optimism that black economic opportunities were steadily improving. In an 1892 letter from Toronto, he noted that blacks were "employed as tradesmen, mechanics, labourers; some are in the service of the government, and a few following professional pursuits, besides the usual quota of waiters, barbers, restaurant and boarding house keepers."[15] It would appear, however, that Abbott was being overly optimistic. Blacks were just as restricted in their range of occupational choices in this city as in the rest of the province.

Another question to be considered is the extent to which the black occupational structure changed over the years. An examination of the censuses of 1871, 1881, and 1901 suggests that the occupational pattern did not change much. As Table 3–5 demonstrates, a study of Windsor, St. Catharines, Hamilton, Toronto, and Amherstburg suggests that the percentage of blacks in skilled and semi-skilled occupations remained fairly constant over the period. The table does suggest that there were considerably more skilled black workers in some cities than in others. These differences can be explained by the fact that each city was unique, and the jobs blacks performed varied according to the opportunities available. There were more skilled workers in Hamilton because of the significant tobacco industry in that city. Amherstburg, on the other hand, had a large number of unskilled workers because the city had numerous marines. The fact that the number of blacks in skilled occupations was not increasing suggests that blacks were being discriminated against. By 1901, most blacks in Ontario had either been born in the province or had lived there for many years since the number of blacks emigrating to Canada from the United States was relatively small in the years following the American Civil War. Despite this fact, blacks were still concentrated in lower-skill occupations.

Nevertheless, some changes were evident. Blacks were steadily losing their dominance of the barbering profession. As can be seen in Tables 3–6 through 3–9, this was true in most areas, although Hamilton witnessed an especially sharp drop in the percentage of blacks who were barbers. Amherstburg and

---

[14] As early as the 1850s this claim had been made by Rev. Ward (1855, pp. 150–151). The historian Daniel Hill noted that "[i]n Toronto ... Blacks met less prejudice since they represented little threat to white residents" (Hill, 1981, p. 105).
[15] Toronto Public Library, Baldwin Room, *A.R. Abbott Papers,* loose clippings, p. 5.

Table 3–5   Percentage of Employed Black Males in Skilled
              and Semi-skilled Work in Selected Towns and Cities
              in 1871, 1881, and 1901*

Town/City	% of workers in skilled or semi-skilled occupations in 1871	% of workers in skilled or semi-skilled occupations in 1881
Amherstburg	27.9	33.0
Windsor	33.2	34.0
St. Catharines	21.4	23.2
Hamilton	69.1	49.4
Toronto	58.2	53.6

* Among the occupations that have been classified as unskilled are the following: labourers, mariners, draymen, servants, whitewashers, waiters, porters, hostlers, drivers, hucksters, bricklayers, servants, and charwomen. Among the jobs that have been classified as skilled or semi-skilled are the following: carpenters, cooks, clerks, barbers, clergymen, tailors, shoemakers, merchants, engineers, plasterers, coopers, blacksmiths, and tobacconists.

Windsor also witnessed sharp declines from 1881 to 1901. The decline was less evident in Toronto, but there was a drop in that city as well. The movement of blacks out of the barbering profession was not restricted to southern Ontario. There was a similar trend in American cities. A study of Cleveland noted that there was a drop in the number of black barbers by 1910,[16] and a study of Detroit shows a steady decline from 1870 to 1920, demonstrating that it was in the late nineteenth century that blacks were being pushed out of the profession. The Detroit study observed that the "declining number of black barbers was due to increased competition from the foreign born, the tightening color line in barbering, and discrimination against black barbershop owners." Technological changes in shaving meant barbers no longer had the stigma attached to them of being in a service occupation, and black barbers in Detroit found themselves reduced to serving a black clientele.[17] A similar trend appears to have been occurring in Ontario.

As can be seen in Tables 3–6 through 3–9, blacks were also not as prominent as carpenters and joiners or as boot- and shoemakers in 1901 as they had been 20 and 30 years earlier. In Ontario, the main growth area for black employment was as porters and, to a lesser degree, as teamsters and drivers. Being a porter on a railway was often the best job a young black male could

16 Kusmer, 1976, pp. 75–76.
17 Katzman, 1973, p. 116.

Table 3–6   Changes in Occupational Pattern from 1871 to 1901
for Employed Black Males in Amherstburg for
Selected Occupations

Occupation	% employed in 1871	% employed in 1881
Labourers	48.8	22.7
Barbers	2.3	5.7
Commercial Clerks	1.2	0.0
Merchants	0.0	1.1
Carpenters and Joiners	7.0	3.4
Boot- and Shoemakers	2.3	2.3

Table 3–7   Changes in Occupational Pattern from 1871 to 1901
for Employed Black Males in Hamilton for Selected
Occupations

Occupation	% employed in 1871	% employed in 1881
Labourers	15.5	25.5
Barbers	14.5	13.1
Commercial Clerks	0.0	2.0
Merchants	0.0	2.0
Carpenters and Joiners	0.9	2.0
Boot- and Shoemakers	5.5	3.3

Table 3–8   Changes in Occupational Pattern from 1871 to 1901
for Employed Black Males in Windsor for Selected
Occupations

Occupation	% employed in 1871	% employed in 1881
Labourers	38.4	39.9
Barbers	3.3	4.9
Commercial Clerks	1.8	0.4
Merchants	1.1	1.5
Carpenters and Joiners	4.4	3.0
Boot- and Shoemakers	1.5	2.2

Table 3–9	Changes in Occupational Pattern from 1871 to 1901 for Employed Blacks in Toronto for Selected Occupations	
Occupation	% employed in 1871	% employed in 1881
Labourers	17.0	18.8
Barbers	18.3	18.2
Commercial Clerks	0.0	0.5
Merchants	0.7	1.6
Carpenters and Joiners	4.6	4.2
Boot- and Shoemakers	5.2	2.1

obtain. In short, blacks were moving from service jobs, such as barbering and, in some cases, waitering to other, less intimate, service jobs, such as portage. For the white community, portage jobs seemed appropriate for blacks because they believed portage was suited to the distinctive black personality. An anonymous writer to *Saturday Night* in 1889 marvelled at black porters when he noted "their inexhaustible stock of politeness and even temper," and wondered how they got those qualities "inside of their clothes without crowding out the rest of 'em." The writer noted that black porters always made themselves useful and agreeable and, because of their carefree ways, "cared not a nap what came next."[18] Blacks were, in this view, naturally suited to being porters. In truth, they were people who were simply providing the service they knew their employers and customers wanted and demanded, one that would provide them with better tips and the least amount of interracial hostility.

Other things had not changed at all. Large numbers of Africans continued to be employed as labourers. Another continuity was that by 1901, blacks had still made no real inroads into white-collar occupations. Blacks were still virtually non-existent as commercial clerks. Toronto had just four black clerks by 1901, while Windsor had just three. There were no black clerks in Hamilton or Amherstburg.[19] Black dentists, doctors, lawyers and other professionals were extremely rare in the province. When they did exist, such as the Amherstburg lawyer Delos Davis, they appear to have been accepted, but were perhaps condescendingly regarded as exceptional. A reference in a Detroit black newspaper, the *Plaindealer,* concerning Davis noted that Canadians "are not only proud of him, but also make him something of a pet."[20] In fact, Davis faced considerable difficulties on his path to becoming a lawyer. Although there were no formal restrictions against blacks becoming lawyers, the resistence based on race was most evident when Davis tried to fulfil the articling requirement. His member

---

[18] *Saturday Night*, June 22, 1889.

[19] Microfilm of 1901 Census Rolls, Toronto, Hamilton, and Essex County.

[20] The *Plaindealer,* May 15, 1891.

of provincial parliament, Hon. W.D. Balfour, had to introduce a special act to the legislature to admit Davis as a lawyer without articling, provided he passed an examination set by the Ontario Law Society. The bill was assented to on March 25, 1884, stating that he had not been able to article "in consequence of prejudices against his color."[21]

In short, the black occupational structure changed very little over these 30 years. The shifts that occurred were caused by changes in the nature of certain occupations rather than improvements in the attitude towards blacks. As the barbering profession became less of a service industry and more of a skilled job, the number of black barbers dropped. As portering and teamster jobs grew, blacks were hired because they were deemed suitable for these low-skill jobs.

In conclusion, the black occupational structure was very different from that of the remainder of the population. Future scholarship is necessary to comprehend and document the obviously profound implications of the racial segregation of labour upon the social, cultural, political and economic lives of these black populations. Blacks were much more likely to be employed in low-skill occupations than were whites. Furthermore, blacks were almost non-existent in white-collar work. What is especially noteworthy is that this pattern held true throughout the province. The situation did not change much over the years. By 1901, blacks were still concentrated in low-skill work and almost non-existent in white collar work, just as they had been 30 years earlier.

References

Census of Canada, 1870–71, Vol. 1. (1873). Ottawa: I.B. Taylor.

Hill, Daniel (1981). *The freedom seekers: Blacks in early Canada*. Agincourt, ON: The Book Society of Canada Limited.

Katzman, David. (1973). *Before the ghetto: Black Detroit in the nineteenth century*. Urbana, Ill.: University of Illinois Press.

Kusmer, Kenneth. (1976). *A ghetto takes shape: Black Cleveland, 1870–1930*. Urbana, Ill.: University of Illinois Press.

Murray, Alexander. (1960). Canada and the Anglo-American anti-slavery movement. Unpublished doctoral thesis, University of Pennsylvania, USA.

Report of the Census of 1881, Vol. 2. Printed by MacLean, Roger & Co., Ottawa, 1884.

Report of the Fourth Census of Canada, 1901, Vol. 1. Printed by S.E. Dawson, Ottawa, 1902.

Silverman, Jason. (1985). *Unwelcome guests: Canada West's response to American fugitive slaves, 1800–1865*. Millwood, N.Y.: Associated Faculty Press.

Simpson, Donald. (1971). Negroes in Ontario from early times to 1870. Unpublished doctoral thesis, University of Western Ontario, Canada.

---

[21] Ontario Archives, *Daniel Hill Black History Research Collection*, Colchester Notes (B), F1416

Stouffer, Allen. (1992). *The light of nature and the law of God: Antislavery in Ontario, 1833–1877*. Montreal: McGill-Queen's University Press.

Ward, Samuel Ringgold (Reverend) (1855). *Autobiography of a fugitive negro*. London: John Snow, 35, Paternoster Row.

Questions for Discussion

1. What is institutional racism? Discuss the three different forms and their application elaborated upon by the essayists.

2. What is the difference between institutional racism and prejudice or discrimination?

3. What does Stewart's "racial devaluation" mean?

4. What is the relationship between occupational and institutional racism?

5. Should the success of a few racially marginalized people be used to deflate the relevance of institutional racism? What is the role of tokenism in the maintenance of institutional racism?

6. According to Stewart, is racism personal? Do you agree or disagree? Why?

7. Is there a necessary correlation between education and anti-racist behaviour?

8. Mizgala discusses the proliferation of Contemporary Native art exhibitions around 1992. What social and cultural transformations would allow for a more sustained and permanent investment in First Nation cultures?

Part 2 Crime and Justice

Crime and justice are often spoken of in tandem. In a society where racism is suspected, one can usually turn to the jurisprudential records, and the criminal dockets and cases in particular, to glean the reality of racism. Typically, the oppressed are subject to disparate treatment at the hands of the criminal justice system. When one speaks of a racially disparate criminal justice system, some of the usual indicia include police brutality, over-policing, disparate periods of incarceration, increased contact with the criminal justice system and its consequences, disparate rates of capital punishment, racial profiling, lack of access to counsel and non-representative juries and judges.

Each of the essays in this Part examines race and its relationship to crime, punishment and justice. The first essay, "Raising Raced and Erased Executions in African-Canadian Literature: Or, Unearthing Angelique", reflects upon the disparate use of executions for black Canadians. The essay further delves into the issue of the relative lack of Canadian prison memoirs and critiques of "criminal injustice literature," that are so prevalent in the United States, especially from African-Americans.

The second essay, "Examining Racism and Criminal Justice: The Advancement of a Defence Based on Section 15(1) of the Canadian Charter Of Rights and Freedoms", focuses on the role of the lawyer in furthering or hampering justice in the representation of black accused. The essay explores the potential of the Charter of Rights and Freedoms as a powerful tool for guaranteeing equality rights to all Canadians and its direct applicability to criminal cases involving potentially racist conduct by police officers.

The last essay in this Part, "Criminological Research on 'Race' in Canada", analyzes race as a social construction and explores the manner in which certain races are associated with crime because of their phenotypic characteristics. The essay documents the processes of racialization that sustains racial hierarchies and prevents inclusive justice.

All the essays in Part 2 are increasingly relevant as we continue to hear questions posed in the media about the disparate treatment of people of colour and First Nations in the criminal justice systems in Canada and the United States. It seems that these questions have been with us for a very long time and it does not appear that the issues manifest in the racialization of the criminal justice system will disappear any time soon.

4

Raising Raced and Erased Executions in African-Canadian Literature
Or, Unearthing Angélique

George Elliott Clarke
English Department
University of Toronto
Toronto

A version of this essay was previously published as "Raising Raced and Erased Executions in African-Canadian Literature: Or, Unearthing Angelique", in *Essays on Canadian Writing* 75 (Winter 2002): 30–61.

George Elliott Clarke

For George Albert Hamilton (1925–49)
and Rufus James Hamilton (1926–49),
Two Africadian Brothers, My Cousins,
Executed for Murder in
Fredericton, New Brunswick, on July 27, 1949.

Preamble

America is not always an enlightening mirror for Canada, and African America
is not always lightning that illuminates the mysterious, shadowy cultures of African Canada. Crucially, one of the distinguishing differences between America
and Canada, as well as between African-Americans and African-Canadians, is
that the former people possess and proclaim a more copious literature of crime
and punishment than do the latter. American and African-American writers are,
dramatically, often criminals or ex-criminals; just as frequently, they heroicize
imprisoned — or executed — charming rogues and impetuous radicals. In contrast, Canadians and African-Canadians are subjects of Her Majesty's allegedly
"Peaceable Kingdom," whose **up**-constitution, the British North America Act
(1867), ordains the drafting of federal laws to promote "Peace, Order, and
good Government".[1] As a result, Canadian and African-Canadian writers are
more apt to be professors than felons (or ex-felons), and prison memoirs and
anti-execution protests are under-represented in Canadian literature. Yet African-Canadians have a history of conflict with white Canadian law enforcement
and the judiciary that should mandate the creation of a race-conscious creative
literature of crime and punishment. However, African-Canadian writers tend to
document injustices in past homelands, not so much Canadian ones. While
many incarcerated — or extinguished — African-Americans, from Nat Turner to
Angela Davis, have emerged as martyr-heroes in African-American literature,
only one — and **proto** — African-Canadian, Marie-Josèphe Angélique, a slave in
Nouvelle-France, has obtained that status in African-Canadian literature — and
only recently. This essay comments on the paucity of "martyrs" in African-
Canadian literature (despite the history of legalized racial injustice) and
explores the use that three African-Canadian writers make of the execution of
Angélique, for arson, in Montréal in 1734.

Under a White-Dominated
Justice System

Incontestably, black conflict with a white-dominated justice system has sparked
many an African-American slave narrative, memoir, poem, blues or chain-gang
or soul or rap song, novel, and drama. Slavery, imprisonment, and punishment

---

[1] Ingle, pg. 131.

66

— these *données politiques* — are the perfect negations of a statist ideology of "freedom" in general, and of freedom from "cruel and unnecessary" pain in particular. Thus, the African-American literary canon flaunts texts by vaunted prisoners and ex-prisoners. Too, the image of the "bad" man or woman, the insurrectionary, or the bro' or sistah who "don't take no shit from nobody" has been a popular and perennial African-American character.[2] Still another recurrent type is the African-American violent martyr, who is a practical, **black** extension of the original American Revolution. Because so many African-American texts feature plots involving men — and women — with revolvers and razors, and who use them in defence of either licence or liberty, this canon comprises an out-and-out "outlaw" literature.

This phenomenon is explained by the need of African-American culture to confront the extralegal horrors of slavery, lynching, police assassinations, and (wrongful) capital punishment in art, in song, in journalism, in film, and in many poems, essays, dramas, and short stories and novels.[3] A hard history has necessitated the illustration of how pernicious laws foster impenitent outlaws and how "for-whites-only" civilization mandates "black criminality". Because African-Americans continue to brave a sanguinary republic, their literature is flush with blood-wet prison cells, incarnadine country roads, and gunned-down, gassed, electrocuted, raped . . . "heroes".

Canada presents, as usual, an alternative story, one seemingly more benign than the American narratives in black and white. The number of heralded "heroic" authors jailed for violent or nonviolent dissent is embarrassingly succinct, headed by the Métis Louis Riel, the leader of two rebellions, who was executed in 1885. True-crime works on notorious Canadian murderers and scandalous killings are popular, however, with Québec being somewhat closer to U.S. cultural practices. (Québec francophones currently support a mass-market tabloid, *Allô police,* which prints lurid stories and macabre photographs of naked or near-naked bodies, dead or alive.) Even so, Canadian "criminal" justice fiction and nonfiction are relatively scarce, save, noticeably, texts generated primarily by French-Canadian writers but also by First Nations, Japanese-Canadian, and some other minority-community authors.[4]

In African-Canadian literature, however, only a minority of writers has dealt with black "criminality" and its punishment by white authority — and only a minority of texts has sought to resuscitate executed black Canadian "heroes". This curious absence of black "crime" texts in Canada is due to several factors.

---

[2] *The Oxford Companion to African American Literature* (Andrews et al., 1997) includes listings for "Badman" and "Bad Woman" as specific types.

[3] In his exploration of the attractiveness of outlaws for American culture, John Fraser (1982) comments, "Naturally, the criminal was almost certain to come from a chivalric-martial group" (178) — that is, a "subgroup" engaged in social struggle (179). African Americans constitute such a group.

[4] I am indebted to Donald Goellnicht and Daniel Coleman, both of McMaster University, for the observation that some minority groups in Canada possess substantial literatures of incarceration and execution. They specify a bevy of First Nations works. Moreover, Goellnicht, in an e-mail (August 21, 2001), writes, "The other Canadian minority literary tradition that is virtually founded on incarceration — of a very political type where the main focus is race — is the Japanese Canadian, where the internment during World War Two is the foundational event." This insight is wise. I suggest that scrutiny of Italian-Canadian, Ukrainian-Canadian, etc., literary canons — that is, the writings of other, once-persecuted ethnicities — will yield relevant bibliographies.

First, the emphasis on peace and order and the legislation of gun control in Canada has meant that black "outlaws" have had restricted opportunities to achieve sustained, "front-page" notoriety.[5] The April 1993 shotgun slaying of a young Greek-Canadian woman, Georgiana Leimonis, in Toronto during the robbery of a popular café by two or more African-Canadian men was one notorious instance of "prominence" being granted to black "outlaws" here.

Second, the abolition of capital punishment in Canada in 1976 and the reconfirmation of abolition in 1985 also restrict, happily, the social territory for martyr narratives.

Third, black violence in Canada is enacted in metropolises mainly against other blacks: these are crimes that media and police forces ignore, and black communities endure. Thus, Jamaican-Canadian essayist Lennox Farrell deplores that black criminals in Toronto "remain unapprehended because of negative relations existing between forces representing [white] 'law and order' and black communities."[6]

Fourth, whatever their antipathies for white Canadian structural racism and Eurocentric imperialism, some African-Canadian writers of Caribbean heritage echo a nostalgic bias towards law and order. Thus, Barbadian-Canadian writer Austin Clarke asserts that "I will admit that the same policemen we sometimes accuse of violent discrimination ... make my life safe and secure in a city bordering on the American syndrome of ghettoized crime" (18). Farrell assaults white police racism, but he also desires strict enough policing to restrict urban "criminals" who "function as would a black arm of the Ku Klux Klan. (A18)" Such "hoods" deserve "neither solace nor sanction."[7] According to Barbadian-Canadian journalist Philip Mascoll, "Jamaicans are basically hard-core, right wingers when it comes to law and order ..." In a November 2000 op-ed piece, he bemoans the difficulties that Jamaica was facing in hanging "six men condemned for first-degree murder."[8] Although officially independent, its highest court remains the anti-death-penalty British Privy Council.[9]

Fifth, there is a fear of contributing to stereotypes about black criminality, for there is no offsetting "badman" or "bad woman" tradition in Canada, partly because such history is suppressed. Repetition of racial stereotypes around "lawbreaking" is spectacularly possible given the inherent biases in court records. This reality is a danger for African-Canadian historians and writers, for legal documents are often the only chronicles available of black Canadian "lawbreakers" and potential "heroes".

---

[5] Despite the media construction of the perpetrators as "Jamaicans" — a denial of their Canadian identities — and the dissemination of racist anti-black discourses, the black community itself viewed the accused men as "thugs." They were no "defiant strugglers against the status quo." Likewise, when Roosevelt (Rosie) Douglas led the destruction of the computer centre at Sir George Williams University in Montréal in 1969, he was accorded "hero" status by only a few.

[6] Clarke, 1992, p.18.

[7] Farrell, 2001.

[8] Mascoll, 2000.

[9] Mascoll mentions Canada in his article, arguing that "the last death sentences commuted in Canada were done by Canada's highest court, not by the British Privy Council." He is mistaken. From the end of the prime ministry of Louis Saint-Laurent to the first abolition of capital punishment in 1976, decisions about death-sentence commutations were made by the federal cabinet.

And sixth, African-Canadian writers are more likely to champion an African-American or African or Caribbean "renegade" than an "indigenous" one. Our poems and plays idolize Rosa Parks, the African-American anti-segregation "lawbreaker" of 1955, not, generally, the unfairly obscure Viola Desmond, imprisoned in Nova Scotia in 1946 for violating segregated seating in a provincial cinema. Or we celebrate Toussaint L'Ouverture, the revolutionary emancipator of Haiti, or Nelson Mandela, the planter of democracy in South Africa, or Harriet Tubman, the liberator of American slaves, but neither black Canadians who have fought injustice and suffered nor those who have committed crimes of either nihilistic or political import.

For example, Trinidadian-Canadian poet Dionne Brand cites the use of executions as assassinations in the demise of Grenada's Marxist government in 1983. In *No Language Is Neutral,* she eulogizes Jacqueline Creft, the minister of education in the People's Revolutionary Government of Grenada, "killed on October 19th, 1983, during a coup":

> in the last
> moment, bullets crisscrossed your temple and your
> heart. They say someone was calling you, Yansa,
> thundering for help.[10]

Another African-Canadian writer, Nigerian-born Ken Wiwa, in his 2000 memoir, protests the trauma of the iniquitous hanging in 1995 of his father, Ken Saro-Wiwa, the enviro-activist, poet, and novelist, by the Nigerian government. Thus, the promotion of "hero" or "martyr" narratives of black Canadian "lawbreakers" is left to spoken-word poets, dub poets, and rappers and to a few left-identified writers, journalists, and intellectuals — in other words, to singers and political activists.[11] One example is dub poet Clifton Joseph's remembrance of "sixteen year old Michael Habbib," who became the victim of "a white racist sniper at Don Mills and Sheppard [in Toronto who] looked out of his high-rise with a high-powered gun and said he was going to shoot the first nigger he saw.[12]" Joseph also recalls the Toronto police "killing of Buddy Evans at the flying disco on king street [in 1978] and of Albert Johnson, in his own house, in front of his young daughter [in 1979]."

The erasure of *le captif noir canadien* in African-Canadian literature is problematic, for the Canadian state has hanged — and the Canadian people have lynched — recoverable "heroes." Their narratives, if unearthed, could bare the "clandestine" racism of Canadian authority and popularize the resistive strategies of African-Canadian communities. Scholars must begin to excavate those occasions when black Canadian "crime" met with white Canadian punishment, particularly because such penalties were usually bloody. Certainly, from Confederation in 1867 until 1962, when the last hangings occurred, of "about 3,000 people ... convicted of crimes punishable by death," Canada executed 701

---

[10] Brand, 1990, p. 11.

[11] Joseph, 2001.

[12] Ibid, p. 18.

of these convicts, reports historian Alan Hustak.[13] The condemned were "subject to a lottery rigged by politics and economics and manipulated by unconscious racism and social prejudice," says Hustak, so "Native people, French Canadians, Canadians of Slavic origin, homosexuals and blacks had a better chance of being executed than did white Anglo-Saxon Protestants."[14] Criminologist Neil Boyd finds that "ethnic and racial origin remained a statistically significant variable in [federal] Cabinet judgements [regarding death sentence commutations]. Native Canadians and French Canadians were more likely to be hanged than English Canadians."[15]

Examining the morbid compilation *Persons Sentenced to Death in Canada: 1867–1976,* edited by Lorraine Gadoury and Antonio LeChasseur, I count 47 men listed as "Negro," or "Colored," or "Mulatto," or "American negro," or "American mulatto" (two occurrences), or "Colored from Bahamas" (one occurrence) who were presumably, in present parlance, black.[16] Of these 47 men (all originally convicted of shooting, stabbing, strangling, axing, slashing, or bludgeoning their victims),[17] slightly more than half of them, or 24, were hanged. Robbery was a chief motive for these crimes. Few of these *damnés* were even regular labourers, let alone skilled workers or professionals. Others received commutations of their sentences, or were, following appeals, convicted on the lesser charge of manslaughter, or were, in a few cases, acquitted at their second trials.[18] Only 23 percent of all persons convicted in capital cases were hanged in Canada, but 50 percent of all blacks so convicted were hanged. Racism may have influenced the federal cabinet to decline mercy in over half the cases where black men faced the noose.[19] Dean Jobb cites the possible influence of racism in the application of the death penalty in Nova Scotia in the 1930s: "Between 1930 and 1937 nine men — six white and three black — were handed the death sentence for murder in the province. Four of the whites were executed, while two of the blacks died on the gallows" (1993, p. 112). Yet, as with the whites, 66.7 percent of the blacks sentenced to die by Nova Scotian

---

[13] Hustak, 1987, p. xv. Criminologist Neil Boyd arrives at a different figure, charging that "Canada hanged 693 men and 13 women..." (p. xi).

[14] Hustak, 1987, p. xv.

[15] Boyd, 1988, p. 60.

[16] Other "ethnicities" registered in this printed necropolis include Chinese, French-Canadian, Ukrainian, Italian, "Indian" [sic], "Half-Breed" [sic], Hungarian, Polish, American, and, of course, British. "Exotic" entries include Acadian, "Mahometan Turk" [sic], German, Belgian, Ruthenian, Yugoslavian, Bulgarian, Dutch, Maltese, Swedish, "Eskimo" [sic], Galician, Doukhobor, Romanian, Armenian, Czechoslovakian, Finnish, Icelandic, Japanese, Greek, Costa Rican, "Hindu" [sic], Serbian, Macedonian, Danish, Jewish, one "American of French Canadian origin," and one "Canadian born in the United States." Canada was, despite its racial biases, an equal-opportunity executioner.

[17] In *Capital Punishment in Canada: A Sociological Study of Repressive Law* (1976), David Chandler notes that, of blacks convicted of capital murder with robbery, between 1946 and 1967, 57.1 percent were executed (p. 217).

[18] Precision on this point is impossible, for Canadian capital case files are often incomplete, containing, say, a note that an order for execution has been filed but no proof that said order was ever executed.

[19] Discussing the last people hanged, province by province in Canada, Allan Hustak (1997) insists that "It is curious and revealing that of the twelve ... two were blacks, four were French Canadians, two were of Eastern European backgrounds, one was part-Indian, one a homosexual and only two were Anglo-Saxon" (p. xv).

courts during the Depression were executed. Jobb remarks that "convicted murderers were hanged in more than three quarters of the cases" in which juries had not recommended mercy;[20] thus, black convicts denied mercy by white juries initially were not likely to receive mercy from white politicians later.

But African-Canadians were dying in executions — fair or foul — even before the Canadian state was born. Worse, some perished for the same reason as did African-Americans — in sacrifice to what Toni Morrison labels a typical form of "white mischief — the kind that surfaces when the opportunity to gaze voluptuously at a black body presents itself."[21] African-Canadian law professor Carol A. Aylward wagers that "[i]n Canada, as well as in the United States, it can be said that law has failed in its purpose of establishing justice for Black members of society."[22] Assuredly, classic white Canadian racism could be as caustic as its U.S. "night rider" counterpart. "In 1911 *Maclean's* magazine published an article," writes Jobb, "that purported to describe the typical black section of a Nova Scotia town. [The article stated that,] 'White people pass it in fear.... It is the abode of little more than innocent shiftlessness, but such places are adapted to the breeding of vice and crime'."[23] Maclean's cast Black Nova Scotians in 1911 in a social role that Morrison saw Simpson compelled to perform in 1994–95: to symbolize "the whole race needing correction, incarceration, censoring, silencing.... This is the consequence and function of official stories: to impose the will of a dominant culture" (xxviii). Aylward lists many "illegal legalities that African-Canadians experience. Citing a 1995 inquiry into systemic racism in the Ontario justice system, she affirms its conclusion that "Black men, women and male youths were overrepresented in the prison system" (15). Additionally, when compared to whites, African Canadians were less likely to receive forgiving treatment from either the police or the courts. (15).

Canadian state narratives about "dangerous black lawlessness" are rooted in African slavery (the Pecuniary Institution), once extant in the eastern provinces (save Newfoundland) of what is now Canada. Aylward registers that "the legacy of slavery still plagues both Canada and the United States" (15). As in the antebellum United States, then, the black slave in Canada was "more answerable for some of his crimes than free whites." Canadian historian Jim Hornby advises, "It is ironic that the slaves' humanity was only recognized by the state."[24] Not surprisingly, then, hangings in "primal" Canada put on display dangling black bodies. The first person hanged in colonial Ontario was "a Negro named Josiah Cutten," states Canadian writer Louis Blake Duff.[25] Caught stealing rum and furs in October 1789, Cutten was damned, in court, as resembling animals that "go prowling about at Night for their prey." Duff also records that "a negro was first in the London District" to be hanged.[26] And the

---

[20] Jobb, 1988, p. 112.

[21] Morrison, 1997, p. xiii.

[22] Aylward, 1999, p. 14.

[23] Quoted in Hornby, 1991, p. xiv.

[24] Hornby, 1991, p. xiv.

[25] Duff, [1949], p. 5.

[26] Ibid., p. 7.

first execution in Welland County, in 1859, "was that of Henry Byers, another Negro," for which "[stands were erected for the spectators and seating was also placed on the roof of a nearby hotel."[27] In Nova Scotia, "Brittain Murray, a black, was hanged for robbery in 1786."[28] Historian Dorothy Dearborn records that in 1798, during the Loyalist settlement of New Brunswick, "a slave of Judge Upham … was tried for the murder of 'the girl West'." Luke Hamilton, who did not enter a plea, "would have had little say in the matter of his guilt or innocence in those days," notes Dearborn, but "was convicted from the marks of the horse shoes on the ground near where the body of the girl was found."[29] He was hanged. In 1815, in Prince Edward Island, writes Hornby, "Sancho Byers was hanged upon conviction of stealing goods described in court as 'one loaf of Bread and one Pound weight and upwards of Butter of the value of one Shilling'." His brother, Peter, was hanged after a coin stolen during a burglary was found in his possession.[30]

In *L'Esclavage au Canada Français*, Québec historian Marcel Trudel documents hangings of blacks in Nouvelle-France (and its post-conquest form, Lower Canada). Jean-Baptiste Thomas was hanged in the Montreal Market, for theft, in the summer of 1735. In 1827, Robert Ellis, convicted of breaking into and stealing from a church, was hanged in front of the prison in Québec City.[31] The most famous black *condamnée* in proto-Québec history is Marie-Josèphe Angélique (discussed below).[32] These blacks, if remembered and written about now, would serve to rend the veil that shrouds Canadian slavery.[33] U.S. historian Robin W. Winks notes that, by the mid-nineteenth century, "writers were maintaining that there had been no slavery in New France at all … and a new popularly held assumption joined those about climate and cotton to obscure any national memory of French slavery" (1997, p. 19). Too, this ignorance about the practice of slavery in what is now Canada is mirrored by the stubborn silence in historical records — of the slaves in Nouvelle-France and in British North America.

---

[27] Ibid., p. 8.

[28] Jobb, 1988, p. 98.

[29] Dearborn, 1999, p. 22.

[30] Hornby, 1998, pp. 49–50. Hornby also suspects that the Byers brothers went to the gallows "to send a message to the public, and perhaps especially to the black population recently released from slavery" (p. 51).

[31] Trudel, 1960/1963, pp. 85, 87. Trudel further comments that "Unfortunately, the press did not preserve for us the spiritual testimony of the negro: we know only that he sustained his innocence until the end and that he submitted to his fate with indifference" (p. 87).

[32] Celebrating the relatively low criminal rate among slaves held in French Canada — 18 criminals found among 3,604 slaves — sin records spanning 15 years, Trudel (1960/1963) opines that such numbers indicate "the normal integration of the slave in French-Canadian society" (p. 97). This mythology of the well-treated black and the "lucky-to-be-in-Canada" slave is one more species of Euro-Canadian propaganda that African-Canadian writers rail against in their depictions of black suffering under white Canadian legal authority.

[33] This suffocating "silence" is real. Although we have few notices in the slaves' own words about their experiences of life, crime, and justice in Nova Scotia, New Brunswick, Prince Edward Island, and the two Canadas, authors like US. historian Robin Winks (1997) are counteracting the sanitization of Slave histories by writers like Miceline Bail (1999, p.383). Winks recalls the slave Olivier Le Jeune whose protest of his baptismal "transformation" pierced a silence that, already in 1632, was obliterating the lives of African slaves from Canadian historical consciousness.

During the post-slavery era (which began, unofficially, in the early nineteenth century and, officially, in 1833), African-Canadians continued to be hanged or lynched. For instance, in "The Charivari" chapter of *Roughing It in the Bush: Or, Life in Canada,* Susanna Moodie records the tale, as told by Mrs. O., of what is in effect the lynching of Tom Smith, somewhere in Upper Canada, sometime before the Moodies' arrival there in 1832. This ex-African-American had had the temerity to marry "not a bad-looking Irish woman." To chastise him for his ill-considered union, a gang had gone "so far as to enter the [newlyweds'] house, drag the poor nigger from his bed, and in spite of his shrieks for mercy, [hurry] him out into the cold air — for it was winter — and almost naked as he was, [ride] him upon a rail, and so ill-[treat] him that he died under their hands." Mrs. O. then tells Moodie that "[t]he ringleaders escaped across the lake to the other side" — presumably the United States — "and those who remained could not be sufficiently identified to bring them to trial." In good Canadian style, Mrs. O. goes on to relate, "The affair was hushed up," though "it gave great uneasiness to several respectable families whose sons were in the scrape."[34] In Moodie's citation of this frontier *"Histoire d'O"*, one sees, in embryonic form, the usual Canadian response to racial violence against so-called visible minorities, whether in Canada or in Somalia: pretend that we are not implicated.[35]

In the twentieth century, "lynchings" may have posed as legal hangings. One possibly "masked" lynching terminated Daniel P. Sampson, aged 49, a Haligonian labourer, in 1935. Convicted of homicide in connection with the stabbing deaths of Edward and Bramwell Heffernan, two white boys aged 10 and 12, in Halifax in 1933, Sampson, if guilty, was a minor version of Nat Turner. Sampson's motive for slaying the children was that they had maligned him with a racist epithet. A Royal Canadian Mounted Police commentary on "The Hefferman [sic] Case" says that Sampson was arrested after "prolonged investigation" and tried twice: in April 1934 and in October 1934. The second trial occurred because "The written confession had been tendered as an exhibit at the Preliminary Hearing but apparently became mislaid in the Prothonotary's office."[36] This circumstance arouses suspicion about Sampson's guilt. Morrison alleges that the "blood" smelled by the media in the 1994–95 O.J. Simpson affair "belonged not to the victims but to the prey — a potent sensation aroused by the site and sight of a fallen, treacherous, violent black body, and sustained by the historical association of such a body with violence as dread entertainment."[37] To what extent, then, was Sampson, guilty or innocent, positioned as the nightmarish black body disrupting facades of white innocence and

---

[34] Moodie, 1852/1989, p. 211.

[35] Tess Chakkalakal's 2000 article "Reckless Eyeballing: Being Reena in Canada" examines what she classifies as the 1997 lynching of the young Indian-Canadian woman, Reena Virk, in Victoria, British Columbia, by a white teen gang (most of them also female). The once-hushed-up torture-murder of a Somali youth by members of the Canadian Airborne Regiment in 1993 was yet another "Canadian lynching".

[36] *Journal of Assembly,* Appendix 27, 1935, p. 10.

[37] Morrison, 1997, p. xiv.

"civilization"?[38] Despite the records of persecutions as prosecutions, suspicious convictions, and suspect hangings, African-Canadian writers have been slow to open ruddy documents and eye past black existence in Canada and the ways of white folk in administering racially unequal "justice." Many "cases" remain "open", and we must sift through their remains. The bodies of our executed must be reclaimed.

Marie-Josèphe Angélique

Marie-Josèphe Angélique is the only African-Canadian executionee to kindle contemplations by several African-Canadian writers and artists. The most famous — though obscure — black victim of execution in Canada has moved African-Canadians to ink, as of 2002, one novel (in French), two plays (in English), and a tribute song (also in English).[39] (The novel *L'Esclave* by the francophone Québécoise writer Micheline Bail is a "white" contribution to the Angélique legend.) Angélique appeals to different black creators for different reasons. By allegedly starting a fire — in the home of her mistress, Thérèse Decouagne — that incinerated, eventually, 46 houses and the convent and church named l'Hôtel-Dieu in *ancien régime* Montréal, Angélique appears in African-Canadian history as a violent resister of slavery. Also, as a black woman who exercised agency in choosing her lovers and in denouncing her accusers, Angélique symbolizes feminist self-actualization. Trudel pegs her as being 21 at the time of her baptism in June 1730,[40] so she was about 25 when she died. Captured in her flight from Québec, condemned as an arsonist, hanged, and then burned on June 21, 1734, in Montréal, Angélique emerges as a classic martyr. Yet she is also, productively for writers and artists, an ambiguous heroine. Before she entered the annals of history and the pages of fiction, Angélique was mainly an acquiescent slave, and no firebrand. Loyal to her owners, she chose to flee only because she feared being sold. Even her "heroic arson" was, perhaps, accidental. If she did set a fire to consume her mistress's mansion, then it was to cover her flight — into the arms of her white lover, Claude Thibault, a fact that complicates her status as a Canadian slave rebel. But the image of her figure (hanging, then burning), martyred in the cause of liberty, **is** irresistible. (Her "Christian" name even encapsulates beings germane to that religion.) She is an African-Canadian version of Joan of Arc, Thomas Hardy's tragic heroine, Tess, and Henry Wadsworth Longfellow's Acadian saint, Evangeline — at least for some of her acolytes.

In his vast history of black Canadians, Robin W. Winks skips every capital case involving "us" save one — that of Angélique. His treatment is catatonically laconic: "a Negress belonging to Mme. François Poulin de Francheville set fire

---

[38] The King v. Farmer is another suspect case. Jobb (1988) notes that black Everett Farmer was hanged in 1937 for the murder of his half-brother partly because he "could not afford a proper defence" (p. 97).
[39] The novel is by Paul F. Brown; the plays are by Lorris Elliott and Lorena Gale, whose works are discussed in this section; the film is by Michael Jarvis; and the tribute song is by Faith Nolan.
[40] Trudel, 1960/1963, p. 92.

to her mistress's house in April 1734, thereby destroying a portion of Montreal ..."[41] Winks neither identifies this "Negress" nor ascribes to her any heroism. To attack the white space — the opaque silence — that shrouds Angélique in Eurocentric histories, Barbadian-Canadian writer Lorris Elliott, "Afro-Acadien"[42] writer Paul Fehmiu Brown, and Afro-Québécoise writer Lorena Gale have published, in turn, a one-act play (an excerpt from a longer play), a juvenile novel, and a full-length play on Angélique. Fittingly, all three authors have Québec connections. Elliott, who died in 1999, was a professor of English at McGill University and active in black arts circles in Montréal; Brown, a native of Acadie, has lived in Montréal for some years; and Gale, a Montréalaise, now lives in Vancouver. The three writers image Angélique in their own terms.[43]

The Image of Angélique in the Eyes of Lorris Elliott, Paul Fehmiu Brown and Lorena Gale

Lorris Elliott: "The Trial of Marie-Joseph Angelique — Negress and Slave"[44]

In his play "The Trial of Marie-Joseph Angelique — Negress and Slave", Elliott repeats the facts of Trudel's history. In his introduction, Elliott writes that Angélique was condemned "for what has been recorded as 'the most spectacular crime committed by a slave in Canadian history'" (55), thus translating Trudel's assertion that "Le crime le plus spectaculaire qu'un esclave ait accompli dans notre histoire, c'est celui de la négresse Angélique ..."[45] Elliott plucks his facts from Trudel, but his usage of Angélique is original. Elliott begins by recounting the history:

> Tortured four times and forced to admit to her "crime", she was allowed to make a confession in prison in the presence of a priest, Navetier. She was then handed over to the Executioner (probably a negro, Mathieu Leveille [sic]), taken to the church to make amends, displayed to the townsfolk and hanged. Her ashes were then spread about. Thus satisfied, the Montrealers began to reconstruct their homes. (55)

(Elliott mistranslates Trudel here, misreading the phrase "c'est probablement le nègre Mathieu Léveillé,"[46] an identification of the executioner, as "probably a negro," an identification of race.) But Elliott jettisons realism in his play, preferring to position Angélique as a time-travelling spirit able to warn future black

---

[41] Winks, 1997, p. 11. In his book, Winks identifies Thérèse Decouagne by her married name.

[42] Paul F. Brown's coinage is discussed in a 1994–95 article by Loic Vennin.

[43] The Nova Scotia-born, Toronto-based singer-songwriter Faith Nolan, whose a cappella song "Marie Joseph Angelique" appears on her second album, Africville (1986), identifies an anti-racist, feminist Angélique in her refrain, "My soul is my own for no man to keep."

[44] Elliott, 1985, pp. 55–65.

[45] Trudel, 1960/1963, p. 92.

[46] Trudel, 1960/1963, p. 95.

immigrants about the innate hostility of Canada. When Angélique first appears on stage, it is 1734; she is in a prison courtyard in Montréal, and she is about to die. Voices shout "Assassin . . . Arsonist," "Hanging's too good . . . burn her alive" (57; ellipses in the original), and "burn the firebrand" (58). The voices assaulting Angélique are sing-songy, childish ("O goody goody . . . we're going to have a hanging" [57]; "We want a burning . . . how about a hanging . . . we want a hanging . . . etc." [58; ellipses in the original]), exposing the congenital savagery of superficially civilized beings. The voices assemble the *brouhaha* of a lynch mob. Before her execution, however, Angélique abandons the eighteenth century for the nineteenth, projecting her spirit through more than a century of time and more than 600 kilometres of space to "haunt" Mary Ann Shadd, "A Black woman, a teacher, founder and editor of The Province [sic] Freeman in Toronto, Windsor, and Chatham, Canada West" (56).

Angélique's spirit odyssey fascinates, but her message to Shadd fulminates. The "arsonist" tells Shadd, the abolitionist newspaper editor and promoter of African-American immigration to Canada West (in the aftermath of the passage of the U.S. Fugitive Slave Bill in 1851), about her life as a **Canadian** slave. "A negress and a slave . . . . a merchant's property," she has been "rooted up, and against my will, brought here to be transplanted . . . here within this snow-cold land . . ." (59; ellipses in the original). Shadd considers Canada a land of liberty: "In fact, the good woman [slave liberator], Harriet Tubman, has brought many a former slave into this country . . . here to live as all others . . . in freedom" (60; ellipses in the original). Angélique soon undermines Shadd's romanticism (or optimism), alleging that "this land [Canada] that uses brother against brother . . . and sister too, is no place to settle in," and Shadd asks, ". . . must I leave Canada to find another country?" (60; ellipses in the original). Angélique answers, while "pointing to the audience," "Do you believe they want us to entrench here, when laws are made against those who would offer us support?" (60).

Her question voices not just her personal, historical despair but, also, the present disgruntlement of black immigrants living in an unwelcoming Canada. Her last words to the audience — and to Shadd — are bitter: "God bless you Canada . . . once I did think that, with Claude, . . . I would find a good life here . . . and freedom . . ." (64; ellipses in the original). She is hanged in view of a Shadd now magically transported to 1734 Montreal. Shadd's last speech reveals her re-education: "O Journey . . . is this true? . . . is this Canada? . . . O Angelique" (65; ellipses in the original). Angélique, as archetypal black immigrant (impotent but rebellious), underlines the persistent agony that white Canadian racism poses for the new black immigrant, whether it be Shadd in the nineteenth century or Elliott and his *confrères* in the twentieth.

Elliott animates Angélique as a wraith generated by Canadian territory and Canadian "terror" — or iniquity. A speaker for indigeneity and racial history, one who will return "[à] *l'état de nature* . . . the very Nature from which she came" (61; ellipsis in the original), Angélique projects the true history of African-Canadian experience out of the landscape itself. In Elliott's extraordinary play, Angélique becomes a Cassandra, one who cries out, "New black immigrants, beware the ingrained Negrophobia of the 'Great White North.'"

Paul Fehmiu Brown: Marie-Josèphe Angélique: Montréal, Québec 21 juin 1734[47]

Opening his eponymously titled novel, *Marie-Josèphe Angélique: Montréal, Québec 21 juin 1734*, Paul Fehmiu Brown declares that "tracer le parcours de Marie-Josèphe Angélique et raconter sa vie, c'est écrire son histoire a l'enverse" (7). He is right. To memorialize this character is to write history inside out or wrong side up. But only an inversion can invest Angélique with the rigour of representative martyrdom. She is, directly, a victim of Nouvelle-France, a slave state. She is the toy of her owners, François Poulin de Francheville and his widow, Thérèse Decouagne, then the credible *vache* of a slave-*taureau* (86), Jacques César,[48] then the plaything of her white lover, Claude Thibault. Occasionally, Brown's Angélique displays anger and mourns her slavery, but these gestures are sporadic and ephemeral. She is willful but frustratingly "loyal." She "belongs to" — and remains with — a household that schemes successfully, through coercion and fraudulent pledges of liberty, to see her impregnated by César, another owner's slave, so that she can bear new slaves to be sold off to pay her owners' debts. This sad destiny is scuttled only because her children, a boy, Eustache, and then twins, Louis and Marie-Françoise, perish in infancy. Angélique contests her slavehood so inconsistently that it is only her stoicism when facing execution that grants her a final, tragic majesty. Angélique possesses a "fausse quiétude" (7): she accepts the degradation and self-denial demanded of slaves because she imagines that she will be freed when she turns 25. At times, she is "assez lucide" — realistic enough — "to consider the present as a universe of shadows" (7). Still, she expects to find "la liberté et la dignité" (7). Angélique demonstrates the patience not of Job, but of Longfellow's *Evangeline*. Longfellow's long poem *Evangeline: A Tale of Acadie* (1847), published in a North American French translation by Pamphile LeMay in 1865, is one of the constitutive myths of Acadian nationalism. Thus, Brown, an Acadian, likely knows the work and its self-sacrificing heroine. She is also, like Evangeline, beautiful and virtuous (though, for a slave, "virtue" is a vagary). While Evangeline is eyed by "[m]any a youth" as "the saint of his deepest devotion" (15), Angélique's beauty leaves no man "indifferent," we are told, "not even the curé" (10). Angélique also staves off coerced intercourse with César until relenting for her own reasons.

Brown's Angélique is "la plus belle" slave woman in Montreal (10), but she is also — albeit only slightly — politically conscious. First, and strikingly, she respects the Afro-Aboriginal alliance that formed when "some Black fugitive slaves, having found refuge among the Aboriginal people, shared with them their communal life, to the great dismay of their former white owners" (31). Second, she appeals — in African custom — to ancestral spirits ("Spirit of my

---

[47] Brown, 1998.

[48] Brown names some of his characters to remind the reader of Québécois personalities. So Jacques César may be a *déclassé* version of Julius Caesar — or a mocking version of notorious former Québec premier Jacques Parizeau. The characters René Bourassa and Jean Péladeau would evoke, for any contemporary Québécois reader, the names of two deceased Québec premiers, René Lévesque and Robert Bourassa, but also Canadian prime minister Jean Chrétien and Québec newspaper publisher Pierre Péladeau, all personages central to recent political discourse in Québec.

ancestors, come and search for me" [41]), thus demonstrating her partial reclamation of her own native culture. Third, Angélique recognizes that New England is freer for blacks than is Nouvelle-France. Hence, when she flees Montréal, she heads for Vermont: "Why? Because this state never practiced in any official or systematic manner the enslavement of Blacks" (99). Her action reverses the Canadian stereotype about a unidirectional, northbound "Underground Railroad." Fourth, she wins over the black hangman who will take her life. Mathieu Léveillé, a character taken from history, is given a Martiniquan origin and the ability to speak "an impeccable French, with a Creole accent" (54). Although he is young, upon arriving in Nouvelle-France he is pressed into service as a hangman. However, he has hanged only one person before Angélique. When he passes the noose around her neck, she maintains "an astonishing calm, causing the young executioner to tremble again" (116). Quivering and looking into her eyes, Léveillé is told by her, "Don't be afraid, my friend, my blood-brother.... It is either my head or yours" (117). Her espousal of a form of pan-Africanist solidarity secures Léveillé's commitment to reunite Angélique with her slave "sister," Marie-Charlotte — on the gallows platform — one last time. And fifth, Angélique is blameless of any crime. She confesses her innocence (the fire was an accident triggered by Thibault) to Marie-Charlotte, who says, "I hope that, from generation to generation, there will always be someone to remember Marie-Josèphe Angélique. History will remember you" (118). Saintly, Christ-like, Angélique commands Marie-Charlotte, "Dry your tears, my friend, I am going to rejoin my ancestors" (118). Angélique ascends to the status of hero-martyr immediately.

Despite all her insight, Angélique has a major flaw. She surrenders easily to the lethal machinery of fate (a gesture reminiscent of Thomas Hardy's Tess): "Slave masters control and rule our lives, but it is Destiny that has the last word" (51; my translation). She repeats this point later: "What I mean is, that Destiny, ours, for you and me, is tragic. It isn't accepting our condition as slaves that is tragic, it is being deprived of dreams" (86).[49] Brown loves the Greek notion that fate demands Angélique's doom and he emphasizes that the "arson" resulting in Angélique's execution was, in fact, sparked by Thibault's failure to close a stove door after setting some logs therein, just before he and Angélique vamoose for Vermont. Brown's Angélique is pristine and preordained to suffer. She is, like Thomas Hardy's Tess, "A Pure Woman", to cite the once-controversial subtitle of *Tess of the D'Urbervilles* (1891/1930). Thus, her arrest in snowy woods mirrors that experienced by Tess Durbeyfield. Angélique has opportunities to thwart her "overlords" and escape her circumstances, but she does too little too late. For example, she calls Decouagne an "old hypocrite" (92), and batters her mistress, knocking her forehead thrice against a table (93). The struggle between them starts a fire, which catches on

---

[49] Angélique awakens to find herself and her lover, the cowardly Thibault, "surrounded by mounted soldiers, who seemed to have appeared from nowhere" (Brown, 1998, p. 100). Likewise, when Tess awakens from her last night of freedom, after sleeping in the open on an "oblong slab" at Stonehenge (Hardy, 1891/1930, p. 511), she faces not only her lover and husband, Angel, but also a group of policemen as still as the [stone] pillars around" (ibid., p. 514). The policemen appeared, one after another, seemingly out of the land itself.

Angélique's skirt (94). But Angélique does not flee; instead, she puts out the fire and continues to live with Decouagne (94), and "answers to the whims of her mistress ..." (95). Angélique is too forbearing — and too fatalistic — for her own good. She knows that it is "illusory to think" that Decouagne will not try to sell her, but she merely awaits "the fatal day nervously" (95). (In sum, Angélique proceeds from *le taureau* [the stud, i.e., César] to *le borreau* [the executioner], pretty much as "fate" ordains.)

Brown's intrusion into the vacant space of the Canadian slave narrative constructs Angélique as a secular Africanist martyr, one who bears witness to black suffering, extends pan-Africanist sympathies to other blacks, sentimentally unites with Aboriginal peoples, and perishes — a wronged innocent — stoically, but one who hesitates to assert any agency. As courageous as Angélique is, her constant expectation that white society will one day allow her liberty amounts to a self-deception that negates effective action. Brown suggests that African-Canadian communities in Québec must remain vigilant in jealously fighting for equality rather than accepting pacifying, rhetorical blandishments about future "bliss," justice, and prosperity.

The cover art of *Marie-Josèphe Angélique* fetishizes the youthful protagonist's beautiful martyrdom. The illustration by Marie-Judith Langlois portrays a svelte and "comely" black woman, chained to a stake, in profile and staring straight ahead — like a figurehead — while flames leap about her form (which Brown says is "naked under her shift" [115]). Yet in the text, before Angélique is bound to the stake, she has been tortured and hanged until dead; she is neither living nor "pretty" now. Her end is brutality that the cover art disavows. The chains that bind her resemble Gucci accessories, not coffle-strength metal.

Lorena Gale: Angélique[50]

The cover art for Lorena Gale's play *Angélique* (2000) is an apposite opposite. Here we see a confident, stern-looking, young black woman, with strong features, gazing directly at us while fire consumes the buildings just behind her. The imagery is not of sexualized martyrdom, but of in-yo'-face terrorism. (Gale's text notes that Angélique is, at her execution, "**barefoot and naked under a rough raw cotton period shirt**" [74].) Elliott and Brown, both men, present Angélique the martyr, but Gale prefers Angélique the rebel. Thus, the cover art by Richard Horne complements the insistently insurrectionary nature of Gale's text (which won the duMaurier National Playwriting Competition in 1995). The two-act play was first produced in Alberta in 1998, then in Detroit and New York City in 1999.

As in Elliott's play, Gale's drama registers that "[t]hen is now. Now is then" (3). The stage directions inform the reader that, "[u]nless otherwise stated, the slaves are working in every scene in which they appear, either in a modern or historical context" (3). Gale describes Angélique pointedly as "[a] slave, in a Canadian history book" (3). Her Angélique summons up a heroine

---

[50] Gale, 2000.

who attests that issues of economic servitude respecting women of colour — and poor whites — remain *au courant*. This Marxist theme infuses the play.

Thus, Gale's version of Thibault — a servant — comments, "I'm just a peon. Like you. Something to pee on" (14). Claude can only work "**quietly in the background**" and not "**watch openly**", as François Poulin de Francheville, his boss and Angélique's owner, undresses her, "revealing period undergarments beneath her modern clothing" (34). After Claude spies his boss "pumping" Angélique "like he's fucking her from behind" (35), he begins to talk to her about escaping "South" to New England, and "[h]e takes her hand and kisses it" (36, 37). His socioeconomic "impotence" drives him to court Angélique by promising her freedom in another land. Their respective class and caste positions would render any union in Nouvelle-France/Québec impossible.[51] At one point, François accuses Claude, in front of Angélique, of "fucking" her, and when Claude the employee denies it, his boss says, "But you want to.... I don't blame you. Everyone should get a taste of brown sugar" (38). (Signifying **her** lack of power, Angélique can only privately curse and surreptitiously spit in the water that she serves François following this incident.) By the play's end, after Claude and Angélique have fled Montréal together, he decides to abandon her while she sleeps. His reasons are tied not so much to race as to class:

> I remember watching my mother's back — always bent, her shirt sleeves rolled above the wrinkles on her elbows. The skin on her arms and hands — rough and red and flaky. She scrubbed laundry for the rich .... Some days I would beg more than she earned .... I've done everything for you [Angélique].... But with you, I'll always be running. And I can't run anymore.... *He runs off.* (71)

Despite his testimony, Claude fulfils a prophecy of Gale's César (here, too, a black stud), who warns Angélique, "There's only one thing worse than a rich white master and that's a poor white who wants to be one. You think he's on your side right now. But watch out. 'Cause in the end they are all white together" (50). Regrettably, she never follows the logic of her own magnificent assertion to Claude that "I'm not willing to bet my body parts on your view of the world" (36).

Earlier, the white mistress, Thérèse De Couagne [sic], beats a hanging tapestry but imagines that she is beating Angélique (thus denying her "sisterhood") for miscellaneous reasons, ranging from "Because the bread didn't rise" to "Because he went to you again last night," or

> Because he stared at you through dinner.
> (smack)
> Because I have to pretend this isn't happening.
> (smack)
> Because I wish you'd disappear.
> (smack)

---

[51] A similar point is made in Michael Jarvis's short dramatic film *Angélique* (1999), written by Peter Farbridge. In this version of the story, Thibault is a successful, libertine artist, Angélique is his model — mistress, Mme. De Couagne [sic] is jealous, César is a would-be rapist, and the executioner is the only true egalitarian. Although Thibault knows that Angélique is innocent of arson (the fire is started by César's attempt at rape), he refuses — out of cowardice — to tell the truth.

Because there is nothing else I can do.
(smack) (30)

Thérèse's excuses for wanting to "smack" Angélique arise from her frustration over her relative impotence as a white wife in a slave society in which African and Aboriginal women may be kept as concubines. Later, after Thérèse is widowed, she berates Angélique for having been her late husband's mistress and curses her as a "[b]lack bitch. Lying whore" who "liked it when he took you" (42). Angélique's defence is that "[t]he master only took from me what you refused to give" (42), an argument that accepts a patriarchal view of marriage. Nevertheless, after the altercation, Angélique promises a bright future for them both: "I know that things haven't been good between us. But that's all going to change now. I'll serve you well. If you will let me" (43). Just as in Brown's novel, Angélique dedicates herself to serving Thérèse. This "solidarity" is shattered when Thérèse designs to sell Angélique — and the latter deigns to flee with Claude. Still, on the day of Angélique's execution, Thérèse recognizes that she herself is — metaphorically — responsible for the fire: "Hang me. It's me" (74). Angélique is her scapegoat.

It is important that Gale's Angélique builds an alliance with Manon, "*a panisse,* a young native [First Nations] slave/servant," and the two women dance together to mingled African and Aboriginal-Canadian drumming and singing (28). Their friendship is complicated by Manon's love for César, who in turn is in love with Angélique. Destructively, Angélique and Manon trade stereotypes about each other's culture (58–59), then deny each other support:

Manon: I don't follow you. Do not follow me.
Angélique: I won't. You have forgotten the way. (59)

Manon later testifies against Angélique (66). But, like Thérèse, by the play's end Manon claims that it was she alone who set the destructive fire (74), thus owning her anger regarding her sociopolitical disenfranchisement.

Gale orchestrates the play's contrasting sex-race-class conflicts so deliberately that by the night of April 10, 1734, when the fire breaks out, five potential arsonists are on hand. Manon appears "**shoveling hot coals into a bucket**"; César "**takes the bucket from Manon and prepares a cigar for smoking**"; Ignace Gamelin, a capitalist who wishes to buy Thérèse's shares in her late husband's factory, "**takes a light from César**" and puffs on another cigar; "**Thérése enters with a candle**"; and Claude "**enters with an oil lamp**" (see 59–61). The sixth suspect is Angélique, who also holds the bucket of hot coals first carried on stage by Manon (62). Even so, the play leaves open two possibilities: (1) that Angélique is innocent of staging the fire (though she has cause to do so); (2) that five characters — including Thérèse herself — have undertaken, independently or in alliances, to set her home ablaze.[52]

When Angélique leaves Montréal with Claude, the mysterious fire — an allegorical representation of their love (62) — consumes 46 houses, a statistic presented as if in a TV news report (63). This statistic recalls a more recent

---

[52] While Angélique may be innocent of arson, she is guilty of murder. Rather than see her infant son grow up to be a slave, she smothers him secretly (26).

fire, well reported internationally, that consumed 61 houses in Philadelphia in May 1985. Triggered by the explosion of a police bomb atop the headquarters of a black-nationalist-cum-back-to-the-earth movement, MOVE, the fire killed 11 people, including five children. *See* Kelley & Lewis, 2000, p. 577. However, Gale may also mean to recall the fire at Montréal's Sir George Williams University (now Concordia University) computer centre in February 1969, as a result of a protest of "racist" grades assigned black students in college courses. Another overlap with the present occurs when a reporter casts the "M.J. Angélique case" as the "O.J." case (69), thus linking Angélique's persecution for alleged arson with Simpson's 1994–97 prosecution for murder. Gale positions Angélique, as do Brown and Elliott, as a model for contemporary "marginals."

By the end of *Angélique,* the protagonist, speaking from the gallows but at a microphone, knows herself to be a forerunner of the day when Montréal will be "swarming with ebony. / There's me and me and me and me . . . / My brothers and my sisters," and she can see them being "Arrested for their difference" (75; ellipsis in the original). She insists on her innocence but also on her interest in *pur et dur* vengeance:

> I will from twisted history,
> be guilty in your eyes.
> If thought is sin
> then I am guilty.
> For I wish that I had fanned the flames that
> lead [sic] to your destruction. (75–76)

She dies amid "**The overpowering sound of drums**" (76), a military-**cum**-multi-cultural sign of her perpetual ability to "light fires of rebellion."

To conclude, Elliott, Brown, and Gale use the execution — or martyrdom — of Angélique to underline their respective political visions. The immigrant writer, Elliott, uses the spectre of Angélique to meditate on the persistence of white Canadian racism. Brown, a native francophone African-Canadian writer, stages his Late Romantic Angélique as a countering black *soeur* of the Acadian nationalist symbol of Evangeline. Gale, a native, bilingual Québécoise, the daughter of an immigrant, identifies Angélique as the radical prophet of a new, multiracial Montréal. The three writers' texts strike dramatic contrasts. Where Elliott's Angélique strives to give future blacks the truth about Canada and set them against settlement, Gale's Angélique prays that Canada will become ever "blacker" and "browner" and thus more accommodating. Elliott's Angélique lectures anglophone blacks primarily, but Brown's Angélique wants to rewrite French-Canadian "racial" history. Intriguingly, both Brown and Gale reprint a legal document declaring Angélique's sentence of torture and death: Brown in French (107), Gale in English (73). The writers stress, then, Angélique's implicit threat to authority, and that authority's explicitly violent response. Yet Brown's Angélique is sentimental, while Gale's Angélique is seditious. All three authorial visions are progressive and useful, for they speak to dilemmas of blackness and racial definition — and indefinition — in Canada, here and now. To establish other versions of these transformative visions of martyrdom, scholars must exhume the bodies of the officially destroyed, the authoritative "Others," of our collective past. We cannot know our history until we know theirs.

Certainly, African-Canadian writers are summoned to banish the disquieting silence around racially biased incarceration and state-sanctioned murder in Canada. We must examine all texts — novels, poems, plays, religious, journalistic, and legal materials — to begin to determine the lives of our "martyrs" in colonial, modern, and postmodern Canada, and to begin to hear their voices speaking back to us. To close with an appropriate, African-American aphorism from Sharon Patricia Holland: "The dead truly acknowledge no boundary, and their unruly universe is worthy of critical examination .... [T]he dead survive and clamor for our recognition."[53]

References

Andrews, William L., et al. (Eds.). (1997). *The Oxford companion to African American literature*. New York: Oxford University Press.

Aylward, Carol A. (1999). *Canadian critical race theory: Racism and the law*. Halifax: Fernwood.

Bail, Micheline. (1999). *L'Esclave*. Montréal: Libre expression.

Boyd, Neil. (1988). *The last dance: Murder in Canada*. Toronto: Seal.

Brand, Dionne. (1990). *No language is neutral*. Toronto: Coach House.

Brown, Paul Fehmiu. (1998). *Marie-Josèphe-Angélique: Montreal, Quebec 21 juin 1734*. Saint-Léonard QC: Editions Publishing 5 Continents.

Chakkalakal, Tess. (2000). Reckless eyeballing: Being Reena in Canada. In Rinaldo Walcott (Ed.), *Rude: Contemporary Black Canadian cultural criticism* (pp. 159–167). Toronto: Insomniac.

Chandler, David. (1976). *Capital punishment in Canada: A sociological study of repressive law*. Toronto: McClelland & Stewart.

Clarke, Austin. (1992). *Public enemies: Police violence and Black youth*. Toronto: Harper Collins.

Dearborn, Dorothy. (1999). *The Gallows of New Brunswick*. Saint John, NB: Neptune.

Duff, Louis Blake. (1949). *The county kerchief*. Toronto: Ryerson Press.

Elliott, Lorris. (1985). The trial of Marie-Joseph Angelique: Negress and slave [Excerpt from "Who All Was There," an unpublished play]. In Lorris Elliott (Ed.), *Other voices: Writings by blacks in Canada* (pp. 55–65). Toronto: Williams-Wallace.

Farrell, Lennox. (2001, August 1) Dead Black Men, Talking. *Toronto Star*, p. A18.

Fraser, John. (1982). *America and the patterns of chivalry*. New York: Cambridge University Press.

---

[53] Holland, 2000, p. 171.

Gadoury, Lorraine, & LeChasseur, Antonio (Eds.). (1992). *Persons sentenced to death in Canada: 1867–1976*. [Ottawa]: National Archives.

Gale, Lorena. (2000). *Angélique*. Toronto: Playwrights Canada.

Hardy, Thomas. (1930). *Tess of the d'urbervilles*. London: Macmillan. (Original work published 1891)

Holland, Sharon Patricia. (2000). *Raising the dead: Readings of death and (black) subjectivity*. Durham NC: Duke University Press.

Hornby, Jim. (1991). *Black islanders: Prince Edward Island's historical Black community*. Charlottetown, PEI: Institute of Island Studies.

———. (1998). *In the shadow of the gallows: Criminal law and capital punishment in Prince Edward Island, 1769–1941*. Charlottetown PEI: Institute of Island Studies.

Hustak, Alan. (1987). *They were hanged*. Toronto: Lorimer.

Ingle, Lorne. (Comp. and Ed.). (1989). The British North America Act. *Meech Lake reconsidered* (pp. 119–141). Hull, PQ: Voyageur.

Jarvis, Michael. (Director). (1999). *Angélique* [Motion picture]. [Montreal:] Rightime Productions.

Jobb, Dean. (1993). *Bluenose justice: True tales of mischief, mayhem, and murder*. Lawrencetown Beach, NS: Pottersfield.

———. (1988). *Shades of justice: Seven Nova Scotia murder cases*. Halifax NS: Nimbus.

Joseph, Clifton. (2001). Recollections: A seventees [sic] Black RAP [Introduction]. In Althea Prince, *Being black* (pp. 13–21). Toronto: Insomniac.

Kelley, Robin D.G. & Lewis, Earl. (2000). *To make our world anew: A history of African Americans*. New York: Oxford University Press.

Longfellow, Henry Wadsworth. (1962). *Evangeline: A tale of Acadie* [Reprint as *Evangeline*]. Toronto: McClelland & Stewart. (Original work published 1847)

Mascoll, Philip. (2000, 15 November). Mother England and her long reach. *Toronto Star*, p. A34.

Moodie, Susanna. (1989). *Roughing it in the bush: Or, life in Canada*. Toronto: McClelland & Stewart. (Original Work published 1852)

Morrison, Toni. (1997). The official story: Dead man golfing [Introduction]. Toni Morrison and Claudia Brodsky Lacour (Eds.), *Birth of a Nation 'hood: Gaze, Script, and Spectacle in the O.J. Simpson sase* (pp. vii–xxviii). New York: Pantheon.

Nolan, Faith. (1986). Marie Joseph Angelique. *Africville* [Album]. [Toronto]: Multicultural Women in Concert.

Royal Canadian Mounted Police. (1935). The Hefferman [sic] case. *Journal of Assembly* (Appendix 27). Halifax: [Nova Scotia Assembly], p. 10.

Trudel, Marcel. (1963). *L'esclavage au Canada français*. Montréal: Les Editions de l'horizon. (Original work published in 1960)

Vernnin, Loic. (1994–95). Les AfroAcadiens. *Le Ven'd'est* [Petit-Rocher, NB]: 16–17.

Winks, Robin W. (1997). *The blacks in Canada: A history*. Montreal: McGill-Queen's University Press. (Original work published 1971)

Wiwa, Ken. (2000). *In the Shadow of a Saint*. Toronto: Knopf.

Examining Racism and Criminal Justice

The Advancement of a Defence Based on Section 15(1) of the Canadian Charter of Rights and Freedoms

Faizal R. Mirza
Lawyer
Toronto

I would like to express my deepest gratitude to Professors Elizabeth Sheehy and Richard J. Iton for their support for my research. I also thank Camille and Charmaine Nelson for their support and generous contribution to the revision of this essay.

Faizal R. Mirza

Equality before and under law and equal protection and benefit of the law

15.(1) Every individual is equal before and under the law and has the right to the equal protection and equal benefit of the law without discrimination and, in particular, without discrimination based on race, national or ethnic origin, colour, religion, sex, age or mental or physical disability[1]

Section

15 of the Charter clearly establishes an equality guarantee among all people. It is the constitutional provision that best addresses racist acts by the police, but it has been profoundly underutilized by defence counsel.

The purpose of this essay is to demonstrate that there is an equality rights crisis in the Canadian criminal justice system caused by the failure of defence counsel to provide the judiciary with the optimal foundation to scrutinize and denounce racist policing; and there is a necessity for lawyers to encourage judges to consider, limit and condemn racist policing through the use of section 15(1) of the Charter.

The essay is divided into three parts. First, recent reported cases[2] with evidence of racist enforcement of the law by the police will be analyzed: *R.* v. *Hamilton* (2000) [Hamilton]; *R.* v. *Gogol* (1994) [Gogol]; and *R.* v. *McCarthy* (1996) [McCarthy]. The facts of these cases possess the necessary requirements to initiate a section 15(1) defence: compelling evidence of racist policing against black[3] accused. These cases are largely representative of the limited Charter arguments that defence counsel employ to address equality-rights infringements by the police. They are selected to elucidate how defence arguments' failure to engage section 15(1) of the Charter permits judges to avoid condemning the racist conduct of the police and addressing the deleterious effects of racism on the recipient.

Second, the cases will be placed in a broader social context by analyzing data that proves racism in Canadian policing is rampant. Third, a viable mechanism for consideration of equality-rights claims, for the protection of black persons subjected to racist policing, will be examined.

---

[1] Canadian Charter of Rights and Freedoms Part, 1 of the Constitution Act, 1982, being schedule B of the Canada Act 1982 (U.K.), 1982, c. 11 [Charter].

[2] "Reported cases" are cases that are published in legal reports, journals and databases and are accessible to persons in the legal community performing legal research. Cases that are considered to be of precedential value because of their discussion of a distinct legal principle or modification of an existing legal principle are more likely to be reported. However, the results of most cases that proceed to trial are unreported. The reported cases discussed in this essay are largely representative of the manner in which defence counsel address racist policing.

[3] The term "black" is used not to endorse the concept of "races" but, rather, to remain consistent with the wording of academic studies and data that demonstrate systemic racism in the criminal justice system.

Racially Discriminatory
Applications of the Law

It is essential that all the members of the criminal justice system strive to protect and preserve the equality rights of accused persons. In the criminal justice system, the police, Crown prosecutor, defence counsel, and judiciary assume distinct, albeit complementary, roles. The police are responsible for investigating crimes and for arresting and charging persons they believe have breached the law. It is the role of the Crown prosecutor to be a minister of justice, to search for the truth and, when necessary, to prosecute the accused. Defence counsel are responsible for vigorously defending their client from state intrusions, challenging the reliability of police-gathered evidence and ensuring that the Crown proves its case beyond a reasonable doubt. Finally, judges preside over trials, review the evidence and legal arguments presented, determine if the legal burdens have been met, and pass sentences.

In criminal law, although the Crown carries the legal burden of proof, it is the defence that carries the persuasive burden of proof when making allegations of racist policing. However, even when the evidence is capable of satisfying the persuasive burden of proof required to demonstrate racist policing, it is apparent from the following cases that defence counsel fail to make constitutional applications based on section 15(1) of the Charter.

R. v. Hamilton

In this case, the defendant was charged with possession of a small quantity of marijuana, assaulting a peace officer with intent to resist arrest, and escape from lawful custody. This case provides a compelling example of how some police officers racially profile[4] black men and subject them to arbitrary detentions, unlawful arrests and excessive uses of force.

Hamilton was walking through a local park in Toronto, on his way to buy a pair of athletic shoes, carrying $200 in cash to make his purchase. On his way to the store he saw some of his friends in the park by picnic tables and went over to visit with them. In contrast to police testimony, Hamilton claimed that during his visit he did not receive a cigar-like object from one of his friends and did not smoke marijuana. A plainclothes officer performing surveillance of the area approached Hamilton and, without saying a word, searched his pockets and seized his money. Hamilton reached with his left hand to retrieve his money but was stopped by a uniformed officer who arrived at the scene and wrestled him to the ground. When Hamilton tried to get up, he was pepper-sprayed in the eyes. An off-duty security guard who was walking with his family in the park at the time observed the encounter and testified that two of the officers called him and the defendants "niggers".[5]

Justice Reinhardt found that, based on the evidence, the police had conducted themselves in an improper manner that violated the accused's rights

---

[4] Racial profiling occurs when certain criminal behaviour is projected onto a specific racial group and is then acted upon by law enforcement when using powers to stop, detain and search.
[5] Hamilton, at para. 16.

under section 10 of the Charter and therefore dismissed the charges.[6] Justice Reinhardt also found that racial slurs were used by the officers and maintained that there was evidence confirming the police had engaged in an unreasonable search, contrary to section 8 of the Charter.[7]

This case was decided on the merits of a constitutional challenge under sections 10(a) and 10(b) of the Charter. Although there was ample corroborating evidence that the police had acted in an overtly racist manner, a section 15(1) Charter application was never argued by defence counsel in this case. The police had racially profiled Hamilton and used excessive force in an attempt to apprehend him. The police considered a group of black men sitting in a park to be sufficient grounds to warrant an aggressive criminal investigation. Indeed, the actions of the police officers were consistent with the racist presumption that the congregation of young black males provides a reasonable suspicion of criminal activity.

Justice Reinhardt's condemnation of the conduct of the police officers was limited to stating that their actions were "unprofessional." The judge did not make any significant effort to condemn the corrupt, unrepentant and morally depraved actions of the police officers. The judicial analysis in this case focused on the unlawful arrest and detention followed by an unreasonable search largely because defence counsel failed to raise a section 15(1) argument. As a result of the limited defence arguments, even though the testimony regarding the use of racist slurs was accepted as credible by the judge, the court was not required to directly address the violation of the accused's equality rights in a case that clearly warranted a powerful statement against racist policing.

R. v. Gogol

This is another case in which there is compelling evidence of racist law enforcement. Defence counsel, on behalf of Gogol, brought an application based on sections 8, 9,[8] and 10 of the Charter to exclude evidence during her trial on a charge of possession of a small quantity of marijuana. Gogol alleged that although she cooperated with the police, she was handcuffed for hours, forced to go to the bathroom while handcuffed, denied her right to counsel, called a "nigger lover,"[9] and had her apartment trashed by the police during the execution of a search warrant.

Gogol testified that an officer at the scene, Constable Lee, said to her, "If you tell anybody what went on here, I'll come back, I'll put a bullet in your head. If not you, I'll get that big black nigger son of yours, and if not him, I'll get your dog."[10] However, Justice Fairgrieve found that the vulgar language and

---

[6] Section 10 states: "Arrest or detention — Everyone has the right on arrest or detention (a) to be informed promptly of the reasons thereof; (b) to retain and instruct counsel without delay and to be informed of that right."

[7] Hamilton at para. 44. Section 8 states: "Search or seizure — 8. Everyone has the right not to be arbitrarily detained or imprisoned."

[8] Section 9 states: "Detention or imprisonment — 9. Everyone has the right not to be arbitrarily detained or imprisoned."

[9] Gogol, at para 14.

[10] Gogol, at para. 8.

the crude sentiments were the product of the accused's efforts to portray her treatment in a more shocking way, and stated that he believed Constable Lee's conduct was not even remotely as violent or hostile towards Gogol as her evidence alleged.[11] Remarkably, Justice Fairgrieve also found that with respect to the use of racial slurs by the police officer:

> I was inclined to believe the evidence of Maureen Forestall which tended to support Ms. Gogol's evidence in this regard. Ms. Forestall, employed by a marketing manager and the sister of a Metro Toronto police officer, testified that her own residence on Marion St. had been searched the same night and that she had been arrested... She was met at the door, she testified, by Cst. Lee, referred to as the red-haired officer with a bandanna, and that he told her to take her son to the Children's Aid where he would be better off than living with drug dealers. Ms. Forestall further testified that when she encountered the same officer at the police station later the same night, he called her a "nigger fucker" and similar names.[12]

Although the judge was ultimately reluctant to accept the testimony of the accused, defence counsel, in addition to the other Charter breaches alleged, should have argued a section 15(1) Charter application that logically connected the evidence supporting racist policing with evidence of police brutality towards the accused. In particular, counsel could have attempted to demonstrate that the actions of the officers at the scene, especially those of Constable Lee, were consistent with unequal application of the law motivated by racism.

Defence counsel did not confront Justice Fairgrieve with a section 15(1) argument; as a result, Justice Fairgrieve was only mandated to evaluate the other Charter breaches alleged, which did not necessarily require a focused judgement regarding whether the police had acted in a discriminatory manner. Indeed, although Justice Fairgrieve agreed that Gogol's Charter rights had been violated and excluded from evidence the small amount of marijuana found at Gogol's home, absent from his reasons was any discussion of the apparent racist motivation by the police for the Charter violations. Specifically, Justice Fairgrieve found that the accused was neither informed of her right to counsel nor provided with a reasonable opportunity to exercise such right, had she wanted to, before being handcuffed. He further ruled that the restraint of the accused in handcuffs for about two hours clearly constituted a detention. This detention was not accompanied by compliance with section 10(a) of the Charter, requiring that the accused be informed of the reasons for her detention, nor by compliance with section 10(b) of the Charter, mandating that the accused be allowed to exercise her right to counsel. Her detention was neither reasonable nor a necessary part of the search authorized, amounting to an arbitrary detention of the kind proscribed by section 9 of the Charter. Further, the search was accompanied by unnecessary damage to the accused's property.

If Justice Fairgrieve had been required to consider a section 15(1) argument, he would have had to consider the credible evidence of the use of racist slurs by the police to determine whether the police applied the law in a discriminatory fashion towards Ms. Gogol. In factual circumstances involving the

---

[11] Ibid.

[12] Gogol, at para. 33.

use of racist slurs by the police and other misconduct, it is important that defence counsel expose and emphasize the serious level of disrespect and hostility demonstrated by the police towards the accused. Without compromise, when police officers use racial slurs, the defence must challenge their ability to enforce the law in a fair manner by exhausting the relevant provisions of the Charter. The courts must be encouraged by defence counsel to perform a vigorous and comprehensive examination of the motivations for misconduct in cases that involve anti-black bias by police officers. In addition, in order to deter and limit racism in policing, it is important that defence counsel convey to the court the "spirit murdering"[13] nature of racism. The Supreme Court of Canada has noted that section 15(1) of the Charter especially applies in circumstances in which a person has been disrespected because of racial animus by a government entity responsible for applying the law. In *Andrews* v. *Law Society* of British Columbia (1990) [Andrews], Justice McIntyre noted that disregard for the inherent human dignity of an individual person goes towards showing a contravention of his/her right to equal treatment under section 15:

> It is clear that the purpose of s. 15 is to ensure equality in the formulation and application of the law. The promotion of equality entails the promotion of a society in which all are secure in the knowledge that they are recognized as human beings equally deserving of concern, respect and consideration.[14]

R. v. McCarthy

Yet another case in which an equality-rights analysis should have been advanced by defence counsel for judicial consideration is *R.* v. *McCarthy*. McCarthy, a black man, was charged with weapons offences. McCarthy's evidence on *voir dire*[15] was that six officers were engaged in the search of his premises for approximately an hour while he sat handcuffed to a chair. He testified that some of the police officers taunted him with racial epithets, hit him across the head several times, shot a toy dart at him and then stuck it on his forehead, and dropped a heavy object next to his bare foot, leaving a dent in the floor. In addition, at some point that night a police officer subjected McCarthy to a mock execution. Specifically, the police officer stated to McCarthy that there was a bullet in the chamber of the gun he was holding, told him, "You're going to fucking die tonight," and then proceeded to point the gun at McCarthy while pulling the trigger.

Strikingly, the evidence of racist police misconduct was unchallenged by the Crown at trial. The Crown called only one police officer on *voir dire,* an officer who had not been named as an abuser by the appellant and who stated that he was primarily with the appellant during the course of the search. The only question put to the police officer by the Crown concerning the allegations of

---

[13] For a discussion of the need for the justice system to acknowledge the psychological impact of racism on persons of colour, *see* Williams, 1994. *See also* Camille A. Nelson, B*reaking the Camel's Back A Constitution of Mitigatory Criminal Law Defenses and Racism-Related Mental Illness*, Michigan Journal of Race and Law, Volume 9, Issue 1, pp. 77–147.

[14] Andrews. *See also* discussion of the Court's application of section 15 of the Charter and discussion of inherent human dignity in Wright, 1996.

[15] A *voir dire* is a hearing held within a trial to determine admissibility of evidence.

abuse was a very tailored inquiry as to whether he had observed McCarthy being struck on the head. The officer said that he did not. Overall, the Crown and the testifying police officer did not offer a satisfactory rebuttal to McCarthy's allegations of misconduct by the police and had not contest the evidence of racist motivation for the abuse. Furthermore, the Crown conceded at trial that the allegations of racist conduct by the officer were as serious as could be imagined and, if accepted as true, would lead to a finding that the search was unreasonable.

Ultimately, on appeal to the Supreme Court of Canada, a new trial was ordered because the trial judge failed to rule on the evidence of racist conduct during the *voir dire*. Hence, the task of resolving allegations of racially inspired abuse was deferred with the hope that the police officers would respond to the evidence at trial. Agreeing with the dissenting opinion of the Court of Appeal, the Supreme Court asserted that McCarthy was entitled to a decision on the merits as they then stood, and the failure to accord him that right entitled him to a new trial.

Despite the compelling evidence of racist policing available to the defence for a successful section 15(1) Charter challenge, counsel only challenged the police misconduct under the guise of a section 8 Charter application. The unchallenged evidence of racist policing clearly indicated that the police officers executed the search warrant in a discriminatory fashion, contrary to McCarthy's rights under section 15(1) of the Charter. In this case there was no legal or strategic reason for defence counsel to limit the Charter advocacy exclusively to unreasonable search arguments. Defence counsel was in an excellent position to meet the persuasive burden of proving racial discrimination.

The McCarthy case indicates that in that in order to protect and, perhaps, restore the dignity of an accused that has been victimized by racist policing, it is imperative that defence counsel, when confronted with evidence of racially inspired police brutality towards their client, provide the court with the optimal legal foundation to publicly denounce and condemn the conduct of the racist officers involved — section 15(1) must be raised and utilized. In situations in which the police subject an accused to an unreasonable search because of anti-black racism, a judicial finding that the actions of the officer(s) involved violated the accused's section 15(1) rights would directly address the emotionally (and sometimes physically) devastating conduct of the police, whereas a judicial finding of a section 8 violation alone may only work to nullify the legality of the search. Indeed, a successful section 15(1) violation argument by defence counsel against racist police officers ensures that racist policing is not subsumed under an inquiry into the search powers of the police.

A finding that the police have violated the section 15(1) rights of the accused may also have broader ramifications for advancing the rights of black persons within the criminal justice system. Judicial findings of equality-rights violations by specific police officers may provide an effective basis for victims of racist policing to pursue civil action against those involved or responsible. In addition, within the policing structure, internal disciplinary bodies should keep track of, investigate and punish police officers who have been found to have flagrantly breached the equality rights of an accused in the course of performing their duties.

Faizal R. Mirza

Consequences of Failure to Engage Section 15

The cases discussed above provide powerful proof that when performing routine duties such as investigative detentions, engaging in searches of property and person, using force and laying charges, police officers discriminate against blacks contrary to their rights under section 15(1) of the Charter.

The underlying purpose of this segment is to highlight section 15(1), the equality-rights clause of the Constitution, which is seldom, if ever, raised by defence counsel when dealing with cases with evidence of racist policing. Consequently, judges are not required to address the motivation for police misconduct and are permitted to sidestep addressing evidence of racist policing by limiting their findings to violations that can be articulated without mentioning the role of racism, such as arbitrary detentions, unreasonable searches and seizures, and unlawful arrests.

Some may contend that the rulings in cases like Hamilton, Gogol and McCarthy demonstrate that under the present criminal law framework, the rights of black persons can be adequately protected by the criminal justice system. In all these cases, the judiciary found in favour of the persons who had been subject to police misconduct.

It is not disputed that the justice system is capable — especially when the facts obviously demonstrate misconduct — of protecting the constitutional rights of black people. However, these and other cases demonstrate that as long as defence counsel fail to provide the court with equality-rights analysis in criminal trials that involve racist policing, there is a substantial risk that racist police officers will walk out of court at the end of trial without having the motivation for their misconduct exposed, denounced and accounted for by the justice system.[16]

By not directly challenging racist policing, counsel fail to tackle directly the right of all persons to be treated equally under the law. It is imperative for the justice system to recognize that many persons who have encountered racist policing have had their lives adversely altered and ambitions stifled — they develop an immense distrust for the justice system. The causes and effects of problems such as racial profiling and the unfair treatment of blacks within the criminal justice system can be addressed through a section 15(1) analysis in addition to other relevant sections of the Charter. Such an analysis would reveal the fundamental nexus between decisions to investigate, arrest, search and detain suspects and the motivating factors of racism and equality-rights infringements.

The profound failure of defence counsel to provide the court with equality--rights advocacy in criminal matters has not gone unnoticed by members of the judiciary. Consider, for instance, that Justice Donna Hackett of the Scarborough Superior Court of Justice has noted that, during a seven-year span, she never had an equality-rights issue raised before her by counsel. She estimates that she

---

[16] For other cases in which a section 15(1) argument could have been advanced on behalf of the accused and considered by the judiciary, *see R.* v. *Richards* (1999), *R.* v. *Burton* (1993), *R.* v. *Lewis* (1992), *R.* v. *Brown* (1998), and *R.* v. *Dunn* (1992).

has presided over approximately 21,000 cases since her appointment.[17] To test the significance of her own experience, Justice Hackett asked six of her colleagues about their experiences and found them to be no different than her own. Remarkably, Justice Hackett together with the other Justices surveyed have collected over 36 years of experience on the bench since 1985, having heard a total of 120,000 cases in the Toronto region.[18]

Racism in Policing

This section will examine a collection of data that demonstrates there is an equality-rights crisis in Canadian criminal law. The cases, literature and studies discussed establish that racism is rampant in Canadian policing. Indeed, the surveys applied and analyzed support the contention that the experiences of the accused in Hamilton, Gogol, and McCarthy do not represent isolated incidents. Many blacks have experienced similar abusive conduct at the hands of police.

Widespread racism in Ontario and its adverse impact on persons of colour, especially blacks, has been judicially noted in *R.* v. *Parks* (1993) [Parks] and *R.* v. *Wilson* (1996) [Wilson]. Parks was charged with second-degree murder and convicted of manslaughter. He appealed the conviction and sentence. Parks was a drug dealer, and the victim was a cocaine user. The offence occurred during a struggle with a knife. The accused successfully argued that the trial judge should have allowed defence counsel to ask prospective jurors whether the fact that the accused was black and the victim was white would adversely affect their ability to impartially perform their duties. In finding that the accused had been denied his statutory right to challenge for cause, which was essential to the appearance of fairness and the integrity of the trial, the court in *Wilson*, the Ontario Court of Appeal extended the opportunity given in Parks for defence counsel to screen jurors for prejudice towards blacks in courts throughout Ontario. The trial judge attempted to limit the findings by Justice Doherty of the Ontario Court of Appeal in Parks regarding anti-black racism to the city of Toronto. According to Chief Justice McMurtry, any distinction based on a geographic boundary between Metropolitan Toronto and other Ontario communities would be arbitrary and should not form the basis of a judicial exercise of discretion to refuse challenge. Given the impact of the media and the fact that racism also occurs in areas in which there is little interaction between blacks and whites, it was unrealistic and illogical to assume that anti-black attitudes stop at the borders of Metropolitan Toronto. Appeal took judicial notice of the existence of anti-black racism in Ontario. In *Parks,* Justice Doherty of the Ontario Court of Appeal concluded that "our institutions, including the criminal justice system, reflect and perpetuate negative stereotypes. These elements combine to infect our society as a whole with the evil of racism. Blacks are among the primary victims of that evil."[19]

---

[17] Hackett, 1998, p. 131.

[18] Ibid.

[19] Parks, pp. 371–372.

Faizal R. Mirza

Judicial notice of the specific tendency of police officers in Nova Scotia to mistreat blacks has been recognized in *R. v. RDS* by the Supreme Court. RDS was a black youth charged with unlawfully resisting an officer in the lawful execution of duty. At trial, RDS and the officer were the only two witnesses, and their accounts of the events differed. Justice Sparks, a black woman, acquitted RDS. In her reasons and in response to Crown submissions, Justice Sparks remarked that police officers have over-reacted when dealing with non-white groups, although she was not referring specifically to the officer in this case. The Crown appealed the case and successfully argued that Justice Sparks' comments gave rise to a reasonable apprehension of bias on her part. The Nova Scotia Court of Appeal ordered a new trial. The Supreme Court of Canada reversed the Court of Appeal ruling and restored Justice Sparks' decision. Specifically, in *RDS,* at the trial level, Justice Sparks used her knowledge of the tendency of police officers to over-react when dealing with visible minorities to determine that a police officer might over-react when dealing with an accused black youth. Supreme Court Justices La Forest, L'Heureux-Dubé, Gonthier, and McLachlin maintained that awareness of the context within which a case occurred is consistent with the highest tradition of judicial impartiality. Justices L'Heureux-Dubé and McLachlin also noted that a reasonable person must be taken to possess knowledge of the local population and its racial dynamics, including the existence in the community of a history of widespread and systemic discrimination against blacks, and high-profile clashes between the police and the black population over policing.[20]

Documented evidence in Nova Scotia and Ontario indicates that there is a perception, especially amongst black people, that blacks are discriminated against by the police. For example, a survey taken in 1989 performed in Nova Scotia for the *Royal Commission on the Prosecution of Donald Marshall Jr.* found that about 60 percent of respondents agreed that police discriminate against blacks.[21] In addition, a survey by the *Report of the Commission on Systemic Racism* taken in the mid 1990s found that 74 percent of black Metro Toronto residents believe that the police treat black people worse than white people.[22] The report found that the black community feels discriminatory treatment from the police is a precursor to the unjustified shooting of black civilians.[23] Since 1978, on-duty police officers have shot at least 16 black people in Ontario, 10 of them fatally.[24] In nine cases criminal charges were laid against the police officers, but none resulted in a conviction.[25] In the past two decades, the number and circumstances of police shootings of blacks in Ontario have convinced many black Ontarians that they are disproportionately susceptible to police violence. The black community has concluded that

---

[20] *See* Justice L'Heureux Dubé and Justice McLachlin, reasons, in RDS.

[21] Head & Clairmont, 1989, pp. 31–33.

[22] Commission on Systemic Racism in the Ontario Criminal Justice System, 1995 [*Report of the Commission on Systemic Racism*], Executive Summary IX.

[23] Ibid., p. 67.

[24] Ibid.

[25] Ibid.

the police are quicker to use their guns against black people and that the shootings are unduly harsh responses to the incidents under investigation. The resulting deaths and injuries have also come to represent the ultimate manifestation of daily discrimination and harassment that many black people experience, especially in interactions with the police. In short the shootings are perceived not as isolated incidents, but as tragedies that affect the entire black community — and as a reflection of the destructive force of systemic discrimination.[26]

Furthermore, studies of black interaction with law enforcement provide compelling evidence of racist policing. Specifically, the data powerfully demonstrates that there is an overpolicing of communities with concentrated black populations, specifically through racial profiling.[27] Racial profiling occurs when certain criminal behaviour is projected onto a specific racial group and then acted upon by law enforcement when using powers to stop, detain and search.[28] The most common forms of racial profiling occur within the context of pedestrian and traffic stops. Under the guise of policing Highway Traffic Act violations, the police routinely stop blacks for criminal investigations.

Statistics analyzed by Scot Wortley of the Centre of Criminology at the University of Toronto demonstrate that black Metro residents (28 percent) were much more likely than white (18 percent) or Chinese residents (15 percent) to report having been stopped by the police between 1993 and 1995.[29] Black residents (17 percent) were also more likely than white (8 percent) or Chinese (5 percent) residents to report multiple stops during this period.[30] Wortley also found that the odds ratio suggests that, after controlling for other variables, blacks are twice as likely as whites or Asians to experience a single stop, are four times more likely to experience multiple stops, and are almost seven times as likely to experience an unfair stop.[31]

The data further revealed that the targeting of black males is particularly striking. Between 1993 and 1995, 43 percent of black male residents, but only 25 percent of white men and 19 percent of Chinese male residents reported being stopped by the police. Significantly more black men (29 percent) than white (12 percent) or Chinese (7 percent) reported two or more police stops during this period.[32]

Wortley has concluded that the statistics reveal that age reduces the probability of being stopped by the police for all racial groups. However, with respect to involuntary police contact, black men and women do not benefit from aging to the same extent as whites and Asians. Indeed, 19 percent of the black respondents over 50 years of age still report that they were stopped by the

---

[26] Ibid.

[27] Ibid., Executive Summary IX.

[28] For a further discussion of racial profiling, *see* Justice Doherty's Ontario Court of Appeal opinion in Richards.

[29] Wortley, 1997, pp. 20–21. *See also Report of the Commission on Systemic Racism.*

[30] Wortley, 1997, pp. 20–21..

[31] Ibid.

[32] *Report of the Commission on Systemic Racism*, Executive Summary IX.

police during this period, compared with only 7.3 percent of the white and Asian respondents in the same age category.[33]

Also, although educational attainment further insulates whites and Asians from police stops, it does not seem to protect blacks.[34] The findings suggest that, unlike whites and Asians, higher educational attainment may not safeguard blacks from being stopped by the police. Cross-tabular analysis reveals that in fact, university-educated blacks are slightly more likely to be stopped (34.0 percent) than blacks with lower educational attainment (27.2 percent).[35] The opposite is true for whites and Asians. Thus, racial differences in police contact are actually more prominent among respondents with a university degree (34 percent vs. 12.4 percent) than among those with less educational attainment (27.2 percent vs. 18.2 percent).[36]

Heightened levels of age and education protect whites and Asians from police contact. While there is a 30 percent chance that young white and Asian males with less than a university education will be stopped by the police, the probability of being stopped drops to 6 percent for older white and Asian males with a university education.[37]

In contrast, for black persons, racist law enforcement transcends economic class. University educated, older black males have almost the same probability of being stopped (40 percent) as young black males without a university degree (44 percent).[38] Ultimately, discriminatory law enforcement, particularly against well-educated blacks, contributes significantly to a mistrust of the criminal justice system by the black population.[39]

Most recently, in October 2002, the findings of a *Toronto Star* newspaper study of Toronto police traffic-offence data dating back to 1996 confirmed that black people are stopped at a disproportionate rate by the police. The study found that a disproportionate number of blacks have been ticketed for violations that emerge only after a traffic stop has been made. These offences, categorized as "out-of-sight" traffic offences, include driving without insurance or a licence. The *Toronto Star* found that in the group where race was listed, 33.6 percent of all drivers charged with out-of-sight violations were black, despite the fact that the black community represents only 8.1 percent of Toronto's population. In contrast, 52.1 percent of whites were charged for out-of-sight offences, although they comprise 62.7 percent of the city's population. Additionally, the *Toronto Star* study further found that black men between the ages of 25 and 34 are especially targeted by the police for out-of-sight offences. Black men in this age category were issued 39.3 percent of tickets for out-of-sight violations, although they represent only 7.9 percent of Toronto's population in that age category, whereas approximately 40 percent of whites in this same age

---

[33] Wortley, 1997, p. 21.

[34] Ibid.

[35] Ibid.

[36] Ibid.

[37] Ibid.

[38] Ibid.

[39] Ibid.

group were charged for similar offences despite comprising over 60 percent of the city's population in that age category.[40] The source for the *Toronto Star* investigation into police crime and race is the Criminal Information Processing System (CIPS), a Toronto database that documents charges laid since 1996. CIPS is used to track arrests and the arrested as the latter enter the criminal justice system and also documents non-criminal offences such as Highway Traffic Act charges and by-law infractions.

The *Toronto Star* study also revealed that among those persons charged with a criminal offence, blacks are treated more harshly than whites by the police. Since late 1996, with respect to simple drug possession charges, whites were released by the police 76.5 percent of the time while blacks were released 61.8 percent of the time. In addition, the study found that since 1997, over 40 percent of blacks charged with a single count of cocaine possession were detained for a bail hearing while only 20 percent of white persons were detained.[41]

Initiating a Section 15 Defence and Remedies

This section will examine the current legal framework regarding section 15(1) of the Charter and attempt to demonstrate how an equality-rights challenge based on racial discrimination can be initiated under this section of the Constitution.

For the purposes of section 15(1) analysis, it is important to note that racism can be operating even if the actors believe themselves to be non-prejudiced. In Canada, the test for unequal treatment is impact, not motive or intention. Institutions such as the police force, courts, and prisons may be found to be in contravention of section 15(1) of the Charter if it is determined that they apply traditionally normal standards in a manner that has a disproportionately adverse effect on persons of colour.[42]

In *Jane Doe* v. *Toronto Commissioners of Police* (1998) [Jane Doe], based on evidence of discriminatory policy decisions by the police during a sexual offender investigation and man-hunt, the court found that the rights of the plaintiff had been violated. In *Jane Doe,* the plaintiff, a victim of a serial rapist, asserted not that only had she been discriminated against by individual officers

---

[40] Jim Rankin, Jennifer Quinn, Michelle Shephard, John Duncanson, and Scott Simmie, *Toronto Star* (October 20, 2002), p. A8. Race is identified in four out of five incidents recorded in the police database (399,922 out of 483,614). For tracking and identification purposes, officers are required to document an arrested person's skin colour, their status in Canada, their employment information, and their country of birth. They also must document how the person is released from police custody. For most arrests for Criminal Code and drug offences, officers recorded all the data required. For lesser offences, such as traffic and city by-law violations, record keeping was less complete, and race was not always indicated. The database also does not throughly document the outcome of arrests once they reach court. The *Toronto Star* singled out 7,511 cases in the database where individuals had been charged with only one count of a traffic offence and focused on the 4,696 cases where skin colour had been noted.

[41] Rankin et al., 2002, p. A12.

[42] MacCrimmon, 1998.

in the investigation of her specific complaint because she is a woman, but that systemic discrimination against women existed within the Metro Toronto Police Force (MTPF) in 1986. This systemic discrimination impacted adversely on all women and, specifically, those who were survivors of sexual assault who came into contact with the MTPF — a class of persons to which the plaintiff belonged. The plaintiff alleged, in effect, that the sexist, stereotypical views held by the MTPF informed the investigation of the serial rapist and caused the investigation to be conducted incompetently and in such a way that the she was denied the equal protection and equal benefit of law guaranteed to her by section 15(1) of the Charter. The judge agreed and found that there existed systemic discrimination towards women in the policing of sexual assault investigations and, therefore, found that the plaintiff's right to equality of treatment had been violated. Section 1, or "the reasonable limits" clause, of the Charter did not apply because the police conduct in issue was not a legislative enactment or common law rule, and the conduct was, therefore, not "prescribed by law." The police also failed to meet the private law duty of care owed to the plaintiff.

Jane Doe stands for the proposition that an officer's conduct, if it demonstrates discriminatory decisions in enforcement, can be challenged under section 15(1) of the Charter. Therefore, discretionary made decisions by an individual officer — for example, to target a black person for criminality while enforcing traffic laws or to use racial slurs and brutal force while executing a search — can be challenged as discriminatory acts that violate protections offered under section 15(1) of the Charter and cannot be saved under section 1.

In addition, part of the precedential value of *Jane Doe* is that the case states section 15(1) protects individuals from systemic discrimination within government structures and institutions. Based on this precedent, a black person that has been illegitimately detained and harassed by the police may be able to successfully advance an equality-rights claim by demonstrating that because of systemic racism in policing, the statute (such as the enforcement of traffic stops and drug offences) was applied in a manner that violated their right to equal treatment under the law. Evidence of widespread and systemic racism within policing (found in the statistical data and academic studies discussed in the previous section) can be introduced in court through expert evidence or be recognized by judicial notice. For instance, in a racial profiling case, the use of statistical data and expert evidence indicating that blacks are stopped and investigated by the police at disproportionate rates could be used by defence counsel to argue that their client was the victim of widespread racist enforcement or racist investigative detentions. Additionally, defence counsel could demonstrate that the actions of the officer(s) are racist and consistent with the widespread police practice and a systemic problem of racial profiling. Therefore, as a consequence of systemic racism in policing and the racist conduct of the officer(s) involved, the accused was denied their Charter rights.

Once a section 15(1) violation has been proven, sections 24(1) and 24(2)[43] of the Charter provide a number of possible remedies to persons who have had

---

[43] Sections 24(1) and 24(2) address enforcement of guaranteed rights and freedoms.

their equality rights infringed upon and are confronted by criminal charges. Section 24(1) of the Charter relates to the enforcement of guaranteed rights and freedoms and states: "Anyone whose rights or freedoms, as guaranteed by this Charter have been infringed or denied may apply to a court of competent jurisdiction to obtain such remedy as the court considers appropriate and just in the circumstances." Under section 24(1) of the Charter, a person who has been subject to unequal treatment can find relief from police misconduct through a stay of proceedings, case dismissal, acquittal and monetary damages.

In *R.* v. *Rehberg* (1994) [Rehberg], the court used section 24(1) to provide relief specific to the accused, who was charged with welfare fraud, when it was demonstrated that the provision she was charged under was seriously flawed and violated section 7[44] of the Charter. The court in *Rehberg* noted that the leading case regarding remedies for Charter violations is *Schachter* v. *Canada* (1992) [Schachter]. In *Schachter* the Supreme Court of Canada confirmed that s. 24(1) of the Charter provides an individual with a remedy for actions that violate their Charter rights. The Supreme Court held that courts should adopt a remedy that is least invasive of the legislative jurisdiction but still provides a suitable remedy for the applicant. In *Rehberg,* it was determined that the most suitable remedy for the applicant under the circumstances would be to grant a stay of proceedings.

Section 24(1) of the Charter would apply if an officer is acting under a constitutionally valid statute and takes action that falls outside the scope or jurisdiction conferred by the statutory provision. For example, when an officer racially profiles and charges a person under a section of the Criminal Code, if defence counsel is able to demonstrate that their client's section 15(1) Charter rights were violated by the police in the course of the investigation, the accused may be entitled to an individual remedy under section 24(1), such as a stay of proceedings, an acquittal, and/or monetary damages for having had their equality rights violated.

Section 24(2) of the Charter may also provide a remedy to an accused who has had their equality rights infringed by the police in the course of an investigation. Section 24(2) of the Charter permits the exclusion of evidence in criminal trials when an accused's Charter rights have been breached and the branches of the Collins test[45] have been satisfied. Following a judicial finding of a section 15(1) violation, under section 24(2) incriminating evidence found pursuant to racist law enforcement tactics can be excluded if the elements of the Collins test are met.

Section 52 of the Charter can also provide a remedy in instances in which the law itself is held to contravene section 15(1). Section 52 permits the court to strike down the legislation or read in or read down provisions in order to

---

[44] Section 7 states: "Life, liberty and security of the person — 7. Everyone has the right to life, liberty and security of the person and the right not to be deprived thereof except in accordance with the principles of fundamental justice."
[45] Collins 1987. In *Collins,* Chief Justice Lamer of the Supreme Court of Canada identified three factors as critical to the question of whether the admission of evidence would bring the administration of justice into disrepute: (1) the nature of the evidence obtained as a result of the Charter violation; (2) the nature of the official conduct; and (3) the effect of excluding the evidence on the administration of justice.

have the legislation comply with the Charter.[46] However, getting to the stage of a section 52 analysis is more difficult than obtaining an individual remedy because proving a piece of legislation is unconstitutional requires the law be found to contravene a Charter right and not be saved under the reasonable limits section of the Charter.[47] In *R. v. Oakes* (1986), Justice Dickson, speaking for the Supreme Court of Canada, which was unanimous on this issue, stated the four criteria that must be satisfied to establish that a limit is reasonable and demonstrably justified in a free and democratic society: (1) sufficiently important objective: the law must pursue an objective that is sufficiently important to justify limiting a Charter right; (2) rational connection: the law must be rationally connected to the objective; (3) least drastic means: the law must impair the right no more than is necessary to accomplish the objective; and (4) proportionate effect: the law must not have a disproportionately severe effect on the person(s) to whom it applies.[48]

Finally, even if a provision or section of a statute does not violate the Charter by itself, the common law position on the provision or section may contravene section 15(1) by facilitating unequal application of the law. In *Retail, Wholesale and Department Store Union, Local 580 v. Dolphin Delivery* (1986), Justice McIntyre stated it is necessary that the courts apply and develop the principles of the common law in a manner consistent with the fundamental values enshrined in the Constitution. For instance, defence counsel could argue that, given the overwhelming evidence of racial profiling in the context of the enforcement of traffic stops by the police, it is necessary that the random stop provision of the Highway Traffic laws be developed to include a common law interpretation of the requirement that in instances in which a *prima facie* case of racial profiling is established by the defence, police officer(s) involved be required to explain the justification and motivation for the stop. In other words, it is arguable that in light of mounting evidence of the prevalence of racist policing, the failure of counsel and courts to have some form of limiting grounds read into the procedures for executing traffic stops has resulted in a situation where the common law of highway traffic procedure is incompatible with the equality-rights guarantees.

Conclusion

In conclusion, racist police conduct is a serious threat to the physical and mental well being of black people. The primary constitutional provision that addresses racist acts by the police has not been adequately engaged by defence

---

[46] *See R. v. M(C)* (1995) in which it was held that section 159 of the Criminal Code was of no force or effect since it violated section 15 of the Charter by potentially denying individuals' liberty for engaging in consensual sexual conduct on the basis of sexual orientation, age and marital status. Section 159 criminalized specific sexual practices unless both parties are over 18 years of age and the acts occur in "private." See also statement regarding the use of section 15(1) in Schachter.

[47] This section states: "Rights and freedoms in Canada — 1. The Canadian Charter of Rights and Freedoms guarantees the rights and freedoms set out in it subject only to such reasonable limits prescribed by law as can be demonstrably justified in a free and democratic society."

[48] For an in-depth analysis of the law of section 1 of the Charter, *see* Hogg, 1998, p. 710.

counsel. Although section 15(1) of the Charter is a powerful provision aimed at guaranteeing the equality rights of Canadians and is directly applicable to criminal cases that involve evidence of racist conduct by the police, it lies largely dormant and unrecognized for its purpose and protections in the criminal law.

It is essential that the persons responsible for administering justice understand that there is a fundamental nexus between racially motivated decisions to arrest, search and detain blacks and the equality rights entrenched in section 15(1) of the Charter. In cases in which there is compelling evidence of racist policing, defence counsel need to take the next logical step in the development of criminal and constitutional law in order to best protect their client and combat systemic racism.

Victims of racist conduct by police officers can only experience true vindication when the courts recognize their experiences and sense of frustration with the criminal justice system. Equality-rights analysis is the optimal way for the courts to hold officers accountable for their improper conduct and to demonstrate an appreciation for the detrimental effects of institutionalized racism.

References

Canadian Charter of Rights and Freedoms Part 1 of the Constitution Act, 1982, being schedule B of the Canada Act 1982 (U.K.), 1982, c. 11, ss. 7, 8, 9, 10, 15(1). [Charter].

Commission on Systemic Racism in the Ontario Criminal Justice System. (1995). *Report of the Commission on Systemic Racism in the Ontario Criminal Justice System*. Toronto, ON: Queen's Printer for Ontario. [*Report of the Commission on Systemic Racism*].

Retail, Wholesale and Department Store Union, Local 580 v. *Dolphin Delivery*, [1986] 2 SCR 573; 33 DLR (4th) 174.

Hackett, Donna (The Honourable Judge). (1998). Finding and following "the road less travelled": Judicial neutrality and the protection and enforcement of equality rights in criminal trial courts. *Canadian Journal of Women and the Law 10*, 129–148.

Head W., & Clairmont, D. (1989, February). *Royal Commission on the Donald Marshall Jr. Prosecution, Discrimination Against Blacks in Nova Scotia: A Research Study 1989*. (Nova Scotia: Royal Commission on the Donald Marshall Jr. Prosecution.

Highway Traffic Act, R.S.O 1990.

Hogg, Peter. (1998). *Constitutional Law of Canada* (1998 Student Edition). Scarborough, ON: Carswell.

Jane Doe v. Toronto Commissioners of Police (1998), 39 O.R. (3d) 487 (Div. Ct.) [Jane Doe.]

MacCrimmon, M. (1998). Generalizing about racism. *Canadian Journal of Women and the Law, 10*, 184–199.

R. v. *Andrews*, (1990) 3. S.C.R. 229. [Andrews].

R. v. *Brown*, (1998) O.J. No 4682 (Gen. Div.). [Brown].

R. v. *Burton*, (1993) O.J. No. 2873 (Ont. C.A.). [Burton].

R. v. *Collins*, (1987) 1 S.C.R. 265, 56 C.R.(3d) 193. [Collins].

R. v. *Dunn*, (1992) O.J No. 685 (Gen. Div.). [Dunn].

R. v. *Gogol*, (1994) O.J. No. 61 (Prov. Div.). [Gogol].

R. v. *Hamilton*, (2000) O.J. No. 2722 (Gen. Div.). [Hamilton].

R. v. *Lewis*, (1992) O.J. No. 2971 (Ont. Ct. Just.). [Lewis].

R. v. *M(C)* (1995), 23 O.R. (3d) 629 (Ont. C.A.).

R. v. *McCarthy*, (1996) 2 S.C.R. 460 [McCarthy], rev'g. [1995] O.J. No. 2006 (Ont. C.A.).

R. v. *Oakes*, (1986) 1 S.C.R. 103.

R. v. *Parks*, (1993), 84 C.C.C. (3d) 353 (Ont. C.A.). [Parks].

R. v. *RDS*, (1997), 118 C.C.C. (3d) 353 (S.C.C.). [RDS]

R. v. *Rehberg*, (1994) N.S.J. No. 35 (N.S.S.C.). [Rehberg].

R. v. *Richards*, (1999) 26 C.R. (5th) (Ont.C.A.). [Richards].

R. v. *Wilson*, (1996), 47 C.R (4th) 61 at 68 & 70 (Ont. C.A.). [Wilson].

Schachter v. *Canada* (1992), 93 D.L.R. (4th) 1 (S.C.C.). [*Schachter*].

The Toronto Star (2002, October and November). [A series of reports based on an investigation into Race and Crime in Toronto, Ontario that began 1999.]

Williams, Patricia. (1994). Spirit murdering the messenger: The discourse of fingerpointing as the law's response to racism. In David Baker (Ed.), *Reading racism and the criminal justice system*. Toronto: Canadian Scholar's Press.

Wortley, S. (1997, November). The usual suspects: Race, police stops and perceptions of criminal injustice. Paper presented at the 48th Annual Conference of the American Society of Criminology, Chicago.

Wright, Nicola Y. (1996, November). Reasonableness, racism and the articulation of bias. Unpublished LLM Degree thesis, School of Graduate Studies and Research, University of Ottawa.

6

Criminological Research on "Race" in Canada

Wendy Chan
School of Criminology
Simon Fraser University
Burnaby

Wendy Chan

Criminological research on the relationship between "race" and crime plays a significant role in shaping our knowledge of the operations of the criminal justice system as well as how we perceive individuals and groups of different racial backgrounds.[1] With recent events bringing concerns about border and national security and terrorism to the forefront, the question of "race" and crime occupies an important place in the politics of contemporary Canadian society. Our ideas about "race" and crime can influence a wide range of public policies and responses. The most recent evidence of this are the debates over the Liberal government's introduction of a new terrorism bill[2] and the question of whether or not the Toronto Police force engages in practices of racial profiling.[3] Moreover, public and political discussions about racial issues are closely tied to concerns around crime, particularly in racially marginalized communities. Given the importance of these issues, we need to understand how knowledge about "race" and crime is organized, structured, and produced, and the implications they have for those living on the margins of Canadian society. This involves examining how we construct and understand social differences, and asking whether or not our approaches to this topic in general, and the concept of "race" in particular, reproduces racial hierarchies and inequalities.

By questioning how the concept of "race" is deployed in criminological research, my aim is to connect this form of knowledge production to the challenges of eradicating racism and other forms of oppression.[4] There is mounting evidence to suggest that in democratic countries like Canada and the United States, non-white individuals and groups are being criminalized at much higher rates, and they are experiencing harsher treatment by the criminal justice system.[5] I argue that criminological research that employs fixed notions of "race" is problematic and cannot adequately address the problems of racism. Instead, greater attention needs to be devoted to the development of critical knowledge

---

[1] In this paper, "race" is put in quotation marks in order to demonstrate that it is an unfounded, ideological category of identity. This argument was made as early as 1918. *See* Locke, 1992.

[2] "Minister likens critics", 2002.

[3] In the Fall of 2002, the *Toronto Star* newspaper ran a series of articles discussing the findings from their study on racial profiling using Toronto police data.

[4] A focus on how "race" is theoretically conceptualized in criminological research is not to suggest that this is the only issue, or the most important issue, in working towards eliminating racism. There are many other important methodological and theoretical questions that can also be asked. *See* Ratcliffe, 2001 and Twine & Warren, 2000 for various discussions on conducting research on "race".

[5] Newspaper articles highlight, on a regular basis, this racial marginalization through detention and imprisonment. *See*, for example, "Muslims endure year of blame", 2002; Macklin, 2002; "Hundreds of Muslims", 2002.

on the topic of "race" and crime, one that involves interrogating the processes by which certain individuals and groups are being singled out for unequal treatment.

Research on "Race" and Crime in Canada

In the last several decades, criminological interest on issues of "race" and racism has been consistent despite its secondary role in shaping research questions.[6] The most notable themes to emerge from this body of work centre on the treatment of Aboriginal people in the justice system; the nature of relations between the police and minority groups; the ascertation of rates of criminality among specific minority communities, particularly immigrants; and, more recently, the debate about the merits of gathering statistics on "race" and crime.

Researchers have paid significant attention to the social control of Aboriginal people at all levels of the criminal justice system.[7] Many scholars working in a variety of social science disciplines have documented the differential treatment of Aboriginal individuals and groups throughout Canadian history and continuing into the present day.[8] For example, several writers highlight how police forces have been responding to an increasing Native militancy across Canada.[9] Confrontations between the police and Native people have been characterized by racism, harassment and, at times, the use of violent force to subdue Native groups fighting for treaty rights and land claims. The Canadian government has recognized the importance of this issue, evident in the establishment of a Royal Commission on Aboriginal Peoples and the publication of several reports addressing the relationship between Aboriginal peoples and the criminal justice system.[10] For many scholars, Aboriginal self-government and the use of non-penal measures, such as restorative justice, are regarded as viable solutions to alleviating the over-representation of Aboriginal peoples throughout the criminal justice system.[11]

Studies documenting how the police treat minority groups remain vibrant. Researchers have queried whether or not the police engage in discriminatory treatment when dealing with minority individuals,[12] and they have attempted to ascertain those factors giving rise to the conflict, distrust and bias affecting

---

[6] The paucity of published scholarly work in this area in Canada suggests that while researchers may discuss issues of "race" in their research, issues of "race" and racism do not appear to occupy a central role in the formation of the research questions.

[7] See, for example, studies by Frideres & Robertson, 1994, and Smandych, Lincoln & Wilson, 1993.

[8] Dell, 2002; Hylton, 2002; Mawani, 2000; Russell, 2000; Backhouse, 1999; Monture-Angus, 1999; Green, 1998; Mosher, 1998; Razack, 1998; McMahon, 1992.

[9] O'Reilly-Fleming, 1994; Anderson, 1992.

[10] Royal Commission of Aboriginal Peoples, 1993, 1995, 1996.

[11] Russell, 2000; Andersen, 1999; Hylton 1999; Monture-Angus 1999.

[12] James, 1998; Pieters, 2001.

minority communities' relations with the police.[13] It is clear from this body of work that many minority communities strongly believe they are subjected to a heavier-handed approach by the police. Moreover, police shootings by white officers of suspects of colour have further exacerbated these sentiments.[14] Efforts to improve police-community relations through the establishment of various task forces and public inquiries often serve merely to further highlight the negative sentiments of suspicion and fear that many communities hold towards the police force.[15] These tensions were publicly revealed when the *Toronto Star* newspaper recently published findings on the use of racial profiling by the Toronto Police force.[16]

Another notable theme is the exploration of the connections between racialized groups and criminal behaviour. This body of research focuses on determining the extent of crime committed by racialized groups, particularly "black" people and immigrants, and examining public perceptions of the links between different racial groups and criminality.[17] Henry, Hastings, and Freer's discussion of public perceptions of "race" and criminality highlights how criminal activities are racialized and the negative impact of these perceptions on the treatment of black offenders in the justice system.[18] They note that while the public believes black people are more likely to engage in criminal behaviour, the empirical evidence does not support this sentiment.[19] Other writers have attempted to unpack the "race-crime" relationship by focusing on specific types of crimes such as homicide,[20] exploring and explaining differences in crime rates among racialized groups,[21] and examining how racial-minority offenders are treated in the justice system.[22]

In response to the concerns about problems and perceptions of discrimination and bias, the Ontario government commissioned a study of systemic racism in the justice system. The Commission found that among the general population in Ontario, there are widespread perceptions that racialized groups suffer from many forms of discriminatory treatment at all levels of the criminal justice system. An extensive series of recommendations, such as organizing consultation sessions with minority groups on criminal justice policy and forming local community policing committees to reform policies and practices within the Ontario

---

[13] James, 1998; Henry, 1994.

[14] *See* Jackson, 1994 for a list of Toronto shootings.

[15] Government of Ontario, 1989.

[16] The findings and subsequent articles concerning this study can be found on the *Toronto Star* newspaper website at: www.thestar.com

[17] Tonry, 1997; Brannigan & Zhiqiu, 1999; Lynch & Simon 1999.

[18] The sample in their study drew from two surveys — a March 1995 Angus Reid poll that randomly surveyed residents in the Toronto area, and a random survey conducted by the authors in October 1995 of 202 adult male and females in the Durham region (Henry, Hastings & Freer, 1996).

[19] Henry, Hastings, & Freer, 1996, p. 472.

[20] Moyer, 1992.

[21] Gordon & Nelson, 1996; Hagan, 1985; Cheung, 1980.

[22] Roberts & Doob, 1997; Doob, 1994; Mosher, 1996, 1998.

justice system, were made to the Ontario government.[23] Whether or not any or all of the recommendations will be adopted remains to be seen.

Finally, there have also been ongoing discussions and debates on whether or not official statistics on "race" and crime should be collected and published. The questions of how such statistics would be used, and for what purposes, shape the positions taken by participants within this debate. A key concern for many who opposed the collection of race-criminal justice statistics revolves around not wanting to reinforce the discrimination of racialized minorities. As well, those in opposition raise a number of methodological problems associated with how people would be racially categorized.[24] On the other hand, those in support of gathering race-criminal justice statistics claim that suppressing this type of information violates the public's right of access to such information.[25] They argue that such information should be made publicly available since the harms do not outweigh the gains to be had from securing access to this type of information. J. Roberts argues for a compromised approach through periodic gathering of "race" statistics under special circumstances.[26] Such an approach would ensure that safeguards are in place to prevent the abuse of this information while also making it possible to have access to "race" statistics. A similar position is shared by S. Wortley, who claims that allowing the collection of race-criminal justice statistics for special studies provides the necessary middle ground to balance the competing interests of those engaged in this debate.[27]

This cursory overview highlights the diverse ways in which "race" issues intersect with the criminal justice system and in our understandings of crime. It is widely recognized within these writings that racial and ethnic minorities, as offenders, victims and workers in the criminal justice system, are subjected to various forms of discriminatory treatment. Many authors acknowledge how criminal justice practices and policies can reinforce problems of racism.[28] This body of work also highlights the dominance of descriptive, empirically oriented and/or quantitative approaches. The emphasis is on providing individualistic and cultural explanations of "race" and crime. With perhaps a few exceptions, the majority of criminological research on race in Canada does not seek to examine the structural factors that contribute to understanding the relationship between racial groups and criminal behaviour or to explore the historical and socially constructed nature of racial groupings.[29] Established definitions of "race" and crime are not generally challenged. Discriminatory practices in the criminal justice sys-

---

[23] Commission on Systemic Racism, 1995.

[24] Hatt, 1994; Johnston 1994.

[25] Gabor, 1994.

[26] Roberts, 1994, pp. 110–111.

[27] Although Wortley (1999) does not specify, such studies might include one-time studies commissioned by various government departments and non-profit organizations like the Canadian Race Relations Foundation.

[28] Brannigan & Zhiqiu, 1999; Jackson, 1999; Anderson & Anderson, 1998; Mosher, 1998.

[29] Exceptions include the work from feminist perspectives, as well as historical and critical research. *See* for example, McCalla & Satzewich, 2002; Sangster, 2001; Backhouse, 1999; Monture-Angus, 1995, 1999; Razack, 1998. Interestingly, many of these scholars are not working directly in the discipline of Criminology, but are in related fields of Sociology, Law, History, Education and Women's Studies.

tem are defined and understood as the over-representation of a racial group. For example, the high rates of incarcerated Aboriginal people or the excessive police attention on young, black youths are regarded as indications of unequal and biased treatment. Where problems of discrimination are recognized, the belief is that further research about crime and criminals will lead to suggestions for improving and fine-tuning institutional practices to reduce allegations of racism. As a result, questions regarding how prevailing stereotypes and myths about racial groups contribute to racism in the criminal justice system are rarely raised, connections between current criminal justice practices and processes of racial categorization to Canada's colonial legacy are rarely acknowledged, and there is no exploration of the relationship between racism and the unequal social, economic and political power dynamics in society. Moreover, our knowledge about how "race" has been deployed by the state to gain legitimacy for repressive crime control strategies is piecemeal at best. Consequently, subtler forms of discriminatory treatment in the criminal justice system remain unexamined. One of the contributing barriers to explaining the complexities of racism in the criminal justice system is the uncritical acceptance of "race" and racial categories as fixed and immutable. As the following section highlights, challenging definitions of "race" is a vital component of a critical approach to the study of "race" and racism.

Problematizing "Race" as an Objective Fact

The idea of "race" as a concept located at the biological level, where racial categories are understood as "natural", and of racial characteristics as concrete and given, continue to be reinforced by positivistic research on "race" and crime.[30] Statistical enquiries, in particular, have been consistent in upholding these views by asking whether or not the criminal justice system discriminates against people on the basis of skin colour or ethnicity.[31] Although critical race scholars have pointed to the limitations of this approach, arguing that "race" is a mythical construct,[32] these arguments have failed to make an impression on researchers conducting positivistic studies on "race" and crime.

Within criminology, only a handful of researchers have raised concerns about how "race" is represented and understood. George Napper, writing in the late 1970s about the situation in America, warned researchers against ignoring the perspectives of minority group members and using racial designations to explain crime rates.[33] He noted:

> If one is told that an overwhelming proportion of people who are arrested are black
> and that the population of the jails and prisons in our country are predominantly and

---

[30] Within the United Kingdom, this type of research is referred to as "administrative criminology". It is, as Barbara Hudson (1999) notes, concerned with conducting applied research with the aim of helping criminal justice agencies develop policies and make decisions.

[31] Hudson, 1999, p. 6.

[32] Miles, 1989, 1993, 2000; Mac an Ghaill, 1999; Guillaumin, 1980, 1988, 1995.

[33] Napper, 1977.

increasingly drawn from the black community, one is forced to conclude that the argument suggesting that blackness and criminality can be used interchangeably has merit.[34]

Almost 20 years later, the failure to heed Napper's advice is evident in Covington's concerns that employing racial classification schemes will reinforce the belief and presence of racialized crime.[35] "Race" differences typically refer to differences between "blacks" and "whites". The problem, as she notes, is that there is no single response or action that can be neatly characterized as either "white" or "black". The diversity between and among different racial and ethnic groups means that there cannot be a straightforward transfer between identification as "black" or "white" and the type of response generated. Without acknowledging this difficulty, racial and ethnic classification is not challenged, the belief that a link exists between one's race and criminal activity is reproduced, and racial meanings are used to explain why "black" or Aboriginal communities have higher crime rates.

Empirical studies on "race and crime" that treat "race" as a discrete variable of analysis have also come under scrutiny. S. Holdaway, in speaking of the British context,[36] notes that

> quantitative studies that have been concerned with racial discrimination within criminal justice institutions have often been unable to move us forward to an adequate explanation. They cannot because they are devoid of a sociological theory to assist an analysis of the social context within which their statistics of outcomes have been constructed.[37]

The failure to make analytical links between wider structural features and, for example, patterns of sentencing is an important concern for Canadian research on "race and crime". The need to go further and explore the social processes that produce discrimination is evident. Failure to examine the wider social context of "race"s can chart out various patterns of behaviour, they cannot explain why specific patterns occur, or the effects they have on legitimating criminal justice practices.

In addition, a number of analytical issues have also been identified in quantitative criminological research on "race". Holdaway argues that treating "race" as a discrete variable reifies the phenomenon of racism as fixed and constant.[38] "Race" becomes a discrete factor among many other discrete parts of a statistical explanation. Such a conceptualization, which disconnects "race" from other processes and treats "race" as an object on its own is inadequate, according to Holdaway, because "race" intersects with other factors, like housing and areas of residence, in ways that are not easily separated.[39] For example, explaining why Vancouver's poorest neighbourhood, the downtown east

---

[34] Napper, 1977, p. 11.

[35] Covington, 1995.

[36] Holdaway, 1998.

[37] Ibid., 1998, p. 81.

[38] Holdaway, 1997b, p. 385.

[39] Ibid., 1997b, p. 385.

side, comprises mostly Aboriginal and other racially marginalized people, involves examining how racism shapes the social and economic opportunities available. Their lack of access to adequate housing, well-paying jobs and good health care highlights how racism is embedded in all types of social practices to sustain their exclusion from mainstream society. Thus, to treat these issues as separate from and in distinction to the category of "race" fails to appreciate how racialized relations are sustained. Viewing "race" as a discrete variable, and the phenomenon of racism as fixed, validates a biologically driven understanding of the concept: it obscures the ways in which racism is constructed and reconstructed over time, and it neglects interpersonal relations by compartmentalizing people's experiences of crime on the basis of "race" rather than understanding them as connected to a larger chain of life experiences.[40] As C. Pope bluntly puts it, "a strict counting and enumeration of variables is not likely to reach any substantive conclusion regarding race and crime . . . such research often portrays minorities as impersonal objects capable of manipulation without regard to their wishes or desires."[41]

Thus, we are in danger of reconstructing racisms, if not reproducing them, by retaining a notion of "race" as a fixed and static entity. Concern that stereotypes and biases against racialized individuals will persist is not without merit. The vast numbers of Aboriginal people in Canadian prisons,[42] or the disproportionate rates of deportation among Jamaican men convicted of criminal offences in Canada,[43] provide strong evidence of the need to rethink how research on "race" and crime is reinforcing, rather than challenging and transcending, "race" and crime myths.

Rethinking the Concept of "Race" in Criminology

The recognition that Canada's colonial legacy has been critical in shaping notions of "race" has led many critical scholars to reject the idea of "race" as an objective fact. As Constance Backhouse notes, "[t]he impermanence and transmutability of 'race' is never clearer than when examined against the backdrop of the past."[44] Furthermore, it has been suggested that the conditions of late modernity are producing multiple forms of racism, thus putting into question the fixed boundaries of a black-white model of racism and the notion that it is possible to clearly delineate who are the "victims" and the "oppressors".[45] The presence of new targets of racism (e.g., national minorities in Eastern Europe, Islamophobia) highlights the weakness of focusing on colour as the marker of racial identity.

---

[40] Ibid., 1997b, p. 387.

[41] Pope, 1982, p. 250.

[42] Cayley, 1998.

[43] Barnes, 2002.

[44] Backhouse, 1999, p. 7.

[45] Mac an Ghaill, 1999; Castles, 1996.

The problematic nature of the term has led many researchers in Canada and elsewhere to eschew its use in exchange for examining the conditions under which differential outcomes are the result of specific processes of racialization.[46] According to R. Miles, racialization refers to "those instances where social relations between people have been structured by the signification of human biological characteristics in such a way as to define and construct differentiated social collectivities."[47] In rejecting the term "race", he concurs with Guillaumin that "the idea of 'race' is *essentially* ideological."[48] Using the term "race" obscures how social reality is constructed by racist practices. As an analytical concept, "race" fails to make known that it is not physical characteristics that create a hierarchy of privilege or prejudice but according significance to those differences and using them to structure social relations.[49] Anti-racist scholar V. Bashi puts it more bluntly, arguing that the issue is not simply about the meanings given to racial categories but that these categories are carved out of racial hierarchies.[50] In addition, a focus on "race" simplifies attitudes and ideologies of racism by creating binary oppositions where, for example, one is either racist or non-racist, when the reality is far more complex. Since there is no agreement over the meaning and significance of terms such as "race" and "racial", these terms will continue to suggest the existence of discrete biological races and imply that anything racial is primarily the result of this fact.[51] The concept of racialization offers an alternative to this impasse.

Other critical race scholars, such as Stephen Small, agree with Miles when he argues that a racialization framework is better able to address the complexities of racism by focusing on how the use of economic, social and political power in contemporary life excludes and denigrates individuals and groups. Small states:

> This framework is a set of assumptions and key concepts which explores the multiple factors that shape what has previously been called race relations. Some of these factors entail explicit reference to race, such as beliefs about the existence of races, prejudice and discrimination based on such beliefs. But other factors — such as competition for economic and political resources (education, jobs, housing elected office) — may seem to have no racial reference. The racialization problematic enables us to draw out the relationship between these seemingly unrelated variables, and, importantly, to begin to assess the significance of each of them.[52]

Unlike the concept of "race", a racialization framework is fluid and dynamic, focusing on those processes that have enabled ideas about "race" to proliferate over time. It involves examining how race is socially and politically constructed in historical, political and institutional contexts. There are many advantages of

---

[46] Small, 1998; Solomos, 1993; Miles, 1989; Banton, 1977.

[47] Miles, 1989, p. 75.

[48] Miles, 2000, p. 137.

[49] Ibid., p. 139.

[50] Bashi (1998) notes that racial categories are the building blocks of racial hierarchies. The changing nature of the categories illustrates prevailing values and ideas about the normative hierarchical order of human beings and where we see ourselves in that hierarchy.

[51] Small, 1998.

[52] Ibid., p. 71.

working within the concept of racialization. First, this framework allows for the inclusion of how gender, sexuality and class also intersect in the development of racialized relations. It can overcome the tendency to treat "race" and gender as separate categories of analysis and give greater attention to how gender, sexual and class distinctions work in simultaneous and interactive ways with "race" to reinforce existing oppressions. Second, racialization highlights how racism is not uniform — different dynamics and conflicts exist and require explanation. Relations between racialized youth and the police in Vancouver are different from those in Toronto or Halifax.[53] The heterogeneous grouping of racial and ethnic groups in Canada means that formations of racialized relations in particular communities can and will vary depending upon the social, economic, and political processes at work in a given context. Developing analyses of these relations involves moving beyond the continuing focus on Aboriginals or black people as the object of inquiry and exploring, for example, how "whiteness" is absent in the signification of "race". Third, examining processes of racialization accepts that "race" is not conceptually fixed and is constantly being negotiated, and that not all forms of racism are constructed exclusively according to skin colour. Culture and religion, for example, can also become symbolic markers of difference, inferiority and undesirability. For instance, Sherene Razack's discussion of criminal cases involving Aboriginal people in the Canadian courts underscores how culture is used to explain and justify racist responses by criminal justice agents.[54] Finally, the concept of racialization encourages consideration of the racialization of whiteness through an examination of the manner in which ethnic groups came to be defined as the "white race" or the "black race". It challenges the notion that "whiteness" has not also been socially constructed. Instead, the political, social and economic circumstances in which the meanings of "white" and "black" are constructed can be explored more fully by a recognition of the agents of racial determination.

If we are to understand the significance of "race" in the functions and operations of the criminal justice system, we need to reflect upon how research in this area contributes to our knowledge about racial differences. Recognizing the unstable and politically contested meaning of "race" and the constructed nature of racial identities through an examination of how people are racialized is at least one alternative in striving for racial justice. By documenting the processes of racialization that construct racist discourses and sustain racial hierarchies, we can begin to challenge the power structures and more effectively address the problems of racism. According to Omi and Winant, one must study both social structure and cultural representation, since race is not only a matter of cultural expression, nor is it simply a set of categories determined by structural positioning.[55] Paying attention to the processes involved in the construction of racialized identities is an important exercise for mapping how institutional arrangements such as those found in the criminal justice system are implicit in upholding social inequalities.

---

[53] Symons, 1999; Ungerleider, 1994.

[54] The cases of Kitty Nowdlok-Reynolds and Donald Marshall are two well-known examples. For a fuller discussion of the culturalization of race, see Razack, 1998.

[55] Omi & Winant, 1994.

References

Anderson, A. (1992). Policing Native people: Native militancy and Canadian militarism. In V. Satzewich (Ed.), *Deconstructing a nation*. Halifax: Fernwood Publishing.

Andersen, C. (1999). Governing Aboriginal justice in Canada: Constructing responsible individuals and communities through "tradition". *Crime, Law and Social Change, 31*(4), 303–326.

Anderson, B., & Anderson, D. (1998). *Manufacturing guilt: Wrongful convictions in Canada*. Halifax: Fernwood Publishing.

Backhouse, C. (1999). *Colour-coded: A legal history of racism in Canada, 1900–1950*. Toronto: University of Toronto Press.

Banton, M. (1977). *The idea of race*. London: Tavistock Publications.

Barnes, A. (2002). The net effect of deportation. In W. Chan & K. Mirchandani (Ed.), *Crimes of colour: Racialization and the criminal justice system in Canada*. Peterborough: Broadview Press.

Bashi, V. (1998). Racial categories matter because racial hierarchies matter: A commentary. *Racial and Ethnic Studies, 21*(5), 959–969.

Brannigan, A., & Zhiqiu, L. (1999). "Where East meets West": Police, immigration and public order crime in the settlement of Canada from 1896 to 1940. *Canadian Journal of Sociology, 24*(1), 87–108.

Castles, S. (1996). The racisms of globalisation. In E. Vasta & S. Castles (Ed.), *The teeth are smiling*. St. Leonards, NSW: Allen and Unwin.

Cayley, D. (1998). *The expanding prison*. Toronto: Anansi.

Cheung, Y.W. (1980). Explaining ethnic and racial variation in criminality rates: A review and critique. *Canadian Criminology Forum, 3*, 1–14.

Commission on Systemic Racism in the Ontario Criminal Justice System. (1995). *Report of the commission on systemic racism in the Ontario criminal justice system*. Toronto: Queen's Printer for Ontario.

Covington, J. (1995). Racial classification in criminology: The reproduction of racialized crime. *Sociological Forum, 10*(4), 547–568.

Dell, C. (2002). The criminalization of Aboriginal women: Commentary by a community activist. In W. Chan & K. Mirchandani (Eds.), *Crimes of colour: Racialization and the criminal justice system in Canada*. Peterborough: Broadview Press.

Doob, A. (1994). *Race, bail and imprisonment: Draft working paper*. Toronto: Commission on Systemic Racism in the Ontario Criminal Justice System.

Frideres, J., & Robertson, B. (1994). Aboriginals and the criminal justice system: Australia and Canada. *International Journal of Contemporary Sociology, 31*(1), 101–127.

Gabor, T. (1994). The suppression of crime statistics on race and ethnicity: The price of political correctness. *Canadian Journal of Criminology*, 153–163.

Gordon, R., & Nelson, J. (1996). Crime, ethnicity and immigration. In R. Silverman et al. (Eds.), *Crime in Canadian society* (5th ed.). Toronto: Harcourt Brace.

Government of Ontario. (1989). *Report of race relations and policing task force*. Ontario: Solicitor General's Office.

Green, R. (1998). *Justice in Aboriginal communities: sentencing alternatives*. Saskatoon: Purich Publishers.

Guillaumin, C. (1980). The idea of race and its elevation to autonomous scientific and legal status. In UNESCO (Ed.), *Sociological theories: Race and colonialism*. Paris: UNESCO.

Guillaumin, C. (1988). Race and nature: The system of marks. *Feminist Issues*, 25–43.

Guillaumin, C. (1995). *Racism, sexism, power and ideology*. London: Routledge.

Hagan, J. (1985). Toward a structural theory of crime, race and gender: The Canadian case. *Crime and Delinquency, 31*(1), 129–146.

Hatt, K. (1994). Reservations about race and crime statistics. *Canadian Journal of Criminology*, 164–165.

Henry, F. (1994). *The Caribbean diaspora in Toronto: Learning to live with racism*. Toronto: University of Toronto Press.

Henry, F., Hastings, P., & Freer, B. (1996). Perceptions of race and crime in Ontario: Empirical evidence from Toronto and the Durham region. *Canadian Journal of Criminology*, 469–476.

Holdaway, S. (1997a). Constructing and sustaining "race" within the police workforce. *British Journal of Sociology, 48*(1), 19–34.

Holdaway, S. (1997b). Some recent approaches to the study of race in criminological research. *British Journal of Criminology, 37*(3), 383–400.

Holdaway, S. (1998). Ethnicity in criminal justice. In I. Mackenzie (Ed.), *Law, power and justice in England and Wales*. London: Praeger.

Hudson, B. (1999). Racism and criminology: Concepts and controversies. In D. Cook & B. Hudson (Eds.), *Racism and criminology*. London: Sage Publications.

Hundreds of muslims rounded up in California. (2002, December 19). *Reuters News*.

Hylton, J. (2002). The Justice system and Canada's Aboriginal people: The persistence of racial discrimination. In W. Chan & K. Mirchandani (Eds.), *Crimes of colour: Racialization and the criminal justice system in Canada*. Peterborough: Broadview Press.

Hylton, J. (Ed.). (1999). *Aboriginal self-government in Canada: Current trends and issues*. Saskatoon: Purich Publishers.

Jackson, M. (1999). Canadian Aboriginal women and their "criminality": the cycle of violence in the context of difference. *Australian and New Zealand Journal of Criminology, 32*(2), 197–208.

Jackson, P. (1994). Constructions of criminality: Police-community relations in Toronto. *Antipode, 26*, 216.

James, C. (1998). "Up to no good": Black on the streets and encountering police. In V. Satzewich (Ed.), *Racism and social inequality in Canada*. Toronto: Thompson Educational Publishing.

Johnston, J.P. (1994). Academic approaches to race-crime statistics do not justify their collection. *Canadian Journal of Criminology*, 166–174.

Locke, Alaine. (1992). *Race contacts and interracial relations*. Washington, D.C.: Howard University Press.

Lynch, J., & Simon, R. (1999). A comparative assessment of criminal involvement among immigrants and Natives across seven nations. *International Criminal Justice Review 9*, 1–17.

Mac an Ghaill, M. (1999). *Contemporary racisms and ethnicities*. Buckingham: Open University Press.

Macklin, A. (2002, November 25). "Myth of crime-prone immigrant persist" *Toronto Star*.

Mawani, R. (2000). In between and out of place: Racial hybridity, liquor, and the law in late 19th and early 20th century British Columbia. *Canadian Journal of Law and Society, 15*(2), 9–38.

McCalla, A., & Satzewich, V. (2002). Settler capitalism and the construction of immigrants and "Indians" as racialized others. In W. Chan & K. Mirchandani (Eds.), *Crimes of colour: Racialization and the criminal justice system in Canada*. Peterborough: Broadview Press.

McMahon, T. (1992). *Aboriginal people and discrimination in the justice system: A survey of Manitoba inmates and related literature*. Unpublished LL.M. thesis, University of Ottawa, Ottawa.

Miles, R. (1989) *Racism*. London: Routledge.

Miles, R. (1993). *Race after race relations*. London: Routledge.

Miles, R. (2000). Apropos the idea of "race" . . . Again. In L. Back & J. Solomos (Eds), *Theories of race and racism: A reader*. London: Routledge.

Minister likens critics to Le Pen. (2002, April 30) *Globe and Mail*.

Monture-Angus, P. (1995). *Thunder in my soul: A Mohawk woman speaks*. Halifax: Fernwood Press.

Monture-Angus, P. (1999). *Journeying forward: dreaming First Nations' independence*. Halifax: Fernwood Press.

Mosher, C. (1996). Minorities and misdemeanors: The treatment of black public order offenders in Ontario's criminal justice system — 1892–1930. *Canadian Journal of Criminology*, 413–438.

Mosher, C. (1998). *Discrimination and denial: Systemic racism in Ontario's legal and criminal justice systems, 1892–1961*. Toronto: University of Toronto Press.

Moyer, S. (1992). Race, gender and homicide: Comparisons between Aboriginals and other Canadians. *Canadian Journal of Criminology*, 387–402.

Muslims endure year of blame. (2002, September 23). *Edmonton Journal*.

Napper, G. (1977). Perceptions of crime: problems and implications. In R. Woodson (Ed.), *Black perspectives on crime and the criminal justice system*. Boston: G.K. Hall.

O'Reilly-Fleming, T. (1994). The Mohawk-Canada crisis: Native peoples, criminalization and the justice system. In D. Baker, (Ed.), *Reading racism in the criminal justice system*. Toronto: Canadian Scholar's Press.

Omi, M., & Winant. H. (1994). *Racial Formation in the United States: From the 1960s to the 1990s* (2nd ed.). New York: Routledge.

Pieters, S. (2001). Racial profiling of black Canadian citizens at port(s) of entry in Canada. Retrieved October 22, 2003, from http://www.geocities.com/CapitolHill/2381/CanadaCustomsandRevenueAgency/cdncustom5.html

Pope, C. (1982). Race, crime and criminological research: Some unintended consequences. *Humanity and Society 6*, 243–256.

Ratcliffe, P. (Ed.). (2001). *The politics of social science research: "Race", ethnicity and social change*. Houndsmill: Palgrave Press.

Razack, S. (1998). *Looking white people in the eye*. Toronto: University of Toronto Press.

Roberts, J. (1994). Crime and race statistics: Toward a Canadian solution. *Canadian Journal of Criminology*, 175–185.

Roberts, J. (2002). Racism and the collection of statistics relating to race and ethnicity. In W. Chan & K. Mirchandani (Eds.), *Crimes of colour: Racialization and the criminal justice system in Canada*. Peterborough: Broadview Press.

Roberts, J., & Doob, A. (1997). Race, ethnicity, and criminal justice in Canada. In M. Tonry (Ed.), *Ethnicity, crime and immigration: Comparative and cross-national perspectives*. Chicago: University of Chicago Press.

Royal Commission on Aboriginal Peoples. (1993). *Aboriginal peoples and the justice system*. Ottawa: Royal Commission on Aboriginal Peoples.

Royal Commission on Aboriginal Peoples. (1995). *Bridging the cultural divide: A report on Aboriginal people and criminal justice*. Ottawa: Royal Commission on Aboriginal Peoples.

Royal Commission on Aboriginal Peoples. (1996). *Report of the Royal Commission on Aboriginal Peoples*. Ottawa: Royal Commission on Aboriginal Peoples.

Russell, D. (2000). *A people's dream: Aboriginal self-government in Canada*. Vancouver: UBC Press.

Sangster, J. (2001). *Regulating girls and women*. Don Mills, ON.: Oxford University Press.

Small, S. (1998). The contours of racialization: Structures, representation and resistance in the United States. In V. Satzewich (Ed.), *Racism and social inequality in Canada*. Toronto: Thompson Educational Publishing.

Smandych, R., Lincoln, R., & Wilson, P. (1993). Toward a cross-cultural theory of Aboriginal crime: A comparative study of the problem of Aboriginal overrepresentation in the criminal justice systems of Canada and Australia. *International Criminal Justice Review, 3*, 1–24.

Solomos, J. (1993). *Race and racism in Britain*. Basingstoke: MacMillan.

Symons, G. (1999). Racialization of the street gang issue in Montreal: A police perspective. *Canadian Ethnic Studies, 31*(1), 124–139.

Tonry, M. (1997). Ethnicity, crime and immigration. In M. Tonry (Ed.), *Ethnicity, crime and immigration: Comparative and cross-national perspectives*. Chicago: University of Chicago Press.

Twine, F., & Warren, J. (Eds.). (2000). *Racing research, researching race: Methodological dilemmas in critical race studies*. New York: New York University Press.

Ungerleider, C. (1994). Police, race and community conflict in Vancouver. *Canadian Ethnic Studies, 26*(3), 91–104.

Wortley, S. (1999). A northern taboo: Research on race, crime and criminal justice in Canada. *Canadian Journal of Criminology, 41*(2), 261–275.

Questions for Discussion

1. To what extent are notions of criminality connected to racial identity?

2. How does the media serve to inform the public about blacks and crime? Does the media have a duty to present a balanced view of black subjects in popular culture?

3. How should factors like social, economic, and political inequity be considered in assessments of criminal culpability?

4. To what extent does racial injustice in the Canadian criminal justice system provoke more criminal activity?

5. How has the discursivity of the literary academy in Canada contributed to an absence of scholarship on race and capital punishment?

6. Debate potential public reactions to the implementation of the defence litigation strategy suggested by Mirza.

Part 3

First Nations — Of Land, Law and Power

This part pulls together information and discussion specific to First Nations communities in Canada. From contact forward to the enactment of the Federal Indian Act, and still today, the government of Canada has had a central role in confining and defining the lives of the First Nations. The legacy, if not the original intent, has been the genocide of some of the First Nations and the near destruction, or impoverishment, of others. At the least, government policy has worked to severely alter indigenous ways of life.

These essays, "Across a Boundary of Lava: Evaluating Race-Based Antagonisms towards the Nisga'a Land Claim Treaty", "Treaty Federalism: Challenging Disciplinary Boundaries, and Bridging Praxis, Theory, Research and Critical Pedagogy in Canadian Political Science"; and "Navigating Discrimination: The Interplay of Context on Native Children's Social Development", explore these issues from many angles and provide information both on historic and contemporary concerns of First Nations communities.

Now that you have been introduced to ways of articulating the concerns of Canadians of colour, we shift your focus to concerns unique to the First Nations in Canada. As the following essays highlight, many social ills were born of battles over property, power and sovereignty. The attempted genocide of First Nations in Canada has created a legacy ripe for critical examination.

On a very basic level, the included works all illustrate the tensions created by the Federal Indian Act, which was enacted and continues to operate, without incorporating the voices of the subjected communities. The three essays provide an insightful look into the consequences of these policies, and they facilitate discussions on past, present, and future efforts to create policies and practices that embrace the needs of the First Nations communities in Canada.

With that in mind, the first essay, "Across a Boundary of Lava: Evaluating Race-Based Antagonisms towards the Nisga'a Land Claim Treaty", reveals the harsh realities of non-indigenous perceptions of the government's treatment of the First Nations community in British Columbia. The essay reveals and explores some of the reactions of Euro-Canadians to the settlements struck between a provincial government and a First Nations tribe. As you read of these sentiments, consider the ideas of the previous Part and examine the role that popular culture plays in creating and perpetuating these sentiments.

The next essay, "Treaty Federalism: Challenging Disciplinary Boundaries, and Bridging Praxis, Theory, Research and Critical Pedagogy in Canadian Political Science", illuminates the political and legal attempts of treaty federalism to respond to the needs of the First Nations communities. The essay examines and deconstructs the policies that contributed to the disparate circumstances facing many First Nations communities in Canada. Constructive policy suggestions are proposed to address these issues. Think critically about the past proposals, as well as the author's suggestions for the future.

The third essay, "Navigating Discrimination: The Interplay of Context on Native Children's Social Development", highlights several methods in which the social ills facing First Nations communities have been addressed. The essay explores the systemically manufactured social ills that plague many Native communities and proposes potential solutions that can be orchestrated both by the government and at the grassroots level.

7

Across a Boundary of Lava
Evaluating Race-Based Antagonism Towards the Nisga'a Land Claims Treaty

Sarah de Leeuw
Geography Ph.D. Candidate
Queen's University
Kingston

A Nisga'a legend explains the unique landscape of the Nass Valley in northwestern British Columbia. Nisga'a park guides working in British Columbia's only co-managed provincial park tell the story. It is etched into a wooden information sign beside the Tseax River, which winds through the remote corner of northwestern British Columbia.

Years and years ago, children living in the Nass Valley were warned to be considerate of the fish and wildlife in their lands. Ignoring the words of their Elders, the children placed lit sticks into the backs of spawning salmon and watched as the salmon swam in brightly coloured circles. Elders reprimanded the children and warned them never to repeat their actions, but the children ignored the direction of their elders and carried on with their antics of placing bits of lit wood into the backs of salmon. As the Elders had warned, repercussions came in the form of a volcanic eruption. The volcano poured lava and fire down to the mouth of the Nass River, creating hundreds of kilometres of gnarled, silver-gray lava beds still visible today.

Hundreds of years later, a new story is being told in the Nass Valley. This one concerns the creation of a land claims treaty, the first modern-day treaty to be signed in British Columbia. The settlement of this treaty, and the backlash against it, is the story of this paper. Reaction to the modern-day treaty has been varied across Canada[1] but can be viewed in microcosm in the small community of Terrace — the closest municipal neighbour to the recently negotiated Nisga'a Territory. Letters to the editor over a three-year period in *The Terrace Standard*, the only weekly newspaper within 400 kilometres of the Nass Valley and the Nisga'a Territory, tell a story of race-based antagonism towards the Nisga'a people and their treaty. This paper examines these prejudices in order to provoke discussion and thought concerning the treatment of, and views toward, First Nations people in Canada, specifically with regards to treaty negotiation and land claim settlements. Resistance to Aboriginal self-government and self-determination takes many forms. It is important to note that it can be equally driven by economic greed or a sense of colonial entitlement: each is problematic in its own right. This paper, however, concentrates primarily on letters containing racist stereotypes about First Nations people and self-government. Correspondence in the Letters to the Editor section of *The Terrace Standard* will provide insight on racist sentiments towards First Nations and their land claim settlements across both British Columbia and Canada. The words appearing in *The Terrace Standard* will thus be evaluated from the perspective that they are indicative of a cultural climate in Canada of racist stereotypes concerning Aboriginal people and the settlement of their land claims.

---

[1] Sterritt et al., 1998.

Sarah de Leeuw

Terrace and New Aiyansh, the largest village within the Nisga'a Territory, are distinct communities and warrant some description in order to facilitate the discussions. Further, a brief outline of the 400-year history leading up to the Nisga'a treaty provides a useful contextualization for the contemporary tensions and disagreement. Finally, an outline of the letters being evaluated, in conjunction with contemporary and historical racism faced by First Nations in Canada, is provided to situate the tensions within a larger context. A conclusion evaluating the lessons taught by the Nisga'a treaty and the responses to it provides insight into possible future community reactions to First Nation land claim treaties.

On Either Side of La*x* Mihl: Communities in the Nass Valley and the Town of Terrace

Terrace and the communities encompassed by the Nisga'a Final Agreement are located in northwestern British Columbia, Canada. Situated over 700 kilometres north of Vancouver, British Columbia's largest urban centre, the communities in the Nass Valley and the City of Terrace are considered rural and have populations below 20,000. Within the Nisga'a territory, there are three predominant communities. Moving southwest along the Nass River they are: Gitlakdamix (New Aiyansh), Gitwinksihlxw (Canyon City), and Laxgalts'ap (Greenville).[2] One community, Gingolx (Kincolith), is situated outside the Nass River watershed on the west coast of British Columbia. A single road, the Nisga'a Highway, links the four communities of Gitlakdamix, Gitwinksihlxw, Laxgalts'al, and (as of December 2002) Gingolx. The same road provides the one continuous link between the Nass Valley and its closest municipal neighbour, the City of Terrace (see Figure 7–1). The original area negotiated in the Nisga'a Final Agreement, the watershed area of the Nass River, encompassed 24,862 square kilometres of land, though the final land allocation was substantially less. A total of 2,500 Nisga'a people, representing almost half the Nisga'a Nation's population, live in the Nass Valley communities and in Gingolx to the west.[3] Gitlakdamix (New Aiyansh) is the home of the Nisga'a's legislative building, Wilpsi'ayuukhl Nisga'a, which opened in September 2000. The community is the largest in the Nisga'a territory, with a population of over 1,000 people.

Terrace is located to the southeast of Gitlakdamix (New Aiyansh) and is separated from the communities in the Nass Valley by an expanse of lava, Lax Mihl. Now a provincial park, called Anhluut'ukwism Laxmihl Angwinga'asanskwhl Nisga'a (the Nisga'a Memorial Lava Bed Provincial Park), the lava beds provide a clear separation between Terrace and the Nass Valley (see Figure 7–2). In order to enter the communities of the Nass Valley from the City of Terrace, one must pass through this tangible geological phenomenon. Terrace has a population

---

[2] Ibid.

[3] From Nisga'a Tribal Council website, *Nisga'a Tribal Council: Hak'ak'a'a'*. Retrieved September 14, 2001 from http://www.schoolnet.ca/aboriginal/nisga1/index-e.html

Figure 7–1

A single road, the Nisga'a Highway, links the three communities of Gitllakdamix, Gitwinksihlxw and Laxgalts'al. That same road provides the one continuous link between the Nass Valley and its closest municipal neighbour, the City of Terrace.

of just below 13,000 and resource-dependent forestry-based economy.[4] The City of Terrace has offices representing both levels of government most closely associated with the Nisga'a land claims treaty: the provincial and federal governments. The City of Terrace was, thus, the closest point of contact, geographically, between people of the Nass Valley and their government representatives. During the final three years (1997–1999) of negotiation on the Nisga'a land claim treaty, both Terrace and the Nass Valley region were represented provincially by Helmut Geisbrecht, member of the New Democratic Party, and federally by Mike Scott, member of the Reform Party of Canada. Scott was a member of the official federal opposition party, and thus not in agreement with the treaty negotiations being executed by the Liberal Party of Canada, the official government of Canada at the time.

One weekly newspaper, *The Terrace Standard*, serves the City of Terrace and outlying regions. The newspaper, central to the discussion in this essay, serves the populations of the Nass Valley and Terrace and is owned by British Columbia community newspaper mogul David Black.[5] The paper's editor and

---

[4] Retrieved September 17, 2001, from *City of Terrace General Information Page, http:www.city.terrace.bc.ca/geninfo.html*
[5] Rose, 2000, p. 183.

Figure 7–2

Now a provincial park, called Anhluut'ukwism Laxmihl Angwinga'asanskwhl Nisga'a (the Nisga'a Memorial Lava Bed Provincial Park), the lava beds provide a clear separation between Terrace and the Nass Valley.

publisher, Rod Link, ran *The Terrace Standard* during the time of the Nisga'a treaty and continued to be its editor as of the writing of this essay. In 1998, the owner of *The Terrace Standard,* David Black, ordered all the newspapers in his chain to oppose the Nisga'a treaty, and decreed further that the editorial content of his newspapers should include no pro-treaty dialogue.[6] In *Spirit Dance at Meziadin*, author Alex Rose notes that "editor Rod Link conceded that he did alter the paper's editorial pages to reflect his boss's edict. 'It's not my newspaper,' [Link] admitted ..."[7] Black's editorial mandate reflects attitudes apparent in letters to the editor written to *The Terrace Standard*, letters that rely heavily on race-based prejudices towards First Nations people. Both Black's editorial stance and the letters to the editor can be read as reflecting the historical opposition faced by the Nisga'a people while negotiating their land claim settlement.

Over 400 Years in the Making:
A Summative Timeline of the Nisga'a Treaty

The Nisga'a people chart the history of their struggle to attain Aboriginal title over land in Nass Valley back 400 years to 1579, the year when Sir Francis

---

[6] Ibid.

[7] Ibid., p. 185.

Drake claimed Canada's west coast for England.[8] The length of time the Nisga'a negotiated with provincial and federal governments is critical to the discussion in this paper about race-based prejudices faced by the Nisga'a, from both their Terrace neighbours and critics across the province. As I will discuss, the denial of historical claim and the lack of temporal contextualization are two key tools used by those residing both inside and outside of Terrace seeking to undermine discussions on Aboriginal title to land. In 1885, 25 years after the newly formed province of British Columbia denied the existence of aboriginal title, three Nisga'a chiefs travelled to Canada's capital to discuss the Nisga'a land claim question with then Prime Minister John A. Macdonald. In 1890, the Nisga'a people established the first Nisga'a Land Committee, only to be met with a prohibition from Ottawa in 1927 stating that Aboriginal people were forbidden to meet for the purposes of discussing the land question.

The Nisga'a Land Committee was re-established in 1955, four years after the federal parliament repealed provisions of the Indian Act that outlawed land claims activities; and in 1968, just over 10 years later, the Nisga'a people took their land question to the British Columbia Supreme Court, culminating in a final 1973 Supreme Court of Canada decision, *Calder* v. *British Columbia* (A.G.) (1973). The Calder decision was central to the claims process in Canada as it forced the Canadian government to acknowledge the existence of Aboriginal title and established that Canada had a legal obligation to settle land-title questions. Nineteen seventy-three marked the beginning of contemporary negotiations for Nisga'a land title in the Nass Valley. What followed was a concentrated and sustained dialogue between the Nisga'a people and governments of British Columbia and Canada, culminating in the year 2000 acceptance of the Nisga'a Final Agreement.[9] In 1976, the Nisga'a began negotiations with Ottawa, and between 1982 and 1991, the government of Canada recognized and affirmed Aboriginal title and the Supreme Court of Canada ruled that two First Nations neighbouring the Nisga'a territory (the Gitxsan and the Wet'suwet'en people) had "'ownership' and 'jurisdiction' over at least some of [their] claimed territory as well as [their] population."[10] In 1991, the provincial government of British Columbia recognized both the Nisga'a right to self-government and Aboriginal title on lands. Between 1996 and 1999, the Nisga'a Tribal Council President, Joseph Gosnell, met with both the provincial and federal governments who were by this time negotiating the Nisga'a agreement in earnest. These meetings and negotiations culminated in the April 1999 provincial ratification of the Nisga'a treaty as well as the April 2000 ratification of the treaty by the Senate of Canada (Bill 51). On September 14, 2000 the Nisga'a legislative building opened (see Figure 7–3). These final four years of negotiations were the years when publicity about the Nisga'a Treaty escalated, and responses to it in the form of letters to the editor in *The Terrace Standard* similarly

---

[8] From Nisga'a Tribal Council Web page *Nisga'a Tribal Council: Hak'ak'a'a'*. Retrieved September 14, 2001, from http://www.schoolnet.ca/aboriginal/nisga1/index-e.html
[9] From Nisga'a Tribal Council Web page *Nisga'a Tribal Council: Hak'ak'a'a'*. Retrieved September 14, 2001, from http://www.schoolnet.ca/aboriginal/nisga1/index-e.html
[10] Bell & Asch, 1997, p. 62.

Figure 7–3

Opening its doors on September 14, 2000, the Wilpsi'ayuukhl Nisga'a is the legislative building of the Nisga'a government.

increased. It is the content and analysis of these letters that will be the focus of the remaining discussion in this essay centring on race-based prejudices.

Voices of Prejudice: Letters to the Editor
in *The Terrace Standard* between 1997 and 1999

I have divided letters to the editor of *The Terrace Standard* about the Nisga'a treaty (which were printed over a three-year period) into three distinct categories: (1) those that support the Nisga'a treaty, (2) those that oppose the treaty but are not premised on racial stereotyping of First Nations people, and (3) those that oppose the treaty and rely upon race-based antagonistic premises. I will focus my attention on this final category, but some comment on the letters as a whole serve to contextualize the discussion. Over 50 letters to the editor pertaining to the Nisga'a treaty appeared in *The Terrace Standard* between 1997 and 1999. This translates into an average of one letter every three weeks. In total, 22 of the letters were clearly in opposition to the treaty, while 18 were clearly in favour of the treaty. Slightly more than 10 letters mentioned the treaty, but they were inconclusive as to a sense from the writer of support for or opposition to the treaty. Of the 22 letters in opposition to the treaty, 11 relied on racial stereotyping of First Nations people while the other 11 did not. Letters in favour of the treaty can be identified in a straightforward manner: they are those in which the author explicitly states their approval of, or support for, the Nisga'a treaty. Letters against the treaty, but not reliant on racial prejudice, are similarly easy to identify. These are letters that take issue with the treaty based on political, ideological, or other multifaceted viewpoints. Issues of race do not enter the discourse of the latter. It should be noted that of these 11 letters, six were written by the same author, a non-Nisga'a resident of the Nass Valley concerned with his property rights. Conversely, the third category of letters, those against the treaty and premised on race-based prejudicial perspectives, were all penned by different authors and are slightly more difficult to define, thus requiring some explanation.

Before a discussion of the sentiments and wording in the letters can occur, the evaluative methodology I am using to determine whether or not a letter relies on race-based prejudice should be clarified. I have found the definition of racism offered in the *Oxford Dictionary of Philosophy* (1999) to be particularly helpful in this regard. The definition of racism offered therein is "the inability or refusal to recognize the rights, needs, dignity or value of people of particular races or geographical origins. More widely, the devaluation of various traits of character or intelligence as 'typical' of particular peoples."[11] Further, discussion and definition of racial prejudice against First Nations people, as put forward by Henry et al. in the book *The Colour of Democracy: Racism in Canadian Society* (2000), has proven useful in my own evaluation of letters to the editors in *The Terrace Standard*. In the book, five discourses are identified as pivotal in a continued view that "... Aboriginal people [are] inherently inferior and incapable of governing themselves."[12] Four of the discourses outlined are:

> *Nationality* (an "other" cannot be tolerated by a society pursuing a unifying national identity grounded on Western values); *paternalism* (a sense of dominance and superiority of a colonial government justifying a civilizing of Aboriginal people, often based on concepts of "Christianizing"); *"blame the victim"* (the present state of affairs for First Nations people, including poverty and unemployment, are focused entirely in the Aboriginal peoples themselves); and finally, *the discourse of a monolithic "other"* (this imposes a common history of "Indianness" as determined and defined by mainstream Canadian society).[13]

The two definitions given by the *Oxford Dictionary of Philosophy* and the text by Henry et al., are illuminating when applied to letters to the editor pertaining to the Nisga'a treaty and appearing in *The Terrace Standard*. These descriptions offered of racism are the basis of my own determination as to whether or not a letter relied on race-based prejudice. As I shall explore, I have found that a number of letters did so rely.

In the April 7, 1999, issue of *The Terrace Standard,* Linda Jean of the City of Terrace had a letter to the editor published. Her letter appears in the Mail Bag section of *The Terrace Standard*, the section in the newspaper wherein the

---

[11] Blackburn, 1996, p. 319.

[12] Henry et al., (2000), p. 119.

[13] Ibid., pp. 139–140.

majority of letters to the editor appear. The letter is entitled "Will Treaty Work?" and in it Jean writes:

> ...[o]ver a hundred years ago, when apparently this all got started, the northwest was just being settled. Now, I wasn't there and neither were they, but forefathers of mine were there just as theirs were, history books recorded it.... So we all basically kind of know what went on over 100 years ago and since.... We [non-natives] knew about metals, buildings, planting harvesting, etc. We could read and write. I imagine we could have been arrogant coming to a new land and finding indigenous people who still chewed animal skins for clothing and hand crafted crockery and weapons for throwing, cooking only over open fires and believing only in their medicine man to cure illness.... There has been a lot of atonement for the past abuses to natives. Limited space does not provide room for listing the privileges natives enjoy that non-natives are not allowed or have to pay for. Not only do we share all of our modern inventions with natives, (right down to bi-focals and false teeth) we also provide them at no cost. We supplement their housing even.... The population of these people we support grows and grows. The more kids they have, the more money we give them.... I don't think more money, just because it is attached to a piece of paper [the Nisga'a treaty] this time, cuts to any real solution.[14]

Jean's letter encapsulates all the elements I have identified as being both in opposition to the Nisga'a treaty and premised on race-based prejudice, or racist, ideologies. Jean's assertion that the northwest of British Columbia was just being settled 100 years ago is not consistent with historical reality. The letter insists upon a benevolent ideal of "settling" as the "settler" pioneer claiming a depopulated or unpopulated land, and Jean thereby erases the inherent violence of colonization practices. Additionally, the letter affirms a Eurocentric notion of civilizing that denies the education of European settlers by Aboriginal populations in the West. As historical geographers Cole Harris and Robert Galois note in their essay "A Population Geography of British Columbia in 1881", the 1881 provincial census indicated a population of over 2,800 Natives in the Lower Skeena River and Nass River region, with a non-native population totalling under 200 — 92 whites and 101 Chinese.[15] Further historical records indicate the populations of First Nations on the west coast of British Columbia were decimated by the smallpox epidemic, suggesting the populations recorded in the late 1800s represented only a fraction of populations existing pre-European contact. Mark Cocker writes that "...it has now been widely accepted that Native Americans declined from an original population of more that 8,000,000 to just 800,000 by the end of the nineteenth century."[16] While these numbers are not specific to the Nisga'a populations, one can extrapolate that the Nisga'a populations of northwest British Columbia prior to European contact were nonetheless substantial and, contrary to Jean's assertion, the northwest was not "just being settled" in the late 1800s. Denial of the Nisga'a's historical connection to the land is not the only premise upon which Jean bases her opposition to the Nisga'a treaty. She also uses, referencing the Henry et al. model, arguments of paternalism and language that "blames the victim". The letter argues that while some abuses were committed against the Nisga'a, these are excusable

---

[14] "Letters to the Editor", 1997–1999, *The Terrace Standard,* pp. 4–5.

[15] Harris, 1998, p. 149.

[16] Cocker, 1998, p. 5.

given the "civilizing" efforts of non-native colonizers and the "atonements" that have since been paid. Jean goes on to suggest that a cycle of poverty exists within the Nisga'a population but focuses her attention on the Nisga'a's responsibility for that cycle, claiming the Nisga'a are wilfully continuing the cycle of systemic poverty. As other letters reveal, Jean is by no means alone in her sentiment toward the Nisga'a treaty and the Nisga'a people.

In the December 30, 1997 issue of *The Terrace Standard,* Martyn Brown of Vancouver, the executive director of the Citizens' Voice on Native Claims, had a letter to the editor published. In the letter, he writes that land claim negotiations will mean that "the province's unfettered title to virtually all crown land in British Columbia is now in question." He goes on to note that

> Regrettably, the court's ruling [on aboriginal title] will likely have the opposite effect to that intended. Instead of leading to more harmonious relations between aboriginal and non-aboriginal Canadians, it will increase racial tensions, particularly in resource-dependent communities.... Instead of leading to greater equality of all Canadians, it will reinforce special status for aboriginal Canadians forever....

Brown's letter is of particular interest because Brown is a Vancouver resident and the executive of a provincial organization. His letter is thus representative of an organization's perspective and speaks of a political constituency beyond his own. His assertion that recognition of Aboriginal title will "increase racial tensions" denotes a belief that racial tensions already exist. Further, his statement that Aboriginal title will "reinforce special status for Aboriginal Canadians forever" suggests that Brown and his organization believe First Nations have had (prior at least to his letter) special status in Canada. Finally, Brown takes special care to reiterate the "Canadianness" of the First Nations of whom he writes, reinforcing the imposed unity grounded on Western ideals to which Henry et al. refer. Again, Brown's perspectives are representative of others' views held on the Nisga'a treaty.

In the April 12, 1999, issue of *The Terrace Standard*, a letter contributed by Garry Edward Schuss of Kitimat, British Columbia (a community 50 km south of Terrace), was published. In the letter he writes,

> I am outraged.... It is time that we treated them [the Nisga'a] as Canadians. It is time to end these upsurges of break away units of small minorities ... and pull this country back together under one constitution which works for all Canadians the same. I have no problem with a group of individuals who want to live in a community together and share traditions and life styles whether they be native, east Indian, native Indian, homosexual or anything else as long as they are treated equally under the same laws and provisions for which all other Canadians also must live.

Schuss's letter represents several fundamental misconceptions concerning both Aboriginal rights in Canada and the concept of equality. His letter suggests a conflation of the concepts of equality and sameness, a conflation not borne out within the context of Canadian practices. For instance, it is understood that individuals within different age groups in Canada have achieved, to an extent, equality with regard to fundamental human rights. This is not to say that youth are treated in the **same** manner as seniors, though a sense of **inequality** would not necessarily apply. It is important to note that Schuss's sense of "equality under the same laws and provisions" is based upon the assumption of the normative body/citizen of a white, male Euro-Canadian and ignores the reality of formal equality, which recognizes and protects difference and specificity within the fabric of Canadian society.

Less than five months prior to Schuss's letter to the editor, Claudette Gosset of Terrace had a letter to the editor published that expressed views similar to those of Schuss. In the November 25, 1998, letter, she writes:

> This treaty business has really got me angry. We were all put on this earth as equals according to the Bible and that is the way I think that things should be. This idea that status [First Nations] people are in so much poverty is a real crock. If a person does not want to work then they will be in poverty but if you want to work there are jobs out there. I am tired of working and paying taxes to support people that are too darn lazy to go to work ... you just want to sit around and be looked after for the rest of your lives and you are bringing up your children to be the same as you.... All land should belong to all Canadians not just a few.

Again, Grosset's and Schuss's letters rely on Henry et al.'s defined foundation of "nationality", wherein an "other" cannot be tolerated by a society pursuing a unifying national identity grounded on Western values. Grosset's alignment of First Nations people with poverty takes responsibility for neither the role of colonial practices in Aboriginal economic disenfranchisement nor the intersection of racism and classism at play in First Nations communities. Her use of Christianity as the model of morality and equality ignores the historical reality of its use as a fundamental part of the colonial apparatus that oppressed (and arguably continues to oppress) Canadian Aboriginal populations from the moment of contact. Further, Grosset's views also encapsulate the criteria of racism outlined by the *Oxford Dictionary of Philosophy,* in that her ideas not only refuse to recognize the needs, rights, dignity or value of the Nisga'a people (and all First Nations people in general), but also devalue the character of First Nations people as "typical" of those she is discussing. Grosset also employs the discourse of "blame the victim" as outlined by Henry et al. Finally, Grosset's premising of her arguments on Christianity is worthy of note given that, as noted by Henry et al., racist dialogue is often premised on the discourse of paternalism in which "Christianizing" plays a key role.

As just explored, over a three-year period between 1997 and 1999, 50 percent of letters to the editor appearing in *The Terrace Standard* and opposing the Nisga'a Treaty are premised on racist assumptions towards not only the Nisga'a people, but also First Nations people as a group. The letters reproduced within this paper are representative of the other letters that voice opposition to the Nisga'a treaty and are premised on racist arguments. The themes in the majority of these letters are: (1) Aboriginal title equates to special rights for First Nations, (2) First Nations people are undeserving of land title due to societal and cultural differences and disadvantages, (3) everyone residing in Canada must live under the same set of regulations and laws and, therefore, First Nations must assimilate, and (4) Aboriginal people have no temporal or historical claim to the land. Several conclusions regarding the cultural climate towards Aboriginal people and the settlement of land claims in Canada can be extrapolated from the letters to the editor appearing in *The Terrace Standard.*

First, a denial of Aboriginal land title and land possession is represented in the letters — a notion predicated on the idea that title of Crown land in Canada rests with non-aboriginal people, and always has. As noted by Peter Kulchyski in *Unjust Relations: Aboriginal Rights in Canadian Courts,* "[Aboriginals] were here first translates into: 'at one time, all of this land was theirs.' We rarely conquered them by force of arms. Now all that land is ours. We owe them something."[17] Second, these letters in *The Terrace Standard* indicate an essential misunderstanding of governance in the Canadian context: several levels of government are already established in this country, including municipal and provincial governments, that are regionally specific. Arguments stating that all Canadians must live by one law ignore present legal realities. Claims that Aboriginal populations have no historical connection to the land, as I have indicated, are ignorant of historical fact. That these misconceptions are present, and that they formed the foundation of 50 percent of anti-treaty letters printed in the newspaper of the Nass Valley's closest municipal neighbour, indicates a climate of racial intolerance and ignorance in conjunction with colonial arrogance towards First Nations land title in British Columbia. The letters, taken as a whole, indicate both the pervasiveness of racist thought towards Aboriginal people and a prevalence of ignorance and hostility to First Nations issues. The question then surfaces: What can be learned from the words printed in letters to the editor of *The Terrace Standard*?

Lessons and Conclusions: Learning from the Letters in a Small Municipal Newspaper

Between 1997 and 1999, the topic of the Nisga'a Treaty generated over 50 letters to the editor in *The Terrace Standard*, the community newspaper operating in closest proximity to the negotiated territory. Of these letters, just under half voiced opposition to the treaty based on the racist and prejudicial perspectives of the authors. The letters can be viewed as representative of three issues: (1) regional opposition, predicated on racism, to the Nisga'a treaty; (2) wider antagonism, also based on racism, towards Aboriginal title in British Columbia; and (3) a general misunderstanding, stemming from race-based prejudices, of First Nations peoples and issues. Within all the anti-treaty letters predicated on racist perspectives, common themes are present. These letters reveal the extent to which responses to Aboriginal land claims will be anchored in common themes of racism within the regional context of Northwest British Columbia and, to some extent, within the province as a whole. The Nisga'a treaty, while unique provincially and nationally, provides insight into future treaty negotiations in the Canadian context. Responses to the treaty similarly provide insight into issues of racism needing to be addressed during treaty negotiation processes.

Having identified common themes of racism in response to the Nisga'a treaty, possible responses to those perspectives might be determined. In the

---

[17] Kulchyski, 1994.

Sarah de Leeuw

case of authors whose letters appeared in *The Terrace Standard,* many of their thoughts laboured under historical and factual misconceptions. It is possible that with a more concentrated education and outreach campaign to neighbouring municipal residents, some of these misconceptions would have been dispelled and the Nisga'a people's possession of, and attachment to the Nass Valley from time immemorial, could have be explained and appreciated. Further, a number of residents who felt compelled to write anti-treaty letters cited anger and outrage as the catalyst for their statements. It is possible that these residents believe themselves to have been excluded from a process in which they wanted to partake; ensuring availability of accessible materials and public forums may have mitigated some residents' anger.

Finally, the racist anti-treaty letters to the editor in *The Terrace Standard* indicate that racial prejudice against First Nations peoples in Canada continues into the twenty-first century. Without concentrated and collective attention to the issue, there remains no clear indication that racism, at least in northwest British Columbia, will subside, particularly with reference to treaty negotiation and Aboriginal title.

References

Bell, Catherine, & Asch, Michael. (1997). Challenging assumptions: The impact of precedent in Aboriginal rights litigation. In Michael Asch (Ed.), *Aboriginal and treaty rights in Canada*. Vancouver, BC: UNC Press.

Blackburn, Simon. 1996. *Oxford dictionary of philosophy*. New York, NY: Oxford University Press.

Calder v. *British Columbia* (A.G.), [1973] S.C.R. 313, [1973] 4 W.W.R. 1, 34 D.L.R. (3d) 145, affirming (1970), 74 W.W.R. 481, 13 D.L.R. (3d) 64 (B.C.C.A.), affirming (1969), 71 W.W.R. 81, 8 D.L.R. (3d) 59 (B.C.S.C).

Cocker, Mark. (1998). *Rivers of blood, rivers of gold: Europe's conquest of Indigenous peoples*. New York: Grove Press.

Harris, Cole. (1998). *The resettlement of British Columbia: Essays on colonialism and geographical change*. Vancouver: UBC Press.

Henry, Frances, et al. (2000). *The colour of democracy: Racism in Canadian society*. Toronto: Harcourt Bracc and Company.

Kulchyski, Peter. (1994). *Unjust relations: Aboriginal rights in Canadian courts*. Toronto: Oxford University Press.

Letters to the Editor. (January 1997 to January 1999). *The Terrace Standard*.

Rose, Alex. (2000). *Spirit dance at Meziadin* Maderia Park, BC: Harbour Publishing.

Sterritt, Neil J., et al. (1998). *Tribal boundaries in the Nass Watershed*. Vancouver: UBC Press.

8

Treaty Federalism
Challenging Disciplinary Boundaries and Bridging Praxis, Theory, Research and Critical Pedagogy in Canadian Political Science

Gina Cosentino
Political Science Ph.D. Candidate
University of Toronto
Toronto

Special thanks to Professor Graham White in the Department of Political Science at the University of Toronto for his consistent and generous support and thorough comments and advice on various versions of this paper. I also thank the four anonymous reviewers for their comments and suggestions. Any shortcomings in this essay remain my own.

Gina Cosentino

Treaty Federalism: Bridging Praxis, Theory, Research and Pedagogy

Self-determination as an international law idea surfaced during the post-war period to assist the process of decolonization of subject national minorities in colonial regimes.[1] As a political, moral, economic and legal concept, self-determination is the basis upon which Indigenous[2] peoples assert their claims for cultural autonomy and revival, which include, among other things, a just resolution of the (mis)appropriation of their lands; state recognition of the political, economic and cultural rights flowing from prior occupancy; and territorial sovereignty over many parts of pre-European-contact North America. At the heart of the project of self-determination then, is the recovery of lands and culture, and the assertion of sovereignty through possible means including, but not limited to, creating a third order of government.[3] As a result, the political/practical means to achieve this is treaty federalism. Treaty federalism can be understood as the ongoing relationship between the state and Indigenous peoples relating to the safeguarding of Aboriginal rights and freedoms, shared territorial management, shared political/legislative authority, and the mutual obligations of the signing treaty partners. It is a concept that reinterprets Canadian socio-political history from the perspective of Indigenous peoples' inherent sovereignty over lands now understood as Canada. It also recognizes that treaties are constitutional instruments that can provide a basis for territorial claims, the protection of Indigenous rights (including self-government and self-determination), and an understanding of Indigenous peoples as constitutional partners of the Canadian nation.[4] This concept, therefore, carries important moral and institutional/practical implications, not the least of which pertain to consultation with, participation by, and representation of Aboriginal peoples in both formal state structures and their own political organizations.

The idea of self-determination became highly politicized by the rise of the modern Indigenous rights movement(s) in the late 1960s, when Indigenous peoples in Canada, New Zealand, Australia and elsewhere applied the concept to

---

[1] *See* Don Wilkinson, 1999.

[2] "Indigenous", "Aboriginal" and "First Nations" are used here interchangeably. First Nations are those who identify themselves as being an original inhabitant of the area now known as Canada. Such groups include, but are not limited to, Indians (including what the Canadian government has classified as status and non-status), Inuit, Métis, and urban Aboriginals. "First Nations" has the added benefit of emphasizing "nationhood".

[3] I thank the anonymous reviewer who highlighted this fact.

[4] It should be noted that not all Indigenous peoples concede to the authority of Canadian governing structures or the Canadian political institutions imposed on them. Some instead prefer a parallel path of institutional coexistence with Canada through their own political institutions.

their goals of "internal decolonization."[5] In Canada, the galvanizing force of the modern Indigenous movement was in part a reaction to the federal Liberal government's discriminatory policy proposal, Statement of the Government of Canada on Indian Policy, 1969 (also known as the 1969 White Paper). The demand for political and social change in Canada by Aboriginal groups intensified over the 1980–1992 period when Canada was involved in three attempts at constitutional change. During this time, Aboriginal groups engaged in social movement activism, launched legal challenges, and sought policy changes. The process of internal decolonization is distinct from the process of "external" decolonization that took place during the "decline of European hegemony,"[6] since the dominating society cannot vacate the colonized territory inhabited by Indigenous peoples in settler societies. Canadian political theorist Charles Taylor calls for a "creative" solution to resolve "the dilemma of exclusion": "Political identities have to be worked out, negotiated, and creatively compromised between peoples who have to or want to live together under the same political roof."[7]

As a result, treaty federalism, or governance issues, are critical to Indigenous peoples in Canada as they struggle to retain and revive their cultures, their lands, and their self-sufficiency. Standard interpretations of Canadian governance (or Canadian federalism) ignore Aboriginal people and their unique constitutional status within the Canadian state. The concept of treaty federalism can reformulate some of the basic political-constitutional relationships that link Aboriginal peoples to the Canadian state. As the report of Royal Commission on Aboriginal Peoples points out, "Treaty federalism is an integral part of the Canadian constitution,"[8] and it offers some guidance for resolving questions regarding the status of Aboriginal peoples within the federation. The settlement of land issues, the recognition of Aboriginal governments as legitimate shareholders of constitutional authority, and the resolution of governance and self-determination issues, flow from the starting point of treaty federalism.

Accordingly, accepting the principles of treaty federalism has profound implications for the realization of Indigenous self-determination and decolonization. It also has important implications for approaching, in Canadian classrooms, issues about the historical and ontological nature of colonialism, Aboriginal-state relations, and treaty politics. By using the discipline of political science as an example, the main purpose of this essay is to challenge academic imperialism, contest accepted disciplinary orthodoxies, open disciplinary boundaries and dialogues, and interject critical perspectives in research and practice

---

[5] I am thankful to Peter Russell for pointing out that there is nothing, in principle, to exclude secession if Indigenous peoples choose it. For an analysis by non-Aboriginal Canadian political scientists of the politics surrounding the Canadian experience with constitutional change on Aboriginal-state relations, *see* Cairns, 1995. *See also* Frideres, 1998. For a comparative perspective on Aboriginal-state relations in Canada and New Zealand, *see* Fleras & Elliott, 1992. For discussion and analysis of the White Paper, *see* Weaver, 1981. For a critical analysis of self-determination and decolonization by an Aboriginal scholar, *see* Alfred, 1999.

[6] Cairns, 1999, p. 23.

[7] Charles Taylor in Cairns et al. (1999), p. 281. He does not offer concrete solutions other than pointing out that some institutional settings may facilitate this process more than others (i.e. some models of federalism).

[8] Royal Commission on Aboriginal Peoples, 1996, p. 194.

Gina Cosentino

vis-à-vis Aboriginal issues in Canada. Like other contributions in this volume, this discussion invites us to question and challenge our disciplinary and intellectual boundaries in order to initiate change from within and without the discipline — to bridge praxis, theory, research and critical pedagogy.

Probing Disciplinary Boundaries and Conventional Approaches

In the Canadian context, it is no coincidence, then, that the drama of Indigenous peoples' relationship with their nation-state has been played out on the stage of constitutionalism, as constitutionalism "affirms not only what has been but what is and what can be."[9] The mixing of identity politics and traditional territorial politics of federalism has provided the site upon which First Nations in Canada have staged some of their struggles for self-determination. Their participation in the politics of contested federalism has forced non-Aboriginal academics, politicians and citizens to rethink federalism: how it originated, what it stands for, and where it should go.

Some Indigenous academics, albeit with reservations, have argued that constitutionalism, or constitutional "dreaming", has a transformative potential.[10] In a post-Charter Canada, Canadian federalism retains heightened importance as federal, provincial and Aboriginal representatives need to determine a way to "accommodate"[11] the inherent right of Aboriginal self-government, and to resolve disputes about conflicting conceptions and interpretations of the Constitution and self-determination.[12] What has defined, or at least guided, this relationship is the challenge to understand the meaning and place of treaties in contemporary Canadian constitutionalism and federalism.[13] The Canadian Charter of Rights and Freedoms was entrenched in the *Constitution Act* of 1982. Sections 25 and 35 pertain to Aboriginal and treaty rights. However, given the vague language of Charter provisions and the politically contested and judicialized nature of Canadian federalism, the Charter and federalism remain important sites of political and judicial contestation for the federal and provincial levels of government, as well as for Aboriginal peoples. The demand for political and constitutional change vis-à-vis Aboriginal-state relations intensified during the last decade, when the Canadian federal system was in constitutional

---

[9] See Dobrowolsky, 2000, p. 2.

[10] Laenui, 2000. For a brief discussion on how constitutional reform has reflected and should reflect the needs, ideas and visions of Aboriginal peoples in Canada, *see* Monture-Okanee, 1991, pp. 28–33. *See also* James Youngblood Henderson (2000) for a discussion of how Aboriginal peoples can "penetrate the colonial legal order of Canada and create a new postcolonial constitutional order" (p. 161).

[11] Monture-Angus (1999) cautions that the idea of accommodation can be and has been tokenistic, as oftentimes the proposed changes do not challenge "the overall structure" (p. 82).

[12] Rasmussen, 1994, p. 94.

[13] RCAP, Vol. I, cited in Abele, Graham, & Maslove, "Negotiating Canada", p. 276 at note 48. For a thorough discussion on Aboriginal policy over the last 30 years, *see* Abele et al., 1999). *See also* Abele, 1999.

flux. Against the backdrop of broader political turmoil over constitutional change, Aboriginal people had a stage upon which to pursue their own constitutional objectives in 1982 and, subsequently, in 1992, after they were effectively shut out from the Meech Lake Accord negotiations in 1987. The series of First Ministers' Conferences dealing with Aboriginal affairs that was initiated by section 37 of the *Constitution Act* of 1982 was also essential in getting Aboriginal self-government issues onto the political/constitutional agenda. Since then, the 1990s saw intensified Aboriginal-state relations marked by violence; contemporary treaty negotiation and resolution, devolution of some government responsibilities to some Aboriginal communities, and court battles over Aboriginal and treaty rights, especially fishing, logging, and land rights. Indigenous leaders during the 1982 Constitutional Accord negotiations introduced self-government as a possible means of achieving Indigenous self-determination. Over the following decade, self-government gained popular appeal among politicians and the public, resulting in, among other things, advances in Aboriginal policy over the past 30 years. These advancements culminated in the inclusion of Indigenous peoples' inherent right to self-government in the 1992 Charlottetown Constitutional Accord. Even though the Accord was rejected in the 1992 referendum, a Royal Commission on Aboriginal Peoples (RCAP) was established in 1993 to look into "issues of land, self-government, and political and social justice for Aboriginal peoples." The Commission was even more salient after the failure of the Meech Lake Accord in 1990 to address Indigenous peoples' concerns in order to deal with national unity concerns with Québec. The Accord ultimately collapsed, due in part to the collective efforts of Aboriginal groups and Aboriginal member of the Manitoba legislature Elijah Harper, as well as other Meech Lake Accord detractors. Almost immediately after Meech, a violent confrontation erupted between the Mohawks of Québec and their allies and the Québec provincial police and the Canadian armed forces. In the end, the Commission argued for the moral and practical principles of treaty federalism: that the relationship between Aboriginal nations and Canada should be based on treaties — those that exist, and modern treaties where required.

However, the normative and practical significance of treaties in Aboriginal-Canadian state relationships has been largely underplayed or absent from Canadian political science.[14] Among some non-Indigenous scholars, the legacy of treaties does not matter much beyond "proving" title extinguishment or proving that Aboriginals have "consented" to the custodianship of the Canadian state. Yet, there is a group of leading academics, primarily Aboriginal scholars and legal and political theorists, committed to forging a normative and substantive link between treaties and Canadian federalism with the hope of transformative ends. This idea is also gaining jurisprudential currency, which is seen in a

---

[14] Hawkes, 1989. When academic works in these areas do address the treaty relationship, most are not refined analyses of how treaties affect Canadian federalism, how they impact Canadian jurisprudence, how they circumscribe Aboriginal-state relationships (especially self-government issues), and how they figure in contemporary land claims and treaty processes. See for example, Morse, 1999 and Pratt, 1989. *See also* Jhappan, 1995.

marked shift in the way the Canadian courts view and interpret treaties.[15] Such interpretation recognizes that treaties distributed constitutional, legal and political norms and responsibilities across Canada. Treaties provide the basis for a (renewed) on-going nation-to-nation relationship that is based on the principles of mutual recognition, intercultural dialogue, sharing, co-existence, partnership, shared sovereignty, Aboriginal consent, Aboriginal rights, and equality.[16] This concept cuts across traditional conceptions of federal-provincial diplomacy by addressing the diplomatic relations engendered by the treaty relationship among nations (both Aboriginal and European and, later, Canadian), and what this means in terms of reaching a just intercultural institutional accommodation.[17] While there are some Canadian political scholars who acknowledge the concept,[18] the leading proponents of this view are legal scholars James Youngblood Henderson, Lawrence Barsh, Patrick Macklem, and political theorist James Tully.[19]

In addition, these scholars argue that students of "federalism in an era of Aboriginal self-government"[20] in Canada have, perhaps unwittingly, overlooked or downplayed the importance of treaties both in the mythologies of Confederation, the distribution of powers in the Constitution, and the legitimacy of Canadian sovereignty more broadly. This is best seen in the socio-political theories of Canadian federalism that underpin Canadian political science research today. For instance, the "dualism theory" of federalism argues that Confederation is a compact between the English and French, and the "contract theory" of federalism views provinces as equal members of the federation. Both the French and English cultural communities, as well as provinces, are seen as the constitutive political actors both at Confederation and in contemporary politics; their saliency figures in the institutional structure of the country. Aboriginal peoples are not seen as such and are often portrayed as another "cultural" group among the many "special interests" who vie for scarce public dollars, media attention, policy consideration or other self-interested pursuits on the "Aboriginal agenda".[21] Even those scholars who are sympathetic to the political concerns of Aboriginal peoples fall short of fully recognizing the impact of the

---

[15] *See* Macklem, 2001 for a comprehensive discussion of the shift in Canadian jurisprudence relating to Indigenous rights, especially chapters 5 and 6.

[16] Andrew Bear Robe (1992) outlines five Aboriginal rights principles that he argues must be respected and recognized by the Canadian people and Canadian Parliament if the idea of treaty federalism is to be operational. *See also* Tully, 1999, pp. 414–415.

[17] Ibid., 413–42.

[18] For example, S.V. LaSelva and Alan Cairns acknowledge the concept but misinterpret it. For example, LaSelva (1996) argues that Aboriginal peoples were not equal partners in Confederation; instead, 'partnership' remains an ideal that needs to be determined and negotiated (151). Cairns (2000) defends a common citizenship regime for all Canadians based on the idea of "citizen's plus' over the idea of a differentiated citizenship inherent in treaty federalism (182).

[19] *See* Barsh & Henderson, 1980 for the first use of the term 'treaty federalism'. *See also* Henderson, 1994b; Tully, 1995; Macklem, 2001. Kiera Ladner also supports this view. For an excellent discussion of treaty federalism as it relates to creating a renewed relationship based on "true" partnership, *see* Ladner, 2001.

[20] This phrase is appropriated from Pratt, 1989. The era of Aboriginal self-government was initiated by Aboriginal peoples' response to the federal Liberal government White Paper policy in 1969 and catapulted into the high-stakes of mega-constitutional change of the 1980s and 1990s.

[21] *See* Flanagan, 2000.

treaty relationship on self-government, constitutionalism and the functioning of federalism.[22] This reproduces epistemological and pedagogical biases of an established (Eurocentric) understanding of treaties vis-à-vis constitutionalism, federalism, minority/cultural politics and national unity issues.

While political science research is emerging under the treaty federalism framework,[23] as a whole, Canadian federalism scholars have not yet tapped into the array of possibilities for research and practice of federalism and constitutionalism under this framework. Even though it is primarily Aboriginal academics, mainly Aboriginal legal scholars, that have used the idea, the concept of treaty federalism is inherently interdisciplinary and is not bound by a rigid methodology from any one discipline. As a result, treaty federalism, a relatively unexplored concept in Canadian political science, must receive greater scholarly attention and consideration since, it broadens research questions, debates, and scholarship to include marginalized perspectives and historical narratives or interpretations of the past. Treaty federalism allows for an incorporation of Aboriginal perspectives detailing Aboriginal conceptions of Aboriginal-Canadian state relations. It can also lead to creative solutions for resolving the "Canadian impasse", or the dilemma of national unity in this country. What we have seen in political science scholarship regarding Indigenous relations with the Canadian state over the past 15 years is much theorizing about Canadian-Indigenous relations without addressing the practical implications of the norms, ideas, and institutions embedded in the historical and current treaty-relationship for Aboriginal self-governance and Canadian-Aboriginal relations.

Reconciling Federalism and Treaty Federalism: Conceptual Compatibility or Conceptual Muddle?

Federalism, in principle, gives us the means to reconcile multiple communities within the boundaries of a nation-state. According to Swinton and Simeon,

> Federalism is at once a set of institutions — the division of public authority between two or more constitutionally defined orders of government — and a set of ideas which underpin such institutions. As an idea, federalism points us to issues such as shared and divided sovereignty, multiple loyalties and identities, and governance through multi-level institutions.[24]

As Swinton and Simeon assert, the theory of federalism embodies the dual idea of the distribution of governmental power on a geographical basis and the **philosophy** that unity and diversity can coexist. There is nothing embedded in the theory of federalism to preclude the application of non-conventional methodolo-

---

[22] *See* Cairns, 2000.

[23] *See* White, 2001; Ladner, 2001.

[24] Simeon & Swinton, 1994, p. 3.

gies (i.e. alternative understandings of the origin and evolution of federalism) for research on Indigenous governance, citizenship and federalism.

Political scientist Roger Gibbins argues that federalism is much more than "governments and their interactions."[25] Federalism, he argues, is also about reconciling diversity. At the level of analysis, the institutional and sociological (identity) dimensions render the study of federalism quite complex. The institutional/sociological/identity/normative nexus of federalism merges with the basic theoretical, practical and transformative concerns of treaty federalism — how to institutionalize diversity in a way that recognizes First Nations as co-sovereign partners in the federation. As a result, a model of federalism that disregards historic (or future) treaty relations denies the realities of accommodating the "difference" that is embedded in the idea of federalism itself.

Treaty federalism, like traditional federalism, can also be explained in terms of institutional and normative dimensions. As an institutional form, treaty federalism is about past, present, and future intra- and intergovernmental relations and the institutional mechanisms and processes between the federal, provincial, and treaty orders of government.[26] The difference between traditional understandings of Canadian federalism and treaty federalism is the interpretation of Confederation and Indigenous-Crown relations. Treaties and, by extension, Indigenous nations are given a different normative and epistemic place within the federation than what a traditional conception of federalism typically ascribes. While traditional federalism scholarship tends to downplay the normative, legal and political authority of treaties in mapping out divisions of powers in the Constitution, treaty federalism reconceputalizes Indigenous peoples as co-sovereign partners in establishing a legal and political order in Canada under the imperial and, later, Canadian state.[27] As Henderson argues, this relationship was not fully or properly implemented due to systemic racism, and it ignored treaty obligations by federal and provincial governments, assimilationist policies, and "interpretative monopolies" of treaties and the law.[28]

The inherent argument within treaty federalism is that if we are to have a democratic, post-colonial, reinvented partnership with Aboriginal peoples, then we need to have a democratic and just institutional and normative basis for dealing with this relationship. The most solid foundation upon which to secure this partnership is a federation that reflects inherent Aboriginal sovereignty, the recovery of lands, and Aboriginal vision(s) about the relationship. The strength of the treaty federalism concept lies in attributing a moral and political force to Aboriginal participation in the creation of institutions and processes that will shape the relationship and on which both Canadian and Aboriginal peoples agree. The focus on Aboriginal consent and legitimation raises important questions relating to issues of social justice, fairness and democracy that many federalism scholars ignore.[29] The role of the treaty relationship is taken seriously

---

[25] Gibbins, 1999, p. 199.

[26] Henderson, 1994a, p. 55.

[27] Ibid. *See also* Webber, 1996; Williams, 1996.

[28] Henderson, 1994a, pp. 55–59. For a similar point, *see also* Turpel, 1989–90; Monture-Angus, 1990.

[29] *See* for example, Flanagan, 2000; Cairns, 2000; LaSelva, 1996; Morse, 1989.

in terms of what it means for envisioning contemporary intergovernmental mechanisms to deal with common interests and conflict as they occur. As a result, there is conceptual overlap between federalism and treaty federalism at both the normative and institutional levels of analysis.

Federalism in Transition: A Shifting Research Paradigm

In order to see where federalism scholarship ought to be headed, it is useful to see where it has been. Canadian political science literature on Canadian federalism and the treaty relationship can be broadly clustered around four broad themes that also fall roughly along the lines of the interpretation of treaties by the courts:[30]

1. **Treaties as Political Accords:** This literature reflects early jurisprudential interpretations of treaties. The material is united by a common normative and interpretive tone about the meaning of treaties, Aboriginal nationhood, and sovereignty that is reminiscent of the early modern Western European understanding of these concepts, which is rooted in the doctrine of discovery and conquest. Some argue that Aboriginal nations are not nations in the Western European sense; therefore, they are not sovereign and, as such, could not have entered into "enforceable" treaties.[31]

2. **Contractualist Vision:** This literature views treaties as a type of ordinary contract that is only enforceable in the context of Crown inaction. The work is mostly formalistic and legalistic, concerned with existing division of powers and the delegation of legislative and administrative authority to Aboriginal nations within the existing federal system. It is united by the broader assumption about the nature of Canadian authority as embodied in the conventional understanding of the principle of parliamentary supremacy over the jurisdictional parameters set out in the Constitution. The fairness and accuracy of the distribution of law-making authority in the Constitution are not questioned. Little attention is paid to issues of Aboriginal agency or the normative and practical implications of Aboriginal participation in treaty-making with Crown and, later, Canadian authorities.[32]

---

[30] I am indebted to Patrick Macklem (2001) here. This is, generally, his conceptual framework of the treaty process (see chapter 5, "Indigenous Difference and the Constitution"). My adoption of this categorization differs from his insofar as I use it to map and organize political science literature in this area.

[31] *See* Flanagan, 1998; Green, 1989.

[32] *See*, for example: Morse, 1989; Pratt, 1989; Smiley, 1977; Jhappan, 1995. Cairns, 2000 and LaSelva, 1996 also reflect this view.

3. **The New Interpretative Framework:**[33] This theme coincides with a **significant** transformation in the judicial understanding of treaties. The scholars here generally reject a strict/positivistic reading of the law and Aboriginal entitlements, and they reject the imperialistic assumptions that are reminiscent of judicial interpretations before World War II. Instead, Aboriginal-government relations are to be based on a new political ethic guided by principles of post-imperialism: fairness, distributive justice, recognition, and meaningful and effective Aboriginal participation rather than legalistic and formalistic interpretations of treaties and federal-provincial division of powers. In addition, Aboriginal cultures are seen as living and must be encouraged to flourish and coexist alongside dominant values, norms and institutions. The work reflects themes like partnership, asymmetrical and multinational federalism, mutual respect, participation, reconciliation, democracy, and institutional and constitutional pluralism that can be achieved through self-government arrangements within Canadian federalism.[34]

4. **Treaties as Constitutional Accords:** This theme is somewhat of an extension of the third, but it has a different normative, epistemic, pedagogic and methodological focus. It attempts to fill the gaps in the dominant legal histories of Aboriginal-Crown relations that typically trace the legal position of Aboriginal people under Canadian law over time. Researchers share a common methodology: they try to understand the treaty relationship as Aboriginal nations would have understood it. Work in this area reflects the treaty federalism thesis that treaties are essential constitutional accords between sovereign nations, and it is united by a common normative concern for ascertaining a just (re)distribution and accommodation of constitutional authority in a post-colonial Canadian state.[35]

Treaty federalism scholars, unlike traditional federalism scholars, offer a different kind of scholarship for federalism, one that seeks to address some of the intellectual gaps left by Western-Anglo, state-centric analyses of federalism. State-centred institutionalism has been the dominant approach in federalism studies since the 1940s.[36] It was not until the late 1960s or early 1970s that Canadian political scientists even took Aboriginal issues as a source of academic inquiry, and even then, Aboriginal peoples were not autonomous actors but appendages of the state with no apparent history, or identity, other than what the state had defined for them. In addition, Aboriginal issues within federalism scholarship are oftentimes subordinated to the more "pressing concern"

---

[33] Macklem, 2001, pp. 144–155.

[34] Fleras & Elliott, 1992; Kymlicka, 1998; Schneiderman, 1998 and Jenson, 1998. *See also* Jenson, 1995. For non-territorial conceptions of self-government, *see* Elkins, 1995. For an opposing view of how constitutional and institutional pluralism can lead to greater social disintegration, *see* LaSelva, 1996 and Cairns, 1995. For an example of a federal government policy initiative under this approach *see Gathering Strength*, 1998.

[35] *See* works by Henderson, 1994b; Macklem, 2001; and Tully, 1995. *See also* the discussion of treaty federalism in the report by the Royal Commission on Aboriginal Peoples, 1996.

[36] *See*, for example, Mallory, 1958.

of quelling Québec nationalist aspirations.[37] In *State, Society and the Development of Canadian Federalism* (1990), political scientists Richard Simeon and Ian Robinson provide an extensive historical political-social-economic analysis of the evolution of Canadian federalism that significantly advances Mallory's schematic of Canadian federalism. Given the breadth of their analysis, it is surprising that their treatment of Aboriginal relations is set within the politics of diversity that seemed to have emerged during the "constitutional federalism" phase of Canadian federalism (their analysis ends with the Meech Lake Accord constitutional debates). Despite Aboriginal-relations issues being, both during and before this time, extremely important to the evolution of Canadian federalism (especially with respect to pre- and post-Confederation treaties), this was not figured in their analysis.

By the early 1980's, with the inclusion of sections 25 and 35 in the Constitution Act of 1982,[38] a new political ethic emerged in the way treaties and Aboriginal sovereignty were viewed by the courts and academics. The courts developed a four-tiered "new interpretative framework" in *Simon* v. *The Queen* (1985) and *R.* v. *Sioui* (1990). This new interpretative (jurisprudential) framework represents a marked change in judicial approach to the interpretation of treaty provisions.[39] As Macklem notes, "[I]t challenges the blind acceptance of the legitimacy of non-Aboriginal norms and values in the process of determining the meaning of vague treaty rights."[40] This framework displaces the earlier narrow, legalistic and textual interpretations of treaties and Aboriginal-state relations. The main charge for political science under this approach is to uncover the "hybridity"[41] of Canadian political institutions, to "discredit the tacit constitutional assumptions that underpin white settler governance,"[42] and to offer an alternative understanding of constitutionalism and federalism.[43]

Similarly, new interpretative scholarship in political science demonstrates an opening up of methodologies and epistemic and normative questions that federalism research raises in relation to Aboriginal peoples. Contemporary federalism methods include neo-institutionalism, society- (or agent-) centred approaches, identity politics, social movement theory, Aboriginal narratives and epistemologies, and interdisciplinary analysis.[44] While there has been definite

---

[37] *See* works by Smiley (1962; 1972; 1974; 1976; and 1987). *See also* McRoberts, 1997; Cairns, 1995; and LaSelva, 1996. In their 1999 article, Simeon and Robinson update their analysis to the late 1990s.

[38] Section 25 states, "The guarantee in this Charter of certain rights and freedoms shall not be construed so as to abrogate or derogate from any Aboriginal, treaty or other rights and freedoms that pertain to the Aboriginal peoples of Canada..." Section 35(1) says, "The existing Aboriginal and treaty rights of Aboriginal peoples of Canada are hereby recognized and affirmed."

[39] This framework is rooted in post-imperial principles of fairness and distributive justice and a flexible and liberal interpretation of the treaty relationship and treaty rights as Aboriginal peoples would have understood them.

[40] Macklem, 2001, p. 145.

[41] Young, 2000.

[42] Maaka & Fleras, 2000, p. 92.

[43] Tully, 2000.

[44] For a discussion of how the politics of identity have injected Canadian political science with new conceptual and methodological approaches, *see* Jenson, 1999.

Gina Cosentino

progress in federalism studies over the past few decades, the main methodological and epistemological limitations of this approach is that it does not offer an alternative understanding of constitutionalism and federalism — it focuses on alternative reconceptualizations of the **existing** federal state without addressing the values, beliefs and ideas that underpins it.[45] The methodological implication of treaty federalism is that it requires the use of agent-centered accounts of how Aboriginal peoples participated in shaping the founding constitutional norms. For example, Iris Marion Young's notion of "hybrid democracy" reflects the discursive and interpretative methods inherent in treaty federalism: "Development of the institutional imagination and commitment to confront the colonial legacy depends partly on rereading the history of modernity, democracy and the building of nation-states from the point of view of colonized peoples considered as actors and not merely as those acted upon."[46]

Applying new interpretative approaches to the "treaties as constitutional accords" view of federalism (the treaty federalism view) enriches federalism scholarship by transcending traditional understandings of federalism and Aboriginal-Crown relations. As a result, treaty federalism scholars are united by a common methodological and epistemological approach: (re)interpreting Canadian constitutionalism and the treaty process, which is retold from "Aboriginal perspectives". Today, judicial and political interpretation dovetails with more contemporary political and social thought on the need to recognize the biases of early interpretations of the treaty relationship and how it has been institutionalized in the very structures and institutions that represent Canadian "democracy".

As a result, embedded in the concept of treaty federalism is a prescriptive element. Treaty federalism tells us how we should approach altering our political practices and institutions to better reflect the central values and principles that have come to define the Canadian political system. Treaty federalism tells us much about the nature of Canadian constitutionalism, about the procedures, values, customs and mythologies that are basic to the Canadian polity. It looks at alternative interpretations of federalism, treaties, and Aboriginal-state relationships as told by Aboriginal peoples. Federalism has been typically defined in territorial and statist terms at the expense of Aboriginal understandings of nationhood. This restrictive understanding of federalism limits the extent to which inherent self-government rights can be creatively conceived in contemporary federalism research.

Despite a shift in the research paradigm, there are Canadian political scientists who continue to dismiss the idea that Aboriginal peoples are co-sovereign partners in the federation. They view Aboriginal self-government as an unworkable, fanciful experiment or, at best, a subordinate government with delegated and limited municipal-like powers.[47] Many federalism scholars are not able to get around a traditional understanding of Canadian federalism and, as a result, treaty federalism is still not seen as a viable alternative for understanding how

[45] *See* Turpel, 1989–90; Henderson, 2000.
[46] Young, 2000, p. 238.
[47] For example, *see* Flanagan, 2000.

Aboriginal participation shaped the founding constitutional and federal norms and what this means for federalism today.

An Emerging Research and Pedagogical Agenda

While the discourse of Canadian political science may find it difficult to accommodate alternative understandings of Canadian political history and Canadian political institutions, the concept of treaty federalism is, nonetheless, viable as an alternative understanding of federalism that establishes the basis upon which to forge a renewed relationship with Aboriginal peoples. The politics of identity, recognition and representation embedded in federalism is made even more salient with treaty federalism. As a result, treaty federalism is more in tune with the realities of contemporary federalism, as Indigenous peoples are pressing to reclaim their histories, lands, governments and autonomy. The moral theory embedded within treaty federalism lies with its democratic premise of constitutionally recognizing the fundamental autonomy of First Nations as political communities, giving voice to their history, identity and desire for nationhood. This theory echoes Patricia Monture-Angus's call for a methodology that "[creates] a space (or spaces) for Aboriginal ways of knowing and understanding to occupy within more mainstream methodologies."[48] Treaty federalism, as a methodological and conceptual lens is interdisciplinary. This has important implications for federalism research in Canadian political science as it takes seriously, as a focus of academic analysis, Aboriginal interpretations of treaties, history, stories and Aboriginal participation in founding political institutions and norms.

The discussion generated by most federalism scholarship about Indigenous-state relations over the past few decades has essentially been monologic: it is one in which Indigenous people are asked (if that) to join in a "non-Indigenous dialogue" about the meaning of the state, federalism, citizenship and Canadian identity. Most times, the participants of the debate, as well as the content, structure, and focus of the debate, are predetermined by non-Aboriginal scholars and ideas without reference to Aboriginal norms, Aboriginal scholarship, history and understanding of Aboriginal people's past, present and future, thereby institutionalizing academic imperialism within the discipline. Subsequently, the discipline of political science needs to develop more self-critical inquiries — about its traditional methodologies, and what is being taught and researched, how, and to whom. Thus far, treaty federalism, as an approach to understanding Canadian federalism and Aboriginal-Canadian state relations and as a conceptual framework, comes closest to accomplishing this goal.

As it stands, when more Canadian political scholars are beginning to discuss the meaning of treaty federalism — regardless of whether they agree to the tenets of treaty federalism — it can, in the end, lead to more self-critical discus-

---

[48] Monture-Angus, 1999, pp. 86–87.

sions about the discipline and pedagogy and the inclusion of Aboriginal scholarship and perspectives in political science. This has been evident in political science, where federalism research and different generations of political scholars have begun to question and broaden the traditional paradigms, frameworks, concepts, methodologies and research questions, as well as broaden the dialogues and debates that political science has conventionally engendered. However, despite the fact that Canadian political science has been forced to deal with the saliency of Aboriginal politics in the post-Charter era, as a discipline it has a long way to go in integrating and legitimating Aboriginal research, epistemologies and methods.[49] Ultimately, if political science, like many other disciplines, is to avoid some of its past epistemological, pedagogical and methodological sins, then scholars must be willing to go beyond the conventional understanding of federalism and embrace some of the diverse methodological approaches inherent in treaty federalism. The challenge then is: How can those perspectives, which challenge prevailing views within and without the existing discipline, penetrate it?

References

Abele, Frances. (1999). The importance of consent: Indigenous peoples' politics in Canada. In James Bickerton & Alain-G. Gagnon (Eds.), *Canadian politics* (3rd ed.) (pp. 443–461). Peterborough, ON: Broadview Press.

Abele, Frances, Graham Katherine A., & Maslove, Allan M. (1999). Negotiating Canada: Changes in aboriginal policy over the last thirty years. In L.A. Pal (Ed.), *How Ottawa spends 1999–2000 shape shifting: Canadian Governance toward the 21st century* (pp. 251–292). Toronto, ON: Oxford University Press.

Alfred, Taiaiake. (1999). *Peace, power and righteousness: An indigenous manifesto*. Don Mills, ON: Oxford University Press.

Barsh, Russell Lawrence, & Henderson, James Youngblood. (1980). *The road: Indian tribes and political liberty*. Los Angeles, CA: University of California Press.

Battiste, Marie. (Ed.). (2000). *Reclaiming Indigenous voice and vision*. Vancouver, BC: UBC Press.

---

[49] I acknowledge and concede to L.M. Findlay's charge that "[s]ignificant numbers of Euro-Canadian scholars have become remarkably good at critiquing the pretensions and practices of modernity and defending marginalized groups, but they do so within institutions among whose faculties Aboriginal peoples are minimally represented" (p. x). However, my aim as a non-Aboriginal Euro-Canadian political science scholar is not to "speak for" Aboriginal people, or "speak to "Aboriginal peoples about themselves" or to anyone else, but to work, in partnership, for our mutual goals of dismantling intellectual hierarchies and forging a post-colonial scholarship and society. This essay, for better or worse, is my small contribution to that effort. For an excellent compilation of essays by Indigenous authors that critiques traditional scholarship, disciplines and research that is situated within the broader project of restoring, respecting and encouraging post-colonial scholarship and Aboriginal epistemologies and methods, *see* Battiste, 2000.

Cairns, Alan. (1995). Aboriginal Canadians, citizenship and the Constitution. In D.E. Williams (Ed.), *Reconfigurations: Canadian citizenship and constitutional change*. Toronto: McClelland & Stewart.

Cairns, A.C. (1999). Empire, globalization and the fall and rise of diversity. In A.C. Cairns et al., *Citizenship diversity and pluralism: Canadian and comparative perspective*. Montreal: McGill-Queen's University Press.

Cairns, Alan. (2000). *Citizen's plus: Aboriginal peoples and the Canadian state*. Toronto: University of British Columbia Press.

Cairns, A.C., et al., (1999). *Citizenship diversity and pluralism: Canadian and comparative perspective*. (Montreal: McGill-Queen's University Press.

Clark, Bruce. (1990). *Native liberty, Crown sovereignty: The existing Aboriginal right of self-government in Canada*. Montreal: McGill-Queen's University Press.

Dobrowolsky, Alexandra. (2000). *The politics of pragmatism: Women, representation, and constitutionalism in Canada*. (Don Mills: Oxford University Press.

Elkins, David. (1995). *Beyond sovereignty: Territory and political economy in the twenty-first century*. Toronto, ON: University of Toronto Press.

Findlay, L.M., "Forward" in Marie Battiste, (Ed.). (2000). *Reclaiming Indigenous voice and vision*. Vancouver, BC: UBC Press.

Flanagan, Thomas. (1998). Does anyone really want an Aboriginal archipelago? In M. Charlton & P. Barker, *Crosscurrents: Contemporary political issues* (3rd ed.) (pp. 9–16). Toronto: ITP Nelson.

Flanagan, Thomas. (2000). *First Nations? Second thoughts*. Montreal: McGill-Queen's University Press.

Fleras, Augie, & Elliott, Jean Leonard. (1992). *The nations within: Aboriginal-state relations in Canada, the United States and New Zealand*. Toronto: Oxford University Press.

Frideres, J.S. (1998). *Aboriginal peoples in Canada: Contemporary conflicts* (5th ed.). Scarborough, ON: Prentice Hall.

Gathering Strength: Canada's Aboriginal Action Plan. (1998). Ottawa: Indian Affairs and Northern Development.

Gibbins, Roger. (1999). "Taking stock: Canadian federalism and its constitutional framework. In L. Pal (Ed.), *How Ottawa spends 1999–2000 shape shifting: Canadian governance toward the 21st Century*. Toronto: Oxford University Press.

Green, L.C. (1989). Claims to territory in colonial America. In L.C. Green & Olive P. Dickason (Eds.), *The law of nations and the new world*. Edmonton, AB: University of Alberta Press.

Hawkes, David C. (Ed.). (1989). *Aboriginal peoples and government responsibility: Exploring federal and provincial roles*. Ottawa, ON: Carleton University Press.

Henderson, James Youngblood. (1994a) Implementing the treaty order. In R. Goose, J. Youngblood Henderson, & R. Carter (Eds.), *Continuing poundmaker and Riel's quest: Presentation made at a conference on Aboriginal people and justice*. (Saskatoon, SK: Purich Publishing.

Henderson, James Youngblood. (1994b). Empowering treaty federalism. *Saskatchewan Law Review, 58*, pp. 241–329.

Henderson, James Youngblood. (2000). Postcolonial ledger drawing: Legal reform. In Marie Battiste (Ed.), *Reclaiming Indigenous voice and vision*. Toronto: UBC Press.

Jenson, Jane. (1995). Citizenship claims: Routes to representation in a federal system. In Karen Knop, et al. (Eds.), *Rethinking federalism: Citizens, markets, and governments in a changing world*. Vancouver, BC: University of British Columbia Press.

Jenson, Jane. (1998). Recognising difference: Distinct societies, citizenship regimes and partnership. In Roger Gibbins & Guy Laforest (Eds.), *Beyond the impasse: Toward reconciliation*. Ottawa: The Institute for Research on Public Policy.

Jenson, Jane. (1999). Understanding politics: Concepts of identity in political science. In J. Bickerton & A-G. Gagnon (Eds.), *Canadian politics* (3rd ed.) (pp. 39–56). Peterborough, ON: Broadview Press.

Jhappan, Rhadda. (1995). The federal-provincial power-grid and aboriginal self-government. In François Rocher & Miriam Smith (Eds.), *New trends in Canadian federalism* (pp. 115–185). Peterborough: Broadview.

Kymlicka, Will. (1998). Multinational federalism in Canada: Rethinking the partnership. In R. Gibbins and G. LaForest (Eds.). *Beyond the Impasse Toward Reconciliation* (pp. 15–50). Montreal PQ: Institute for Research on Public Policy.

Ladner, Kiera. (2001). "Is negotiated inferiority inevitable? Treaty federalism and the Royal Commission on Aboriginal Peoples vision of a renewed relationship. *American Review of Canadian Studies* (Spring/Summer).

Laenui Poka (Hayden F. Burgess). (2000). Processes of decolonization. In Marie Battiste (Ed.). *Reclaiming Indigenous voice and vision*. Toronto: UBC Press.

LaSelva, S.V. (1996). *The moral foundations of Canadian federalism: Paradoxes, achievements and tragedies of nationhood*. Kingston: McGill-Queen's University Press.

Maaka, Roger, & Fleras, Augie. (2000). Engaging with indigeneity: Tino Rangatiratanga in Aotearoa. In Duncan Ivison et al., *Political theory and the rights of Indigenous peoples*. (New York: Cambridge University Press.

Macklem, Patrick. (2001). *Indigenous difference and the Constitution of Canada*. Toronto: University of Toronto Press.

Mallory, J.R. (1958). Five faces of federalism. In P.-A. Crepeau and C.B. Macpherson (Eds.), *The future of Canadian federalism* (pp. 3–15). Toronto: University of Toronto Press.

McRoberts, Kenneth. (1997). *Misconceiving Canada: The struggle for national unity*. (Toronto: Oxford University Press.

Monture-Angus, Patricia. (1999). Standing against Canadian law: Naming omissions of race, culture and gender. In E. Comack et al., *Locating law: Race/class/gender connections* (76–97). Halifax, NS: Fernwood Publishing.

Monture-Okanee, Patricia. (1991). Seeking my reflection: A comment of constitutional renovation. In D. Schneiderman (Ed.), *Conversations among friends/entre amies: Proceedings of an interdisciplinary conference on women and constitutional reform* (pp. 28–33). Edmonton, AB: Centre for Constitutional Studies.

Morse, Bradford. (1989). Government obligations, Aboriginal peoples and section 91(24). In David C. Hawkes, *Aboriginal peoples and government responsibilities: Exploring federal and provincial roles* (pp. 59–92). Ottawa, ON: Carleton University Press.

Pratt, Alan. (1989). Federalism in the era of Aboriginal self-government. In David C. Hawkes (Ed.), *Aboriginal peoples and government responsibility: Exploring federal and provincial roles* (pp. 19–58). Ottawa, ON: Carleton University Press.

Rasmussen, Merrilee. (1994). Self-government and intergovernmental relations. In R. Gosse, J. Youngblood Henderson, & R. Carter (Eds.), *Continuing poundmakers and Riel's quest: Presentations made at a conference on Aboriginal peoples and justice*. (Saskatoon, SK: Purich Publishing.

Robe, Andrew Bear. (1992). Treaty federalism. *Constitutional Forum, 4*(1), 9–10.

Robinson, Ian, & Simeon, Richard. (1999). The dynamics of Canadian federalism. In James Bickerton & A.-G. Gagnon (Eds.), *Canadian politics* (3rd ed.) (pp. 239–262). Peterborough, ON: Broadview Press.

Royal Commission on Aboriginal Peoples. (1996). *Report of the Royal Commission on Aboriginal Peoples* (Vol. 2). Ottawa, ON: Supply and Services Canada.

Schneiderman, David. (1998). Human rights, fundamental differences? Multiple charters in a partnership frame. In R. Gibbins and G. LaForest (Eds.). *Beyond the Impasse Toward Reconciliation* (pp. 147–185). Montreal PQ: Institute for Research on Public Policy.

Simeon, Richard, & Robinson, Ian. (1990). *State, society and the development of Canadian federalism*. Toronto, ON: University of Toronto Press.

Simeon, Richard, & Swinton, Katherine. (1994). Introduction: Rethinking federalism in a changing world. In K. Knop et al., *Rethinking federalism: Citizens, markets and governments in a changing world*. Vancouver: UBC Press, 1994.

Simon v. The Queen, [1985] 24 D.L.R. (4th) 390 (S.C.C.); and *R. v. Sioui*, [1990] 1 S.C.R. 1025.

Smiley Donald V. (1962). The Rowell-Sirois report, provincial autonomy and postwar Canadian federalism. *Canadian Journal of Economics and Political Science, 28*, pp. 54–69.

Smiley Donald V. (1972). *Canada in question: Federalism in the seventies*. Toronto, ON: McGraw-Hill Ryerson.

Smiley Donald V. (1974). *Constitutional adaptation and Canadian federalism*. Document 4, Royal Commission on Bilingualism and Biculturalism. Ottawa, ON: Queen's Printer.

Smiley Donald V. (1976). Canada and the quest for a national policy. *Canadian Journal of Political Science 8*, pp. 40–62.

Smiley, Donald V. (1977). Federal-provincial conflict in Canada. In Peter Meekison (Ed.), *Canadian federalism myth or reality*. Toronto: Methuen.

Smiley, Donald V. (1987). *The federal condition in Canada*. (Toronto: McGraw-Hill Ryerson.

Tully, James. (1995). *Strange Multiplicity: Constitution in an Age of Diversity*. New York: Press Syndicate of the University of Cambridge.

Tully, James. (1999). Aboriginal peoples: Negotiating reconciliation. In J. Bickerton & A-G. Gagnon (Eds.), *Canadian politics* (3rd ed.) (pp. 434–442). Toronto: Broadview Press.

Tully, James. (2000). The struggles for and of freedom. In Duncan Ivison et al., *Political theory and the rights of Indigenous peoples* (pp. 36–59). New York, NY: Cambridge University Press.

Turpel, Mary Ellen. (1989–90). Aboriginal peoples and the Canadian Charter: Interpretative monopolies, cultural differences. *Canadian human rights year book* (pp. 3–45). Ottawa: University of Ottawa, Human Rights Research and Education Centre.

Weaver, Sally. (1981). *Making Canadian Indian policy: The hidden agenda, 1968–1970*. (Toronto: University of Toronto Press.

Webber, Jeremy. (1996). Relations of Force and Relations of Justice: The Emergence of Normative Community between Colonists and Aboriginal Peoples. *Osgoode Hall Law Journal* v33(4), pp. 623–60.

White, Graham. (2001). A fourth order of government? Treaty federalism through claims-mandated co-management and regulatory boards. Paper prepared at the annual meeting of the Canadian Political Association, L'Université Laval, Québec, May.

Wilkinson, Don. (1999). The meaning of self-determination. *Quadrant*. March.

Williams, Robert A., Jr. (1996). "The people of the state where they are found are often their deadliest enemies": The Indian side of the story of Indian rights and federalism. *Arizona Law Review* v38, Fall, pp. 981–97.

Young, Iris Marion. (2000). Hybrid democracy: Iroquois federalism and the postcolonial project. In Duncan Ivison et al., *Political theory and the rights of Indigenous peoples* (pp. 239–247). New York, NY: Cambridge University Press.

9

Navigating Discrimination
The Interplay of Contexts on Native Children's Social Development

Wendy L. Hoglund
Life-span Development Psychology Ph.D. Candidate
University of Victoria
Victoria

Wendy L. Hoglund

The sociocultural, historical, political and socioeconomic milieux in which Native and non-Native children are developing play prominent roles in shaping their social development.[1] Ideals for healthy socialization patterns (i.e., ways parents, elders, and community members model, teach, and instill respected values in children) and social development trajectories (i.e., capacities for constructive and adaptive intellectual, behavioural, and emotional functioning across a variety of social settings) can differ across peoples, communities and nations. These differences can be rooted in sociocultural practices, historical experiences, political relationships, and socioeconomic positions. While the interplay of sociocultural, historical, political, or socioeconomic forces can create notably different contexts in which and ways that all children are socialized, an understanding of the healthy (as compared with problematic) socialization and developmental patterns among groups of Native children is often situated in theories devoid of sociocultural, historical, political or socioeconomic meaning.[2]

The term "Native" is used for simplicity to include persons of the many diverse First Nations, Métis, and Inuit heritages who live on and off reserves in Canada, as it is beyond the scope of this paper to discuss each group or nation individually. It is recognized that Native peoples in Canada are heterogeneous groups of peoples and nations in terms of culture, opportunities, political position, and history. There are, however, certain similarities in terms of world views, wisdom, cultural values, customs, perspectives, and forces of oppression that unite these distinct nations of Native peoples. The objective of this paper is to highlight how some of the overarching systemic barriers and discrimination may influence some Native children's social development across these Nations rather than to focus on the unique cultures and political, social, and economic positioning of each specific nation of Native peoples in Canada.

Ecological systems theory argues that the socialization and development of children can best be understood by considering the multiple levels of dynamic, interacting systems or contexts surrounding them.[3] Ecological models propose that children are nested within a series of contextual levels in which they develop, including their families, neighbourhoods, and communities. For example, characteristics of individual children, such as competence, optimism and emotional well-being, are thought to be directly influenced by family-level factors, including parental nurturing and connectedness to their culture, and community-level factors, including cohesiveness and availability of quality social services and cultural activities. These more proximal contexts are, in turn,

---

[1] Clarke, 1997; McLoyd, 1998b; Obgu, 1987; Pagani, Boulerice & Tremblay, 1997.

[2] Smith, 1999, pp. 19–37.

[3] Bronfenbrenner, 1977.

enveloped by a series of overarching societal forces that include sociocultural, historical, political, and socioeconomic systems. Such distal overarching systems are considered an indirect influence on children's socialization and development through their effects on the more proximal arenas that children are embedded in, such as their families and communities. The interplay of these proximal and distal systems can operate to support or interfere with children's capacity to successfully navigate social and developmental challenges.

This paper explores how the interplay of sociocultural (discourse, theory and continuance of culture), historical (colonial policies and systems),[4] political (treaty negotiations, land claims and court decisions), and socioeconomic (components and mechanisms of poverty) contexts can interactively influence Native children's socialization and developmental patterns. This paper discusses how institutionalized racial discrimination grounded in historical and ongoing colonialism has blemished the discourse on Native children's socialization and development and precludes examination of Native children who show positive and encouraging developmental pathways despite growing up in socioculturally biased, historically and politically oppressed, or socioeconomically disadvantaged circumstances. One goal of this paper is to set the stage for more holistic, contemporary visions of Native children that capture the complexity of their lives and the sociocultural, historical, political, and socioeconomic conditions that can serve as ongoing challenges for many Native children.

Ways Sociocultural Contexts Can Challenge Native Children

Cultures are primary, overarching systems that offer a sense of connectedness to groups of peoples or nations in terms of shared values, beliefs, traditions, teachings, and so forth. Cultures also represent significant social contexts in which children learn and express various behaviours, emotions, and so forth.[5] In Canada, the cultural diversity and richness of the heterogeneous nations of Native peoples represent distinct social contexts that can meaningfully affect the patterning of Native children's experiences and development. The continuity of Native cultures and its influence on Native children is inextricably intertwined with the cultures' social experiences, history, political relations, and socioeconomic conditions, all of which can be powerful agents in the socialization and development of Native children.

Portrayals of Native children's socialization and development have been, and continue to be, influenced by mainstream theories and analyses that invariably discriminate against Native children in their comparisons with non-Native children and children who grow up amid vastly different sociocultural, historical,

---

4 While the colonization of Native peoples is rooted in history, the adverse forces of colonization are ongoing, as seen, for example, through discriminatory sociocultural forces, political relations and socioeconomic conditions.
5 Johnson-Powell, 1997.

political contexts.[6] Culturally inappropriate and incompetent research methodologies have also contributed to the distorted lens through which Native children's socialization and development are often viewed.[7] The majority of research about Native children has pathologized Native children, families and communities by singularly focusing on problem behaviours and social maladaptation while overlooking the mechanisms and processes that facilitate positive behaviours and outcomes, such as the experiences of Native children who become community leaders, or communities that have retained or reclaimed levels of cultural continuity.

Focusing on differences between groups, such as comparisons between Native and non-Native children, can lead to an underestimation of the resources, strengths and skills of Native children, families and communities when mainstream socialization practices and developmental patterns are assumed to be the standards for all children. In mainstream developmental theories, social development generally constitutes a process of developing cognitive, behavioural, and affective skills, such as accurate interpretation of social cues and realistic anticipation of one's actions, that enable one to adapt to diverse contexts and challenges.[8] Deviations from mainstream standards are often construed as evidence that Native children's achievements are less than optimal and inferior to those of their mainstream peers rather than viewed as equitable and congruent developmental pathways.[9] Conventional developmental definitions may be limited in their application to Native children if salient aspects of the contexts where Native children are developing are not incorporated.

Theories and examinations of Native children's development that are constructed from perspectives not cognizant of or thoughtful about the meaning of Native peoples' cultures, values, beliefs, traditions or histories can perpetuate racialized interpretations of Native children's social development when weaknesses (e.g., problem behaviours) rather than strengths (e.g., competent behaviours) are illuminated.[10] Limited interpretations of Native children's social development fail to capture Native children's accomplishments, successes, and promising futures or to illustrate the positive developmental trajectories that are common for the majority of Native children.

On the other hand, theories grounded in perspectives that celebrate the cultural diversity of Native peoples and nations and that are mindful of the significance of cultural values, belief systems, traditions and ongoing colonial oppression advance an understanding of the meaning that Native peoples' cultures, histories, political relations, and socioeconomic circumstances hold for how Native children's healthy social development is defined, encouraged and achieved.[11] While there are many Native children from poor and non-poor families who do well in school, receive athletic awards, have rewarding relationships

---

[6] Smith, 1999, pp. 78–90.

[7] Cauce, Ryan, & Grove, 1998; Dumas, Rollock, Prinz, Hops, & Blechman, 1999; McLoyd, 1998a.

[8] Consortium on the School-Based Promotion of Social Competence, 1996; Dodge & Price, 1994; Masten & Coatsworth, 1998.

[9] Cauce et al., 1998; Dumas et al., 1999; McLoyd, 1998a.

[10] Cauce et al., 1998; Dumas et al., 1999; Mitchell & Beals, 1997; Smith, 1999, pp. 78–90.

[11] Dumas, Rollock, Prinz, Hops, & Blechman, 1999; Stanfield, 1998; Smith, 1999, pp. 123–137.

with peers, are promising artists, and contribute to the development of Native communities and nations, little is heard about these Native children's life stories, mentors, and self-perceptions or what Native heritage or colonial oppression means to them. Several Native youth organizations, such as the Aboriginal Youth Network,[12] Manitoba First Nations Youth Council,[13] and Aboriginal Youth Business Council,[14] were initiated, developed, or continue to be supported by Native youth. Yet the skills, accomplishments, and developmental pathways of these Native youth are rarely portrayed by non-Native researchers, policymakers, educators, or the media.

Often, important regional, historical, political and socioeconomic differences found within the heterogeneous groups of Native peoples, communities and nations are more extensive than those found between Native and non-Native peoples.[15] For example, research from Chandler and Lalonde found that Native communities in British Columbia with jurisdiction over multiple public and social services (e.g., education, welfare, child care) have considerably lower youth suicide rates than Native communities with little control over these services.[16] This research indicates that resources and strengths such as reclaimed self-governance systems within Native communities can indeed play a significant role in shaping Native children's developmental pathways. Yet, diversity in terms of contextual influences on Native children's development is not always reflected in non-Native developmental theories, research directions, policy decisions, or program development.[17]

Native families, communities and nations all play fundamental roles in fostering Native children's well-being. Focusing discourse on characteristics of Native communities and families that promote culturally valued markers of "success" and strengths in Native children is essential for reducing the social hegemony that has restricted portrayals of Native children to deficit-focused models. Recognizing that Native children's social behaviours are likely promoted by unique sociocultural, historical, political, and socioeconomic mechanisms (including culturally competent programming, land claims and treaty settlements and poverty) may refocus the lens through which Native children's social development is evaluated and understood. Non-Native academics, educators, policymakers, and service workers, for example, have in various ways (e.g., theoretically, historically, and politically) contributed to restricted visions of Native children. Images of Native children can be amended when Native families, communities and nations play the prominent role in socializing Native children, and when the ongoing colonialism, historical and political oppression, and socioeconomic discrimination facing many Native families, communities and nations are adequately recognized and understood.

---

[12] *See* Youth Network website: http://www.ayn.ca

[13] *See* First Nations Youth Council website: http://www.mfnyc.mb.ca.

[14] *See* Youth Business Council website: http://www.aybc.org

[15] Dumas et al., 1999.

[16] Chandler & Lalonde, 1998.

[17] Cauce et al., 1997; Dumas et al., & Blechman, 1998; McLoyd, 1998a; Smith, 1999, pp. 42–53.

Wendy L. Hoglund

Ways Historical Contexts Can
Challenge Native Children

In 1755 the Canadian federal government established the first Indian Department, a precursor of the Department of Indian and Northern Affairs Development (DIAND), to administer social, health and welfare services to "Indians" registered under the Indian Act.[18] Even though the values, belief systems, customs, languages, teachings and practices of Native peoples have historically and fundamentally differed from those of non-Native peoples, the services provided by the Department of Indian Affairs (DIA) were often insufficient and void of any recognition of Native cultures, languages, traditions, religions, or ceremonies.[19]

By acting in direct conflict with the systems of Native peoples, many historical practices and policies imposed by European colonizers suppressed the continuity of Native cultures and abrogated Native peoples' rights to determine preferred ways of knowing and living.[20] The appointment of non-Native DIA commissionaires restricted the continuity of traditional Native socialization practices and health and well-being promoting models through the assimilationist policies implemented by officers of the Indian Department.[21] For example, the abolishment of Potlatch ceremonies among coastal Native communities by Duncan Campbell Scott, Commissioner of Indian Affairs in the early 1900s, bridled the cultural continuity of coastal communities.[22] Historically, cultural distinctiveness among Native cultures was only valued by the DIA when it constituted forms of what Eurocentric commissioners deemed ethnographic art appropriate for display in museums, such as ceremonial regalia or staged photos of Native peoples.[23]

One of the most prominent forms of colonial desegregation in the history of the DIA was the support for and initiation of the residential school system for Native peoples. Federal and church control of Native peoples' schooling under the auspices of the Indian Act of 1869 aimed to engender Native peoples' education but became assimilationist policy that eradicated Native peoples' rights to determine valued teachings.[24] It has been widely documented that the establishment of the residential schooling system affected the continuity of Native socialization practices within Native families and communities through the forcible removal of Native children from their homes and communities to attend these schools.[25] Through the experience and legacy of the residential schools which abolished traditional native education systems, Native children

---

[18] Department of Indian and Northern Affairs Development [DIAND], 1997.

[19] Fisher, 1998; Monture-Angus, 1999; Royal Commission on Native Peoples, 1996; Venne, 1997; Waldran, 1997.

[20] Monture-Anugs, 1999; Royal Commission on Native Peoples, 1996.

[21] Fisher, 1998; Monture-Angus, 1999.

[22] Fisher, 1998.

[23] Ibid.

[24] Monture-Angus, 1999; Royal Commission on Native Peoples, 1996; Venne, 1997.

[25] Fisher, 1998; Monture-Angus, 1999; Royal Commission on Native Peoples, 1996; Venne, 1997; Waldran, 1997.

experienced the suppression of their cultural knowledge, languages and pratices; were left without the training to be effective parents in their communities; and were indoctrinated with a sense of cultural inferiority that infiltrated successive generations.[26] While the majority of residential schools closed in the mid-1970s, their destructive legacy on Native children's development still reverberates through Native communities, as evidenced, for example, by high rates of suicide attempts, suicides, and engagement in risk behaviours such as substance abuse and dropping out of school among contemporary Native children and youth.[27]

The residual effects of prejudiced colonial systems and policies such as the residential schools on the socialization and the health and well-being of many contemporary Native children is often underestimated.[28] Current discourse and scholars critical of ongoing colonialism suggest that the prevailing social and political hegemony of colonial times has not ceased in contemporary times.[29] The historical and ongoing colonial hegemony has sprouted the racialized discrimination that many contemporary Native children encounter in terms of sociocultural misunderstandings, restricted political standing, poor socioeconomic conditions and assumptions of compromised futures.[30] The ongoing, eroding effects of historical and continued colonial policies and practices on traditional cultural and family systems and on Native children's social development is slowly being revealed. As Native families, communities and nations recover from genocidal policies and confront ongoing colonial practices and discrimination, the potential threats of mainstream, non-Native practices to the survival of Native cultures and traditional socialization practices must be addressed.

Rethinking and renewing political relationships between Native nations and Canadian municipal, provincial and federal governments are necessary steps to ensure that Native children grow up in social, political and economic contexts that competently foster their well-being. These contexts need to be moulded by Native families and communities to ensure that Native children are socialized in ways that recognize how the healthy development and healing of many Native children, families and communities are embedded within the continuance of Native cultures, languages, teachings, beliefs, procurement of secure land bases, and equitable treaty settlements and court decisions.

Ways Political Contexts Can Challenge Native Children

Political (and legal) relationships that continue to influence Native children's social development are embedded within historical and current treaty negotiations, land claims and court decisions, and the exercise of authority over Native

[26] Fisher, 1998; Monture-Angus, 1999; Royal Commission on Native Peoples, 1996; Waldran, 1997.

[27] Monture-Angus, 1999; Morgan, 1998; Royal Commission on Native Peoples, 1996.

[28] Royal Commission on Native Peoples, 1996; The Children's Commission, 1999, p. 78.

[29] Alfred, 1999, pp. 80–89; Monture-Angus, 1999; Royal Commission on Native Peoples, 1996; Venne, 1997; Smith, 1999, pp. 19–37.

[30] Monture-Angus, 1999; Royal Commission on Native Peoples, 1996; Smith, 1999, pp. 42–53.

peoples by Canadian governments in terms of defining minimum delivery standards for Native-designed and -implemented programs. The signing of the Royal Proclamation in 1763 between Native peoples and the British monarchy was the foundation of the current relationship between Native peoples in Canada and the Canadian state.[31] Although the earliest relationships may have been predicated on mutual trust and respect, it is apparent in historical treaty negotiations (e.g., *Baker Lake v. Minister of Indian Affairs and Northern Development* [1980])[32] that a relationship built on trust, respect, and peace was not always upheld by the Canadian state.[33]

The Royal Proclamation recognized Native peoples in Canada as distinct societies that were socially and politically organized. This Proclamation also bound representatives of sovereign powers external to Native societies to enter into formal agreements with Native peoples prior to settling lands occupied by Native peoples. However, the Proclamation did not validate Native peoples in Canada as representative of nations as defined by international law.[34] This invalidation enabled the Crown and, subsequently, the Canadian government to assert jurisdiction over Native peoples and the land they occupied under the claims of *terra nullius*.[35] This derogatory argument paved the way for subsequent ethnocentric legal precedents (e.g., Baker Lake [1980]) to commandeer the rights of peoples who do not adhere to the cultural way of life of the colonizer, most commonly Europeans.[36]

The political and legal relationships between Native nations and the Canadian governments continue to be colonial, as evidenced by current treaty and land negotiation processes and legal precedents that include the controversial treaty referendum in British Columbia in 2002; tensions over Native fishing rights at Burnt Church, New Brunswick in 2000; confrontations over ceremonial lands at Oka, Québec in 1990, Gustafsen Lake, British Columbia, in 1995, and Ipperwash, Ontario, in 1995; and the *Delgamuukw* v. *British Columbia* (1997)[37] and *Van der Peet* (1996)[38] court cases. In *Van der Peet* (1996), Justice Lamer emphasized that Native rights are only recognized and affirmed on the basis of a distinct way of life — meaning unique from non-Native ways of being — which

---

[31] Morgan, 1998; Venne, 1997.

[32] In *Baker Lake* v. *Minister of Indian Affairs and Northern Development* (1980), Justice Mahoney developed a culturally pejorative test to determine whether a culture had Native rights. This test relied on determining whether a cultural group and their ancestors were indeed an organized society based solely on comparisons to the structure of the colonizing (generally European) society (Asch, 2000; Bell & Asch, 1997).

[33] Asch, 2000; Asch & Bell, 1994; Bell & Asch, 1997; Monture-Angus, 1999; Venne, 1997.

[34] Venne, 1997.

[35] The argument of *terra nullius* claims that sovereign states need not enter into agreements over lands unoccupied or occupied by peoples considered to have no political or social organization (Asch, 2000).

[36] Asch, 2000; Asch & Bell, 1994.

[37] In *Delgamuukw* v. *British Columbia* (1997), Justice McEachern set a precedent whereby to establish the right to titlement over lands, Native communities must prove exclusive occupation prior to European settlement. As Asch states, this proof relied on ethnocentric reasoning where societal organization was established through comparison with colonizing societies (Alfred, 1999, pp. 121–128; Asch, 2000; Asch & Bell, 1994).

[38] Bell & Asch, 1997; Asch, 2000; Asch & Bell, 1994

must be demonstrated by each Native community seeking to have their rights recognized by the courts. The Van der Peet and Delgamuukw decisions distinguished Native peoples' rights exclusively on how culturally distinct they were from non-Native cultures and other Native communities and, in the process, disregarded any mention of political rights. Not acknowledging Native peoples' political rights has enabled the courts to avoid allegations that the sovereignty Canada asserted over Native peoples was illegitimate. In current times, some of the strongest support for land claims and rights to self-governance has been procured by the Nisga'a nation in British Columbia[39] and the founding of Nunavut territory.

Currently, programs, services, and policies that affect Native children and families who are "registered" under the Indian Act are generally administered by DIAND, a department of the federal government whose authority over program development and funding is, in most cases, delegated by the federal government.[40] While the Constitution Act of 1867 gave the federal government exclusive jurisdiction over "registered" Native peoples and the lands reserved for them, provincial governments have jurisdiction over property and civil rights, municipal institutions, and the authority to enact changes in programs and services that affect Native and non-Native peoples.[41] Thus, it becomes ambiguous whether federal or provincial governments have jurisdiction over the development and delivery of programs and policies that affect Native children and families. These unresolved jurisdictional debates likely interfere with Native communities' capacities to develop and implement competent social programs for Native children.

Generally, jurisdiction over programs and services offered by Native governments is delegated[42] by provincial and federal governments in areas that are not deemed culturally specific, such as social welfare policies and programs, by requiring that programs and services maintain the delivery standards defined by the provincial or federal systems.[43] In some systems, improvements have been made in the level of control awarded to Native governments. For example, some school districts now have a First Nations Education Division that has delegated authority over curricula and educational services that affect Native children. These divisions are better equipped to provide culturally competent curricula for Native children than many non-Native run school districts.[44] However, the resources to implement and sustain programs that serve children and families who are "registered Indians" are allocated by block-budgets from the federal government (most notably the DIAND) to Native communities, organi-

---

[39] See chapter 7 by Sarah de Leeuw in this volume.

[40] DIAND, 2001a; Morgan, 1998.

[41] Morgan, 1998.

[42] With delegated jurisdiction, the authority of Native governments is granted, and can be restricted or withdrawn, by the federal and provincial levels of government (Morgan, 1998).

[43] British Columbia, 1996; DIAND, 2001a; DIAND, 1995a; Morgan, 1998.

[44] Culturally competent programs respectfully incorporate and recognize differences in Native cultures, languages, traditions, teaching, and beliefs, and focus on addressing the history and political and economic positioning, needs and priorities of local communities.

zations, and governments.[45] Thus, the reach of these programs and services can be at the discretion of federal and provincial governments' funding priorities and accountability requirements.

Both the federal and provincial governments have constitutionally based jurisdiction,[46] while the territories have delegated jurisdiction and fall under the authority of the federal government. That the territorial governments have only delegated authority while the provincial governments are privileged with constitutionally based authority, is problematic, as a large proportion of Inuit and other Native people reside in the territories. The territories, like many recognized Native governments or governing boards, have limited power in enacting laws of general application for programs and policies that serve Inuit and Native peoples in the North.

Delegating Native peoples' authority over program development and implementation perpetuates the patriarchal and colonial system of governance that has plagued Native peoples since colonization. It also undermines Native peoples' competence in judging acceptable standards for programs that provide social, educational, or economic services to Native children and families. As witnessed by research in British Columbia, Native peoples' jurisdiction over services that affect Native children and families is essential for the cultural continuity of Native communities and fostering Native children's positive developmental pathways.[47] For Native children living in poorer Native communities, communities that have not been able to negotiate control over local services, or communities whose cultures are no longer intact, support from external Native and Canadian governments may be needed. However, it is inherent,[48] rather than delegated, jurisdiction over rights to self-govern that must be recognized and affirmed by the provincial and federal governments. One step towards gaining inherent jurisdiction lies in rethinking the current political and legal relationships between the heterogeneous groups of Native nations and the Canadian governments.[49] Changes in these relationships could potentially further the reach of Native-sponsored policies, programs, and services and improve the biased sociocultural and socioeconomic positioning of many Native children and families.

Ways Socioeconomic Contexts Can Challenge Native Children

Systemic socioeconomic disadvantages that challenge all children, and Native children in particular, must be adequately recognized and understood. Improv-

---

[45] DIAND, 2001a; Morgan, 1998.

[46] Constitutionally based jurisdiction is secured from the Constitution Act of 1867 and can only be transformed through constitutional amendments. This form of jurisdiction enables governments to determine the scope of their own laws and policies (Morgan, 1998).

[47] Chandler & Lalonde, 1998.

[48] Inherent jurisdiction recognizes that Native peoples' authority to be self-governing nations is not granted by other levels of governments but, rather, emerges from the existence of self-governing entities among Native peoples prior to European settlements (Morgan, 1998).

[49] Asch, 2000; Bell & Asch, 1997.

ing socioeconomic conditions among children, families and communities is one key to the survival of both Native and non-Native peoples. As socioeconomic conditions are linked to a plethora of educational, social, physical, emotional and intellectual outcomes, strengthening the socioeconomic status of Native children, families and communities may foster Native peoples' capacities for achieving goals of self-determination and, in turn, foster the healthy social development of Native children. The future leadership of Native communities and nations depends on Native children's healthy development and capacity to secure a skill base in the areas of cultural knowledge, customs, languages, values and beliefs.[50] As Taiaiake Alfred cogently argues,

> today [Indigenous] survival depends on the emergence of new Native leaders who embody traditionalism as a personal identity and at the same time have the knowledge and skills required to bring traditional objectives forward as the basic agenda of the political and social institutions they work within.[51]

In Canada, the overall socioeconomic condition, including poverty and unemployment rates, of many Native peoples is consistently described as poor or, at best, marginal.[52] High rates of poverty, unemployment, school dropouts, low-paying jobs and poor health status are but some of the risk factors recognized as contributing to disparities in socioeconomic standing among many Native peoples.[53] Addressing these socioeconomic risks as well as diversity in the contexts in which Native children are developing (e.g., rural versus urban centres) is essential to programs, services, and policies that influence Native children's developmental trajectories. National Native organizations, working with the National Children's Agenda, have identified eradicating prevalent poverty among Native children as a top priority to support Native children's healthy development.[54]

Young children have a higher risk of living in poverty than any other age group, which has significant implications for their social development.[55] Risks for living in poverty are strikingly higher for Native children when compared with non-Native children. According to Statistics Canada census reports, 44 percent of Native persons lived below the low-income or poverty cut-off line in 1996 compared with 20 percent of non-Native persons, with even higher rates for Native persons living on-reserve and in the Yukon and Northwest Territories, including Inuit peoples.[56] For children under age 15, the percentage living in poverty increases to 52 percent for Native children, and 23 percent for non-Native children. For children under the age of six, the poverty rate rises to 60 percent for Native children and to 25 percent for non-Native children.[57] Again,

---

[50] Alfred, 1999, pp. 128–145; Boyer, 1989; Deloria, 1990; Simpson, 1995.

[51] Alfred, 1999, p. 137.

[52] DIAND, 1995b; Royal Commission on Native Peoples, 1996; Statistics Canada, 1998a.

[53] Ibid.

[54] DIAND, 2001b.

[55] Duncan, Brooks-Gunn & Klebanov, 1994; Duncan, Yeung, Brook-Gunn & Smith, 1998; McLoyd, 1998b.

[56] Statistics Canada, 1998b.

[57] Ibid.

these poverty rates are likely higher for Inuit children and Native children who live on reserves and in northern communities. Conversely, these statistics suggest that approximately 48 percent of Native children under age 15, on average, do not live in poverty and, conceivably, do not experience the level of economic stressors that poor Native children do. However, commonalities between poor and non-poor Native children, such as historical and political oppression, social discrimination across the course of their lives or culturally incompetent public services, may exist and operate similarly, regardless of Native children's socioeconomic positioning.

Children living in socioeconomically disadvantaged families, neighbourhoods and communities are more likely than children from more affluent families, neighbourhoods and communities to experience both acute and chronic stressors. These stressors include impoverished neighbourhood and housing conditions; parental unemployment or low-paying, low-status, stressful employment; limited social supports; low-quality public and social services; few educational opportunities; and inappropriate adult and peer role models.[58] With increasing amounts of adverse and chronic stressors, children's risk for social adjustment problems, such as behavioural or academic problems, rises.[59] Experiencing persistent poverty in early childhood can also interfere with children's capacity for developing competent behaviours and skills, such as self-regulation and cognitive skills, that may be important for school entry, academic success or leadership roles.[60] However, these markers of "success" may not adhere to valued developmental goals ascribed to Native children by Native parents, communities, and so forth. The accumulation of hardships associated with persistent poverty, such as ongoing poor nutrition, and limited access to resources, such as necessary and high-quality health care services, can also interfere with families' and communities' abilities to actively identify options or obtain services that could lessen the stressors associated with poverty.[61]

Aside from tarnished reports of Native children who live in remote or poor communities, surprisingly few studies have examined how acute or persistent poverty affects valued socialization and developmental patterns among Native children and within families and communities. Missing are investigations of what individual, familial, community, or cultural strengths are available to support the development of socioeconomically disadvantaged Native children and how these supports operate. Interestingly, research in the United States with Native American children aged 9 to 13 years found that living in poverty did **not** increase Native American children's risk for emotional or behavioural problems.[62] This finding is contrary to the body of research that has shown poverty to be a risk for non-Native children's healthy social development.[63]

---

[58] Attar, Guerra & Tolan, 1994; McLoyd, 1998b; Pagani et al., 1997.

[59] Ibid.

[60] Duncan, Brooks-Gunn & Klebanov, 1994; Duncan, Yeung, Brooks-Gunn & Smith, 1998; Masten & Coatsworth, 1998; McLoyd, 1998b; Pagani, Boulerice & Tremblay, 1997.

[61] McLoyd, 1998b.

[62] Costello, Farmer, Angold, Burns & Erkanli, 1997.

[63] Attar et al., 1994; Duncan, Brooks-Gunn & Klebanov, 1994; Duncan, Yeung, Brooks-Gunn & Smith, 1998; Pagani, Boulerice & Tremblay, 1997.

It is likely that many mechanisms, including connections to traditional cultures and extended family members and levels of self-governance, interactively operate as stress-reducing buffers to alleviate the negative effects of poverty within some Native communities and families.[64] For example, living in the proximity of extended family members can ameliorate the stressors associated with parenting in the context of poverty when extended family members are available, reliable and competent caregivers and can provide alternative, pro-social role models for children.[65] In many Native communities, extended family networks provide support, guidance, and cultural continuity for children and families.[66] Additional mechanisms that could support Native children's favourable social development in the context of poverty include access to culturally competent services that are developed and administered by Native communities.[67] However, access to these services and support systems may be limited for Native families or children disconnected from their communities or cultures.

Variations among groups of Native children, families, communities and nations in terms of sociocultural, historical, political, and socioeconomic contexts potentially create differences in culturally valued ways that Native children are socialized and develop over time. It is also likely that there are important individual, family, community, and cultural factors that protect some Native children from the unfavourable effects of living in the context of poverty, social discrimination, historical or political oppression, or colonialism.[68] These factors within group differences demand greater understanding. What internal and external supports are available to Native children who show positive developmental trajectories in spite of living amid adversities like poverty and social and political discrimination? Why is so little heard about the Native children who graduate from high school, who contribute to the development and continuance of Native communities and nations, or who challenge the assumptions of deficit-focused developmental models? Future investigations of differences within Native families, communities and nations in terms of normative socialization and developmental patterns, strengths, resources, and opportunities may help to dispel many of the myths that pervade racialized discourse and tarnish images of Native children. Understanding the mechanisms by which familial, community, and cultural resources, supports and strengths influence the social development of Native children who live in poor and non-poor contexts, urban and rural contexts, communities with and without Native governments, and so forth would lead to a more holistic understanding of Native children's socialization and developmental patterns. Understanding how contextual mechanisms foster as well as challenge Native children's healthy social development is essential for generating informed, strengths-based research priorities and supporting Native-sponsored policy and program developments.

---

[64] Chandler & Lalonde, 1998; Clarke, 1997; Costello, Farmer, Angold, Burns & Erkanli, 1997.

[65] McLoyd, 1998b.

[66] Royal Commission on Native Peoples, 1996.

[67] Clarke, 1997; Machamer & Gruber, 1998.

[68] Chandler & Lalonde, 1998; Health Canada, 2000; Royal Commission on Native Peoples, 1996.

Wendy L. Hoglund

Implications for Native-Sponsored Research, Policy, and Practice

Recognition of the complexity of the sociocultural, historical, political and legal, and socioeconomic forces that may challenge Native children as they navigate childhood is crucial for the development and implementation of unbiased research, policies, and programs. Theories of Native children's social development that are rooted in an ecological approach may be better equipped to detail how the interplay of sociocultural, historical, political and legal, and socioeconomic factors can meaningfully shape Native children's socialization and developmental patterns. It is becoming conspicuously clear that programs and policies that affect Native children need to be developed, implemented and examined amid the discrimination and oppression Native children and families may be navigating. Increased support and funding is particularly needed for high-quality, culturally competent programs that are developed and administered by Native communities and governments. For example, through the First Nations reinvestment component of the National Child Benefit program, Native communities that administer social assistance to low-income Native families receive adjustment funds from the federal government.[69] However, these families need to be identified through the government as "status" or "registered Indians", which presents significant barriers to the reach and effectiveness of these programs. An important ingredient of the reinvestment program is that local Native communities determine the specific needs and priorities of Native families and children and reinvest the funds into culturally competent, community-based programs. Many of these reinvestment programs have addressed issues related to poverty, including nutrition programs at schools and clothing programs, have supplemented child care or Aboriginal Head Start programs; or have worked to build competence and workplace skills among Native youth.

Aboriginal Head Start initiatives are federally funded programs (for "registered Indians") that are sponsored by Native not-for-profit organizations, such as Native Friendship Centres.[70] These programs aim to foster Native children's development prior to school entry. However, funding for these programs is generally only available to children and families who are "registered Indians", which sharply constricts the ability of other Native families and children to access these services when needed. Specific components of Aboriginal Head Start programs include learning in Native cultures and languages, education, health promotion, nutrition, social support, and support for parental involvement. Other Native-sponsored programs have welcomed community elders into the school system to afford Native children (particularly children who have limited access to traditional cultures) the opportunity to learn cultural traditions, languages, and belief systems from respected elders.[71] The inclusion of Native community elders in educational programs also provides Native children with

---

[69] DIAND, 2001c.

[70] Health Canada, 2000.

[71] Armstrong, 2000; DIAND, 2001c; Health Canada, 2000.

166

positive role models and mentors and can assist in building bridges between Native parents and non-Native educational systems.

At the post-secondary level, provincially accredited Native Studies and Native-specific degree or diploma programs at both Native colleges and institutes, such as the Saskatchewan Indian Federated College, and traditional universities, such as the University of Victoria (which offers the Indigenous Governance Master's program), are on the rise. There is also a movement towards Native-sponsored alternative justice projects, such as healing circles and restorative justice programs, that focus on reconnecting alienated individuals with the community through opportunities to amend harm done to other persons or their communities.[72] Restorative justice programs can build communities through developing the social skills and understanding of the children and communities affected by the harm. These types of programs can also offer an effective way to create culturally and socially effective conflict-resolution skills among children.

One of the most unequivocal sources of support for fostering the healthy development of Native children lies within local Native communities and nations and their success in securing land-base structures and reclaiming rights to self-determination. Native communities that have been able to reclaim rights to nationhood and secure a stable land base may be the most effective vehicles for paving healthy developmental paths for Native children. However, for Native communities whose culture is no longer intact, whose resources are drained, or who have not yet been able to garner a secure land base or governance system, additional support from outside Native organizations, such as the Native Healing Foundation or Assembly of First Nations, or government agencies, such as DIAND, may be needed.

Refocusing theories, programs and policies, as well as reworking political and legal relationships between Native nations and the Canadian governments is necessary for greater breadth in visions of Native children's socialization and developmental patterns. Contemporary practices, policies and relationships have the power to remove the racialized barriers that obstruct many Native children's capacity for healthy, positive developmental trajectories when the many influential contexts surrounding Native children, families and communities are acknowledged. Informed documents on systemic barriers that can challenge Native children and the mechanisms through which Native-sponsored policies, practices and political relationships can competently foster Native children's social development need to reach non-Native researchers, scholars, educators, service providers, and policymakers.

This review underscores the necessity for strengths-based research with Native children, families and communities that examines how sociocultural, historical, political, legal and socioeconomic characteristics are linked and can affect Native children's normative and healthy developmental trajectories. Overcoming the multiple discriminatory adversities that have marginalized many Native children can best be achieved when Native communities and nations actively control the educational, social, economic, and political systems in which

---

[72] LaPrairie, 1998.

Native children are socialized. Researchers, educators, service providers, and policymakers need to look beyond Western European models of successful development to adequately understand favoured socialization and developmental processes within the sociocultural, historical, political, legal and socioeconomic contexts of Native children's lives and the families and communities in which Native children live.

References

Alfred, T. (1999). *Peace, power, righteousness: An Indigenous manifesto*. Don Mills, ON: Oxford University Press.

Armstrong, J. (2000). A holistic education, teachings from the dance house: We cannot afford to lose one Native child. In M.K.P.A. Nee-Benham & J.E. Cooper (Eds.), *Indigenous educational models for contemporary practice: In our mother's voice* (pp. 35–43). Mahwah, NJ: Lawrence Erlbaum Associates.

Asch, M. (2000). First Nations and the derivation of Canada's underlying title: Comparing perspectives on legal ideology. In C. Cook & J.D. Lindau (Eds.), *Aboriginal rights and self-government* (pp. 148–291). Montreal, QC: McGill-Queen's University Press.

Asch, M., & Bell, C. (1994). Definition and interpretation of fact in Canadian title litigation: An analysis of Delgamuukw. *Queen's Law Journal, 19*(2), 503–550.

Attar, B., Guerra, N., & Tolan, P. (1994). Neighbourhood disadvantage, stressful life events, and adjustment in urban elementary-school children. *Journal of Clinical Child Psychology, 23*, 391–400.

Baker Lake (Hamlet) v. *Minister of Indian Affairs and Northern Development*, [1980] 1 F.C. 518; (1979), 107 D.L.R. (3d) 513 (F.C.T.D.).

Bell, C., & Asch, M. (1997). Challenging assumptions: The impact of precedent in Native rights litigation. In M. Asch (Ed.), *Native and treaty rights in Canada: Essays on law, equality, and respect for difference* (pp. 38–74). Vancouver, BC: UBC Press.

Boyer, E.L. (1989). *Tribal Colleges: Shaping the Future of Native America*. Princeton, NJ: Carnegie Foundation for the Advancement of Teaching.

British Columbia, Ministry of Aboriginal Affairs. (1996). *British Columbia's approach to treaty settlements self-government*. Retrieved October 23, 2003, from BC Ministry of Aboriginal Affairs website www.aaf.gov.bc.ca/aaf/pubs/s-gsumm.htm

Bronfenbrenner, U. (1977). Toward an experimental ecology of human development. *American Psychologist, 32*, 413–531.

Cauce, M., Ryan, K.D., & Grove, K. (1998). Children and adolescents of color, where are you? Participation, selection, recruitment, and retention in developmental research. In V.C. McLoyd & L. Steinberg (Eds.), *Studying minority adolescents: Conceptual, methodological, and theoretical issues* (pp. 147–166)). Mahwah, NJ: Lawrence Erlbaum Associates, Inc.

Chandler, M.J., & Lalonde, C. (1998). Cultural continuity as a hedge against suicide in Canada's First Nations. *Transcultural Psychiatry, 35*, 191–219.

Children's Commission, The. (1999). *1998 Annual report of the Children's Commission*. Victoria, BC: The Children's Commission.

Clarke, I.A.S. (1997). The American Indian child: Victims of the culture of poverty or cultural discontinuity? In R.D. Taylor & M.C. Wang (Eds.), *Social and emotional adjustment and family relations in ethnic minority families* (pp. 63–81). Mahwah, NJ: Lawrence Erlbaum Associates.

Consortium on the School-Based Promotion of Social Competence. (1996). The school-based promotion of social competence: Theory, research, practice, and policy. In R.J. Haggerty, L.R. Sherrod, N. Garmezy & M. Rutter (Eds.), *Stress, risk, and resilience in children and adolescents: Processes, mechanisms, and interventions* (pp. 268–316). New York, NY: Cambridge University Press.

Costello, E.J., Farmer, E., Angold, A., Burns, B.J., & Erkanli, A. (1997). Psychiatric disorders among American Indian and white youth in Appalachia: The Great Smoky Mountains study. *American Journal of Public Health, 87*, 827–832.

Delgamuukw v. *British Columbia,* [1997], 3 S.C.R. 1010.

Deloria, V. (1990). Knowing and understanding. *Winds of Change, 5*, 12–18.

Department of Indian and Northern Affairs Development. [DIAND] (1995a). *Federal policy guide on Native self-government: The government of Canada's approach to implementation of the inherent right and the negotiation of Native self-government*. Retrieved October 23, 2003, from DIAND website www.inac.gc.ca/pr/pub/sg/plcy_e.html

Department of Indian and Northern Affairs Development. [DIAND] (1995b). *Highlights of Aboriginal conditions 1991, 1986: Demographic, Social and Economic Characteristics*. Ottawa: DIAND.

Department of Indian and Northern Affairs Development. [DIAND] (1997, December). *The Department of Indian Affairs and northern development*. Retrieved October 23, 2003, from DIAND website http:/www.ainc-inac.gc.ca/pr/info/info108_e.html

Department of Indian and Northern Affairs Development. [DIAND] (2001a). *Funding agreements*. Retrieved October 23, 2003, from DIAND website http:/www.ainc-inac.gc.ca/ps/ov/agre_e.html

Department of Indian and Northern Affairs Development. [DIAND] (2001b). *National children's agenda*. Retrieved October 23, 2003, from DIAND website http:/www.ainc-inac.gc.ca/pe-cp/nca_e.html

Department of Indian and Northern Affairs Development. [DIAND] (2001c). *National Child Benefit*. Retrieved October 23, 2003, from DIAND website http:/www.ainc-inac.gc.ca/pe-cp/122_e.html

Dodge, K.A., & Price, J.M. (1994). On the relation between social information processing and socially competent behavior in early school-aged children. *Child Development, 65*, 1385–1397.

Dumas, J.E., Rollock, D., Prinz, R.J., Hops H., & Blechman, E.A. (1999). Cultural sensitivity: Problems and solutions in applied and preventive intervention. *Applied and Preventive Psychology, 8*, 175–196.

Duncan, G., Brooks-Gunn, J., & Klebanov, P. (1994). Economic deprivation and early childhood development. *Child Development, 65*, 296–318.

Duncan, G., Yeung, W. Brook-Gunn, J., & Smith, J. (1998). How much does childhood poverty affect the life chances of children? *American Sociological Review, 63*, 406–423.

Fisher, A.D. (1998). Anthropology and education in Canada, the early years (1850–1970). *Anthropology and Education Quarterly, 29*, 89–102

Health Canada. (2000). *Children making a community whole: A review of Aboriginal head start in urban and northern communities.* Retrieved October 23, 2003, from Health Canada website www.hc-sc.gc.ca/dca-dea/publications/pdf/cmacw_final_e.pdf.

Johnson-Powell, G. (1997). The culturologic interview: Cultural, social, and linguistic issues in the assessment and treatment of children. In G. Johnson-Powell, J. Yamamoto, G.E. Wyatt & W. Arroyo (Eds.), *Transcultural child development* (pp. 349–364.). New York, NY: John Wiley & Sons, Inc.

LaPrairie, C. (1998). The 'new' justice: Some implications for Native communities. *Canadian Journal of Criminology, 40*, 61–80.

Machamer A.M., & Gruber, E. (1998). Secondary school, family, and educational risk: Comparing American Indian adolescents and their peers. *Journal of Educational Research, 91*, 357–369.

Masten, A.S., & Coatsworth, J.D. (1998). The development of competence in favourable and unfavourable environments: Lessons from research on successful children. *American Psychologist, 53*, 205–220.

McLoyd, V.C. (1998a). Changing demographics in the American population: Implications for research on minority children and adolescents. In V.C. McLoyd & L. Steinberg (Eds.), *Studying minority adolescents: Conceptual, methodological, and theoretical issues* (pp. 3–28). Mahwah, NJ: Lawrence Erlbaum Associates, Inc.

McLoyd, V.C., (1998b). Socioeconomic disadvantage and child development. *American Psychologist, 53*, 185–204.

Mitchell, C.M., & Beals, J. (1997). The structure of problem and positive behavior among American Indian adolescents: Gender and community differences. *American Journal of Community Psychology, 25*, 257–288.

Monture-Angus, P. (1999). *Journeying forward: Dreaming First Nations independence* (pp. 21–39). (Halifax, NS: Fernwood Publishing.

Morgan, N.A. (1998). *Legal mechanisms for assumption of jurisdiction and control over education by First Nations.* Victoria, BC: The First Nations Education Steering Committee. Retrieved October 23, 2003, from BC Ministry of Education website www.fnesc.bc.ca/publications/pdf/legalmechanisms.pdf

Obgu, J.U. (1987). Variability in minority school performance: A problem in search on an explanation. *Anthropology and Education Quarterly, 18*, 312–335.

Pagani, L., Boulerice, B., & Tremblay, R. (1997). The influence of poverty on children's classroom placement and behavior problems. In G. Duncan & J. Brooks-Gunn (Eds.), *Consequences of growing up poor* (pp. 311–339). New York, NY: Russell Sage Foundation.

R. v. Van der Peet, [1996] 2 S.C.R. 507.

Royal Commission on Native Peoples. (1996). *Report of the Royal Commission on Native Peoples*. Ottawa, ON: Royal Commission on Native Peoples. [Also available: www.indigenous.bc.ca.]

Simpson, V. (1995). Tribally controlled schools: A realization for self-determination. In G.E. Thomas (Ed.), *Race and ethnicity in America: Meeting the challenge in the 21st century* (pp. 13–26). Washington, DC: Taylor & Francis.

Smith, Tuhiwai. (1999). *Decolonizing methodologies: research and Indigenous peoples.* London, UK: Zed Books.

Stanfield, J.H. (1998). Ethnic modeling in qualitative research. In N.K. Denzin & Y.S. Lincoln (Eds.), *The Landscape of qualitative research: Theories and issues* (pp. 333–358). Thousand Oaks, CA: Sage Publications.

Statistics Canada. (1998a, January 13). 1996 Census: Aboriginal data. *The Daily*. Retrieved October 23, 2003, from Statistics Canada website www.statcan.ca/Daily/English/980113/d980113.pdf

Statistics Canada, (1998b, May 12). 1996 Census: Sources of income, earnings and total income, and family income. *The Daily*. Retrieved October 23, 2003, from Statistics Canada website www.statcan.ca/Daily/English/980512/d980512.pdf

Venne, S. (1997). Understanding Treaty 6: An Indigenous perspective. In M. Asch (Ed.), *Indigenous and treaty rights in Canada: Essays on law, equality, and respect for difference* (pp. 173–207). Vancouver, BC: UBC Press.

Waldran, J. (1997). The Native peoples of Canada: Colonialism and mental health. In I. Al-Issa & M. Tousignant (Eds.), *Ethnicity, immigration, and psychopathology* (pp. 169–187). New York: Plenum Press.

Questions for Discussion

1. Review the definitions of racism and racial prejudice offered by de Leeuw. How does she apply these definitions to the letters she discusses? Do you agree or disagree?

2. To what extent was the racism displayed in the letters quoted by de Leeuw informed by a literal ignorance of the history of First Nations in Canada?

3. Are there creative ways to negotiate a peaceful compromise within the circumstances of land claim negotiations?

4. Choose a specific letter that de Leeuw has quoted and formulate a rebuttal that considers the context and perspectives of First Nations peoples.

5. In the de Leeuw essay, the letter writers complained that Aboriginal Canadians were receiving special status. But Consentino begins her paper with the idea of self-determination, which Indigenous peoples are using to assert their just place in the modern nation-state. Are these notions reconcilable?

6. Consentino quotes Charles Taylor in her introduction. Review that quote. Does history show that everyone wants to live under the same political roof? Do Indigenous people have historical reasons for shying away from such attempts at harmonious living?

7. Discuss the benefits and costs of each of the four interpretations of treaties by the courts. Is one better than the others? Why or why not?

8. As Hoglund points out, the reality is that many Aboriginal communities are economically and socially depressed. Even so, non-aboriginal Canadians, as demonstrated in de Leeuw's work, perceive an overcompensation to the Aboriginal community. How can we account for this disconnect?

9. All three essays demonstrate that racial privilege and marginalization are deeply connected to Western notions of property. Discuss.

Part 4 Race, Place and Nation

This part explores the expanse of nationhood as a concept capable, in its interaction with race and ethnicity, of defining, relegating and othering. Interconnected with the examination of intersectionality and performance, these essays recognize that the manner in which one's nationality is (de)constructed may not necessarily comport with one's racial identity. With increasing globalization and the shifting of borders and boundaries, the inclusion and exclusion of people can be instantaneously prescribed, enforced and monitored solely on the basis of national status. These created places of Nation are particularly deserving of study as an obvious construct with political weight. Each essay in this Part recognizes the complexity of racial identity when foreignness and "alien" status are added to the equation. These essays highlight race as a construct that is dependent upon geographic-national context.

The first essay, "Adrift in the Diaspora: Reflections on Loss of Home and Self", explores the sense of homelessness and the quest for belonging common to many immigrants who leave their homes in search of better lives for their families. The essay raises the disconcerting issue of assimilation as a barrier to (re)acceptance in one's nation of origin in such a way that an immigrant is possibly left adrift between a country that does not accept them due to racial identity or foreignness and a country where resettlement is difficult due to the stigma of inauthenticity.

The second piece, "Racism between Jews: Israeli Women in Calgary", examines intragroup discrimination. The essay explores the role of relocation, immigration and assimilation in differentiating and in excluding immigrants from the same country. Interviews are used as the basis for examining the challenges faced by recent immigrants in being accepted in a foreign land by people of their own racial/ethnic/religious group.

The third piece, "Local Colour: The Spectacle of Race at Niagara Falls", explores the exploitative role of tourism in maintaining "raced" perceptions that appeal to travellers. The essay examines the "primitive" depiction of the First Nations at Niagara Falls in order to further the frontier appeal of Canadian tourism. A raced discourse of the First Nations was perpetuated — one that prevented conceptualizing Indigenous populations as modern contemporary shapers of their own destiny and portrayed them rather as people to be observed, depicted and consumed as frozen artifacts from Canadian history.

Therefore, the expansiveness of the nature of nationhood is considered in this part. The forces simultaneously pushing and pulling, confining and defining, constructing and deconstructing identity-based belonging on the basis of race centre the examinations in this part.

10

Adrift in the Diaspora
Reflections on Loss of Home and Self

Camille A. Nelson
School of Law
Saint Louis University
Saint Louis

Introduction

I often wonder where home is. I am constantly negotiating between home and abroad, native culture and adopted culture, assimilated and/or hyphenated existence.[1] Having felt that my various places of residence in Canada were never truly my home, I am left to ponder this question even more now that I have heard of the increasing violence[2] against "Returnees" on the island of my birth, Jamaica.[3] The Returnees of whom I speak are those ambitious people who emigrated from Jamaica seeking a better life and greater economic opportunity for themselves, their elders and their children. Like members of other "voluntary"[4] immigrant and migrant groups, many Jamaicans who left home did so with the expectation that the short-term sacrifices would be outweighed by the long-term benefits.[5]

The long tradition of Caribbean migration to foreign lands began at the start of the twentieth century, first to Panama to assist in the construction of the canal and to other Caribbean and Central American countries such as Cuba, Costa Rica and Nicaragua, and then to the United States starting in the 1920s and continuing in the 1930s. Nearly half of the people of Jamaica go abroad to work in North America and Europe. (Kasinitz, 1992, p. 64) Few societies on earth have been as shaped by the movement of their people as those of the Caribbean. Subject to chronic overpopulation, scarce resources, seclusion, and limited opportunities of small island nations, West Indians have utilized migration as a survival strategy whenever they have been able to do so. (Lewis, 1997, p. 561, n.3) Most Jamaicans presently living abroad have taken up

---

[1] Professor Hope Lewis states: "Where is home" for Jamaican women? In my experience, it was East Flatbush, Brooklyn, as well as Kingston, Jamaica." (Lewis, 1997, p. 570; Minh-ha, 1994, p. 9.)
[2] "Island Dream Ends", 2001; Hunt, 1999; McGrory, 2000; Broad, 1999; "Wealth Clue", 1999; Syal, 2000; Taylor, 1999.
[3] Jamaica, the name of which was derived from the country's Arawak Indian name "Xaymaca," means "the land of wood and water." An island in the Caribbean Sea, Jamaica is an island 146 miles from east to west and 51 miles at its widest point from north to south. After being a colonial possession of the United Kingdom for 300 years, Jamaica gained independence from Britain on August 6, 1962, and is now a constitutional monarchy and member of the Commonwealth.
[4] Although no explicit directive or policy requiring migration existed, Returnees viewed the economic, social and educational disparities in a way that made the desire to stay economically precarious.
[5] Lewis, 1997, p. 596. Immigration is not just movement from one country to another or a change in the place of residence and work. It connotes expectations on the part of those in the host country that the newcomer will become a part of the society. Such expectations of assimilation and acculturation are not necessarily the norm for migrant workers who are expected to return home (Heisler, 1998, p. 560).

residence in the United States, Canada and the United Kingdom.[6] Indeed, rates of migrancy in the Caribbean are the highest in the world.[7] Despite these statistics, many Jamaicans never intended their ultimate destination to be any place other than Jamaica. Even Jamaicans who have obtained foreign citizenship maintain a close tie with the island, making Jamaica what Professor Orlando Patterson has called "a transnational state."[8]

The Returnees who spent years abroad often endured the compounded travails of economic hardship, isolation, racial violence and harassment in their adopted homes, resulting in an idealized Jamaica transformed by longing. They dealt not only with the pain of separation from family and loved ones, but often with the resentment of populations hostile to immigrants in their adopted homes.[9] Certainly in Canada and England, the problem of race is often perceived to be co-extensive with "the immigrant problem." In addition to racial hostility from majority white populations in their adopted homes, Caribbean immigrants and migrant workers who view themselves as Black may additionally be regarded as "other" by people of African descent in their adopted homes. A sense of national pride and responsibility is revealed in the fact that Jamaicans abroad send commodities[10] and money home[11] in amounts second only to tourism in contributing to the economy's net foreign earnings.[12] The majority of such shipments come from the United States and Canada, where most of the estimated 2 million émigrés reside. Due to the effect of structural adjustment policies (SAPs), devaluations of the Jamaican currency meant large price increases for the Jamaican people. These increases had a large impact on the

---

[6] The United States is the primary host country for migrant Jamaicans, followed by Canada and the United Kingdom. There are nearly as many Jamaicans living abroad as in the country. Multilateral Investment Fund [MIF], 2001. *See also* Patterson, 2001 (the author is a professor of Sociology at Harvard, and the former special advisor for social policy and development to Jamaica's late Prime Minister Michael Manley, from 1972–1980).

[7] Chaney & Sutton, 1992, pp. 8–9 (noting high rates of emigration from the entire Caribbean to Europe and North America and that the rate reached 16 percent of Jamaica's population in the mid-1970s.)

[8] Patterson, 2001.

[9] *See* Lewis, 1997, p. 574 (noting that although most Jamaican women identify themselves as Black, they are still regarded as "other" by some Americans, including some African Americans. Conversely, the particularity of their experience may be subsumed under an externally imposed essentialized definition of "blackness"); Gladwell, 1996 (discussing competing images of Caribbean immigrants as "different Blacks" in the United States and Canada). For additional information on racism and immigration in Canada *see* http://saxakali.com/index.htm (website addresses racism and immigration through its "Issues of Color" section); Matas, 1996; Richmond, 1994. *See also* information provided by the Canadian Race Relations Foundation website: http://www.crr.ca/EN/default.htm ("The Foundation is committed to building a national framework for the fight against racism in Canadian society.

[10] French, 1994, pp. 165, 167 *cited in* Lewis, 1997, p. 569, n.9. For a discussion of the political impact of SAPs on Jamaican politics *see* Manley, 1990 (epilogue, written in 1989, discussing changes in Jamaican political economy since the original edition of the book in 1975).

[11] *See* the discussion of remittances at note 34.

[12] With nearly as many Jamaicans residing abroad as at home, remittances have long played a vital role in the economy. On a per capita basis, Jamaica receives the highest remittance inflows of any country in the region. Annual remittances for 1999 were estimated to total more than 50 percent of the country's income from exports and 63 percent of the revenues from tourism and is almost 35 times greater than the amount of official development assistance received (MIF, 2001).

cost of imported items. Accordingly, immigrants and migrants abroad were informed by their relatives of the scarcity and expensiveness of staple goods and the practice of sending such items home became commonplace. Despite being a land with tremendous natural resources, Jamaica is an island of stark contrasts — a dreamy tropical escape for most visitors, who frolic carefree at the island's luxurious resorts, and a land of grinding poverty for many Jamaicans.[13]

A recent article in the *London Times* chronicling the targeting of Returnees left me adrift in sorrow as I read of the violent demise of 50 Returnees to Jamaica in recent years.[14] The peaceful existence many Returnees expected has been elusive. Being torn between the realities of living like a caged animal within a home fortified by bars, on one hand, and risking armed violence on the other, Returnees often become disenchanted. Now in their senior years, Returnees have laboured abroad for a good part of their lives and amassed modest amounts of money in order to retire "back home". Although not naïve, Returnees may not have expected to become targets in their native land. Returnees who, while living abroad, were quick to defend and support their island paradise have found themselves the objects of jealousy, envy and, even, scorn as their return signals the very embodiment of the developed world within the developing world. While this juxtaposition of the "First World" within the "Third" is not uncommon to native Jamaicans, the often flawed class-based alignment of the body of the returnee with the body of the wealthy and leisured tourist has provoked reminders of the exploitative consequences of globalization and evidences the gap between rich and poor.

The Returnee as personification of privilege resonates with the historical weight of the house-slave versus field-slave dichotomy. House slaves, as inhabitants of the Big House, were often seen as "selling out", and all too eager to do the master's bidding.[15] This intentionally exploitative and constructed slave hierarchy served the purpose of creating division among slaves and furthering the master's agenda of physical and psychic control. But another colonial dichotomy must be recognized — that of the West as aligned with the master, and the rest aligned with the body of the slave. Thus, by going to live amongst the "masters" in the West and by reaping the rewards of the "master's" world, Returnees have often become the subjects of resentment grounded in the legacy of colonial history. Hence, we must account for the complicity of Returnees in the devastation of our lands, based upon a seeming acquiescence or participation in foreign markets that function, to a large extent, on the expectation and actualization of an ordering of worlds — First, Second and Third — with its corresponding economic, financial and lifestyle implications. Globalization has been referred to broadly as

> the economic phenomenon — the internationalization of production, of financial and banking services, and of neo-liberal economic policies promoting privatization and lib-

---

[13] *See The Economy,* Jamaican Information Service: An Executive Agency of the Government of Jamaican, http://www.jis.gov.jm/information/economy.html For additional information on the economy of Jamaica *see* Lake, 1998, p. 37; Bolles, 1996, p. 105 (discussing economic developments in Jamaica since the 1970s); Danielson, 1993.

[14] McGrory, 2000.

[15] Child & Yellin, 1987; Berlin et al., 1998.

eralization, all of which are facilitated by advances in technology that have completely transformed traditional understandings of time and space.[16]

Despite the difficulties of generalizing about a phenomenon as complex and contradictory as globalization, considerable evidence suggests that globalization intensifies inequalities both within and between states and that, on the whole, it further undermines the precarious position of the poorest and most vulnerable, the vast majority of whom live in Third-World countries.

Alternatively, the violence that some Returnees encounter may be attributable to the dysfunction of family — family members are often the ones we abuse the most and take for granted since alternative venues for the release of frustration have more serious repercussions and are not as easily accessed.[17]

The primary aim of this essay is to consider what, if any, impact we "privileged"[18] "inter/nationals"[19] might have upon the homelands we cherish and to which we seek a safe return. I acknowledge that middle- and upper-class persons who were born into poverty and have remained in their countries of origin but who have taken up residence in more affluent surroundings might experience similar sentiments regarding their places of origin. For instance, middle-class African Americans who might have left the inner-city neighbourhoods of their childhood for residence in predominantly white suburbs may have analogous concerns about conceptions of "home", loss of community and the possibility of return. With each passing generation there is a greater psychological, cultural and economic distance that may impede the ability of these "Returnees" to reclaim their past homes as well. Are we, by virtue of our acquired cultural and economic "otherness", unwelcome outsiders, forever unable to reinsert ourselves into our homes with legitimacy and credibility? And what of individuals like me, born in Jamaica and raised abroad in countries like Canada, that were never fully offered unconditional belonging? Do we have any standing to make demands or suggestions after our long absences? These questions have interdisciplinary implications for the burgeoning academic and social interests in the politics of identity and other critical discourses, including what Cornel West has dubbed "the new cultural politics of difference." The new cultural politics of difference consists of creative responses to the precise circumstances of our present moment — especially those of marginalized First-World agents who shun degraded self-representations, articulating instead their sense of the flow of history in light of the contemporary terrors, anxieties and fears of highly commercialized North Atlantic capitalist cultures (with their escalating

---

[16] Anghie, 2000, p. 246.

[17] *See* bell hooks' discussion of black-on-black violence as abuse and frustration that cannot be directed against white America without serious consequences (hooks, 1995, p. 163). For information about self-destructive behaviours in Black communities, *see* Kirk, 1996, p. 3 (the author contends that stress is significantly related to the degree and amount of power perceived by an individual within the societal context and that, consequently, Blacks experience a great deal of stress).

[18] I feel it is imperative that I acknowledge my acquired privilege, based largely upon the sacrifices of generations of my family. As an academic, I have the luxury to contemplate these issues in relative peace.

[19] I appreciate Professor Hope Lewis' use of this term to suggest the existence of dual national and cultural identities, as well as an international and transnational identity going beyond traditional conceptions of nationality. *See* Lewis, 1997.

xenophobia against people of colour, Jews, women, gays, lesbians and the elderly). These theories are "distinct articulations of talented (and usually privileged) contributors to culture who align themselves with demoralized, demobilized, depoliticized and disorganized people in order to empower and enable social action...."[20] It is within this framework that a candid exploration of the predicament confronting the Returnee will be undertaken. I have used song lyrics as a vehicle that conveys contemporary social and political discourse relevant to these issues. These songs represent but a portion of the contemporary cultural response that is representative of the politicized roots of Jamaican music. They narrate from the heart, addressing relevant experiences affecting their lives and their families — things lived and suffered. Part I discusses the plight of the Returnees. Part II examines the impact of globalization upon Jamaica and other developing countries. Part III concludes with a search for solutions. Such articulation is but the first step in the move from theory to action, arguably the foundation of any post-colonial intervention or project.[21] This is but one such call to action — an attempt to recognize, problematize and seek resolution.

Plight of the Returnee

It should come as no surprise that Returnees might find readjustment from their adopted homes to their native homes difficult, or at least not without challenge. Longing and reminiscing necessarily give way to a reality that is not as rose coloured and impeccable as the recollections generated during nostalgic flights of fancy. Indeed, this disconnect between the "real" and (re)imagined Jamaica is a strategy of self-preservation for the immigrant abroad. Socially isolated and victims of recurring racism, for immigrants the goal of returning to an idealized homeland is often the vehicle of emotional and psychic preservation.[22] Social psychiatry presents a disturbing picture of the situation confronting many Returnees.[23] Some literature from the United Kingdom has identified patterns of psychiatric morbidity of Afro-Caribbean immigrants, with schizophrenia being identified as the most common diagnosis.[24] While it has been suggested that these statistics relate to the increased likelihood that British psychiatrists will over-diagnose non-white patients,[25] other studies have deter-

---

[20] West, 1990.

[21] *See,* e.g., Lewis, 1997, p. 567; Johnson, 2000, p. 753; Romero, 2000, p. 837; Carbado, 1997, p. 237; Calmore, 1992, p. 2129; Chang, 1993, p. 1241; Chew, 1994, p. 1; Thomas, 1999, p. 1; Valdes, 1996, p. 1; Volpp, 1996, p. 1573; Young, 1997, p. 907.
[22] Said, 1999.

[23] *See* Hickling, 1991. This research indicates that Jamaican people who have lived as migrants in the U.K., U.S.A. or Canada for a number of years are diagnosed with schizophrenia with much greater frequency than a similar group of Jamaicans who had not migrated, and that on their return from overseas, the migrants have moved from one difficult situation to another. The Jamaicans who had been living in First-World countries for long periods of time had almost twice the rate of schizophrenia than a similar group of Jamaicans who had never migrated.
[24] Kiev, 1965; Gordon, 1965; Bagley, 1971a, 1971b; Dean et al., 1981.

[25] Dean et al., 1981; London, 1986.

mined that the increased rates may be due to sociopolitical stresses, such as racist discrimination encountered by immigrants of colour in their adopted homes.[26] Stressors, like new modes of communication, racialized social interaction and economic hardship, coupled with status striving where opportunities are racially organized, may influence or exacerbate the onset of schizophrenia, depression and anxiety in Afro-Caribbeans.[27] Indeed, Charles Lam Markmann has described some of the migration to colonial and neo-colonial metropolises as dysfunctional and counterproductive in the first place.[28] He argued that such migration represents a yearning to reject familiar cultural forms in exchange for a wholehearted but ultimately disappointing adoption of those of the colonizer.[29] Indeed, Bob Marley, while narrating the quest of diasporic Africans for a better life, dealt with the theme of an exodus from an oppressive regime (Babylon) to liberation in the homeland. The central message of his 1977 song *Exodus* was a vision of a glorious end to the suffering of all "Jah's"[30] people:

> Exodus, movement of Jah people
>
> Open your eyes and look within
> Are you satisfied with the life you're living?
> We know where we're going; we know where we're from
> We're leaving Babylon, we're going to our fatherland.[31]

Freedom, liberation, salvation, peace and, simply, relaxation form part of the Returnees' desire to return home to Jamaica.[32] Yet this desire for home is disrupted by the challenge of (re)adjusting to a culture from which they have been absent for many years, to the accompanying charges of "foreignness" and the danger posed by seeming to have too much money.[33] Returnees face the dilemma of having to assert and perform their "Jamaicanness", a racialized identifier that the savvy immigrant may have learned to disguise and suppress in their adopted homes.

Imagine the disillusionment of living abroad in a foreign land, being marginalized, discriminated against and told to go home. You agree — who

---

[26] Hashmi, 1968; Littlewood & Lipsedge, 1982; Baumgartl & Favell, 1995; Oakley, 1996; Merkl & Weinberg, 1997.

[27] Bagley, 1971a; Carter, 1994, p. 543 (for literature detailing increased levels of depression, anxiety and somatic illness due to racism); Falk, 1996, p. 774 (stating that the majority of social scientists agree that black individuals' mental and physical health suffer negative effects as a result of racism, *citing* Pierce, 1974, p. 512).

[28] Markmann, 1967.

[29] Ibid.

[30] Term often used to reference God.

[31] Thirdfield.com, *Exodus* lyrics, retrieved October 25, 2003, from http://www.thirdfield.com/html/lyrics/exodussong.html

[32] Speaking within the "community", many Jamaicans, even after living abroad for decades, still refer to Jamaica as home.

[33] BBC Monitoring Latin America, "Jamaica Foreign Minister denies Jamaicans who come home are persecuted" [hereinafter "Jamaica Political Report"], January 12, 2001. (Report documenting radio broadcast in which Returnees spoke out about the treatment meted out to them by fellow citizens who often referred to them as "foreigners." The Returnees said they were fed up with the level of crime and the generally low level of respect shown to them by other members of the Jamaican society).

wants to die in this cold place anyway? You send money[34] home to your relatives over the years, educate your children, make your retirement plans, and head back home once you have managed to "scrimp and save" enough to guarantee a certain lifestyle that you have worked so hard to achieve. Having taken few, if any, vacations, you yearn for the island breeze that your colleagues describe in their appreciative voices upon their return from Jamaican vacations. Envious of the liberties they take when on the island, you mention that you have actually never been to many of the tourist attractions they have mentioned, and that you have not had the opportunity to return home in some time — not since you were home for a funeral a few years ago. You make a silent pledge to yourself that, some day, you will return home, "live the life," breathe easy, and truly "walk good".[35] Many Returnees specifically, and immigrants generally, have never felt completely at home, accepted or appreciated in their adopted countries.[36] They look back and reminisce about happier, perhaps simpler, times in their homeland. As Madam Sarup has opined:

> Millions of people in the world today are searching for "roots", they go back to the town, the country or the continent they came from long ago. They try and learn something of that culture, that history. These are the people [who] in some way have found it difficult "to form roots", to become firmly established. By learning about their "roots" they (hope) to gain a renewed pride in their identity.[37]

I believe the above description will resonate for many of us set adrift in the African Diaspora. The threat of inevitable homelessness looms — we never feel completely at ease within our natural (albeit not truly original) habitats. Does anyone really have such a habitat anymore? Questions of home, exile and the expatriate experience overlap. To claim a home is not only a territorial process, but also an emotional and psychic one. Clearly, it is not just we Jamaicans seeking to return to our homelands who might be affected and afflicted with sentiments of longing and ambivalence. As Edward Said has stated, exile on the twentieth-century scale is "strangely compelling to think about but terrible to experience"; as a phenomenon it is "irremediably secular and unbearably historical."[38] Writes Trinh Minh-ha:

---

[34] Remittances, the money that migrants and immigrants earn working abroad and then send back home to their countries of origin, are one of the most visible impacts of the migration phenomenon. The flow of remittances to families and communities "back home" are not unique to Latin Americans and Caribbeans but, rather, occurs throughout the world, with over $71 billion estimated in remittances worldwide in 1990 and over $5.7 billion in the Latin America/Caribbean region (Russell, 1995, *cited* in Meyers, 1998).
During the first six months of 2000, remittances transfers of US $394.8 million entered Jamaica, an increase of US $48.4 million over the corresponding period last year. Bohning, 1995 (noting that "remittances from Jamaicans abroad ... account for as much as $500 million annually of the incoming foreign exchange surpassing even tourism," according to the Jamaican Finance Minister), cited in Lewis, 1997, p. 599, n.123.

[35] Jamaican dialect.

[36] The experience of the Jamaican in Canada can be viewed through the lens of Canadian cultural definition. Much of the rhetoric around the Canadian state stems from a recognition of the two founding nations, Britain and France, to the exclusion of the First Nations and many racialized immigrants who do not hail from those two nations. *See* Delgado & Stefancic, 1998.

[37] Sarup, 1994, p. 96.

[38] Said, 1990, pp. 357–358.

> For people who have been dispossessed and forced to leave for an uncertain destiny, rejected time and again, returned to the sea or to the no man's land of border zones: for these unwanted expatriated, it seems that all attempts at exalting the achievements of exile are but desperate efforts to quell the crippling sorrow of homelessness and estrangement. The process of rehabilitation, which involves the search for a new home, appears to be above all a process by which people stunned, traumatized and mutilated by the shifts of events that have expelled them from their homelands learn to adjust to their sudden state of isolation and uprootedness.[39]

This is the essence of the African Diaspora. For 400 years, millions of Africans were forcibly dislocated from their homes and dispersed throughout the globe under colonizing programs of an Imperial Europe. For these descendants of the enslaved, home is necessarily a complex and traumatic concept. Perhaps Minh-ha is correct in articulating this phenomenon as a rehabilitative process — a quest for healing by a return to that which is familiar and comfortable.[40] However, after years abroad, — 20, 30, 40 years — one cannot return unchanged. Racial and cultural assimilation and acculturation has ensured our survival;[41] we return out of touch with the issues facing our brothers and sisters back home. Perhaps worst of all, because of our financial ability to rejoin our respective communities and surpass our previous social status, we are economically privileged. We have accumulated capital abroad from the same systems that have impoverished our brothers and sisters back home.[42]

The violence inflicted on us upon our return home is not surprising given that in some ways we may embody those very qualities we traditionally associate with colonial exploitation. We are not those we seek to leave behind, but we now embody and perform much of what is alien, what is foreign. "But not my family," I cry; "We have done you no harm." Sound familiar?[43] This harm, however, is unavoidable, as we have profited from the system that mandates the ordering of race, culture and nations. Indeed, the reason many of us moved in the first place was to improve our positions in the global order. Although our departures *en masse* were tantamount to a plundering of the island, we put our well-being and that of our immediate families first, above our concerns for the nation-state — to do otherwise would likely have been foolhardy, given that part of the reason we sought to leave Jamaica is that it, too, left much to be desired in terms of politics, class oppression, race relations, caste and social systems.

---

[39] Minh-ha, 1994, p. 12.

[40] Ibid.

[41] Nelson, 2001.

[42] For instance, while Returnees might have profited from investment portfolios, pensions or mutual funds geared towards investment in large multinational corporations, these same multinationals profit from shifting economies of scale, often assisted by free-trade zones, tax-free zones and cheap and/or child labour that effect dire consequences for countries like Jamaica.

[43] *See* body of literature against claims for reparations for slavery. Among the arguments is a claim that present generations should not be held accountable for the actions of those who were slave owners or who profited from the institution of slavery. *See*, generally, Parker, 2000 (author states that "[a]t this point in history, the problem facing black Americans has nothing to do with the legacy of slavery and, as a result, cannot be ameliorated by 'reparations'"); Horowitz, 2001.

While we might seek to distinguish ourselves from the other oppressors, the colonizers[44] who have exploited our people for generations, by having gone to live among these same exploiters, have we not to a certain extent become like them? We start to speak "their" language; we even dress like "them" and eat what "they" eat. We previously pledged to uphold our "roots", and to abide by our culture. Yet, the words of Peter Tosh in his 1978 song *Mystic Man* taunt us, reflecting how we have partaken of some of the forbidden West in the name of "fitting in":

> I man don't
> I don't drink no champagne
> . . . .
> I don't sniff them cocaine
> . . . .
> Don't take a morphine
> . . . .
> I don't take no heroin
> No no no
> . . . .
> I man don't
> Eat up your fried chicken
> . . . .
> Eat up them frankfurters
> . . . .
> I man don't
> Eat down the hamburger
> . . . .
> I man don't
> Drink pink, blue, yellow, green soda. . . .[45]

We deny it, but our native brothers and sisters call us "English", "American", and "Canadian" behind our backs — an insult that questions our cultural identity and authenticity by refuting our national belonging.[46] We have become quasi-foreigners.

> Am I British? Yes, I have, as a friend pointed out, a "white man's house", and I've forgotten my mother tongue, but I do not feel British? I think of myself as an exile and it's painful here, and there in India when I return for short visits. I don't have the confidence to become, as some have suggested, cosmopolitan. But like so many others, I am preoccupied by ideas of home, displacement, memory and loss.[47]

Furthermore, the repurcusssions for violence against Returnees may not be as immediate as those for violence against "tourists", a disincentive that also affects the plight of Returnees. Posters all over Jamaica proclaim, "Treat Our Tourists Right." This same campaign does not apply with equal vigour to

---

[44] On the history of colonization of Jamaica by Spanish then English rule, *see* Long, 1972; Gardner, 1909; Goodwin, 1946.

[45] Retrieved October 25, 2003, from http://www.fortunecity.com/tinpan/metallica/471/MysticManMain.html

[46] *See* "Jamaica Political Report", 2001 (noting that some returning residents spoke out on radio "about the treatment meted out to them by fellow citizens, who often referred to them as foreigners [saying] they were fed up with the level of crime and the generally low level of respect shown to them by other members of [Jamaican] society."

[47] Sarup, 1994, p. 93. *See also* Minh-ha, 1994, p. 16.

Returnees, who are not as prized an economic vehicle. Returnees are also far more accessible, as we often seek out the genuine experience of home that so many tourists never wish to see. While Returnees generally mingle with the people, live among the locals and seek out the Jamaica of their childhoods, many visitors to Jamaica do not stray too far from their luxurious resorts — neither the hotel chains nor the tourists themselves wish to ruin their vacations with the stark contrasts of the "real" Jamaica. Indeed, I believe it is the preference of many hotel operators, manifested by passive and active discouragement of venturing "out there," that the tourists remain on the compounds and spend their valuable currency in the resort rather than sharing the wealth with the locals who clamour outside the security gates. Accordingly, Returnees whose posture is away from the tourist traps and their accompanying security and towards an authentic Jamaican experience may prove easy targets indeed by sheer virtue of accessibility and the systematic enticement of tourist dollars away from Jamaican communities and towards the largely foreign-owned tourist.[48]

What truly distinguishes us from our sisters and brothers we left behind but our temporary separation from and desire to return to the locales of our youth? Does our economic and cultural difference rupture any chance of belonging, or can the stain of foreign otherness be overcome?

Dr. Frederick W. Hickling of the Department of Psychiatry at the University of West Indies provides a relevant case study.

> The patient, who was seen by the author in 1978, was a 22-year-old black male, dreadlocked Rastafarian musician who had been born and raised in rural Jamaica by his maternal grandparents. He attended school in Jamaica and was considered a "bright" student.... His parents had migrated to the United Kingdom when he was an infant and were divorced in that country. When he was aged 11, he joined his mother and stepfather in the UK and entered the school system there. He was one of few black children in his school and reported many harassing experiences of racial hostility and discrimination at the school and in the environment in which he was growing. His own conduct became increasingly rebellious, and he began to get into serious trouble with the school by the educational authorities; he was soon arrested by the police. He continued to have trouble with police and social authorities, and he was sent to Jamaica by his parents. *As a cockney-speaking dreadlocked Rastafarian he was viewed with suspicion in Jamaica and his behaviour became increasingly abnormal as he tried to reconnect with his family, who had accepted his return reluctantly.* He was finally brought to the author by some friends who had grown up with him in England and relocated to Jamaica themselves once they had attained adulthood. They provided a comprehensive history of his life and described the difficulties he was having re-settling in Jamaica....[49]

Impact of Globalization on "Home"

The romanticized notions of home that sustained us all these long, cold nights in a foreign land were likely but a sliver of the truth, an almost spiritual yearn-

---

[48] Taylor, 1993; Barry, 1984; "Tourism Sector Update" 2001 ("These resorts are self-contained entities that provide all accommodations, food, entertainment, and amusements. Guests never need to leave the confines of these secure compounds"); James, 2001 ("Many of the estimated 1.3 million tourists who visit Jamaica each year stay in all-inclusive resorts.").

[49] Hickling, 1991, pp. 84–85 [emphasis added].

ing so glorified and sugar-coated as to be unrealistic and, often, historically inaccurate. The idea of home and belonging is complicated by global colonization and ideals of citizenship and nationhood, which are racialized. Having roots is not simply a matter of knowing one's cultural or national history, nor, even, residing in the place of one's birth. If this were so, many hyphenated and racially marginalized Canadians would not consistently suffer from feelings of dislocation, and many European Canadians arguably would. The Returnees' longing for a home other than Canada speaks to the racial exclusiveness of Western citizenship.

This isolation and marginalization of the "new" Canadian is coupled with guilt. We were deserters, leaving when they/we were most in need. Many of the "best and the brightest", who were, often, the educated fled — because they/we could.[50] Beginning in the 1950s the "first world" actively solicited our skilled labourers and university graduates.[51] The West sought out our educators, health care practitioners, skilled labourers and other professionals.[52] Indeed, it has been noted that Jamaica lost 50% of its university graduates in the country between 1980 and 1986 and had the highest rate of emigration in the world during the 1980s. The BBC noted the epidemic proportions of teacher recruitment from Jamaica, with headlines that stated, "School systems in developing countries are being ransacked by teacher recruitment agencies to fill staff shortages in England. Jamaica is the latest to feel the effect." "Last year 600 teachers left the island to work abroad, mostly in the USA and England. More have already gone this year. One high school head teacher told the BBC the recruitment raids amounted to 'rape and pillage'."[53] Such statistics generated concern in the Jamaican government about "exporting" trained professionals to the United States.[54] In the 1950s and 1960s, the British Government issued an appeal for labour from the British colonies, particularly in the areas of health and transportation.[55] Other governments similarly sought out and recruited

---

[50] Migration from the Caribbean to Canada, the United States and United Kingdom after World War II was spurred by labour shortages in those host countries following the war. *See* Marshall, 1983, pp. 120–121.

[51] *See* Barnes, 1995 (noting that "Jamaica ... lost 50 percent of university graduates in the country between 1980 and 1986"), cited in Lewis, 1997, p. 570, n.13; French, 1992 (noting that Jamaica had the highest rate of emigration in the world during the 1980s, and noting the Jamaican government's concern about "exporting" trained professionals to the United States), cited in Lewis, 1997, p. 599, n.123.

[52] In the 1950s and 1960s, the British government issued an appeal for labour assistance, particularly in the areas of health and transportation. *See* Hickling, 1991.

[53] *See* Barnes, 1995; Baker, 2002.

[54] Maxwell Nelson, B.Sc. (Econ.), M.E.D., M.B.A., M.I.R., C.M.A., C.F.P.) (personal communication, July 16, 2001). Again, this sentiment has been echoed by current Jamaica's minister of education, Senator Burchell Whiteman, who has stated that the loss of such experienced teachers was putting the Jamaican school system "at risk". The principal of Shortwood, one of Jamaica's largest teacher training colleges, believes that "one solution for countries like Britain is to put something back into the Jamaican system — by helping to fund teacher training there." In this way, she says, "we can serve the needs of both the countries that are recruiting and those they are recruiting from" (Baker, 2002).

[55] Maxwell Nelson (Telephone interview, July 16, 2001): Explaining that migration from the Caribbean to Canada, the United States and Britain after World War II was spurred by labour shortages in those host countries following the war; *see also* Marshall, 1983, pp. 120–121.

"qualified" Jamaicans to supply labour in areas of shortage. Canada, for instance, recruited teachers, college graduates and nurses.[56] Indeed, in a conversation that made me realize I did not know nearly as much about my parents as I had thought, my father confirmed these efforts as the manner in which he was recruited by the Canadian government.

As an honours graduate of the major teacher's college in Jamaica and of the University of the West Indies, my father had heard the 1965 graduation speech given by then Prime Minister of Canada Lester B. Pearson. My father recalls Prime Minister Pearson's invitation — "any qualified Jamaican would find that the application process for Canadian citizenship had been considerably eased."[57] This invitation whetted my father's appetite. Like other graduates, he was becoming disenchanted with low wages and limited prospects for career advancement on the island. Interestingly, part of the limited ability to advance was due to his status as a poor "outside child".[58] The Jamaican class and caste system has its own restrictions that prevent easy movement between classes — this system limits status mobility and encourages ambitious Jamaicans to seek more equitable considerations for advancement elsewhere.

Upon learning from a fellow teacher's college graduate that the Canadian government was recruiting out of a Kingston hotel, my father attended one of the meetings, which he described as "secret." When I asked why such meetings would be secret, my father replied that "There were no advertisements; it was all word of mouth. You know how in Jamaica word of mouth is even faster than the telephone. Besides, the Canadian government didn't want the Jamaican government to know it was recruiting its teachers. The Jamaican government had paid for many of our teaching degrees and here we were running off to covert meetings with another government."[59]

In retrospect, it is beyond curious that an official representative of the Canadian Ministry of Immigration and Citizenship would meet with so many graduates under an almond tree at a fancy Kingston hotel. In my father's mind, there is no doubt that these meetings were for active recruitment, but were subversively arranged. My father's recollections index the extent to which the Jamaican government was never reimbursed or rewarded for its support of the university education of its citizens. This covert recruitment eventually became a sore point for the Jamaican government which sought to limit the loss of their most educated and qualified citizens. This history of deliberate social sabotage has clarified for me the dominant middle-class orientation of many of the Canadian-Jamaicans with whom I was raised. Teachers, nurses, or administrators — these were the people actively sought by foreign governments. Beyond a "brain-drain", this was a "brain suck".

---

[56] Ibid.

[57] Ibid.

[58] Jamaican dialect for a child born outside of wedlock and, therefore, illegitimately.

[59] Maxwell Nelson (Telephone interview, July 16, 2001).

Transnational corporations, international economic agencies and Western governments enabled these practices, acting as new imperial powers[60] constructing systems whereby millions of people and dollars move from South to North in the name of capital.[61] An example of such capital is the flow of remittances between developed and developing nations. Nowhere is this movement of money more apparent than in Latin America and the Caribbean, where migration has created a situation where remittances constitute a critical flow of foreign currency to the majority of countries. The implications for national economies are vast and include major financial, development and labour issues throughout the West Indies and Jamaica specifically.[62]

> [M]igration to these countries [the USA, U.K. and Canada] has been restricted to the highest skilled and trained West Indian professional, and the offspring of Afro-Caribbeans presently resident in those countries. Thus historically these Afro-Caribbean migrants have been highly motivated and often highly skilled people who have fled the harsh economic realities of the British colonial territories in which they grew up, and who, in the main, have been very industrious and highly successful in the countries to which they have migrated.[63]

But who did these "highly skilled migrants" leave behind? While many emigrants diligently send money and commodities back to our homelands, poverty on the island of Jamaica is still overwhelming.[64] With impoverishment comes desperations and despair, which, in turn, may foster criminality.[65] By recruiting and actively soliciting much of our burgeoning middleclass,[66] did the developed world essentially leave us even more impoverished than immediately following decolonization? Post-coloniality, then, is more a useful theoretical construct than a political or social reality, since we can trace the kind of "brain suck" that took place in the 1950s and 1960s, with its ongoing and cumulative effects that continue to resonate. The 2000 dance-hall[67] hit song *LOOK* by Bounty

---

[60] Cahn, 1993, p. 159 (Discussing the increasing influence of international financial institutions in shaping both domestic and international law); Sassen, 1993, p. 61; Rohter, 1997, p. A1 (discussing the detrimental impact of the North American Free Trade Agreement [NAFTA] on Caribbean economies).

[61] Lewis, 1997, p. 571 (noting that transnational corporations move freely from country to country to find low-cost labour and less-restrictive government regulations and to encourage migrant labourers to follow).

[62] *See,* generally, MIF, 2001.

[63] Hickling, 1991.

[64] Approximately 34 percent of Jamaicans are living below the poverty line (*see* Central Intelligence Agency [CIA], 2003).

[65] For information on the link between poverty and crime, *see* Massey, 1995, p. 1203 (developing "a theory that links high rates of black crime to two features of U.S. urban society: high rates of black poverty and high levels of black segregation"); Bailey, 1984, p. 531 (linking black crime to economic deprivation).

[66] While many Returnees experienced a decrease in social class upon leaving Jamaica, the money made abroad, even for lower-status positions, was greater. In the First-World countries to which the Returnees migrated, they were likely to be employed at a lower occupational class level than their social (occupational) class level of origin, although the money earned was at a higher level than what they were accustomed to in Jamaica. *See* Foner, 1985 (discussing a former teacher who worked as a companion in the hope of putting her daughter through school); Hickling, 1991, p. 88.

[67] Dance-hall forms part of the contemporary evolution of reggae music. In many ways it is similar to African-American hip-hop in its danceability and tendency to tackle difficult urban issues.

Killer (a.k.a. Rodney Basil Price) addresses some of the effects of disenfranchisement and marginalization. It is a startlingly candid commentary on the effects of economic oppression on increased criminality from the perspective of those left behind.

> Look into my eyes, tell me what you see?
> Can you feel my pain? am I your enemy?
> Give us a better way, things are really bad,
> The only friend I know is this gun I have.
>
> ...
>
> Look into my mind, can you see the wealth?
> Can you tell that I want to help myself?
> But if it happen that I stick you for your ring
> Don't be mad at me it's a survival t[h]ing.
>
> ...
>
> Look into my life, can you see my kids?
> Let me ask you this, do you know what hungry is?
> Well in this part of town, survival is my will
> For you to stay alive you've got to rob and kill.
> Look into my house would you live in there?
> Look me in the eyes and tell me that you care,
> Well I've made up my mind to end up in the morgue
> Right now I'd rather die, 'cause man a live like dog.
>
> Look down on my shoes, can you see my toes?
> The struggle that we live nobody really knows
> Stop and ask yourself, would you live like that?
> and if you had to then, wouldn't you bus gun shot?
> Look into the schools, tell me how you feel?
> You want the kids to learn without a proper meal
> Den what you have in place to keep them out of wrong?
> If they drop out of school dem a go bus dem gun.[68]

This song speaks eloquently of the resentment of those left behind, the failure of the government to provide credible alternatives to crime and the vast economic disparities between social groups. Is it, therefore, any wonder that Returnees have become targets? Moving targets, literally speaking. Jamaica, like much of the developing world, is a desperately poor country.[69] The economic prospects of Jamaican workers, farmers, entrepreneurs and even government officials are deteriorating, while local violence is increasing substantially.[70] Jamaica now has vast shantytowns, unemployment at depression levels, high rates of economic inequality, one of the highest crime rates among non-warring nations, and significant drug abuse.[71] The situation in the capital city of

---

[68] Retrieved October 25, 2003, from www.reggaejams.com/lyrics.htm

[69] World Bank, 1999; Patterson, 2001. There were more than 900 murders on the island in 1996. Most occurred in the urban ghettoes of Kingston and had their roots in political conflict, the international trade in guns and drugs, and widespread poverty.

[70] Patterson, 2001. *See also* Green, 1997.

[71] Patterson, 2001; D'Aguilar, 1997 (citing tatistics on crime levels in Jamaica and includes information on recent violence in Tivoli Gardens, Kingston, which left over 27 dead); Portes, Dore-Cabral & Landolt, 1997.

Kingston, the concrete jungle, is particularly grim for its less affluent residents. This grinding poverty shackles many residents and prevents the realization of potential. As Bob Marley noted in his hit *Concrete Jungle*, many residents of Kingston slums are captive to poverty:

> No sun will shine in my day today
>
> ...
>
> The high yellow moon won't come out to play
>
> ...
>
> Darkness has covered my light
> And has changed my day into night
> Now where is this love to be found, won't someone tell me?
> 'Cause life, sweet life, must be somewhere to be found, yeah
> Instead of a concrete jungle where the livin' is hardest
> Concrete jungle, oh man, you've got to do your best, yeah.
>
> No chains around my feet, but I'm not free
> I know I am bound here in captivity
> And I've never known happiness, and I've never known sweet caresses
> Still, I be always laughing like a clown
> Won't someone help me?
> Cause, sweet life, I've got to pick myself from off the ground, yeah
> In this here concrete jungle,
> I say, what do you got for me now?
> Concrete jungle, oh, why won't you let me be now? . . . .[72]

Without a doubt, there are many factors contributing to poverty in developing nations. However, the role of the International Monetary Fund (IMF), the World Bank, and other such international, quasi-governmental, Western dominated economic institutions in the predicament of developing nations such as Jamaica has been identified and criticized.[73] These lending and development institutions, dominated by the world's richest nations, exact a steep price from developing nations that accept or refuse aid.[74] Critics routinely accuse the Bretton Woods institutions of eroding not only national sovereignty but also the labor and environmental interests guarded by national legislation."); "IMF & World Bank", 2000 (noting that despite IMF and World Bank's role of "bail[ing] out governments with troubled economies" ... critics are upset because

---

[72] BobMarley.com, *Concrete Jungle* lyrics, retrieved October 25, 2003, from http://www.bobmarley.com/songs/songs.cgi?concrete

[73] For articles criticizing quasi-governmental institutions, such as IMF and World Bank, *see* The IMF & the World Bank from Fairness & Accuracy in Reporting [FAIR] website: http://www.fair.org/issues-news/imf-worldbank.html (last visited September 23, 2002) (Carbado, 2000, p. 117). *See also* Patterson, 2001.

[74] U.S. voting power has steadily declined to current levels of 19.1 percent in the IMF and 17.22 percent in the World Bank. The IMF and the World Bank differ from most public international organizations because they follow a weighted voting system. Voting is based on quotas related to economic criteria. Quotas are based upon a complex formula that considers such relative economic strength factors as gross domestic product, external reserves, and variability of exports. The final agreement reached for the IMF and the World Bank gave each nation 250 basic votes, with a weighted voting of one additional vote for each part of a nation's quota equivalent to US$100,000 (Gianaris, 1991).

"[t]he IMF and the World Bank only provide money to governments under certain conditions, usually bound to strict currency and trade agreements. These imposed conditions, say critics, often make the situation worse in poor countries.").

The late prime minister of Jamaica, Michael Manley,[75] believed that the energy crisis of the early 1970s forced his government to commit to loans to cover the rising expenses of fuel-based imports.[76] As Jamaica had only recently emerged from colonialism, the economy was already particularly vulnerable.[77] Since private banks do not make such loans, Manley went to the IMF and World Bank. Developing nations have challenged, or have reluctantly accepted, the domination of international trade and lending agencies by developed countries, Jamaica is but one example.[78] The combination of external economic shocks to the island's major economic industries and the Manley government's agreement to the introduction of SAPs led to the election of a new conservative government under former Prime Minister Edward Seaga of the Jamaica Labour Party in the violent elections of 1980. The present government is again led by the People's National Party under Prime Minister P.J. Patterson. Joan French notes that SAPs in Jamaica have led to "a widening gap between electorate and government as the latter acts more and more as a mere middle-level manager for the implementation of policies designed in Washington."

I recognize that to blame the problems of developing nations exclusively on colonization and the global economic order is to disempower, to some extent, the nations themselves and to discount their agency. There is, I am sure, also blame to be laid on the governments of many a developing nation — corruption, incompetence and lack of interest are accusations voiced in an effort to provoke change. Professor Devon Carbado, addressing Jamaican migration to England, states "Of course, Jamaican workers, as a replacement labor force, were being exploited in England. But they were also being exploited in Jamaica as well." In this way, he recognizes the simultaneous push and pull implicit in many migration scenarios.

The Jamaican government has met many of the conditions imposed by the IMF in return for much-needed loans. However, in this predicament, meeting payments on foreign debt takes precedence over satisfying the basic human needs of much of the Jamaican populace. Jamaican public debt is nearly 160 percent of the gross domestic product, and interest consumes more than half of all government expenditure.[79] Understandably, little money is left to "trickle down", a situation that fuels social problems such as crime, poverty and a lack

---

[75] Manley, who died in 1997, was head of the leftist People's National Party of Jamaica and a leading figure in international Third World politics.

[76] French, 1994. See Documentary Film from Stephanie Black, Life and Debt, discussing Jamaica's economic woes. Life and Debt opened the 2001 Human Rights Watch Film Festival, and premiered Tuesday, August 21, 2001 on PBS.

[77] Boyd, 1988.

[78] Henkin et al., 1987, pp. 1186–1188 (discussing the internal structure of the International Monetary Fund, weighted voting, and criticisms of the voting structure by developing countries).

[79] Patterson, 2001. Jamaica has carried one of the largest foreign debt loads per capita in the world. See also Klak, 1996, pp. 352–387 (noting that Jamaica's "foreign debt/GDP ratio was 147 percent as of 1991").

of educational and employment opportunities. "The term 'trickle-down' effect refers to the theoretical phenomenon by which sustained economic growth that may occur initially with a country's wealthy class will eventually spread to the entire economy"[80] For instance, the country has a stable annual inflation rate of 5.8 percent, falling interest rates and adequate international reserves. Facing exclusion from the world's dominant financial and trade markets, many developing nations like Jamaica acquiesce to involving such economic institutions and become compromised by debt and reduced social services. They gear production to export markets, rather than local consumption, and provide incentives to attract foreign investment, such as tax-free zones, limited environmental restrictions, reduced labour and employment standards, etc.

The gap between rich and poor has devastating consequences for both the "haves" and the "have-nots."[81] The "haves" seek to shield themselves from the poverty surrounding them and retreat into armed enclaves designed to keep the "have-nots" at bay. The "have-nots" see the posh mansions on the hillsides, recognize the designer attire and the cushiness of affluence — even the additional weight borne on the thighs, hips and waistlines of the "haves" is a sign of prosperity, indulgence and excess.[82] Homi Bhabba recognizes that:

> "a crisis of identification is initiated in the textual performance that displays a certain "difference" within the signification of any single political system... It becomes crucial to distinguish between the semblance and similitude of the symbols across diverse cultural experiences ... and the social specificity of each of these productions of meaning as they circulate as signs within specific contextual locations and social systems of value.

In this scheme of manufactured economic disparity, labour is as fluid and portable as other economic goods, is as disposable or expendable as the proverbial widget, and does not trigger recognition of the implications for that individual, their family, and the nation.

The contemporary economic crisis confronting ordinary Jamaicans is the inheritance of a colonial legacy.[83] The systematic pillaging of much of the island's middle-class by developed Western powers is consistent with a history steeped in such theft of labour, from the enslavement of Arawak Indians (most of whom were worked to death at the hands of the Spanish and English) to the English victors' transportation of African slaves to the island — indeed, the

---

[80] Adelman & Robinson, 1988, pp. 949, 952; Ackerman & Alstott, 1999, p. 249 (the author notes that trickle-down economics has utterly failed and will continue to fail in the globalizing economy of the future. The past is prologue: By 1995, the top 1 percent owned 38.5 percent of the nation's disposable wealth, up from 33.8 percent in 1983.).

[81] The United Nations Population Fund states that "People around the world are migrating in search of better lives on a scale unknown in history, creating a crisis for both industrialized and developing nations." "Tensions are growing as the haves and have-notes and different ethnic groups rub shoulders to a greater extent than ever before" (Lederer, 1993). *See also* Honeywell, 1983.

[82] Bhabba, 1994, pp. 1, 23, 172; Butler, 1993; Hall, 1997; Hall & du Gay, 1996; Blackwell Cultural Studies Resources, at http://www.blackwellpublishers.co.uk/cultural/; University of Iowa Cultural Studies Resources, at http://www.uiowa.edu/~commstud/resources/culturalStudies.html; Ethnic and Cultural Studies Resources, at http://www.educationindex.com/culture/; Cultural Studies Central, at http://www.culturalstudies.net/

[83] Patterson, 1969; Williams, 1944; Shepherd, & Beckles, 2000; Sherlock & Bennett, 1998; Burton, 1997; Campbell, 1988; Flanagan, n.d.

legacy of Jamaica as an island refuge of pirates further corroborates this history.[84] Bob Marley addressed this history of racial exploitation and its legacy in his *Redemption Song,* when he sang:

Old pirates yes they rob I
Sold I to the merchant ships
Minutes after they took I from the
Bottomless pit
But my hand was made strong
By the hand of the almighty
We forward in this generation triumphantly
All I ever had is songs of freedom
Won't you help to sing these songs of freedom
Cause all I ever had redemption songs, redemption songs. . . .[85]

Presently constructed as a place for affluent, mainly white, Westerners to enjoy an "anything goes" vacation, as a place of rum and reggae, cocoa, sugarcane and ganja, the interests of the average Jamaican become subsumed within a complicated global matrix of economies of scale, market efficiency and consumer demand. This construction is about power. Capital moves about the globe and creates what Sarup has called *hierarchies of places* — the complex relationship between rich and poor nations emerging under the rubric of globalization.[86] Jamaica was not, and is not, near the top of this hierarchy. Hence, the possibilities for many Jamaicans are manipulated by externalities in a manner that may leave some feeling resentful and desperate. This sentiment is echoed by reggae and dance-hall singer/poet Buju Banton, whose debut album broke all sales records on the island and earned him more number one singles than any other reggae artist, including Bob Marley.[87] In *Destiny,* Banton sings:

The rich man's wealth is in the city
Destruction of the poor is his poverty
Destruction of your soul is vanity
Do you hear
I and I, I wanna rule my destiny
I and I, I wanna rule my destiny. . . .[88]

The destructive impact of economic globalization on the lives and livelihoods of the population of this once self-sustaining nation requires further study.[89] Like many developing nations, Jamaica suffers from its placement near

---

[84] For historical information on the Arawak Indians, Jamaican slavery and pirates, see "A Brief History of Jamaica", retrieved October 25, 2003, from http://home.earthlink.net/~prestwidgew/jamaicanhistory.html; Olsen, 1974; Farabee, 1967.
[85] Song Lyrics.co.nz, Bob Marley, *The Redemption Song,* retrieved October 25, 2003, from http://www.songlyrics.co.nz/lyrics/b/bobmarley/redemption.htm
[86] Sarup, 1994, p. 96.
[87] Retrieved October 25, 2003, from http://www.bujubanton.net/biography.html
[88] ReggaeSound.com, *Destiny,* retrieved from http://www.reggaesound.com/lyrics/destiny.html
[89] "Globalization expands and accelerates the movement and exchange of ideas and commodities over vast distances" (Global Policy Forum, n.d.). Globalization has been defined as "the growing economic interdependence among countries as reflected in increasing cross-border flows of goods, services, capital, and know-how." Farrar, 1999, p. 930. *See also* Rubin, 1995; Kozul-Wright & Rowthorn, 1998; Lecraw, 1998, p. 338; Patnaik & Chandrasekhar 1998; Crotty et al., 1998.

Camille A. Nelson

the bottom of this global hierarchy, and many of the ambitious natives who had the means or the connections fled and/or were lured to developed countries near the top of the global hierarchy of places. The Returnees similarly bear the trappings of relative affluence gained during their sojourn in the developed world; they reap the rewards from the "elevated" places to which they have migrated. Didn't the acquisition of such privilege and power have something to do with why they/we left in the first place?[90] Indeed, this "acquisition" of privilege is a mixed blessing. We have cut off our noses to spite our faces.

Searching for Solutions

I have no happy resolution. Part of the experience of being adrift in the Diaspora is not only the sense of homelessness, but also the sense of disembodiment that comes with shifting selves and negotiated existences.[91] As Minh-ha has noted:

> Colonized and marginalized people are socialized to always see more than their own points of view, and as Said phrases it, "the essential privilege of exile is to have, not just one set of eyes but half a dozen, each of them corresponding to the places you have been.... There is always a kind of doubleness to that experience, and the more places you have been the more displacements you've gone through, as every exile does. As every situation is a new one, you start out each day anew."[92]

One's identity is attached to one's knowledge, body and sense of home. If one is without a home, one's identity is compromised. Either one is identity-less, or one is multiply constructed across time, space and location. The situation is compounded when one's dislocation is forced or less than fully free, and one's relocation is complicated by rejection based on racism. It is a daring proposition to operate under exponential identities.[93] Identities are not free-floating; they are limited and expanded by borders and boundaries.[94] I would add, however, that identity does have a temporal component that resonates through time, making historical legacy tangible and relevant today. Bob Marley spoke of this confluence of identity and history unfettered by time and space in his remarkable song *Slave Driver*:

For information concerning violence at G7 and G8 summit meetings, *see* Crampton, 2001; "Protesters Rampage", 2001 (President Bush said that "although the protesters claimed to represent the poor, they were embracing policies that "lock poor people into poverty and that is unacceptable to the United States'"); "Summit Protests Rage", 2001 (despite pleas for calm from leaders at a global summit and from protest organizers, riots raged for a second day).

[90] Admittedly, the power is relative and limited. Indeed, many of the Returnees are Black or Asian and were never fully accepted abroad in their adopted homelands.

[91] Cornel West has stated that the state of perpetual and inheritable domination the Diaspora Blacks had at birth produced the modern Black Diaspora problematic of invisibility and namelessness (West, 1990, p. 26).

[92] Minh-ha, 1994, p. 16.

[93] It is hardly surprising, then, that when identity is doubled, tripled, multiplied across time, cultures, generations and space, and "when differences keep blooming within despite the rejections from without, she dares, by necessity" (Minh-ha, 1990, p. 329).

[94] Sarup, 1994, p. 95.

Ev'ry time I hear the crack of the whip
My blood runs cold
I remember on the slave ship
How they brutalised our very souls
Today they say that we are free
Only to be chained in poverty
Good god, I think it's all illiteracy
It's only a machine that make money

...

Slave driver the table is turned baby now
Catch a fire so you can get burned baby now
Slave driver the table is turned
Catch a fire so you can get burned

...

Oh god have mercy on our souls.[95]

In this song, the "I" doing the hearing can be read as both an ancestral slave and a contemporary black subject still mired in the racism of this colonial legacy. But difficulties arise from these colliding selves when the realities of one's present situation force the submergence or repression of other cherished identities. Emotions converge in confusing and complex ways. Writes Minh-ha:

> Love, miss and grieve. This I can't simply deny. But I am a stranger to myself and a stranger now in a strange land. There is no arcane territory to return to. For I am no more an "overseas" person in their land than in my own. Sometimes I see my country people as complete strangers. But their country is my country. In the adopted country, however, I can't go on being an exile or an immigrant either. It's not a tenable place to be.[96]

Home, for many of those adrift in the Diaspora, can hardly be more than a transitional or circumstantial and fleeting place since the (semi)"original" home cannot be recaptured, nor can its presence/absence be entirely reconciled in the "remade home".[97] My parents and other first-generation emigrants have a powerful sense of home. As my "home", Jamaica is but a whisper of a recollection — something intangible, yet visceral. It is the (re)creation of memory and the "insisting call from afar, back home."[98] Minh-ha references this frustration of living a difference that has no name, yet too many names.[99] Straddling the centre and the margins, North and South, developed and developing relegates one to the fringes definitionally. As Sarup observed, home becomes a challenging concept to negotiate:

> It is usually assumed that a sense of place or belonging gives a person stability. But what makes a place home? Is it wherever your family is, where you have been brought up? The children of many migrants are not sure where they belong. Where is home? Is it where your parents are buried? Is home the place from where you have

---

[95] Marley, 2001.

[96] Minh-ha, 1994, p. 16.

[97] Cantave, 2001, p. 164.

[98] Ibid., p. 15.

[99] Minh-ha, 1994, p. 327.

been displaced, or where you are now? Is home where your mother lives? And, then, we speak of "home from home". I am moved when I am asked the phenomenological question "Are you at home in the world"? In certain places and at certain times, I am. I feel secure and am friendly to others. But at other times I feel that I don't know where I am.[100]

Our longing is born of a strong affinity, the first true experience of comfort, but also from desperation and yearning for acceptance, to de-hyphenate our segregated, assimilated selves. This desire and longing for what has been called "future memory" reflects the mode of dwelling experienced when one navigates the back and forth between what once was and that which is yearned for once more.[101] Minh-ha observes:

> If it seems obvious that the history of migration is one of instability, fluctuation and discontinuity, it seems also clear for many Third World members of the Diaspora that their sense of group solidarity, of ethnic and national identity, has been nourished in the milieux of the immigrant, the refugee and the exiled. Here, identity is a product of articulation. It lies at the intersection of dwelling and travelling and is a claim of continuity within discontinuity (and vice-versa).[102]

In the case of the Returnees, such articulation cannot be the product of one individual or one interested party. Rather, the dialogue on how to accommodate and, let us hope, welcome Returnees must necessarily be generated by all involved persons and groups: the government (which has an obvious stake in the monies Returnees invest and spend on the island), the Returnees themselves (who may feel vulnerable), the Church,[103] (which has traditionally been the centre of Jamaican community and family life), and the masses (who may underestimate the contributions Returnees have made and continue to make to their homeland) must all be involved in addressing these issues. The statistics clearly demonstrate the Returnees' safety as a national crisis that warrants national dialogue lest Jamaica suffer yet another economic setback brought on not by global institutions, but by Jamaicans abroad who may be inclined to sever their relationship with the island. We must admit that there is a problem, whether it is poverty coupled with resentment, jealousy, classism, or privilege. In this way, an education campaign similar to the "Treat Our Tourists Right" movement may be in order, given the reciprocal interests at stake — the Jamaican economy needs the infusion of capital brought by the Returnees, and the Returnees desire and long for a peaceful return to their homeland.

Returnees did not leave their island home with ill will; they have always kept in touch with family and friends, have supported and sustained the island on a level second only to tourism, and have, generally, considered themselves Jamaicans first and foremost. The Returnees felt compelled to seek opportunities that were not as readily available in Jamaica. The *choice* to return home reflects profound love. Many, if not all, of the Returnees could have decided to

---

[100]Sarup, 1994, p. 94.

[101]Minh-ha, 1994, p. 12 (referencing Jelloun). *See also* Hyppolite, 2001, p. 3.

[102]Minh-ha, 1994, p. 14.)

[103]Jamaica is one of the smallest islands in the Caribbean but has more churches per square feet than any other nation (Ham, 2000).

relocate to Florida, St. Lucia, St. Kitts, the Bahamas, etc., or they could have decided to stay in their adopted countries. They chose, however, to come home because they love and miss their country. They want to enjoy their homeland with the good will of their brothers and sisters. They believe they are worthy of reacceptance, not derision and violence.

For second-generation Jamaicans, being raised or born abroad does not, in our own minds, make us any less Jamaican. The culture mediates our lives: I grew up in a Jamaican home in Canada. My parents would not have known how to proceed in any other way. From the ackee and saltfish, reggae and dance-hall music, from the dominoes and the bush jackets to the Appleton and Red Stripe and the "labrish",[104] the community and the culture were always Jamaican. We were taught to be proud of our heritage. Together with our parents, we have never forgotten home, and we, too, have a desire to return.

References

Ackerman, Bruce, & Alstott, Anne. (1999). Your stake in America. *Arizona Law Review, 41*, 249–260.

Adelman, Irma, & Robinson, Sherman. (1988). Income distribution and development. In Hollis Burnley Chenery, T.N. Srinivasan & Jere R. Behrman (Ed.), *Handbook of Development Economics Volume 2*. New York, NY: Elsevier Science Pub. Co.

Anghie, Antony. (1993). The heart of my home: Colonialism, environmental damage, and the Nauru case. *Harvard International Law Journal, 34*, 445–278.

Anghie, Antony. (2000). Time present and time past: Globalization, international financial institutions, and the third world. *New York University Journal of International Law & Politics, 32*(3), 246–505.

Antrobus, Peggy. (1995). Women in the Caribbean: The quadruple burden of gender, race, class and imperialism. In Achola O. Pala, (Ed.), *Connecting across cultures and continents: Black women speak out on identity, race, and development*. New York, NY: United Nations Development Fund for Women.

Bagley, C. (1971a). Mental illness immigrant minorities in London. *Journal of Biosocial Sciences, 3*, 449–459.

Bagley, C. (1971b). The social aetiology of schizophrenia in immigrant groups. *International Journal of Social Psychiatry, 7*, 292–304.

Bailey, William C. (1984). Poverty, inequality, and city homicide rates. *Criminology, 22*, 531–550.

Baker, Mike. (2002, March 15). UK "poaching" Jamaican teachers. *BBC News*. Retrieved October 25, 2003, from http://news.bbc.co.uk./1/hi/education/features/1871706.stm

---

[104]Jamaican for dialogue and conversation.

Barnes, Corinne. (1995, August 18). Caribbean women find it's fertilizer that makes the grass green. *Inter Press Service*.

Barrels of hope for Jamaicans. (1992, May 24). *Chicago Tribune*, p. 7B.

Barry, Tom et al. (1984). *The Other Side of Paradise: Foreign Control in the Caribbean*. New York: Grove Press.

Baumgartl, Bernd, & Favell, Adrian. (Eds.). (1995). *New xenophobia in Europe*. London: Kluwer Law International.

Baynes, Leonard M. (1996). Who is black enough for you? The stories of one black man and his family's pursuit of the American dream. *Georgetown Immigration Law Journal, 11*, 97–101.

Baynes, Leonard M. (1997). Who is black enough for you? An analysis of Northwestern University Law School's struggle over minority faculty hiring. *Michigan Journal of Race & Law, 2*(2), 205–233.

BBC Worldwide Monitoring. (2001, January 12). BBC Monitoring Latin America: Jamaica: "Foreign Minister denies Jamaicans who come home are persecuted" [Jamaica Political Report]

Berlin, Ira, et al. (Eds.). (1998). *Remembering slavery: African Americans talk about their personal experiences of slavery and emancipation*. New York: New York Press.

Bhabba, Homi K. (1994). *The Location of Culture*. New York: Routledge.

Black, Stephanie. (Dir.). (2001) *Life and Debt*. Jamaica: Tuff Gong Pictures.

Bolles, A. Lynn. (1996). *Sister Jamaica: A study of women, work, and households in Kingston*. Lanham: University Press of America.

Bohning, Don. (1995, February 26). Better days dawn for Jamaica. *Dallas Morning News*, p. 26A.

Boyd, Derick A.C. (1988). *Economic management, income distribution, and poverty in Jamaica*. New York: Praeger.

Briguglio, Lino. (Director). (1997). Island and Small States Institute. *Small Island Developing States and their Economic Vulnerabilities*. Retrieved October 25, 2003, from The Island Gateway website http://www.geic.or.jp/Islands/docs/lino.html

Broad, Ian. (1999, September 18). murder gangs threaten dream retirement isle. *Evening Standard, p. 18*.

Burton, Richard D.E. (1997). *Afro-Creole: Power, opposition, and play in the Caribbean* (pp. 13–46). Ithaca, New York: Cornell University Press.

Butler, Judith. 1993. *Bodies the Matter: On the Discursive Limits of Sex*. New York: Routledge.

Cahn, Jonathan. (1993). Challenging the new imperial authority: The World Bank and the democratization of development. *Harvard Human Rights Journal, 6*, 159–198.

Calmore, John O. (1992). Critical race theory, Archie Shepp, and fire music: Securing an authentic intellectual life in a multicultural world. *Southern California Law Review, 65*, 2129–2225.

Campbell, Mavis C. (1988). *The maroons of Jamaica, 1655–1796: A history of resistance, collaboration & betrayal* (*passim*). Granby, MA: Bergin & Garvey.

Cantave, Sophia. (2001). Home is… In Edwidge Danticat (Ed.), *The butterfly's way: Voices from the haitian dyaspora in the United States*. New York: Soho Press.

Carbado, Deven W. (1997). Motherhood and work in cultural context: One woman's patriarchal bargain. In Adrien Katherine Wing (Ed.), *Critical race feminism: A reader* (pp. 237–254). New York: New York University Press.

Carbado, Devon. (2000). Motherhood and work in cultural context: One woman's patriarchal bargain. In Adrian Katherine Wing (Ed.), *Global critical race feminism: An international reader* (pp. 115–129). New York: New York University Press.

Carter, James H. (1994). Racism's impact on mental health. *Journal of the National Medical Association, 86*, 543–547.

Carter, W. Burlette. (2000, July/September). Race and religion: Revising "America's most segregated hour. True reparations. [Panel Discussion.] *Governing two cities: Civil law and religious institutions. A symposium. George Washington Law Review, 68*, 1021–1119.

Carty, Anthony. (1992). Critical international law: Recent trends in the theory of international law. *European Journal of International Law, 3*, 66–93.

Central Intelligence Agency of the United States. [CIA] (2003). Jamaica. *World Fact Book 2003*. Retrieved October 25, 2003, from http://www.odci.gov/cia/publications/factbook/geos/jm.html (last updated August 1, 2003).

Chaney Elsa M., & Sutton, Constance R. (Eds.). (1992). *The context of Caribbean migration in Caribbean life in New York City: Socio cultural dimensions* (pp. 8–9).

Chang, Robert S. (1993). Toward an Asian American legal scholarship: Critical race theory, post-structuralism, and narrative space. *California Law Review, 81*, 1241–1323.

Chen, Jim. (2001). Epiphytic economics and the politics of place. *Minnesota Journal of Global Trade, 10*, 8–85.

Chew, Pat K. (1994). Asian Americans: The "reticent" minority and their paradoxes. *William & Mary Law Review, 36*, 1–79.

Child, L. Maria, & Yellin, Jean F. (Eds.). (1987). *Harriet A. Jacobs: Incidents in the life of a slave girl*. Massachusetts: Harvard University Press.

Crotty, James, et al. (1998). Implications of globalization for macroeconomic theory and policy in developing countries. In Dean Baker et al. (Eds.), *Globalization and Progressive Economic Policy*. Cambridge, MA: Cambridge University Press.

Crampton, Dave. (2001, July 23). Debt campaign survives G8 violence. *Scoop*. Retrieved October 25, 2003, from http://www.scoop.co.nz/mason/stories/HL0107/S00134.htm.

Cummings, Scott L., & Eagly, Ingrid V. (2001). A critical reflection on law and organizing. *UCLA Law Review, 48*, 471–472.

D'Aguilar, Lloyd. (1997, March 19). Jamaica — crime: Killing frenzy draws fear and concern. *Inter Press Service*.

Danaher, Kevin. (Ed.). (1994). *50 years is enough: The case against the World Bank and the International Monetary Fund*. Boston: South End Press.

Danielson, Anders. (1993). *The political economy of development finance: Public sector expansion and economic development in Jamaica (passim)*. Boulder: Westview Press.

Dean, G., et al. (1981). First admission of Native-born and immigrants to psychiatric hospitals in south-east England. *British Journal of Psychiatry, 139*, 506–512.

Delgado, Richard, & Stefancic, Jean. (Eds.). (1998). *The Latino/a condition: A critical reader (Parts III & IV)*. New York: New York University Press.

Falk, Patricia J. (1996). Novel theories of criminal defense based upon the toxicity of the social environment: Urban psychosis, television intoxication, and black rage. *North Carolina Law Review, 74*, 774–854.

Farabee, William Curtis. (1967). *The central Arawaks*. Oosterhout, Netherlands: Anthropological Publications.

Farrar, John H. (1999). Symposium. Law-based nature of the new international financial infrastructure: The new financial architecture and effective corporate governance. *International Lawer, 33*, 927–954.

Fitzpatrick, Joan, & Kelly, Katrina R. (1998). Gendered aspects of migration: Law and the female migrant. *Hastings International & Comparative Law Review, 22*, 47–104.

Flanagan, Erik. (n.d.). *Black struggle in colonization*. Retrieved October 25, 2003, from The Dread Library website http://debate.uvm.edu/dreadlibrary/flanagan.html

Foner, Nancy. (1985). Race and color: Jamaican migrants in London and New York City. *International Migration Review, 19*, p. 708.

French, Howard W. (1992, May 6). Caribbean exodus: U.S. is constant magnet *New York Times*, p. A1.

French, Joan. (1994). Hitting where it hurts most: Jamaican women's livelihoods in crisis. In Pamela Sparr (Ed.), *Mortgaging women's lives: Feminist critiques of structural adjustment*. London: Zed Brooks.

Gardner, W.J. (1909). *A history of Jamaica, from its discovery by Christopher Columbus to the year 1872*. London: Unwin.

Gianaris, William N. (1991). Weighted voting in the International Monetary Fund and the World Bank. *Fordham International Law Journal, 14*, 919–923.

Gladwell, Malcolm. (1996, April 29). Black like them. *The New Yorker*, p. 74.

Global Policy Forum. (n.d.) A closer look: Cases of globalization. Retrieved October 25, 2003, from http://www.globalpolicy.org/globaliz/special/index.htm

Goodwin, William Brownell. (1946). *Spanish and English ruins in Jamaica*. Boston: Meador Publishing Co.

Gordon, E.B. (1965). Mentally ill West Indian immigrants. *British Journal of Psychiatry, 111*, pp. 877–887.

Green, Charles. (Ed.) (1997). *Globalization and survival in the black diaspora: The new urban challenge*. Albany: State University of New York Press.

Greenhouse, Steven. (1999, October 9). Labor, revitalized with new recruiting, has regained power and prestige. *New York Times*, p. A14.

Hall, Stuart, & du Gay, Paul. (Eds.). (1996). *Questions of Cultural Identity*. London: Sage.

Hall, Stuart. (Ed.). (1997). *Representation: Cultural Representations and Signifying Practices*. London: Sage in association with Open University.

Ham, Ken. (2000, November 17). Jamaica — Vacation or evangelism? *Answers in Genesis Ministries*. Retrieved October 25, 2003, from http://www.answersingenesis.org/docs2/4406news11-17-2000.asp

Hashmi, F. (1968). Community psychiatric problems among Birmingham immigrants. *British Journal of Psychiatry, 3*, 196–201.

Heisler, Martin. (1998). Contextualizating global migration: Sketching the sociopolitical landscape of Europe. *UCLA Journal of Internal and Foreign Affairs, 3*, 560.

Henkin, Louis, et al. (1987). *International Law: Cases and Materials* (2d ed). St. Paul, Minn.: West Publishing Co.

Hickling, Fredrick W. (1991). Double jeopardy: Psychopathology of black mentally ill returned migrants to Jamaica. *International Journal of Social Psychiatry, 37*, 80–89.

hooks, bell. (1995). *Killing rage: Ending racism.* New York: H. Holt and Co.

Honeywell, Martin. (Ed.). (1983). *The Poverty Brokers: The IMF and Latin America.* London, UK: Latin America Bureau.

Horowitz, David. (2001, January 3). Ten reasons why reparations for blacks is a bad idea for blacks — and racist too. *FrontPageMagazine.com.* Retrieved October 25, 2003, from http://www.frontpagemag.com/articles/printable.asp?ID=1153

Hunt, Jon. (1999, September 13). Jamaican "returnees" targeted by criminals. *Birmingham Post*, p. 3.

Hurwitz, James D. (1985). Abuse of governmental processes, the First Amendment, and the boundaries of Noerr. *Georgetown Law Journal, 74*, 65–136.

Hyppolite, Joanne. (2001). Dyaspora. In Edwidge Danticat (Ed.), *The Butterfly's Way: Voices from the Haitian Dyaspora in the United States.* New York: Soho Press.

IMF & World Bank. (2000, April). *CBC News Indepth.* Avaiable from http://cbc.ca/news/indepth/imfworldbank

IMF, World Bank face tough questions on corruption. (2000, October 2). *Radio Free Europe/Radio Liberty.* Available from http://www.globalpolicy.org/socecon/bwi-wto/imf/2000/corrupt.htm

Island dream ends in ambush and murder. (2001, July 16). *Times (London)*, p. 13.

Issues — Slavery and Reparations. *The Multiracial Activist.* Retrieved October 25, 2003, from http://www.multiracial.com/issues/issues-slavery.html

James, Ian. ((2001, July 21). Jamaican resorts far from violent. *Associated Press.*

Johnson, Kevin R. (1997). "Melting pot" or "ring of fire"?: Assimilation and the Mexican-American experience. *California Law Review, 85*, 175–225.

Johnson, Kevin R. (1998). Race, the immigration laws, and domestic race relations: "A magic mirror" into the heart of darkness. *Indiana Law Journal, 73*(4), 1111–1170.

Johnson, Kevin R. (2000). Celebrating LatCrit theory: What do we do when the music stops. *University of California at Davis Law Review, 33*, 753–785.

Jordan, Ann D. (1996). Human rights, violence against women, and economic development (The People's Republic of China experience). *Columbia Journal of Gender and Law, 5*, 240–244.

Kasinitz, Philip. (1992). *Caribbean New York: Black immigrants and the politics of race.* New York: Cornell University Press.

Kiev, A. (1965). Psychiatric morbidity of West Indian immigrants in an urban group practice. *British Journal of Psychiatry, 111*, 51–56.

Kirk, Alton R. (1986). Destructive behaviours among members of the black community with a special focus on males: Causes and methods of Intervention. *Journal of Multicultural Counseling and Development, 14* (1), 3.

Klak, Thomas. (Ed.). (1996). *Globalization and Neoliberalism: The Caribbean Context* (pp. 352–387). Lanham, MD: Rowman & Littlefield.

Kozul-Wright, Richard, & Rowthorn, Robert (Eds.). (1998). *Transnational Corporations and the Global Economy* (*passim*). New York: St. Martin's Press.

Kundnani, Arun. (2001, October 1). From Oldham to Bradford: The violence of the violated. Retrieved October 25, 2003, from Institute of Race Relations website http://www.irr.org.uk/2001/october/ak00003.html

Lake, Obiagele. (1998). *Rastafari women: Subordination in the midst of liberation theology*. North Carolina: Carolina Academic Press.

Lecraw, Donald J. (1998). Bargaining power, ownership, and profitability of transnational corporationsin developing countries. In Paul W. Beamish (Ed.), *Strategic alliances* (p. 338). Northampton, MA: Edward Elgar Publishing.

Lederer, Edith M. (1993, July 6). Unprecedented migration creating crisis for rich and poor nations. Associated Press.

Lewis, Hope. (1997). Lionheart gals facing the dragon: The human rights of inter/national black women in the United States. *Oregon Law Review, 76*, 570–630.

Littlewood, R., & Lipsedge, M. (1982). *Aliens and alienists* (*passim*). London, UK: Routledge.

London, M. (1986). Mental illness among immigrant minorities in the United Kingdom. *British Journal of Psychiatry, 149*, 265–273.

Long, Edward. (1972). *The history of Jamaica*. New York: Arno Press.

Manley, Michael. (1990). *The politics of change: A Jamaican testament* (2d ed.) (pp. 219–255). Washington, D.C.: Howard University Press.

Markmann, Charles Lam. 1967. *Black skin, white masks* (Frantz Fanon, Trans.) (*passim*). New York: Grove Press.

Marley, Bob. The Words of Bob Marley, Slave Driver, available at: http://www.bobmarley.com/songs/song.cgi?slave (last visited Fed 22, 2004).

Marshall, Dawn I. (1983). Towards an understanding of Caribbean migration. In Kritz, Mary M. (Ed.), *U.S. Immigration and Refugee Policy* (pp. 120–121). Massachusetts: Lexington Books.

Massey, Douglas S. (1995). Getting away with murder: Segregation and violent crime in urban America. *University of Pennsylvania Law Review, 143*, 1203–1235.

Matas, David. (1996). Racism in Canadian immigration policy. In Carl E. James (Ed.), *Perspectives on racism and the human services sector: A case for change* (pp. 93–103). Buffalo: University of Toronto Press.

McGrory, Daniel. (2000a, August 2). Fatal homecoming in paradise. *Times Newspapers Ltd.*, p. 28.

McGrory, Daniel. (2000b, August 3). Jamaica "returnee" 50th to be murdered. *Times (London)*.

McWhorter, John H. (2001, July 23). Against reparations. *The New Republic*. Retrieved October 25, 2003, from http://www.tnr.com/072301/mcwhorter072301_print.html.

Menjivar, Cecilia, et al. (1998). Remittance behavior among Salvadoran and Filipino immigrants in Los Angeles. *International Migration Review, 32*, 97–126.

Merkl, Peter H., & Weinberg, Leonard. (Eds.). (1997). *The revival of right-wing extremism in the nineties* (*passim*). London: F. Cass.

Meyers, Deborah Waller. (1998, May). Migrant remittances to Latin America: Reviewing the literature. A working paper published by Inter-American Dialogue and the Tomas Rivera Policy Institute.

Minh-ha, Trinh R. (1990). Marginalia: displacement and resistance. In Russell Ferguson et al. (Eds.), *Out there: Marginalization and contemporary culture*. New York: MIT Press.

Minh-ha, Trinh T. (1994). Other than myself/my other self. In George Robertson et al. (Eds.), *Travellers' tales: Narratives of home and displacement*. London & New York: Routledge.

Multilateral Investment Fund. [MIF] (2001, May 17 and 18). *Remittances to Latin America and the Caribbean: Comparative statistics* (Part 3, p. 17). Regional Conference on Remittances as a Development Tool, Washington, DC. Retrieved October 25, 2003, from Inter-American Devlopment Bank website http://www.iadb.org/mif/v2/files/comparativeremittan2.pdf

Nelson, Camille A. (2001). Breaking barriers: Strategically assimilated or assimilated strategically. Paper presented at the Black Law Students of Canada Conference, February 15 to February 18, Ottawa, Canada. [Draft manuscript on file with author.]

Oakley, Robin. (1996). *Tackling racist and xenophobic violence in Europe* (*passim*). New York: Manhattan Publishing Co.

Olsen, Fred. (1974). *On the trail of the Arawaks*. Norman, OK: University of Oklahoma Press.

Parker, Jay. (2000, February). An apology and reparations for slavery? *The World & I*. Retrieved October 25, 2003, from http://www.worldandi.com/public/2000/April/repcon.html

Patnaik, Prabhat, & Chandrasekhar, C.P. (1998). Globalization, transnational corporations, and economic development: Can the developing countries pursue strategic industrial policy in a globalizing world economy? In Dean Baker et al. (Eds.), *Globalization and Progressive Economic Policy*. Cambridge, MA: Cambridge University Press.

Patterson, Orlando. (1969). *The sociology of slavery* (*passim*). Madison, NJ: Fairleigh Dickinson University Press.

Patterson, Orlando. (2001, July 23). The roots of conflict in Jamaica. *New York Times*, p. A17.

Pierce, Chester M. (1974). Psychiatric problems of the black minority. In Arieti Silvano (Ed.), *American Handbook of psychiatry*. New York: Basic Books.

Portes, Alejandro, Dore-Cabral, Carlos, & Landolt, Patricia. (Eds.). (1997). *The Urban Caribbean: Transition to the New Global Economy*. Baltimore, MD: Johns Hopkins University.

Public funds, private agendas [Editorial]. (1996, February 23). *Investor's Business Daily*. Available from National Center for Policy Analysis website http://www.ncpa.org/pd/govern/govcc.html

Radin, Charles A. (2000, April 13). Critics say IMF, World Bank leave struggling nations dependent. *Boston Globe*. Available from http://www.globalpolicy.org/socecon/bwi-wto/wbank/bwi00-1.htm

Ramsaran, Ramesh F. (1992). *The challenge of structural adjustment in the Commonwealth Caribbean (passim)*. New York: Praeger.

Remittances boosted sales during 2000 Christmas season. (2001, January 28). *The Jamaican Gleaner*. Retrieved October 25, 2003, from http://www.jamaica-gleaner.com/gleaner/20010128/business/business1.html

Richmond, Anthony H. (1994). *Global apatheid: Refugees, racism, and the new world order (passim)*. Toronto: Oxford University Press.

Rohter, Larry. (1997, January 30). Caribbean reels in NAFTA's wake. *New York Times*, p. A1.

Romero, Victor C. (2000). Aren't you Latino?: Building bridges upon common misperceptions. *University of California at Davis Law Review, 33*, 837–849.

Rubin, Seymour J. (1995). Transnational corporations and international codes of conduct: A study of the relationship between international legal cooperation and economic development. *American University Journal of International Law & Policy, 10*, 1275–1290.

Russell, Sharon Stanton. (1995). *The impact of international migration on sending countries*. Presented at State Department Conference on Latin American Migration: The Foreign Policy Dilemma.

Said, Edward. (1990). Reflections on exile. In Russell Ferguson et al. (Eds.), *Out There, marginalization and contemporary culture* (pp. 357–358). New York: MIT Press.

Said, Edward. (1999). *Out there: A memoir*. New York: Alfred A. Knopf Inc.

Sarup, Madan. (1994). Home and identity. In George Robertson et al. (Eds.), *Travellers' tales: Narratives of home and displacement*. London & New York: Routledge.

Sassen, Saskia. (1993). Economic globalization: A new geography, composition and institutional framework. In Jeremy Brecher et al. (Eds.), *Global visions: Beyond the new world order* (pp. 61–66). Boston: South End.

Scanlan, John A. (1994). Symposium, global migration and the future of the nation-state: A View from the United States — social, economic, and legal change, the persistence of the state, and immigration policy in the coming century. *Indiana Journal of Global and Legal Studies, 2*, 83–85.

Sellgren, Katherine. (2002, March 28). Third world schools sucked dry. *BBC News*. Retrieved October 25, 2003, from http://news.bbc.co.uk./1/hi/education/1898800.stm

Shepherd, Verene A., & Beckles, Hilary McD. (Eds.). (2000). *Caribbean slavery in the Atlantic world: A student reader*. Princeton, NJ: Marcus Weiner Publishers.

Sherlock, Philip, & Bennett, Hazel. (1998). *The story of the Jamaican people (passim)*. Princeton, NJ: Markus Weiner Publishers.

Suro, Roberto. (1989, July 16). Employers are looking abroad for the skilled and the energetic. *New York Times*, p. 4.

Syal, Rajeev. (2000, July 2) Jamaican returnees warned of violence by High Commission. *Sunday Telegraph (London)*, p. 13.

Symposium, (1997). Symposium, citizenship and its discontents: Centering the immigrant in the international imagination. *Oregon Law Review, 76*, 207.

Taylor, Frank Fonda. (1993). *To hell with paradise: A history of the Jamaican tourist industry*. Pittsburgh: University of Pittsburgh Press.

Taylor, Kenneth. (1999, March 19). Paradise lost; a spate of savage killings has shocked Jamaica. The 29 victims are all elderly, returning "from Britain and America to the rural idylls they remember from their childhoods. But times have changed and they're not welcome anymore . . . ." *The Indep. (London)*, p. 1.

Thomas, Chantal. (1999). Causes of inequality in the international economic order: Critical race theory and postcolonial development. *Transnational Law & Contemporary Problems, 9*, 1–16.

Tourism sector update. (2001, April 1). *Caribbean Update*.

Trimble, Philip R. (1990). International law, world order and critical legal studies. *Stanford Law Review, 42*, 815–849.

United States Commission on Immigration Reform. (1995) *Legal Immigration: Setting Priorities*. (1995 Executive Summary). [Report to Congress.] Washington, DC: U.S. Government Printing Office. Also available from www.utexas.edu/lbj/uscir/exesum95.html

Valdes, Francisco. (1996). Latina/o ethnicities, critical race theory, and post-identity politics in postmodern legal culture: From practices to possibilities. *La Raza Law Journal, 9*.

Volpp, Leti. (1996). Talking "culture": Race, nation, and the politics of multiculturalism. *Columbia Law Review, 96*, 1573–1621.

Wealth clue to Jamaican death spree. (1999, September 13). *Birmingham Evening Mail*, p. 16.

West, Cornel. (1990). The new cultural politics of difference. In Russell Ferguson et al. (Eds.), *Out there: Marginalization and contemporary cultures*. New York: MIT Press.

Williams, Eric. (1944). *Capitalism and slavery* (p. 51). New York: Russell & Russell.

World Bank, (1999). Country report. Jamaica. *World development report 2000/01: Consultations with the poor*. East Sussex, UK: Oneworld Development Network. Retrieved October 25, 2003, from http://www.worldbank.org/poverty/voices/reports/national/jamaica.pdf

Young, Donna E. (1997). Culture confronts the international. *Albany Law Review, 60*, 907–918.

Biblography

Blackwell Cultural Studies Resources, at http://www.blackwellpublishers.co.uk/cultural/; University of Iowa Cultural Studies Resources, at http://www.uiowa.edu/~commstud/resources/culturalStudies.html; Ethnic and Cultural Studies Resources, at http://www.educationindex.com/culture/; Cultural Studies Central, at http://www.culturalstudies.net/

A Brief History of Jamaica. Available at http://home.earthlink.net/~prestwidgew/jamaicanhistory.html (last visited October 25, 2003).

11

Racism
Between Jews
Israeli Women
in Calgary

Melanie Fogell
Faculty of Communication and Culture
University of Calgary
Calgary

> Before the Law stands a gatekeeper. To this gatekeeper comes a man from the coun-
> tryside and requests admittance to the law. But the gatekeeper says that he cannot
> admit him just now. (Kafka, "Before the Law")[1]

Several

years ago I attended a presentation by The Women of Colour Collective in Calgary.[2] The purpose of the workshop was to raise awareness and sensitivity about one's own racist attitudes. The presenters encouraged participation and feedback from the audience, and the workshop seemed to be very effective. However, when I mentioned my experience of anti-Semitism, I was told that my experience did not really count as racism. I knew that from their point of view I did not look like a member of a "visible" minority; but the feeling of being silenced was painful, nonetheless. My experience did count for me.

This essay is based on a larger project that focused on narrative and Jewish identity.[3] The research was not undertaken with the specific aim of studying racism; however, discrimination between Canadian Jews and Israeli immigrants was one of several themes that emerged. My interest in issues of Jewish identity stems from my own Jewish, immigrant background. As one of the third generation of East European Jewish immigrants, I grew up with stories of the **pogroms** in Russia and Poland from which my grandparents escaped.[4] Stories about concentration camps are also etched upon my childhood memories. For many years, I thought my parents and grandparents were exaggerating about the existence of anti-Semitism. Why would they be afraid of Nazis when it happened, in my mind, so long ago?

Growing up in the post-Holocaust 1950s, my upbringing and education was imbued with Zionist ideals, so I feel a strong, albeit confused, connection to Israel. The State of Israel stood for Jewish strength and hope for the future. What does it mean, then, when Jews leave Israel? My focus on Israeli women is related in part to my own conflict with Zionism as well as my own struggle with Jewish identity.

---

[1] Kafka, 1993, p. 249.

[2] Women's Studies course, "Contemporary Issues in Feminism", University of Calgary, July, 1993.

[3] Fogell, 2003.

[4] "The first series of attacks, or pogroms, erupted in 1881 and lasted until 1884. They consisted of assaults on Jewish quarters accompanied by rapes, looting, and some killing.... The impact of these pogroms lasts to the present day. They signified to many Jews that Russia would never grant them legal emancipation. The result was the beginning of a vast immigration movement which between 1900 and 1914 saw 1.5 million Jews leave Russia" (Smith, 1992, p. 28).

Melanie Fogell

Reflexive Methodology

In the larger study I referred to several theoretical perspectives to guide me through the murky territory of interpretative research, hoping that seeing through the lens of other perspectives would help to expand my interpretation. This is not the same as making it more truthful. Alvesson and Sköldberg refer to the process of "reflecting on several levels or directed at several themes" as "reflexive research."[5] In discussing the advantages of this kind of research, they assert that

> [re]flection can, in the context of empirical research, be defined as the **interpretation of interpretation** and the launching of critical self-exploration of one's own interpretations of empirical material (including its construction).[6]

They also point out that "it is difficult, if not by definition impossible, for researchers to clarify the taken-for-granted assumptions and blind spots in their own social culture, research community and language."[7] I have taken up the challenge of investigating a topic that, for me, is emotion-laden.

This anthology focuses on racism, specifically looking at the intersections of race and nationality. My essay on racism among Jews in Calgary[8] does not fit neatly into all the definitions provided in the Introduction. The inclusion of my essay raises questions about whether anti-Semitism belongs in the category of racism because the persecution of Jews is usually referred to as anti-Semitism. However, the goal of the genocide during the Holocaust was to eliminate a race of subhumans, so using the Holocaust as a historical precedent, Jews are sometimes referred to as a race. Thus, anti-Semitism is, for some, a form of racism. Although post-colonial theory has much to offer in the discussion of identity, its contested nature makes the already complex issue of Jewish identity too unwieldy for the purpose of this essay.[9]

Calgary has a well-established Jewish community, which has been in existence since approximately 1875. It has four congregations: Orthodox, Conservative and Reform, as well as Chabad House, which is the outreach program of the Lubavich Chassidic Movement. The Jewish community has its own community centre, two Hebrew day schools, funeral chapel, cemeteries, and many volunteer organizations. It is difficult to know exactly how many of the Jews in Calgary are Israelis because of the ambiguous nature of questions in the census concerning religion and ethnic or cultural group. The distinction between race and religion when it comes to Jews is unclear for both Jews and non-Jews. Some Jews would argue vehemently that being Jewish has to do with religion

---

[5] Alvesson & Sköldberg, 2000, p. 5.

[6] Ibid., p. 6.

[7] Ibid., p. 7.

[8] Canadian Census, 1996. According to the 1996 census, there are a total of 2,925 Israelis in Canada. Of these, 1,255 are female and 1,670 are male. In Calgary there are a total 260 Israelis, and of these 150 are male and 110 are female. It is difficult to judge the accuracy of these statistics, because individuals may identify their ethnic group as Jewish, Canadian, or Israeli. During the interviews, the participants in my study were definite about both their Israeli and Jewish identities, but I did not ask them how they would identify themselves in a census survey.

[9] Ashcroft, Griffiths & Tiffin, 1995, p. xv.

alone, whereas others identify themselves as "secular" or cultural Jews. Because of the ambiguity in the way the choices are provided for religion and ethnic origins in the 1996 census, it is difficult to ascertain the actual number of Israelis in Canada. According to Torczyner and Brotman:

> Respondents to the census are permitted to choose only one religion. They may choose up to four ethnic affiliations. These ethnic responses however are not reported in order of priority. Consequently, one can only make note of the number of persons who selected "Jewish" as their ethnic origin as well as other ethnic choices, which they may have indicated.[10]

Yet, in the 1996 census there were a total of 35 male Israeli responses and 30 female responses. Of those, 15 of the male responses were "single", and 20 were "multiple". Of the female responses, 10 were "single", and 25 were "multiple". The Canadian census definition of single and multiple responses is as follows: "A 'single' response occurs when a respondent gives one ethnic origin only. A 'multiple' response occurs when a respondent provides two or more ethnic origins. 'Total responses' indicate the sum of single and multiple responses." It is possible that some Israelis respond only as Jewish for ethnic group, and it is also possible that they do not identify themselves at all with an ethnic group or religion.

In the larger study on which this essay is based, I examined Jewish identity through the lenses of hermeneutics, narrative theory, and feminist post-structuralism. It is not within the scope of this essay to address all of these approaches, so I will rely mostly on Judith Butler's feminist post-structural notion of interpellation, which has much to offer in any discussion of identity.[11] Interpellation, simply put, is the act of naming combined with the act of answering to that name. In this way the subject is called into being by society, and she must answer that call. Butler points out:

> This suggests that such a subject in language is positioned as both addressed and addressing, and that the very possibility of naming requires that one first be named. The subject of speech who is named becomes, potentially, one who might well name another in time.[12]

This idea applies to the Jewish Israeli female subjects in my research. For example, a Canadian Jewish woman may "name" an Israeli woman in a particular way. However, that same Canadian woman has already been called into being by society's discourse. The Israeli woman in this example will likely go on to name others at another time. The Jewish Diaspora Zionist discourse differs from the Israeli Zionist discourse, so that both of the women in this example have already been called into being through other discourses. Any agency these subjects may have is in answering the call of a particular discourse.

Butler discusses lived lives as a performance, but only as it applies to gender. She looks back on her theory of performativity and gender and attempts to clarify her ideas in the preface of the 1999 publication *Gender Trouble* and

---

[10] Torczyner & Brotman, 1996, p. 15.

[11] Butler, 1997, p. 29.

[12] Ibid.

explains that she originally drew on Jacques Derrida's post-structural interpretation of Kafka's "Before the Law."[13] There the one who waits for the law, sits before the door of the law, attributes a certain force to the law for which one waits. The anticipation of an authoritative disclosure of meaning is the path by which that authority is attributing and installed: the anticipation conjures the object.[14] Following this thinking, Butler speculates that perhaps the notion of gender is a "similar expectation." In other words, the meaning of gender is proscribed by those with power and, in waiting "before the door", we in society are waiting to be defined. In doing so, this "expectation ends up producing the very phenomenon that it anticipates."[15] Derrida's notion of the expectation of judgement actually producing that anticipated outcome applies to women and to Jews. Butler points out that "the question of whether or not theory of performativity can be transposed onto matters of race has been explored by several authors."[16] In the case of Diaspora Jews, it is the stereotyped Jew, defined by those with power, who sits before the "door of the law." The anticipation of the power is what produces the Other. It is my contention that Israeli Jews are the Other to Diaspora Jews, and vice versa. Stereotypes about Jews in the Diaspora differ from stereotypes of Israeli Jews. In relation to Jews, the Diaspora is defined as "the dispersion of Jews among Gentile nations, all those Jews who live outside the biblical land of Israel."[17] Elazar and Weinfeld point out that "today the existence of diasporas is no longer unique to the Jewish people."[18] The dispersion of the Jewish people has been going on for more that 2,000 years and the Jewish people today live in countries all around the world. However, as Elazar and Weinfeld point out, "Since the establishment of the State of Israel, either parts or all of these diaspora communities have resettled in Israel, yet the vast majority of world Jewry lives in the diaspora."[19] I will not go into a discussion of the many stereotypes, but the fact that Israeli Jews must negotiate different stereotypes when they migrate to Canada complicates the situation further.

Racism/Anti-Semitism

Hamilton comments that "the social relations of racism have pervaded the country's history from its inception, creating sustained and shifting categories of "otherness" — those defined for all practical purposes as outside the Canadian polity."[20] Although she explains that "the process of racialization rationalizes

---

[13] Butler, 1999, p. xiv.

[14] Ibid.

[15] Ibid.

[16] Butler lists several scholars who have taken up the notion of performativity and race: Saiiya Hartman, Lisa Lowe, Dorinne Kondo, Homi Bhabba (Ibid., p. xvi).

[17] Brown, 1993, p. 663.

[18] Elazar and Weinfeld, 2000, p. 5.

[19] Ibid.

[20] Hamilton, 1996, p. 131.

the creation and sustaining of social and economic inequalities," Hamilton stresses that "it is a mistake to think that racializing the other is dependent upon these hierarchies."[21] To paraphrase, the racialized other is a socially constructed concept that does more than just perpetuate social and economic inequalities. The racialized other is created within a historical context. Hamilton argues that

> [w]ho gets included in the category of racial minority is historically specific, and race is not a subset of ethnicity. Racism is more properly identified as a system of power relations that rationalizes and normalizes differential treatment at an institutional level.[22]

When this system of power is normalized, racism becomes part of everyday common sense and is not seen as a power that excludes. Rather, it is just the way things are naturally. Thus, the racialized other can be constructed in several ways.

Bannerji echoes this idea in her discussion of the Canadian use of the term "visible minorities."[23] She argues that the use of this term implies that "some people are more visible than others."[24] As she explains,

> There must be something "peculiar" about some people which draws attention to them. This something is the point to which the Canadian state wished to draw our attention. Such a project by the state needs a point of departure which has to function as the norm, as the social average of appearance. This well-blended, average, "normal" way of looking becomes the base line, or "us" (which is the vantage point of the state), to which those others marked as "different" must be referred, and in relation to which "peculiarity" is constructed. The "invisibility" of these men and women depends on the state's view of them as normal, and therefore, their institution as dominant types.[25]

Bannerji also points out that "in situations where visibility was ostensibly lacking in physical terms, as in Nazi Germany, it has been constructed by the forced pinning-on of symbols which marked people out, and cut them apart from the rest of society."[26] Here she is referring to the yellow Star of David worn by Jews, the red star worn by communists, and the pink triangle worn by homosexuals as "ways of producing visibility."[27] There are, in fact, some Jews who can be distinguished from the dominant white majority by colour; however, the point Bannerji puts forward is that "visibility" is socially constructed.[28]

Providing a background for anti-Semitism in Canada, Hamilton discusses anti-Semitism in Europe. As she explains,

---

[21] Ibid.

[22] Ibid.

[23] Bannerji, 1993, p. 148.

[24] Ibid.

[25] Ibid.

[26] Ibid., p. 150.

[27] Ibid.

[28] Ibid.

> The history of anti-Semitism in Europe ... was nourished by envy for the perceived political and economic success of some Jewish people and the political opportunity presented for scapegoating such people for the ills of society.[29]

In reference to the social and historical construction of anti-Semitism and racism, Gershbain and Rubin write that "although the light-skin of many Jews grants us a relative degree of privilege, when this no longer serves the purposes of the state our access to it may simply be revoked."[30] The authors mentioned above stress the constructed nature of racism. As Bannerji suggests, racism can be present whether or not the minority is a different colour than the dominant group. Sometimes the similarities between racism and anti-Semitism make them indistinguishable. It is my contention that the topic of ethnic discrimination belongs in a collection of essays on racism. Trying to differentiate ethnic, national and racial categories, Anthias and Yuval-Davis explain that

> [w]hile each of the groups and their [sic] designation require [sic] a historically specific analysis it is not possible to distinguish in an abstract way between ethnic, racial or national collectivities but rather one can distinguish their different discourses and projects.[31]

They further explain that these categories are changeable, and "in different social and historical contexts, a process of re-labelling or redesignation may occur."[32] Anthias and Yuval-Davis stress that what is common to all of these categories "is that they involve the social construction of an origin as a basis for community or collectivity."[33] More simply stated, the question of ethnicity/race and nationality overlap and may change within cultural and historical contexts. In their view, "the specificity of racism lies in its working on the notion of ethnic groupings," and that "it is a discourse and practice of inferiorizing ethnic groups."[34] Following this line of thinking, anti-Semitism can also be placed in the category of racism. As a Jew, I find it distressing to use the word "racism" when looking at relationships between Jews; however, following this definition, the term "racism" unfortunately does apply in the treatment of some Israeli Jews by some Canadian Jews, as I found in my interview research.

Focusing on immigrants' self-perceptions, Moghaddam, Taylor, Pelletier, and Shepanek refer to a study on visible-minority women that discovered "that the longer these women lived in Canada, the more they felt that they were viewed by the majority group as outsiders."[35] Although my research does not specifically concern "visible" minorities, I do explore immigrants' perceptions of themselves as well as look at how they think they are viewed by the host society in Calgary, Canada. According to these authors, the labels "Canadian" and "immi-

---

[29] Hamilton, 1996, p. 132.

[30] Ibid.

[31] Ibid.

[32] Anthias & Yuval-Davis, 1996, p. 3.

[33] Hamilton, 1996, p. 4.

[34] Ibid.

[35] Moghaddam, Taylor, Pelletier & Shepanek, 2000, p. 268.

grant" are indicative of "different levels of 'inclusion' and 'exclusion.'"[36] When applying these ideas to a study of Israeli women, the issues become even more complex. Israeli Jews may be seen as outsiders by Canadian Jews, and Canadian Jews may be perceived as outsiders by the majority society. Perceptions of all the individuals and groups may not coincide. My study is limited in that I am not investigating the actual perceptions of the host society; however, by exploring how an immigrant perceives herself in the context of her situation, the larger host community may learn something about itself.

My research is based primarily on tape-recorded and fully transcribed open-ended interviews that I collected with Jewish Israeli women in Calgary over the course of approximately three years between April 1999 and July 2002. During this time I conducted 11 interviews that ranged from one and a half hours to three hours in length. I tried to recruit participants by placing an advertisement in the Calgary Jewish community newspaper. I did not get the response I had hoped for, so I asked an Israeli friend to suggest some women who might be interested. She gave me the names of two women who, in turn, recommended others. Eventually I was able to recruit 11 research participants. The women interviewed have resided in Calgary for periods ranging from one to 20 years. In no way can this be considered a representative sample of the population; however, questions are raised about how the dominant society relates to those considered outsiders. They signed consent forms concerning anonymity at the time of the interviews and again before excerpts of the interviews were to be printed. All but one of the women agreed to sign a second consent form. Some of the participants wanted more anonymity than the pseudonyms and descriptions I provided, so I made revisions accordingly. It is beyond the scope of this essay to examine all the interviews, so I have only referred to those where the issue of discrimination was raised. To afford anonymity, I combined segments from several interviews to create one composite participant. The words are verbatim; however, the woman with the pseudonym Noam is a fictional character based on a combination of several interviews.

During the course of the research I came to better understand the ways in which I am attached to the epic Jewish narrative as well to the Zionist discourse. The parameters of this essay do not allow me to expand on the ways my own narrative intersects with those of the participants. I consider myself both the author and the researcher, and I make no claims of objectivity. Usher addresses the impossibility of separating the researcher from the research.[37] He suggests that "Both research and literature as practices of writing construct worlds and are therefore 'fictional.'"[38] However, he does not mean that fictional is the equivalent of untrue. Many versions of the "truth" are possible. My research draws on the notion that "time becomes human time to the extent that it is organized after the manner of a narrative; narrative, in turn, is mean-

---

[36] Ibid., p. 269.

[37] Usher, 1996, p. 35.

[38] Ibid.

ingful to the extent that it portrays the features of temporal existence."[39] That is, until a story is put into words, it is unknowable.

At the core of this research is what Warnke refers to as "social identity."[40] The identity to which I refer is always located within a context of culture and history within society. Warnke defines social identity as "the identities we have as Blacks, Caucasians, women, Latinos, gays and so on, identities that we grow up as, assert as struggles for recognition, or try to eliminate and avoid."[41] I would add Jewish identity and Israeli identity to this list. For Warnke, the perception of our social identities as interretations works well when exploring narratives. The perception of our social identities as interpretations works well when exploring narratives. Jewish identity has a different meaning for individual Jews in the Diaspora and for individual Jews in Israel. The non-Jewish world also has many interpretations of Jewish identity.

There are several issues to consider in approaching research by giving weight to personal stories. Haug points out that "one of the difficulties is that past feelings and thoughts may be distorted by present-day value-judgements."[42] In discussing personal narratives, she maintains that it is possible to get past these distortions with "practical questioning."[43] In contrast to Haug, I do not believe that distortions can be avoided; they can only be acknowledged.

Israeli Emigration

Since the establishment of the State of Israeli in 1948, very little research has been done on Israeli emigration and the scholarly work written specifically about Israelis and migration has been done mostly in the United States.[44] In his seminal work on Israeli immigrants in New York, Shokeid cites the *Harvard Encyclopedia of American Ethnic Groups* in its short reference to Israelis in the United States:

> Israeli immigrants pose a problem for the Jewish community: they have chosen to leave the land that every Jewish American has learned to regard as a haven, the guardian of Jewish survival, and the center of Hebraic culture. The ambiguity toward *yordim* ... has expressed itself in the absence of formal recognition of the Israelis as a Jewish immigrant group.[45]

The Hebrew word *yordim* refers to those who have left Israel. As Linn and Barkan-Asher explain, "*aliya* (immigration to Israel) usually has positive connotations, while *yerida* (emigration from Israel, the emigrant being a *yored* — plural *yordim*) implies a rejection of Israeli life." *Aliya* translated means "to go

---

[39] Ricoeur, 1983, p. 3.

[40] Warnke, 2002, p. 306.

[41] Ibid., 307.

[42] Haug, 1999, p. 71.

[43] Ibid., p. 69.

[44] Shokeid, 1988, p. 2.

[45] Ibid.

up," while *yerida* means "to go down." Linn and Barkan-Asher further point out that "every loss of a citizen through emigration is conceived as a weakening of the defence of the country," and that emigrants are "acutely aware" that "the term *yordim* has a pejorative connotation ... and are consequently subject to feelings of vulnerability and guilt."[46] Israeli emigrants, then, are subject to suspicion from Jews in the Diaspora; they also feel insecure about their own position in a new society.

Sobel studied Israeli emigrants while they were still in Israel. He explains that Israelis see emigration as a serious problem. He points out that "while a demographic emergency in a purely objective sense might not exist, it is clear that a psychological emergency does."[47] He asserts that

> [w]hatever the "facts" of the matter, large numbers of Israelis — the man in the street as well as establishment figures — **perceive** emigration as a problem and one of serious dimensions. Emigration has in some respects come to be treated as a national emergency. Government figures, academic authorities and media gurus have all commented.[48]

Sobel explains that the emigration of yordim causes insecurity among Israelis. The creation of the Jewish State was dependent on Jewish immigration or *aliyah,* and its importance became "paramount":[49]

> In a broader context, this stigmatization reflects Zionist ideologies which encourage immigration, or aliya to Israel and discourage departure, or yerida. These beliefs, internalized by most Israelis, are shattered by the act of emigration and, until recently, have supported stigmatization of the migrant or yored.... The yored develops a myth of return which defuses the guilt of departure and authenticates the status of permanent expatriate. It is this myth that contributes to the social construction of a distinct Israeli ethnicity.[50]

Israeli Jews in Canada can be considered a separate ethnic group from Jews born in Canada or anywhere else in the Diaspora.

The Interviews

Noam is in her early thirties and has lived in Canada for approximately five years. Her job puts her in daily contact with both Canadian and Israeli Jews. When I asked her how she is treated by Canadian Jews, she admitted, "It's hard when I'm talking to you because I know you are a Canadian Jew." I tried to push her on this by explaining that this was exactly the type of information I was interested in, and so she continued:

> I'm going to be totally honest with you. Because I think we do come from a different culture. We do come from a different country, and as much as Canada is a country of

---

[46] Linn & Barken-Asher, 1996, p. 7.

[47] Sobel, 1986, p. 14.

[48] Ibid.

[49] Ibid.

[50] Ibid.

immigrants who are supposed to accept different person [sic], so why can't they accept us as we are? Why are they like that? What is it in them that we can maybe adopt? I adopt many people things that I think are nice and good and maybe we should learn from it.

Noam is painfully aware that she is not accepted by the Canadian Jews with whom she has had contact, but she is willing to try and be more like them. I tried to push her further on this topic by asking, "How do you get this message?" She explained that some Canadian Jews seem to think that Israelis are just "using" Canada, even though she points out, "I don't even use Canada or use what it has." She then continued to tell me how she believes Canadian Jews perceive her:

Also we're more barbaric, the way we speak, the way we talk, the way we behave. Our demands are sometimes not logical even, even in terms of education. We're not supposed to educate kids in terms of behaviour or manners.

At this point I was having difficulty understanding what she meant, so I asked how she got this idea.

I notice by the attitude, by the way I am judged. My work is judged. By the way they would look at my car that stands out in the parking lot. By the way they would, when I tell them where to come to my house for my son to play with or where she lives, they wouldn't take a step further.

In other words, Noam has noticed that Canadian Jews treat her as if she is somehow inferior to them. Her car is not expensive enough and she does not live in what might be considered a desirable Jewish neighbourhood. Noam felt judged by Canadian Jews. I asked her if people had actually come right out and said this to her. She replied, "Yes, they do. And the feeling they give you is that you are barbaric and uneducated. Your kids are wild. They have no manners whatsoever." I asked her to speculate about why Canadian Jews behaved this way towards Israelis.

They would not associate with you because they look down on you because they are insecure. It is not because they think that they are better than you. They know they are not. They are insecure because many feel that we should have stayed there. Fight our wars and they send the money and it's kind of also a guilt feeling for them that they are sitting on the fat of the land and on the big bucks criticizing what Israel is doing but they don't do anything about it. And they feel — many of them feel as if we come in to take away their security, take away their positions.

Noam was quite bitter as she told her story. Having lived in several other countries, she also suggested that this behaviour was a particularly Canadian phenomenon. When I asked Noam how she coped with these Canadian attitudes, she explained she has learned to laugh it off. When she said this, however, she did not seem to be in a laughing frame of mind. Continuing, she explained: "I actually look at them with pity. I really pity them because they don't grow out of this *shtetl* mentality."[51] In her introduction to Zborowski and Herzog's book *Life is with People*, Barbara Kirshenblatt-Gimblett, discusses the

---

[51] Ibid.

book's popular success when it was first published. Though a great popular success, the book poses several vexing problems, among them the identification of East European Jewish culture with the *shtetl*. During the fall of 1948, as researchers struggled with what to call the culture they had been studying, they identified *shtetl* with the prototypical "enclave community" that carried the "core culture" of East European Jews. In other words, Noam looks at many of the Jews in Calgary as an unfortunate throwback to the past. She explained that she is "extremely grateful" that her parents brought her up "as a proud Jew and a proud Israeli." She is "not afraid of the Gentile," and she is not afraid to say what she "feels or thinks," and she is not afraid to "rock the boat."

When referring to the *shtetl* mentality, Noam is again attributing Canadian Jewish behaviour to self-hatred and fear. *Shtetl* is a Yiddish word describing the insular Jewish communities in Eastern Europe that existed before World War II. Jews lived in these communities both by choice and because they were not permitted to live among the non-Jews. Although many of the Israeli women interviewed came from families that originated in Eastern Europe, the move to Israel was seen as a break with the insular traditions of the *shtetl*.

The scope of this essay does not permit an in-depth discussion of the ways in which Zionism has an impact on hostile feelings between Israeli Jews and Jews in the Diaspora. It was mentioned earlier that there are often negative feelings towards those Israelis who emigrate. In Israel, Jews in the Diaspora are considered to be in Exile:[52]

> The highly negative perception of Exile often turned from *sheililat ha-galut* (the repudiation of the state of living in exile) to *shelilat ha-gola* (the condemnation of the people who live in exile), the product of its demeaning and regressive lifestyle. According to this view, life in exile turned the Jews into oppressed, submissive, weak, and fearful people who passively accept their fate, hoping to be saved by God or by Gentiles' help.[53]

According to Yael Zerubavel, above, Israelis are taught from childhood to see themselves as the "New Hebrews," an improvement over the Jews in the Diaspora. Israelis who then decide to live in the Diaspora are likely to have negative feelings about themselves and about the Jews already living in the Diaspora. The Jews in the Diaspora are also aware that these feelings exist. With these layers of unresolved resentment, it is difficult for both Canadian and Israeli Jews to make sense of their identities.

When I asked Noam how being Jewish in Israel is different from being Jewish in Calgary, she explained that her ideas on this subject have changed over time. She explained that in Israel "the lived experience deceptively means that … you don't have to think about being Jewish," rather than that "you're Jewish because you're living in Israel." She further explained that there is no Hebrew equivalent of the word "abroad" by which to refer to everywhere other than Israel:

---

[52] Kirshenblatt-Gimblett, 1995, p. xiv.

[53] Zerubavel, 1995.

> There is no such expression, "abroad." It's outside — *haslet alit*. Outside of the *alit*. *Alit* is the country. There is only one "the country." It's Israel. The land. Outside "the land" is outside of Israel.

I realized that this would indeed be a very different way of looking at the world. She went on to further describe the experience of growing up in Israel. She explained that when she was young, she believed that Israel was the centre of the earth:

> Look at the word Mediterranean. Medi, terra, right? The centre of the earth, right? So Israel is the centre, Jerusalem is the centre. That's a given. Right? Nobody actually says it, but you grow up with that, and not to mention the chosen people issue.

It was clear that she was in conflict about her choices. If a person grows up believing that her country and her people are at the centre of the universe, it must be very painful to realize it might not be so.

I asked Noam whether she has made friends in the community, and she replied, "Yeah, we have a lot of friends, but mostly Israeli, from the Israeli community. It seems harder to get in contact with the Canadians." When I asked the reason for this she answered,

> Maybe because they [Canadians] see friendship as something different. I have a few friends [Canadian] but I don't see them. It's not the same relationship as with the Israelis because we're used to, as friends in Israel, to meet everyday, to talk on the phone every day. Maybe Canadians aren't that open to that. So I meet with them [Canadians], but it's not the same relationship can't say it's friends but maybe because I see friendship as something more intense.

I found it interesting that she visits or talks to her friends every day. There are times when I barely even talk to my children and husband every day, and they live in the same house with me. It was clear that Noam feels constrained in her relationships with Canadians. She worries that Canadians might find her strange if she were to act like herself. When I asked when she felt this, she responded,

> Well, just when I talk. Whatever I want, or say what ever I want, you know. People here are more, it seems like, programmed. You have to act a certain way. You have to talk a certain way. You have to be polite.

I got the sense that when she used the word "polite," what she meant was closer to "detached" or "frigid." Noam interpreted Canadian behaviour as unfriendly, and she was very much aware of how she had to perform with Canadians. I also asked her about her connection to the Jewish community in Calgary. In her words,

> I feel like it's — the Jewish community is split by three parts. There is a Canadian Jewish community. There is an Israeli Jewish community and there's a Russian Jewish community. And each one is polite to another but not more than. There is no interaction between these parts.

She said that she felt most comfortable with the Israeli community. With each question, she started with a positive-sounding answer, and I sensed that she was trying to be careful not to insult me, a Canadian. Although she misses Israel, she "loves" Canada. She went on, "I like the fact that people respect each other. At least they show respect to each other. They're patient with each other." I wondered if she really had respect for me, or if she felt compelled to perform in a respectful way.

When Noam commented further on life in Canada, I was struck by her words: "I like the space you know; we don't sit on each other's souls. I love this privacy. Sometimes in Israel, it's impossible because of the lifestyle." I told her that her statement about sitting on each other's souls was very powerful. She had translated this from Hebrew. It struck me that in Israel, they really were sitting on each other's souls. The country is much more crowded but, more important, the history of the country is visible in the many layers of civilization that have built societies, one on top of the other. Canadians do not have to bear the same weight.

Interviewing the participants in this study allowed me to peek into how other women play out their social identities. The tension between Jews in the Diaspora and Jews in Israel has become clearer to me. I can see now that the tension I have always felt is real. My last conversation with Noam, when I asked for her consent the second time, reinforced my feeling about this tension. She explained that since the interview two years earlier, she has started to understand just how different living in the Diaspora is than living in Israel. She mentioned a new awareness of anti-Semitism. She was very distressed about a very public anti-Semitic comment made by David Ahenakew, the former head of the Assembly of First Nations, even though Ahenakew made a tearful public apology. Gatehouse, commenting on Ahenakew's blunder, wrote, "Sometimes 'I'm Sorry' doesn't quite cut it. Suggesting that it was a good and necessary thing that Adolph Hitler 'fried' six million Jews in the Holocaust is one of those occasions."[54] Like many others, Noam was shocked by this statement. She found it frightening. I was a bit confused by her reaction because I assumed that growing up in Israel she would be used to Arab anti-Semitism. However, she explained that the Arab hatred is always there, so they take it for granted. There is nothing surprising about a situation that has been going on for so long. She was shocked that there was such virulent anti-Semitism outside of Israel. Having grown up in Israel, in a Jewish majority, she had not experienced the fear that accompanies anti-Semitism.

Butler's notion of interpellation, or naming, is a powerful concept. Although she uses it only in the context of gender, there are many aspects of identity that benefit from a closer look at how we are named and how we name others. There are many assumptions we make about each other and I have become aware of how much I do not know.

References

Alvesson, Mats, & Sköldberg, Kaj. (2000). *Reflexive methodology*. London: Sage.
Anthias, Floya, & Yuval-Davis, Nira. (1996). *Racialized boundaries*. New York: Routledge.

---

[54] Gatehouse. 2002, p. 37.

Ashcroft, Bill, Griffith, Gareth, & Tiffin, Helen. (1995). *The post colonial studies reader*. London: Routledge.

Bannerji, Himani. (1993). Popular images of south Asian women. In Himani Bannerji (Ed.), *Returning the gaze: Essays on racism, feminism and politics*. Toronto: Sister Vision Press.

Brown, L. (Ed.). (1993). *The new shorter Oxford english dictionary*. Oxford: Clarendon Press.

Butler, Judith. (1997). *Excitable speech*. New York: Routledge.

Butler, Judith. (1999). *Gender trouble*. New York: Routledge.

Census Nation Series. (1996). Retrieved October 25, 2003, from http://datalib.library.ualberta.ca/data/census/1996/nation/index.html

Elazar, D.J., & Weinfeld, M. (Eds.). (2000). *Still moving: Recent Jewish migration in comparative perspective*. New Brunswick, NJ: Transaction Publishers.

Fogell, Melanie. (2003). Broken promises and refigured selves: Narrative and Jewish identity. Unpublished PhD dissertation, University of Calgary.

Gatehouse, J. (2002, December 30). No Real Excuse. *Maclean's*. pp. 37–38.

Hamilton, Roberta. (1996). *Gendering the vertical mosaic: Feminist perspectives on Canadian society*. Toronto: Copp Clark Ltd.

Haug, Frigga. (1999). Memory work. In Frigga Haug et al., *Female sexualization: A collective work of memory*. London: Verso.

Kafka, Franz. (1993). Before the law. *The great short works of Franz Kafka*. New York: Schocken.

Kirshenblatt-Gimblett, Barbara. (1995). Introduction. In Mark Zborowski & Elizabeth Herzog, *Life is with people: The culture of the Shtetl*. New York: Schocken. (First published 1952)

Linn, R., & Barker-Asher. N. (1996). Permanent impermanence: Israeli expatriates in non-event transition. *The Jewish Journal of Sociology, 38*(1), 5–16.

Moghaddam, F., Taylor, D., Pelletier, P. & Shapanek, M. (2000). The warped looking glass: How minorities perceive themselves, believe they are perceived, and are actually perceived by majority-group members in Quebec, Canada. In M. Kalbach & W. Kalbach (Eds.), *Perspecitves on ethnicity in Canada*. Toronto: Harcourt Canada.

Ricoeur, Paul. (1983). *Time and narrrative, Volume 1*. Chicago: University of Chicago Press.

Shokeid, Moshe. (1988). *Children of circumstances*. Ithaca: Cornell University Press.

Smith, Charles D. (1992). *Palestine and the Arab-Israeli Conflict* (2nd ed.). New York: St. Martin's Press.

Sobel, Zvi. (1986). *Migrants from the promised land*. New Brunswick, NJ: Transaction Books.

Torczyner, James L., & Brotman, Shari L. (1996). *Weaving diverse strands: Demographic challenges transforming the fabric of Jewish communal life in Calgary*. Calgary: McGill Consortium for Ethnicity and Strategic Planning.

Usher, Robin. (1996). Textuality and reflexivity in educational research. In D. Scott & R. Usher (Eds.), *Understanding educational research*. London: Routledge.

Warnke, G. (2002). Social identity as interpretation. In J. Malpas, U. Arnswald & J. Kertscher (Eds.), *Gadamer's century: Essays in honor of Hans-Georg Gadamer*. Cambridge: The MIT Press.
Zeruabavel, Yael. (1995). *Recovered roots*. Chicago: University of Chicago Press.

Bibliography

Barsky, Robert F. 1996. Refugees from Israel: A threat to Canadian Jewish identity? In Howard Adelman & John Simpson (Eds.), *Multiculturalism, Jews, and identities in Canada*. Jerusalem: Magnes Press.
City of Calgary. Civic Census. Available at: www.gov.calgary.ab.ca.
Dua, Enakshi. (1999). Introduction. In Enakshi Dua & Angela Robertson (Eds.), *Scratching the surface: Canadian anti-racist feminist thought*. Toronto: Women's Press.
Gold, Gerald, & Cohen, Rina. (1996). The myth of return and Israeli ethnicity in Toronto. In Howard Adelman & John H. Simpson (Eds.), *Multiculturalism, Jews, and Identities in Canada*. Jerusalem: The Magnes Press.
Weinfeld, Morton. (2001). *Like everyone else ... But different*. Toronto: McClelland & Stewart.
Zborowski, Mark, & Herzog, Elizabeth. (1995). *Life is with people: The culture of the Shtetl*. New York: Schocken. (First published in 1952)

12

Local Colour
The Spectacle of Race at Niagara Falls

Karen Dubinsky
History Department
Queen's University
Kingston

This essay was previously published as "Vacations in the Contact Zone: Race, Racism and the Tourist Industry at Niagara Falls", in Nupur Chaudhuri and Ruth Pierson (Eds.), *Nation, Empire, Colony: Historicizing Gender and Race* (Bloomington: Indiana University Press, 1998). It was revised and expanded as "Local Colour: The Spectacle of Race at Niagara Falls", in Antoinette Burton (Ed.), *Unfinished Business: Gender, Sexuality and Colonial Modernities* (London: Routledge, 1999).

Tourism

is about difference. As British sociologist John Urry has established, the tourist gaze is constructed primarily "in relationship to its opposite, to non-tourist forms of social experience and consciousness."[1] Indeed, the quest for difference is a fundamental aspect of modern Western tourism; so much so that the designation "tourist" has become a term of embarrassment, something almost everyone is but no one wants to be. "One among some fifty million globe trotters," Trinh T. Minh-ha observes, "the traveller maintains his difference mostly by despising others like himself."[2]

Scholars of imperialism and culture have expanded our understanding of the construction of difference in travel to include those on the receiving end of the gaze. Travel writing by Europeans helped to produce Europe's "differentiated conceptions of itself in relation to 'the rest of the world'," as Mary Louise Pratt has put it in her fine study, *Imperial Eyes*.[3] A host of recent studies have probed the relationship — historical and contemporary — between travel, imperialism and racism. Native North Americans, Africans and Caribbeans are, in and of themselves, big tourist draws. A poster that appeared in Dominica in the early 1980s exhorted locals "Smile. You are a walking tourist attraction." Viewed from the comfort of air-conditioned tour buses, Black neighbourhoods from South Africa to Harlem have been transformed into apparently harmless tourist spectacles. The grand old days of colonialism are evoked — and purchased — in hotel bars in British Columbia and on the beach at Club Med. In most North American cities, Chinatowns and gay ghettoes alike have been refurbished from places of vice and crime to upscale shopping and dining areas. Whole land masses and economies in the Caribbean have been appropriated for European and North American tourism. Even in the poorer regions of North America — the Canadian Maritimes in particular — tourists are encouraged to search out and enjoy the "simple folk". In the face of all this, the popular cliche that travel broadens the mind seems difficult to sustain.[4]

This essay considers the relationship between travel and the creation of racial/ethnic hierarchies at one specific tourist destination, Niagara Falls. Niagara has been, for almost 200 years, a world-famous resort. For nineteenth-century visitors especially, it was an overwhelming spectacle, summoning great feelings and provoking voluminous discussions of its wider meaning. As one guidebook advised visitors in the 1890s, "[i]t is not merely what we see, but

---

[1] Urry, 1990, p. 2. Other useful studies of the social meaning of tourism are Wilson, 1991; Robertson et al., 1994; and Shields, 1991.

[2] Minh-ha 1994, p. 22.

[3] Pratt, 1992, p. 5.

[4] *See,* for example, Anderson, 1991; Buntman, 1996; Furlough, 1993; Francis, 1992; Jasen, 1995; McKay, 1994; Phillips, 1991; Rassool & Witz, 1996; Pattullo, 1996; Taylor, 1993.

Karen Dubinsky

what impression has been wrought upon the mind? What new idea and inspiration has arisen in the soul? ... Sit! Ponder! Contemplate! This is no place for butterflies, but earnest thinking souls."[5] Fortunately for historians, a good many visitors expressed themselves in print, and through the volumes of published travellers' accounts, guidebooks and other writings, it is possible to reconstruct the multiple and often-changing meanings of Niagara.[6]

At Niagara, as at many other notable North American tourist stops, travellers encountered a powerful natural spectacle, which they tended to find both alluring and terrifying. But they also found new human curiosities. As one particularly indignant tourist described it, "vendors of Indian beadwork, itinerant philosophers, camera obscura men, imitation squaws, free and enlightened negroes, guides to go under the Cataract — who should have been sent over it — spiritualists, phrenologists and nigger minstrels have made the place their own."[7] These encounters were described by Europeans in a variety of ways — in terms of fear, humour, sometimes pity — and we only have access to one side of the conversation. Nobody published or preserved the opinions of the Native souvenir seller or the Irish hack driver. Furthermore, lots of different kinds of people travelled in the nineteenth century, and acquired, as James Clifford explains, "complex knowledge, stories, political and intercultural understandings," without producing travel writing. Some of Niagara's visitors would have brought along their own servants, for example, whose reactions to the waterfall, as much else, are unrecorded in existing travel narratives.[8]

But my point is that these encounters were a kind of conversation — even though one voice was louder — not a monologue. These tourist experiences take place in what Pratt has termed the "contact zone", the space in which people who are "geographically and historically separated come into contact with each other ... usually involving conditions of coercion, radical inequality and intractable conflict." In the context of dramatic and unequal relations of power, the relationship between colonizer and colonized (or traveller and "travellee") is not one of separateness and apartheid, but rather "copresence, interaction, interlocking understandings and practices."[9]

Why was the spectacle of racial difference so interesting to white Europeans and North Americans? How can we explain the apparently paradoxical world views of the colonizers, who at once deplored the "savages" in their midst and made them central characters in their museums, exhibitions, fairs and literature?[10] Is Western fascination with things "primitive", as Mariana Torgovnik has posited, really about "imagining us," a revelation of the self that is inherent in the act of defining the other?[11] Nineteenth-century travellers'

---

5 Rev. J.W. Wilson, cited in Morse, 1896, p. 12.

6 The social meaning of Niagara in the nineteenth century has been analyzed by several scholars. *See,* for example, Irwin, 1996; Jasen, 1995; McKinsey, 1985; McGreevy, 1994; and Sears, 1989.

7 Butler, 1872, p. 25.

8 Clifford, 1997, p. 34.

9 Pratt, 1992, pp. 6–7.

10 *See,* for example, Coombes, 1994; McClintock, 1994; Rydell, 1993; Lutz & Collins, 1993; Moyles & Owram, 1988; Phillips, 1997.

11 Torgovnick, 1990, p. 11.

tales provide compelling evidence about the complicated and peculiar relationship between white people and "the rest of the world'.

Many people, especially literary scholars, have found travel writing a compelling source of information about the cliches, conventions and stereotypes Westerners developed as they attempted to understand what appeared to them as the strange realities of the non-Western world.[12] My approach differs from the way most literary scholars have used travel narratives, however, for I have collected a variety of writings about one location, and I have placed these writings in the context of the tourist industry. In what follows, I connect tourism-as-gaze with tourism-as-industry, an approach to travel writing that reveals that the re-enforcement of racial hierarchies through travel had a significant (and underanalyzed) foundation. Racial hierarchies have been inscribed in the political economy and power relations of the tourist industry. The rhetorical strategies of nineteenth-century visitors to Niagara helped render the natural and human wilderness of the New World knowable and, thus, able to be appropriated. These acts of appropriation were produced discursively — creating Niagara Falls as an icon of the untamed — *and* economically entrenching racial and ethnic hierarchies into the bricks and mortar of the tourist industry itself.

Native People as Tourist Attractions[13]

One reason travellers came to Canada in the nineteenth century was to see Native people. From travellers' descriptions of the sight of their "first Indian", to the variety of invented stories of native tragedy and sacrifice associated with the Maid of the Mist "legend", to the construction of an "authentic" Indian village in the 1950s, Native people have been woven into the natural history of the area. Along with waterfalls and wax museums, Native people were thus established as tourist attractions, extensions of the natural landscape. The tourist gaze, as Jonathan Culler has suggested, is constructed by symbols, and the practice of tourism might be thought of as the collection of signs.[14] And nothing was a more important signifier of North America than Native people.

Throughout the nineteenth century, Native people signified wilderness, the opposite of civilization. Like the explorers, traders, missionaries and invading armies before them, European tourists patrolled the civilization/wilderness border carefully. They had a firm sense of the side they occupied, but they also evinced a strong curiosity about what, and who, lay on the opposite shore. By the nineteenth century, the civilization/wilderness boundary had acquired a meaning specific to the project of expanding the British Empire. Following McClintock, we can posit that a visit to the wilds of North America was understood as a trip through "anachronistic space: prehistoric, atavistic and irrational,

---

[12] Influential analyses of travel writing include Hall, 1998; Spurr, 1993; and Stowe, 1994.

[13] A note on language: I use the term "Indian" when quoting from historical sources and the contemporary term "Native" otherwise.

[14] Culler, 1981.

inherently out of place in the historical time of modernity."[15] As Canadian historian Patricia Jasen has recently documented, the quest for "wild things" brought hundreds of thousands of tourists to Ontario in the nineteenth century. Niagara was no different than many other nineteenth-century North American tourist destinations in this respect; it was tame enough to accommodate the standards of daily comfort demanded by the European upper class (by the mid-nineteenth century at least six luxurious hotels stood on both sides of the river), yet wild enough to be interesting. The Tuscarora Indians, forced to migrate from the Carolinas in the early 1700s, resettled 10 miles away from the Falls, near Lewiston, New York. The community served, as Jasen has noted, as "a sort of laboratory ... where visitors could assess the residents' capacity for civilization while picking up souvenirs at the same time."[16] This particular contact zone, then, gave European visitors a close-up look at one of the century's great binaries: the difference between "progress" and "degeneration". As McClintock has explained, degenerate types of people were necessary for the self-definition of the European middle class, for "the distance along the path of progress traveled by some portions of humanity could be measured only by the distance others lagged behind."[17]

Thus, the sight of one's "first Indian" on the shores of the Niagara River was regularly noted in travel writings, sometimes in a tone that rivalled the excitement at seeing the waterfall. As soon as composer Jacques Offenbach arrived at Niagara, his guide insisted, "you would like to see the Indians." And George Sala captured his first Indian in his travel diary in much the same way as he might have recorded sighting a bird: "[H]e was the first North American Indian, in his own land, I had seen."[18]

Like virtually all travellers, both Sala and Offenbach were disappointed with what they saw. In fact, in most accounts of first sightings of Native people, we can glimpse what I think of as the moment of "racial panic" as travellers let loose a volley of invectives at the spectacle of race before them.[19] Travellers' descriptions of Niagara's Native inhabitants ran the gamut of nineteenth-century stereotypes: they were too ferocious or too tame, romantic figures or pathetic drunkards, uncivilized and unChristian, boring or ridiculous in their attempts to mimic white lifestyles. Some felt cheated; as early as 1855 Ida Pfeiffer complained that the Tuscarora reserve was "now scarcely worth going to see, as the inhabitants, who have become Christians, go dressed like the whites, and build and cultivate their fields just like their neighbours."[20] This conflict between the assimilationist aims of modern government policy and the demands of tourism for difference and exoticism explains the popularity of stage managed "Indian events" at Niagara Falls in the 1870s and 1880s, such as the Indian Burial Cer-

---

[15] McClintock, 1994, p. 40.

[16] Jasen, 1995, pp. 42, 70.

[17] McClintock, 1994, p. 46.

[18] Sala, 1865, p. 184; and Offenbach, 1875, p. 74.

[19] I am using this term in the same sense that Eve Kosofsky Sedgewick has used the term "homosexual panic," in order to emphasize the permeability of boundaries, a central feature of relations between observer and observed in the contact zone. See Sedgewick, 1990, pp. 19–22.

[20] Pfeiffer, 1855, p. 244.

emony and Great Buffalo Hunt, organized by the Niagara Falls Museum. Such events, however, did not stem the tide of tourist disappointment and cynicism, and one way of presenting oneself as a knowing, world-weary traveller was to question the authenticity of the Indians one met. The "Oriental Dancing Girls" and "Indian Snake Charmers" at North American circuses in this era were often played by heavily made-up white people, and rumour had it that some of Niagara's Indians were also theatrical inventions. Offenbach, in 1875, wrote that he "expected to find savages, but they showed me pedlars, men who produced articles de Paris ... were they really Indian? I rather doubt it."[21] Edward Roper, visiting Niagara for a second time in the 1890s, noted "there are the same Indians about as of old; they say the squaws come generally from 'ould Oirland'." Many complained about "Irish Indians" or "Indian curiosities" made in New York [or England, or France, or later, of course, Japan], and, by the 1890s, guidebooks, such as the popular series edited by Karl Baedeker, advised readers that "the bazaar nuisance [at Niagara] continues in full force.... Those with Indian curiosities should buy from the Indians themselves."[22] From savage to boring to fake, Natives as tourist attractions generally disappointed, but they always drew.

The sight of Native people provoked more than the desire to gaze. While the European gaze itself is proprietary (the "master-of all-I-survey," as Pratt calls it), visitors claimed possession through a variety of other gestures. The other was consumed both imaginatively — when Europeans wrote their own scripts for fantasy conversations — and literally — when Europeans purchased Native-crafted souvenirs. In both of these encounters — imagining Native people, and buying from them — we can glimpse the two-sided nature of relationships in the contact zone: exchange and appropriation.

Consider, for example, Sala's long discussion of his "first Indian," which happens, he claims, as the two are gazing at the waterfall together. Sala begins with a familiar diatribe: the Indian is a "shiftless and degraded vagrant, who does not wash himself, who is not at all scrupulous about taking things which do not belong to him, who will get blind drunk on rum or whisky whenever he has a chance." Yet after this outpouring he returns to their mutual fascination with the waterfall, and the Native man changes from a human object of scorn to one of nature's victims. "I wonder what he's thinking, as we look at the Falls together; maybe he is thinking that all this used to be mine," Sala muses. Adopting the voice of what Pratt calls the anti-conquest (in which European subjects "secure their innocence in the same moment as they assert European hegemony"), Sala narrates his Indian fantasy: "All this belonged to me, and now I am a vagrant and an outcast and the white man charges me for the birds I have slain." Sala ends his reflection with a return to the explicit imperial voice, but his tone has changed from disgust to pity: "Poor copper hued child of the wilderness!"[23] We might read this as imperial guilt, genuine com-

---

[21] Offenbach, 1875, p. 74; Davis, 1993.

[22] Roper, 1891, p. 419; Baedeker, 1893/1971, p. 200.

[23] Sala, 1865, pp. 184–185; Pratt, 1992, p. 7; Spurr, 1993, p. 128.

passion or the reinscription of racism, but the point is that it's an exchange that can function only because of the imagined silence of one party.[24]

The passion for collecting Indian "curiosities" also signals the cultural comingling — within hierarchical relations — that characterizes the contact zone. Why were Europeans and white North Americans so fond of Native souvenirs when they were clearly so ambivalent about the people who made them? Indeed, most visitors to Niagara commented on the "grotesque and gaudy" style of Native handicrafts, even as they purchased them. (One visitor even claimed to have seen a "real scalp of an Indian, duly labelled and consisting of a triangular piece of skin" for sale in an Indian bazaar.)[25] By purchasing souvenirs, travellers could prove that they'd made the journey, and perhaps they could also pretend to have attained a certain level of "Indianness". Art historian Ruth Phillips argues that European fondness for Native souvenirs in North America reflects Europeans' love/hate relationship with Native culture, as though by collecting and consuming Indian artifacts white people might displace real, live aboriginals.[26] The effect of this exchange on Native people is less clear. Women and children especially secured employment as makers and sellers of Native crafts, and the participation of Native people in the tourist economy was, perhaps, one way for them to make the best of a bad situation. But the manufacture and sale of tourist commodities was, at best, a rear-guard defence against dispossession of land and assimilationist government policies.[27]

Unlike some other feminists who have written on this topic, I see little evidence that female travellers rejected the voice of colonial authority or found a common identity with the other.[28] Far more persuasive is the argument that nineteenth-century European women invented a voice of imperial female authority, disparaging the other in order to become part of the self. But gender certainly framed European encounters with Niagara's others. The paradigmatic "first Indian" who provided a moment of panic and, sometimes, further reflection, was always male, which likely indicates more about European notions of fitting representatives of culture than the sex of the Native person one actually first saw. Travellers always spoke of Native souvenir sellers as female — an "army of persistent saleswomen" as one guidebook put it — which increased the possibility that ones' "first Indian" would be a woman.[29]

Native women were not, however, ignored by Europeans, as the centuries-old fascination with the Maid of the Mist "legend" at Niagara indicates. Dating (possibly) from a story that circulated among fur traders in the 1750s of an Iroquois man caught above the Falls in a current and swept over, the tale changed form through the nineteenth century to conform to European conventions of drama, romance and sexuality. Tales of sexual relations between whites and

---

[24] It is also an exchange with enduring cultural significance in North America. On the legacy of Blacks as visual but voiceless icons, from anti-slavery images to Rodney King, see Baker, 1993, pp. 38–48.

[25] Jackson, 1886, p. 131.

[26] Phillips, 1991, p. 20. *See also* Phillips, 1997.

[27] Jasen, 1995, p. 81; Phillips, 1991, p. 5.

[28] Mills, 1991; Melman, 1992; Foster, 1990; and Birkett, 1989.

[29] *The Humbugs,* 1884, p. 7.

Natives were standard fare in nineteenth-century adventure fiction, and "Indian maids" were always popular. But the white male who is charmed by the Native woman is doomed, and the only escape is the death of the Native woman, which of course allows the white man to concentrate on his real mission — to conquer the land.[30]

These "legends" are merely the nineteenth and twentieth-century versions of a long-standing cliche of colonial history. The "uncertain continents," as Anne McClintock has termed Africa, the Americas and Asia, "were always eroticized by Europeans, and 'travellers' tales abounded with visions of the monstrous sexuality of far-off lands ... a fantastic magic lantern of the mind onto which Europe projected its forbidden sexual desires and fears."[31] In this case, the Iroquois man became an "Indian maid", named Lelawala, forced by her unfeeling father, the chief, to descend the Falls in a canoe to appease angry gods. Sometimes the father, in a moment of remorse, joins her; in other versions, she is joined by her lover and rescued by him at the bottom of the Falls.[32] Various versions of this story have been told — in guidebooks, travellers' accounts, and tourist industry promotional literature — for centuries. The story has added, as I have argued elsewhere,[33] to the commonplace nineteenth-century discursive practice of gendering the Falls female and has figured centrally in the imaginary geography of Niagara as a place of romance, danger and sexuality.[34] Many travellers, especially men, claimed they could "trace in the outlines the indistinct shape of a woman, with flowing hair and drooping arms, veiled in drapery," in the waterfall. Those lacking in imagination were assisted by tour promoters; a 1915 Canada Steamship Lines brochure, for example, invited tourists to imagine that "instinctively we see the Indian maid in her flower-bedecked canoe approach the apex of the Falls, her body erect, her demeanour courageous." Images of naked Native women going over the waterfall adorned postcards, promotional brochures, as well as high art for two centuries.[35] Stories like this gave North America a dash of romance and adventure. But these tales also fit well with white people's preconceived ideas about their presence in the New World. Colonial domination is understood as a good thing, for it reins in "the natural excesses and the undirected sexual energies of the colonized."[36] It was only in the summer of 1996 that the Maid of the Mist Steamboat Company finally listened to the protests of Native groups and ceased telling this tale as fact.

---

[30] Goldie, 1989, pp. 71–72.

[31] McClintock, 1994, p. 22. *See also* Spurr, 1993, p. 171.

[32] Of many versions and origins of this story, one is credited to Lieut-Col. Frederick C. Curry (Curry, 1946).

[33] Dubinsky, 1999.

[34] Ibid., pp. 19–52.

[35] William Howard Russell, *Canada: Its defences, condition and resources*, 1865 (as cited in Dow, 1921, p. 318); Canada Steamship Lines, 1915, p. 7.

[36] Spurr, 1993, p. 172.

Karen Dubinsky

Serving Colonialism: Waiters, Drivers and Guides

The contrast between civilization and wilderness was also played out in travellers' accounts of their perceptions of the Niagara labour force. While the waterfall itself was a beloved icon of the sublime, its "handlers" were detested. Complaints about the "disgustingly obtrusive civilization that crawls over its (Niagara's) sides," were nearly universal at Niagara, and almost every visitor had a story to tell of an importuning hackman or swindling tour guide.[37] The "hateful race of guides ... miserable little peepshows and photographers, bird stuffers, shell polishers, and collectors of crystals," destroyed what many considered the proper appreciation of nature, and such concerns about the debasement of Niagara figured centrally in the campaign, waged by politicians, conservationists and intellectuals, to "free Niagara" through the creation of public parkland in the 1880s.[38]

The first suggestion of racial or ethnic conflicts between visitors and the tourist industry came as early as the 1840s. Two businessmen, Thomas Clark and Samuel Street, local merchants and mill owners owned the ferry service, which took people back and forth across the river until the Upper Suspension Bridge was built in 1869. These businessmen managed to move in on a thriving Native-run ferry service, for Native men had taken passengers across the river in canoes since the 1820s.[39] Clark and Street drew from two other disparaged labour markets, black and Irish men, to make the trek across the river, and some travellers did not enjoy the ride. In 1842, a petition circulated, complaining that the ferrymen were "addicted to habits of intemperance" and were thus "unaccommodating and uncivil to passengers" and "in the habit of extorting from persons larger sums than their employers advertised." The ferry rides continued as a novelty excursion in the 1880s, though travellers still grumbled about the "surly Canadian Charon" who took them across.[40]

Since the 1830s, black men from the community of nearby Drummondville found steady employment in Niagara's hotel industry.[41] Encounters with Black waiters at hotels sometimes caused the same momentary racial panic as the sight of one's "first Indian". European hotel guests remarked that they "could not get used to the negroes' attendance, I am always afraid lest they soil all they touch." Others found them objects of novelty, "pleasant, funny creatures," or "good, grinning curly pated Sambos," particularly when dressed in white servant's jackets. Some (especially the English) inverted prevailing racial hierarchies to contrast blacks favourably to the Irish: "awkward, stupid, noisy and

---

[37] Southesk, 1875 (as quoted in Dow, 1921, p. 268).

[38] Sala, 1865, p. 136. On the Niagara preservation campaign, see Killan, 1975; Runte, 1973; and Welsh, 1977.

[39] *Niagara Falls*, 1890, p. 15.

[40] Greenhill & Mahoney, 1969, p. 111; Jackson, 1886, p. 126.

[41] Winks, 1971, p. 146. See also Thomas, 1995, p. 15. U.S. sources suggest that black men accounted for approximately one quarter of the restaurant labour force until the 1930s. See Cobble, 1991, p. 18. Few references exist to the presence of black women in the Niagara tourist industry, with the exception of an account of a trip to the Cave of the Winds in the 1880s, which suggests that a "bright eyed mulatto girl" worked at the change room ("Cave of the Winds", 1880s).

slow, I confess they (blacks) are more bearable and amenable to counsel than their fair skinned brothers.... Irish waiters abound, and their character is by no means improved by being 'citizens of a free country.'"[42]

Just as the presence of Native people lent an air of drama and exoticism to the surroundings, the presence of Black tour guides, particularly at several dangerous excursions around the waterfall, intensified the experience of "doing" Niagara. Two of the most popular attractions through the nineteenth century were the Table Rock and Cave of the Winds tours, where travellers suited up in oilskin costumes and made their way through torrents of water to literally go, as it was advertised, "behind the Falls." When Isabella Bird entered Table Rock House in the 1850s, she recoiled at the notion of having to disrobe, and when she saw herself decked out in oilskin, she was shocked to behold "as complete a tatter-demallion as one could see begging upon an Irish highway." Her process of transformation is experienced completely in racial terms; she loses her Englishness. As she left the dressing rooms, "a negro guide of most repulsive appearance awaited me," then she began her (literal and metaphoric) descent. At the most difficult part of the passage,

> heavy gusts almost blew me away; showers of spray nearly blinded me ... I wished to retreat and essayed to use my voice to stop the progress of my guide. I raised it to a scream, but it was lost in the thunder of the cataract. The negro saw my incertitude, and extended his hand. I shuddered even there as I took hold of it, not quite free from the juvenile idea that "the black comes off." He seemed at that moment to wear the aspect of a black imp leading me to destruction.[43]

Other visitors voiced similar fears about their guides — "great ugly blacks", as Lord Acton remembered in the 1880s; "strapping specimens of negro or mulatto, in thick solid ungainly boots," wrote another. Trying, perhaps, to repress such fears, other male visitors turned their guides into silly children. W. G. Marshall was annoyed that his guide, whom he constantly referred to as "my darkie," kept interrupting his own reverie about God and nature: "Look, colonel, look at it! Hain't it mighty, hain't it glorious?"[44] Table Rock and Cave of the Winds guides of all nationalities — and there were some non-blacks employed there — were described as rugged, hypermasculine creatures, "in the prime of manhood, large and well built" as one visitor wrote.[45] Indeed, escalating complaints from visitors that Table Rock's owner, Saul Davis, employed "negroes who used profane language and spoke very excitedly" in order to harass customers and extract more money from them led the Ontario government to appoint a Royal Commission in 1873 to investigate "ill-treatment or extortion ... practised upon visitors to Niagara Falls."[46] Yet, like the steamship journeys or wilderness excursions led by Native guides elsewhere in Ontario, the combination of human and natural dangers heightened the adventure for Europeans. The rushing water or roaring rapids were almost indistinguishable

---

[42] Golovin, 1856, p. 15; Monck, 1891, p. 161; Hughes, 1895, p. 150; and Day, 1880, p. 150.

[43] Bird, 1856/1966, pp. 231–234.

[44] *NFR*, 25 January, 1922; Russell, 1865 (as cited in Dow, 1921, p. 323); Marshall, 1881, p. 81.

[45] Tyndall, 1873.

[46] Killan, 1975.

Karen Dubinsky

from the ferocious men who navigated them.[47] Male visitors' narratives of their passage through Niagara Falls reflects a clear sense of pride and pleasure, such as that of Frederic Almy, who spoke of the water "foaming and rushing about your knees, and lugging at you with an invitation that is irresistible. I have," he declared, "seen grave men frolic in the water, their trousers and sleeves swelled almost to bursting with the imprisoned air.... To play so with Niagara is indescribable." Others spoke of the "delightful, novel and strange sensation, of commingled terror and safety."[48]

Tourists were no more inclined to recognize the irony of their position — that their comfortable existence at Niagara was facilitated by the presence of the waiters, guides, souvenir sellers and drivers whom they despised — than were middle- and upper-class Europeans who encountered the Other in their households, their workplaces, their Empires. The tourist gaze at Niagara was firmly trained on the boundary between civilization and wilderness, progress and degeneration, which let the European imagination roam freely through fear, annoyance, hatred, desire and, always, the assertion of power.

As we have seen, these excursions to the contact zone were narrated by the traveller. Yet "walking tourist attractions" might occasionally take matters into their own hands, and I do not wish to understate their agency or their ingenuity. In the 1920s, the U.S. government passed a law that reversed centuries-old Native treaty rights to cross the U.S./Canada border without impediment. Clinton Rickard of the Tuscarora band was one of many Natives who became involved in the campaign against this discriminatory law. He found, to his surprise, that the mythical tourist Indian could serve as an effective political weapon in this battle. Rickard spent a summer donning traditional dress and visiting tourist camps at Niagara Falls. As he was posing in headdress and buckskin for photographs, he also lobbied tourists about this unjust law and persuaded many to write to authorities in protest. The law was eventually repealed.[49] In the contact zone, exchange and appropriation went hand-in-hand.

References

Almy, Frederick. (1893). What to see. In William Dean Howells (Ed.), *The Niagara book: A complete souvenir of Niagara Falls*. Buffalo: Underhill and Sons.

Anderson, Kay. (1991). *Vancouver's Chinatown: Racial discourse in Canada, 1875–1980* (pp. 211–244). Montreal, PQ: McGill Queen's University Press.

Baedeker, Karl. (1893/1971). *The United States* (Reprint edition). New York, NY: Da Capo Press. (First published 1893)

---

[47] Jasen, 1995, p. 72.

[48] Almy, 1893, p. 37, *The Complete Illustrated Guide*, 1880, p. 33; Roper, 1891, p. 418.

[49] Rickard, 1971, p. 71.

Baker, Houston A. (1993). Scene ... not heard. In Robert Gooding-Williams (Ed.), *Reading Rodney King, reading urban uprising.* New York, NY: Routledge.

Bird, Isabella. (1856/1966). *The Englishwoman in America* (Reprint edition). London, UK: Toronto, University of Toronto Press. (First published 1856.)

Birkett, Dea. (1989). *Spinsters abroad: Victorian lady explorers.* Oxford, UK: Basil Blackwell.

Buntman, Barbara (1996). Bushman images in South African tourist advertising: The case of Kagga Kamma. In Pippa Skotnes, *Miscast* (pp. 271–279). Cape Town: University of Capetown Press.

Butler, William. (1872). *The great lone land,* London, UK: Sampson.

Canada Steamship Lines, Ltd. Passenger Department. (1915). *Niagara to the Sea.*

Cave of the Winds. (circa 1880s). *Providence, Rhode Island Journal.*

Clifford, James. (1997). *Routes: Travel and translation in the late twentieth century.* Cambridge, MA: Harvard University Press.

Cobble, Dorothy Sue. (1991). *Dishing it out: Waitresses and their unions in the twentieth century.* Urbana, IL: University of Illinois Press.

Complete illustrated guide to Niagara Falls and vicinity, the. (circa 1880). Niagara Falls, : N.Y. Gazette Printing Company.

Coombes, Annie E. (1994). *Reinventing Africa: Museums, material culture and popular imagination in late Victorian and Edwardian England.* New Haven: Yale University Press.

Culler, Jonathan. (1981). Semiotics of tourism. *American Journal of Semiotics, 1*(1–2), 127–140.

Curry, Frederick C. (1946). The discovery of the cave of the winds. *Ontario Historical Society Papers and Records, 27,* 19–22.

Davis, Janet. (1993). Spectacles of South Asia at the American circus, 1890–1940. *Visual Anthropology, 6,* 127–133.

Day, Samuel Phillips. (1880). *Life and society in America.* London, UK: Newman and Co.

Dow, Charles Mason. (Ed.). (1921). *Anthology and bibliography of Niagara Falls* (Vol. 1). Albany, NY: J.B. Lyon.

Dubinsky, Karen. (1999). *The second greatest disappointment: Honeymooning and tourism at Niagara Falls.* Toronto, ON: Between the Lines.

Foster, Shirley. (1990). *Across new worlds: Nineteenth century women travellers and their writing,* New York, NY: Harvester.

Francis, Daniel. (1992). *The imaginary Indian: The image of the Indian in Canadian culture.* Vancouver, BC: Arsenal Pulp Press.

Furlough, Ellen. (1993, Spring). Packaging pleasures: Club Mediterranee and French consumer culture, 1950–1968. *French Historical Studies, 18*(1), 65–81.

Hall, Catherine. (1998). Going a-trolloping: Imperial man travels the empire. In Clare Midgley (Ed.), *Gender and imperialism* (pp. 180–199). Manchester, UK: Manchester University Press.

Hughes, Thomas. (1895). *Vacation rambles.* London, UK: Macmillan.

The humbugs of Niagara Falls exposed. (1884). Niagara Falls, New York: Suspension Bridge Company.

Goldie, Terry. (1989). *Fear and temptation: The image of the Indigene in Canadian, Australian and New Zealand literature*. Montreal, PQ: McGill-Queen's University Press.

Golovin, Ivan. (1856). *Stars and stripes, or American impressions*. London, UK: W. Freeman.

Greenhill, Ralph, & Mahoney, Thomas. (1969). *Niagara*. Toronto, ON: University of Toronto Press.

Irwin, William. (1996). *The new Niagara: Tourism, technology and the landscape of Niagara Falls, 1776–1917*. University Park, PA: Pennsylvania State University Press.

Jackson, Moses. (1886). *To America and back: A holiday run*. London, UK: McQuordale.

Jasen, Patricia. (1995). *Wild things: Nature, culture and tourism in Ontario, 1790–1914*. Toronto, ON: University of Toronto Press.

Killan, Gerald. (1975, June). Mowat and a park policy for Niagara Falls, 1873–1877. *Ontario History, 70*, 115–135.

Lutz, Catherine A. & Collins, Jane L. (1993). *Reading national geographic*. Chicago: University of Chicago Press.

Marshall, Walter Gore. (1881) *Through America*. New York: Arno Press. (Original work published 1881)

McClintock, Anne. (1994). *Imperial leather: Race, gender and sexuality in the colonial contest*. New York, NY: Routledge.

McGreevy, Patrick. (1994). *Imagining Niagara: The meaning and making of Niagara Falls*. Amherst, MA: University of Massachusetts Press.

McKay, Ian. (1994). *The quest of the folk: Antimodernism and cultural selection in twentieth-century Nova Scotia*. Montreal, PQ: McGill-Queen's University Press.

McKinsey, Elizabeth. (1985). *Niagara, icon of the American sublime*. Cambridge, MA: Cambridge University Press.

Melman, Billie. (1992). *Women's orients: English women and the Middle East, 1718–1918*. London, UK: Macmillan.

Mills, Sara. (1991). *Discourses of difference: An analysis of women's travel writing and colonialism*. London, UK: Routledge.

Minh-ha, Trinh T. (1994). Other than myself/my other self. In George Robertson et al. (Eds.), *Travellers' tales: Narratives of home and displacement*. London, UK: Routledge.

Monck, Frances E. (1891). *My Canadian leaves*. London, UK: Richard Bentley.

Morse, S.D. (1896). *Greater Niagara*. Niagara Falls, Ontario: Gazette Printing House.

Moyles R.G., & Owram, Douglas. (1988). *Imperial dreams and colonial realities: British views of Canada, 1880–1914*. Toronto, ON: University of Toronto Press.

Niagara Falls: Nature's grandest wonder. (circa 1890). Buffalo: Matthews and Northrup.

Offenbach, Jacques. (1875). *America and the Americans*. London, UK: William Reeves.

Pattullo, Polly. (1996). *Last resorts: The cost of tourism in the Caribbean*. London, UK: Cassell.

Pfeiffer, Ida. (1855). *A lady's second journey round the world*. London, UK: Longman Brown.

Phillips, Richard. (1997). *Mapping men and empire: A geography of adventure*. London, UK: Routledge.

Phillips, Ruth B. (1991). Consuming identities: Curiosity, souvenir and images of indianness in nineteenth-century Canada. David Dunton Lecture, Carleton University, Ottawa, Ontario.

Phillips, Ruth. (1995) Why not tourist art? Significant silences in Native American museum representations. In Gyan Prakash (Ed.), *After colonialism: Imperial histories and postcolonial displacements* (pp. 98–125). Princeton, NJ: Princeton University Press.

Pratt, Mary Louise. (1992). *Imperial eyes: Travel writing and transculturation*. New York, NY: Routledge.

Rassool, Ciraj, & Witz, Leslie. (1996). South Africa: A world in one country, moments in international tourist encounters with wildlife, the primitive and the modern. *Cahiers d'Etudes africaines*, 143, 335–371.

Rickard, Clinton. (1971). *Fighting Tuscarora: The autobiography of Chief Clinton Richard*. Syracuse, NY: Syracuse University Press.

Robertson, George, et al. (Eds.). (1994). *Travellers' tales: Narratives of home and displacement*. London, UK: Routledge.

Roper, Edward. (1891). *By track and trail: A journey through Canada*. London, UK: W.H. Allen

Runte, Alfred. (1973, January). Beyond the spectacular: The Niagara Falls preservation campaign. *New York Historical Society Quarterly*, 57(1), 30–50.

Rydell, Robert W. (1993). *World of fairs: The century-of-progress expositions*. Chicago: University of Chicago Press.

Sala, George. (1865). *My diary in America in the midst of the war*. London, UK: Tinseley Brothers

Sears, John. (1989). *Sacred places: American tourist attractions in the nineteenth century*. New York, NY: Oxford University Press.

Sedgewick, Eve. (1990). *Epistemology of the closet*. Berkeley, CA: University of California Press.

Shields, Rob. (1991). *Places on the margin: Alternative geographies of modernity*. London, UK: Routledge.

Spurr, David. (1993). *The rhetoric of empire: Colonial discourse in journalism, travel writing and imperial administration*. Durham, NC: Duke University Press.

Stowe, William. (1994). *Going abroad: European travel in nineteenth-century American culture*. Princeton, NJ: Princeton University Press.

Taylor, Frank Fonda. (1993). *To hell with paradise — A history of the Jamaican tourist industry*. Pittsburgh, PA: University of Pittsburgh Press.

Thomas, Owen A. (1995). *Niagara's freedom trail: A guide to African-Canadian history on the Niagara Peninsula*. Thorold, ON: Region Niagara Tourist Council.

Torgovnick, Mariana. (1990). *Gone primitive: Savage intellects, modern lives*. Chicago: University of Chicago Press.

Tyndall, John. (1873, July). Niagara Falls. *Eclectic Magazine of Foreign Literature, Science and Art*, XVIII, p. 26.

Karen Dubinsky

Urry, John. (1990). *The tourist gaze leisure and travel in contemporary societies*. London, UK: Sage.

Welsh, Thomas. (1977). The early years of the Queen Victoria Niagara Falls Parks Commission. Unpublished M.A. Thesis, Queen's University.

Wilson, Alexander. (1991). *The culture of nature: North American landscape from Disney to the Exxon Valdez*. Toronto, ON: Between the Lines.

Winks, Robin. (1971). *The blacks in Canada: A history*. Montreal: McGill-Queen's University Press.

Questions for Discussion

1. Query the possible invisibility of Jewishness as a bodily marker. Does invisibility create the potential for certain privileges that "visible minorities" cannot attain or is invisibility just another machination of racism?

2. How are nations invested in the creation and proliferation of intergroup racism? How do economic, immigration and social policies contribute to intra/intergroup racism?

3. Nelson's definition of home is informed by the emotional state of the subject and their psychic connectedness to a geographical site. To what extent can diasporic migrants return "home"?

4. The term "primitive" has been based upon an absence of cultural relativity? What is "primitive", and who defines it? Can Western Culture be seen as primitive?

5. How can we account for the simultaneous marginalization of the First Nations and the exploitation of their culture for commercial gain? Is there something inherently colonial about tourism?

6. What are some modern-day contact zones?

7. To what extent do we encourage civilizations to perform a static racialized notion of their culture for a touristic gaze?

8. Dubinsky notes that although marginalized subjects (Natives, Blacks, Irish, etc.) would have had some degree of agency and potential for resistance with the contact zone(s) of nineteenth-century Niagra Tourism, recouping their thoughts and voices is difficult due to the absence of literary and scholarly evidence. Are there alternative methods or sources for recouping the voices of the marginalized within this context?

9. Nelson uses music lyrics to demonstrate cultural resistance. How can other art forms be harnessed for liberatory ends? Is such "use" of art problematic?

5

Complexity of
Intersectionallity
and
Performance of
Racial Identity

Race

 cannot be thoroughly analyzed in the abstract, nor in a vacuum, ignoring the impact of other social constructs and forces that operate to either minimize or exacerbate the consequence of race. Race intersects with just about every other variable one can conceptualize, including, gender, religion, ethnicity, sexual orientation, class, immigration status, language, culture, age, ability and any other social categorization and construction. This part examines this intersectionality in the Canadian context and also addresses the appropriation of a racial identity through performance — how one can adopt a set of performative tropes, be it speech, dress, posture, etc., associated with a certain racial, national and cultural identity.

The first essay, "Speak White! Language and Race in the Social Construction of Frenchness in Canada", explores the intersection of language and race. By examining the historical stigma surrounding the French language in Canada, this essay reveals a raced dynamic in the contested construction of Canadianness. This essay illustrates that language and race are two axis used to center discriminatory practices. Josée Makropoulos explores both the British marginalization of white French populations and the later white French marginalization of Black (people of colour) French populations. Important questions are raised: linguistically, who gets to be Canadian and racially, who gets to be French?

The next essay, "Jack Canuck Meets John Chinaman: Race, Nation, Class and the Masculine Dimensions of Chinese Racialization in Canada to 1923", highlights the intersection between race, gender and sexuality. This essay recognizes the gendered historical distinction made between white Anglo Saxon males and Chinese males in Canada on the basis of race, culture and ethnicity.

The third essay, "Performing Desire: Hip-Hop, Identification, and the Politics of Becoming Black", examines the intersection of race, nationality, language and gender and focuses on the way in which young recent immigrants from Africa attempted to "become black". This essay maintains that societal perceptions of racial identity are disseminated through the media, assessed by young people, modified and adopted in order to perform some version of racial identity. As Awad Ibrahim argues, the possibilities for such racial performance are often imposed upon subjects from the outside in.

Considered in total, the essays reveal the complexity of racial categorization. The contributors essentially explore the fiction of a pure racial articulation. That is, the essays reveal just how truly constructed — be that socially, culturally, gender-wise and politically — race really is.

13

Speak White!
Language and Race in the Social Construction of Frenchness in Canada

Josée Makropoulos

Sociology and Equity Ph.D. Candidate
Ontario Institute for Studies in Education
of the University of Toronto
Toronto

I wish to thank the editors, Camille Nelson and Charmaine Nelson, for providing excellent feedback and suggestions on the previous version of this text. My sincere thanks to the two blind reviewers for their insightful comments, as well to Fred Dufresne for his commentaries on the earlier draft of the paper.

Josée Makropoulos

Introduction

While the concept of race is not biologically determined in scientific terms, it is widely used as a social category among English-speaking academics in Canada.[1] Racial identities are understood in relation to locations of structural advantage and disadvantage in society. From this viewpoint, the societal issue of race must be understood and acknowledged in order to resist and challenge racism, imperialism and (neo)colonialism.

The social understanding of race permeates all aspects of Canadian life, and significantly influences the dominant operational definition of "Frenchness" in the country. For lack of a better term, I have coined "Frenchness" as a social construction where race and the French language play a predominant role in setting up the boundaries of identification, recognition and participation in Francophone life. The concept of Frenchness also involves intersectionality with other social categories, like religion, class, ethnicity, sexual orientation and gender.

In many ways, I outwardly correspond to the normative understanding of Frenchness as a result of my whiteness and because I learned French as a "mother tongue". My baptism as a Roman Catholic also coincides with the traditional religious/racial origins of French Canadians. At the same time, I do not meet the definition of *Franco-Ontarien de souche* (Old-stock Franco-Ontarian), nor of *Francophone pure-laine* (Francophone made of pure-wool), since my father is Greek. I also learned English as a complementary home language and was exposed to the Greek language and culture while growing up.

This essay will illustrate in greater scope how Frenchness integrates whiteness and the nativity of the French language to maintain the status quo. This goal will be accomplished through the discursive analysis of Frenchness; it is defined and deployed in a variety of contexts, like legislative texts, political speeches, government publications, association documents, literary productions and newspaper articles. These examples will be discussed in relation to three discursive ideologies identified by Heller and Budach[2] (**traditional**, **modernizing** and **globalizing**) that shape what it means to be a minority Francophone living in the Canadian context.

---

[1] *See* Dei, 1996; Razack, 1998; Solomon & Rezai-Rashiti, 2001.

[2] Heller & Budach, 1999.

Beginnings: Frenchness as a Common Experience of Marginalization

The **traditional** discourse identified by Heller and Budach[3] is imbedded in the early life experiences of French-Canadian settlers. The traditional discourse is characterized by a common experience of marginalization that was accompanied by the stigmatization of Frenchness and the need to maintain good relations with the English majority. This discourse also emphasizes the need to develop internal forms of solidarity in order to confront the dominance introduced by the English-speaking majority. Traditional discourses on Frenchness incorporate the notion of race to identify a group of people who shared a common language, religion and cultural practices. The experience of racism at the hands of the English majority also gave rise to different brands of French-Canadian nationalism that, in turn, integrated racial categorizations.

Several historical examples illustrate the early marginalization of French Canadians. For instance, the expulsion[4] of the Acadians exemplifies their racialized treatment at the hands of the British, even though both groups shared white European origins. The Acadians (also known as the French Neutrals) had settled in the Maritimes from the onset of the seventeenth century. Acadians were ordered to take an unqualified oath of allegiance to the British Crown in 1755, and their refusal to comply was interpreted as a sign of treason by the British. Over 10,000 Acadians, or about 75 percent of the population, were deported between 1755 and 1763. This tragic event has not yet been recognized or addressed in a formal apology by the British Crown.

Lord Durham, who was appointed the title and functions of High Commissioner and Governor General of British North America, also upheld the notion of British superiority over the French. The following excerpt, cited from his 1839 report[5] illustrates that Lord Durham considered the English a superior race that could dominate the French at the intellectual, economic, social and physical levels. He felt it was important to put an end to French nationalism in order to "integrate" French people into the English race.

> It will be acknowledged by every one who has observed the progress of Anglo-Saxon colonization in America, that sooner or later the English race was sure to predominate even numerically in Lower Canada, as they predominate already by their superior knowledge, energy, enterprise, and wealth. The error, therefore, to which the present contest must be attributed, is the vain endeavour to preserve a French Canadian nationality in the midst of Anglo-American colonies and states.

The idea that the French could become English citizens was essentially based on the desire to build on their whiteness while suppressing their language and culture. An example that illustrates this desire is the implementation of Regulation 17 in Ontario schools from 1912 until 1927. The provincial government introduced this repressive policy in order to impose English on all stu-

---

[3] Ibid.
[4] Paratte, 1998; Dow, 1986.
[5] Lucas, 1912.

dents, especially those attending French and bilingual schools. This transitional "bilingual" program essentially discouraged the general usage of French as a language of instruction beyond grade two, and only allowed one hour of French instruction in upper grades.

The general mobilization against Regulation 17 gave rise to a collective memory of Franco-Ontarian identity based on a common struggle and victory.[6] For instance, Francophones became involved in political-legal contestations and public forums organized with the French Catholic clergy. The Québec government came to their aid by transferring funds to help support French-language instruction in Ontario. The racialized condition of Franco-Ontarians became apparent in the establishment of clandestine French classes. The fight against the anti-French movement also involved the active contribution of philanthropic Anglophones of the *Unity League,*[7] who fought for French language rights and the abolishment of this law.

In spite of French-English alliances, sentiments of antagonism against the French persisted in Ontario during the 1940s and 1950s. Personal narratives[8] of Franco-Torontonians indicate that they were often the target of racial slurs and remarks. They were reprimanded by English speakers about the inadequacy of their language when they spoke French in public areas like tramways or at work. Some Francophones were asked why they did not speak the "White people language", or were simply told to "Speak White." These comments reinforced the view that English was the only legitimate "voice" of whiteness, and that French should not be heard in public.

These examples indicate that several attempts were made to take the "French" out of "Frenchness" and, eventually, "assimilate" White Francophones into English. These conditions set the groundwork for the emergence of different brands of French-Canadian nationalism that, in turn, offered competing perspectives on the traditional understanding and boundaries of Frenchness.

The hanging of Métis leader Louis Riel in 1885 instigated a traditional form of French-Canadian nationalism. The aftermath of his execution was accompanied by a growing sense of nationalism among Canadians of French origin who identified with Riel as a martyr and a hero. French-Canadian statesman Louis-Honoré Mercier reinforced this sentiment of indignation by proclaiming, "Our brother, Louis Riel, is dead."[9] This appeal calls for a sense of unity between the French and the Métis (French/Native ancestry) as "brothers" in the same "family" or "blood line" who have a common struggle. The stirring of nationalist sentiments also provided Mercier with the opportunity to win the premiership of Québec (1886–1892), during which he developed the autonomist stand of the province in its relations with the federal government, which promoted English interests.

Another important leader in the promotion of French-Canadian unity is Henri Bourassa, who won the Québec elections in 1911. Quotations taken from

---

[6] *See* Choquette, 1987; Welch, 1988; Gervais, 1996.

[7] Choquette, 1980.

[8] Trudelle & Fortier, 1987.

[9] An Act to Revoke the Conviction of Louis David Riel, November 22, 1996, H-C (Bill C-297).

a 1912 speech[10] shed light on Bourassa's conception of Frenchness, which values language as an important vehicle to preserve a race:

> When a race ceases to express its thoughts and feelings in its own language, the language that was grown with it and been formed along with its ethnic temperament, it is lost as a race. The preservation of language is absolutely necessary for the preservation of a race, its spirit, character, and temperament ...
>
> I have proved that the Canadian Confederation is the result of a contract between the two races in Canada, French and English, based on equality and recognizing equal rights and reciprocal duties. Canadian Confederation will only last as long as this equality of rights is recognized as the basis of the public right in Canada, from Halifax to Vancouver.

In the first passage, the concept of race is broadly defined as a national group with a distinct set of values and emotional characteristics. The descriptors of race ("spirit", "character", "ethnic temperament", "thought" and "feelings") stir feelings and sentiments that are difficult to evaluate in objective terms. In the second passage, the notions of race and language are explicitly linked to the modern framework of Canadian citizenship. Bourassa challenges the "not-quite-white" status of French in relation to English and emphasizes the importance of equal and reciprocal duties. This discourse implicitly refers to the preservation and protection of the white race in the Canadian Confederation and in particular, to the place reserved for Whites of French origin.

The idea of racial and linguistic purity as markers of Frenchness is explicitly formulated in the traditional discourse set forth by the Abbé Lionel Adolphe Groulx (1878–1967), who is renowned as the "spiritual father" of modern Québec.[11] This traditional discourse developed the ideological groundwork for Québec nationalism based on the notion of territorial sovereignty. The doctoral research conducted by Esther Delisle exposes Groulx's legacy of anti-Semitism that was also apparent in various French nationalist circles during the 1930s.[12] The following two quotations from Groulx's book *La naissance d'une race*[13] [*The Birth of a Race*] exemplify the tensions of his traditional understanding of Frenchness that wants to move towards modern autonomy:

> And that disposes enough of that so-called *métissage* of our ancestors with the Red-Skins of Canada, *métissage* whose legend continues to spread in intellectual and academic circles where we attempt to establish, with the help of this lie, our character as an inferior race. The most astonishing and hurtful for us is that this legend obtained and maintains a great deal of credit even in France ... (My translation, p. 23).
>
> It is crucial to show that the small group of our ancestors possessed a great strength: a perfect homogeneity. Ethnic, social, religious and moral homogeneity, homogeneity and intrinsic values, nothing lacking to constitute a seed of elites ..] (My translation, p. 19)

---

[10] H. Bourassa., *La Langue française et l'avenir de notre race* (Discours prononcé devant le Premier Congrès de la Langue Française au Canada, à la 6e séance générale, le 28 juin, 1913, extrait du compte rendu du Congrès. Québec, Imprimerie de l'Action sociale).

[11] Claude, 1967.

[12] Delisle, 1992.

[13] Groulx, 1919.

The traditional condition of the French as a marginal group is apparent in the first passage through its association with the notion of "inferiority" that, according to Groulx, is sustained by the English and in France. This brings Groulx to negate the existence of the Métis, which he considers a "legend" that undermines the "purity" and legitimacy of French-Canadian whiteness. In the second passage, Groulx promotes the idea of a modern French elite that shares common ethnic, social, religious and moral values. In this regard, Groulx's view of Frenchness involves the racial demarcation of whiteness.

Another example of traditional French-Canadian nationalism concerns *l'Ordre de Jacques Cartier*, commonly referred to as *La Patente*. This secret society was founded in 1926 by Francophone civil servants with the help of the French-Catholic clergy. The society remained active for almost 40 years and worked towards the attainment of rights for French Canadians and the advancement of national prosperity.[14] However, *La Patente* was not representative of all segments of French-Canadian society. No women were admitted into this secret society that was only open to practising Catholic men who embraced their ideals. The emphasis on Roman Catholicism also reinforced the racial boundaries of Frenchness that excluded Jews[15] and other denominations.

Promoting Frenchness within the Realm of Whiteness

The **modernizing** discourse identified by Heller and Budach[16] emerges during the 1950s, when the francophone elite began to develop modern strategies of mobilization to promote the French language as a common rallying point. The modern vision of the Québec government promotes the idea of unilingual French zones at the institutional and territorial levels. Francophones outside Québec similarly embraced the modern ideal of establishing autonomous French spaces. These changes significantly influence the conceptualization of Frenchness in Canadian society. The modernizing discourse of the State minimizes the acknowledgement of race as a social reality in order to appear more inclusive and democratic. At the same time, the racialized condition of Frenchness as a victimized condition surfaces in modern literary and academic productions, thus suggesting that Frenchness is not fully white through its identification with, and appropriation of, blackness.

Early modernizing discourses on Frenchness exemplify the tensions between the traditional conception of race and the need to develop modern principles of democracy. An example that illustrates these tensions is the manner in which Prime Minister Lester B. Pearson responded to the mobilization of the French-

---

[14] *See* Reglement des C.O.J.C., août 1935.

[15] *See* Cyr, 1964.

[16] Heller & Budach, 1999.

speaking majority of Québec during the Quiet Revolution.[17] Pearson embraced modern ideals of democracy by appointing the Royal Commission on Bilingualism and Biculturalism (1963) to inquire into linguistic and cultural representation in the country. Meanwhile, the Royal Commission's mandate incorporated a traditional conception of race that is closely allied to Henri Bourassa's notion of equal French and English citizenship rights. This dichotomy is illustrated in the description of its mandate in the Commission's Preliminary Report:

> ... inquire into and report upon the existing state of bilingualism and biculturalism in Canada and to recommend what steps should be taken to develop the Canadian Confederation on the basis of an equal partnership between the two founding races, taking into account the contribution made by the other ethnic groups to the cultural enrichment of Canada ...[18]

The creed of the "two founding races" is developed in traditional terms through its association with language and culture as complementary forces. Colour and physical attributes are not explicitly stated, but the referral to "bilingualism" and "biculturalism" positions French and English as equal partners within the realm of whiteness. The modern discourse of inclusion is manifested through the desire to take into account "other ethnic groups", and recognize the cultural contribution of difference. This discourse, however, affirms the centrality of French and English whiteness and relegates everything else to the realm of "otherness". Furthermore, no attention is explicitly directed to the "place" or "role" of First Nations in the process of nation-building.

Despite these ambivalences, the Royal Commission developed a series of recommendations for promoting the French and English languages in Canada while recognizing the contribution of cultural diversity. Prime Minister Pierre Elliot Trudeau subsequently adopted the 1969 Official Languages Act,[19] which provided official language status to both French and English. In 1971, Trudeau also introduced the multicultural policy within a bilingual framework.[20] This policy refuted the "bicultural" thesis that was reproduced in the very name of the Royal Commission on Bilingualism and Biculturalism. By treating language and culture as two exclusive entities, the modern discourse on multiculturalism appeared inclusive of people of immigrant origin by attributing equal value to all cultures. At the same time, this allowed the government to restrict the role of "other" languages outside the parameters of the "official" bilingualism reserved for the two European languages of colonization.

The federal policy of multiculturalism within a bilingual framework was widely contested in the province of Québec. Several French Québeckers disliked

---

[17] For a brief history of the Quiet Revolution, see Québec history website of Marianopolis College as maintained by Claude Bélanger: http://www2.marianopolis.edu/quebechistory/readings/lesage.htm
[18] B&B Commission, 1965.

[19] This Act was replaced by the Official Languages Act, L.R. (1985), ch. 31. This legislation favoured the notion of transportable language rights across Canada developed from a personality approach. This did not take into account the notion of "bilingual districts" that was suggested by the Royal Commission.
[20] Government Response to Volume 4 of the report of the Royal Commission on Bilingualism and Biculturalism, Commissioners André Laurendeau and Davidson Dunton, to the House of Commons, October 8, 1971. Appendix to Hansard, October 8, 1971.

the notion of multiculturalism since biculturalism would have recognized French as one of the official national cultures in Canadian Confederation.[21] There was also the concern that the official bilingual framework presupposed the asymmetry of French and English, given their traditional inequalities. Subsequently, in 1981, the Government of Québec devised its own provincial plan, entitled *Autant de façons d'être Québécois*[22] (As many ways to be a Québecker). The mandate is reproduced below:

> This is inspired by a triple objective: assure the maintenance and the development of cultural communities and their specificity, sensitize Francophone Quebeckers about the contribution of cultural communities to our common heritage, and favour the integration of cultural communities in the society of Quebec and especially in sectors where they have until now been under-represented, particularly in the Public Service, a subject that the program addresses and proposes measures of improvement. (My translation, p. ii)

This passage does not explicitly refer to race but highlights the whiteness of French as a common language and important link to the "common heritage" of Québec, which benefits from "the contribution of cultural communities". This discourse promotes Habermas' notion of "living together" that calls for the intercultural understanding among communities who share the common goal of nation building. This plan also recognizes the concept of equity to assure the integration and social participation of historically under-represented citizens in the public service.

On a critical note, this ministry document uses ambiguous concepts that implicitly suggest that non-White people of French descent are not "real" Québeckers. Even though the title, *As many ways to be a Québecker*, suggests there are many ways to identify with Québec society, the terms "Francophone Québeckers" and "cultural communities" are used as two mutually exclusive terms. This discourse does not discuss the role of First Nations in this modernizing project, nor does it explain the place of Anglo-Québeckers who are white or of colour. In this regard, it is not obvious if French-speaking citizens of immigrant origin are "Francophone Québeckers" or how many generations it takes cultural and/or racial minorities to become "legitimate" members of Québec society. Of course, the negative comments made by Jacques Parizeau following the 1995 Québec referendum revealed that some provincial leaders believed, just as he did that Québec "belongs" only to Whites of French-European descent.

In spite of the State's attempts to avoid racial terminology, the modern ideology of the racialized condition of Frenchness permeated public discourse. A striking example is the concept of race and victimology that is captured in the expression "White Niggers of America," introduced as the title of Pierre Vallières' political manifesto.[23] This manifesto presents the ideological preoccupations of Vallières, who embraced an extreme left-wing vision of Québec revo-

---

[21] Labelle, Rocher & Rocher, 1995.

[22] Québec, 1981.

[23] I am indebted to professor Sharene Razack for pointing out to me the concept of "White Niggers", introduced in radical French nationalist discourses to describe the condition of whites of French ancestry as "second-class whites". Any interpretation errors remain my own. *See* Vallières, 1968; Pinkham, 1971.

lution during his involvement with the *Front de libération du Québec* (FLQ).[24] For instance, Vallières explains that his participation in the FLQ was motivated by the fact that he could no longer "bear to be a nigger" and wished to "free" French Canadians from their "condition as niggers in America" (p. 281). He also lamented the condition of "White niggers" who suffer the consequences of "white racism", which makes it difficult for them to "overthrow imperialism, and found a new society on a completely different basis from that of the present society" (p. 53).

Vallières appropriates racist imagery to denounce the social conditions of the Francophone Québécois and, in particular, the working class of French white ancestry. In this respect, Vallières recognizes the intersectionality of racial identity and social class in the politics of the modern industrializing economy. As Clarke points out, Vallières was likely unaware that Thomas Chandler Haliburton (1796–1865) had used the concept of "White Niggers" to describe the poor white Nova Scotians who were "sold annually on sessions day, to the lowest bidder for a year."[25] However, both references to the "White Nigger" emphasize the "blackening" of labour performed by lower-class Whites.

In his manifesto, Vallières denounces white racism against French Whites at the expense of racism exerted against visible minorities living in Québec. He argues that "in Quebec there is no "black" problem" (p. 21), in spite of the presence of long-established African-Canadian communities and Caribbean immigration from the late fifties onward.[26] In most cases, Francophone Black immigrants come from former French colonies that share a history of slavery, imperialism and colonialism. Several studies also discuss the relationship between Québec nationalism and racism directed towards visible minority groups in the province, including Blacks of French- and English-speaking backgrounds.[27]

Another example of a racialized discourse on Frenchness is the poster pocm *Speak White,* written by Michèle Lalonde at the height of the Quiet Revolution of Québec. The title reintroduces the racial slur "Speak White", which that was traditionally used by Anglophones to denigrate French. However, Lalonde appropriates the notion of "Speak White" and uses the technique of code switching to challenge English oppression and to develop a sense of pride and unity among Francophones.

> Speak white
> Tell us that God is a great big shot
> And that we're paid to trust him
> **Speak white**

---

[24] Members of the FLQ promoted a socialist vision of revolution in order to secure Québec independence. Although most members were pacifists, there did exist radicals that became involved in terrorist actions involving bombings and kidnappings, which escalated during the October Crisis in 1970.

[25] Clarke, 1994, p. 35. Clarke does not mention if these poor Nova Scotians were of Acadian descent, but historical evidence does indicate that some Nova-Scotian Acadians who avoided the Deportation by fleeing into the woods were later imprisoned and worked as unpaid labourers in extreme poverty (*see* Paratte, 1998).

[26] Statistique Canada, 1999.

[27] Labelle, Salée & Frenette, 2001.

c'est une langue riche
pour acheter
mais pour se vendre
mais pour se vendre à perte d'âme
mais pour se vendre[28]

In this quote, Lalonde presents English as the language of authority that imposes itself as racially superior to French. The French response offers a voice of *résistance* that describes English as a language for the "rich" and "buying", but one that involves "selling oneself" and "one's soul". In this respect, the relationship between English and French in this poem incarnates traditional racial inequalities between both languages. At the same time, the use of code switching from English to French asserts the need to develop a modern sense of French autonomy. This is illustrated in the conclusion of the poem, which declares, "We're doing fine, we are not alone", in English and then addresses the Francophone in French to say, "We know that we are not alone" (my translation).

Thomas Maxwell's book *The Invisible French: The French in Metropolitan Toronto* also presents racial imagery to describe Frenchness as a state of invisibility.[29] A central argument in this book is that cultural assimilation undermines the retention of the French ancestral heritage that was "invisible" in English-speaking multicultural Toronto during the 1960s and 1970s. Maxwell elaborates this idea through a comparative analysis between Franco-Torontonians and the structural pattern of "invisible ethnic minorities" identified by Abner Cohen, who conducted most of his research in Africa.[30] Maxwell's use of the social metaphor of invisibility is, however, limited, since French Whites are not different from English Whites in ways that are (in)visible to the eye. The racial difference resides in the marginal voice of French that is traditionally silenced by English.

A classic account of invisibility as a racial condition is presented in Ralph Ellison's novel *Invisible Man,* which concerns the traditional Black American experience.[31] Ellison's story is narrated in the first person by a nameless educated black man who experiences oppression as a result of his condition of invisibility in a white world. In the prologue, the narrator introduces the concept of invisibility as a metaphor to describe how he is perceived in the beholder's inner eye. The concept of social invisibility is acknowledged as a condition that is imposed upon him as a result of his blackness. This blackness goes beyond the so-called "biochemical accident to [his] epidermis" to justify why he is not "seen" as a whole person. The narrator ultimately identifies himself as invisible to challenge oppression imposed by a white world.

Another version of the *Invisible Man* is depicted by Franco-Ontarian writer Patrice Desbiens in his narrative account *L'Homme Invisible/The Invisible Man: Un recit/A Story,* which describes the minority French condition in modernizing

---

[28] Lalonde, 1974.

[29] Maxwell, 1977.

[30] Cohen, 1974, pp. 91–98.

[31] Ellison, 1952/1990.

times.[32] The main protagonist in Desbiens' story is another nameless man referred to as *l'Homme Invisible*/The Invisible Man, who searches for his identity in a country where he feels invisible. A slightly different version of the same truth is exemplified in the story by presenting a French version on the left side of the page and an English version on the right side of the page. This literary technique signals the inability to translate the French experience into English and vice versa. The duality of the French and English worlds exemplifies the Franco-Ontarian condition as one that has two languages and two identities, and is torn between two worlds. This story also offers a literary critique of the federal promotion of official bilingualism by showing that the protagonist's French side is fading, thus contributing to his death (or assimilation) in English-speaking Ontario.

Normalizing Frenchness and Reclaiming Blackness

The third type of discursive orientation identified by Heller and Budach[33] is the **globalizing** discourse that emerged in the early eighties and is currently in full development. The globalizing discourse is characterized by the neo-liberal orientation of the State and the massive restructuring of the traditional economic base that directly impacts Francophones. These social changes bring into question the minority status of Francophones living outside of Québec, who are increasingly perceived as occupying a privileged status in the global market because of their knowledge of French and English.

Anthony Giddens also points out that globalization exemplifies the tensions of modernity, as the need to normalize diversification is confronted with the need to maintain the authenticity of local identities and affiliations.[34] These tensions are embodied in global discourses on Frenchness. On one hand, the State articulates a normalized discourse on Frenchness based on the criterion of Canadian citizenship and the knowledge of French as a first language. On the other hand, the authenticity of race is claimed by Francophone visible minorities whose blackness constitutes an additional layer of marginality.

A globalizing discourse on Frenchness was introduced in 1982 through the adoption of Section 23 in the Canadian Charter of Rights and Freedoms.[35] This constitutional provision was the first to officially provide collective citizenship rights to the two official language minority groups of the country that include Anglophones in Québec and Francophones in the rest of Canada. The overall objective of Section 23 is to guarantee official-language minority education at

---

[32] Desbiens, 1981.

[33] Heller & Budach, 1999.

[34] Giddens, 1990.

[35] Canadian Charter of Rights and Freedoms, Part 1 of the Constitutional Law of 1982, Annex B.

the primary and secondary levels across Canada.[36] However, this legal framework adopts a normalizing conception of Frenchness that excludes many French-speaking minorities from being recognized as legitimate Right-Holders to minority French education.

Minority Language Educational Rights
23.(1) Citizens of Canada
(a) whose first language learned and still understood is that of the English or French linguistic minority population of the province in which they reside, or
(b) who have received their primary school instruction in Canada in English or French and reside in a province where the language in which they received that instruction is the language of the English or French linguistic minority population of the province, have the right to have their children receive primary and secondary school instruction in that language in that province.

(2) Citizens of Canada of whom any child has received or is receiving primary or secondary school instruction in English or French in Canada, have the right to have all their children receive primary and secondary school instruction in the same language.

(3) The right of citizens of Canada under subsections (1) and (2) to have their children receive primary and secondary school instruction in the language of the English or French linguistic minority population of a province
(a) applies wherever in the province the number of children of citizens who have such a right is sufficient to warrant the provision to them out of public funds of minority language instruction; and
(b) includes, where the number of those children so warrants, the right to have them receive that instruction in minority language educational facilities provided out of public funds.

The discursive analysis of Section 23 reveals that it does not consider language and race as interlocking forms of oppression.[37] This disposition also requires Canadian citizenship and the knowledge of French as a mother tongue, and/or a "family" relationship with French primary and/or secondary schools in Canada. Landed immigrants and refugees are not recognized as Right-Holders. Section 23 might still not recognize Francophone immigrants who do acquire Canadian citizenship, especially if they received their primary education outside Canada and if their native tongue is not French.

The constitutional framework regulating access to minority French education is incorporated in the legal definition of who is a Right-Holder to Franco-Ontarian education. More specifically, Section 23 is integrated in Subsection 288 of the 1990 Education Act of the province of Ontario to define the concepts of "French-speaking ratepayer" and "French-speaking person".[38] These definitions of Frenchness subsequently exclude immigrant parents as well as "French-speaking" Canadians who speak a language other than French or English as their first language.

---

[36] An implicit objective of Section 23 was to introduce the "Canada" clause that directly challenged the legitimacy of Bill 101. The Supreme Court of Canada subsequently ruled that Québec could not impose French-language education on children whose parents had received their primary schooling in English elsewhere in Canada. However, the French school requirement is maintained for immigrants.
[37] Makropoulos, 2002.
[38] R.S.O. 1990, c. E-2, s. 292.

Immigrants and ethnic minorities who want to send their children to French schools can be evaluated on a case-by-case basis. Subsection 289 of the 1990 Education Act states that students who do not meet the "French-speaking person" criterion can be admitted to French minority language programs at the discretionary power of a three-member admission committee appointed by the school board or school authority. This provision was established to accommodate Anglophone families who want to enrol their children in a minority French school.[39] However, the idea of subjecting children of French immigrant backgrounds to admission committees[40] contradicts equity and multicultural principles recognized by Section 15 of the Canadian Charter of Rights and Freedoms and the 1988 Multiculturalism Act.[41]

Another barrier imposed on immigrant Francophones is the reluctance to allow the utterance of "ethnic voices" in the Franco-Ontarian educational system. More precisely, the language-planning policy for minority French schools insists on the primacy of French as the main language of teaching and communication. This policy is similar to the Québec intercultural model insofar as Franco-Ontarian schools aim to promote openness to cultural diversity through the means of French as a common language. The 2000 curriculum guideline of the Ontario Ministry of Education and Training insists on **only French** as a general rule of conduct in the school:

> **French, language of teaching**
> It is important to insist on the mastery of French in all courses, with the exception of language courses other than French. Hence, the French language will be used in all educational programs and learning activities, if they take place in school or outside of school, and will use French didactic material for students with the exception of the following cases:
> - for the teaching of a language other than French;
> - when the expectations and the learning contents of the program guidelines require the usage of another language;
> - in particular circumstances, like the visit of an invited personality or in emergencies when the health or the securities of students are in danger. (My translation, p. 4)[42]

According to this policy, non-official languages, such as heritage languagesor indigenous languages, are not "admitted" in Ontario French-language schools, with the exception of the enumerated cases. [43] Heller points out that attempts to counteract the assimilatory pressures of English sometimes lead to exclusionary practices towards students of immigrant backgrounds.[44] Her research in a Toronto French high school shows that many teachers repeat the well known phrase "Parlez français!" [Speak French!] in classrooms and in the

---

[39] Heller, 1994.

[40] Concerns have been raised in Saskatchewan about the access to French language schools for children of Francophone immigrants. *See* Jedwab, 2002, p. 37.

[41] Canadian Multiculturalism Act, R.S., 1985, c. 24 (1988, c. 31).

[42] Ministère de l'Éducation et de la Formation, 2000.

[43] The concept of heritage languages is currently used in the Canadian context to designate languages other than English and French that are spoken by members of multicultural communities. The term "heritage language" is not used in the context of indigenous languages spoken by First Nations.

[44] Heller, 1999.

hallways. The underlying ideology of this position is reiterated in the saying *L'anglais, ça s'attrappe*, which means that it is easy to "catch" the English language the way you would catch a cold. In this sense, Heller draws a vivid parallel by suggesting that school authorities go to much effort to ward off the English virus by creating quarantined French-language zones.

The saying, "Parlez français," or "Speak French," can also be compared with the saying "Speak White" insofar as minority languages are silenced in order to favour their assimilation into the dominant language(s) of whiteness. The main difference between the ideologies concerns the location of whiteness. The saying "Speak White" positions English as the language of whiteness, and French is silenced. The saying "Speak French" attempts to counteract the omnipresence of English by insisting on the right to speak French, at the risk of making it obligatory. French subsequently becomes white vis-à-vis ethnic and/or native voices that are relegated to silence. The process of imposing French as the only language of legitimacy in Franco-Ontarian schools also reproduces colonial relations of power that characterize the history of French linguistic imperialism.

The racial disadvantage of being of Francophone immigrant origin is apparent in their lack of visibility and integration in the Franco-Ontarian educational system. An emerging literature addresses the everyday manifestation of racist practices in Francophone institutions and in the area of minority French education.[45] A great deal of emphasis is placed on the need to develop multicultural curricula and inclusive teaching practices. Another concern is the pressing need to implement equitable hiring practices, since there is a low proportion of black teaching staff in French schools.

The ability to implement change through equitable provincial government programs has become increasingly problematic since 1995, when the conservative government of Mike Harris introduced the Job Quotas Repeal Act.[46] This law counteracts employment equity policies that recognize the concept of equity to favour the notion of equal opportunity. Provincial school boards are therefore not required by law to establish equitable hiring practices in order to ensure racial diversity among teaching and administrative personnel. The Ontario Ministry of Education and Training has adopted a "laissez-faire" policy with matters concerning anti-racist education by leaving this issue up to the discretion of local school boards, principals and individual teachers.

These social conditions led to a public outcry from community organizations and local groups who identify themselves as both Francophones and members of racial and ethnocultural minority groups. The discourse of reclaiming French blackness was officially formulated in 1995, with the foundation of the *Conseil pour l'intégration des francophones-minorités raciales* [Council for the integration of Francophones of racial minorities]). This council was mainly composed of Francophones of Black African descent who were established in Ottawa, Toronto and Windsor.[47] Their vision offers a new outlook on

---

[45] *See* Mujawamariya, 2002; Mianda, 1998; Berger, 1998; Dufresne, 2000.

[46] Job Quotas Repeal Act, Statutes of Ontario, chapter 4, 1995.

[47] Muse, Brihmi & Pierre, 1999.

Frenchness by reclaiming the authenticity of blackness in order to gain visibility in Franco-Ontarian institutions traditionally dominated by Whites of French ancestry.

An important project undertaken in 1998 by French-speaking visible minority community leaders was the creation of a Working Committee of Ethnocultural Francophone Communities of Ontario on Education.[48] This Committee consulted over 300 visible minority Francophones in Ontario about their preoccupations concerning the future of Franco-Ontarian education. The results presented in their report show that fully qualified visible minority Francophone teachers are over-represented in the area of supply work, but rarely secure permanent positions due to institutional racism. The report also discusses the "assets" of Francophones of immigrant backgrounds who want to contribute to the overall advancement of Francophone life in Canada and abroad.[49]

In January 2003, some Black Francophone activists presented a court challenge to ask the federal government to formally recognize French-speaking Blacks and racial and ethnocultural minorities as "Francophones" in the Canadian context. The excerpt reproduced below presents the main arguments at stake in this case:

- The Official Languages Act is inclusive in its reference to Francophones. It refers to two communities with equal rights: one of French language expression, and the other of English language expression.
- In the application of this law, only the people whose maternal language is French and their children are counted as Francophones.
- Canadians and immigrants, who come from countries whose national or official language is French, but whose maternal language is not French, are not recognized as Francophones. Their maternal language is a local foreign language, like Fon, Creole, Swahili, Lingala or Wolof for example.
- Because these people are not counted among the Francophone population, the allotment of resources for their integration does not take into account their needs for establishment, integration, development and actualization. (My translation)[50]

When coming to Canada, these people thought they were going to integrate into a French-language community; but, outside Québec, the services and resources in place cannot help them to integrate into the Francophone community.

This discourse contests the pervasiveness of whiteness in the Canadian Government's definition of who constitutes a "Francophone" in the country. The State's reluctance to admit French speakers whose native tongue is a foreign local language (like Creole or Lingala) helps maintain the status quo of French whiteness at the expense of Black and visible minority groups. This translates into additional layers of exclusion for Francophones of immigrant and visible minority groups whose needs and realities are not taken into account by current public policies and social services.

---

[48] Comtois, 1998, p. 8.

[49] Comité de travail des communautés ethnoculturelles francophones de l'Ontario sur l'éducation, 1998.

[50] Conseil économique et social d'Ottawa-Carleton, 2003.

Josée Makropoulos

Conclusion

"Speak White" is a central theme in this essay, as it illustrates the salience of language and race as two complementary forces in the social construction of Frenchness. In many ways, "Speak White" embodies the traditional experience of marginality and racism directed towards Whites of French ancestry. Modernizing public discourses on Frenchness integrate "Speaking White" as part of their racial heritage and, in some instances, also appropriate blackness and invisibility experienced by people of colour.

The modern notion of "Speak White" was democratically translated by the State into speaking English and French as the two official voices of bilingual whiteness in Canada, while the Québec Government strove to promote a French provincial voice. The voice of whiteness was not extended to First Nations or to heritage-language communities. However, visible minority Francophones are currently claiming their right to "Speak French" in institutions and networks where they lack visibility and recognition.

"Speaking White" has several implications for public reform in the Canadian context. First of all, it is important to acknowledge all forms of racism and exclusion experienced by members of *la francophonie*. This includes racism directed towards Whites of French ancestry, as well as linguistic and racial discrimination against Francophones of heritage-language communities and visible minority groups. All forms of oppression experienced by Francophones in Canada need to be addressed in order to counteract multiple facets of marginalization and their intersectionality with other social locations of disadvantage like religion, nationality, social class, ethnicity and race.

References

B&B Commission. (1965). *A preliminary report of the Royal Commission on Bilingualism and Biculturalism*. (Ottawa: Queen's Printer.

Berger. M-J (1998). Vers l'inclusion de l'évaluation égalitaire de la pluriethnicité francophone minoritaire. *Revue du Nouvel-Ontario, 21*), 115–133.

Choquette. R. (1980). *'Ontario français, historique*. Montréal, Québec: Éditions Études Vivantes.

Choquette, R. (1987). *La foi gardienne de la langue française en Ontario, 1900–1950*. Montréal: Éditions Bellarmin.

Clarke, G.-E. (1994). White niggers, black slaves: Slavery, race and class in T.C. Haliburton, *The Clockmaker. Nova Scotia Historical Review, 14*, 13–40.

Claude. R. (May 24, 1967). Le père spirituel du Québec moderne. *Le Devoir*. Republié dans *le Devoir* du 30 janvier 2000, à l'occasion du 90e anniversaire du journal.

Cohen, A. (1974). *Two-dimensional man* (pp. 91–98). Berkeley and Los Angeles: University of California Press.

Comité de travail des communautés ethnoculturelles francophones de l'Ontario sur l'éducation. (1998, June). *Saisir l'opportunité. Les états généraux complémentaires de l'éducation élémentaire et secondaire de langue française en Ontario. L'école franco-ontarienne de l'avenir*. Rapport de travail.

Comtois, M. (1998, May 4). Les afro-francophones veulent plus de professeurs. *Le Droit*, p. 8.

Conseil économique et social d'Ottawa-Carleton. (2003, January). *Une requête devant les tribunaux demande au gouvernement fédéra; de reconnaître en tant que francophones les membres des communautés noires, de minorités raciales et ethnoculturelles qui viennent de pays francophones*. Communiqué.

Cyr. R. (1964). *La Patente*. Montréal: Éditions du Jour.

Dei, G. (1996). *Anti-racism education: Theory and practice*. Halifax: Fernwood.

Delisle, E. (1992). *Le Traître et le Juif: Lionel Groulx, Le Devoir, et le déclin du nationalism d'extrème droite dans la province du Québec, 1929–1930*. Outremont, PQ: L'Étincelle. [Translated: *The traitor and the Jew: Anti-Semitism and the delirium of extremist right-wing nationalism in French Canada from 1929–1939*. Outremont, PQ: Robert Davies Publishing.

Desbiens, P. (1981). *L'Homme invisible/The invisible man. Un récit/A Story*. Sudbury, ON: Éditions Prise de Parole.

Dow, J-E. (1986). *The deportation of the Acadians* Ottawa: Minister of Supply and Services Canada.

Dufresne, F. (2000). *Les besoins des minorités ethnoculturelles et raciales en matière d'intégration dans le système judiciaire canadien*. Rapport pour la Clinique juridique communautaire de l'Université d'Ottawa, Ottawa, Ontario.

Ellison, R. (1990). *Invisible man*. Toronto: Random House of Canada. (Originally published by Random House in 1952)

Gervais, G. (1996). Le Règlement XVII (1912–1927). *Revue du Nouvel-Ontario, 18*, 123–192.

Giddens, A. (1990). *The consequences of modernity*. Stanford, CA: Stanford University Press.

Groulx, L.A. (1919). *La Naissance d'une race*. Montréal: Bibliothèque de l'action française.

Heller, M. (1994). *Crosswords: Language, education and ethnicity in French Ontario*. Berlin, NY: Mouton de Gruyter.

Heller. M. (1999). *Linguistic minorities and modernity: A sociolinguistic ethnography*. London, UK: Longman.

Heller, M. & Budach, G. (1999). Prise de parole: la mondialisation et la transformation des discours identitaires chez une minorité linguistique. *Bulletin suisse de linguistique appliquée, 69*(2), 155–166.

Jedwab, J. (2002). *Immigration and the vitality of Canada's official language communities: Policy, demography and identity*. Report prepared for the Office of the Commissioner of Official Languages, Canada.

Labelle, M., Rocher, F., & Rocher, G. (1995). Pluriethnicité, citoyenneté et intégration: de la souveraineté pour lever les obstacles et les ambiguïtés. *Cahiers de recherche sociologique, 25*, 213–244.

Labelle, M., Salée, D., & Frenette. Y. (2001). *Incorporation citoyenne et/ou exclusion? La deuxième génération issue de l'immigration haïtienne et jamaïcaine*: Fondation canadienne des relations raciales.

Lalonde, M. (1974). *Speak white*. Montreal: L'Hexagone.

Lucas, C.P. (Ed.). (1912). *Lord Durham's report* (Vols 1–3). Oxford, England (Original work published 1839).

Makropoulos, J. (2002). Les cadres juridiques relatifs à l'intégration professionnelle des minorités immigrantes dans le contexte scolaire. In D. Mujawamariya (Dir.) *L'intégration des minorités visibles et ethnoculturelles dans la profession enseignante: Récits d'expérience, enjeux et perspectives* (pp. 101–119). Outremont, PQ: Les Éditions Logiques.

Maxwell, T. (1977). *The invisible French: The French in metropolitan Toronto* Waterloo, ON: Wilfrid Laurier University Press.

Mianda, G. (1998). Être une immigrante noire africaine francophone à Toronto: Vécu et perception des rapports de genre. *Reflets, 4*(1), 34–53.

Mujawamariya D. (dir.) (2002). *L'intégration des minorités visibles et ethnoculturelles dans la profession enseignante. Récits d'expérience, enjeux et perspectives*. Outremont, Québec: Les Éditions Logiques.

Muse, R., Brihmi, M. & Pierre, M. (1999). *Réflexion et concertation: le développement des minorités raciales et ethnoculturelles francophones*. Document de travail présenté à PCH-Ontario.

Ministère de l'Éducation et de la Formation (2000). *Planification des programmes et évaluation. Le curriculum de l'Ontario de la 9e à la 12e année*. Toronto: Gouvernement de l'Ontario.

Paratte, H-D. (1998). *Acadians. Peoples of the Maritimes*. Halifax, NS: Nimbus Publishing.

Pinkham, J. (Trans.) (1971). *White niggers of America*. Toronto: McLelland and Stewart Limited.

Québec, Ministère des Communautés culturelles et de l'Immigration. (1981). *Autant de façons d'être Québécois: Plan d'action du gouvernement du Québec à l'intention des communautés culturelles*.

Razack, S. (1998). *Looking white people in the eye: Gender, race and culture in courtrooms and classrooms*. Toronto: University of Toronto Press.

Solomon, R.P., & Rezai-Rashiti, G. (2001, July). *Teacher candidates' racial identity development and its impact on learning to teach*. Report funded by The Canadian Race Relations Foundation.

Statistique Canada (1999). *Recensement de 1996, Caractéristiques ethnoculturelles et sociales de la population canadienne*. Série dimensions, catologue 94F0004 XCB.

Trudelle, C. & Fortier. P. (1987). *Toronto se raconte: La Paroisee du Sacré-Coeur*. Toronto: La société d'histoire de Toronto.

Vallières, P. (1968). *Nègres blancs d'Amérique: Autobiographie précoce d'un «terroriste» québécois*. Montréal: Éditions Parti Pris.

Welch, D. (1988). The social construction of Franco-Ontarian interests towards French language schooling, 19th century to 1980s. Unpublished PhD thesis, University of Toronto, Toronto, Ontario.

14

Jack Canuck Meets John Chinaman
Race, Nation, Class and the Masculine Dimensions of Chinese Racialization in Canada to 1923

G. Bruce Retallack
History Ph.D. Candidate
University of Toronto
Toronto

G. Bruce Retallack

Canada's

1923 Chinese Exclusion Act[1] marked the culmination of a series of increasingly draconian laws at all levels of government designed to limit the participation of Chinese immigrants in the political, economic and social life of the nation. Although racism clearly formed the basis for these measures, the discourses through which they were debated, enacted and contested frequently invoked notions of normative masculinity and its deviances. The centrality of masculine gender prescriptions to anti-Chinese agitation in this era was partly a reflection of the overwhelmingly male composition of the Chinese immigrant community. With a male/female ratio of 15:1 in 1921, the early Chinese in Canada were almost universally characterized as a "bachelor society,"[2] and day-to-day observation of the Chinese would have subliminally reinforced a race/gender conflation in the minds of white-Canadian observers. From the first appearance of the Chinese in British Columbia in the 1850s, one of the most common descriptive identifiers used across Canada was "John Chinaman",[3] a distinctly male epithet that was occasionally applied to even non-male Chinese: "Two of the Johns intend 'returning in the spring', bringing their families of female Johns and demi-Johns with them."[4] The fact that this kind of gender-specific nomenclature was not applied to other groups such as the Japanese, Italians, Ukrainians or, most important, to "Canadians" of British or French origin, reinforces the idea that the resident white population tended to think of the Chinese in Canada in exclusively male terms from the outset.

This perception was further buttressed by prevailing notions of nation and class. Central to both categories in Canada were concepts of "whiteness" — or more specifically, Britishness — and, in some ways, of "manliness". As Kay Anderson has commented, "[i]n the minds of whites, 'race' and 'nation' became interchangeable idioms around which socio-political units were built."[5] More specifically, participation in the political life of the Canadian nation was itself an entirely white-male prerogative until 1918, and early legislation that restricted Asian immigrants from participating in the body politic of the fledgling nation therefore challenged not only their citizenship but also their mascu-

---

[1] The official name is the Chinese Immigration Act (An Act Respecting Chinese Immigration) Statutes of Canada 1923, c. 38.

[2] Wright, 1988, p. 9. This ratio represents a national average: local variations could vary significantly. *See* Wickberg, 1979, p. 91. It is also important to note that "bachelor" is used in the sense of "solitary male", and not necessarily "unmarried". Some commentators, in fact, employ the more cautious phrase "married bachelors", although none pursue the implications of this construction. See for example, Tan & Roy, 1985, p. 4.

[3] For an interesting speculation on the origins of this term, *see* Lai, 1991, pp. 26–27.

[4] *The Victoria Gazette*, October 22, 1859 (as cited in Lai, 1991, p. 26).

[5] Anderson, 1991, p. 110.

line identities.[6] Similarly, the earliest and most enduring complaint about "John Chinaman" was that he presented an unfair economic challenge to "Canadian" (i.e., white-male) labour. It is, therefore, not surprising to find that while one set of discriminatory laws aimed to exclude the Chinese from the political life of the country, another set was clearly intended to limit their economic participation. Such proscriptions, however, were not applied universally, and pointed to a strong class division **within** the Chinese community. In all of the federal "Head Tax" enactments,[7] for example, as well as the Exclusion Act itself, merchants were specifically exempted from the exclusions, presumably on the basis of their financial contributions to government coffers. Thus, the "Chinaman" who informed both racist agitation and legislative action was consequently understood to be a single, sojourning male labourer or small businessman.[8] There was no necessity to spell out this specificity in detail: it was merely "common sense", and obvious to the middle-class gaze.

However, while the Chinese were pre-defined as male workers by circumstance, by legal constraints, and by intersecting conceptions of race, class, and nation, there was considerably less consensus about their masculinity, or "manliness". On the one hand, as Mariana Valverde has argued, the white host society considered the Chinese as being "so uncivilized that they had degenerated ... [resulting in] a loss of manhood and [a] consequent need for drugs to induce sexual desire."[9] At the same time, there was a seemingly contradictory conception of Chinese males as dangerous sexual predators, despite the fact that under the first construction, "white [women] ... ought to have been seen as relatively immune from coercive sexual advances."[10] Several scholars have noted this apparent paradox, but only one has attempted to address the problem head-on. In her 1996 essay "Like a Chinese Puzzle: the Construction of Chinese Masculinity in 'Jack Canuck'", Canadian historian Madge Pon proposed to reconcile the "emasculation and feminization of Chinese men" with "the contradictory belief that Chinese men posed a moral and sexual threat to white women," by analyzing the relevant articles in a muckraking Toronto newspaper of the day.[11] The evidence for the "sexual predator" construction is well documented in Pon's essay and elsewhere, but the assertion of a generically "feminized Chinaman" has proved rather more elusive. In fact, Pon fails to demonstrate — or even seriously pursue — her claim that Chinese males in Can-

---

[6] British Columbia disenfranchised the Chinese in 1875, and Saskatchewan in 1908. Further legislation also explicitly barred them from voting in provincial or municipal elections. Since federal voting rights were dependent on the provincial franchise, such legislation also effectively barred the Chinese from participation in federal politics and from holding any public office. For a brief summary of this issue *see* Li, 1998, pp. 32–33.

[7] First imposed in 1885, the Head Tax was initially set at $50, increasing to $100 in 1900 and $500 in 1903.

[8] Most scholars agree that many Chinese never intended to remain in Canada, and there is considerable evidence to support this contention. A few historians, however, assert that this is merely another "construction" imposed on the Chinese by the host community. *See* in particular Chan, 1981.

[9] Valverde, 1991, p. 111. The opium trade played an important part in anti-Chinese agitation, as exemplified by the quasi-scientific 1922 expose of Emily F. Murphy (*see* Murphy, 1922/1973).

[10] Backhouse, 1999, p. 141.

[11] Pon, 1996, pp. 88–89.

ada were necessarily or universally "feminized".[12] This is not to suggest that no such feminization occurred, but that as a generalization, and as a contradiction, this construction obscures the varieties of masculinities at work from both the host and immigrant perspectives.

There are two related theoretical problems in Pon's formulation. First, the notion that the white-Canadian majority "constructed" Chinese masculinity is tenuous at best. What was constructed was a **representation** of Chinese manhood in terms of, and for the consumption of, that white majority. It was, if you will, a measurement of deviation, revealing as much or more about the implied standards of white masculinity as about the Chinese "other". The experiential realities of Chinese masculinities remain invisible from this perspective. The second problem lies in Pon's use of the singular in referring to "masculinity", even as she proposes to deal with two specific variants. In attempting to parallel a "feminization" process with a fear of masculine sexuality, Pon conflates the first category (gender) with the second (sex), thereby creating an artificial and irreconcilable dilemma. The assumption of a coherent, unitary construction masks the complex and contingent interactions at work. Although Chinese males were clearly seen as not being properly "manly" in the eyes of white-Canadian observers, this does not mean that they were all 'gender constructed' in the same way, nor that they necessarily accepted these categorizations in whole or in part. Chinese immigrants undoubtedly carried their own masculine gender prescriptions that variably cohered with or opposed the host models. The contours of these various masculine constructions and subjectivities are mostly lacking from current historiography, but when the textual evidence is augmented with the visual record, a suggestive pattern emerges. Images, both graphic and photographic, provide a useful and underutilized means of identifying symbolic markers of race, class and gender in an historical context, and the existing imagery of the early Chinese in Canada certainly points to a more varied and complex set of masculine identities than has been suggested in Canadian historical literature to date.[13]

Of particular importance are the Canadian illustrations and cartoons of the nineteenth and early twentieth centuries that dealt with the issue of Asian immigration, since they had considerably more representational flexibility than did the photographs of the period.[14] The period under discussion has been called the "Golden Age of the Press in Canada," and the press was the primary source of visual images for the bulk of the population. Although photography was increasingly popular, it remained an essentially private art form, and the main popular vehicle for the representation of public figures was engraved or lithographed portraits in the illustrated magazines and papers. These images

---

[12] Apart from suggesting that this construction has "been noted by historians" (Ibid., p. 89), Pon's account of "emasculating images of Chinese men as 'unmanly,' 'bland,' 'cowardly,' and 'yellow," (Ibid., p. 95) relies on a single article from the September 16, 1911 issue of *Jack Canuck*.
[13] This study is based on an examination of some 150 images, or more than half of the visual record of the Chinese in Canada up to 1923, according to their foremost analyst. *See* Wright, 1988, for an excellent cross-section of this material.
[14] On the history of the press in Canada, *see* Kesterton, 1979; Rutherford, 1982; Sutherland, 1989. Dewalt, 1995, remains the best source for the technical history of graphic reproduction. On cartooning and its influence, *see* in particular Press, 1981 and Desbarats & Mosher, 1979.

Figure 14–1

The Heathen Chinee in British Columbia by James L. Weston. *Canadian Illustrated News,* April 26, 1879. Courtesy of Thomas Fisher Rare Book Repository, University of Toronto.

strove to conform to the principles of "high art" in the Western tradition. The new art of cartooning, by contrast, was perceived to be a "low" populist genre, and not to be taken seriously. The three modes of representation — the photograph, the illustration and the cartoon — therefore functioned in quite different ways, although all were important facets of the visual surround of everyday life. Most of these images presented their Chinese subjects in a deliberately demeaning fashion, and they conveyed that evaluation primarily by contrasting normative white manhood with its perceived Chinese variant, using markers of difference that revolved around matters of size, posture, clothing and grooming. These distinctions can all be found in what is probably the most famous of these illustrations — the 1879 cover of the *Canadian Illustrated News* entitled *The Heathen Chinee in British Columbia* (Figure 14–1). Here the traditional Chinese garb of loose, flowing tunic and black slippers provides an immediate contrast to the more restrictive formal "masculine" apparel of the white figure. This obvious difference served to make exotic or "Orientalize" the Chinese figure to white observers at first glance and invoked at least a suggestion of the feminine.[15] Hair plays a role here by contrasting the traditional sleek Chinese hairstyle, including the signature queue, with the thick short hair and flowing patriarchal beard favoured by many elite white men at the time.[16] In addition to these outward cultural signs of difference, however, there are other, less obvious, signifiers at work in this image. The white figure is significantly taller than his Chinese counterpart, and is made more so by his top hat. Moreover, his erect, purposeful stance dominates the other's twisted submissive posture while further emphasizing the height difference. These markers of size and posture were regularly used at the time to differentiate between idealized white manhood and subordinate "others", including both women and children, and they are still often associated with representations of femininity today.[17] Their near-universal application in images of Chinese-Canadian males, therefore, reinforces the fact that "feminization" was not merely a rhetorical device, but a cultural perception based on visual gender signifiers, and it is dressed thus, with queue flying, that Chinese men were invariably portrayed in drawings and cartoons of the era. This persistent graphic disempowerment (in white Western terms) had the effect of symbolically licensing dominant white males to manhandle the unruly "John Chinaman".

It is important to reiterate in this context that the opposite of "masculine" is not necessarily "feminine". As several gender historians have suggested, up to and including the period in question, "**[m]anhood** ... had historically been seen as the opposite of **childhood**."[18] Thus, while sex differentiation is undoubtedly significant, there is also an important dialogue based on age — or, more precisely, on maturity — at work here. Sexual immaturity is often, and erroneously, subsumed under the rubric of "feminization", whereas in fact they often represent two distinct differentials from normative (white) adult manhood. These intersecting categories of age and sex difference found their clearest expression in discourses surrounding "the houseboy". The word itself clearly invokes a metaphor of immaturity from the outset, regardless of the actual age of the person involved. Historian Peter Ward cites as an example that "[a]s Mrs. Goodfellow remarked, 'ours was a good boy and it wasn't long before he was quite a help.' Help he was, but boy he was too."[19] Chinese domestic help was

---

[15] On the concept of "orientalization", *see* in particular Said, 1979.

[16] Ironically, the shaved forehead and queue were originally imposed as a symbol of servitude and submission in China by the Manchu dynasty. *See* Wright, 1988, p. 9.

[17] The best analysis of this differentiation remains Goffman, 1979.

[18] Kimmel, 1997, pp. 119–120.

[19] Florence Goodfellow, *Memories of Pioneer Life in British Columbia,* p. 14 (as cited in Ward, 1990, p. 26).

thus often constructed as boyish as much as feminine, providing a particular inflection of masculine identities from the perspective of white males, for whom the "gendered distinctions drawn between men and boys were meaningful."[20]

Although domestic workers rarely appeared in the cartoons and graphic illustrations of the period, the photographic record suggests, albeit inconclusively, that some "houseboys" of any age may have retained traditional Chinese forms of dress that, to Western eyes, look like women's clothes rather than "proper" manly attire. In an 1893 portrait of Lee Pin Kam, *Celestial Washy Washy* to the Bruce family of Calgary (Figure 14–2), with its condescendingly

Figure 14–2

Our Celestial Washy Washy. Photograph of Lee Pin Kam by R. Randolph Bruce, 1893. Courtesy of Glenbow Archives, NA-2307-32.

---

[20] Stiles, 1998, p. 103.

"humorous" inscription, Lee's smooth face, "pig-tail" and flowing robe all semiotically signalled "female" in North American culture at the turn of the last century, and the impression was reinforced by the fact that domestic tasks were firmly identified as "women's work". In performing such duties, Chinese males unwittingly invoked prevailing gender stereotypes in the minds of white observers.[21] Nor was this ascription restricted to houseboys. Chinese laundry and restaurant workers in all-male mining towns, for example, who "regularly and exclusively performed 'women's work,' ... were not perceived as being masculine."[22] The triple signifying layers of language, image and function ensured that the feminization paradigm would be an extremely powerful one with respect to some Chinese Canadians. In practice, however, "neither age nor feminization could completely erase the fact that the Chinese [houseboy] was a masculine ... presence,"[23] nor alleviate concerns over "the supposed sexual danger they posed to women in town."[24] Thus it was that Jack Kong, a 17-year-old Chinese domestic worker accused of murder, could be characterized by the media as being of "...'so slight a frame as to appear girlish,' thereby instantly mark[ing] him as something other than a 'normal man.'"[25]

At the centre of this apparent contradiction was an underlying perception of men's "natural" sexuality, and some modern commentators continue to suggest that "[p]rostitution, gambling, and opium smoking were prominent features of Chinese social life largely **because** the community was transient and overwhelmingly male" [emphasis added].[26] The basic assumption is that single males will inevitably turn to such socially proscribed activities, since they lack the "steadying" influence of wives and families. This, of course, was precisely the assertion of anti-Chinese agitators at the turn of the last century, and it found its clearest expression in a group of laws known collectively as the "white women's labour laws." Ostensibly intended to protect (white) women workers from any danger, in practice these laws specifically identified the Chinese employer as a moral and sexual threat to white womanhood, invoking once again the triple categories of race, class, and gender.[27] The sexual fears underpinning these debates were based on a pre-existing perception of the Chinese male that reflected a complex interaction of cultural constructions and signifying systems. Racial essentialism was the scientific and cultural orthodoxy of the day and fostered concerns in the popular imagination over racial purity and the need to "stick to one's own kind". The eugenics movement in particular, with

---

[21] That Chinese males were willing to perform such work certainly served to reinforce their "femininity" in the eyes of contemporaries, but the notion is occasionally taken up unproblematically by historians asserting that the Chinese were "'forced" to take "women's work". The real question is whether the **Chinese** considered these tasks women's work or not: did it, in other words, impact on their own masculine self-identification?

[22] Forestell, 1998, p. 262.

[23] Dubinsky & Givertz, 1999, p. 76.

[24] Forestell, 1998, p. 262.

[25] Dubinsky & Givertz, 1999, p. 73. The embedded quote is from the *Vancouver Sun*, April 4, 1914.

[26] Ward, 1990, p. 18.

[27] Saskatchewan was the first province to pass such legislation, followed by Manitoba, Ontario and British Columbia. For details, *see* Walker, 1997, pp. 50–56.

Figure 14–3

MISS CANADA WILL GUARD THE YUKON AGAINST YELLOW INVASION.

Miss Canada Will Guard the Yukon against Yellow Invasion, by unknown artist. *The Klondike Daily Nugget,* March 27, 1901.

its social Darwinist underpinnings, lent a "scientific veneer" to racial fears about "debasing the stock" through miscegenation or rape.[28] In this context, inevitably, "race and gender [became] ineluctably intertwined, through the primacy of heterosexuality in reproducing the former and defining the latter."[29] Although such quasi-scientific perceptions may not have been universally accepted in the 1850s and 1860s, by the time the first "white women's labour law" was enacted in 1912, the construction was complete, ingrained, and such "common sense" as to preclude any possibility of serious debate.

[28] Valverde, 1991, p. 107. The best account of the eugenics movement in Canada remains McLaren, 1990.
[29] Dyer, 1997, p. 30. Note the parallel use of "gender" and "heterosexuality" as if the two terms were interchangeable.

G. Bruce Retallack

The symbolic foundation of this race/nation/sex conflation is reflected clearly in a 1901 cartoon (Figure 14–3), which contrasts the figures of two Chinese workers with both the upright, contained image of the Mountie and the looming presence of "Miss Canada". Note, however, that Miss Canada is **not** truly guarding the Yukon in this representation, but merely presiding over affairs. She is purely allegorical, and represents not a particular person or group, but rather the country itself. The symbolic equation "Canada = White Womanhood" forms an important recurring theme in the racial rhetoric of the time. The master metaphor by which women represent the body physical of the country and men the body politic had significant implications for the manner in which national issues were conceptualized and debated. As Ronald Takaki commented, "[t]he entire history of white America has been one of penetration into the 'virgin land.'"[30] Within the terms of this sexual metaphor, any threat to the nation automatically becomes a masculine attack on white womanhood. Race, nation and gender thus combined at a symbolic level to predispose white Canadians towards the construction of "John Chinaman" as a potential sexual danger, even while they simultaneously drew derogatory comparisons between his "manhood" and that of white Canadians, represented in idealized form by the figure of the Mountie — "Jack Canuck" himself.

As a symbol of Canadian masculinity, the figure of Jack Canuck faded from view after 1950, but for the period in question he was very much in evidence. The origins of the "Jack Canuck" figure remain obscure. Originally applied as a pejorative reference to French Canadians, it was adopted in the 1870s and '80s to characterize ideal (white) Canadian manhood, and eventually the body politic itself. By the end of the nineteenth century, "Jack" had become closely identified with the image of the Mountie (an officer of the Royal Canadian Mounted Police), and almost always appeared in that guise until the 1950s. Regardless of the representational details, however, Jack was always depicted as a clear-eyed, broad-shouldered, erect and controlled young white male.[31] As this image suggests, he was invariably portrayed as a figure of phallic power: note the rifle, the erect posture, the inflated chest and the military attire. These are all typical symbols of masculinity in Western representation, denoting readiness, effectiveness and control. The issue of control, in particular, is highly important. The outward signs displayed here — the posture and the uniform — were taken as reflections of an inner discipline that has been referred to as the "Iron Cage."[32] Rationality, and particularly sexual control, were important components of white manhood throughout the period in question. Good men, true men — **white** men — were expected to have enough self-control to restrain themselves from succumbing to their "animal passions". They were also expected to defend the honour of their women (and their nation), who were thought to be unable to protect themselves against the uncontrolled sexual depredations of the "lesser

---

[30] Takaki, 1979, p. 265.

[31] There is, sadly, no published analysis of this fascinating part of Canada's symbolic history.

[32] There are a number of excellent recent studies on the subject of nineteenth-century constructions of normative masculinity in Britain and the United States, although little in a specifically Canadian context. *See* Bederman, 1996; Mangan & Walvin, 1987; and particularly Rotundo, 1993. Richard Dyer makes much the same point with reference to race in Dyer, 1997.

races", in this case the Chinese. Note that all of the markers of difference and diminishment noted in Figure 14–1 above reappear here. It is precisely here, where visual and verbal discourses intersect, that the contradictions between the feminized Chinaman and the sexual predator are symbolically fused; but it must be stressed that the contrast is essentially intramasculine. While it is possible to read some "feminine" characteristics into traditional Chinese male garb, or into the frequent portrayal of "submissive" postures, the overall distinction is between dominant and subordinate masculinities, not between the masculine and the feminine. It is within this construction that the discourses surrounding Chinese racialization must be contextualized, and in terms of which the apparent contradictions noted by Pon disappear.

Symbolically, then, the concept of the Chinese as a sexual hazard could indeed sit quite comfortably alongside images of Chinese males as diminished, emasculated, "feminized" and, in both gendered and political terms, impotent. This was, in fact, the precise discourse that the Canadian host society constructed and articulated in both graphic and rhetorical representations. But this is not the entire story. The photographic record provides other, significantly different views of Chinese-Canadian males in this era. Most of the pictures preserved in Canadian archives are casual snapshots, showing groups of all-Chinese or mixed White/Chinese composition going about their normal business in Chinatown or in a variety of work and public settings.[33] Although many of the Chinese men in these photos do indeed appear to be somewhat shorter and slimmer than their white North American counterparts, there is a striking tendency for them to be dressed in Western attire in many public situations where both races are present. Thus, while host illustrators insisted on retaining a traditional visual stereotype for artistic or political effect, the Chinese themselves appear to have frequently adopted the outward trappings of Western manhood when interacting with the host community. Within the confines of the home or the streets of Chinatown, however, there is a striking reversion to traditional forms of dress and posture.

Two posed portraits of "Lee Wah, James, Chinese convert" demonstrate both the clothing shift and the critical posture change. The first image (Figure 14–4) shows the "traditional legs-spread dominant pose" that is typical of much Chinese male portraiture in the period under consideration and stands in marked contrast to the Anglophone tradition of the closed, erect profile that is reflected in the second picture (Figure 14–5). Although one Canadian historian has referred to these as "before-and-after" shots, there is no particular reason for making such an assumption, unless of course one believes that the normative Western model is indeed more "advanced", and unlikely to be rejected once achieved.[34] The visual record clearly suggests that Chinese males often appeared in Western clothes and postures in public, while shifting to traditional forms in private circumstances. This at least presents the possibility that Chinese males may have adopted multiple forms of masculine self-representation,

---

[33] The largest collections are held by the Vancouver Public Library (British Columbia) and the Glenbow Archives (Alberta). Both collections have been reviewed *in toto* and augmented with images from the Metro Toronto Reference Library (Ontario).

[34] *See* Wright, 1988, p. 108.

Figure 14–4

Lee Wah, James — First Chinese Convert. Photograph by Thomas B. Straiton Studio, 1892. Courtesy of Vancouver Public Library, Special Collections, VPL8588.

some designed for consumption by the host community, and some for "at home". It is the definition of that "at-home" masculinity that is lacking from our historical record to date, but there are some suggestive clues scattered through the existing historiography.

In his influential 1982 study *Gold Mountain*, Anthony B. Chan clearly characterizes the Chinese family, in Canada as elsewhere, as "a patriarchal hierarchy,"[35] a conclusion that is amply borne out by first-hand accounts.[36] This would certainly tend to strengthen a cross-racial identification of normative maleness, but the specific dimensions of that patriarchy, and particularly its perceptions of "natural" male-female relations, might also create barriers to that identification. It would be enormously productive to know how Chinese men — and women — have perceived white-Canadian masculine prescriptions over time. Did they find Canadian men overly controlled? Dominated by their women? Sexually inadequate? The problem, obviously, is to determine just what, pre-

---

[35] Chan, 1983, p. 100.

[36] For oral histories of the Chinese in Canada, *see* Huang, 1992; Women's Book Committee, 1992; Chong, 1995.

Figure 14–5

Lee Wah — Chinese Convert. Photograph by J.L. Browne Studio, 1892. Courtesy of Vancouver Public Library, Special Collections, VPL8585.

cisely, was "practice", and how well it accorded — or not — with the stereotypes of the host society. In other words, while it is unquestionably revealing and productive to delineate an increasingly nuanced account of white-Canadian "construction" of Chinese masculinities, it is also true that we will not fully understand the prevailing dialectic until we can uncover the **Chinese** construction of Chinese masculinities and the Chinese perceptions of **white** masculinities. Since such prescriptions are involved with social performance and self-identity, understanding their contours can help illuminate how and to what extent they have historically been negotiated in the context of inter-cultural encounters.

By incorporating both textual and visual evidence, we can begin to see that the Canadian "construction" of Chinese masculinities in the pre-Exclusion era were visual/visceral as much as textual/rational, were deeply informed by conceptual categories of race, class and nation; and were organized around a normative model of white-Western masculinity. The same evidence, however, suggests that Chinese males themselves carried their own gender prescriptions that intersected with those constructions in complex and variable ways. If we are to fully understand the phenomenon of Chinese racialization in Canada, we

need to unwrap both the critical components of white-Canadian masculine stereotypes, and the specific gender prescriptions of Chinese immigrants in an historical context. Only then will we at least begin to understand, in an historical
sense, where cultural practice informs racism. Certainly the existence of a separate Chinese-Canadian vision of "ideal" masculinity can serve as a salutary
reminder that, in our quest to uncover our own negative constructions of
minority groups, it is perhaps "unhelpful to suggest a vision that turns the
Other into the Same."[37]

References

Anderson, Kay J. (1991). *Vancouver's Chinatown: Racial discourse in Canada,
1875–1980*. (Montreal: McGill-Queen's University Press.

Backhouse, Constance (1999). *Colour-coded: A legal history of racism in Canada,
1900–1950*. Toronto: University of Toronto Press for The Osgoode Society
for Canadian Legal History.

Bederman, Gail. (1996). *Manliness & civilization: A cultural history of gender and
race in the United States, 1880–1917*. Chicago: University of Chicago Press.

Chan, Anthony B. (1981). "Orientalism" and image making: the sojourner in
Canadian history. *The Journal of Ethnic Studies, 9*(3), 37–46.

Chan, Anthony B. (1983). *Gold mountain: The Chinese in the new world*. Vancouver: New Star Books.

Chong, Denise. (1995). *The concubine's children*. Toronto: Penguin.

Desbarats, Peter, & Mosher, Terry. (1979). *The hecklers: A history of Canadian
political cartooning and a cartoonists' history of Canada*. Toronto: McClelland
& Stewart.

Dewalt, Bryan. (1995). *Technology and Canadian printing: A history from lead
type to lasers*. Ottawa: National Museum of Science and Technology.

Dubinsky, Karen, & Givertz, Adam. (1999). "It was only a matter of passion":
Masculinity and sexual danger. In Kathryn McPherson, Cecilia Morgan et
al. (Eds.), *Gendered pasts: Historical essays in femininity and masculinity in
Canada*. Don Mills, ON: Oxford University Press.

Dyer, Richard. (1997). *White*. New York: Routledge.

Forestell, Nancy M. (1998). Bachelors, boarding-houses, and blind pigs: Gender
construction in a multi-ethnic mining camp, 1909–1920. In Franca Iacovetta,
Paula Draper et al. (Eds.), *A nation of immigrants: Women, workers, and
communities in Canadian history, 1840s–1960s*. Toronto: University of
Toronto Press.

Goffman, Erving. (1979). *Gender advertisements*. Cambridge, MA: Harvard University Press.

Huang, Evelyn. (1992). *Chinese Canadians: Voices from a community*. Vancouver: Douglas & McIntyre.

Kesterton, W.H. (1979). *A history of journalism in Canada*. Toronto: Macmillan.

---

[37] Anderson, 1991, p. 15.

Kimmel, Michael. (1997). *Manhood in America: A cultural history*. New York: The Free Press.

Lai, David Chuenyan. (1991). *The forbidden city within Victoria: Myth, symbol and streetscape of Canada's earliest Chinatown*. Victoria, BC: Orca Book Publishers.

Li, Peter S. (1998). *The Chinese in Canada*. Toronto: Oxford University Press.

Mangan, J.A. & Walvin, James. (Eds.). (1987). *Manliness and morality: Middle-class masculinity in Britain and America, 1800–1940*. Manchester: Manchester University Press.

McLaren, Angus. (1990). *Our own master race: Eugenics in Canada, 1885–1945*. Toronto: McClelland & Stewart.

Murphy, Emily F. (1973). *The black candle*. Toronto: Coles Publishing Company. (First published 1922 by Thomas Allen, Toronto, Ontario)

Pon, Madge. (1996.) Like a Chinese puzzle: The construction of Chinese masculinity in "Jack Canuck". In Joy Parr & Mark Rosenfeld (Eds.), *Gender and history in Canada*. Toronto: Copp Clark Ltd.

Press, Charles. (1981). *The political cartoon*. Toronto: Associated University Presses.

Rotundo, E. Anthony. (1993). *American manhood: Transformations in masculinity from the revolution to the modern era*. New York: BasicBooks, a division of HarperCollins Publishers, Inc.

Rutherford, Paul. (1982). *A Victorian authority: The Daily Press in late nineteenth-century Canada*. Toronto: University of Toronto Press.

Said, Edward W. (1979). *Orientalism*. New York: Vintage Books.

Stiles, Deborah. (1998). Martin Butler, masculinity, and the North American sole leather tanning industry: 1871–1889. *Labour/Le Travail, 42*, 103.

Sutherland, Fraser. (1989). *The monthly epic: A history of Canadian magazines 1789–1989*. Toronto: Fitzhenry & Whiteside.

Takaki, Ronald T. (1979). *Iron cages: Race and culture in nineteenth-century America*. New York: Alfred A. Knopf.

Tan, Jin, & Roy, Patricia E. (1985). The Chinese in Canada. *Ottawa: Canadian Historical Association*.

Valverde, Mariana. (1991). *The age of light, soap, and water: Moral reform in English Canada, 1885–1925*. Toronto: McClelland & Stewart.

Walker, James W. St. G. (1997). *"Race," rights and the law in the Supreme Court of Canada: Historical case studies*. Toronto & Waterloo: The Osgoode Society for Canadian Legal History and Wilfrid Laurier University Press.

Ward, W. Peter. (1990). *White Canada forever: Popular attitudes and public policy towards Orientals in British Columbia*. Montreal: McGill-Queen's University Press.

Wickberg, Edgar. (1979). Some problems in Chinese organizational development in Canada, 1923–1937. *Canadian Ethnic Studies/Etudes Ethniques au Canada, 11*(1), 88–98.

Women's Book Committee. Chinese Canadian National Council. (1992). *Jin Guo: Voices of Chinese Canadian women*. Toronto: Women's Press.

Wright, Richard Thomas. (1988). *In a strange land: A pictorial record of the Chinese in Canada, 1788–1923*. Saskatoon, SK: Western Producer Prairie Books.

15

Performing Desire
Hip-Hop, Identification, and the Politics of Becoming Black

Awad Ibrahim
Educational Foundations and Inquiry Program
Bowling Green State University
Bowling Green

This essay was first published as Awad Ibrahim, "'Hey, ain't I Black too?' The Politics of Becoming Black" in Rinaldo Walcott (Ed.), *Rude: Contemporary Black Canadian Cultural Criticism* (Toronto: Insomniac Press, 2000).

The argument I want to make to you is that race works like a language. And signifiers refer to the systems and concepts of classification of a culture, to its making meaning practices; and those things gain their meaning not because of what they contain in their essence, but in the shifting relations of difference which they establish with other concepts and ideas in a signifying field. Their meaning, because it is relational and not essential, can never be finally fixed. But it is subject to the constant process of redefinition and appropriation. ... The meaning of a signifier can never be finally or transhistorically fixed. That is, it is always, or variously always, a certain sliding of meaning; always a margin not yet encapsulated in language and meaning; always something about race left unsaid; always someone, a constitutive outside, whose very existence the identity of race depends on, and it is absolutely distinct to return from its expel and abject position outside the signifying field, to trouble the dreams of those who are comfortable inside.

Stuart Hall[1]

Introduction: Towards a Becoming of Being

Subject in progress (or process), *sujet en procès,* or becoming of being, or being as a continuous act of becoming, is the central contention of this essay. It is a Kristevan[2] notion that assumes not fixity, but performativity[3]; not being in thetic and static sense, but being as being that is never complete; and for this essay, it assumes a being that is becoming Black. Based on a "critical ethnographic research project"[4] that engages this notion as its backdrop, this essay will trace how a group of continental francophone African youth, living in an urban metropolitan city in southwestern Ontario, Canada, were in the process of becoming Blacks.

The youth come from places as diverse as Democratic Republic of Congo (formerly Zaïre), Djibouti, Gabon, Senegal, Somalia, South Africa, and Togo. And the process of becoming Black was on the one hand, marked by an **identification** with and a **desire** for North American Blackness[5]; and it was, on the other, as much about gender and race as it was about language and cultural

---

[1] My own transcription of a videorecorded seminal lecture on race by Stuart Hall (Hall, 1996); *see also* Hall, 1997.

[2] Kristeva, 1974; *see also* Nietzsche, 1977, p. 197.

[3] *See* Butler, 1999.

[4] *See* Ibrahim, 1998.

[5] According to Russell Simmons, the impact of African-American culture is no longer in the margin; on the contrary, it is where the cool and hip mainstream culture and music are set (Simmons, 2001; *see also* Smitherman, 2000, p. 31). My current research on the impact of Black popular culture, especially hip-hop, on White youth in rural areas in Québec, is another proof of this claim. I am finding that in a town of 95 percent Whites, hip-hop (as an urban Black cultural form) is the most popular cultural form among young people.

performance. I shall delineate these youths' desire for and identification with Blackness through language. North American Blackness is an encompassing multicultural, multilingual, multiethnic and multinational category. It is a category whose skin color is black and who — for social, historical, and political reasons — either defines itself or is defined as "Black." I use "Black" interchangeably with "African" in my work; Paul Gilroy refers to them as "The Black Atlantic."[6] In Canada, this category includes indigenous African-Canadians whose presence dates back to 1600s;[7] African Caribbeans/West Indians who came to Canada en masse during the 1950s and 1960s; and continental Africans who started arriving in Canada in considerable numbers in the late 1980s. Although the presence of Blackness in Canada dates back to early 1600s, significantly, given their sheer numbers, politics, and history, North American Blackness, in the popular imaginary, is equated with African-Americans. Their cultural, linguistic, artistic, musical, political and historical impact is palpable, not only on other North American Blacks — including Canadians — but also on mainstream culture. Those young people were learning Black English as a Second Language (BESL).[8] Geneva Smitherman defines "Black English" as "... the most dynamic language of U.S. slave descendants, more commonly known as African Americans. [And] Terms for this language vary — Black Talk, African American Vernacular English, Black or African American Language, Black English, Black Dialect, Ghetto Speech, Street Talk, Ebonics, and others."[9] It is an oral language that has its own grammar and syntax and is spoken by all sectors of African Americans. She writes, "Black Talk crosses boundaries of age, gender, region, religion, and social class because it all comes from the same source: the African American Experience and the oral tradition embedded in that experience."[10] (See also the section on "Research Subjects, Method, and Site" in this essay.) The youth studied accessed BESL through Black popular culture, namely rap music. Besides rap, they also took up and performed hip-hop cultural identity. The paper is an ensemble of snapshots narrating how they were becoming Black.

The social categories of race and gender were central to this process of becoming Black. In the case of the African youth, for instance, although both male and female verbalized a strong identification with Blackness during interviews, the situation was different when it came to the intensity of bodily performance. That is, whereas all male students articulated and performed a strong identification with and a complete appropriation of hip-hop and rap through their dress, posture, walk, and talk, female students, depending on their age,

---

[6] Gilroy, 1993.

[7] Prince, 2001.

[8] "Black English as a Second Language (BESL)" is a term I coined that refers to the process of learning the language (*see* Ibrahim, 2001). Here, I argue that learning BESL by African youth is an act of affinity and desire towards the North American Black community. This act does not require a full mastery of the language, but banks on ritual expressions such as "whassup" or "whassup homeboy." I call this "Black Stylized English (BSE)". In actuality, BESL and BSE are interchangeable; both refer to the learning of Black English through ritual expressions for purposes larger than language per se.

[9] Smitherman, 1994–2000, p. 1.

[10] Ibid.

tended to be more postmodernly eclectic. The younger girls (12–15 years old) had the same linguistic and cultural practice and performance as the boys in their appropriation of rap and hip-hop while the older girls (16–18 years old) tended to be more selective. They combined, for example, hip-hop with different styles of African "traditional" dress without any sense of contradiction. This non-contradictory combination of cultural practices, in the final analysis, became the law, the social order, that allowed the youth to form **their own** culture. The product of this combination is what I term, following Sartre and Bhabha, **the third space**.[11] This combination, however, is not fixed, but performative: it is shifting, modified, and ever changing.

Borrowing from Judith Butler,[12] the idea of performativity is central to my research. Again, it is a concept that assumes not fixity but repetition, parody and continual acts of becoming. Following Simone de Beauvoir, Butler took gender, or the category "woman", as an example. (Note the synonymity between gender and race within Butler's conception.) She argues that one is not born a woman; one, in fact, becomes one. Gender, therefore, for Butler, is the repeated stylization of the body, a set of recurrent acts, words, gestures, or what Roland Barthes[13] calls complex semiological languages. These are signs that are open for signification and different readings since they cannot produce verbal utterances yet are ready to be spoken. For Butler, these complex languages are produced and performed on the surface of our bodies: in and through our modes of dress, our walk, in our hair, *maquillage,* lip gloss; also in how we shape and articulate space and representation.

I am contending, accordingly, that we perform our identities, desires, and investments, at least in part, in and through these complex semiological languages of our dress, walk and talk. This is what I have termed **ethnography of performance**.[14] As a research methodology, ethnography of performance also argues that ethnographers' best access to research subject's inner selves is their subject's verbal and non-verbal performance. That is, the juxtaposition of what people actually and materially perform on and through their bodies with what they say and think about those performances combine to give ethnographers a more complete picture of their research subjects' identities.

For Butler,[15] performativity also assumes agency — the ground where questions of choice circulate, questions like: who do we, as social subjects, identify with? who and what do we desire **to be**? what choices do we make? are they purely ours? how do they come about? what shape or form do they take, and why? However, by now we know "[t]he source of personal and political agency" — as Butler convincingly noted —

> comes not from within the individual, but in and through complex cultural exchanges among bodies in which identity itself is ever-shifting, indeed, where identity itself is

---

[11] Sartre, 1980; Bhabha, 1990; for full discussion, *see* Ibrahim, 1998, 2000c.

[12] Butler, 1999.

[13] Barthes, 1983.

[14] Ibrahim, 1997, 1999, 2000a, 2000b, 2000c.

[15] Butler, 1999.

constructed, disintegrated, and recirculated only within the context of a dynamic field of cultural relations.[16]

To put it simply, our agency is governed, in the Foucauldian sense,[17] by the sociocultural context in which we live: which, in turn, governs our investments in who we want to be and what we want to become. **Being** is being distinguished here from **becoming**. The former is an accumulated memory, an understanding, a conception and an experience upon which individuals interact with the world around them, whereas the latter is the process of building this memory of experience. (And "memory" is seen here as a reservoir of experiences that allows one to feel and live through the familiar and unfamiliar.) For example, as a continental African, I was not considered Black in Africa; other terms served to patch together my identity, such as **tall, Sudanese**, and **basketball player**. However, as a refugee in North America, my perception of self was altered in direct response to the social processes of racism and the historical representation of Blackness, whereby the antecedent signifiers became secondary to my Blackness and my being was (re)translated: I became Black.

In what follows, I discuss, first, my research, its contentions, propositions, and questions and then, secondly and succinctly, introduce its methodology, site and subject. I then offer examples of African youth speech to demonstrate the interplay between subject formation, identification and BESL learning. I also offer students' reflections and narratives on the impact of identification and becoming Black, and conclude with remarks on the need to deconstruct this panoptic gaze that limits, as we will see, African youth social life.

Research Subjects, Method, and Site

This project constitutes part of a larger critical ethnographic research[18] I conducted at Marie-Victorin[19] between January and June 1996, which made use of my newly developed methodological approach, **ethnography of performance**. The research, which took place in an urban, French-language high school in southwestern Ontario, Canada, looks at the lives of a group of continental Francophone African youth and the formation of their social identity. Besides their gendered and raced experience, their youth and refugee status were vital in their **moments of identification:**[20] that is, where and how they saw themselves reflected in the mirror of their society (questions of agency within this metaphor are explored below). Put otherwise, once in North America, I con-

---

[16] Butler, Ibid., p. 127.

[17] Foucault, 1980.

[18] For R. Simon and D. Dippo (1986), "critical ethnographic research" is a set of activities situated within a project that seeks, and works its way towards, social transformation. This project is political as well as pedagogical, and who the researcher is and what his or her racial, gender, and class embodiments are necessarily govern the research questions and findings.
[19] All names are pseudonyms.

[20] *See* Bhabha, 1994.

tend, these youth were faced with a social imaginary[21] in which they were already Blacks. This social imaginary was directly implicated in how and with whom they identified, which in turn influenced what they linguistically and culturally learned and how they learned it. What they learned, I demonstrate, is Black Stylized English (BSE), which they accessed in and through Black popular culture. They learned by taking up and repositing the rap linguistic and musical genre and, in different ways, acquiring and rearticulating the hip-hop cultural identity.

BSE is Black English (BE) with style; it is a subcategory. BE is what Smitherman refers to as "Black Talk", which has its own grammar and syntax.[22] BSE, on the other hand, refers to ways of speaking that do not depend on a full mastery of the Black Talk. It banks more on ritual expressions, such as "whassup," "whadap," "whassup my Nigger," and "yo, yo homeboy," which are performed habitually and recurrently in rap. The rituals are more an expression of politics, moments of identification, and desire than they are of language or of mastering the language per se. It is a way of saying, "I too am Black," or, "I too desire and identify with Blackness."

By Black popular culture, on the other hand, I refer to films, newspapers, magazines and, more important, music such as rap, reggae, dance hall, pop, and rhythm and blues (R&B). The term **hip-hop** "is the overall naming apparatus" that "comprises everything from music, to clothing choices, attitudes, language, and an approach to culture and cultural artifacts positing and collaging them in an unsentimental fashion."[23] More skeletally, I used hip-hop to describe a way of dressing, walking, and talking. The dress refers to the myriad shades and shapes of the latest **fly gear**: high-top sneakers, bicycle shorts, chunky jewellery, baggy pants, and polka-dotted tops.[24] The hairstyles, which include high-fade designs, dreadlocks, corkscrews, and braids, are also part of this fashion. **The walk** usually means moving the fingers simultaneously with the head and the rest of the body as one is walking, and it is more observable in the boys than in the girls. **The talk**, however, is BSE. Significantly, by patterning these behaviours African youth enter the realm of becoming Black. As an identity configuration, the latter is deployed to talk about the **subject-formation project** (i.e., the process and the space within which subjectivity is formed) that is produced in, and simultaneously is produced by, the process of language learning, namely, learning BESL. More concretely, becoming Black meant learning BESL, as I show below; yet the very process of BESL learning produced the epiphenomenon of becoming Black.

The central working contention of the research was that once in North America, continental African youth enter a **social imaginary**: a discursive or symbolic space in which they are already constructed, imagined, and positioned, and thus treated by the hegemonic discourses and dominant groups, respectively, as Blacks. Here, I address the White (racist) everyday communicative

---

[21] *See* Anderson, 1983; and Fine, Powell, Weiss & Wong, 1997.

[22] Smitherman, 1994–2000.

[23] Walcott, 1995, p. 5.

[24] Rose, 1991, p. 277.

state of mind: "Oh, they all look alike to me!" This positionality, which is offered to continental African youth through net-like praxis in exceedingly complex and mostly subconscious ways, does not acknowledge the differences in the students' ethnicities, languages, nationalities, and cultural identities. Frantz Fanon sums up this net-like praxis brilliantly in writing about himself as a Black **Antillais** coming to the metropolis of Paris:

> I am given no chance, I am overdetermined from without. I am the slave not of the "idea" that others have of me but of my own appearance .... I *progress* [italics added] by crawling. And *already* [italics mine] I am being dissected under white eyes, the only real eyes. I am *fixed*. Having adjusted their microtomes, they objectively cut away slices of my reality. I am laid bare ... When people like me, they tell me it is in spite of my color. When they dislike me, they point out that it is not because of my color. Either way, I am locked into the infernal circle.[25]

In other words, continental African youth find themselves in a racially preoccupied society that, wittingly or unwittingly and through fused social mechanisms such as racisms and representations, asks them to racially fit somewhere. To fit somewhere signifies choosing or becoming aware of one's own being, which is partially reflected in one's language practice. Choosing, as we have already seen, however, is a question of agency, which itself is governed and disciplined by social conditions. For example, to be Black in a racially preoccupied society, like the Euro-Canadian or U.S. society, means that one is expected to be Black, act Black, and so be the marginalized Other.[26] Under such disciplinary social conditions, as it will become clear, continental African youth express their moments of identification in relation to African-Canadian and African-American cultures and languages, thus becoming Black. That they take up rap and hip-hop and speak BSE is by no means a coincidence. On the contrary, these actions are articulations of the youth desire to belong to a location, a politics, a memory, a history and, hence, a representation.

The site of the research was a small Franco-Ontarian intermediate and high school (grades 7–13): Marie-Victorin (MV). MV had a school population of approximately 389 students from various ethnic, racial, cultural, religious, and linguistic backgrounds. Although it is a French-language school, the language spoken by students in the school corridors and hallways was predominately English; Arabic, Somali, and Farsi were also spoken at other times. The school had 27 teachers, all of whom were White, and its archives show that up until the 1990s, students were also almost all White, except for a few students of African (read: Black) and Middle Eastern descent.

For over six months, I attended classes at MV, talked to students, and observed curricular and extracurricular activities two or three times per week. Because of previous involvement in another project in the same school for almost two years, at the time of this research I was well acquainted with MV and its population, especially its African students, with whom I was able to develop a good communicative relationship.

---

[25] Fanon, 1967, p. 116.

[26] *See* Hall, 1991; and hooks, 1992.

Being the only Black adult, with the exception of one counsellor, and being a displaced subject, a refugee, and an African myself had given me a certain familiarity with the students' experiences. I was able to connect with different age and gender groups through a range of activities, initially "hanging out"[27] with the students and, later, playing sports with various groups. I was also approached by these students for both guidance and academic help. Because of my deep involvement in the student culture, at times my status as researcher was forgotten, and the line between the students and myself became blurred; clearly, we shared a **safe space** of comfort and trust that allowed us to open up, speak and engage freely.

Significantly, at the time of this research, students who (or whose parents) were born outside Canada made up 70 percent of the entire school population at MV. Continental Africans constituted the majority within that figure and, indeed, within MV's population in general, although their numbers fluctuated slightly from year to year. On its part nonetheless, the school continued to emphasize the theme of unity within this multicultural and multiethnoracial population. The slogan that the school advertised, for instance, was *unité dans la diversité* (unity in diversity). This discourse of unity, however, remained at the level of abstraction and had little material bearing on the students' lives, and the absence of people of colour from school personnel was a case in point. Indeed, it was the Frenchness of the school that seemed to be the capital of its promotion. That is, the French language, especially in Canada, represents a form of extremely important **symbolic capital** that, according to Bourdieu,[28] can be the key for accessing **material capitals** — jobs, business, and so on. Given their post-colonial educational history, most African youth, in fact, come to Franco-Ontarian schools already possessing a highly valued symbolic capital: *le français parisien* (Parisian French).

My research subjects encompassed these youth and part of a growing continental francophone African population in Franco-Ontarian schools, to which I refer as **Black Franco-Ontarians**. Their numbers have grown exponentially since the beginning of the 1990s. The participants varied: first, in their length of stay in Canada (from one to two, to five to six years); second, in their legal status (some were immigrants but the majority were refugees); and, third, in their sex, class, age, and linguistic and national backgrounds. As already noted, they came from places as diverse as Democratic Republic of Congo (formerly Zaïre), Djibouti, Gabon, Senegal, Somalia, South Africa, and Togo. With no exception, all of the African students in MV were at least trilingual, speaking English, French, and mother tongue or first language, with various (post-colonial) histories of language learning and degrees of fluency in each language.

On my return to MV in January 1996 to conduct my research, I spent the first month talking to, and spending time with male and female African youth of different age groups — with their permission as well as their parents' and the

---

[27] This means staying somewhere to familiarize oneself with the place, its people, and their ways of "being" in that space. In the school, these sites are informal, and include hallways, the schoolyards, the school steps, the cafeteria, and the gymnasium, places where the people in them are comfortable enough to speak their minds.

[28] Bourdieu, 1991.

school administration's. After a month, I chose 10 boys and six girls for extensive ethnographic observation inside and outside the classroom and inside and outside the school, and interviewed all 16. I conducted two types of interviews: individual and group. All interviews were conducted on the school ground, except for one group interview with the boys, which took place at one of the students' house. The individual interviews extended between an hour and a half to two hours and a half; the group interviews — one with the boys, and one with the girls — extended beyond three hours. I used open-questions where I asked the participants to explain certain patterns or verify certain conclusions.[29] Of the 10 boys, six were Somali speakers (from Somalia and Djibouti), one was Ethiopian, two were Senegalese, and one was from Togo. Their ages ranged from 16 to 20 years. The six girls were all Somali speakers (also from Somalia and Djibouti), aged 14 to 18 years. The students chose the language in which the interviews were conducted (English or French), and I translated the French-language interviews into English. The only Black counsellor and the former Black teacher were also interviewed.

Becoming Tri- or Multilingual: Sites and Sides of BESL Learning

Since these youth find themselves in a context where English is the medium of everyday interaction, this inescapability translates into a will to learn English rapidly. Elsewhere,[30] I offered popular culture, especially television, friendship and peer pressure as three mechanisms that hasten the speed of learning. The African students felt peer pressure, especially in their early days in the school, when they were denigrated for not speaking English. Franco-Ontarian students, Heller explains, use English in their everyday interaction, especially outside class.[31] If African students want to participate in schoolwide as well as in-and-outside class activities, they have no option but to learn English. Once it is learned, English becomes, on the one hand, as much a source of pride as it is a medium of communication; on the other, it allows African students to make friends and to fully participate in dominant markets and public spaces.

Yet, making friends, and even learning English, are influenced by the popular imaginary, representation, and culture: television. I asked students in all of the interviews "Où est-ce que vous avez appris votre anglais?" [Where did you learn English?]. "*Télévision,*" they all responded. However, within this télévision, a particular representation — Black popular culture — seems to **interpellate**[32] African youth identity and identification. Because African youth have few African-American friends and have limited daily contact with them, they access

---

[29] Ibrahim, 1998.

[30] Ibrahim, 1999.

[31] Heller, 1994; 1992.

[32] The subconscious ways in which individuals, given their genealogical history and memory, identify with particular discursive spaces and representations and the way this identification participates thereafter in the social formation of the Subject (*see* Althusser, 1971).

Black cultural identities and Black linguistic practices in and through Black popular culture, especially rap-music video-clips (accessed through MuchMusic, MuchVibe, and BET [Black Entertainment Television]), television programs, and Black cinematic representations (referring mainly to U.S. Black cinema). In the following excerpt, I inquired about the last movies Najat (14, F, Djibouti) saw:[33]

> Najat: I don't know, I saw *Waiting to Exhale* and I saw what else I saw, I saw *Swimmer*, and I saw *Jumanji*; so wicked, all the movies. I went to *Waiting to Exhale* wid my boyfriend and I was like "men are rude" [laughs].
>
> Awad: Oh believe me I know I know.
>
> Najat: And den he [her boyfriend] was like "no women are rude." I was like we're like fighting you know and joking around. I was like, and de whole time like [laughs], and den when de woman burns the car, I was like "go girl!" You know and all the women are like "go girl!" you know? And den de men like khhh. I'm like "I'm gonna go get me a popcorn" [laughs]. (individual interview, English)

Besides showing the influence of Black English in the use of "de," "den," "dat," and "wicked," as opposed to, respectively, "the," "then," "that," and "really really good," Najat's answer shows that youth bring agency and social subjectivities to the reading of a text. These subjectivities, it is important to note, are embedded in history, culture, and memory. Two performed aspects of subjectivity that influenced Najat's reading of *Waiting to Exhale* were her race and gender identities. Najat identified with Blackness, embodied in a female body; the Black/woman (played by Angela Bassett), in burning her husband's car and clothes, interpellates Najat.[34]

Another example (a videotaped moment) in a different context demonstrates the impact of Black popular culture on African students' lives and identities. Just before the focus-group interview with the boys. Picture this: *Electric Circus,* a Toronto-based television music and dance program that plays mostly Black music (rap/hip-hop, reggae, soul and R&B) began. "Silence!" one boy requested in French. The boys started to listen attentively to the music and watch the different fashions of the young people on the program. After the show, the boys' code switched among French, English, and Somali as they exchanged observations on the best music, the best dance, and the cutest girl. Rap and hip-hop music and the corresponding dress were obviously at the top of the list.

The moments of identification in the above examples are significant in that they point to the process of identity formation that is implicated, in turn, in the

---

[33] Each student name is followed by age, gender (F=female, M=Male), and country of origin; each extract is followed by the type of interview (individual or group) and the language in which it was conducted. The following transcription conventions are used:

<u>underlined text</u>   English spoken within French speech or French spoken within English speech

[ ]   Explanation or description of speaker's actions

[...]   Text omitted

[34] Much interesting critical assessment could be made of the role of films and other genres of popular culture, but I leave this interesting opportunity for further assessment elsewhere.

linguistic norm to be learned. The Western hegemonic representations of Black-ness, Hall shows,[35] are marginalizing, displacing, etc., and tend to work along-side historical and subconscious memories that facilitate their interpretations by members of the dominant groups. Once African youth encounter these repre-sentations, they look for Black cultural and representational forms as sites for empowered/centred identity formation and identification.[36] An important aspect of identification is that it works over a period of time and at the subconscious level. In the following excerpt, Omer (18, M, Ethiopia) addresses the myriad ways in which African youth are influenced by Black representations:

> Black Canadian youth are influenced by the Afro-Americans. You watch for hours, you listen to Black music, you watch Black comedy, Mr. T.,[37] the *Rap City,* there you will see singers who dress in particular ways. You see, so. (Individual interview, French)

Mukhi (19, M, Djibouti) explored the contention of identification by arguing that

> We identify ourselves more with the Blacks of America. But, this is normal, this is genetic. We can't, since we live in Canada, we can't identify ourselves with Whites or country music you know [laughs]. We are going to identify ourselves on the contrary with people of our colour, who have our lifestyle you know. (Group interview, French)

Mukhi evokes biology and genetic connection as a way of relating to Black America, and his identification with it is clearly stated. For Mukhi and all the students I spoke to, this identification is certainly connected to their inability to relate to dominant groups, the public spaces they occupied, and their cultural forms and norms. Alternatively, Black popular culture emerged not only as a site for identification but also as a space for language learning.

"A'ait, Q7 in the House!"

Rap, for African students, was an influential site for language learning. However, since rap was more prevalent in the boys' narratives than in the girls', this raises the question of the role of gender in the process of identifica-tion and learning.

In rap style, one starts a performance by "checking the mic": "One two, one two, mic check." Then the rapper either recites an already composed lyric or otherwise "kicks a free style," displaying the spontaneity that characterizes rap. The rapper begins the public performance by introducing herself or himself with a true or made-up name — "yo this is Shapir" — and thanks her or his "main man," or best friend, who often introduces the rapper to the public. Spe-cific to gangster rap, one represents not only oneself but a web of geophysical and metaphorical spaces and collectivities that are demarcated by people and territorial spaces: "represen'in Q7," "a'ait, this is Sam represen'in AQA." At

---

[35] Hall, 1990.

[36] *See* Kelly, 1998.

[37] Master T. was an M.C. of a local Canadian rap-music television program called *Rap City* (Much Music) that continues to air mostly American rap videos.

the end of the performance, when the recitation or freestyle is completed, again one thanks the "main man" and "gives peace out" or "shad out" (shout out) to the people.

On many occasions, the boys performed typical (gangster?) rap language and style, using linguistic as well as bodily performance, including name calling. What follows are just two of the many occasions on which students articulated their identification with Black America through the re/citation of rap linguistic styles.[38]

Sam: One two, one two, mic check. A'ait [aayet], a'ait, a'ait.

Juma: This is the rapper, you know wha 'm meaning? You know wha 'm saying?

Sam: Mic mic mic; mic check. A'ait you wonna test it? Ah, I've the microphone you know; a'ait.

Sam: [laughs] I don't rap man, c'mon give me a break. [laughs] Yo! A'ait a'ait you know, we just about to finish de tape and all dat. Respect to my main man [pointing to me]. So, you know, you know wha 'm mean, 'm just represen'in Q7. One love to Q7 you know wha 'm mean and all my friends back to Q7... Stop the tapin boy!

Jamal: Kim Juma, live! Put the lights on. Wordap. [Students talking in Somali] Peace out, wordap, where de book. Jamal 'am outta here.

Shapir: Yo, this is Shapir. I am trying to say peace to all my Niggas, all my bitches from a background that everybody in the house. So, yo, chill out and this is how we gonna kick it. Bye and with that pie. All right, peace yo.

Sam: A'ait this is Sam represen'in AQA [...] where it's born, represen'in you know wha 'm mean? I wonna say whassup to all my Niggas, you know, peace and one love. You know wha 'm mean, Q7 represen'in for ever. Peace! [Rap music]

Jamal: [as a DJ] Crank it man, coming up [rap music]. (Group interview, English)

Of interest in these excerpts is the use of Black stylized English, particularly the language of rap. On the other hand, when Shapir offers "peace to all" his "Niggas," all his "bitches," he is firstly re/appropriating the word **Nigger** as an appellation that is common in rap/hip-hop culture. That is, although no consensus, friends, especially young males, commonly call a Black friend **Nigger** without its traditional racist connotation. Second, however, Shapir is using the sexist language that might exist in rap.[39] These forms of sexism have been challenged by female rappers Lil' Kim, Queen Latifa, Missy Elliott, and Salt 'N Pepa and were critiqued by fellow female and male students. For example, in my interview with the girls, Samira (16, F, Djibouti) expressed her dismay at the sexist language found in some rap circles:

OK, hip-hop, yes I know that everyone likes hip-hop. They dress in a certain way, no? The songs go well. But, they are really really, they have expressions like fuck, bitches, etc. Sorry, but there is representation. (Group interview, French)

---

[38] The names cited in the extracts are Sam (19, M, Djibouti), Juma (19, M, Senegal), Jamal (18, M, Djibouti), and Shapir (17, M, Somalia).
[39] *See* Rose, 1991.

Here, Samira is addressing the impact that these expressions might have on the way society at large relates to and perceives the Black female body, which in turn influences how it is represented both inside and outside rap/hip-hop culture. Hassan (17, M, Djibouti) as well expressed his disapproval of this abusive language: "Occasionally, rap has an inappropriate language for the life in which we live, a world of violence and all that." (Individual interview, French)

The boys were clearly influenced by rap lyrics, syntax and morphology (in their broader semiological sense), especially by gangster rap.[40] Depending on their age, the girls, on the other hand, had an ambivalent relationship to rap, even though both boys and girls used the same three strategies in learning ESL (English as a Second Language) in general and BSE in particular through music: listening, reading and reciting. Jamal, in the above cited extract, for instance, was listening to the tunes and lyrics while reading and following the written text. Acting as a DJ, he then repeated not only the performer's words and expressions, but also his accent.

For their part, the girls also used similar strategies to Jamal's. For example, during a picnic organized by a mixed group of males and females, the females listened to music while following the written text and reciting it (complete with accents) along with the singer. The girls' choice of music (including Whitney Houston and Toni Braxton) differed in that it was softer than that chosen by the boys and contained mostly romantic themes.

For the most part, the older females (16–18 years old) tended to be more eclectic in how they related to hip-hop and rap. Their eclecticism was evident in how they dressed, and in what language they learned. Their dress was either elegant middle class, partially hip-hop, or traditional, and their learned language was what Nourbese Philip calls "plain Canadian English."[41] The younger females (12–14 years), on the other hand, like the boys, dressed in hip-hop style and performed BSE.[42]

Performing Acts of Desire

I have identified rap and hip-hop as influential sites in African students' processes of becoming Black, which in turn affected what and how they learned. Their narratives also significantly show that the youth were quite cognizant of their identification with Blackness and the significance of race in their choices. In the following conversation, Mukhi reflected on the impact of rap (as just one among many other Black popular cultural forms) on his life and other lives around him:

---

[40] Gangster, or Gangsta Rap is a form of rap that does not know censorship; it speaks its mind using socially defined "obscene" language. According to Smitherman (2000, p. 142), "gangster" refers to "(1) any event, activity, behavior, person or object [or language] that represents a rejection of mainstream society's standards. (2) A rebellious, nonconformist person, a social 'outlaw' who refuses to buckle under to white authority and white norms and is thus revered. Both meanings reflect a resurfacing and extension of the 1960s/70s concept of **gangsta**, referring to street life and street culture."

[41] Philip, 1991.

[42] For full analysis of gender identity difference among African youth, *see* Ibrahim, 2000b.

Awad: But do you listen to rap, for example? I noticed that there are a number of students who listen to rap, eh? Is ...

Sam: It is not just us who listen to rap, everybody listens to rap. It is new.

Awad: But do you think that that influences how you speak, how ...

Mukhi: *How we dress, how we speak, how we behave.* [italics added] (Group interview, English)

These linguistic patterns and dress codes that Mukhi addresses are accessed and learned by African youth through Black popular culture. As I already noted, these patterns do not require mastery and fluency. Indeed, they are performative acts of desire and identification. As Amani (16, F, Somalia) contended:

We have to wonder why we try to really follow the model of the Americans who are Blacks? Because *when you search for yourself, search for identification, you search for someone who reflects you, with whom you have something in common.* [italics added] (Group interview, French)

Hassan supported Amani as follows:

Hassan: Yes yes, African students are influenced by rap and hip-hop because they want to, yes, they are influenced probably a bit more because it is the desire to belong may be.

Awad: Belong to what?

Hassan: To a group, belong to a society, to have a model/fashion [he used the term *un modèle*]; you know, the desire to mark oneself, the desire to make, how do I say it? To be part of a <u>rap</u> society, you see. It is like getting into <u>rock and roll</u> or <u>heavy metal</u>. (Individual interview, French)

Hence, **one invests where one sees oneself mirrored**. Such an investment includes linguistic as well as cultural behavioural patterns. In an individual interview, Hassan told me it would be unrealistic to expect to see Blackness allied with rock and roll or heavy metal, as they are socially constructed as White music. On the other hand, he argued emphatically that African youth would have every reason to invest in basketball — constructed as a Black sport — but not hockey, for example.

Conclusion: Towards a Pedagogy of the Imaginary

When it encounters resistance from the other, self-consciousness undergoes the experience of desire — the first milestone on the road that leads to the dignity of the spirit ... As soon as I desire I am asking to be considered. I am not merely here-and-now, sealed into thingness. I am for somewhere else and for something else. I demand that notice be taken of my negating activity insofar as I ... do battle for the creation of a human world — that is, of a world of reciprocal recognition.[43]

---

[43] Fanon, 1967, p. 218.

The desire on the part of African youth, particularly the boys, to invest in basketball is analogously no different from their desire to learn BESL. Learning is hence neither aimless nor neutral, nor is it without the politics of identity. As I have shown, a second-language learner can have a marginalized linguistic norm as a target, depending on who is learning what, why and how. I have also discussed how these youth were becoming Black, which meant learning BESL. Becoming Black, I have argued, was an identity signifier produced by and producing the very process of BESL. To become Black is to become an ethnographer who translates and looks around in an effort to understand what it means to be Black in Canada, for example. To understand what it means to be Black in Canada, African youth felt the need to look outside the country. Significantly, this was a negation neither to the everyday struggle of local Black communities, nor to their strong presence. Their identification with African-Americans speaks, on the one hand, to the history of Blackness in Canada — the present that is made absent, nowhere to be seen or heard, especially in the school and the media. And, on the other, it articulates the global impact of Black/African-American popular culture, especially hip-hop — what might be called "the Afro-Americanization of youth." In becoming Black, the African youth were interpellated by rap and hip-hop as sites of identification. Gender, however, was as important as race in what was being chosen and translated, and by whom and how it was chosen and translated.

Choosing the margin, I emphasize, is simultaneously an act of investment, an expression of desire, and a deliberate counterhegemonic undertaking. Choosing rap, especially, must be read as an act of resistance. Historically, rap has been formed as a voice for voicelessness and performed as a prophetic language that addresses silence, the silenced, and the state of being silenced. It explores the hopes and the human, political, historical, and cultural experience of the *Black Atlantic*.[44] As Jamal argued,

> Black Americans created rap to express themselves; how do I say it? Their ideas, their problems, [and] if we could integrate ourselves into it, it is because rappers speak about or they have the same problems we have. (Individual interview, French)

Such problems may include human degradation, police brutality, and everyday racisms.[45] Above all, rap is a conscious attempt to make visible that which is made invisible and to address the impact of being under the hegemonic White gaze. Of course, the gaze is invisible, as we know, which renders any attempt to addrcss it or deconstruct it even more formidable.[46] As a mechanism and technology of panopticism and power, the gaze is felt but not seen. This is because, in the exercise of power, **the economy of invisibility** — panopticism, the gaze — is more yielding than the traditional notion of power in producing docile bodies and in getting the desired results. Traditionally, Foucault argued, power is defined as what is seen, shown, and manifested.[47] According to the

---

[44] Gilroy, 1993.

[45] *See* Essed, 1991 and Anthias & Yuval-Davis, 1992.

[46] I am invoking the invisibility of the gaze, therefore, to address the present that can only be felt but not seen, a present that polices and regulates our bodies and identities.

[47] Foucalt, 1984.

economy of invisibility, this is no longer, and never was, the case. The mechanism and mechanic of power, again, Foucault argued, is "exercised through its invisibility."[48] And those on whom this mechanism was exercised "could remain in the shade; they received light only from that portion of power that was conceded on them, or from the reflection of it that for a moment they carried." In power, "it is the subjects who have to be seen," not the mechanism of its exercise — the gaze. And for these subjects, the gaze is not something they see; they only feel "its effects — in replica, as it were — on their bodies."[49] Nonetheless, I would like to undertake such a task by proposing what I want to term a "pedagogy of the imaginary":[50] a critical pedagogy aims and points at a way of deessentializing and decolonizing public spaces, both represented and imagined. For me, the imaginary is that combined space that leans more towards the unconscious than the conscious; a space that allows us to know what to expect. The imaginary is the subject's internalization of **images** — mental representations, memories, conceptions, perceptions — that are mostly subconscious. These imagoes preferentially orient the way in which the subject apprehends the Other.[51] It poses the following questions: how do we as a nation, as groups, and as individuals imagine ourselves as well as others; what impact does it have on others, and how can we, as pedagogues, work with this imaginary to make people imagine themselves as well as others differently?

The African students, it seems to me, were casualties of fixity. That is, they were already fixed in an identity, already slotted in an imaginary, which in complex ways limited how and where they circulated, performed, and articulated their identities. In so being, they were erased and made invisible. This (fixed) identity is not based on who one **is**: one's own social-cultural, national, and linguistic identity. It is based, on the contrary, primarily on how one appears, one's racial identity: "Oh, they all look alike to me!" This state of mind is thus largely dependent on the already circulating colonial discourses and hegemonic representations of Blackness. Hence, such fixed identities do not depend upon how one sounds when speaking; all they require is visual observation and scrutiny of a body.

It is this imposed fixity that we need to further reckon with. For now, I want to argue that it is an act of symbolic violence that requires no intentionality. Intentionally or not, symbolic violence had been exerted on African students, for example, by denying them their full identities, which encompassed more than their racial identity. Put differently, African students appeared to have fallen prey to this fixity, which imposed on them the already

---

[48] Ibid., p. 199.

[49] Ibid.

[50] Without entering in a full debate about the Lacanian language, a signifier that hardly anybody seems to fully signify (Letche, 1994), I use "the imaginary" as an expression of everyday life. The imaginary is not simply the place where images are produced or where the subject engages the pleasures of the imagination. In effect, the imaginary is where the subject misrecognizes (*méconnaît*) the nature of the symbolic. The imaginary is thus the realm of illusion, but a necessary illusion (Ibid.).

[51] In the imaginary mode, Jane Gallop contends, one's understanding of the Other is shaped by one's imagoes and, in the final analysis, the perceived Other is, in fact, at least in part, a projection (*see* Gallop, 1985).

established North American order, discourses, and historical representations of Blackness. What we visibly "see" can be deceiving; and although we may all project preconceived identities on others in one way or another in our everyday interactions, when this imposition is coupled with power, its consequences can be traumatic, if not injurious.

The pedagogy of the imaginary addresses those who can manoeuver those socio-historical structures that allow them to exert such violence. Paulo Freire[52] has called them the oppressors: those who possess the power to represent, structure and restructure nations and narrations, and thus write and rewrite. It is important that in formulating a pedagogy, though, we need to discuss, position, observe, and imagine race as well as gender as categories of visible subjects that occupy sites recognizable only through an actual, ethnographic, and **material encounter**, and not an imagined one. In such sites, Blackness may refer to a homosexual, a middle-class person, a writer, a university professor subjects; gender may refer to a lesbian, an upper-middle-class person, a company executive, and so on. In other words, we need to imagine subjects' categories as always occupying different and multiple sites, albeit perhaps not in abundant numbers in some sites. Since the public imaginary has been colonized by the self-serving power bloc representing only their own kind, these categories have rarely been represented in heterogeneous ways and discussed as ever-changing.

The pedagogy of the imaginary in this context, then, is a hopeful yet critical pedagogy that "allows us to affirm multiple black identities, varied black experience. It also challenges colonial imperialist paradigms of black identity which represent blackness one-dimensionally in ways that reinforce and sustain white supremacy."[53] It is a pedagogy that will eventually help us to imagine, in the case of African students, for example, that Blackness has cultural, national, religious, and linguistic repertoires that differ from those evident in North American Blackness, which is itself far more diverse and complex than African-American rap/hip-hop culture. Blackness is **de facto** multicultural, multilingual, and multiethnic.

Within this pedagogy, another form of encounter is of a particular significance in rupturing the normative and normalizing gaze: **symbolic encounter**. Here, the emphasis is on texts, art, and cinematic and other forms of symbolic representations. Specifically, I am proposing rap, hip-hop, and Black popular culture in general as pedagogical moments, "sites of symbolic encounter," with Blackness in the classroom. In so doing, I am pointing to the horizon of possibilities of using Black cultural productions, particularly musical, literary, and cinematic representations, as moments of rupture of what hooks called "colonial imperialist paradigms" where Black identities are represented "one-dimensionally." As we have seen, Black popular culture (rap and hip-hop in particular) are curriculum sites where learning takes place and where identities are invested.

---

[52] Freire, 1993.

[53] hooks, 1990, p. 28; *see also* hooks, 1994; and Willinsky, 1998.

In the language of antiracism education,[54] proposing Black popular culture as a curriculum site is, on the one hand, a call to centralize and engage marginalized subjects, their voices, and their ways of being and learning. And it raises the following question, on the other: In the case of African students, whose language and identity are best pedagogues teaching and assuming in the classroom if they do not engage rap or hip-hop? This proposition, then, entails a legitimization of a form of knowledge otherwise perceived as illegitimate.[55]

The encounter with Black cultural forms, moreover, is and must be seen as a moment of critical examination instead of passive consumption. Because Black popular cultural forms are also social and historical productions, they are as much sites of hope, celebration and acknowledgement as they are sites of critique. Rap and hip-hop, as noted, are not exceptions to dominant discourses of sexism and homophobia.[56] They should, therefore, not be unproblematically consumed, but should be critically framed, studied, and engaged. Yet, rap and hip-hop are also sites of hope, a hope that will eventually broaden the horizon of possibility;[57] the possibility that Blackness is seen and imagined for what it is: multiple, complex, and multilayered. A hope that will allow all students, but particularly those from dominant groups, to be introduced to, and be able to "see," multiple ways of speaking, being, and learning. In Paulo Freire's[58] language, introducing rap and hip-hop in class, especially in the case of African students, is done with the hope of linking their world, identities, desires, and investments with their words.

References

Althusser, Louis. (1971). *Lenin and philosophy*. London: New Left Books.

Anderson, B. (1983). *Imagined communities: Reflections on the origin and spread of nationalism*. London: Verso.

Anthias, F., & Yuval-Davis, N. (1992). *Racialized boundaries*. London & New York: Routledge.

Barthes, Roland. (1983). *Elements of semiology*. New York: Hill & Wang. (Original work published 1967)

Bhabha, Homi. (1990). The third space: Interview with Homi Bhabha. In J. Rutherford (Ed.), *Identity community, culture, difference* (pp. 26–33). London: Lawrence & Wishart.

Bhabha, Homi. (1994). *The location of culture*. London & New York: Routledge.

---

[54] *See* Dei & Calliste, 2000; Dei, 1996; James, 1995; Ibrahim, 2000b; and Chideya, 2000.

[55] Ibrahim, 2000b and 1999.

[56] *See* Rose, 1991, and Walcott, 1995.

[57] *See* Simon, 1992.

[58] Freire, 1993.

Bourdieu, Pierre. (1991). *Language and symbolic power* (G. Raymond & M. Adamson, Trans.). London: Polity Press.

Butler, Judith. (1999). *Gender trouble: Feminism and the subversion of identity.* New York: Routledge. (Original work published 1990)

Chideya, F. (2000). *The color of our future: Race for the 21st century.* New York: Quill William Morrow.

Dei, G.J., & Calliste, A. (Eds.). (2000). *Power, knowledge and anti-racism education.* Halifax: Fernwood.

Dei, G.J.S. (1996). *Anti-racism education: Theory and practice.* Halifax: Fernwood.

Essed, P. (1991). *Understanding everyday racism: An interdisciplinary theory.* Newbury ParK, CA: Sage.

Fanon, Frantz. (1967). *Black skin white mask.* New York: Grove Weidenfeld.

Foucault, Michel. (1980). *Power/knowledge: Selected interviews and other writings.* New York: Pantheon Books.

Foucault, M. (1984). *Foucault reader.* New York: Pantheon Books.

Fine, M., Powell, L., Weiss L., & Wong, L.M. (Eds.). (1997). *Off white: Readings on race, power and society.* New York: Routledge.

Freire, P. (1993). *Pedagogy of the oppressed.* New York: Continuum.

Gallop, Jane. (1985). *Reading Lacan.* Ithaca & London: Cornell University Press.

Gilroy, Paul. (1993). *The black Atlantic: Modernity and double consciousness.* London & New York: Routledge.

Hall, Stuart. (1990). Cultural identity and diaspora. In J. Rutherford (Ed.), *Identity, community, culture, difference* (pp. 222–237). London: Lawrence & Wishart.

Hall, Stuart. (1991). Ethnicity: Identity and difference. *Radical America, 13*(4): 9–20.

Hall, Stuart. (1996). *Race: The floating signifier.* [A videorecording produced, directed, and edited by Sut Jhally.] Northampton, MA: Media Education Foundation.

Hall, Stuart. (Ed.). (1997). *Representation: Cultural representations and signifying practices.* London: Open University.

Heller, Monica. (1992). The politics of codeswitching and language choice. *Journal of Multilingual and Multicultural Development, 13*(1&2): 123–142.

Heller, Monica. (1994). *Crosswords: Language, education and ethnicity in French Ontario.* Berlin & New York: Mouton de Gruyter.

hooks, bell. (1990). *Yearning: Race, gender, and cultural politics.* Toronto: Between the Lines.

hooks, bell. (1992). *Black looks.* Boston, MA: South End Press.

hooks, bell. (1994). *Teaching to transgress: Education as the practice of freedom.* London & New York: Routledge.

Ibrahim, Awad. (1998). *'Hey, whassup homeboy?' Becoming black: Race, language, culture, and the politics of identity. African students in a Franco-Ontarian high school.* Unpublished doctoral dissertation, OISE, University of Toronto, Toronto, Ontario.

Ibrahim, Awad. (1999). Becoming black: Rap and hip-hop, race, gender, identity, and the politics of ESL learning. *TESOL Quarterly, 33*(3), 349–369.

Ibrahim, Awad. (2000a). "Hey, Ain't I Black Too?" The politics of becoming black. In R. Walcott (Ed.), *Rude: Contemporary black Canadian cultural criticism* (pp. 109–136). Toronto: Insomniac Press.

Ibrahim, Awad. (2000b). "Whassup homeboy?" Black/popular culture and the politics of "curriculum studies": Devising an anti-racism perspective. In G.J.S. Dei & A. Calliste (Eds.), *Power, knowledge and anti-racism education: A critical reader* (pp. 57–72). Halifax: Feronwood.

Ibrahim, Awad. (2000c). Trans-framing identity: Race, language, culture, and the politics of translation. *trans/forms: Insurgent Voices in Education, 5*(2), 120–135.

Ibrahim, Awad. (2001). Race-in-the-gap: Émigrés, identity, identification, and the politics of ESL learning. *Contact, 27*(2), 67–80.

James, Carl E. (1995). Multiculturalism and antiracism education in the Canadian context. *Race, Gender and Class, 2*(3), 31–48.

Kelly, J. (1998). *Under the gaze: Learning to be black in white society*. Halifax: Fernwood.

Kristeva, Julia. (1974). *La révolution du langage poétique* [Revolution in Poetic Language]. Paris: Lautréament et Mallarmé.

Letche, J. (1994). *Fifty key contemporary thinkers*. New York: Routledge.

Nietzsche, Friedrich. (1977). *A Nietzsche reader* (Selected and translated with an introduction by R. J. Hollingdale). New York: Penguin Classics.

Philip, Marlene N. (1991). *Harriet's daughter*. Toronto: The Women's Press.

Prince, A. (2001). *Being black*. Toronto: Insomniac Press.

Rose, Tricia. (1991). "Fear of a black planet": Rap music and black cultural politics in the 1990s. *Journal of Negro Education, 60*(3), 276–290.

Sartre, Jean-Paul. (1980). *Being and nothingness: A phenomenological essay on ontology* (Hazel E. Barnes, Trans.). New York: Pocket Books.

Simon, R.I. (1992). *Teaching against the grain*. New York: Bergin and Garvey.

Simon, R.I., & Dippo, D. (1986). On critical ethnography work. *Anthropology & Education Quarterly, 17*(3), 195–202.

Simmons, Russell. (2001). *Life and def: Sex, drugs, money, and god*. New York: Crown.

Smitherman, Geneva. (2000). *Black talk: Words and phrases from the hood to the Amen corner*. Boston: Houghton Mifflin. (Original work published 1994)

Walcott, Rinaldo. (1995). *Performing the postmodern: Black Atlantic rap and identity in North America*. Unpublished doctoral dissertation, OISE, University of Toronto, Toronto, Ontario.

Willinsky, John. (1998). *Learning to divide the world: Education at empire's end*. Minneapolis: University of Minnesota Press.

Questions for Discussion

1. How do race, language, and culture intersect with one another?

2. What does the phrase "speak white" mean according to Makropoulos?

3. Discuss the dichotomization between White-male and Chinese-male identity in nineteenth- and early-twentieth-century British Columbia? How does Retallack argue that gender has informed racialized identity in the stereotypes of "Jack Canuck" and "John Chinaman"?

4. According to Ibrahim, what are the processes and the reference points involved in becoming black?

5. Describe what the phrase "ethnography of performance" means as stated by Ibrahim?

6. Retallack argues that we must examine the representation of Chinese men in terms of "dominant and subordinate masculinities." What previous model of inquiry is he disrupting and how might his approach open new possibilities of interpretation?

7. Makropoulos and Ibrahim both use the term "Franco-Ontarian". Discuss how and why they each mobilize this term.

8. Both Nelson, in "Adrif in the Diaspora" (Part 4), and Ibrahim, in "Performing Desire", address a longing for belonging. Explore the similarities and differences of this quest.

Part 6 Popular Culture

The depiction of racial and ethnic identity within popular culture is complex insofar as it highlights the tensions inherent in any marketable (re)presentation. Popular cultural representations are unique since their medium generally allows for mass-production, dissemination and consumption. Film, radio and television are each media capable of reaching hundreds, thousands, millions or even more consumers simultaneously. Hence, their potential power is not only their immediacy (the ability to experience something "as it is happening") but their reach. This reach not only raises question about how Canadians construct themselves for other Canadians, but for external consumption.

Popular culture is also seductive because it is often consumed *casually*, that is in private or otherwise non-officious spaces which do not appear to direct, regulate or confine consumption in obvious ways. The distinctiveness of the consumption of popular culture, which is often associated with leisure activities or fun, is historically different from the assumed contemplative or intellectual endeavour of "high" art consumption. Arguably, it is the *fun* of popular culture which may seduce consumers into uncritical consumption practices.

For the majority to embrace popular culture, stereotypical depictions, iconography and symbolism might be more appealing than more compelling, nuanced and heterogeneous portrayals. Popular culture helps to produce racial stereotypes which in turn become embraced, even demanded, by audiences. Arguably then, any media portrayal, which represents ethnic and racial identity in a way more consistent with mainstream perceptions, may be more likely to be financially successful; hence, the frequent claim from television, film and music/radio executives, that they are simply "giving the people what they want".

The essays in this Part reveal, however, that the salience of popular Canadian culture is controlled not only by the whims of an (un)informed and fickle audience but also by both subliminal and overt political, social and economic motivations. The three essays included in this essay, "Race In/Out of the Classroom: Degrassi (Junior) High as Multicultural Context"; "Other Canadian Voices: The Development of Ethnic Broadcasting in Canada"; and "(Re)Visioning Histories: Racism in Early Prairie Cinema", all reveal the social and political construction of race within Canadian popular culture.

These essays force the reader to consider several important questions. First, what constitutes pluralistic, heterogeneous racial identity within popular culture? Second, do such identities "sell"? And perhaps most important, are we, as the audience and consumers of popular culture, thinking critically about the complex political, social, and even moral messages about race and ethnicity that we are ingesting? If popular culture is to provide an educative role, majority perceptions of racial and ethnic identity must be informed ones that include and are transformed by the voices of those depicted and portrayed. The following essays are designed to introduce you to the rhetoric and ideas through which you can tackle your new task. The opening essay, "Race In/Out of the Classroom: Degrassi (Junior) High as Multicultural Context", focuses on a contemporary Canadian teen television show and discusses the characters, their relationships, and their problem resolution. The show, which will be familiar to many of you, was designed to be a progressive look into Canadian teenage culture that transcended racial barriers. Examine its storylines closely to determine whether they function as designed.

The next essay, "Other Canadian Voices: The Development of Ethnic Broadcasting in Canada", refocuses the lens of analysis on radio broadcasting. This essay traces the history of the Canadian Broadcasting Corporation as it relates to notions of racial and ethnic identity. The behind-the-scenes politics of this media are revealed and problematized.

Part 6 closes with "(Re)Visioning Histories: Racism in Early Prairie Cinema", an essay that examines the early depiction of racial minorities in Canadian cinema. This essay reveals the political impetus and propagandistic importance behind some early Canadian cinema. Significantly, such films are responsible for helping to construct the very racial "others" which they then sought to assimilate.

This Part examines popular culture as a politicized site where assimilationist and conformist strategies are often deployed, intentionally or not, through the use of racial stereotyping. The power of popular culture is its *everywhere* quality, which provides an immediacy and saturation unparalleled by other forms of cultural production or communication. It is this power that allows it to influence our behaviours, impressions, perceptions, assessments and opinions, often without our knowledge.

By critically examining a variety of media, including television, radio and cinema, both official and unofficial Canadian policy is unearthed as it implicates race, ethnicity and gender. Accordingly, these authors encourage a cautious and critical digestion of popular culture, which mandates an understanding of the power of popular culture to shape our perceptions of ourselves and others.

16

Race In/Out of the Classroom
Degrassi (Junior) High as Multicultural Context

Michele Byers
Department of Sociology and Criminology
Saint Mary's University
Halifax

Identity is a complicated matter. Everyone has one, rarely are we aware of how we got one.

Howard Ramos[1]

Why

is there so little written about Canadian television? Why have so many scholars (including myself) consistently made the focus of our inquiries American television? Even in a recent text called *Media and Minorities: Representing Diversity in a Multicultural Canada*, the authors use *The Cosby Show* as their case study.[2] The lack of attention paid to Canadian television makes it a relatively untapped source for study. For the purposes of this essay, I will focus on one program that represents a departure from the representations of multiculturalism and diversity offered by other youth-oriented texts. The *Degrassi* series, while trying to maintain a certain National ambiguity — presumably to broaden the appeal of the show south of the Canadian border — has come to be recognized as excessively Canadian, almost to the point of cliché (as are, for example, poutine, saying, "Eh," and The Tragically Hip). What is it about the show that makes it resonate so strongly with ideas about Canadian identity and culture? Can we read this not as mere abstraction, but as a concrete representational and performative vision? What is this vision, and what is there about it that made *Degrassi* so popular and has allowed it to maintain this popularity in the decade since its last episode aired?

Degrassi Junior High (later *Degrassi High*) emerged slightly ahead of the moment when youth-oriented media overtook North America in the early 1990s. Though the Spelling-driven *Beverly Hills, 90210* is often considered the grandparent of the "genre," in fact, *Degrassi* was there a year earlier. Moreover, there is a myth (one whose "truth" I have never been able to prove) that Spelling approached the producers of *Degrassi* during its first year. Apparently, he was interested in buying the show's concept, though he wanted to move it to Los Angeles and, of course, recast. It was after his offer was declined that he developed the *90210* series and, certainly, there are some similarities between the two. But *Degrassi* offered a very different vision of adolescent social life, one that is quite unique in its Canadianness. Though the series earned much praise and critical acclaim from the first, very little has been written about it outside of the popular press. In what follows, I will take an indepth look at *Degrassi* and what it said (and says) about the construction of

---

[1] Ramos, 2001, p. 104.

[2] Fleras & Hunz, 2001, Chapter 5.

racial identity — in terms of not only race and ethnicity as minority issues, but also the intersection of marginalization and privilege — in urban Canada.

When we think about Canadian television, it is often within a rather problematic hierarchy; that is, positioned beneath the monolithic American media industry. The fear that Canadian media products will be lost in the vortex of U.S. products is nothing new. Neither is the desire to combat this cultural invisibility by creating products that are uniquely — recognizably — Canadian. But this drive is equally problematic, because what does it mean to produce something that is recognizably Canadian? Although Americans are by no means a homogeneous group, they are often felt to possess a sense of "Americanism" that is absent in our more fragmentary Canadianness.[3] What this really raises are two distinct questions: What does it mean to make "Canadian television"? And why do we, or why does everyone, seem to prefer American-style programming?

I think we have to take these questions separately in order to do them each justice. I want to start with the second first, because it appears to have the easiest and most obvious answer. American programs are prolific and dominate not only their own airwaves and ours but, increasingly, the global airwaves as well. This has created a lot of panic, here as elsewhere, about the loss of cultural identity and the need for media products that reflect the concerns, values and moralities of particular viewing populations. Additionally, it appears that American media products have become the standard for our disparate viewing pleasures. This is, in part, because of their sheer number, allowing them to be more easily (and cheaply) disseminated. In almost any area of programming, most people will tune in to American television; sometimes I even find myself watching American news because it seems to be more interesting than my local stations. Another thing that allows American programming to set standards is finance. That is, they are able to saturate the airwaves, creating a situation where the look and feel of their products comes to be identified as superior. (One often hears comments that Canadian programs "look" Canadian — meaning inferior.) There is a feeling that "if a series is too Canadian, if it has a special Canadian flavour, then it won't be marketable."[4] There is a huge media network to fill (cable, digital cable, satellite), and much of it is filled with American products (whether new or in syndication). Hence, another reason we watch American media so often is that it takes up most of our mediated spaces most of the time.

The second question is a lot more difficult to answer. What is Canadian television, and what makes it recognizable? First, Canadian production values often seem different from American ones. There is a different look to Canadian television (in the texture and in the narrative style) that often makes it recognizable, especially to those of us who are Canadian (and prone to being a little self-deprecating) and say, "Oh, **look** at that it has to be Canadian." But there are other things that are, if not unique to Canadian television (and little is), rather pronounced within its narratives. One of these things is diversity.

---

[3] Audley, 1983.

[4] Taras, 2001, p. 193.

Diversity (racial and ethnic in this instance) is, as I have said, not unique to Canadian television programming. There are many American television shows that offer some diversity in terms of racial and ethnic representation. But there has been a tendency to omit diversity in youth programming in favour of racially segregated series development. This was true of shows such as *Beverly Hills, 90210* and *The Fresh Prince of Bel-Air,* which aired at roughly the same time as *Degrassi.* It has continued to be true of more recent series like *Buffy the Vampire Slayer, Dawson's Creek, Friends* and *Moesha.* It seems that the idea of a show that focuses on teenagers in ethnically and racially diverse environments (including high schools and communities) is not seen as viable at this time. That is not to say these shows never engage questions of diversity and discrimination, but that they are produced in very specific ways: usually to teach the audience about racial tolerance through the tropes of parental, peer or community intolerance of such issues as interracial dating. Often, these themes are not intrinsic to the greater narrative structure, lasting merely an episode or two (at which point the characters who represent a departure from the racial or ethnic status quo disappear). Race is employed in the service of its own invisibility within the dominant culture as well as called upon to act as a voyeur of that culture.[5] But in some Canadian shows like *Degrassi* (as well as *Ready or Not* and *Madison*), diversity is integrated more comprehensively into the show. That is not to say diversity is not mobilized in the service of addressing issues of discrimination and prejudice, but that having a racially and ethnically diverse core cast extends beyond this function. Characters of different racial and ethnic backgrounds are shown to be part of a common and collective community, one that allows them to have characteristics that extend beyond a focus on their race and/or ethnic affiliation. This, perhaps, bears out the idea that youth-oriented programming is more "diversity-friendly," at least in Canada.[6]

The cast of *Degrassi* is primarily white, though it includes characters of African-Canadian and Asian descent. There are also characters identified as Italian, Greek, Jewish, Latin, Irish, Lebanese, Eastern European and Catholic. This diversity is organized as a natural part of the characters as they go to school and about the business of their everyday lives. This is different from attempts to use diversity (especially in terms of race) to make a show more profitable by allowing it to seem more "correct."[7] Here, diversity does not function in the service of profit, but in the service of representation. The stories that enact issues of prejudice and discrimination grow out of relationships that appear to develop naturally in the community the text represents. That is, the plot does not bring in diverse characters in order to allow brief, heated storylines. These storylines, when they appear, grow out of the relationships between characters who already exist. And the televisual community represented seems to bear a much more honest relationship to the community that produced it and where it was produced (in this case, the very diversified landscape

---

[5] Hoechsmann, 1996.

[6] Fleras & Hunz, 2001, p. 88.

[7] DuCille, 1996.

of inner-city Toronto). This is a great departure from the series that represent diverse spaces as televisually homogeneous (for example, the New York of *Friends*). *Degrassi* actually seems to live in the community in which it was produced rather than some bleached version of it.

The other central marker of this show as Canadian, one that can be linked directly to its ability to represent diversity, is the fact that the show was produced for the Canadian Broadcasting Corporation (CBC); that is, public broadcasting. Within the sphere of public broadcasting there is less anxiety about production than is often found in the regular — for profit — networks. Because public broadcasters do not rely on advertising revenues in the same way that other broadcasters do, they do not have to toe the lines (financial and moral) set out by the advertising industry and the producers of consumables they serve. D'Acci provides an excellent practical illustration of how this sort of thing can work. In her article about *Cagney & Lacey* (a slightly controversial female cop/buddy show that aired in the mid-1980s), she described their attempt to introduce a storyline in which one of the characters ponders whether to have an abortion.[8] Recall that this period was more politically neutral than the current period, and yet advertisers were pressured by right-wing groups to pull their support for the show if the network went through with its plan to run the episode. Unable to risk the revenue necessary to keep the network running, the episode was shelved.

A public broadcaster like the CBC may not feel the same sort of pressure. In fact, *Degrassi* has aired two major storylines in which teenaged characters chose to have abortions. They also followed (and continue to follow into the new series, *Degrassi: The Next Generation,* first aired in October 2001) the story of a pregnant eighth grader who successfully fought to be allowed to remain in her junior-high class while pregnant. Perhaps these storylines also say something about the relationship between this show and Canadianness. They suggest that there is a link between Canadian identity and a belief in liberalism, a sense of greater equality and tolerance (especially in relation to our neighbours to the south). The affiliation of *Degrassi* with the CBC is an instrumental part of its Canadianness, because the CBC, more than any other Canadian television station, must meet standards that are specifically linked to Canadianness. As described by Siegel, these include: addressing the needs of Canadian society as a whole, fostering communication between and among cultures and regions, and "contributing to the development of national unity and provision for a continuing expression of Canadian identity."[9] This last criterion articulates rather clearly that *Degrassi* is a very Canadian show, made by a network that is especially concerned with Canadianness. As Taras suggests, the CBC "has been not only the major chronicler of Canadian life, but one of its defining features."[10] *Degrassi* has these liberal sensibilities embedded deeply within it, sensibilities that emerge in the show's treatment of difficult and often taboo issues, includ-

---

[8] D'Acci, 1992, pp. 169–202.

[9] Siegel, 1983, Chapter 8.

[10] Taras, 2001, p. 117.

ing sex, death, racism and prejudice, the latter two being those with which I will be concerned for the rest of this essay.

I am concerned with the specificity with which the Canadian subject matter of *Degrassi* is constructed. If *Degrassi* belongs to a certain tradition — leftist public broadcasting with an aim towards egalitarianism and education — then, are questions of race, ethnicity, privilege and prejudice dealt with within its narratives? I will investigate this question by examining some of the storylines that focus on these issues as they arise within the more general narratives and character development of the series. I will also explore how certain characters (and not others) are mobilized to carry the weight of issues of race and ethnicity. That is, although *Degrassi* is embedded in a discourse of diversity — in the sense that it is itself diverse in terms of cast — only certain characters are coded racially and/or ethnically in the sense that their identities are marked as such by the narrative. Why is it, for instance, that the character BLT (Dayo Ade) is defined foremost by his race (Black), while the character Lucy (Anais Granofsky, who is multiracial) is more powerfully defined by her gender and political affiliations? Why, further, is diversity in this text, as in most others, defined in the absence of the acknowledgement of privilege? Why is whiteness, even if sometime defined along ethnic lines, not racialized? Why is race so often essentialized on the basis of colour?[11]

I would like to begin by looking at two *Degrassi* narratives that feature questions of race, prejudice and discrimination. The first concerns Arthur (Duncan Waugh) and Yick (Siluck Saysanasy), two best friends who must negotiate their relationship despite differences embedded in race and class. The second follows an ongoing romantic relationship between Michelle (Maureen McKay) and BLT, who must deal with the resistance they encounter to their interracial relationship. Especially poignant is Michelle's slow realization of her position of privilege as well as the racist attitudes that surround her and actually come from some of the people she loves best in the world: her parents. Finally, I will analyze some other examples of how ethnic identity is organized within the *Degrassi* narrative.

Arthur and Yick have been best friends of rather opposite physical appearances since the first days of *Degrassi Junior High*. The rotund Arthur is a smart, upper-middle-class White kid. Yick is a diminutive Vietnamese immigrant; in his own words, a "boat person." Although some of Yick's struggles develop out of his ambivalent feelings about his immigrant status, they are often articulated in terms of class. That is, Yick articulates his dissatisfaction first in terms of his ability to consume in a class-conscious North American society and his anger at his friends' (especially Arthur's) inability to recognize his multiple positioning on the basis of race, class and nationality, nor their own privilege. Second, Yick's dissatisfaction is tied intimately to his desire to give value to his past in terms that seem to be defined strictly through a financial materiality that it is difficult, if not impossible, for him to negotiate.

---

[11] DuCille, 1996.

In the episode "Smokescreen,"[12] Yick faces a dilemma when he is asked to do a class presentation about his family. His anxiety stems from his feeling that he is worthless and that his family history is of less value than those of his peers. Yick explains this in terms of his immigrant status, which he feels makes him valueless, as he asks: "Who wants to hear about being poor and living in a big house with about a million relatives?" Part of the reason for Yick's feeling that he, his family and their history are valueless is that they have come to Canada without any tangible — that is material — artifacts of their family history. Without the consumable artifacts of culture (or items that are accorded value, whether economic, cultural or emotional), Yick feels that he, and his family history, are also devoid of value. What is interesting is that this story emerges as Yick and his classmates listen, rapt, to their classmate, Susie (Sarah Charlesworth), who is African-Canadian. Susie expresses her family history in terms of the changes that have occurred in the lives of "Black people," drawing on the story of her uncle, a NASA astronaut. Susie's family artifact, a NASA badge, has enormous cultural currency among her classmates, and it is this event that creates so much of a sense of devaluation in Yick about his own life. He states: "Who cares about refugees? I need something interesting, like Susie's badge. Otherwise I'll be boring."

In order to circumvent this problem, Yick decides to fabricate a history that emerges from a material object that will be recognizable, and of recognizable value, to his peers and teachers during his class presentation. Because his is of Asian descent, Yick draws on popular knowledge of dynastic traditions when deciding on an appropriate and "authentic" product with which to demonstrate/designate the materiality of his racial and cultural heritage. What he does is make his way to a "junk shop" in order to purchase a very inexpensive "Asian-looking" vase. Yick hopes that this material product will identify the value of his racial and cultural heritage to his peers at school, that this value-laden materiality will alleviate the embarrassment he feels about being poor and an immigrant. In a sense, the vase will allow him to transcend this status — or so he thinks — by tying him to a rich (in both senses of the word) cultural heritage in some originary or dynastic space ("Ming" or "Manchu" he says) that the others will recognize as being of value. The vase thus comes to stand in for what Yick feels are the only things that count as valuable within the discourse of race, culture and class within Canadian society, a discourse Arthur helps validate when he continually insists that Yick should have the vase appraised to discover its "actual" worth. At this point, Yick does not see his stories as valuable artifacts of race and culture; he wants the material goods he associates with Canadian affluence. Yick's desire to meet this expectation is what prompts the fabrication of this story in the first place.

In the end, the vase ends up broken. Since Yick cannot afford another one, Arthur encourages him to tell the class the actual story of his and his family's journey to North America:

Yick: Now I don't have anything to show.

---

[12] *Degrassi Junior High.* "Smokescreen". Dir. by John Bertram.

Arthur: Just tell them how you and your family got here.
Yick: Who cares about boat people?
Arthur: But it's a great story ... and it really happened.

While Arthur is necessary to Yick's move to value his own experience (to see its value), the centre of this scene is Yick and his ambivalence in anticipation of the potential cruelty (mockery, boredom) of his audience. But — of course — they are more rivetted by Yick's true story (which includes action, suspense and adventure) than they ever could have been with his fake "Ming" vase:

Yick: We were at sea for more than a month. We hardly had anything to eat. One time, we saw another ship, but they told us to lie down on the deck because it might be a pirate ship. They go around looking for boatloads of people to rob and sometimes take the pretty girls with them. They didn't see us and we finally got to a safe port. My whole family was safe and sound, which wasn't true for everyone. We were very lucky, but all we escaped with was our clothes and that's why I don't have anything to show. Thank you.

Yick thus learns a valuable lesson about his self-worth while he treats his classmates to a lesson of their own about a very particular type of immigrant experience.

This episode tells us several things. It tells us how much emphasis is put on the material, and how problematic it is to live without the material products of one's cultural history. This is familiar to many immigrants and refugees who fled their homes during times of war and/or persecution. This is something many people understand or come to understand, especially in a culture like ours that puts so much emphasis on the materiality of the past. I can give you an example from my own life. My mother's family are survivors of the Shoah (the systematic extermination of groups such as Jews, Poles, Roma, homosexuals and persons with disabilities by the Nazis, primarily during the late 1930s and 1940s), and we have very few material artifacts from that part of my family; the few pictures and paintings we have really are treasures. I did not give it much thought until I met my husband's family, who have lived in the same area of Nova Scotia for many generations and have a literal archive of materials that chronicle their family history (from diaries and letters to pictures and paintings, houses and furniture and businesses). The very abundance of their material history underscored both the dearth of mine, as well as the value of this history. In this episode, Yick must learn (as many of us have) that his history itself, his story, is of material value, as much as a vase or a book or a ring.

What this episode also indicates is that many people recognize the value of history, even divorced from the materiality of artifacts. But it does not mean that Yick suffers from some kind of false consciousness that Arthur and the others must help him overcome, or that he suffers from some false consciousness that they, for some reason, are immune to. If Yick is anxious about sharing his experiences, if he feels that they are not of value, these feelings must be grounded in some reality. Even though this episode allows all involved to learn a lesson — Yick learns the value of his story and that others can recognize its value; his classmates learn that the story is more important than the artifact — there is, in this episode, a subtle reminder that we continue to put value on the ability to articulate cultural history through the ownership and display of material goods. It also tells us how our educational system, with its emphasis on "show and tell," often participates in this elevation of material goods over the stories of lived experience. It suggests the lengths to which students may go to perform in ways they feel are sanctioned by their schools, even if it means fabricating a history for themselves.

This episode also tells us something about the hierarchy of race and ethnicity that exists in Canadian society, especially as it is experienced by new immigrants. Yick understands his racial/ethnic identity as being inextricably linked to his destiny, especially in terms of the way he thinks he will be interpreted, understood and judged by his peers, whom he sees as being above him in some sort of race/ethnicity/class hierarchy.[13] The question of the commodification of culture is also important here.[14] Although there is no real attempt on Yick's part to commodify himself, he sees commodity culture as an intrinsic part of the valuation process of race/ethnicity and historiography. His story on its own has no value, except in the manner in which it can be punctuated by the demonstration of ownership of cultural capital in the form of historical artifacts (like Susie's NASA badge). Without this tangible link to the past, the past itself seems to be rendered inert and empty.

The main problem with this episode is that Yick relies so heavily on others to validate the value of his own experience. His expectation is that his experience will be seen as boring and valueless by the majority of his classmates (the majority of whom he sees as more "Canadian" than he is), and that makes him see his experiences that way. In the end it is Arthur, a white male (not an insignificant fact), who validates and legitimizes Yick's experience, who insists that Yick recognize the intrinsic value (and uniqueness) of his experiences. Yick goes along with Arthur, even though he remains doubtful about the reception his story will receive. It is only the response of his classmates (repeating words like "excellent" and "amazing" as they leave the classroom) that seems to open Yick's eyes to the value of his own experiences. The questions this raises are whether all children/adolescents take such a belittling view of the narratives of their family histories, or, more likely, whether this is the experience of groups that see their experiences as more marginal (and thus of less value) than those of their more mainstream-centred peers. This question of the social construction of race and ethnicity is a very important one.[15]

Perhaps a more traditional storyline, but one that is interesting in its scope, is the romantic storyline that follows the relationship between Michelle and BLT (a.k.a. Bryant). Although this storyline stretched over several seasons, two episodes are especially instructive in a reading of interracial relationships and

---

[13] Freedman, 1990, p. 59.

[14] DuCille, 1996.

[15] James, 2001, pp. 1–7.

the problematic issues they raise for many young people. The first episode in question, "Black and White", which takes place when the characters are in grade eight, focuses most insistently on the need to confront and combat racial ignorance, prejudice and discrimination everywhere, including within the peer group and family.[16] Though the tone is sometimes didactic, there is a real sense that the show is trying to deal with these issues systematically, and in as broad a manner as possible, by drawing on characters already known to the audience, though not necessarily in terms of their race or ethnic affiliation. And although the central story in this episode is one of a White girl and an African-Canadian boy, wider diversity is also drawn on to illustrate the complexity of issues of racial and ethnic discrimination.

Degrassi wastes no time attacking the question of racism. In the opening moments of this episode, BLT, walking out of class to catch up with his friend Michelle, is bumped into by another boy who calls him "N——r." BLT retaliates, and both boys are eventually dragged off and punished for fighting. A discussion with his friends Snake (Stefan Brogran) and Wheels (Neil Hope) is revealing in that it shows how positions of privilege allow racial prejudice to continue unchallenged. Snake suggests that BLT should simply let the incident go, rather than fighting back. But BLT challenges him by suggesting this is only an option for his white friend because "no one's ever called you N——r." For BLT race is, as Pellegrini suggests, "a lifelong process and training" that "receives continual and often painful reinforcement from without."[17] Operationalizing privilege, which BLT does in this episode (and which, as we shall see, other characters do later) is extremely important, because it is done so rarely on television. When this sort of event happens on a show like *Beverly Hills, 90210,* the character who challenges the privilege of whiteness is almost always a marginal character, while the character being challenged, because they are central to the narrative, can only be problematically critiqued because, in the end, they have to at least give the appearance of being "good." But privilege is always at work within the television narrative, as well as in its production; that *Degrassi* uses central characters of different races and ethnic backgrounds to play out questions of diversity and prejudice means privilege is, at least, addressed somewhat in production as well as in performance. This is one of the few places where images of difference are not wholly absent from the "social mirror."[18] It is also a place that demonstrates the body is connected to a past that is inextricably linked to hierarchies of privilege.[19]

The incident with BLT sparks an instructive and complex discussion as Michelle and her girlfriends sit down for lunch:

Alexa:	...and he's a great dancer, of course, that goes without saying...
Lucy:	S'cuse me?
Alexa:	Well, he is Black.

---

[16] *Degrassi Junior High.* "Black and White". Dir. by John Bertram.
[17] Pellegrini, 1997, p. 80.
[18] DuCille, 1996, p. 13.
[19] Judith Butler, cited in Schneider, 1997, p. 21.

L.D.:	Alexa! That's pretty racist.
Alexa:	Racist?
Lucy:	That's like saying all Black people are great athletes.
Alexa:	Well, he was captain of the basketball team.
Lucy:	That's not because his skin's dark. It's because he has talent and he works hard.
Alexa:	Sorry, sorry. It was just a comment. I mean, my parents would die is they found out I went out with a Black guy. They don't even like me going out with Simon.
L.D.:	Why not?
Alexa:	He's not Greek.
L.D.:	Whoa!
Lucy:	Sounds pretty prejudiced to me.
Alexa:	They can't help it. They still think they live in a village back in Greece.

The peer group here (Lucy, L.D. [Amanda Cook] and Alexa [Irene Courakos] performs a very important function in terms of sanctioning and education. Michelle, at this point, does not participate in the conversation, but the camera repeatedly moves to her as she takes in what is being said. The young women spell out several important things in this scene: First, that commonly held attitudes and beliefs about different racial and ethnic groups can be racist; second, that anyone can be prejudiced, even members of one's own family; third, that conversations about race need not be avoided and racist statements can be challenged; fourth, that prejudice is not simply an issue between "black" and "white," but one that constitutes a complex web of relationships between persons of different races, ethnic groups, generations and classes.

Later, still thinking about the lunchtime discussion, Alexa looks to Lucy for more information:

Alexa:	Lucy, have you ever been discriminated against?
Lucy:	Yeah, lots of times. I get it both ways because I'm only half Black, right. So I get called Oreo or half-breed. Really nice stuff.

This is an interesting scene for Alexa, because it shows her making the leap from being somewhat ignorant about what constitutes prejudice and discrimination to a position in which she realizes that people close to her may have been discriminated against. Lucy's giving voice to her own experiences of racism by both the Black and White communities is also interesting because of how she is positioned within the narratives of this show. Unlike BLT, who is heavily racialized, Lucy is much less often involved in storylines where her race/ethnicity is at issue. In fact, this is one of the few episodes in which she speaks to her racial identity. It suggests that since the focus of this episode is race, specifically, various perspectives were mobilized to paint as broad a picture of this subject as possible (by mobilizing Black, White and multiracial voices), even though the racial identity of characters like Lucy is not at issue at other times.[20]

Michelle has some heavy revelations of her own when her parents refuse to let her go to the graduation dance with BLT. Though they insist it has nothing to do with BLT'so being Black, Michelle remains somewhat sceptical, remembering perhaps, how her father would not shake the hand BLT had offered him that afternoon. Quick to defend her parents when BLT asks "Is it because I'm Black?" she is not so clear when she says to Lucy:

Michelle: But they're my parents.
Lucy: Just because they're your parents doesn't mean they're perfect.

Michelle still is not convinced. When she goes home, she asks her mother, point blank, whether the reason she is prohibited from attending the dance with BLT is because he is Black. In a discussion that is quite difficult to watch because it is so full of prejudicial cliches, Michelle's mother insists: "We believe in equal opportunity, but not everyone is like us," this is "to protect you," "imagine you got married and had children," and, "different cultures have different values." Michelle, of course, can (and does) counter her mother's assertions with her own: for instance, that she wants to go to a dance, not get married, and that BLT was born "here" just like her and, thus, is just as "Canadian" as she is.[21] But in the end, she is the child, and her mother's position seems to suggest that she is naïve, ignorant of the world, and simply unable to understand until "she grows up." But instead of complying, Michelle goes to school and tells BLT that he was right about her parents, but that she would like to go to the dance with him anyway.

I like that this episode raises the issue of how difficult it is to learn that the people close to you, whether they are family or friends, have racist views. *90210* dealt with this issue too, briefly, when Donna (Tori Spelling) dated a U.C. athlete named D'Shawn (Cress Williams): something that enraged her mother. But on *90210*, Donna and D'Shawn never really had a relationship and, although the incident allowed Donna to stand up to and expose her mother's prejudices, their relationship never seemed to be worth more than this revelatory note. Here, by contrast, Michelle actively defies her parents by choosing to pursue a relationship with BLT. She arrives at the conclusion that the reason her parents have given for forbidding the relationship (that she is too young to date) merely masks their true feelings (fear of what will people think if their daughter dates someone of another race) and does reflect a position that she can adhere to. It is rare that a television show creates storylines where acting against parental authority results in something positive rather than some painful lesson. And yet, Michelle does not fully recognize her own condi-

---

[20] Actually, Lucy's character is primarily defined in terms of gender. She is an outspoken feminist who often speaks to issues of women's and human rights, including sexism and the right to abortion.
[21] James, 2001.

tion as oppressor within these regimes of power — only of being oppressed because of her age.[22]

Michelle and BLT continue their relationship (presumably keeping it secret from her parents), and seem relatively happy until the issue of race surfaces again two seasons later, on the eve of Michelle's 16th birthday (in the two-part episode "Sixteen").[23] This episode focuses on Michelle rather than BLT, making the central theme of this episode the fight for personal independence and values rather than prejudice. It is unfortunate, as it would have been interesting if BLT had been given a stronger voice in this episode, instead of making him the motivating factor in Michelle's strivings for voice and space. On the other hand, this episode picks up where "Black and White" left off, in the sense that it continues to question the transmission of racist values within the family and how one young woman chooses to fight against it. The episode also expands this issue to include racist perceptions within the community.

When "Sixteen" begins, Michelle is living with her father after her parents have divorced and her mother has moved to Calgary. Although it is her 16th birthday, her father will not let her go out with friends because it is a school night. BLT walks Michelle home and kisses her goodbye while Michelle's father watches from the front window. When she enters the house, he confronts her about her relationship with BLT. She insists that they are just friends, but her father counters that she should "find another friend," to which she responds, "You mean someone white. You're a racist!" A fight ensues during which the father utters a fairly familiar version of "not under MY roof," to which Michelle responds by throwing all her clothes into a suitcase and running to her best friend Alexa's, to whom she explains, as the front door opens, "I've left home." This statement is very important — because it underscores that Michelle is not running away, she is leaving.

Of course, staying at Alexa's is not an option, so Michelle sets out to get an apartment and find a part-time job. Alexa, Simon (Michael Carry) and BLT accompany her on her search. The company is not always beneficial, such as when they are told that an apartment is taken — after the landlady has had a good look at BLT. As they near the next listing, BLT chooses to wait on the street, musing, "I think I'll stay here this time." The others simply smile and nod, suggesting they agree that this might be the best idea. There is no critical reaction to these events, which is strange considering that Michelle is leaving home because her father is racist. Finally, Michelle finds an adequate room, and BLT's father helps them move her in, underscoring the difference between their parents. Michelle pawns her grandmother's ring (given to her by her father for her birthday) to pay her first and last months' rent, underscoring her severing of family ties.

What Michelle does not anticipate is that her newfound emancipation will come at a cost. She cannot handle work and school, and her roommates keep her up at night. She falls asleep in class, and her grades plummet. She has too many responsibilities and no time for her friends. Her friends are worried, as is

---

[22] Fuss, 1989.

[23] *Degrassi Junior High*. "Sixteen". Dir. by Kit Hood.

her father, who finally seeks BLT's help in order to get Michelle back home. They seem to form an uneasy truce, but there is no simple, Hollywood ending where the two become friends, or where Michelle's father suddenly rejects his bigotry and embraces BLT. Instead, he seems to understand that being nice to BLT is the only thing that will allow him to reconnect with his daughter. While it seems clear that BLT only helps out of his concern for Michelle, the story does not go much further. Michelle and her father slowly reconcile, and she eventually moves back home, though on her terms. Over the summer, the two teens drift apart. When Michelle returns from visiting her mother in Calgary, she finds that BLT has a new girlfriend: a fellow athlete who, though it is never really commented upon, is also Black. Although BLT's new girlfriend is Black and Michelle begins to date Snake (who is White), the show does not devolve into the suggestion that these pairings provide a resolution to the racial issues their relationship has raised. Rather, Michelle and BLT, like most adolescent couples, must face the fact that they have changed and grown apart.[24]

Michelle and BLT's story is a complex and interesting one. There are storylines within this narrative that focus on issues other than race. In some sense, this is, again, a story of Michelle's growing recognition of the prejudice that surrounds her as well as her position of privilege. Specifically, she enjoys many privileges, including the possibility of not recognizing the prejudice of those around her (her parents, friends, neighbours) until it directly impacts on her life. This is what Diamond refers to as the privilege "of being able to leave home."[25] BLT, on the other hand, is less the focus of these stories, perhaps because these lessons are already well known to him. Further, vis a vis Michelle, his function is not to educate. He is a boy who likes a girl and yet, as we are shown, it is never as simple as that, even in a country as diverse and supposedly tolerant as Canada. Another lesson that we can cull from this narrative is that, as Canadians, we have to attend to racial prejudice in our own selves, homes, schools and communities, and question our own positions of privilege. Too often, we ignore the possibility of racism and bigotry in Canada, and assume ourselves to be "better," especially in comparison to our neighbours to the south. This storyline addresses questions of racial prejudice from a variety of perspectives, and allows a wide range of voices to be heard. The issue that is least taken up, and that I pointed to at the end of the last paragraph, is worth repeating: In the end, Michelle and BLT's relationship ends.

Ethnicity (as well as race) is produced and hierarchized within the discourses employed by this show. The most important is the lack of interrogation of positions of privilege, especially those associated with race and ethnicity. In one sense, the privileging of certain categories of social experience is criticized as, for example, in Yick's story, where the student himself is shown to disprivilege his own heritage — although Yick is shown to be the only person

---

[24] It is interesting to note that the two-hour series finale, "School's Out", ends with Alexa and Simon's wedding. In "Black and White"," Alexa raises the issue that her parents do not approve of Simon because he is not Greek. The question of ethnicity or interethnic relationships is scrutinized less than the question of race. However, it would have been interesting to watch the unfolding of Simon and Alexa's relationship in relation to their parents.
[25] Diamond, 1997, p. 48.

who negatively assesses his experience. On the other hand, just because the others see value in Yick's experience does not mean that they enter a position where they can (or do) interrogate their own privilege.

Yick continually reminds Arthur of his class privilege, forcing him to think about many of the things he takes for granted, and how he is allowed to do because of this privilege. But for the most part, privilege — whether in terms of class, race, ethnicity, sexuality, or ability — is made secondary to a reflection on the lower end of the hierarchical binary of privilege. For example, Maya (Kyra Levi, who is Jewish, but also has Charcot-Marie-Tooth disease [CMT] and uses a wheelchair) has to explain her position as disabled and non-Christian. Her "job" is to make the others think about HER, which is important, but often allows them not to look at themselves. It allows them to forgo their interrogation the privileges of ability and Christianity accorded them and denied to her. Once again, the order of privilege is left intact. That is not to underestimate the benefits of television shows that actively interrogate hierarchies of race and ethnicity; challenge racism, prejudice and discrimination; and engage in discussions of diversity in the home, school and community. But these examples do not represent the culmination of critical possibilities for how media texts can take up questions of race and ethnicity. And one of the most important overlooked areas here is the question of privilege, especially racial and ethnic privilege.

If students who belong to minority groups see themselves as lower on the social hierarchy then their peers, then they cannot be alone in this perception. Sometimes the values of one character (or their family), because of ethnic affiliation, are seen as in conflict with the majority. For instance, Voula's (Niki Kemeny) father forbids her from attending a dance because he does not approve of Canadian attitudes about sex and dating.[26] Voula wants to explain to her father that the dance is being held in honour of a school project to sponsor a child — a project that was her brainchild — but feels as though she is speaking to a brick wall whose rules are "old fashioned." Similarly, Diana's (Chrissa Evodolou) acting out is aimed specifically at transgressing the rules of her very strict Greek parents and older brother. She circumvents these rules in order to go to parties and experiment with tobacco, drugs and alcohol. In both of these cases, peer groups encourage the defiance of parents because the parents' rules do not conform to what the peer groups feel is the Canadian norm.

Ethnicity is traditionally featured less than race in television. The examples provided employ the trope of ethnic diversity only as a way to show the problematic relationship of young people caught between immigrant parents and assimilated peers. Like racially diverse counterparts, however, ethnically diverse characters are not simply brought into the text to stimulate discussion about ethnicity or race. Instead, the characters are already there, activate in the text, and these incidents are part of the way they are constructed. For some characters, ethnicity and/or race comes to the fore as it is dictated by the particularities of the narratives (i.e., Voula, Alexa, BLT, Yick, Diana). Other characters

---

[26] Voula's ethnic background is never made explicit, but I would suggest that she is Eastern European.

may be inscribed racially or ethnically, though this plays only a very minor part in their stories (i.e., Lucy, Tessa, Bronco, Tabi, Nick). What is important is that race and ethnicity, while forming an integral part of each of these characters, does not provide their only function within the greater structure of *Degrassi*. None of the characters are pushed off the show after they have fulfilled their "teaching" function.

Television as an institution is built upon assumptions of white, "Americanized" (i.e., Anglo-Saxon, Judeo-Christian) privilege. Canadian television often seems to buy into the "image of Canada as a 'white country.'"[27] That is, as a heavily structured and hierarchical institution, it was developed to employ, entertain and inform specific populations. Even though television has expanded to include a slightly wider range of actors and issues, the structure of the medium itself and its underlying structure have not really changed. Yet shows like *Degrassi* suggest that it is possible for television to move in a more critical direction. Achieving this means addressing critical issues and opening up texts to include more diverse characters, whose race (or ethnicity, gender, sexual orientation, nationality, religion, class, age, ability) is not incidental to the text but, simultaneously, is not the exclusive reason why they merit being "produced" for television in the first place.

One of the most important issues surrounding the production of television shows for the CBC is that the CBC is mandated to produce shows that address Canadians as a whole, in all their diversity.[28] *Degrassi* moved in this direction by employing a cast that included characters who were Black and White, but also Asian, Latin, Irish, Greek, Italian, Jewish, Catholic, Eastern European and biracial. The cast also included characters with epilepsy, AIDS, leukemia and bulimia. Many of the characters were middle class, but others were wealthy, working class and poor. Some were born in Canada, and others came to Canada as immigrants. For some, English was their first language, and for others it was not. Being Canadian born and educated in an urban centre, the images I have seen in this show resonate with my own experiences of diversity in and out of the classroom. That is, the people I grew up and went to school with were diverse racially, ethnically and religiously, and though this diversity sometimes created tension, it was not the only or necessarily the defining aspect of our lives and interactions. It was no utopia in which racism, prejudice, discrimination and intolerance were completely absent. And yet, it was not a place in which people were defined by a single term, either.

The refusal to portray one dimensional characters who are defined by single and often marginal characteristics is an important one. It means that just because a character is Black or Asian, race does not become the only aspect of that character's production. Such characters are also defined by their relationships, activities and activism. This does not diminish the impact that race/racism has on the character or the show, it just means that the context within which

---

[27] Shadd, 2001, p. 12.

[28] It has been very interesting to watch the new series, *Degrassi: The Next Generation*, which first aired in October 2001. *Degrassi* producer/creator Linda Schuyler is back at the helm of the series with her production company. But the new series is being produced for CTV, not the CBC. I am not ready to say much about it yet, but so far it is not bad.

these narratives are produced is wider. Specifically, *Degrassi* allowed its characters, no matter what their racial or ethnic affiliation, to be central parts of the text. The show did not provide a homogeneous cast periodically interrupted by the arrival of a minor character who played a one-dimensional role and served to briefly illuminate issues of racism, prejudice and intolerance; to educate the core cast; and, finally, to reassure the viewer that neither they nor their producers were themselves racist, prejudiced or intolerant. Instead, it selected an ensemble or collective that represented a rather more diverse vision of contemporary urban populations than we have been used to seeing in youth-oriented programming.[29]

This is not to suggest that this show, or Canadians in general, have a more enlightened attitude about race and ethnicity than anyone else, or that we, somehow, are more tolerant and less prejudiced. What it does suggest is that a combination of public broadcasting and "liberal" or "left" values helped to produce a show that evidenced great diversity. It allowed questions of racism in the context of the individual, couple, family, peer group, school and community to be critically addressed. It did not reduce issues of race and ethnicity to moments of racism and prejudice, even if the interrogation of these topics was of crucial importance. It demonstrated that character diversity did not have to be a temporary thing rooted in the desire to address issues of racism; that characters who represent diverse perspectives do not have to be minor players who appear to tell a specific story, and then depart.

On the other hand, this show, like most others, never fully raised the question of privilege. Thus it replicated some of the problems associated with most other television shows that examine only one side of racism. And yet questioning privilege is an integral component in really understanding how and why racist attitudes are perpetuated. Even from this Canadian-public-television-with-a-mandate-towards-diversity perspective there is a reluctance to critically engage with the question of privilege. Why? Perhaps it is easier to fight obvious examples of racial and ethnic oppression, suggesting that while it is something that still happens, it is limited in scope and example. Further, it suggests that most people (usually represented by the television show's key players) are basically good, if at times misinformed and lacking in experience about issues of diversity. It suggests that all "we" need is an encounter with an "Other" to set us on an unencumbered and more enlightened path. Until we are ready to interrogate positions of privilege as well as oppression, we will only be hearing one side of the story.

---

[29] Adult programming, especially in the form of the dramatic series (i.e., *E.R.*, *The West Wing*, *The Practice*, *Boston Public*, *Law & Order* and *NYPD Blue*), use diversity in somewhat similar ways. Other Canadian shows aimed at youth (i.e., *Ready or Not*, *Madison*) work similarly to *Degrassi*, though they have not established the same sort of following. Most American television series aimed at youth (i.e., *Felicity*, *Dawson's Creek*, *Roswell*, *Sabrina*, *Friends*) tend to be much more homogeneous, as well as much more pedantic. That is, some simply never interrogate their lack of diversity (and so never address critical questions of racism and prejudice), while others instrumentally employ diversity in order to make points about racism, prejudice and privilege in momentary, rather than ongoing, ways.

References

Audley, Paul. (1983). *Canada's cultural industries*. Toronto, ON: James Lorimer & Company.

D'Acci, Julie. (1992). Defining women: The case of *Cagney & Lacey*. In Lynn Spigel & Denise Mann (Eds.), *Private screenings: Television and the female consumer* (pp. 169–202). Minneapolis: University of Minnesota Press.

Diamond, Elin. (1997). *Unmaking mimesis*. London & New York: Routledge.

DuCille, Ann. (1996). *Skin trade*. Cambridge, MA: Harvard University Press.

Fleras, Augie & Hunz, Jean Lock. (2001). *Media and minorities: Representing diversity in a multicultural Canada* (Chapter 5). Toronto: Thompson Educational Publishing, Inc.

Freedman. Barbara. (1990). Frame-up: Feminism, psychoanalysis, theater. In Sue-Ellen Case (Ed.), *Performing feminisms: Feminist critical theory and theater*. Baltimore & London: Johns Hopkins University Press.

Fuss, Diana. (1989). *Essentially speaking: Feminism, nature & difference*. New York & London: Routledge.

Hoechsmann, Michael. (1996). I am white, male and middle-class in a global era: Marketing (to) generation x. In M. Pomerance & J. Sakeris (Eds.), *Pictures of a generation on hold: Selected papers*. Toronto: Media Studies Working Group.

James, Carl E. (2001). Introduction: Encounters in race, ethnicity, and language. In Carl E. James & Adrienne Shadd (Eds.), *Talking about identity: Encounters with race, ethnicity and language* (pp. 1–7). Toronto: Between the Lines.

Pellegrini, Ann. (1997). *Performance anxieties: Staging psychoanalysis, staging race*. New York & London: Routledge.

Ramos, Howard. (2001). It was always there? Looking for identity in all the (not) so obvious places. In Carl E. James & Adrienne Shadd. (Eds.), *Talking about identity: Encounters in race, ethnicity, and language*. Toronto: Between the Lines.

Schneider, Rebecca. (1997). *The explicit body in performance*. New York and London: Routledge.

Shadd. Adrienne. (2001). "Where are you really from?" Notes of an "immigrant" from North Buxton, Ontario. In Carl E. James & Adrienne Shadd (Eds.), *Talking about identity: Encounters in race, ethnicity, and language*. Toronto: Between the Lines.

Siegel, Arthur. (1983). *Politics and the media in Canada* (Chapter 8). Toronto: McGraw-Hill Ryerson.

Taras, David. (2001). *Power & betrayal in the Canadian media*. Peterborough, ON: Broadview Press.

17

Other Canadian Voices
The Development of Ethnic Broadcasting in Canada

Ryan Edwardson
History Ph.D. Candidate
Queen's University
Kingston

The Canadian broadcasting system was founded as a nation-building force of identity creation and dissemination, a solution to the division between Anglo-Celtic and French Canadians and a bulwark against Americanization. Comprising both publicly and privately owned stations, the public service has focused on its bicultural mandate while privately owned stations have served commercial interests, including overlooked and profitable ethnic markets.[1] The increase in immigration from non-traditional areas after World War II led to a federally instituted broadcasting policy designed to integrate these audiences — both pre-existing and recent — into the dominant national project. The ethnic challenge to bicultural dominance during the 1960s, however, resulted in new ideas of Canadian identity and the institutionalization of a multicultural ethnic policy. While the national service has increasingly reflected Canadian diversity, third-language broadcasting has remained limited to privately owned stations and market-driven consumption.

Broadcasting in Canada emerged in the early twentieth century as a contested sphere of economic interests, consumer desire, and nationalism. Originally consisting of privately owned stations and signal overflow from the United States of America, the domestic market was primarily served by local programming and American entertainment products. The private station interest in providing marketable material, however, resulted in an abundance of American programming, especially of an entertainment and mass cultural form, that nationalists viewed as a threat to the national identity. The Canadian Radio League led a movement for a publicly owned national broadcasting system, styled on the British Broadcasting Corporation, as a means of limiting American material and fostering Canadian identity. The federal government's response was one of nationalization: the 1929 Royal Commission on Radio Broadcasting recommended a public system, federal jurisdiction over broadcasting was upheld in 1931–32 court challenges, and in 1932 the Canadian Radio Broadcasting Act was established alongside the Canadian Radio Broadcasting Corporation (restructured into the Canadian Broadcasting Corporation [CBC] in 1936). The tremendous cost of creating a broadcasting service that spanned the nation required using the CBC in addition to privately-owned stations, however, both of which (as well as a second private network established in 1959) came under state regulation, first by the CBC itself and, later, by a separate regulatory body. While the CBC was nationally funded, private stations had to rely

---

1 Although "ethnic" could be used to refer to any ethnic group in Canada, it has been commonly used by both government and broadcasters to refer to groups other than Anglo-Celtic, French, and Native Canadians. For the sake of clarity, then, this essay will use it in its established context. Due to Native-Canadian broadcasting's unique history, it will not be dealt with in this essay.

Ryan Edwardson

on advertising revenue and were, thus, subject to consumer desire and program marketability.[2]

As an easily accessible form of media capable of transmitting large amounts of informational and entertainment programming, broadcasting quickly became an important part of daily life for many Canadians. It also served nation-building purposes as an efficient way of disseminating national myths, symbols, stories, and experiences. In doing so, broadcasting helped to provide many Canadians with a national sense of place, the type of "imagined community" Benedict Anderson has explored.[3] The process was not without its racial implications, however, as national broadcasting systems, and the myths and symbols they disseminate, often carry with them ethnic ties. Sociologist and theorist of ethno-nationalism Anthony D. Smith, for example, has shown how ethnic hegemonies are entrenched even in civic states that promote themselves as culturally open or multicultural.[4]

The success of using broadcasting and similar consumer-based media for nation-building purposes depends on control of distribution and content. Privately owned broadcasting stations and the use of non-state-selected material facilitates the distribution of other identities and alternatives to the dominant national project. As Kosaku Yoshino has argued in "Rethinking Theories of Nationalism: Japan's Nationalism in a Marketplace Perspective," nationalism exists in a "cultural 'marketplace' in which ideas of national distinctiveness are 'produced', 'reproduced', 'distributed' and 'consumed'."[5]

While the Canadian public broadcasting system was focused on fulfilling its nationalist mandate, private stations — often criticized as being carriers of American entertainment programming and for putting profit before nationalism — provided ethnic communities with their first broadcasting opportunities. Post-WWII immigration, especially to established metropolitan ethnic areas, fostered sizable broadcasting audiences and economic markets. Stations were able to access the often overlooked markets in return for providing those groups with programming unavailable elsewhere. Grocery store owner Johnny Lombardi, for example, began a weekly one-hour Italian music program on CHUM Toronto in 1946 that became a focal point for Toronto's Italian community. Twenty years later Lombardi established his own station, CHIN Toronto. Jan van Bruchen hosted a weekly Dutch program on CKBB Barrie in 1952, and also went on to establish his own station 20 years later, CJVB Vancouver.

These early programming achievements were surpassed in 1957 when Casimir Stanczykowski applied to the CBC for the third-language broadcasting station licence, a category that did not exist at that time. The Board of Broadcast Governors (BBG) took over the CBC's regulatory powers in 1958 and, due to the lack of a third-language policy, it took Stanczykowski until 1962 to receive a licence for Canada's first multilingual radio station, CFMB Montreal. The BBG's 1962 "Foreign Language Broadcasting" policy was designed to inte-

[2] For an overview of early Canadian broadcasting history, *see* Peers, 1969, 1979.
[3] Anderson, 1983.
[4] *See,* for example, Smith, 1983; 1986; 1995; 1998; and 2000.
[5] Yoshino, 1999.

grate the "great influx of immigrants in the years since 1945," a need predicted to "gradually disappear unless there is a continuing heavy influx of immigrants." Integration was to be accomplished by requiring third-language licence holders to broadcast programs about Canadian history, politics, society, and English-and/or French-language courses in conjunction with their usual programming. Obtaining a third-language license was not an easy task. A third-language broadcasting licence was not a new broadcasting category but an amendment to the existing licences, allowing licence holders to increase the maximum 15 per-cent third-language material upwards of 40 percent, measured between 6 a.m. and 12 p.m.[6] Stations requesting to do so required special permission following a public hearing and were limited to areas with an audience of at least 150,000–200,000; and the licensee had to serve all of the third-language groups in the area (unilingualism was prohibited).

The availability of ethnic broadcasting increased during the 1960s, providing established communities and recent immigrants with programming unavailable on the national network. A one-week survey conducted in 1955 by the Canadian Association of Radio and Television Broadcasters noted over 60 hours of programming on 27 stations; by 1958 it had increased to approximately 144 hours, and by 1966 it was 211 hours on 50 stations. The 1966 survey recorded 21 stations in Ontario (broadcasting 110 hours during the survey week), 10 in Québec (60 hours), six in Alberta (18 hours), four in Manitoba (16 hours), four in Saskatchewan (four hours), and five in British Columbia (three hours). CFMB Montreal (the only multicultural station in Canada at that time, broad-casted 48 hours), CHWO Oakville (30 hours) and CKFH Toronto (20 hours) made up almost half of all hours broadcast, with Ontario and Québec together making up approximately 80 percent of the national amount.[7] Creating pro-gramming material was difficult, however, due to the limited access to produc-tion facilities, small pools of talent, absent financing, and a market often too small to cover recording, production, and distribution costs. While these prob-lems existed for mainstream program producers, they were even greater for third-language and non-traditional program production.

The increase in ethnic broadcasting reflected shifting ethnic demographics and the greater influence of the marginalized communities. It also coincided with a greater governmental recognition of Canada as a multicultural society. The federal government's 1963–1970 Royal Commission on Bilingualism and Biculturalism (B&B), originally an attempt to appease French-Canadian nation-alism by examining the relationship between the "two founding races," provided other ethnic groups with an opportunity to renegotiate their position in the nation. Charged with discrimination and racism by increasingly powerful ethnic lobby groups, the commission changed "two races" to two "founding peoples,"

---

6 Board of Broadcast Governors (BBG), "Foreign-Language Broadcasting," Public Announcement, January 22, 1962. According to the "BBG Public Hearings" of May 13, 1959, both the BBG and Stanczykowski wanted a policy that would help immigrants adjust to their "new home".
7 Canadian Association of Radio and Television Broadcasters (predecessor to the Canadian Associ-ation of Broadcasters), 1955 survey; 1958 figures from the Canadian Radio and Television Commis-sion (CRTC), 1974; 1966 figures from a one-week survey in February 1966, stated in the Royal Commission on Bilingualism and Biculturalism (B&B), Book Four, (1969), p. 187.

and by that point the place of "other ethnic groups" in the national project was a popular public issue.[8]

The national broadcasting service's focus on the two dominant ethnic groups was not spared from criticism. The CBC relied on private broadcasters to provide third-language programming because it was already under tremendous pressure to unite English and French Canada — a task complicated by the separate and highly regionalized English- and French-language networks, which provided not bilingual but dual unilingual services. As the CBC explained to the B&B Commission, "it is natural that some of these groups should want broadcasts in their own language, but the Corporation is not in a position to meet this demand." Indeed, the CBC pointed out that they were "a Federal agency, the statutory creation of Parliament.... Parliament recognizes only two official languages."[9] Broadcasting legislation, however, was unclear. Section 3(g)(iii) of the 1968 Broadcasting Act stated that "the national broadcasting service *should* be in English and French," while in Section 3(g)(iv) the CBC was to "provide for a continuing expression of Canadian identity."[10] In its recommendations, the B&B Commission called for the CBC to "remove its proscription on the use of other languages in broadcasting."[11]

In addition, the B&B Commission recommended that the Canadian Radio and Television Commission (CRTC)[12] — the broadcasting regulator that replaced the BBG in 1968 — remove the 1962 third-language broadcasting regulations, undertake studies into the portrayal of other cultural groups, and assess the role of broadcasting in maintaining ethnic languages and cultures.[13] As with the CBC, however, the CRTC interpreted its task as one of nation building before market demands and maintained a policy of promoting a multicultural Canada through bilingualism and nation-promoting programs. During Johnny Lombardi's CHIN Toronto third-language-licence renewal hearing in 1970, for example, the CRTC accused Lombardi of failing "to assist the newcomers to learn English or French by special programs that have this end in view; stimulate the listener's pride in Canadian citizenship; and generally make them feel at home in Canada."[14] Lombardi defended his station, explaining that they "try to sort of integrate gradually. We do not try to jam it down their throats."[15] CHIN served 23 language groups, he explained to the commission: "We are providing a platform for those minority groups who, without us, would be absolutely voiceless."[16]

Developments in multicultural policy placed new obligations on governmental institutions, including the public broadcasting service. "Many Canadians are

---

[8] B&B, Book One, pp. xxi–xxv. Also *see* B&B, Book Four.

[9] B&B, Book Four, p. 183.

[10] The 1968 Broadcasting Act, Sections 3(g)iii and iv., italics added.

[11] B&B, Book Four, pp. 183, 191.

[12] Renamed the Canadian Radio-Television and Telecommunications Commission in 1976.

[13] B&B, Book Four, pp. 190–194.

[14] CRTC, 1970, Vol. 1, p. 215.

[15] Ibid., p. 226.

[16] Ibid., p.187.

looking at national bodies and feeling that they are not fulfilling the national function," a member of the Standing Committee argued in 1970, "because we are pretty occupied with our founding races and are not fulfilling the national fabric which is supposed to be the mosaic."[17] While bilingualism was reaffirmed by the federal government's 1969 Official Languages Act, Canada's ethnic diversity was laid out in the 1971 policy of "multiculturalism in a bilingual framework," the creation of a Minister of State for Multiculturalism portfolio, a Multiculturalism Directorate in the Department of the Secretary of State and, in 1973, the Canadian Consultative Council on Multiculturalism. It was a hopeful solution to Canada's increasingly complex ethnic composition. "The multicultural nod to ethnic minorities," Augie Fleras and Jean Lock Kunz noted in *Media and Minorities: Representing Diversity in a Multicultural Canada*, "was envisioned as a potential counterbalance to neutralize (or de-politicize) an excessively bicultural focus of Canada."[18] It also provided a contrast to the American melting pot, helping to create the image of a unique Canadian mosaic and "peaceable kingdom."[19] "A better use of ... domestic multicultural resources," the CRTC explained during the CBC's 1974 licence renewal, "could be a healthy corrective to the continuing imbalance of foreign [American] influences in Canadian life"[20] — the irony of the passage seems lost on the commission.

Although the CBC increasingly reflected Canada's official multiculturalism, it was still criticized for its lack of third-language programming. The situation worsened in 1973 when the CBC acquired CKSB in St. Boniface, Manitoba, and ended its weekly Ukrainian-language program. In that same year, the CBC also eliminated spoken-language (but not recorded music) Gaelic from the program "Island Echoes" at a station in Cape Breton. Both situations erupted into controversy, but the CBC defended its actions to the Standing Committee on Broadcasting, Film, and Assistance to the Arts. "The work we are doing in French and English is far from complete," CBC President Laurent Picard explained. "The demands to fulfil our mandate in French and English ... are extremely great." Accordingly, "French and English are the mandate of the corporation and no other language."[21] In fact, the CBC argued that multiculturalism necessitated a bilingual service. CBC Executive Vice-President Lister Sinclair explained that all Canadians needed to learn about the diversity of heritages, "and therefore they should know about it in either English or French, which are the only two languages common to everybody."[22] The CBC needed to maintain its focus on multiculturalism in a bilingual framework, then.

CRTC president Pierre Juneau supported the CBC's position on third-language programming. According to Juneau, the national service was to perform

---

[17] Standing Committee on Broadcasting, 1970, pp. 32–33.

[18] Fleras & Kunz, 2001, p. 13.

[19] The term was popularized by William Kilbourn in *Canada: A Guide to the Peaceable Kingdom*.

[20] CRTC Decision 74-80.

[21] Picard, 1973, 13–14. Note that in 1977 Pierre Elliott Trudeau called for an investigation into the CBC's failure to fulfil its English and French mandate, forming the Committee of Inquiry into the National Broadcasting Service.

[22] Standing Committee on Broadcasting, Film and Assistance to the Arts, 1973, p. 23:24..

nation-building tasks and not to provide programming — especially of a type that could be viewed as specialty or audience-specific — that could be provided by private stations. He told the committee that there was no problem with private stations bearing the "load" of third-language broadcasting as long as it did not place them in bankruptcy. "If the service is provided anyway, then it would seem to me that people benefit," Juneau argued.[23]

A number of groups appeared before the committee, including the Ukrainian Canadian Committee and the Italian Business and Professional Men's Association of Ottawa, to argue for third-language broadcasting on the CBC. The demand for airtime on the CBC was not just about broadcasting availability, it was about the national broadcaster's obligation to serve the diversity of groups that made up Canada. Much like the B&B Commission, the Standing Committee on Broadcasting, Film, and Assistance to the Arts concluded that the lack of third-language programming on the CBC was due not to legislation but to the CBC's interpretation of its mandate.[24] Interestingly, the CBC's International Service had been broadcasting across Europe in over a dozen languages since 1945 as part of its program "to provide information about this country to listeners in other lands."[25]

The use of non-traditional languages, and even multiculturalism itself, was especially controversial in Québec. Radio-Canada, the French-language wing of the Canadian Broadcasting Corporation, had an important role in disseminating the Québécois challenge to the national status quo. Television, Richard Collins noted in *Culture, Communication & National Identity: The Case of Canadian Television,* acted as "an agency of progressive change, calling into existence the Québec of the Quiet Revolution: a secular, modern, and self-confident society experiencing itself as 'chez soi'."[26] The failure to consolidate a bicultural Canada during the 1960s and the election of separatist governments led to the institutionalization of a distinct Québécois ethnic direction. Despite the national policy of multiculturalism, the Québec government's language legislation and cultural policy direction affirmed the primacy of French unilingualism and Québécois national identity and culture.[27]

While the CBC struggled with both its English- and French-Canadian mandate and the new multicultural direction, audiences were able to access an increasing amount of ethnic programming on private stations. Private initiative — and not government funding — helped create an ethnic and third-language broadcasting industry.[28] Along with the four multilingual radio stations established by 1973 (CFBM Montreal, CHIN-AM and CHIN-FM Toronto, and CJVB Vancouver), each broadcasting in approximately 20 languages, at least 49

---

[23] Standing Committee on Broadcasting, Film and Assistance to the Arts, 1973, p. 32.

[24] Standing Committee on Broadcasting, Film and Assistance to the Arts, 1974, p. 5

[25] CBC, 1962.

[26] Collins, 1990, p. 198.

[27] *See,* for example, the Government of Québec's 1978 "A Cultural Development Policy For Québec."

[28] In contrast, Rosalind Patterson has found that in Australia "multilingual and multicultural broadcasting have received considerable support in the form of legislation and funding from both Labor and conservative governments" (Patterson, 1999, p. 65).

others were broadcasting third-language programming.[29] The multilingual stations were joined by CJKS Winnipeg in 1975, which served an audience that included those abandoned by the CBC in St. Boniface. While some private television stations provided airtime for ethnic programs, including a weekly CHIN program on CITY-TV Toronto, the first multilingual television licence was awarded in 1978 to Toronto-based Multilingual Television Ltd. Cable and satellite technologies also provided increased opportunities for ethnic television broadcasting, including World View (a Pay-TV network in British Columbia) in 1982, and Latinovision and Chinavision in 1984.[30]

The increase in program selection reflected the trends in Canadian ethnic diversity and identity. According to the 1981 census, Canadians reported their heritage as 40.2 percent British, 26.6 percent French, and 33.2 percent "other."[31] During this period the federal government further entrenched the official multicultural identity through the passing of the Charter of Rights and Freedoms (1982) and the Canadian Multicultural Act (1988). For its part, the CRTC released "A Broadcasting Policy Reflecting Canada's Linguistic and Cultural Diversity" and a system of program classification that made it easier to provide multicultural and multilingual broadcasting.[32] Despite these changes, however, the revised 1991 Broadcasting Act maintained that Canadian broadcasting was largely one of "linguistic duality." The public service was to "be in English and French, reflecting the different needs and circumstances of English and French linguistic minorities" while also "reflect[ing] the multicultural and multiracial nature of Canada."[33]

While broadcasting has increasingly reflected Canada's diverse composition, the nature and requirements of media consumption have often worked against multicultural goals. As Edna Fainaru, Communications Adviser for the League for Human Rights of B'Nai B'rith Canada, reported to the Standing Committee on Communications and Culture in 1985,

> The typical Canadian or Quebecer is depicted without an 'accent', white and of British or French origin, in other words 'dyed in the wool' or 'of native stock'. The content of television programs for the general public (series, shows, et cetera) gives a truncated vision of Canadian society.... Those who are outside the norm, with an accent of a strange name, are often stereotyped and socially isolated. Most programs dealing with multicultural 'reality' or 'current events' focus on the customs and the folklore of the countries of origin. The tendency is to centre on religious festivals and holidays, as well as traditional recipes and arts and crafts.[34]

---

[29] Standing Committee on Broadcasting, Film and Assistance to the Arts, 1973, 26, p. 12.

[30] CRTC Decisions 84-444 and 84-445.

[31] CRTC, 1985, p. 51.

[32] CRTC, Cable Regulations (SOR/86-831), Radio Regulations (SOR/86-982) and Television Regulations (SOR/87-49). While these measures were overly complex, they were simplified in 1999, with ethnic programming defined as "programming directed to any culturally or racially distinct group other than one that is Aboriginal Canadian, or from France or the British Isles. Such programming may be in any language or combination of languages." See CRTC, Public Notice 1999–117.

[33] See Sections 3(d)(iii), 3(b), 3(m)(iv), and 3(m)(viii) of the 1991 Broadcasting Act.

[34] Standing Committee on Communications and Culture, 1985, p. 48.

The process of affirming and representing national diversity, then, is difficult in a media that emphasizes representational myths and symbols and views dominant ethnicities as the norm.

By the end of the twentieth century, ethnic broadcasting had moved from the margins to, if not the mainstream, at least a distance from the earlier integrationist legislation. Occasional programs on private stations were gradually replaced by entire stations dedicated to multicultural and multilingual programming. It has been a slow process, including competing identities and challenges to national ethnic policies, with certainly more changes to come. "Canada has become a more culturally and linguistically diverse country," the CRTC noted in 1998. "Almost 80% of the one million immigrants who arrived in this country between 1991 and 1996 reported a mother tongue other than English or French."[35] Nevertheless, while the Canadian broadcasting system has slowly shifted from dualistic to pluralistic, the question of ethnic and third-language broadcasting's proper place on the public service is still up in the air.

References

Anderson, Benedict. (1983). *Imagined communities.* London: Verso.

Canadian Broadcasting Corporation (CBC). *Broadcasting in Canada: History and development of the national system.* CBC Information Services.

Canada. Board of Broadcast Governors (BBG). *Foreign-language broadcasting, public announcement, Jan. 22, 1962.* Ottawa: BBG.

Canada. Parliament. House of Commons. Standing committee on broadcasting, film, and assistance to the arts. Vol. 23. 1973. Ottawa: Queen's Printer.

Canada. Royal Commission on Bilingualism and Biculturalism. (B&B). Report. Vols.1-4. 1967-69. Ottawa: Queen's Printer.

Canadian Radio and Television Commission. (CRTC). (1970). Public Hearings, February 10–13. Ottawa: CRTC.

Canadian Radio and Television Commission. (1974). *Multilingual broadcasting in the 1970s.* Ottawa: Information Canada.

Canadian Radio and Television Commission. (1985, March). Ethnic broadcasting, public hearings. Ottawa: CRTC.

Collins, Richard. (1990). *Culture, communication & national identity: The case of Canadian television.* Toronto: University of Toronto Press.

Fleras, Augie, & Kunz, Jean Lock. (2001). *Media and minorities: Representing diversity in a multicultural Canada.* Toronto: Thompson Educational Publishing, Inc.

Kilbourn, William. (1975). *Canada: A guide to the peaceable kingdom* (1st Laurentian Library ed.). Toronto: Macmillan of Canada.

Patterson, Rosalind. (1999). "Two nations, many cultures: The development of multicultural broadcasting in Australia and Canada", *International Journal of Canadian Studies,* Vol.19, 61–83.

---

[35] CRTC, Public Notice 1998–135.

Peers, Frank. (1969). *The politics of Canadian broadcasting, 1920–1951.* Toronto: University of Toronto Press.

Peers, Frank. (1979). *The public eye: Television and the politics of Canadian broadcasting, 1952–1968.* Toronto: University of Toronto press.

Smith, Anthony D. (1983). *Theories of nationalism* (2nd ed.). New York: Holmes & Meier.

Smith, Anthony D. (1986). *The ethnic origins of nations.* Oxford & New York: B. Blackwell.

Smith, Anthony D. (1995). *Nations and nationalism in a global era.* Cambridge, UK: Polity Press.

Smith, Anthony D. (1998). *Nationalism and modernism: A critical survey of recent theories of nations and nationalism.* London & New York: Routledge.

Smith, Anthony D. (2000). *The nation in history: Historiographical debates about ethnicity and nationalism.* Hanover, NH: Brandeis University Press (a partner in the University Press of New England consortium).

Standing Committee on Broadcasting. (1970, May 12). Film and assistance to the arts. 24: 32–33.

Standing Committee on Broadcasting. (1974, January 7). Film and Assistance to the Arts, Report to the House, 32:5.

Standing Committee on Communications and Culture. (1985, June 6). 23:48 [translation].

Yoshino, Kosaku. (1999). "Rethinking theories of nationalism: Japan's nationalism in a marketplace perspective. In Kosaku Yoshino" (Ed.), *Consuming ethnicity and nationalism: Asian experiences.* Honolulu: University of Hawaii Press.

18

(Re)Visioning Histories
Racism in Early Prairie Cinema

Sheila Petty
Media Studies
University of Regina
Regina

Special thanks to the Mendel Art Gallery, Saskatoon, Saskatchewan, for providing me the opportunity to do initial work on these films in conjunction with the 1998 exhibition "Plain Truth: Prairie Photographers and Filmmakers, 1858–1950." Thanks also to D.L. McGregor.

Visions

of Canada as a nation have frequently see-sawed between imaged of the country as one of the most racially tolerant countries in the world and one where intolerance is systemic, deeply imbedded and dangerously subtle in its expression. This duality is further complicated by a popular view of Canadian history that focuses on the influence of Britain and France and sidelines other historical national identities to marginalized positions that, although connected to the main thrust of the nation's evolution, are minor in their effects upon it. As a result, racist incidents in the course of Canada's history tend to be viewed as anomalous events rather than actions that are foundational to the way in which dominant white-Canadian society has developed.

In describing the experiential essence of the term, "Black Canadian," Rinaldo Walcott outlines a process of becoming that is "constituted from multiple histories of uprootedness, migration, exchanges and political acts of defiance and self-(re)definition".[1] Drawing on Walcott's position, this essay explores the tension between notions of dominant culture and the existence of multiple histories through an examination of early Canadian prairie cinema. In particular, this work will probe the existence of racist stereotypes in three films: *Nation Building in Saskatchewan: The Ukrainians* (Dick Bird, Saskatchewan, 1920, 20 min.), *Heap Busy Indians* (B.E. Norrish, Alberta, 1922, 8 min.), and *Tuffy and Our Gang* (S. Fox, Saskatchewan, 1930, 3 min.). Focusing on a close analysis of aesthetics, the essay will explore how such films were the site of racist narratives that continue to influence Canada as a nation today.

In terms of documenting social histories, the medium of film occupies a significant place in the twentieth century. The ability to view culture as a series of moving images creates a relationship between time and space that is unique in its ability to preserve ideological and cultural constructs with social contexts that retain a measure of their original dynamicism. Furthermore, because film is a product of decision and artistic construction, it reveals as much about its authorship as it does about its subject. As film historian Peter Morris observes, "it seems to have been realized almost from the beginning in Canada that film could be used for more than just entertainment."[2] From as early as 1898, all levels of the Canadian government and private industry recognized film's potential to disseminate propaganda or advertise goods and services. Developed by governments and other organizations, "sponsored industrial documentaries" arose as a means to disseminate issues, values and standards to large populations in dispersed circumstances.[3] One such example is *Nation Building in Sas-*

---

[1] Walcott, 1997, p. 121.

[2] Morris, 1978, p. 33.

[3] Ibid., p. 6.

katchewan: The Ukrainians, which was produced by the Saskatchewan Department of Education in order to encourage Ukrainian immigrants to send their children to school.

The influence of British immigrants on the Canadian Prairies cannot be underestimated: along with the structure of government and legal institutions, these immigrants also brought racial attitudes that shaped how such institutions determined what was socially and culturally acceptable in Canada.[4] With later waves of immigrants, governments and other organizations sought out means of inculcating those of other cultures with "acceptable values." However, this was often a hotly contested process in which racism against newcomers played a powerful role in shaping the dynamics of the relationships between different groups of immigrants and the more established British Canadians.

It is generally acknowledged that the first Ukrainian immigrants arrived in Canada in 1891.[5] In the period between 1896 and 1914, over 200,000 Ukrainian immigrants poured into Manitoba, Alberta and Saskatchewan.[6] Fleeing difficult economic conditions, these Ukrainian-Canadian settlers came from the peasant class, which "had very little opportunity for education in the Ukraine. Of these, 50% were illiterate, and as late as 1921, the Ukrainians were the most illiterate people in Canada."[7] In addition, the practical and economic difficulties in establishing homesteads "kept many children out of school because every pair of hands was needed in the very fight for existence."[8] This created a strain in the educational system across the prairies as these systems attempted to balance the need to educate the Ukrainian population with the hardships they faced.

This wave of immigration did more than present a challenge to the education system; it also challenged the Anglo-Saxon establishment's sense of proprietorship over the western provinces.[9] As Myrna Kostash has observed, unless British civilization "prevailed against 'the alien invasion' and the mass of 'human dregs' from Eastern Europe, one's family life, one's career, one's self-esteem would be dragged about in the muck of the foreigners' culture."[10] This reflected the British attitude that although the Ukrainians were industrious, "they were not 'white' and were certainly very inferior to English-speaking people."[11] This type of judgement was based on a concept of degrees of whiteness that privileged Anglo-Saxon heritage and culture over those of East Europeans.[12] As Constance Backhouse writes, "the doctrines of natural selection and 'survival of the fittest,' promulgated by Charles Darwin and Herbert Spencer, laid the intellectual framework for an intensified stratification of racial

---

[4] Shepard, 1997, p. 69.

[5] Skwarok, 1959, p. 9.

[6] Ibid., p. 53.

[7] Ibid., pp. 53–54.

[8] Ibid., p. 55.

[9] Kostash, 1977, p. 34.

[10] Ibid., p. 35.

[11] Ibid., p. 37.

[12] Ibid.

typology."[13] This type of rationalization reinforced a sense of privilege among those descended from white European stock who regarded their culture as "well above the more 'primitive' racial stages of 'simple savagery' and 'barbarism.'"[14] Certainly, the sense of racial entitlement framed the perspective with which Slavic immigrants were viewed, for, as Kostash writes acerbically, "what could have been further from the Anglo-Saxon ideal of blond-haired manhood than these swarthy, high-cheeked, long-haired, buxom people in skins."[15] In addition, at this time in Saskatchewan's history, questions of race, immigration and the protection of the dominant white Anglo-Saxon privilege were highly contentious on a number of fronts. For example, the recruiting success of the Ku Klux Klan in the province and the struggle of the Chinese community against the racist White Women's Labour Law, which seriously restricted the right of Chinese entrepreneurs to hire white women for their businesses, are well documented.[16] Such events demonstrate the deep entrenchment of racism as a justified means of "defending" white "Anglo-Saxon civilization" against a rising tide of colour.[17]

The racism encountered by Ukrainian Canadians led to the development of what Kostash describes as identities that were either inscribed in a romantic mythology of Ukrainian origin or politicized by resistance to the debasement of those same origins. The Anglo-Saxon majority's desire to assimilate the interlopers unquestionably met with stiff resistance from the Ukrainian Canadians as noted by Skwarok, who comments that "their whole historical background was a struggle for the preservation of their national identity."[18] Hence, education, perceived by both parties as "the greatest instrument of assimilation," became a ground of contestation for both sides of the conflict.[19]

Nation Building in Saskatchewan: The Ukrainians is a sponsored industrial documentary[20] that deals with this tension through a narrative approach that, on its surface, appears to respect Ukrainian culture, but subtly disparages it against the values of British-Canadian society. In particular, the film advances two central premises. First, continued attachment to traditional Ukrainian cultural ways is equated with being old-fashioned and economically deprived. Second, assimilating to Canadian society as defined by British precepts is equated with progress and prosperity. The silent film begins with an overview of Ukrainian immigration to Canada. Textual intertitles, appearing between shots depicting arriving Ukrainian immigrants, describe them as "thrifty, hard-working

---

[13] Backhouse, 1999, p. 42.

[14] Ibid.

[15] Kostash, 1977, p. 36.

[16] See, for example, Backhouse, 1999, Chapter 5, pp. 124–172.

[17] Kostash, 1977, p. 35.

[18] Skwarok, 1959, p. 54.

[19] Ibid.

[20] Sponsored industrial documentaries were frequently commissioned by all levels of governments in order to promote certain social values and standards. On the Prairies, and particularly in Saskatchewan, this genre of early film was created by government departments such as Agriculture and Education to take rural/agricultural issues into churches and grange halls around the province. *See* for example, Morris, 1978, p. 66; and James, 1977, pp. 23–24.

farmers that have brought under cultivation thousands of acres of our fertile prairie land." Although a seemingly positive statement, the use of the possessive "our" evidences a subtle form of proprietorship, as if the Ukrainian settlers are serfs working on someone else's land.

In a later section, intertitles describe the settlers' first homes as being "patterned after European models — mud walls, usually whitewashed, small windows and thatched roofs." The long shot that follows reveals a home that is distinctly Eastern European in its appearance. This shot is contrasted with the next set of intertitles that state, "modern Canadian homes followed," offering the "fine residence of a prosperous merchant" as an example. Followed by a shot of a timbered, English-style home with an upper balcony and front porch, this depiction suggests that in order for Ukrainian immigrants to be successful and achieve prosperity in Canada, they must leave "old world" Eastern-European ways behind and embrace the "new world" Anglo-Saxon values of 1920s Saskatchewan.

A further development of this line of argumentation occurs in the next section of the film. Beginning with an intertitle that proclaims, "Canadian millinery has no attraction for the older women," the film illustrates its point through a series of medium and medium long shots of older women and children wearing babushkas and the embroidered clothing typical of traditional Ukrainian dress. The next intertitle asserts that "younger men and women — many of them Canadian-born — present a different picture," and supports its contention by a medium shot of schoolchildren in contemporary dress smiling into the camera. Here, the ideological point is twofold: First, it draws a distinction between those born in the Ukraine and those born in Canada, seeming to suggest that having a Canadian origin naturally means moving away from Ukrainian roots. Second, it implies that those who retain strong links to their cultural heritage are somehow incapable of change. Thus, rather than portraying the retention of Ukrainian culture in a positive light, the narrative strategy subtly disparages it by insisting that progress can only be achieved by becoming more "Canadian" than Ukrainian.

The film's next section presents the story of a young boy identified as "John W" as he moves through the education system from grade school to university. The intertitles purport that John was born in western Canada of Ukrainian heritage, clearly marking him as belonging to the second category of citizenship outlined above. A medium shot depicts John and his mother arriving at the school in a horse-drawn wagon. Both the wagon and the babushka worn by the mother link her to a Ukrainian old-world lifestyle. This is contrasted by John's knickerbocker British-style school suit, reinforcing the sense that he belongs to a more contemporary, Canadian generation. The intertitles that follow imply that waiting to meet the teacher is naturally stressful for both mother and child. The stress is alleviated a few shots later when, in a medium shot, John's mother and the male teacher smile and talk to each other easily. The teacher bends and greets John eye to eye, patting him on the head reassuringly and then leading him inside. The dialectical purpose of this exchange is to diffuse the cultural tension inherent in such a meeting between polarized cultures by valorizing teachers and, through them, the education process as non-threatening.

This premise is carried further in the next section of the film, which focuses on the benefits of participating in the education system. For example, John is portrayed as an enthusiastic student in a close-up shot in which he demonstrates his proficiency in English by the ease with which he spells "hieroglyphics." The sequence culminates in John's convocation from university, presented in a long shot as he and other students participate in a graduation parade. The accompanying intertitle exhorts, "What he did, **you** can do!" capping off a positive portrayal of assimilation that slickly sidesteps any challenge to its validity as a strategy of identity. As with previous examples, John's prosperity and progress is linked to eschewing traditional Ukrainian culture and embracing British value systems. This presentation delimits Ukrainian culture as a positive societal force and, ultimately, supports a view of that culture as being inferior to that of British Canadians.

In addition to governments and institutions, Canadian corporate entities were early participants in the use of film for propagandistic purposes. One of the first, and most prolific, users of the new medium was the Canadian Pacific Railway (CPR), which used film as a marketing tool to draw tourists to prairie and other domestic destinations along its railway. Aggressively advancing its own corporate interests, the CPR was a major pioneer in the development of an early film genre known as "scenics": often taking the form of personal essays, these short films presented the prairies, and particularly Banff, Alberta, as a place of high adventure situated amid breathtaking scenery.

Heap Busy Indians was produced in 1922 as part of a series of CPR scenics known as **Kinograms**, short travelogues intended to promote CPR travel destinations.[21] Directed by B.E. Norrish, *Heap Busy Indians* "documents" a gathering of the Blackfoot First Nation at Gleichen, Alberta. Aimed at attracting tourism, this short film offers a stark example of how white dominant society appropriates, reconfigures and distorts First Nations culture as entertainment.[22] The commodification of First Nations culture by Western civilization has a long history rooted in colonial imperatives that justified the collecting and displaying of Indian peoples and cultural artifacts for white consumption.[23] It is critical to note that the experience of First Nations peoples under colonization cannot be equated with that of other histories of colonization in Canada. Forcibly displaced from their land, "having never ceded it by treaty or other instrument of consent," First Nations peoples have faced physical and cultural genocide on a scale unprecedented in Canadian history.[24] Furthermore, the dominant role played by British immigrants in the Canadian Prairies ensured that British views of their racial superiority became institutionalized in government departments.[25]

---

[21] Morris, 1978, pp. 223–225.

[22] This essay deals with a very narrow subject area, but it is crucial to recognize that the historical context of the appropriation of First Nations culture takes place against the wider backdrop of the centuries-long struggle by First Nations peoples to assert their socio-political, economic and spiritual rights. For a detailed discussion of these issues and their relationship to cultural appropriation in media, *see* Churchill, 1998.

[23] Crosby, 1991, p. 267. For further discussion on collecting and displaying cultures, *see* Clifford, 1990.

[24] Churchill, 1998, p. x.

[25] Shepard, 1997, p. 69.

Sheila Petty

This led to a view of First Nations peoples as biologically less developed than the dominant white society.[26] As Richard Hill suggests, these attitudes were "evolutionist in construction, [and] propped up by scientific, rationalist thought."[27] Later supported by ethnographic and anthropologic approaches that privileged white cultural imperatives, these attitudes systematically entrenched paternalistic notions that diminished the cultural validity of First Nations peoples.

Hill has suggested that the lack of First Nations access as agents of their own self-representation to mass media has resulted in a representation of these cultures that is "filtered through a white person's sensibility first."[28] Ultimately, this creates texts that are more evocative of the dominant culture in which they were produced than the cultures they purport to represent. The fact that films such as *Heap Busy Indians* reflect colonial attitudes that were "acceptable" within the historical context in which the film was made does not present a satisfactory defence of their inherent racism: in fact, such films provide strong documentary evidence of the roots of the discrimination that still exists in Canadian society and institutions.

Heap Busy Indians is presented in an anecdotal style, and quickly establishes its white Anglo-Saxon viewpoint by referring in intertitles to its subjects as "gentle redskin[s]" who make a business out of "posing" as Indians for tourist consumption. The first visual images, medium and long shots of two Blackfoot men pitching hay into a wagon, subtly advance a white precept that places more value on assimilation than on the retention of indigenous culture. This is reinforced by the next set of intertitles, which read, "The popular demand is for a regular old time Injun in paint and feathers — the kind you read about." Taken together, the image and intertitle sequence seem to suggest that the Blackfoot people were assimilated into white society by day and were Indians only in their spare time. Such an assertion exposes a long-standing history of cultural appropriation by white society, which distorted and conflated First Nations cultures by misrepresentation in mythical constructions created by white imagination to suit white precepts and entertainment needs.[29] One of the most striking examples of this apporpriation in the film occurs during a sequence in which town officials greet a visitor to Gleichen. The intertitle indicates that when important visitors arrive, the Blackfoot Nation is called out in "the ancient finery to supply the local colour and excitement," indicating an attitude that negates their contribution as an expression of culture by reducing it to a form of exoticism. This is followed by a medium long shot of white dignitaries parading past on horseback, accompanied by a First Nations man in full cere-

---

[26] Hill, 1992. For an in-depth discussion of race definition in a Canadian context, *see* Backhouse, 1999, pp. 18–55. For a broader context, *see* Jahoda, 1999, pp. 63–74.
[27] Hill, 1992, p. 15.
[28] Ibid., p. 17. Additional viewpoints on this issue can be found in Bowles, 2001; Nelson, 1998; and Jahoda, 1999, pp. 113–127.
[29] *See* Kilpatrick, 1999, p. 1. Constance Backhouse suggests that such opportunities created conflicted attitudes among First Nations people towards "performance" of their culture for white entertainment. For example, there was the natural resentment created by the resulting devaluation of culture. In other cases, performances mocked white expectations. Finally, such performances afforded the potential of economic gain and fame (*see* Backhouse, 1999, p. 64.)

monial attire, reinforcing the sense of display for white entertainment and cultural tourism purposes. In a later sequence, a long shot depicts a white dignitary receiving a ceremonial headdress from a First Nations participant. The accompanying intertitle then disparages the symbolism of the act by suggesting that the recipient receives "no voting powers and no dividends — you get the feathers." This depiction underscores white society's total disregard for First Nations culture as a viable community force by valuing it only as a means to servicing white imperatives.

The final section of the film is devoted to a portrayal of a Blackfoot Sun Dance, which is described in the intertitles as "something between a cabaret and an 'Old Home Week'." Immediately, this description deprives this event of its sacred cultural context and, instead, presents it solely within a white construct of amusement and spectacle.[30] Later, the arrival of the Blackfoot participants is depicted in a series of long and medium long shots, which are intercut with long shots of prairie chickens competing in a mating dance. This is followed by a long shot of Blackfoot in traditional dress, posed for a portrait. The sequence links the gathering of the Blackfoot people to that of the birds, implying a connection between their ceremony and the wildness of nature. In effect, Norrish is portraying the Blackfoot as "noble savages," an image popularized by the eighteenth-century French philosopher Rousseau in which indigenous peoples were viewed to be more directly connected to nature and, thus, more in touch with their basic instincts.[31] Although such an argument seems palatable on its surface, it reduces "elaborate and various cultures to mere 'forces of nature.'"[32] Furthermore, in the context of *Heap Busy Indians*, the portrayal demonstrates a distinct paternalism that ultimately exoticizes the culture and brings it in line with a white imaginary that is less concerned with accuracy and respect than it is with novelty.

Another consequence of western Canada's Eurocentric British inheritance is a "powerful bias against blackness, and dark-skinned peoples."[33] Although Britain had abolished slavery in 1834, the worldwide advancement of the British Empire, based on technological superiority, confirmed British views of racial supremacy.[34] Reinforced by the arrival of African-Americans emigrating from Oklahoma and other areas earlier in the nineteenth and twentieth centuries, racist treatment of black people took a wide variety of forms, from racist stereotypes portrayed in western Canadian newspapers, advertisements and minstrel shows to segregation in public places, such as bars.[35] Furthermore, racist depictions in Hollywood films and serials such as the *Our Gang* series contributed to the development of a hostile environment.

---

[30] There is a grim irony in this appropriation of the Sun Dance, given its locus as a means of resistance against white assimilation. *See* Pettipas, 1994 and Gresko, 1974.

[31] Ibid.

[32] Ibid.

[33] Shepard, 1997, p. 17.

[34] Ibid., p. 69.

[35] Shepard, 1997, pp. 71–72, 112. Shepard offers a number of journalistic and visual examples of racism directed towards African-Americans who immigrated to western Canada (Shepard, 1997, pp. 66–101). *See also,* Nelson, 1998.

Sheila Petty

On September 3, 1930, the *Regina Leader-Post* announced on its front page that a Hollywood director had arrived in town to make a *Leader-Post/Broadway Theatre* movie comedy that would feature local talent. Producer Sammy Fox, who purported to have worked with Hal Roach, intended to create his own version of the popular *Our Gang* series entitled *Tuffy and Our Gang,* focusing on the comedic adventures of a group of children. Recruiting local children to play the series characters, Fox shot some disjointed scenes for an episode entitled "A Free Ride" and then left town under questionable circumstances, allegedly having failed to pay either his cinematographer or his hotel bills.[36]

The film is worthy of consideration despite its unfinished state because it demonstrates the existence of clearly articulated racist stereotypes in popular media in the early twentieth century. The central character in the film is Farina, played by Cecil States, an African-Canadian youth.[37] Fox apparently lifted the character directly from Roach's *Our Gang* series, and his version of Farina drew on the "lovable little pickaninny" stereotype of the original character.[38] This is supported by promotional material from the *Leader-Post*, which describes Farina's character in *Tuffy and Our Gang* as "the black cloud of the Leader-Post theatre local gang comedy."[39] In this context, it is clear that Farina's character is defined primarily on the basis of his racial identity as a troublemaker.

The surviving footage demonstrates a telling binarism between black and white cultures. In terms of dress or behaviour, there are no significant cultural differences among the white children. However, Farina's portrayal is distinctly different, featuring "pickaninny twisted pigtails" drawn from the original character as a signifier of race.[40] This difference is emphasized during a series of shots in which the children first peer into the window of a music store at the goods, and then decide to beg in order to get money to purchase an item, resulting in Farina leading a shuffle dance to entice passersby to contribute to their cause. This effectively marginalizes Farina and his culture and, although the others join in, it remains a blackface performance of what is, essentially, a white stereotype of black culture.

In another significant section, Farina is hit in the face with a cream pie, an event characterized in the *Leader-Post* as an extremely coal black boy being suddenly changed into "a laughing white-faced youngster."[41] Depicted in a medium shot, Farina and the other children are at the rear of a building, where a pie is cooling on a barrel. One of the boys forces Farina's face into the pie: in effect, Farina is forced to don the "white mask". The comedic effect is based on the ironic racing of Farina's body, which emphasizes the impossibil-

---

[36] *See* the television program, *Regina, Miracle of the Plains*, CKTV (1978), courtesy of the Saskatchewan Archives Board.

[37] Very little is known about the recruitment of the children. However, the front page of the *The Leader Post* acted as a "casting call" in the article, "Pictures of 'Our Gang' Planned for Children of City," September 30, 1930.

[38] Bogle, 1991, p. 20.

[39] *The Leader Post,* September 22, 1930.

[40] Bogle, 1991, p. 20. For an in-depth discussion on the cultural significance of black hair, *see* Mercer, 1994, pp. 97–128.

[41] *The Leader Post*, September 4, 1930.

ity of the situation. As a black child in a white mask, he can be nothing other than a pretender.

The re-examination of early prairie films such as *Nation Building in Saskatchewan: The Ukrainians*, *Heap Busy Indians*, and *Tuffy and Our Gang* offers an important opportunity to connect contemporary racisms with historical expressions of them. In speaking of the depictions of North American First Nations in film, Jacquelyn Kilpatrick has stated, "Films have been around for only a century, but the stereotypes within them have their origins in over five centuries of perceptions — and misperceptions."[42] The issues raised by these films continue to have meaning today and challenge us to examine our past and present in a critical light.

References

Backhouse, Constance. (1999). *Colour-coded racism: A legal history of racism in Canada, 1900–1950.* Toronto: University of Toronto Press.

Bogle, Donald. (1991). T*oms, coons, mulattoes, mammies, and bucks: An interpretive history of blacks in American films.* New York: Continuum Publishing Company.

Bowles, John P. (2001, Winter), Blinded by the white: Art and history at the limits of whiteness. *Art Journal, 60*(4), 39–41.

Churchill, Ward. (1998). *Fantasies of the master race: Literature, cinema, and the colonization of American Indians.* San Francisco: City Lights Books.

Clifford, James. (1990). On collecting art and culture. In Russell Ferguson, Martha Gever, Trinh T. Minh-ha & Cornel West (Eds.), *Out there: Marginalization and contemporary cultures* (pp. 141–169). New York and Cambridge, MA: New Museum of Contemporary Art and the MIT Press.

Crosby, Marcia. (1991). Construction of the imaginary Indian. In Stan Douglas (Ed.), *Vancouver anthology: The institutionalized politics of art.* Vancouver: Talon Books.

Gresko, Jacqueline. (1974). White "rites" and Indian "rites": Indian education and Native responses in the West, 1870–1910. In A.W. Raporich (Ed.), *Western Canada past and present.* Calgary: McClelland & Stewart West.

Hill, Richard. (1992). "One part per million: White appropriation and Native voices. *Fuse, 15*(3), 12–22.

Jahoda, Gustav. (1999). *Images of savages: Ancient roots of modern prejudice in Western culture.* New York: Routledge.

James, C. Rodney. (1977). *Film as national art: NFB of Canada and the film board idea.* New York: Arno Press.

Kilpatrick, Jacqueline. (1999). *Celluloid Indians: Native Americans and film.* Lincoln & London: University of Nebraska Press.

Kostash, Myrna. (1977). *All of Baba's children.* Edmonton: Hurtig Publishers.

---

[42] Kilpatrick, 1999, p. 1.

Leader Post, 27(207) (September 4, 1930), Regina Saskatchewan.

Leader Post, 27(207) (September 22, 1930), Regina Saskatchewan.

Mercer, Kobena. (1994). *Welcome to the jungle: New positions in black cultural studies.* London & New York: Routledge.

Morris, Peter. (1978). *Embattled shadows: A history of Canadian cinema, 1895–1939.* Montreal: McGill-Queen's University Press.

Nelson, Charmaine. (1998). *Through an-other's eyes: White Canadian artists — black female subjects.* Oshawa, ON: The Robert McLaughlin Gallery.

Pettipas, Katherine. (1994). *Severing the ties that bind: Government repression of Indigenous religious ceremonies on the Prairies.* Winnipeg: University of Manitoba Press.

Pictures of "Our Gang" planned for children of city. (1930, September 30). *Leader Post.*

Regina, miracle of the plains. (1978). CKTV, courtesy of the Saskatchewan Archives Board.

Shepard, R. Bruce. (1997). *Deemed unsuitable.* Toronto: Umbrella Press.

Skwarok, J. (1959). *The Ukrainian settlers in Canada and their schools.* Toronto: Basilian Press.

Walcott, Rinaldo. (1997). *Black like who?* Toronto: Insomniac Press.

Questions for Discussion

1. Writing on *Degrassi*, Byers questions the Canadian preference for programming American-style. Survey your class: Is there a real preference for American programming? What are the reasons given for preferring either type of programming?

2. Are there reasons, outside of economic dominance, that account for the popularity of American programming?

3. Byers writes that in *Degrassi*, diversity does not function in the service of profit, but in the service of representation. Would it be wrong for diversity to function as profit? Should we have a moral or ethical problem with profit-driven diversity programming? Why or why not?

4. Edwardson reports that regulations were introduced to foster integration of the Canadian population. Discuss the assimilatory power of the media.

5. Former CBC Executive VP Lister Sinclair stated in the past that "it was important that everybody in the country should know about the diversity of heritages and therefore they should know about it in either English or French, which are the only two languages common to everybody." Explain why you agree or disagree with this statement. Is it fair to have an expectation that immigrants should conform to the use of the dominant languages?

6. How would you describe the goals of the three films discussed by Petty? To what extent can they be read as assimilationist? Now consider *Degrassi*. Taking into account the different dates of production, are there significant similarities and issues that have remained?

7. When Petty discusses the final section of *Heap Busy Indians*, she writes that the Blackfoot Sun Dance is described as "something between a cabaret and an "Old Home Week". Is this an example of how inadequately English can be used to discuss a primarily non-English culture? Considering Edwardson's discussion of multi-lingual radio, what aspects of a culture are lost when they are translated and broadcast in another language?

Part 7

Production and Representation

This Part explores the disconnect between the majority's perception of Canadian people of colour and First Nations and the self-perception of those individuals and groups. Through four essays in this Part, the reader will be encouraged to delve into the concerns of Canadian people of colour and First Nations when likenesses, that are neither completely true nor completely false, are presented by people with varying degrees of education and familiarity about the objects of their assessments.

In the first essay, "Each Sentence Realized or Dreamed Jumps Like a Pulse with History and Takes a Side: Dionne Brand's 'Telling' Stories", your attention is drawn to the written word regarding Canadian people of colour. Here, Lynda Hall explores the complexities of a black Canadian writer using her artistic voice as a vehicle for social progress.

The second essay, "Articulating Spaces of Representation: Contemporary Black Women Artists in Canada", shifts focus from written to visual art yet continues in its exploration of the discrepancy between production and representation. Likewise, there is a shift in the cultural background of the essayist. Here, a Chinese-Canadian examines how black Canadians have represented themselves. Pay attention to what Alice Ming Wai Jim sees and says for she is discussing black women as they have artistically discussed themselves.

The third essay, "The 'Hottentot Venus' in Canada: Modernism, Censorship and the Racial Limits of Female Sexuality", further develops the notion of black images represented by non-blacks, and Charmaine Nelson offers a discussion about white artistic representation of black women. Here, not only will you discover the politics that underlie what is classified as an artistic impression, but you will also be offered an in-depth look at the historical exploitation of black women, in which the brilliance of black beauty and sexuality was dulled by animalistic, side-show representations.

The part closes with "Racial Recognition Underpinning Critical Art", an essay in which a white artist explains her cultural and racial explorations and considers the challenges she faces in representing those of another race in her own way. Here we have the benefit of Joanne Tod's words as an accompaniment to her art.

The essays included here all explore the racialized aspects of cultural production and representation as a powerful mechanism for both oppression and liberation. The creation of "art" is not a neutral endeavour, nor is the representation of a people an apolitical possibility. This Part seeks to unveil and explore these issues as they are encountered in the world of the visual arts.

19

Each Sentence Realized or Dreamed Jumps Like a Pulse with History and Takes a Side
Dionne Brand's "Telling" Stories

Lynda Hall
English Department
University of Calgary
Calgary

I would like to thank AnaLouise Keating and Sima Rabinowitz for their generous and insightful comments on drafts of this essay. As well, I would like to thank Charmaine Nelson and Camille Nelson for initiating this collection and for their superb editorial advice.

I have tried to keep my throat gurgling like a bird's. I have listened to the hard gossip of race that inhabits this road.... I have tried to write this thing calmly even as its lines burn to a close. I have come to know nothing is simple. Each sentence realized or dreamed jumps like a pulse with history and takes a side. What I say in language is told in faultless knowledge of skin, in drunkenness and weeping, told as a woman without matches and tinder, not in words and in words and in words learned by heart, told in secret and not in secret, and listen, does not burn out of waste and is plenty and pitiless and loves.

Dionne Brand[1]

Racism is a collective experience, a social experience.

Dionne Brand[2]

Trinidad-born

Toronto writer and scholar Dionne Brand persistently demonstrates the pervasive racism in Canada in her many volumes of autobiographical poetry and fiction and her collections of essays. Her work embodies a powerful journey of struggle in the search for identity and existence for herself and for others. Brand's writings make visible the layering of institutionalized social power and knowledge regimes that reinforce each other, layers that Michel Foucault identifies as networks that perpetuate "capitalist exploitation."[3] Brand's work exemplifies Foucault's claim that "to force the institutionalized networks of information to listen, to produce names, to point the finger of accusation, to find targets, is the first step in the reversal of power and the initiation of new struggles against existing forms of power."[4] Foucault identifies the need to embrace the "power to speak,"[5] and Brand's emphasis on language, memory, and writing to clearly speak out about and expose layers of oppression is the focus of this essay. In particular, with reference to Brand's *Bread Out of Stone* and *No Language Is Neutral,* I examine her documentation of the systemic racism that is perpetuated through the institutions of education, law (immigration, police, employment), and popular culture. Combining the personal and the political, she refuses to separate the public from the private, the private body from the body politic. Her 1994 collection of essays *Bread Out of Stone* engages racism in relation to capitalism, culture, education, immigration, and employment. Brand's 1990 *No Language Is*

---

1 Brand, 1998, p. 31.
2 Brand, 1990.
3 Foucault, 1977, p. 216.
4 Ibid., p. 214.
5 Ibid.

Neutral most crucially engages the profound connections between writing, living, and political activism. In *No Language Is Neutral*, her sixth book of poetry, Brand's narrative, documentary, autobiographical writing addresses her cultural roots in Trinidad, the lives of her mother and grandmother, her experiences as an immigrant in Toronto, and the affirmation of her lesbian sexuality. While this essay focuses specifically on Brand's critique of the racism that imbues society, her writings also address oppression related to gender, sexuality, class, and other related issues.

Before directly engaging *No Language Is Neutral* and *Bread Out of Stone*, I will briefly situate them in the context of Brand's oeuvre, and the wider context of black writers. Due to the breadth of coverage of her work, Brand is one of Canada's most respected and widely read writers, and her works are included in university curricula in several disciplines. She is a major Canadian writer whose evocative, sensual, and poignant work is widely recognized for its beauty and its honesty. This essay focuses on the topic of racism and does not convey in any way the magnificence or variety of her publishing, nor does it discuss Brand's many other important activities, such as teaching, lecturing, readings, video directing, and community work.

Brand is critically acclaimed for her literary merit, her social commentary, and her political work. Her two most recent novels, *At the Full and Change of the Moon* (1999), and *In Another Place, Not Here,* (1996), are poetically infused and offer autobiographically inflected fictional meditations that complement the works I engage in this essay. Her latest book, *A Map to the Door of No Return: Notes to Belonging* (2001), is an autobiographical exploration of the relevance and nature of identity and belonging in a culturally diverse and rapidly changing world. When asked about the meaning of *A Map to the Door of No Return* in an interview by Maya Mavjee, Brand replied, "Beyond the meaning of existence in the black Diaspora, it's how one defines one's own existence within history, within a specific place."[6]

Brand's writings form an essential part of the rich milieu of black Canadian writers. Here, I just mention two prominent black Canadian writers whose works also comprise excellent literary sources for the analysis of racism in Canada. George Elliott Clarke was born in Windsor, Nova Scotia, in 1960, and is a seventh-generation Canadian of African-American and Mi'kmaq Amerindian heritage. Clarke's publications include two verse collections, *Saltwater Spirituals and Deeper Blues* (1983), and *Lush Dreams, Blue Exile* (1994); a verse-novel, *Whylah Falls* (1990 & 2000); and two verse plays, *Whylah Falls: The Play* (1999 & 2000), and *Beatrice Chancy* (1999). His opera *Beatrice Chancy*, with music by James Rolfe is about slavery in the Nova Scotia of the early 1800s. He wrote the screenplay for the feature film *One Heart Broken into Song* (Dir. Clement Virgo, 1999). Clarke continues to publish poetry with three chapbooks: *Provençal Songs* (1993 & 1997), *Gold Indigoes* (2000), and *Execution Poems* (2001). His new collection of poems is *Blue* (2001). Another Toronto-based writer, Makeda Silvera, was born in Jamaica and has lived in Canada for over 30 years. She is the co-founder and managing editor of Sister Vision Press, and

---

[6] Brand, 2001.

is the author of two collections of short stories, *Her Head a Village* (1994) and *Remembering G and Other Stories* (1990). She is the editor of *The Other Woman: Women of Colour in Contemporary Canadian Literature* (1994), *Ma-Ka: Diaspora Juks* (1997), and the frequently referenced *Piece of My Heart: A Lesbian of Colour Anthology* (1991). *The Heart Does Not Bend* (2002), set in Canada and Jamaica, is her first novel.

Brand's writings, which blend contemporary black life with the historical and include works of fiction and essays, are also complementary to the works of two black American women writers, Alice Walker and Toni Morrison. Alice Walker's works include the novels *The Third Life of Grange Copeland* (1970), *In Love and Trouble* (1973), *Meridian* (1976), *You Can't Keep a Good Woman Down* (1981), *The Color Purple* (1982), *The Temple of My Familiar* (1989), *Possessing the Secret of Joy* (1992), and *By the Light of My Father's Smile* (1998); three books of poetry; and two collections of essays, *In Search of Our Mother's Gardens* (1983), and *Living by the Word: Selected Writings 1973–1987* (1988). Toni Morrison's novels explore the black experience in the United States, with a multi-generational compass that echoes with Brand's work. Morrison's novels include: *The Bluest Eye* (1970), *Sula* (1974) *Song of Solomon* (1977), *Tar Baby* (1981), *Beloved* (1987), *Jazz* (1992), *The Dancing Mind* (1997), and *Paradise* (1998). Morrison's theoretical *Playing in the Dark: Whiteness and the Literary Imagination* (1992) offers a critical analysis of black presence in American literature. Her analysis reverberates with Brand's critique in *Bread Out of Stone* of cultural stereotyping and the usually ignored racism that imbues many artistic endeavours. In *A Map to the Door of No Return: Notes to Belonging,* Brand discusses Morrison's work. She further elaborates on the overlap between her work and Morrison's in the Maya Mavjee interview:

> Morrison's issue is with America — the black presence and the nature of freedom in America. I think that space is the space I'm actually talking about. The journey to Africa is not a temporal journey to a physical homeland but a journey to a spiritual one which has elements of a past that was broken and tragic.[7]

Engaging issues of race, ethnicity, class, geography, and sexuality in both *Bread Out of Stone* and *No Language Is Neutral*, Brand insists on the intricate interconnections of all these aspects of her self/selves; no one part is privileged over the other, while each part is exposed as dominant in different life experiences. The dramatic impact of language and social prescriptions on the individual often triggers a desire to write, assume a voice, and "talk back" to negative stereotypes and racist remarks; in a 1990 interview Brand explained:

> I was "born into my subject" as some writer has said. That has immense possibilities and implications. It's the same as being a lesbian. There are very real strictures, the human rights things. But you also know you are opposed to that, so you struggle against it.[8]

As these words illustrate, her rich, evocative writings evince political motivations for social change.

---

[7] Brand, 2001.

[8] Kirchhoff, 1990.

Brand emphasizes memory and history in creating present identity and future possibilities. For that reason, one lens through which I examine *No Language Is Neutral* and *Bread Out of Stone* is Gloria Anzaldúa's theoretical notion of "autohistoria." Gloria Anzaldúa is an American Chicana writer whose collections of essays, such as *Borderlands/La Frontera,* and edited collection, *Making Face, Making Soul/Haciendo Caras: Creative and Critical Perspectives by Women of Color,* have played a major role in revisions of U.S. feminisms, ethnic studies, queer theory, and post-colonial theory. Anzaldúa explains the origin of her term "autohistoria":

> I call it "auto" for self-writing, and "historia" for history — as in collective, personal, cultural, and racial history — as well as for fiction, a story you make up. History is fiction because it's made up, usually made up by the people who rule.[9]

Brand's entire body of work exemplifies the dynamic of "autohistoria." Brand critiques what she calls the "official Canadianness" that involves immigrants in the "intricate mental trick of forgetting what is called 'their past.'"[10] She notes, "One is supposed to empty oneself of the past/place and fill oneself with the present/place"; however, in reality, she says, "we come full of ourselves — who we were and are and will become."[11] Her writings resist silencing and insist upon bringing the past to its proper place in creating the present and promoting future possibilities. In terms of Anzaldúa's "autohistoria," Brand's work brings the past to light and offers a sense of presence for herself and for her readers. Socially prescribed loss and absence are replaced with presence, and a more accurate history is created through collective efforts.

No Language Is Neutral interweaves stories of her history and the history of the black people in Trinidad with several more layers of colonialist racism experienced over the three decades since she came to Canada in 1970. The past and the present are a palimpsest, and the history is not possible to forget, informing the present and creating and shaping possibilities for the future. Her poetic language and use of dialect make the experiences immediate and real for the reader. She recalls first coming to Canada and her disbelief at "race conscious landlords and their jimcrow flats," salespersons who ignore her money on the counter, and being in Canada "doing the work nobody else wants to do."[12] She records the psychological damage she suffered due to the racist treatment she received: "I became more secretive, language seemed to split in two, one branch fell silent, the other argued hotly for going home."[13]

My title for this essay, "Each sentence realized or dreamed jumps like a pulse with history and takes a side", appears as part of the extended poem, "No Language Is Neutral."[14] This line demonstrates Brand's determination to interweave the past, present and future, and the embodied nature of her lan-

---

[9] Anzaldúa, 2000, p. 242.

[10] Brand, 1994, p. 137.

[11] Ibid., p. 138.

[12] Brand, 1998, p. 28.

[13] Ibid.

[14] Ibid., p. 31.

guage, with the "pulse" of life jumping rather than being stagnated into no movement and no change. Her work addresses issues within the debate over the concept of hybridity. One critical issue within the concept of "hybridity," as identified by literary theorists Bill Ashcroft, Gareth Griffiths, and Helen Tiffin in their *Key Concepts in Post-Colonial Studies*, is that it "has frequently been used in post-colonial discourse to mean simply cross-cultural 'exchange.'" They continue, "this use of the term has been widely criticized, since it usually implies negating and neglecting the imbalance and inequality of the power relations it references."[15] When problematizing hybridity as more than just "crossings" (as in border crossings), Brand's work exemplifies the complex of associations and the fault-lines or seams that arise around issues of race, gender, sexuality, and class, as well as resource distribution and power, and their representation and construction in culture. Not just exposing the "crossings" that disrupt any notion of universalization and the given supremacy of a dominant culture, Brand transgressively eschews notions of "cross-cultural exchange" and names the imbalances of power. Identifying the role the media play in perpetuating racism through negation, Brand notes that the newspapers say, "When people come here they just have to leave their culture behind and become Canadian."[16] She encourages an opening up of cultural possibilitics, and social possibilities, to change the status quo.

Provoking change, rather than just a replacement or shifting of the demarcations, borders, and divisions that fragment society, Brand recognizes frames for what they are: artificial barriers that serve to perpetuate the oppressions such as racism, homophobia, sexism, and classism. She questions assumptions of white racial superiority that ground Canadian institutions such as the Canadian Broadcasting Corporation, the National Film Board, and the Canada Council — institutions that control funding for formal cultural production.[17] Looking at the National Ballet and the Toronto Symphony gives a glimpse of the "white skin" that becomes the "signifier for socio-economic opportunity and privilege."[18] Viewed through Brand's eyes, we become aware of the racism imbuing Canadian "formal culture" and register that race is significant, as well as "class, gender, and sexuality," in terms of organizing society around "maleness, class and heterosexual privilege."[19] As well, she exposes the racist ideology that sets unjust values on cultural work of black artists that are not used to evaluate "white work,"[20] such as whether the work is a representative portrayal, or whether it is "sense making" for society. Brand encourages analysis of cultural products as a legitimating forcc and of the racist ideologies that inform Canadian society.

Brand demarcates the racism of cultural representations and the power imbalance in cultural exchanges. Cultural imperialism is examined from diverse

---

[15] Ashcroft, Griffiths & Tiffin, 1999, p. 119.

[16] Brand, 1994, p. 61.

[17] Ibid., p. 124.

[18] Ibid., p. 125.

[19] Ibid., p. 124.

[20] Ibid.

arenas, particularly in one chapter: "Whose Gaze, and Who Speaks for Whom." White film productions of black people for white audiences create a situation replete with cultural appropriation and racial misrepresentation. For instance, she recalls watching a documentary about Thelonious Monk, in which Monk goes mad, and the white audience laughs. The film says nothing about why Monk goes mad, "Not a word about the shape of blackness in America."[21] Brand cites the film *Round Midnight,* about the black saxophonist Dexter Gordon. In the film, a white French man watches Gordon throughout, creating the white man's gaze upon Gordon as object of the gaze, and as the gaze the viewer assumes in a kind of "universal transparency."[22] The white man assumes the power-laden role of knowledge holder and interpreter. She suggests these films depict their subjects, who become the objects of our gaze, as objects of doom and pity.

Taking her analysis to another level, she examines her position as a viewer. She recalls that, sitting in the audience,

> I feel under scrutiny; I, too, feel his gaze and the gaze of the knower communicating with the screen. I identify this gaze as the gaze of liberal racism, which codifies Black genius as tragic but somehow energizing for the white man who steps into "agency" at the genius's dissolution.[23]

In her personal narratives Brand writes of vivid experiences as the target of racism, and her accounts are a reality check for those of us inclined to embrace a decidedly less racist history in Canada. In terms of popular culture in general, she condemns the commercial films that offer a revised picture of the past, such as *Mississippi Burning* and *Driving Miss Daisy,* films complicit in "melting down and eroding"[24] the gains made by the 1960s Black revolution.

The complexities of deciding what cultural productions should be approved are obvious when Brand explores in depth the choice to produce *Show Boat* in Toronto. Studying the event from both the conservative and liberal points of view, she exposes the racism grounding *all* excuses for supporting a show that depicts "Classic racism."[25] Brand suggests the choice to continue with the show indicated a case of "White racial memory," a sense of "Nostalgia, a deep longing for a racist past."[26] She delves into the psychology of racism and the desires fuelling racism. Her rendering of this particular incident in our recent cultural past is an excellent example of the value of Brand's writing in terms of "talking back" and encouraging examination of events otherwise ignored. She speaks of "white ignorance, white denial, white fear, white apathy, white lies, white power disguised as concern for censorship."[27] Wilful ignorance can be attacked through critical analysis of events such as this. Brand claims this inci-

---

[21] Ibid., p. 115.

[22] Ibid., p. 114.

[23] Ibid.

[24] Ibid., p. 60.

[25] Ibid., p. 118.

[26] Ibid., p. 119.

[27] Ibid.

dent is a fine example of what cultural historian Michelle Wallace names as "the production of knowledge [that] is constantly employed in reinforcing intellectual racism,"[28] a quotation that appears in Wallace's 1990 *Invisibility Blues*. Brand's work speaks back to those who are in denial about the pervasive racism and homophobia grounded in culture and supported linguistically. She consistently makes visible the power held, and the effects of the power held, by those who control cultural productivity.

Popular culture produced by black people has mixed effects, according to Brand. On the positive side, she states that songs such as Wilson Pickett's "When a Man Loves a Woman" validates black women's "sense of Black desire, Black desire not white desire as we had been fed and which derogated ours in the popular culture."[29] However, she decries the song's sexist implications that shape black women's notions of romance, desire, and sexuality. Patriarchal and heterosexist power structures still limit possibilities for women: "Defined for so long within white culture as outside of feminine norms, we accepted a competing iconography of feminine sexuality within a taken-for granted patriarchy."[30] In a double bind, black women are either limited to low-paying and laborious jobs, or if they succumb to the "romance of Black desire", they could land as "single mothers or on the walk."[31] She also identifies the pervasive cultural stereotyping of white women as embodying femininity and black women as embodying masculinity and strength, stereotypes providing impossible and damaging models that are often internalized.

On the other hand, Brand offers a picture of experiences that blend a sense of some positive factors intermingling with the negative. She recalls working at the post office: "Here is escape at least from femininity,"[32] which indicates her relief at escaping the norms of white femininity through the atmosphere of the post office. But there is no escape, even in the post office, from "the envy of colony, education, the list of insults for this, better than, brighter than, richer than, beginning with this slender walk against the mountainous school."[33] There is comfort in the community of black people she works with, and she recalls leaving work, when "Each night, the black crowd of us parts in the cold darkness, smiling."[34]

Brand's work exposes the systemic racism occurring as all the major institutions mesh into one. The legal system and police enforcement comprise another powerful institution with drastic impact on the black community. Police brutality and surveillance of people of colour are a fact of life in Canada, and Brand provides ample evidence. She speaks of "Toronto the Good, that sets the police on [black children] for hanging on the streets, for appearing in their own skins

---

28 Ibid., p. 120.
29 Ibid., p. 67.
30 Ibid.
31 Ibid.
32 Ibid., p. 29.
33 Ibid.
34 Ibid.

in malls and parking lots."[35] The racism the children encounter is exacerbated in adulthood. Exposing a circular dynamic, one that is hard to escape, Brand notes, "young Black men in Toronto are shot by police and shoot each other at will today, and young Black women are brutalized, some get shot by cops, too, and answer to the names 'bitches' and 'hos'."[36] Here, she clearly exposes hierarchies of colour *and* of gender in terms of physical violence and linguistic naming. The black women are victimized by white *and* black men.

Racial archetypes and stereotypes impact all people, and it is difficult not to internalize negative representations, such as the media-emphasized connection between blacks and violence and crime, she explains. Violence within the black community is exacerbated by social conditions and by the racism that continues to imbue police forces. Brand's description of racist actions and reportings surrounding the "Just Desserts" case in 1994, and of the speculations that had long-term effects on black teenage boys, reverberates intolerably in stories on the newscasts today.[37] The statistics on prison populations support Brand's criticism of the justice system, since people of colour are incarcerated in numbers disproportionate to their populations. Injustice perpetuates itself at all levels of society, and this is mirrored in each level of the justice system itself. The forces of economics and the police state interplay, and she notes that "The new order fills up the jails with unemployed, underemployed, unemployable. So an ideological war presages the economic war on Black people."[38]

Brand also condemns the official policies and rules that govern immigration in Canada. The frequently expressed fear that immigrants take away jobs from white people combines with wilful blindness to the fact that immigration policies are all about "the economy and cheap labour," according to Brand.[39] Since every encounter with immigration is layered in racism, Brand states that she rarely leaves Canada. The hassles at the border are too difficult to continue to confront. She relates how her partner, who is black and was born in Halifax, was strip-searched at the border because in the eyes of the immigration officers and the general public, "all Blacks are recent immigrants and always suspect."[40] An ongoing dynamic is the immigration rules encouraging women of colour to come to Canada for a limited period of time to serve as maids, nannies, or factory workers, but not allowing them to bring their own children to Canada. The ability to send much-needed money home to support the family is suffered at the expense of the children left behind. This practice is a continuation of slave relations, where black women were forced to care for white children above their own. Brand notes that black women workers who were encouraged to come to Canada in the 1960s and 1970s to serve in the "kitchens and factories" were told not to bring "their appendages [children] in the first place,"[41] and

---

35 Ibid., p. 61.

36 Ibid., p. 67.

37 Ibid., p. 64.

38 Ibid., pp. 72–73.

39 Ibid., p. 73.

40 Ibid., p. 122.

41 Ibid., p. 61.

now the mothers who have stayed and had children must suffer the consequences. She discursively connects generations of racism.

In her fiction and essays, Brand draws a vivid picture of the effects of such social structuring as the "Jane-Finch projects". Brand describes Toronto as a city that piles mothers and children "up in low-ceilinged projects where your heart squeezes into your throat and there's no room to breathe in the corridors, much less think yourself out of this good, good city."[42] Poor diet, lack of educational encouragement, the deadliness of local malls, police surveillance, and the "fakery of commodified dreams" filling the entertainment media and advertisements hold young people back from attaining their potential, Brand argues.[43] Caught between options of being a "superstar or criminal,"[44] children are filled by the media with false images of the potential to be super sports stars or musicians.

All levels of education are rampant with racist actions that create barriers. The resulting lack of education holds individuals back from achieving their highest potential. Racism in the schools translates into a general atmosphere where black children are "classified either as behavioural problems or as learning-disabled."[45] Even the physical environment in the schools is detrimental to the black children's ability to succeed. Brand comments on the "desolate schoolyards and lunch-rooms"; the miserable physical environment is exacerbated by bullying and racist remarks: "the sand-lots are full of racial epithets that children must shrug off or be found too thin-skinned."[46] She details her own experiences with post-secondary education in Canada. Lack of readings by and about people of colour in the university English reading curricula, and the Eurocentric, racist and sexist ideologies embedded in the institutions in the 1970s discouraged her from continuing to complete a Ph.D. at that time. While conditions have improved to some extent, her observations definitely demand attention and rectification today. University course offerings and faculty appointments do not reflect the student population.

These brief moments in Brand's *No Language is Neutral* and *Bread Out of Stone* provide some evidence of the acute and critical gaze Brand brings to her writings. Her depictions of the material realities of racism in Canada in these two volumes combine to embody a valuable resource for general readers and for classes in diverse subjects. Bringing her own experiences to ground her insightful analyses makes the readings immediate and powerful. Brand addresses racist situations still all too familiar today, as in the past, and her evocative writings force each reader to examine stereotypes, blind spots, and ignorance and to take a leading role in participating in the social transformation she incites. The racism that imbues society must be rectified. Looking to the future, Brand hopefully sees the "vibrant possibilities" of the multitude of voices emerging in Canada: "These voices see the imagination as transformative, as

---

[42] Ibid., p. 62.
[43] Ibid., p. 66.
[44] Ibid., p. 62.
[45] Ibid., p. 122.
[46] Ibid., p. 61.

leading out of the pessimism of colonial discourse, as making new narratives...."[47]

References

Anzaldúa, Gloria. (2000). *Interviews/entrevistas* (AnaLouise Keating, Ed.). New York: Routledge.

Ashcroft, Bill, Griffiths, Gareth, & Tiffin, Helen. (1999). *Key concepts in post-colonial studies*. New York: Routledge.

Brand, Dionne. (1990, October). The language of resistance (Interview by Beverley Daurio). *Books in Canada*, 14.

Brand, Dionne. (1994). *Bread out of stone: Recollections, sex, recognitions, race, dreaming*. Toronto: Coach House Press.

Brand, Dionne. (1998). *No language is neutral*. Toronto: McClelland & Stewart.

Brand, Dionne. (2001. Fall). Beyond the door (Interview by Maya Mavjee). *READ magzine*. Retrieved from http://www.randomhouse.ca/readingmag/page28.htm.

Foucault, Michel. (1977). *Language, counter-memory, practice* (Donald F. Bouchard, Ed. and Trans.). Ithaca: Cornell University Press.

Kirchhoff, H.J. (1990, October 17). Finding poetry in possibility. *Globe and Mail*, C4.

---

[47] Ibid., p. 131.

20

Articulating Spaces of Representation
Contemporary Black Women Artists in Canada

Alice Ming Wai Jim
Curator
Vancouver International Centre
for Contemporary Asian Art
Vancouver

Introduction

The last two decades have been witness to a maturation of cultural race politics in Canadian art. In her recent book, *Other Conundrums: Race, Culture and Canadian Art,* Monika Kin Gagnon provides extensive coverage of "this explosion and proliferation of work by artists of colour and First Nations artists in Canada during the 1980s and 1990s in the visual arts, film, video, and writing."[1] Marked by changes in the ways that Canadian artists — First Nations, of colour, and white — organized and produced art in recognition of the problems of multiculturalist tenets of the 1970s and the detrimental effects of institutionalized racism in Canada and its impact on, among other sectors, the arts, this movement brought along with it a steady stream of conferences, festivals, screenings, workshops, publications, and exhibitions focusing on identity politics with an intensity, activism, and presence never felt before.[2]

This essay looks at two exhibitions that were embedded in the specificities of this historical moment in Canadian cultural race politics: *Black Wimmin: When and Where We Enter,* which was presented in five different gallery spaces across the country in 1989, and its follow-up in July 1997, *Women's Work: Black Women in the Visual Arts,* which was presented in conjunction with CELAFI, the Celebrating African Identity Festival, held every five years in Toronto. The former set two precedents, each of which mark it as a significant example of anti-racist and anti-sexist work in the arts as well as an important cultural development in Canadian art history: it was the first group exhibition of work by Black women artists in Canada, and it was the first to be coordinated by Black women curators. The latter is a reprisal and re-examination of the agenda of the former within a more focused curatorial theme centring on women's work. Both involved a conscious naming of oneself as an agent of one's own cultural production.

Through this process of self-authorization, or as Trinh T. Minh-ha writes, "authorized voices authorizing themselves to be heard," the staging of these exhibitions not only challenged stereotypical constructions of Black women, Black women artists, and their artistic production, but also produced critical sites of resistance, moments that French spatial theorist Henri Lefebvre referred to in his book *La production d'espace,* written in 1974, as "spaces of representation."[3] For Lefebvre, spaces of representation, or lived spaces, are constituted by social relations encountered in everyday life and are constantly in the process of produc-

---

1 Gagnon, 2000, p. 21.

2 Lai, 2000, p. 15.

3 Minh-ha, 1991, p. 188; Lefebvre, 1984.

tion and negotiation. More important, they are also political and ideological: hence, potential sites for the articulation of counter-discourses.

I first met the curators and artists involved in these two exhibitions when I began my research on Black-Canadian women artists in 1994 and my later involvement writing the exhibition essay for *Women's Work*. As a young researcher and writer of colour, I found myself immersed in a very exciting moment in the development of Black-Canadian art, both politically and artistically. Networks were being formed, critical discourse was being called for, and alliances were being forged between groups of artists of colour as well as within them, in a growing awareness of the cultural politics of difference. Within this context, I saw my own intervention as an emerging art historian as part of this activity. Faced with the paucity of published materials on artists of colour in Canadian art history, as well as grappling with my position as a first-generation Canadian-born Chinese, I too was working, and continue to work, from a perspective fully embedded in my personal experience of the internal structures of race and racialization in Canada. It was at this time that I became more fully aware of the power of representation in terms of both image production and writing practice. Indeed, it is through the many different modes of articulation that bring forward the variability and changeability of spaces of representation that interventions can be and are being made in Canadian cultural politics. The three sections that follow here, compiled over a period of six years and each about a specific moment in the history of Black-Canadian art ranging from 1989 to 2002, comprise part of my efforts in this project.

1989: Black Wimmin — When and Where WE Enter[4]

> Only the BLACK WOMAN can say "when and where I enter, in the quiet undisputed dignity of my womanhood, without violence and without suing or special patronage, then and there the whole Negro race enters with me."
>
> Anna Julia Cooper, *A Voice of the South* (1892)[5]

Black Wimmin: When and Where We Enter was conceived and organized by Buseje Bailey and Grace Channer, two Black women activist-artists who, along with other collaborators, subsequently founded the Diasporic African Women's Art Collective (DAWA), a non-profit community network of Black women artists formed in 1984 to promote Black women's culture in Canada.[6] With the

---

[4] An extended version of this section appears in "An Analysis and Documentation of the 1989 Exhibition *Black Wimmin: When and Where We Enter*", published in the *Canadian Art Review*, which in turn was drawn from my 1996 M.A. thesis by the same title at Concordia University, Montreal, Quebec in 1998.

[5] Giddings, 1984.

[6] DAWA was disbanded in late 1989, soon after the exhibition. The African diaspora in Canada has resulted largely from three main phases of migration: (1) the importation of slaves in Upper and Lower Canada during the seventeenth and eighteenth centuries and the escape of Blacks from slavery in the United States; (2) the pre-confederation Black settlement in the Maritimes and, to a

participation of 11 artists from Toronto, Ottawa, Kingston, Montreal and Edmonton, the exhibition, which was also accompanied by seminars and talks, began its tour at Toronto's A Space Gallery on January 28, 1989, and travelled to Houseworks Gallery in Ottawa, XChanges Gallery in Victoria, Galerie Articule in Montreal, and Eye Level Gallery in Halifax, where it closed on September 23, 1989.[7]

The exhibition title, drawn from the inspiring words of turn-of-the-century Black activist Anna Julia Cooper, boldly asserted the project's political trajectory of centring the Black woman in its artistic inquiry. Bringing forward issues of historicity and spatiality, the exhibition presented itself as a challenge to dominant, traditional Eurocentric politics of aesthetics and representation and its various undercurrents existing in the Canadian art arena, which, in its denial of difference in the name of multiculturalist liberalism, habitually ignored the contributions of artists of colour. In response, the project as event provided a space for the articulation of Black women's experiences where there was none previously, and as a result, represented an important moment in Canadian art history. Theu, the "when" in the title not only brought forward the historicity of the project, its actual implementation and execution, but also marked the point of entry for Black women artists into the Canadian art scene.

Clearly, then, the issue of location, in the sense of making spaces of representation, or the situating of "home," was an equally important aspect of the exhibition's political impetus. Situating the "where" of its interrogation was connected to an awareness of how the historical displacement of diasporic subjects and their subsequent "migratory subjectivity" (to use Carole Boyce Davies' term) has not only contributed to their invisibility but has also problematized the development of a politics of location.[8] Consequently, the notion of "home" for many members of the diaspora often involves a metaphor of migration or spatial construct rather than a fixed geographical point. For example, Black feminist writer bel hooks speaks of a "homeplace" as "the construction of a safe place where black people could affirm one another and by doing so heal many of the wounds inflicted by racist domination."[9] For Black women, as well as other women of colour and immigrant women whose diasporic experiences, from slavery to current exploitative work structures, have historically forced them to work in homes other than their own, the notion of "home" becomes a particularly crucial site of resistance.[10]

For the organizers, in conjunction with this reclamation of a "homeplace" as a site of resistance was the activity of making other spaces of experience, such as the Canadian art scene, feel like home. The exhibition thus sought to

---

lesser extent, in Southern Ontario; and (3) in the last 20 to 35 years, the emigration of people from various places of origin, including Britain, the Caribbean, and the African continent. The use of the term "Black" in this essay refers generally to all these diasporic categories.

[7] The 11 artists were: Buseje Bailey, Claire Carew, Grace Channer, Dzian Lacharité, Khadejha McCall, Kim McNeilly, Folukë Olubayo, Chloë Onari, Barbara Prézeau, Suli Williams, and Winsom.

[8] Davies, 1994, p. 1.

[9] hooks, 1990, p. 42.

[10] Brand, 1993, p. 272; hooks, 1990, p. 47. This view would differ from the early (white) feminist writings that located home as a crucial site of oppression for (white) women, while work outside the home was considered liberating.

create political and spatial interventions within the art world as well as discrete pockets of "homes," or subtexts of resistance, through the work and participation of the individual artists.[11] This curatorial concern to address both the historicity (when) and location (where) of Black women can be seen to be reinforced most openly by Dzian Lacharité's *Right Time, Right Place*, a fragile installation of a dwelling made of bamboo branches and light cloth, inside which one could walk barefoot on cool sand to experience the feelings embodied by terms such as "refuge", "shelter" and "home". In effect, each body of work included in *Black Wimmin: When and Where We Enter* could be seen as both a site of resistance and a juncture point in which to raise issues of significance to members of the African diaspora.

Given the context, it was no surprise that identity politics was the primary issue explored. Notions of representation were examined, challenged, re-envisioned and/or reaffirmed through various methods of re-/presentation. Key examples included the works by Khadejha McCall, Buseje Bailey, and Grace Channer. In their attempt to redefine the parameters of representation for the Black female body, they challenged racial and gender stereotypes of women of African descent — ritualized fertility goddesses, versions of the mammy figure — that have been constructed by colonial and neo-colonial discourses. McCall's elaborately screen-printed and batiked textiles explored different perceptions of women of African descent. Her *Strong Black Woman* (Figure 20–1), depicting the figure of a Black "super mom," challenged the predominantly white male role in the commercial world, while *One Day Soon* interrogated the historical and current status of Black women in North American society. Bailey's mixed-media triptych, *The Black Box*, addressed the image of Black motherhood through a tribute to her female family members and Black women's history. Channer's *Ba Thari* (a South African phrase meaning "women from whom generations come"), a floor sculpture made of twigs, driftwood, and messages on pieces of shredded cloth, not only addressed Black women's self-image but also paid homage to their "resilience echoed by that of the driftwood which had passed through many eras and touched many shores but still survived to tell its stories" (Figure 20–2).[12]

In sum, however, it was the bringing together of these diverse articulations in the form of a group exhibition, in the political act of taking possession of a space to articulate previously marginalized voices, that *Black Wimmin: When and Where We Enter* was able to intervene most forcefully in the racial Eurocentric biases of the mainstream Canadian art scene and Canadian cultural politics in general. For example, there were moments in which the location of the venue became just as, if not more, important than the presentation of work inside, and an equal test of the project's curatorial tenacity. Rephrased, the dynamics surrounding these spaces of representation, culturally speaking, reflected, to a degree, the external social realities outside the art world. That the curator-artists continued to assert the project's Black feminist agenda, whether it was in a predominantly white-populated space (such as the venue in Victoria) or in a pre-

---

[11] Participation here is understood as a form of activist cultural practice. *See* Felshin, 1995, p. 12.

[12] Channer, letter to the author, January 1996.

Figure 20–1

Strong Black Woman, Khadejha McCall, 1989. Copyart, silkscreen, handprinting, and painting on unstretched canvas, 48 × 36 inches. Photo: artist.

Figure 20–2

Ba Thari, Grace Channer, 1989. Mixed-media floor sculpture. Photo: artist.

dominantly Black one (such as in Halifax), in the process placing themselves and the exhibition in direct confrontation with the various discourses of cultural difference existing in these communities, undeniably spoke to the urgency and necessity of such an act in the first place. In this sense, the exhibition can be read as embodying a kind of postcolonial strategy that extended beyond the walls of the gallery space in which it was originally physically confined to address the cultural politics of representation in Canada itself.

1997: Women's Work — Black Women in the Visual Arts

Eight years later, curator-artist Buseje Bailey went on to coordinate *Women's Work: Black Women in the Visual Arts* at the YYZ Artists' Outlet in Toronto in July 1997. In contrast to the all-encompassing approach to Black women's artistic production of the earlier exhibition, *Women's Work* applied a more focused curatorial strategy. The theme of this exhibition examined, challenged, and subverted prevailing definitions of women's work through the art of nine female artists of African descent, again from across Canada, but none of whom were in the 1989 exhibition. Presenting a diversity of media ranging from two-dimensional and sculptural pieces by Donna-Lee Bolden, Marie-Denise Douyon, Paulette Hawkins and Charmaine Lurch to three time-based works by Tanya Hamilton, Donna James and Lillian Allen, it was an effort to re-articulate the presence of Black women artists in contemporary Canadian art and highlight once again the diversity, creativity and span of their cultural production. [13]

For centuries, domestic labour such as cooking, cleaning and child rearing has been considered "women's work." However, because of the great disparity in Western history between the type of domestic work considered suitable for white women and that which has been relegated to Black women, the realm of the domestic remains to this day a site of oppression for the latter, despite recent changes in the way gender roles are constructed. For instance, ubiquitous racial stereotypes of women of African descent as mammies and encumbered servants continue to influence hiring practices in other fields of employment such as management, social work, and the arts. In response, the exhibition sought to destabilize these stereotypical notions by emphasizing that Black women's work occupied a much larger domain than that which is perceived. In its exploration of the category "women artists of African descent" as both a site of resistance and a site of empowerment, it attempted to show Black women's art/work to be constantly in a process of development and transformation, refuting any idea of a monolithic definition for this production.

In view of Black feminist notions of home and migrant subjectivity, important themes in *Black Wimmin: When and Where We Enter*, were also explored in several of the works included in *Women's Work*. For example, the creative, whimsical mixed-media pieces by Chrystal Clements reformulated notions of

---

[13] For an extended description, see my exhibition essay written for *Women's Work: Black Women in the Visual Arts*, Toronto, YYZ Artists Outlet, July 1997.

women's work through a subversive reading of everyday domestic objects, children's rhymes and familiar proverbs (Figure 20–3). In their creative uses of word play and repeating images, each tableau encouraged an exchange of ideas, stories and anecdotes about family and life in general, suggesting an intimate relationship between familial domestic culture and the act of storytelling, a metaphor for keeping cultural histories and traditions alive. Linguistic expressions embedded with cultural meaning also played a part in Hamilton's short film *The Killers* about a young Jamaican girl named Biebel who, left in the care of her grandmother, tries to keep her ailing grandfather alive with lizard bones collected after an old wives' tale in the hope that this will ensure the return of her mother who is away in America. Haunting and moving at the same time, the film looked at the people left behind by women like Biebel's mother who migrate overseas to find work with the intentions of sending for their children later. Finally, Melinda Mollineaux's photomontage series of abstracted tree limbs, landscapes and family members explored the female diasporic condition from the perspective of a migrant subject, prompting viewers to question the ways in which history, memory and Black female identity are inscribed onto a cultural landscape that is geopolitically unlimited in the context of transnational migrations, yet socially circumscribed on every other level (Figure 20–4).

Certainly the focus of this exhibition on the specificity of women's work in relation to women artists of African descent signalled a maturity in the discourses surrounding identity politics in its recognition of the limits of organizing events based solely on the participant's racial self-identification. However, it is also of crucial importance to acknowledge the historical moments from which the articulation of a specific identity category for this exhibition and its earlier edition emerged, especially considering the presentation of the former in conjunction with the second installment of the city-wide Celebrating African Identity Festival and other smaller exhibitions of work by artists of colour that occurred across the country, particularly at artist-run centres, within this eight-year period. For example, the anti-racist movement of the 1980s, as Tariq Modood writes, "consisted of (in the case of white people, a solidarity with) an oppositional blackness based on an inversion of the racist white-black/coloured divide, together with a celebration of the positive elements of the black diasporic African heritage of struggle, and of the achievements of the contemporary bearers of that heritage."[14] With vestiges of this conflation of the "political solidarity of all non-whites and a black diasporic African ethnicity" still at large in the 1990s, it can be observed that the tensions between alliances of anti-racist groups and the celebration of difference within these groups remain an issue of contention to this day.[15] A historical consideration of feminist intervention in the arts would bring forward similar disjunctures concerning identity and difference inseparable from issues of race and ethnicity. Thus, with respect to discussing forms of anti-racist interventions such as these two exhibitions, among others, it is necessary, as Gagnon suggests, "to think of cultural race politics as a transformative process," one that is determined by the specifics of the moment being discussed

---

[14] Modood, 1997, p. 159.

[15] Ibid.

Figure 20–3

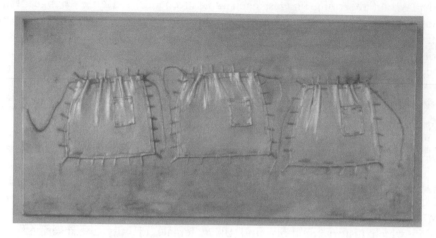

ArmHer, Chrystal Clements, 1997. Mixed-media on panel board. Photo: curator.

Figure 20–4

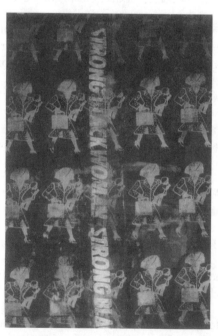

Day by Day Goes By, Melinda Mollineaux, 1997. Photomontage series, 5 of 100 images, each 4 × 4 inches. Photo: artist.

rather than seen as one "homogenous and containable mass or problem."[16] In this way, a recognition can be afforded, not only of the ways in which processes of identification are fluid and contingent, presenting what may seem incessant challenges for the social body, but also of how much has been accomplished through the articulation of spaces of representation within the framework of activism in the arts.

2002: What Now?

Since *Black Wimmin: When and Where We Enter* and *Women's Work: Black Women in the Visual Arts*, many more exhibitions have involved the curatorship and artistic production of Black Canadian women, with the most recent being *Sister Visions III: Through Our Eyes*, which took place at the Art Gallery of Nova Scotia in Halifax in 2000, and *Black Body: Race, Resistance, Response*, which took place at the Dalhousie Art Gallery in 2001, also in Halifax. However, the situation for the arts in Canada has greatly changed since the 1980s and 1990s. Funding cuts, processes of amalgamation, and general negligence of the cultural landscape at the level of governmental bodies has impacted the productivity and continuation of cultural activities in dire and detrimental ways. On the occasion of writing this essay, I had the opportunity to get a sense of the current issues at stake for Black women artists from a very personal perspective through email communications with Buseje Bailey, the curator involved with both the exhibitions I discuss here.[17] This brief but candid exchange is published in its entirety by way of conclusion.

AJ: What are your thoughts about some of the major undertakings over the last twenty years with respect to funding, equity and politics? Have they had any effect?

BB: Despite some major undertakings over the years ... and despite the initiatives undertaken in the past to address equity, there are some issues that these initiatives failed to address, or could not address. One of which is sustainable support. What do I mean by that? Well, artists need the support of community and society at large. They need time, which is money, and space, which is money, to develop and sustain that development in their practice and production. They also need the support of the art institutions at different levels. If this field is a constant uphill battle and the support is sporadic and uncertain, the result of which is an unsustainable practice, then growth/development is sure to fail.

AJ: What about artists' networks and arts festivals that have taken place, things that seemed to signal that there has been work in activism that should have alleviated such problems?

---

[16] Gagnon, 2000, p. 30.

[17] Our email conversations took place between November 3, 2001 and December 6, 2001.

BB:	I am assuming that you are speaking of "the community." The community and its institutions are more interested in its own survival, and have abandoned any attempts to support our development, proceeding instead with the status quo. The community-network of CAN:BAIA, which I was part of when I curated the *Women's Work* exhibition in conjunction with its CELAFI festival, was on its last leg, and later declared bankruptcy.
AJ:	Perhaps we can go back in time and trace how the situation has come to this point?
BB:	It is not very difficult to understand, and we don't have to go back very far; it is like yesterday. This culture is not an avid supporter of the arts; and the arts that have government support are typically Euro-centric or mainstream. Does that sound trite to you?!
AJ:	What about in the academic world?
BB:	Because you are involved from an institutional perspective, and the writing that exists lags behind what is actually happening now, by the time you get the text/narrative, it seems like the changes that appeared to have taken place are long-lasting or are still in effect. But the changes that need to happen are structural, not mere add-ons during this time of plenty.

In the era when the Conservatives swept into power, organizations and institutions that were able to support diversity in culture had their funding cut. So they (the government and affiliated institutions) needed to cut back — what they cut back were the frills, the add-ons — support to the arts, specifically funds towards developing diverse communities in the arts. True support would give the participants a period of maturation in which to grow and develop their practice. The current half-hearted support and activity shows us that it is possible to give support to the artist, but what is needed is true consciousness, not superficial solutions.

Part of the romantic mystique is to believe that an artist will make art no matter what, but the economics of this great global world have changed. We do not find art material in the garbage heap any more. Technology is a big part of art today — nobody is giving that away. Art comes full circle, back to the place of requiring economic support.

Networking is good if the people who are networking have some funds. The true cost of those events (conferences, festivals, touring exhibitions, etc.) was never tallied. The conferences and festivals never supported us. The arts that were showcased at these events took us years to put together, and some of the networks were formed by the artists themselves. In fact, some of these events merely exploited the communities and did not offer a strong foundation for us to stand on. Then the storm of conservatism came and washed their superficial support away.

AJ:	So things are not better.
BB:	Things are not better, we are working twice as hard. We cannot even get back to or produce the work as we used to. Artists are usually the poorest sector of society. Moreover, a lot of the com-

munity links have dried up or changed their mandate to fit government funding solutions.

AJ: So I guess you don't think highly of exhibitions that get put on
only during Black History Month in February.

BB: Yes, I have to say that Black History month art exhibitions are
an excellent venue for emerging Black artists; but when this is
the only venue for Black artists, then I find great issue with the
lack of inclusion of Black/African art in any or all other venues.

AJ: Can you say a few words about some recent projects you have
been involved in, for example, the *Black Body: Race, Resistance,
Response* exhibition in Halifax?

BB: I was asked to participate in *Black Body* by the curator, Pamela
Edmonds, who was familiar with my past work and the premises
behind it. As these fell within her curatorial theme, she asked
me to participate. I exhibited my 1992 video *Blood* (Figure 20–5)
and my installation *Body Politics* from 1991–2001. In that geographical location that kind of work is needed again and again.

AJ: What do you think of comments that refer to self-representa-
tional work as self-victimization, be it in terms of race, gender,
class, and other socially constructed forms of difference?

BB: Only someone who represents the establishment could say such a
statement. Those of us who have had to speak our own truth
know better. I really do not want to dignify that assault. I would
also need more specific information about particular representational work that is considered victim art in order to respond.

Also, what happened to the voices that said self-representation brings our
world into reality? No one has spoken our truth or has spoken or can speak
for us. Self-representation means bringing forward a vast missing contribution
from a significant section of the community to engage in the development of a
diverse art.

AJ: Are you working on anything now?

BB: Well, not much in the pursuit of art making. I am sorry to dis-
appoint you. Most of us cannot live in the "white" romantic definition of the artist. We must live in the present, very
conservative, very controlled art arena. With all the rhetoric
about and in this arena, there is a very practical side to making
art. It takes money, and lots of it, to play the very insatiable
game. I have no money. And what little I get these days, I use
to survive. However, I am working on few experimental pieces
that involve multimedia work on the computer. But that kind of
thing, again, takes money. So right now I am basically working
on the logistics. So in terms of end products, I don't know when
these would be ready.

AJ: Is this new body of work conceived in terms of a certain theme
in mind?

Figure 20–5

Blood, Buseje Bailey, stills from videotape, 5:54 mins. Photo: artist.

BB: Essentially I am exploring images, so I am not working on a particular theme but pushing the limits to see what I can achieve aesthetically, but they do concern women, the environment, things that can be suggestive of other things.... I have also compiled a selection of topical images from the media, from newspapers and magazines, for example, illustrating the most headlined stories these days, housing, fighting terrorism, collaging them together not knowing where I am going with it.

AJ: Can you offer any positive views on the situation of the arts at this point?

BB: Things are difficult, but it comes and it goes, maybe sometime down the road things will turn around ... but artists, what do we do in the meantime, making art despite audience absenteeism, working in isolation just to cut it? It's not just about artists, but audiences too. There is a lot to be done in developing audiences for the arts in Canada. While most mainstream art is being supported by government funding, a hell of a lot needs to be done to support broad-base art in Canada, Canadian home-grown production.

AJ: What is your advice to emerging artists?

BB: I would never dissuade a person who wants to be an artist, but you always have to have something to fall back on. For people who participate in sports, for example, everybody tells them to get an education so that if they break an arm or strain something, they will be able to do something else. This is similar in the arts, but of course there is always the one in a million chance that you will be really successful, not only financially but having fulfilled your dreams and with the respect of your peers, since money is not the only objective in making art. People have to find their own fulfilment; for artists, this has much to do with creating something that others can relate to in some kind of meaningful way. Art is a powerful tool to communicate ideas.

AJ: Thank you very much, Buseje, for taking the time to participate in this email interview.

References

Brand, Dionne. (1993) A working paper on black women in Toronto: Gender, race and class. In Himani Bannerji (Ed.), *Returning the gaze: Essays on racism, feminism and politics*. Toronto: Sister Vision.

Davies, Carole Boyce. (1994). *Black women, writing and identity: Migrations of the subject*. New York: Routledge.

Felshin, Nina. (1995). *But is it art? The spirit of art as activism*. Seattle: Bay Press.

Gagnon, Monika Kin. (2000). *Other conundrums: Race, culture and Canadian art*. Vancouver: Arsenal Pulp Press and Artspeak Gallery; Kamloops: Kamloops Art Gallery.

Giddings, Paula. (1984). Epigraph. *When and where I enter: The impact of black women on race and sex in America*. New York: W. Morrow.

hooks, bell. (1990). *Yearning: Race, gender and cultural politics*. Toronto: Between the Lines.

Jim, Alice Ming Wai. (1998). An analysis and documentation of the 1989 exhibition *Black Wimmin: When and Where We Enter. Canadian Art Review (RACAR) 23*(1–2), 71–83.

Lai, Larissa. (2000). Foreword. In Monika Kin. Gagnon, *Other conundrums: Race, culture and Canadian art*. Vancouver: Arsenal Pulp Press and Artspeak Gallery; Kamloops: Kamloops Art Gallery.

Lefebvre, Henri. (1984). *The production of space* (Donald Nicholson-Smith, Trans.). Oxford: Blackwell.

Minh-ha, Trinh T. (1991). *When the moon waxes red: Representation, gender and cultural politics*. New York: Routledge.

Modood, Tariq. (1997). "Difference", cultural racism and anti-racism. In Pnina Werbner and Tariq Modood (Eds.), *Debating cultural hybridity: Multi-cultural identities and the politics of anti-racism*. London: ZED Books.

21

The "Hottentot Venus" in Canada
Modernism, Censorship and the Racial Limits of Female Sexuality

Charmaine A. Nelson
Department of Art History
and Communication Studies
McGill University
Montreal

There is an indelible mark in my memories of my undergraduate education as a student of Western art history in Canada.[1] If I had been given a penny for every time a professor had lectured on Edouard Manet's *Olympia* (1863, Figure 21–1), only to refuse to discuss the conspicuous presence of the black maid, I would be quite a wealthy woman today. Noting the historical compulsion to erase her presence, Lorraine O'Grady has argued that:

> She is the chaos that must be excised, and it is her excision that stabilizes the West's construct of the female body, for the 'femininity' of the white female body is ensured by assigning the not-white to a chaos safely removed from sight.[2]

Figure 21–1

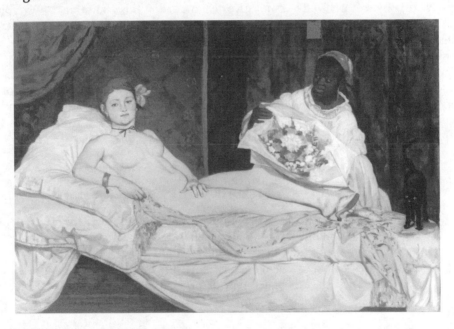

Edouard Manet, *Olympia* (1863), oil on canvas, Musée d'Orsay, Paris, France, Réunion des Musée Nationaux/Art Resource, New York.

---

[1] I am using the term "Western" to indicate original European traditions and their colonial permutations in countries such as Canada, the United States and Australia.
[2] O'Grady, 1991, p. 153.

Charmaine A. Nelson

While my claim may seem like an extraordinary exaggeration, when art historical discursivity, especially its Modernist permutations,[3] are scrutinized for their
ability or willingness to accommodate race, my point as a comment on the
dominating Eurocentrism of art historical disciplinarity becomes painfully clear.
Modernism refers to a cultural movement and an historical moment but, more
important for art history, to a specific artistic practice generally designated by a
dominating, often formalistic interest in issues of style and aesthetic concerns.
Modernism, however, must also be acknowledged as a specific art historical discourse that dictates the limits of art production and interpretation. Historically,
Western Modernism has privileged painting above all other media and has further privileged aesthetic practices that reinforced and celebrated the two-
dimensionality of painting. This explicit focus upon materiality has often elided
social, historical and political issues from the discourse. The Modernism of
visual culture has also historically been the exclusive domain of white-male
artistic production centred around notions of urbanity, voyeurism and bohe-
mianism. Ironically, Modernism's obvious dependence upon the bodies of
transgressive female subjects (often prostitutes or courtesans) and the appropriation of African, Native and Oceanic arts has only recently been given critical
attention. Manet's *Olympia* is not an arbitrary choice on my part.[4] The utter
disavowal of race as a valid issue of art historical inquiry is evidenced in T.J.
Clark's otherwise archivally exhaustive chapter on this painting, "Olympia's
Choice". Clark's social art historical analysis of the painting is fundamentally
based upon class identity. Griselda Pollock has noted his unwillingness to deal
with the obvious gender and sex issues that are latent within the painting.[5]
However, my concern is with his almost complete disregard for the racially
"other" subject of the painting — the black maid who is clearly visible. For a
student of art history or the uninitiated, the uncontested value of this painting
is indexed by the extent to which scholars of art history need not identify it for
their canonically indoctrinated audiences. As Pollock has warned:

> Canonical art history may be defined as a kind of border police, monitoring the visi-
> bility of which links, which borrowings, which genealogies are to be acknowledged,
> while others, [sic] become aberrant, ignorant, incorrect or plain invisible.[6]

Although Manet's name and the basic formalistic and stylistic concerns of
the art object as a seminal painting that marked the celebrated beginnings of
Western Modernism need not be restated, I would argue that what has been
consistently disavowed, and what needs now to be urgently examined and
retrieved, is the body of the black female maid, her colonial context and the

---

[3] For an understanding of Modernism within the visual arts *see* Greenberg, 1994. For a feminist
critique of this tradition *see* Pollock, 1988.
[4] T.J. Clark quotes a nineteenth-century source that perverts the black maid's representation as
that of a "hideous negress", uncritically used the Hottentot Venus as a barometer of the grotesque,
and included contemporaneous "humourous" engravings of *Olympia* that radically burlesqued and
mammified Manet's demure, even pretty, black maid. However, he fails to address the core issues
of race and racialized sexuality as an obvious theme compelled by the deliberate juxtaposition of
the white and the black female bodies (Clark, 1984, pp. 92, 93, 96, 97).
[5] *See* Pollock, 1998.
[6] Pollock, 1999, p. 187.

psycho-social constraints that have facilitated the erasure of her obvious presence and significance in the first instance. Elaborating upon the focus of her book *Negrophilia: Avant-garde Paris and Black Culture in the 1920s* (2000) and its decidedly post-colonial methodology, Petrine Archer-Straw has written:

> I was aware that although art historians discussed black culture's influence on the Parisian avant-garde there was no text that looked at the avant-garde's motivations outside of *artistic imperatives*. Redressing this imbalance called for an examination of rarely considered tropes within European art history that reinforced negative stereotypes of blacks, especially in respect to primitivism. (Italics mine)[7]

We need to ask what art historical discourse, especially its Modernist permutations, makes possible and suppresses and through what logic and apparatus its borders are policed.[8] In other words, we need to examine the historical suppression of issues of race, colour and colonialism within art historical discursivity, and create a space for post-colonial interventions within cultural practice and analysis. Just as feminist interventions have made it possible to discuss gender and sex issues within the context of patriarchy, a post-colonial intervention within art history would privilege discussions of race, colour and culture within a colonial context. A post-colonial art history also creates a space for the discussion of the production of Native, black, Asian and other traditionally marginalized artists. This intervention would also fundamentally take up representation as a process of identification and, therefore, position visual culture as colonial discourse, a site where racial identities are produced and deployed.

Critical theory, especially feminist interventions, have provided clear and effective strategies for cultural transformation of the traditionally patriarchal disciplinarity of art history.[9] However, recent criticisms of white feminist practice have contested the extent to which the deployment of an essentializing category of Woman, coupled with the silence around race/colour, have re-entrenched the colonial privilege of the white female body. Post-colonial scholarship, particularly its manifestations within Cultural Studies, is helping to provide the theoretical and material structure for a racial intervention within art history, one that acknowledges culture as a site of colonial discourse and, thus, a generative source of racialized identities and racism.[10]

---

[7] Archer-Straw, 2000, p. 10.

[8] A significant tactic used in the policing of traditional art historical hegemony is to control which questions may or may not be formulated in the face of an art work. A fitting recent and personal example occurred in a review of my art exhibition *Through An-Other's Eyes: White Canadian Artists — Black Female Subjects* (1998), in which I employed a post-colonial feminist perspective to explore the three century-long fascination of white Canadian artists with black female subjects. In a review by Henry Lehman in *The Gazette*, rather than critique the exhibition within its own stated thesis and discourse, Lehman belittled the very premise of the show by demonstrating its difference, and implied inferiority and exteriority, to the discourse of Modernist art history and its singular and supposedly universal concerns with formal analysis and "pure" aesthetics. In so doing, Lehman also effectively dismissed the possibility and legitimacy of anything other than a white male viewing body (*See* Lehman, 2000; *see also* Nelson, 1998 and 2000).

[9] Pollock & Parker, 1981, and Pollock, 1999.

[10] Two recent and excellent examples of a post-colonial art history are Pollock's *Differencing the canon* (1999), and Wood's *Blind Memory* (2000). In the Canadian context, Gagnon's *Other Conundrums* (2000) and Acland's "Elitekey" (1998) have set a high standard.

Charmaine A. Nelson

Post-colonial scholarship has also informed the recent racial interventions within the overwhelmingly colonial discourses of anthropology, ethnography and museology. Recent critical contributions to the study of culture have interrogated Western colonial histories of exhibition and human display.[11] Within the institutionalized museum practices of ethnographic display, human anatomical and skeletal remains often served as "primitivizing" markers of the racial identification of colonial subjects: evidence of the supposed evolutionary inferiority of colonized populations. Exceeding museum practices in their mass appeal to broad middle- and lower-class populations, the more socially accessible spectacles of fairs, circuses and open-air exhibitions often replaced skeletal remains with the living bodies of colonized subjects.[12] As Rosemary Wiss has argued, "European discourse on the perception of difference was partially informed by exhibits of indigenous people brought back to Europe by colonial scientists and entrepreneurs during the eighteenth and especially nineteenth centuries."[13] Ccolonial subjects framed within the Eurocentrically biased and artificially imposed boundaries of reconstructed and anthropologically "authentic", "primitive" villages were made to perform their cultures and also, significantly, their races, for the entertainment of white audiences.

The colonial practice of human display distanced the white observer, both literally and figuratively, from the primitivized bodies of colonial subjects. Safely behind the carefully demarcated boundaries of the exhibitions and fairgrounds, the space of the colonial "other" was clearly separated from the privileged space of the white viewer/"self". The deliberately cultivated material and psychic distance was a part of the colonial apparatus that visually objectified the exhibited human subjects and racialized the bodies of the exhibited and spectators alike within colonial binaries.

Colonial Exhibition Practices

It is within the colonial space of the West that the "Hottentot Venus" emerged, an iconic sexual and racial identity that resulted from the transatlantic imperialist regimes of global colonization.[14] The term "Hottentot" is present within nineteenth-century Western human sciences as a name for a group of people or tribe and, sometimes, even for a distinct race. Whereas Hottentots were often considered a subcategory of the Negro/Negroid race, the nineteenth-century human scientist James Cowles Prichard went so far as to distinguish them as a separate and inferior race to Negroes. To append Venus to this term has both general implications in its referencing of ancient mythology and more specific implications in its referencing of nineteenth-century cultural and social ideals of female sexuality and beauty. Since Venus, which has most frequently in Western art been represented as white female subjects, has widely

---

[11] *See*, for example, Clifford 1989; Lavine & Karp, 1991; and Coombes, 1988.

[12] Hinsley, 1991.

[13] Wiss, 1994, p. 12

[14] *See* Prichard, 1851, p. 109.

been read as an idealization of female beauty, to affix the term "Hottentot" is an ironic or cruelly "humorous" gesture that substitutes a racially "othered" body — the grotesque — for the expected beautiful white female body. Saat-Jee/ Saartje/Saartjie, or Sarah Baartman, as she was named by her Dutch owner/ agent, was one of several South African women who were displayed naked throughout Europe for the sexual titillation of white audiences.[15] It is important to note that although the legal status of these women as slaves is in dispute, the nature of their interaction and relationships as African women with European men during a colonial period where slavery and scientific racism were prolific makes it easy to assume at the very least a fundamentally inequitable and exploitative engagement based upon dominant ideals of racial and sex/gender difference. Taken from South Africa in 1810 by Hendrick Cezar (the brother of her Dutch "master") and the Englishman Alexander Dunlop (a ship's surgeon and trader in "museum specimens"),[16] Saat-Jee was exhibited in London, toured throughout England and, finally, taken to Paris.[17] The colonial regime that transfigured Saat-Jee into the "Hottentot Venus" relied upon the dissolution not only of her individuality, but also of her humanity since, as part of an animal act, Saat-Jee's humanness was fundamentally questioned through her constant juxtaposition with animals.[18] The "Hottentot Venus" was a colonial stereotype that attempted to homogenize representations of black female sexuality as "primitive" and pathological.

Within the practices of colonial ethnographic exhibition, the living Saat-Jee was publicly displayed to curiosity seekers who were "...amazed and affrighted by the sight of her naked body with its enlarged buttocks and elongated genital flap."[19] It is critically important to note that it was these corporeal signs, the buttocks and the flap, that were seized upon and reified as intrinsic signs of a deviant sexuality. As such, these signs of corporeal excess became fundamentally connected not only with blackness but also with the pornographic. It is the visibility of these signs, and their legibility as racially specific, that provoked the cultural censorship that I will discuss in detail below.

Other Hottentot women suffered fates similar to that of Saat-Jee. As the entertainment at dinner parties of the social elite, their naked bodies became a sexual spectacle for the titillation and curiosity of white viewers. The sexual exploitation of black women within Western exhibition practices worked to dichotomize the Hottentot body with the ideals of white bourgeois womanhood. This coerced public performance was an integral part of the racial and sexual othering of the black female body within the cultural imagination of the modern West. The sexual and racial objectification of Hottentot women was a matter of life and death. Besides being exhibited as scientific specimens, subhuman examples of racial and sexual difference, Hottentot women had autopsies per-

---

[15] Wallace, 1990, p. 45.

[16] Wiss, 1994, p. 13.

[17] Jounnais, 1994; Wiss, 1994, pp. 11, 13.

[18] Within the scientific discourse of the body, the Hottentot's increasing viability as a "missing link" between the animal kingdom and human beings is consistent with Saat-Jee's bestialization and display as part of a stable of animals.

[19] Gould, 1982.

formed on them by Western scientists in a deliberate search for a source of pathology that would confirm colonial theories of sexual and racial identity as biologically based and, thereby, fixed and essential.[20] Saat-Jee died in 1815 of an inflammation. Her body was subsequently autopsied by the revered comparative anatomist Cuvier and, post-dissection, ceded to the Musée de l'Homme in Paris, where its scientific efficacy as a racial and sexual specimen became institutionally sanctioned. The museum displayed her skeleton, genitalia and brain until 1974. Saat-Jee's remains were finally repatriated 186 years after her death in Paris. Indigenous leaders of the Khoisan people, or "Bushmen" (widely believed to be the original inhabitants of the southern tip of Africa), heralded her repatriation as a symbolic act that could aid in the reclamation of Khoisan identity.

The "Hottentot Venus" in Canada

Although Hottentot women were never (to my knowledge) "imported" to Canada, the Hottentot Venus did make a significant appearance within early-twentieth-century Canadian culture — an appearance that, despite the vast geographical distance between Canada and Europe, clearly indexes the prolific circulation and normalcy of colonial ideals of blackness and their saturation of Western consciousness. The Hottentot's representation and legibility in Canada is significant not only for the way this identifiably iconic anatomical type indexed racialized and sexualized conceptions of the body, but also for the way it speaks to the social and psychic constitution of difference within the colonial politics of identity. It is the hierarchization of racialized bodies and their cultural policing that must be interrogated if Modernism's investment in coloniality and, indeed, blackness is to be understood.

Within a conservative cultural milieu, Canadians embraced censorship as a means of enforcing the arbitrary social boundaries of artistic production. However, this censorship was not universally applied. Rather, it was practised within historically Eurocentric hierarchies that racialized concepts of beauty and sexuality. In April, 1927, Max Weber's *Contemplation* (ca. 1923, Figure 21–2) and *Retirement* (ca. 1921, Figure 21–3) and Alexandre Archipenko's *The Bather* (date unknown) were secretly removed from the walls of the *International Exhibition of Modern Art* hosted by the Art Gallery of Toronto.[21] To acknowledge this censorship as a racially motivated action within a colonial cultural framework calls for an understanding of the conservatism of early-twentieth-century Canadian figure painting, the simultaneous politics of representation and censorship, and the historical pathologization of blackness and black female sexuality. But since colonial stereotypes are not only polarized but also parasitic, we must hold these factors in tension with the white female body and its liminality — its proximity to the so-called primitiveness of the black body and the subse-

---

[20] *See* Allie, 2002; Jounnais, 1994; Wiss, 1944, p. 11.

[21] The Art Gallery of Toronto is today known as the Art Gallery of Ontario. I will henceforth refer to this institution by the abbreviation "AGT".

Figure 21–2

Max Weber, *Contemplation/Compostition of Nude Figures* (ca. 1923). Oil on Canvas, 30 × 40 inches. The France Lehman Loeb Art Center, Vassar College, Poughkeepsie, NY, USA. Gift of Mrs Helen M Davis (Helen Miller, class of 1920). 1940.5

Figure 21–3

Max Weber, *Retirement* (ca. 1921). Oil on Canvas, 32 1/4 × 40 1/8 inches. Rose Art Museum, Brandeis University, Waltham, Massachusetts. Gift of Mrs. Weber and her children Maynard and Joy, Great Neck, New York, in memory of Max Weber.

quent threat to white male identity. It is within this colonial matrix that the "Hottentot Venus" made an appearance within the Canadian cultural landscape.

Adherence to Traditions

In 1931 the Canadian artist and critic Bertram Brooker called the Canadian art community puritanical, and over 15 years later the Montreal-based painter Louis Muhlstock deemed the lack of artistic freedom to be the result of an "excess of prudery."[22] Although these established Canadian artists were more directly concerned with the state of figure painting in Canada, their opinions appropriately surmised the conservative climate of Canadian artistic production in general.

Early Canadian artists commonly emulated European models to validate their art within the youthful colony. However, this emulation did not extend itself to Modern European trends. Rather, twentieth-century Canadian artists embraced established historical styles of recognized European artistic schools. This colonial dependence was fostered by art patronage and art education that celebrated and rewarded artists who patterned their work after canonized Western art. The resulting lack of innovation was evidenced, to varying degrees, within the different genres of painting.[23] This traditionalism was partially maintained through the practice of museum censorship that was used to eliminate potentially offensive representations of the human (particularly female) body. Within this realm, the "offensive" paintings were usually those that broke from such traditional and idealized visions of the white female body as the nude.[24] "The nude" and "the naked" are two specific art historical terms that have most often been applied to representations of the female body in Western art. The nude, which dominated French nineteenth-century academic tradition, has historically needed a *raison d'etre*. Generally pandering to a heterosexual male gaze, it has been the more conventional of the two categories, and is associated with the Beautiful and "high art". The naked is aligned with limitlessness, sexuality and impropriety, while the nude is often allegorical, or a body that is *always already* unclothed. The naked often points up the process of undressing, the social and biological body and, therefore, is generally aligned with the Sublime and the pornographic.

Lack of allegory, of contrived womanly innocence, or of nature's canopy generally provoked controversy and, inevitably, censorship. Paintings that represented naked, as opposed to nude, women were said to pose moral threats to the viewing public. Censorship was used in an effort to monitor and carefully delimit the boundaries of female sexuality. However, this practice was not arbitrary but directed specifically at representations of the white female body in an

---

[22] Brooker, 1931; Muhlstock, 1947.

[23] Twentieth-century Canadian landscape painting, although heavily dependent upon Dutch art, was decidedly more progressive than figure painting. While many landscape artists, including the acclaimed Canadian Group of Seven, aggressively pursued a Modern vision of the vast Canadian wilderness, figure painters adhered more rigidly to nineteenth-century European prototypes.

[24] *See* Clark, 1972; and Nead, 1994.

effort to protect the idealization of white womanhood through a policing of the arbitrary divide between art and pornography.

Representations of the black female body in Canadian culture have historically received no such paternalistic concern. Overtly sexualized images of black women were condoned, even praised, while comparatively innocuous paintings of white women were actively censored.[25] Within this colonial practice, the Canadian museum community was enforcing deterministic ideals of race and sexuality by participating in the construction and perpetuation of a Eurocentric womanhood. As such, black women were constituted as "other" by the white artistic community at the centre.

The Canadian museum community, whether sanctioning or censoring female nudes, participated in the construction of whiteness. As Ruth Frankenberg has illustrated:

> ...whiteness refers to a set of locations that are historically, socially, politically, and culturally produced and, moreover, are intrinsically linked to unfolding relations of domination.[26]

The paradigmatic nature of whiteness within colonial discourse provided, and continues to provide, a protection to white women not historically extended to black women. But within any dichotomous relationship there is an interdependence and, thus, the identity of the white woman is constructed not only in her presence, but in her absence; her "other" — that is, Black Woman. It is crucial, then, to examine not only what was representable at any given moment, but also what was beyond representation.

Controversy, Censorship and White Female Nudes in Canadian Painting

During the late 1920s and early 1930s, white female nudes regularly incited controversy and provoked censorship within the Canadian art milieu. Censorship was generally enacted under the guise of a "public service" imposed by museum officials, who, as the purveyors of an authoritarian knowledge, acted for the greater benefit and protection of the community. Serving two main agendas, the censorship of white female nudes functioned simultaneously to protect the museum audience from the social threat of pornography and to preserve the ideals of white womanhood and the definitions of femininity and sexuality at its core. Yet, censorship was not limited solely to Canadian art works, but extended to art works exhibited in Canada.

Non-Canadian artists were targeted by censors during the first Canadian exhibition of international Modern art at the AGT. Three paintings of female nudes were removed from the *International Exhibition of Modern Art*: Max Weber's *Contemplation* (ca. 1923) and *Retirement* (ca. 1921) and Alexandre Archipenko's *The Bather*. The exhibition (also known as the Brooklyn Exhibi-

---

[25] Nelson, 1995.

[26] Frankenberg, 1991, p. 6.

Charmaine A. Nelson

tion for its original site) was assembled by the Société Anonyme, largely owing to the efforts of Katherine Dreier. As president of the society, Dreier was a vigorous supporter of Modern art and had earlier founded the society with the assistance of Marcel Duchamp and Man Ray.[27] According to Ruth Bohan:

> ...[t]he Brooklyn Exhibition was both the largest and most comprehensive exhibition of modern art shown in this country [United States of America] in the 1920s and the Société Anonyme's grandest achievement.[28]

American audiences had been better prepared than their Canadian neighbours to consume these Modern art works. As Bohan has noted, the occurrence of several other exhibitions of Modern art had laid the foundation for the *International Exhibition.* The *Armory Show,* the *Forum Exhibition,* and the several other smaller exhibitions of Modern art held at Alfred Stieglitz's gallery at 291 Fifth Avenue had injected Modernism into the consciousness of the American audiences, even if those audiences had not yet been ready to embrace it.[29]

Contrarily, the *International Exhibition of Modern Art* marked the first direct exposure of Canadian audiences to the international Modernism of twentieth-century artists. To all but those intimately acquainted with current European artistic trends, these Modernist art works, many of which had begun to embrace abstracting principles, would have seemed "alien" to the conservative Canadian audience. That the exhibition opened in Canada at all is due in large part to the diligent individual efforts of a Canadian familiar with artistic developments in the international art arena, Lawren Harris.[30] After much determined negotiation with officials at the AGT, Lawren Harris' relentless efforts resulted in the exhibition's showing in Toronto. A successful Canadian artist and patron, Lawren Harris' nationalist ideology embraced Modernist art as a vehicle for the articulation of a uniquely Canadian cultural identity. As a member of the Canadian Group of Seven, Harris' painting, though considerably more conservative than that of his counterparts in the *International Exhibition*, reflected his belief in the need for Canadian artists to embrace the possibilities of Modernism.

Toronto was the final venue of the *International Exhibition.* The show had opened at the Brooklyn Museum on November 18, 1926. From there it had travelled to the Anderson Galleries, New York, and the Albright Art Gallery, Buffalo, before concluding its journey in Toronto.[31] The presence of the Weber and Archipenko nudes in the original AGT catalogue is evidence of the original intention to include the pieces and the hastiness of their withdrawal once in Toronto.

According to a first-hand account, the exhibition organizer, Miss Dreier, had overseen the hanging of the exhibition, but upon returning to the gallery the same evening for the private opening, she found that works by Weber and

---

[27] Bohan, 1980, p. iii.

[28] Ibid., p. ii.

[29] Ibid.

[30] Ibid., 1980, p. 140.

[31] Pfaff, 1984, p. 80.

Archipenko had been removed in the interim.[32] Though a local report noted that "...the exclusion of these nudes may not be an instance of prudery,"[33] another explanation located the nexus of sexual and racial motivations that had provoked their censorship. The report stated:

> These that the censor has consigned to the coal regions are physical.... They are readily identifiable as women.... One of Weber's nudes, "Contemplation" might win a prize in a Hottentot beauty contest.[34]

The reference to the Hottentot bodies as the catalyst for censorship situated the network of racialized anatomical codes that governed the representational practices of the body at this historical moment.

Negrophilia and Modernism: Black Woman as Subject

Throughout the 1920s and 1930s, both Weber's and Archipenko's female nudes possessed the so-called fleshy, excessive, spectacular Hottentot anatomy described by this Canadian newspaper reporter. Both artists were active within European Modernism, the undisputed capital of which was Paris, at a moment when *les choses africain* dominated the consciousness of Western cultural production. The colonial origins of Modernism must be examined within the context of negrophilia, the social and cultural phenomenon of white fear/desire for the black body. Beyond recognizing negrophilia as a phenomenon through which blackness, as supposedly primitive, was revealed and celebrated, we must scrutinize it as a generative force and interrogate it as the very process through which Africanness and blackness were othered, and the white body/self located as "civilized", beautiful, rational and intelligent. As Petrine Archer-Straw has commented upon the avant-garde cultural scene of 1920s Paris:

> The negrophiles who fraternized with blacks cultivated a shadowy world of nightclubs and bohemianism; their interests were in conflict with mainstream, "traditional" values. 'Blackness' was a sign of their modernity....[35]

James Clifford situates this Modernist preoccupation with African art and peoples within the framework of the colonial power structure that facilitated the appropriation and fetishization of the colonial subject as "other":

> Picasso, Leger, Appollinaire, and many others came to recognize the elemental, "magical" power of African sculptures in a period of growing *negrophilie*, a context that would see the irruption onto the European scene of other evocative black figures: the jazzman, the boxer (Al Brown), the *sauvage* Josephine Baker. To tell the history of modernism's recognition of African "art" in this broader context would raise ambigu-

---

[32] Brooker, 1931, p. 94.

[33] Ibid.

[34] "Paintings of Nudes", 1927.

[35] Archer-Straw, 2000, p. 19.

ous and disturbing questions about aesthetic appropriation and non-Western others, issues of race, gender, and power.[36]

Modernist practice, then, was as much about the West's colonial fascination with African cultural production as it was the racist surveillance, representation and consumption of African bodies as "primitive" objects themselves.

Early in his career, Max Weber spent three formative years in Paris, then the centre of Western artistic activity. While studying at the Academie Julian, Weber became active in Parisienne contemporary life, socializing with other avant-garde artists, among them Henri Matisse, Robert Delaunay, Henri Rousseau and Pablo Picasso.[37] The artistic community within which Weber circulated was full of young, white, male Modernists who actively appropriated so-called primitive art forms, African and otherwise. It was within this context that Weber, as William Gerdts has noted, "...[a]lso became acquainted with African Negro sculpture, then newly discovered and highly popular with young moderns in Paris."[38]

Alexandre Archipenko's experience with the "primitive" art of Africa parallels that of Max Weber's. Arriving in Paris from Russia in 1908, Archipenko quickly became associated with the Parisienne artistic vanguard.[39] By 1910 Archipenko was exhibiting with the Cubist painters at the *Salon des Independants*. Although Archipenko did not embrace all of the Cubist idioms, a kinship was forged through a mutual fascination with African art. The following year, Archipenko's debt to the "primitive" was directly revealed in the title of his bronze sculpture *Negro Dancer*.[40]

The preoccupation of Modern European artists with African art has been historically rationalized as a purely superficial interest based mainly upon formal aesthetic concerns. This narrow assessment has been perpetuated throughout art historical discourse, attributing the overwhelming influence of African art on twentieth-century Western culture to a mere formal reactionism to dominant artistic styles. It is the Eurocentric exclusivity of art historical discourse and its inability to accommodate questions of race, colour and colonialism that have effectively suppressed the colonial context of Western Modernism within the discipline. Contemporary art historians have continued to replicate these beliefs. According to Katherine Janszky Michaelson:

> In their search for alternatives to impressionism, painters and sculptors alike employed these "primitive" sources to arrive at the new vocabulary of clear massive forms that became the point of departure for cubism. With a new emphasis on formal and structural problems ... subject matter began to lose the importance it had in the nineteenth century, as is demonstrated by the many generically titled works by Archipenko and others.[41]

---

[36] "Histories of the Tribal and the Modern" in Clifford, 1988, p. 197.

[37] Gerdts, 1959, p. 7.

[38] Ibid.

[39] Michaelsen, 1986, p. 19.

[40] The bronze sculpture *Negro Dancer* (1911) is in the Schueler Collection, Stockholm, Sweden.

[41] Michaelsen, 1986, p. 20.

This statement not only frames Modernism as a superficial search for a new aesthetic vocabulary, it blatantly refuses the obvious colonial context of Modernism's preoccupation, appropriation and exploitation of African cultures and peoples. Weber, Archipenko and their contemporaries shared not only a fascination with African art and objects, but with Africanness and blackness as they had been defined in terms of white contact with "primitive" peoples of African descent. This fascination, fuelled by white male artists' interaction with African art and their experiences with the "primitive" presence of black people (primarily as artistic performers in nineteenth- and twentieth-century Paris) was largely played out through representations of black women. That Weber and Archipenko were participants within this negrophilia reveals itself in their construction of the female body as Hottentot.

Both Weber's *Contemplation* (ca. 1923) and *Retirement* (ca. 1921) are compositions that incorporate several female forms represented with thick limbs; rounded stomachs; wide hips; heavy, circular breasts; and large buttocks. Similarly, Archipenko's female bathers of this period exhibit sturdy proportions and fleshy bodies that were categorically opposed to more traditional Western notions of female beauty. Weber clearly represented the "Hottentot" bodies of his women as white.

While the presence of the four male figures in Weber's *Retirement* (ca. 1921) may also be located as a source for the disturbing reception of this painting, the Hottentot anatomy of the women must be understood as a device that could mediate this otherwise unacceptable presence. The bodies of Weber's women mark them as possessing a "primitive" black sexuality and, through this inscription, normalized the otherwise problematic presence of the men. Weber's painting recalls Manet's *Déjeuner sur l'herbe* (1863), whose representation of a naked white woman with two fully clothed white men can be read as a commentary on the role of class in the social construction of female sexuality within the social structures of nineteenth-century Paris. When Manet painted *Déjeuner sur l'herbe,* Paris was erupting with controversial debates about prostitution, and the human "sciences" were actively engaged in a search for a visual vocabulary of the body that would identify and fix the body of the white prostitute as an essential site of sexual deviance. Class, then, as race, would be revealed as a predetermined physical marker of sexual behaviour and deviance.

Manet's juxtaposition of the black body of the maid with the white body of the prostitute in *Olympia* (1863) located the conflation of race and sexual deviance within the nineteenth-century discourses of female sexuality. As two separate bodies, the maid and the prostitute reflect two different sides of the same coin. They were both viewed as sexually deviant in an essential way that implicated their very biology. But whereas the white woman's sexual deviance allowed for the possibility (however slim) of transcendence or redemption, the black woman, physically marked by the stain/colour (and other anatomical and physiognomical signs) of her racial difference, could never transcend her "primitive" sexuality. Part of the problem of *Olympia*'s reception was her elusiveness to class categorization, a commentary by Manet on the increased social confusion of prostitutes and "proper" women by men in Paris. The hysteria around the (in)visibility of the prostitute indexed concern for the spread of syphilis and its problematic and sexist alignment with the female bodies of prostitutes as opposed to the male bodies of their clients. But the cool reception of this painting must also be examined in terms of Manet's rupturing of the fantasy of the prostitute as Desire for a heterosexual male gaze, a fantasy dependent upon the subsumption of the economic exchange of money for sex, a fact revealed by the placement of Olympia's hand securely over her genitals and the fixing of her ambiguous gaze outward to the implied John whose position we (the viewer) now occupy.

Through the proximity of the two bodies, Manet clearly referred to a significant trope within the annals of Western figure painting through which a "black sexuality" was transferred onto the body of a white female subject, or the black female subject acted as a surface to reinforce the unquestioned beauty and racial superiority of the white female subject.[42] As Deborah Willis and Carla Williams have described:

> Exotic but rarely exalted, the black female image frequently functioned as an iconographic device to illustrate some subject believed to be worthier of depiction, often a white female. When she appeared at all, she was a servant in the seraglio, a savage in the landscape, "Sarah" on the display stage, but always merely an adjunct.[43]

However, I would argue that part of the overwhelming rejection of Manet's *Olympia* was based precisely upon its refusal to reinforce this colonial dichotomization of black and white female identity and sexuality. It was the white female body within *Olympia* that was read as naked, dirty, dead, and sexually uncontrollable.[44] Juxtaposed with the fully clothed demure presence of the black maid, Manet effectively reversed and problematized the stereotypical racial positions to which these two bodies were generally assigned. The rejection of Weber and Archipenko at the AGT in Canada was based on a similar refusal — the destabilization of a presumed colonial racing of female sexuality.

For Picasso, the bodies of the black woman and the white prostitute became conflated into a single iconic Hottentot anatomy in his drawing *Olympia* (1901), after the earlier painting.[45] Unclothed on a bed, she is ready to service not one (as Manet's *Olympia* implied), but two white men (one of them, arguably, Picaso himself). Black Woman, always already sexually promiscuous, uncontrollable, feral, is represented as a prostitute.[46] The grave irony here is, of course, that within the colonial history of slavery, black women did not have the privilege of exchanging their sexuality for personal economic benefit, as such an exchange was premised upon the legal and material ownership and control of one's body. Disenfranchised by colonial legal discourse, black female

---

[42] *See,* for example, Dante Gabriel Rossetti, *The Bride or The Beloved* (1865–66); Jean Léon Gérôme, *Moorish Bath* (ca. 1870); Lilly Martin Spencer, *Dixie Land* (1862); John Lyman, *Sun Bathing 1* (1955).

[43] Willis & Williams, 2002, p. 1.

[44] Clark, 1984.

[45] Pablo Picasso, *Olympia* (1901), pen and coloured crayon, private collection, Paris, France.

[46] The institutionalization of breeding practices that effectively encouraged the rape of black female slaves for the economic benefit of the white plantocracy must be scrutinized with regard to the de-/regendering of black bodies within slavery.

slaves were property, and the rights to economic benefit from their labour and procreative capacities were invested with their white owners.

The iconic stature of the Hottentot body as a marker of black sexual deviance and availability was evidenced in Matisse's *Blue Nude (Souvenir of Biskra)* (1907), a work whose inspiration Archer-Straw traces to the artist's North African trip the previous year.[47] Although the artist chose non-flesh colours to represent the body of the female subject, the arbitrary nature of this selection is undermined by the geometric and Africanized mask-like face that refutes the otherwise indiscriminate palette by signifying a black body. The thick limbs and full circular breasts are accompanied by deliberately enlarged, overemphasized buttocks that manage to reveal themselves to the viewer despite the fact that this blue woman is positioned with her body frontally aligned with the viewer in a reclining pose.

This is the same point at which Weber's and Archipenko's representations of women are inserted into the Modernist dialogue. Unlike Manet's *Olympia,* with the separate bodies of the black and white women, or Picasso's *Olympia,* which still constituted the represented female body as black, the works of Matisse, Weber and Archipenko share a moment in which the signification of race at the level of skin colour was unnecessary to establish the race of the represented body. The woman could be white, as in the images of Weber, or even blue, as with Matisse's *Blue Nude (Souvenir of Biskra),* yet the viewer was able to read race into these bodies despite the ambivalence of skin. It is clear, then, that anatomical and physiognomical signs of the body were as important as colour in the identification of race. It is also clear that race was not only visual but also, crucially, what was visible when taken as a sign of what was beyond vision — since, regardless of skin colour, the Hottentot anatomy signalled that deep down within the body, in the biology and the "essence" of these women, they were all black. And blackness was not just a racial position, but also a sexual one.

Conclusion

Weber's and Archipenko's representations of the Hottentot body locate the colonial fascination of Western artists with blackness and Africanness, particularly as it has been manifested within representations of black women. By the twentieth century, the Hottentot body type was intimately connected with a Western artistic consciousness that perceived black women as sexual "primitives". The iconic nature of the Hottentot body provided a concrete visual language for this perception, which could then be constituted in a specific, representable, physical body.

The censorship of Max Weber's and Alexandre Archipenko's female nudes from the *International Exhibition of Modern Art* at the AGT was a reaction that perpetuated the dichotomous perception of black and white female sexuality within colonial discourse. The representation of the "Hottentot" body type of

---

[47] Archer-Straw, 2000, p. 56.

itself was not enough to seal the fate of Weber's and Archipenko's final subjects. The represented female bodies were offensive not because they depicted the so-called anatomical irregularity of the Hottentot anatomy but because they dared to construct this body for women who were not definitively identifiable as black. This ambiguity recalled the Freudian preoccupation with white women as the "weak evolutionary link" and their constant danger of backsliding into the "primitive" state of black sexuality, a threat that a patriarchal logic registered mainly in terms of the inevitable danger to the white male body. Although idealized as the paradigm of beauty and sexual purity, within the phallocentric West, the impossibility of female sexual difference as anything but black led to white women's precarious and liminal position, which was further destabilized by associations with the "primitive".

Within Freudian psychoanalysis, white female sexuality has been located as a site of "primitive" fear/desire. The inscription of female sexuality as danger has aligned white female sexuality with colonial representations of blackness. Accordingly, white women were seen as the most immediate threat to the imagined "purity" of white men and the heterosocial sanctity of Western civilization. It is the liminality of the female body that Weber and Archipenko works recalled, breaching the racialized standards of social propriety as they marked the tenuous boundaries between art and pornography.

The Weber and Archipenko works, in representing the iconic Hottentot body, recalled the "primitive" site of a black sexuality. But also, as a white or racially unfixed body, they recalled the instability of white female sexuality, and threatened the idealization of white womanhood. While the marks and assigned meanings of the Hottentot body seemed essentially appropriate for the representation of "black sexuality", when applied to the white female subject they became foreign, offensive, potentially pornographic and worthy of cultural policing.

References

Acland, Joan. (1998). Elitekey: The artistic production of Mi'Kmaq women. *Canadian Art Review, 25*(1–2), 3–11.

Allie, Mohammed. (2002, May 6). Return of 'Hottentot Venus' unites bushmen. *BBC News*. Retrieved October 25, 2003, from http://news.bbc.co.uk/1/hi/world/africa/1971103.stem

Archer-Straw, Petrine. (2000). *Negrophilia: Avant-garde Paris and black culture in the 1920's*. New York: Thames & Hudson,

Bohan, Ruth Louise. (1980). The Société Anonyme's Brooklyn Exhibition, 1926–1927: Katherine Sophie Dreier and the promotion of modern art in America. Unpublished Ph.D. dissertation, University of Maryland, College Park, Maryland.

Brooker, Bertram. (1931). Nudes and prudes. *Open House*. Ottawa: Graphic Publishers Limited.

Clark, Kenneth. (1972). *The nude: A study in ideal form*. Princeton: Princeton University Press.

Clark T.J. (1984). Olympia's Choice. *The painting of modern life: Paris in the art of Manet and his followers*. London: Thames & Hudson.

Clifford, James. (1988). *Predicament in culture: Twentieth-century ethnography, literature and art*. Cambridge: Harvard University Press.

Coombes, Annie. (1988). Museums and the formation of national and cultural identities. *The Oxford Art Journal, 11*(2), 58–68.

Frankenberg, Ruth. (1991). *White women, race matters: The social construction of whiteness*. Minneapolis: University of Minnesota Press.

Gagnon, Monika Kin. (2000). *Other conundrums: Race, culture, and Canadian Art*. Vancouver: Arsenal Pulp Press.

Gerdts, William H., Jr. (1959). *Max Weber: Retrospective exhibition October 1st — November 15th, 1959*. Newark: The Newark Museum.

Gilman, Sander. (2002). The Hottentot and the prostitute: Toward an iconography of female sexuality. In Kymberly N. Pinder (Ed.), *Race-ing art history: Critical readings in race and art history*. New York: Routledge.

Gould, Stephen. (1982). The Hottentot Venus. *Natural History, 91*, 20–27.

Greenberg, Clement. (1994). Modernist painting. *Art in theory 1900–1990: An anthology of changing ideas*. Oxford: Blackwell.

Hinsley, Curtis M. (1991). The world as marketplace: Commodification of the exotic at the world's Columbian exposition, Chicago, 1893. In Ivan Karp & Steven D. Lavine (Eds.), *Exhibiting cultures: The poetics and politics of museum display* (pp. 344–365). Washington: Smithsonian Institution Press.

Jounnais, Jean-Yves. (1994, May). The Hottentot Venus. *Art Press, 191*, 34.

Lavine, Steven D., & Karp, Ivan (Eds.). (1991). *Exhibiting cultures: The poetics and politics of museum display*. Washington: Smithsonian Institution Press.

Lehman, Henry. (2000, March 4). Artists' vision coloured by prejudice? *The Gazette*, p. J2.

Michaelsen, Katherine Janszky. (1986). *Alexander Archipenko: A centennial tribute*. Washington: National Gallery of Washington and Tel Aviv Museum.

Muhlstock, Louis. (1947). An excess in prudery. In Robert Ayre & Donald W. Buchanan (Eds.), *Canadian art: Christmas–New Year, 1947–48* (Vol. 5, No. 2). Ottawa: Canadian Art.

Nead, Lynda. (1994). *The female nude: Art, obscenity and sexuality*. London: Routledge.

Nelson, Charmaine. (1995). Coloured nude: Fetishization, disguise, dichotomy. *Canadian Art Review, 22*(1–2), 97–107.

Nelson, Charmaine. (1998). *Through an-other's eyes: White Canadian artists — black female subjects*. Oshawa: Robert McLaughlin Gallery.

Nelson, Charmaine. (2000, March 11). Art critic called misinformed. *The Gazette*, p. J5.

O'Grady, Lorraine. (1991). Olympia's maid: Reclaiming black female subjectivity. In Joanna Frueh, Cassandra L. Langer & Arlene Raven (Eds.), *New feminist criticism: Art, identity, action*. New York: Harper Collins Publishers (Icon Editions).

Paintings of nudes consigned to cellar. (1927, April 4). *The Toronto Daily Star*, p. 22.

Pfaff, L.R. (1984). Lawren Harris and the international exhibition of modern art: Rectifications to the Toronto catalogue (1927), and some critical comments. *Canadian Art Review, 11*(1–2).

Pollock, Griselda. (1988). Modernity and the spaces of femininity. *Vision and difference: Femininity, feminism and the histories of art*. London: Routledge.

Pollock, Griselda. (1999). *Differencing the canon: Feminist desire and the writing of art's histories*. London: Routledge.

Pollock, Griselda, & Parker, Roszika. (1981). *Old mistresses: Women, art and ideology*. London: Pandora.

Prichard, James Cowles. (1851). *Researches into the physical history of mankind* (4th ed., 3 vols.). London: Houlston and Stoneman.

Wallace, Michelle. (1990). Modernism, postmodernism and the problem of the visual in Afro-American culture. In Russell Ferguson, Martha Gever, Trinh T. Minh-ha & Cornel West (Eds.), *Out there: Marginalization and contemporary cultures*. New York: The New Museum of Contemporary Art.

Willis, Deborah, & Williams, Carla. (2002). *The black female body: A photographic history*. Philadelphia: Temple University Press.

Wiss, Rosemary. (1994) Lipreading: Remembering Saartjie Baartman. *Australian Journal of Anthropology, 5*(1–2), 11–40.

Wood, Marcus. (2000). *Blind memory: Visual representations of slavery in England and America*. London: Routledge.

22

Racial Recognition Underpinning Critical Art

Joanne Tod
Artist and Lecturer
Toronto

Though

Though he worried over my decision to become an artist, my father offered practical assistance and made suggestions that helped in the development of my career. The loathed business course he insisted I take in high school, for example, taught skills that enabled me to work in art galleries for several years before becoming self-sufficient as an artist. My father was intelligent, rational and he voted NDP.

Thus I reminisced as I stood in the mist of the open freezer door, contemplating several rock hard Brazil nuts enshrouded in a Ziploc bag. They're easier to crack when frozen solid, so the story goes. Niggertoes. It was true, that's what daddy called them. This strange word had no context for me, a white, middle-class child of the suburbs, and my father never used any other racial epithets.

My mother, on the other hand, voiced biased opinions about English people, whose hygiene and cuisine she mocked. Her oft-repeated remarks puzzled me. My childhood social sphere included several first-generation British people and based on my observations, her criticisms seemed unfounded. And besides, wasn't my maternal grandmother from Glasgow? Maybe it was Scottish nationalism. My grandmother's Glaswegian brogue seemed an authentic testament to her ethnic roots. Strange, though, not only was Grandma's maiden name Lithuanian, but so had been the names of her two husbands. Even odder was that it took so long to register the obvious: My grandmother was Lithuanian. When I asked why this information had been suppressed, my mother assured me that in Canada during the war, "you couldn't get a job unless you had a WASP surname." She had many stories of discrimination that seemed to corroborate this statement. Further questioning led to the discovery that her family had Jewish ancestors as well (*see* Figure 22–1). It was fascinating for me, as an adult, to have a logical explanation for the delicious lunches my mother would prepare back then, while I was still in public school and came home at noon. A far cry from the peanut butter of my schoolmates, I was lovingly served, on rye with chopped onion, chicken liver fried in grievella, or matzoh farfel. Jewish specialties.

I loved peanut butter, too, of course, and I recall reading in the *Golden Book Encyclopaedia* that botanist George Washington Carver had worked with peanuts. I remember the colour illustration of Carver, who looked distinctly green in reproduction. It did not correspond with the deep blue black skin of the first black man I ever saw, at Malton Airport, in the late 1950s. This dazzling person in a scarlet hat and jacket captivated me. He was a Skycap.

The new medium of television introduced a first generation of black entertainers who suddenly caught the attention of a huge, predominantly white, audience. Television and radio defined my own experience of black culture almost exclusively. The glamour of Harry Belafonte and Sammy Davis Jr., though, had

Figure 22–1

Approximation, 1988, 120 × 78 inches, oil on canvas.

In this painting, Royal Doulton Toby jugs, ceramic items emblematic of Britain, are turned on their sides. This inversion attempts to portray my feeling of being "turned around" upon discovering my mother's true ancestry. The portrait in the centre is Mary Kelly, a well-known artist who, although American, has spent much time in England. She has a British accent and, not incidentally, resembles my mother.

Joanne Tod

nothing to do with what I witnessed personally. We took several vacations to the United States when I was young, and I observed that black people there were usually serving my family or me in some capacity. I began to learn something about the history of slavery and its consequences first hand.

The only black student at my Port Credit high school was Dave Mann, son of a famous football player. Everyone else was white. When I think of this now, I find it quite astounding. Even Ontario College of Art (OCA), which I attended in the early 1970s, was not the racially diverse place it is now. But at college, I finally met some Jewish people. In spite of my family history, I didn't know any Jews except for Billy Pomeroy, who, in grade 7, was excused from Religious Education class. So I was delighted to learn about "jewishness". As well, there were several Chinese people I became friends with while at OCA. One guy, Andrew, was a very gifted wood block printer whose English was practically non-existent. It was difficult for him, as there weren't a lot of other Chinese-speaking students at the time. But people recognized his ability and encouraged him while he learned the language. And it was worth the wait. Over a delicious home cooked meal prepared by Andrew, he told us that he'd escaped from China while serving in Chairman Mao's Red Army. He jumped ship and swam to Hong Kong. His family lost everything in the Cultural Revolution, and his mother had committed suicide. It was tragic and dramatic, yet Andrew persevered and did well. However, I remember an instructor at OCA openly ridiculing him and mimicking his accent in front of the class. Ironically, it was a class in contemporary art issues. I was angry and embarrassed for Andrew, who knew, along with everyone else, exactly what was happening. I regretted not pointing out this racist behaviour to the instructor at the time. But I may still take the opportunity retroactively, since I continue to cross paths with this individual in the art community.

Just after graduating from OCA, I made a painting based on an image from a Japanese bondage magazine. I knew nothing of this practice of sexual macramé, but I was intrigued by the photographs. One series featured a naked woman bound and tied upside down in a traditional Japanese kitchen. To me, the "exoticism" implied by the culturally specific location was completely overridden by the fact that the bound figure was female. This struck me as a perfect, if extreme, metaphor for women's lot in life, confined to domestic drudgery in spite of feminism's liberating effects. This was a seminal work for me because it presaged the many paintings I would produce that dealt directly with my perception and critique of sexism, racism and social injustice (Figure 22–2).

It was my mother's experience of unfair treatment based on ethnicity that first made me aware of discrimination. I was outraged on her behalf and, perhaps because of this, began to notice, and look for, other examples of social inequity. By identifying, pointing out and then making art about these issues, I intended to pull them into the light of day and nail them to the gallery wall for public scrutiny (Figure 22–3).

Sometime in 1979, I went to see Peter MacCallum performing at a West African drumming workshop. Peter is a respected Toronto photographer, and I was curious to see what he was up to. It was a memorable event that was to shape my future dramatically. I was very moved and excited by this music, and

388

Figure 22–2

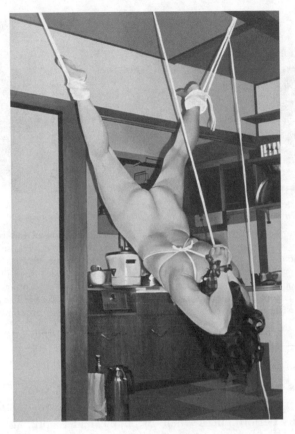

In the Kitchen, 1975, 36 × 54 inches, acrylic on canvas.

I wanted to learn more. I went to the next rehearsal, led by percussionist Bob Becker, a brilliant musician whose specialty is xylophone and who had studied with Ghanaian master drummer Abraham Adzenyah. The session was to have taken place in the percussion department of the Royal Conservatory, but the studio was flooded due to a recent storm. Instead, our lesson was held in Marshall McLuhan's office, a secluded gatehouse on the University of Toronto campus. McLuhan had died just the week before, and it was poignant for us to be there representing the Global Village.

My interest in learning traditional Ghanaian music continued for many years, and I was privileged to study and perform with many fantastic musicians. I studied mainly percussion, but this music involves singing and dancing as well. It is complex and requires physical co-ordination and stamina. During this time, I became friends with several Ghanaians. We founded a group, "Flaming

Figure 22–3

Shh... They own this Restaurant, 1984, 48 × 120 inches, oil on canvas.

This work acknowledges the ubiquity of prejudice. The focal point of this panoramic interior is a group of Asian people seated at a table. The title of the work suggests ambiguity of attribution—who is making this comment: the artist, the viewer, or someone at another table within the composition of the painting? In the foreground, a bowl of oranges functions as a codified reference to Edouard Manet's painting *A Bar at the Folies-Bergéres,* except here the viewer is placed in the position of the barmaid. This further complicates the reading of the work by suggesting the idea of economic disparity.

Dono," that was to perform semi-professionally for 10 years. We shared many exhilarating intervals playing music together. We also shared many "green rooms" at various performances when 20 people had to prepare for a costumed event. We got to know each other on an intimate level. For me, this is ground zero as far as racism is concerned: Intimacy diffuses racism. Together, we stripped off our sweat-soaked costumes, then partied and drank beer together. I learned that Rahima's waist-length dreadlocks had to be washed, "like a fine wool sweater" and also how to swear in Ga, which seems to favour detailed anatomical description. Sam, who grew up in Accra, entertained us with stories of his youth. With the British influence still prevalent, he and his classmates would be marched around dressed in khaki uniforms while singing European-style marching songs. These rhythmic tunes, sung mainly in Ga, were an opportunity to display publicly a hilarious lack of respect for the white drill sergeant. A translation of one such ditty:

> Sergeant Major, your mother,
> Sergeant Major, your father,
> Sergeant Major, Sergeant Major,
> Your mother's vagina.

The irreverence of these amusing anecdotes struck a chord. The very notion of mockery appealed to me, because as an artist, I felt that part of my

Figure 22–4

Mrs. Sue Mukherjee, 1997. 96 × 64 inches, oil on canvas.

This painting is based on a photograph I took at a wedding reception in Markham, Ontario. It was the marriage of our friend Leena Roy, a young woman we've known since she was a child. Leena is the Canadian-born daughter of Bengali parents, and the event was a traditional Hindu ceremony. I made several paintings based on guests resplendent in formal Indian attire. The series, called *New Society Paintings* alluded to John Singer Sargent's full-figure portraits of well-dressed individuals.

job was to question authority. And the jokes demonstrated a sexist humour that seemed all too familiar to me.

Fraternizing and bonding with people from a different community, over time, allowed me to penetrate through formality to a deeper level of understanding and trust. And when making art, I felt that sometimes I could pre-

sume to speak on behalf of someone else, exposing critical issues, because
these concerns had already been endorsed by "the other", my friends.

What began as a shared interest in music led to my lifelong relationship
with Bob Becker. Bob and I also studied tabla drumming with a virtuoso player
from Banares, India, Pandit Sharda Sahai. We traveled to India on two occasions and stayed with his family, with whom we became very close. The children we met in India 20 years ago are now adults living in Europe and North
America. Padma, one of these children, is now a happily married computer
programmer living in Miami (Figure 22–4).

Canada's multicultural programs have been somewhat successful in responding to an ethnically diverse population, and many of these programs are genu-
inely altruistic in their mandates. But distribution of funds is still determined by
councils and boards that are primarily white, in spite of the fact that growing

Figure 22–5

New York, New York, 2001, 39 × 58 inches, oil on canvas.

There is a wonderful old apartment building in midtown Manhattan where I stay when I
visit New York. I have grown to appreciate the building's distinctive charm and have documented the elevator waiting areas on each level. The floors and doors have all been
painted with shiny black enamel. Each landing has a different arrangement of tables,
chairs and ornaments; leftovers that have become little shrines to past inhabitants of the
apartment. The highly reflective surfaces create wonderful, aqueous mirroring. I began
this painting on September 8, 2001. In light of subsequent events, the title, in addition to
identifying a location, attempts to reflect the duality of the architectural disaster that took
place there.

numbers of cultural producers are not. If Canada has begun to lose its manners, and its reputation for tolerance, surely this indicates the need for re-evaluating the idea of equity. Open criticism is necessary. I was dismayed to hear about several incidents of racial discrimination that have taken place in the past few months involving people I know. In one instance, my friend has hired a lawyer to fight her case. She would not elaborate on the nature of it, saying only that the matter is not resolved and is too painful to discuss. She also revealed that she has experienced racist treatment in the past. How many times, I wondered, having never been subject to it myself.

I can only speculate on the repercussions of recent world events post-September 11th and how they will affect our own nation. In my opinion, the only way out of our current dilemma is to work assiduously to understand, communicate with and love our neighbours. We must strive to overcome our fear and suspicion in these difficult times (Figure 22–5).

Questions for Discussion

1. Hall quotes Brand in saying that she was "born into [her] subject." Are there limits to the artist's ability to produce and represent subjects of other cultures? If so, what are these limits? In the case of Joanne Tod, a white Canadian artist who frequently represents people of colour, how would this theory unfold?

2. Hall writes that today, "black women are victimized by white and black men." To what extent is this sexual and racial victimization better or worse than in the days of the Hottentot Venus?

3. Hall discusses Brand's contestation of institutional racism and racism in the justice system. How do these arguments coincide with issues raised in Parts 1 and 2?

4. Both Jim and Nelson point to an institutional racism and sexism that affect the place and value of people as subjects and producers of art. Discuss.

5. Jim's status as Canadian-born Chinese removes her from her subject. Are there racial empathies that transcend the distinctions between Asianness and blackness in this case?

6. Nelson writes that Saat-Jee was constantly juxtaposed with animals. Why do you think it was such an easy comparison for the white colonists to make? How is the concept of cultural relativity related to the process of colonization?

7. According to Nelson, how was censorship used as a regulatory device to produce a sexual and racial ideal of a female body?

8. Tod writes that for her, intimacy diffuses racism. First, define the kind of intimacy of which Tod speaks; then, ask yourself whether you agree. If the intimacy is sexual, is it problematic given the colonial histories of the sexual pathologization of black women (i.e., the Hottentot Venus in the West)?

9. All four essays discuss the intricacies of race and representation. They all coincide at the complex issue of how race impacts who is socially authorized as a producer of culture and who is marginalized as an object of representation. Dicuss.

Part 8 Multiculturalism

wishin

I'm not wishin' i were you. . .who knows what you're wishin about me.
but the government, in its wisdom, thinks that there has to be
someway we can live "mul-ti-cul-tur-ally."

now the government didn't ask you. . .the government has never consulted me
and under the "mul-ti-cul-tu-ral" guise,
a problem is manifesting.

see, i never wanted to be you. . .i just want to be free
but it feels like you're wishin the country could be free of me.

Anonymous

As the poet points out, though the motivations of multiculturalism may be admirable, this official Canadian policy is not without its challenges and controversies. Foremost among these is multiculturalism' construction with a bilingual and bi-cultural framework that privileges the British and French as the normative and founding identities of Canada. But how do First Nations and Whites of non-Anglo or non-Franco heritage fit in? And what about people of colour, or even more complex and in line with issues raised in essay 15 by Awad Ibrahim, what of those people of colour who consider themselves to be British or French? The next four essays explore some of these issues and provide a synthesis of some of the debate surrounding Canadian multiculturalism.

This part explores the impetus behind this constitutionally protected policy and the foundation for its development. The concept of multiculturalism is exploded as neutral and entirely benevolent towards First Nations and Canadians of colour. Rather, the essays "But Where Are You REALLY From: Reflections on Immigration, Multiculturalism, and Canadian Identity", "Social Cohesion and the Limits of Multiculturalism in Canada"; and "Racializing Culture/Culturalizing Race: Multicultural Racism in a Multicultural Canada", all reveal some of the "raced" underbelly of the policy. Does multiculturalism helps to constitute a normative ideal of Canadian identity as white? The essays address the myth of Canadian multiculturalism and reveal it as a discourse that is not absolutely progressive. Rather, the policy of multiculturalism is problematized and critically analyzed. Suggestions are made on whether the policy should be retained and, if so, how it can be transformed in order to fulfil its true promise.

The first and second essays, "But Where Are You REALLY From: Reflections on Immigration, Multiculturalism, and Canadian Identity" and, "Social Cohesion and the Limits of Multiculturalism in Canada", address the limits of multiculturalism on both a personalized and theoretical level, respectively. The third essay, "Racializing Culture/Culturalising Race: Multicultural Racism in a Multicultural Canada", further details multiculturalism's limitations and challenges the reader to acknowledge the potential for the policy of multiculturalism to perpetuate Canadian racism. The fourth essay, "Rearticulating Multiculturalism: Transcending the Difference-Blind Liberal Approach", offers ways to salvage the idea of multiculturalism, and highlights positive ways in which multiculturalism can add to Canadian society.

These essays, like the others included in this anthology, expose the reader to deconstructionist thought with the goal of illuminating the benefits and costs of a given policy, theory, action, or occurrence. However, as you assess the true value of multiculturalism, do so in light of all of the information presented in the parts preceding this one. Bold social questions have been posed and any condemnation or praise of multiculturalism is best made with consideration of some of the debates and dialogues opened and examined throughout this anthology and with contemplation of the questions posed throughout this book. However, as you end this part, and close this book, do not abandon the ideas herein. These essays facilitate a dialogue in which we must be willing to partake in order to ensure the splendor and the benefits of Canada for all Canadians.

23

But Where Are You REALLY From?

Reflections on Immigration, Multiculturalism, and Canadian Identity

Melanie C.T. Ash
Lawyer
New York

Introduction

So... uh... where are you from?

A white lusty man asks hoping for a delicious exotic entree...... He has not asked my white woman friends / only me.

Assumption: Plain white wrappers come from nowhere but here but plain brown wrappers must be from someplace else / Not from here definite — ly
Not from here.

Baines[1]

There is an ironic coming of age for all Canadians of colour: the moment when you first become aware that you are not seen as a Canadian. That you will forever have to justify your presence in your country in a way that white Canadians, and even newly-arrived white immigrants, never will. Sadly, the question I am asked becomes a familiar refrain: "What island are you from?" — a reference to the West Indies, from which the bulk of Black immigrants came to Canada.[2] "Well, where were you *born*?" There are innumerable variations. Sometimes it's, "You're not *from here,* are you?" asked with incredulity. "Okay, but where are *your parents* from?"[3]

As frustrating as it is to many Canadians of colour, the mainstream perception among Canadians is that Canada is a white country and that Canadian is synonymous with white. This perception, constructed throughout the country's history, is the result of historical forces: legislative enactments, government policies, social choices, legal determinations, racism, and xenophobia. It is especially ironic in light of the fact that Canadian policies espouse "multiculturalism within a bilingual framework"[4] and 44 percent "of the Canadian population reported at least one ethnic origin other than British, French or Canadian in the 1996 Census."[5]

The startling disjunction between the common self-perception that Canadians are white, and the reality that Canadians are multicultural and come from a large variety of ethnic and racial origins is deserving of study. In the face of Canada's proclamation of multiculturalism, how does Canadian identity remain a white identity? Is Canada's largely liberal democratic history inconsistent with

---

[1] Baines, 1994, p. 151.

[2] Department of Heritage, 2000, p. 6 (discussing the results of the 1996 Census). *See also,* Foster, 1996, pp. 18–30.

[3] *See* Foster, 1996, pp. 33–34.

[4] Department of Heritage, 2000.

[5] Department of Heritage, 1999, p. 5.

multiculturalism? This last question is one that has been explored in some depth by Canadian philosopher Will Kymlicka. Kymlicka is internationally regarded as an innovative thinker based on his work *Multicultural Citizenship: A Liberal Theory of Minority Rights*, which purports to have reconciled the operation of multiculturalism with the fundamental tenets of liberalism. According to the *American Political Science Review*, *Multicultural Citizenship* is "a very important book, one that is indispensable for the present discussion of multiculturalism.... It ought to be compulsory reading for all those who want to carry on the debate in this area."[6] Canadian multiculturalism, as articulated by the Multiculturalism Act, R.S.C. 1985, c. 24, s. 3, is the Canadian government's policy of, among other things, "foster[ing] the recognition and appreciation of the diverse cultures of Canadian society and ... promot[ing] the full and equitable participation of individuals and communities of all origins in the continuing evolution and shaping of all aspects of Canadian society and assist[ing] them in the elimination of any barrier to that participation." Kymlicka's work, which makes a strong case for the compatibility of liberalism and multiculturalism using the Canadian experience as an example, is an appropriate context within which to examine and critique the specifics of Canadian multiculturalism.

Kymlicka's *Multicultural Citizenship:* The Liberal Vision

Will Kymlicka is viewed as one of liberalism's foremost thinkers on multiculturalism.[7] His tome *Multicultural Citizenship* explores the extent to which multiculturalism can coexist with liberalism's tenets of "individual liberty, democracy, and social justice."[8] According to Kymlicka, liberalism is the social, political and economic framework that best fosters the goal of individual choice, freedom and self-fulfilment and, therefore the framework to which all societies should aspire.

Kymlicka defines as multicultural a society that includes within its midst minority groups. He identifies two possible variants of minority groups, distinguishable by the means by which they became incorporated into new communities: (1) the conquest/colonization of previously sovereign communities, or (2) voluntary immigration to a society.[9] These two methods of incorporation, Kymlicka holds, result in two very different types of cultural diversity. The first

---

[6] Review: Multicultural Citzenship: Will Kymlicka, retrieved October 25, 2003, from Oxford University Press (USA) website, http://www.us.oup.com/us/catalog/general/subject/Politics/PoliticalTheory/PoliticalPhilosophy/?view=usa&ci=0198290918#reviews

[7] Oxford University Press describes Kymlicka as "the most original and influential scholar in the field of multiculturalism" and emphasizes that he is "widely regarded as the most influential and original theorist of the rights and status of ethnocultural groups in liberal democracies" (Description: Multicultural citizenship: Will Kymlicka, retrieved October 25, 2003, from Oxford University Press (USA) website: http://www.us.oup.com/us/catalog/general/subject/Politics/PoliticalTheory/PoliticalPhilosophy/?view=usa&ci=0199240981#titledescription).

[8] Kymlicka, 1995, p. 6.

[9] *See* Kymlicka, 1995, pp. 21, 24–25.

is "the coexistence within a given state of more than one nation, where 'nation' means a historical community, more or less institutionally complete, occupying a given territory or homeland, sharing a distinct language and culture."[10] Although Kymlicka acknowledges that not all minority groups fit neatly into this categorization scheme, he rejects the adoption of a less rigid dichotomy. The second is the immigration of "large numbers of individuals and families from other cultures," and the decision to permit them "to maintain some of their ethnic particularity," resulting in a "polyethnic" state.[11]

Though Kymlicka acknowledges that colonialists/conquerors are technically "immigrants", he nevertheless groups them with aboriginal nations, distinguishing them from what he describes as "voluntary immigrants" on the basis that colonial settlers

> came not as migrants entering an alien society, forced to acquire a new national identity, but as a colonial vanguard that would create a new England in the image of the one they left behind. ... There was a fundamentally different set of expectations accompanying colonization and immigration — the former resulted from a deliberate policy aimed at the systemic recreation of an entire society in a new land; the latter resulted from individual and familial choices to leave their society and join another existing society.[12]

As a result, Kymlicka sees colonial settlers as founders of "nations" rather than members of "ethnic groups".

Having clarified the boundaries of his project by defining his vision of multiculturalism, Kymlicka addresses the challenge of reconciling the operation of multiculturalism within a liberal society: the accommodation of "these national and ethnic differences in a stable and morally defensible way," so as to give effect to the fundamental principles of liberalism and permit individual attainment of the good life.[13]

Kymlicka's discussion of reconciling the seemingly conflicting principles of multiculturalism and liberalism begins with the acknowledgement that some form of accommodation is needed for cultural difference, given that cultures are essential to the realization of human potential. He identifies two types of acceptable accommodations for group-cultural difference. First, for national minorities, Kymlicka envisions self-government rights, whereby political power is devolved to a political unit centred in a geographical territory in which members of the minority group form the majority. Second, Kymlicka endorses polyethnic rights intended to allow ethnic groups and religious minorities both practise to and to celebrate their cultural heritage and participate in "mainstream" political and economic institutions.[14] In Kymlicka's theory, national minorities are entitled to enact external protections vis-à-vis the majority culture in order to preserve the integrity of their culture. On the other hand,

---

[10] Ibid., p. 11. In Canada, Kymlicka identifies as national minorities the French, the English and the Aboriginal nations (pp. 12–13).

[11] Ibid., pp. 13–14.

[12] Ibid., pp. 95.

[13] Ibid., p. 26.

[14] Ibid., pp. 27–32.

Melanie C.T. Ash

Kymlicka's liberalism is much more skeptical of placing internal restrictions on a nation in order to protect the culture of ethnic minorities.

Though cognizant of criticism that the latter position amounts to "a new version of the old ethnocentrism, ... which sets the (liberal) majority culture as the standard to which minorities must adhere,"[15] Kymlicka justifies his position by distinguishing members of immigrant ethnic groups from "colonists". Thus, in the Canadian context, he would distinguish the group-based rights owed to both First Nations as the original inhabitants of this country and the French Canadian national minority (specifically, *les Québécois*) by virtue of their history as a 'colonial vanguard' who arrived in North America with the intention of re-creating their society and institutions from those owed to other ethnic groups who arrived as "voluntary immigrants" knowingly joining an existing society. As a result, Kymlicka's vision of a multicultural society within a liberal framework is a society in which national minorities are entitled to self-government rights to enable protection from external influences, while ethnic minorities are permitted to retain their culture[16] but are, nevertheless, expected to integrate into the "mainstream" liberal society.

Multiculturalism in Canada — Challenging the Myths Inherent in Kymlicka's Liberal Perception

If the ongoing "Heritage Minutes" ad campaign is to be believed, Canada is a country of harmoniously mixed cultures: welcoming runaway slaves to the last stop on the underground railway; allowing Irish orphans to keep their names even while becoming Québécois; inviting Chinese immigrants into the country to build the transcontinental railroad; and adopting a First Nations word to give Canada its name. This is the ideal country that the Canadian government so proudly proclaims.[17]

But reality is in striking discord with the romanticized vignettes the government creates to sustain the myth of multiculturalism. Canada at one time embraced the institution of slavery.[18] It pursued a policy of "civilizing" and assimilating its First Nations, then, later, imposed upon them the segregative policy on which South Africa's apartheid was based.[19] It imposed a head tax on

---

[15] Ibid., pp. 153.

[16] For example, by exempting Jews and Muslims from Sunday closing legislation, and exempting Sikhs from motorcycle helmet laws (Kymlicka, 1995, p. 97).

[17] This series of vignettes, known as the Heritage Minutes program (but now also referred to as Historica Minutes), is funded by, among others, the CRB Foundation and Canada Post Corporation, and operates to mythologize particular events in Canadian history through historical re-creation accompanied by crescendos of inspirational music. ("The Heritage Minutes", retrieved October 25, 2003, from Historica website, http://www.histori.ca/minutes/default.do)

[18] *See* Walker, 1997, p. 124. *See also* Mendes, 1995, pp. 1–4 to 1–8.

[19] *See,* for example, Kulchyski, 1994; Walker, 1997, pp. 28–30.

Chinese people seeking to enter the country.[20] It interned Japanese Canadians during World War II, and dispossessed them of their property.[21]

Such instances of overt racism are not only memories from the past. In 1995 the Vancouver Police Board ruled that being Black constitutes reasonable and probable grounds to be stopped and searched.[22] In the late 1980s and early 1990s, Members of Parliament fought a bitter struggle to prevent baptized (turbaned) Sikhs from becoming members of the RCMP under the guise of protecting the country's heritage as reflected in the police red dress uniform.[23] Former Quebec Premier Jacques Parizeau lashed out at "the ethnic vote" following the narrow defeat of his separatist option in the 1995 referendum, while Lucien Bouchard urged nationalist women to increase the birth rate of white babies.[24] These gritty vignettes reflect a Canada different from the harmonious multicultural model touted in the Heritage Minutes.

It is this reality of racial and ethnic disharmony that I will explore in the next section of this essay by means of a critique of Kymlicka's vision of multicultural citizenship within a liberal framework.

The Myth of the "Colonial Vanguard": The Deliberate Construction of an English Nation

In articulating the multicultural rights to which minorities are entitled, Kymlicka draws a distinction between national minorities and ethnic groups. The propriety of this distinction is far from clear. Kymlicka's theory accepts without question the inevitability of the current multicultural dynamic (whereby the western European heritage of the early settlers formed the foundation of modern Canadian society), thus predetermining the type of minority rights that should be provided. However, the multicultural dynamic was far from inevitable. It was the product of, and replicates, historical racism and discrimination as manifested in Canadian immigration law and policy.[25] To base a system of multiculturalism on demographics that were orchestrated in a racially discriminatory manner raises serious concerns. This point deserves some elaboration.

Kymlicka appears to operate on an understanding of Canadian immigration patterns that identifies British and French colonial settlers as the colonial vanguard, arriving and establishing settlements in the images of their homelands, and relegates all "others" who arrived later to the status of mere voluntary immigrants who abandoned their own institutions on departure from their

[20] Walker, 1997, p. 63.

[21] Order in Council establishing regulations respecting the British Columbia Security Commission, P.C. 1665, C. Gaz. 1942 (Extra). *See also* P.C. 2483, C. Gaz. 1942 and P.C. 469, C. Gaz. 1943.

[22] In the Matter of the Police Act and In the Matter of a Public Inquiry Into a Complaint Made by Cornelius Muojekwu (March 1995) (Vancouver Police Board).

[23] Black, 1994, p. 8.

[24] *See*, for example, "Parizeau blames loss", 1995; Warwick, 1995; Came, 1995.

[25] See notes 33–38 and accompanying text.

homelands.[26] In reality, a more careful examination of immigration policy is required. As Walker has noted:

> For a country such as Canada, immigration is undoubtedly the most fundamental policy a government can set. Immigrants provide the raw material for the national identity. The nature of the country itself, and what it is to be in the future, is determined by the kind of people who are allowed to enter. An immigration policy is a conscious screening mechanism enabling the current occupants of the territory to select their partners in the building of the nation.[27]

Kymlicka's bifurcation of minorities into ethnic and national is an extraordinarily naive treatment of the Canadian immigration debacle when, in fact, potential "colonial vanguards" were deliberately prevented from settling in the new territory in order to ensure an envisioned British/French racial purity. In fact, according to Catherine Dauvergne, the distinctly European flavour of the colonial vanguard is reflective of the fact that "Canadian immigration law was anglo-conformist, seeking to construct the new nation as predominantly British."[28] As a result, it is inappropriate to simplistically measure the rights of immigrants based on a model of white European ethnic assimilation given that, as Enid Trucios-Haynes has argued, this "ignores the history of immigration law, which targeted specific racial groups for exclusion...."[29]

The long history of visible minorities in Canada must call into question the validity of drawing an absolute distinction between the rights of so-called "national minorities" and those of mere "ethnic groups".[30] Beginning in 1628, enslaved Blacks were transported into the country by the "vanguard" of colonial settlers. Other Blacks arrived in Canada as free people: in 1783, Black Loyalists who fled the United States for Canada after the American Revolution relied on the British government's promises of freedom and equality; in 1812 a group of "Refugees" fled slavery to fight for the British in the War of 1812 and arrived in Canada seeking the fulfilment of promises of land and freedom.[31] On this basis alone, the suggestion that the colonial vanguards were solely of British and French heritage is called into question.

Furthermore, there is evidence that the relative absence of visible minorities and other ethnic minorities among the colonial vanguard was certainly not a matter of happenstance, but rather was deliberately orchestrated. In particular, in 1885 the federal government imposed a "head tax" on Chinese immi-

---

[26] Kymlicka does acknowledge one exception to this pattern — the particular circumstances of Hutterite, Mennonite, and Doukhobour communities that immigrated based on promises they would be permitted to re-create their society within the Canadian nation. *See* Kymlicka, 1995, pp. 25, 41, 119–120.

[27] Walker, 1997, p. 246.

[28] Dauvergne, 1997, p. 340.

[29] Trucios-Haynes, 1997, p. 387. While the author makes this observation with respect to the United States, it is equally applicable to the Canadian context.

[30] By use of the uniquely Canadian term "visible minorities", I intend to distinguish minorities who are people of colour from other ethnic minorities who have been constructed as white. I do not, however, intend to include First Nations peoples, whose claim to political and land rights extends back to time immemorial.

[31] *See* Walker, 1997, pp. 124–125. *See also* Winks, 1971; Walker, 1992; Grant, 1990.

grants to discourage Chinese immigration.[32] In 1923, the government repealed the head tax and substituted a prohibition on Chinese immigration that stood until 1947.[33] The prohibition on Chinese immigration, combined with the head tax,

> had profound and longstanding detrimental effects upon individuals and families in the Chinese Canadian community. These effects include the inability of Chinese Canadian families to form, develop and live normally, ... significant financial loss, hardship, emotional distress, family separation, loss of companionship of spouse, child and parent, loss of opportunity and injury to dignity.[34]

Further, to deter immigrants originating from beyond the British Isles or France, the government adopted an immigration act that permitted the use of race as a ground for admission or exclusion,[35] and immigration regulations passed pursuant to that act selectively admitted people based on their country of origin (Britain, Australia, South Africa, America, France, etc.) and excluded people based on their "peculiar customs, habits, modes of life, and "probable inability to become readily assimilated."[36] In 1907, the Canadian government negotiated a "Gentleman's Agreement" with Japan limiting the number of Japanese immigrants to Canada. In 1914, in an effort to eliminate Indian immigration, the Canadian government instituted the "continuous journey" rule requiring immigrants to arrive in Canada by unbroken journey from the country of origin, at a time when there was no possibility of direct travel between India and Canada.[37] "In these various ways, each one designed to meet specific circumstances [that the government perceived as a 'threat' to the maintenance of a white nation,] policies excluded immigrants deemed unassimilable. By the 1930s [those government policies had succeeded, as] practically no persons of African or Asian origin were entering Canada."[38]

Based on the circumstances under which Kymlicka's "national minorities" and "ethnic groups" came to, or were deliberately prevented from coming to, Canada, it is disingenuous to rely on that distinction as the basis for granting rights, because it simply serves to replicate the racism of the past. Kymlicka, by his silence on the existence of race-based immigration policies and his reification of the inevitability of European culture constituting Canadian "national" culture, becomes an apologist for liberal ethnocentrism and, perhaps unknowingly, implicates himself in the perpetuation of ongoing historical racial wrongs.

---

[32] Chinese Immigration Act, S.C. 1885, c. 71.

[33] Chinese Immigration Act, R.S. 1923, c 38.

[34] *Mack v. Attorney General of Canada* (2001) 55 O.R. (3d) 113 at 118 (per Cumming J.) (recognizing the repugnancy of the Chinese Immigration Act, even while striking the class action claims by surviving payers of the head tax, and surviving spouses and descendants of deceased payers of the head tax).

[35] Immigration Act, S.C. 1910, c. 27. *See also* Walker, 1997, p. 27.

[36] *See,* for example, *P.C.* 1351, *C. Gaz.* 1954.

[37] *P.C.* 32, *C. Gaz.* 1914.

[38] Walker, 1997, p. 28.

Melanie C.T. Ash

The Myth of Liberal Multiculturalism

Multiculturalism is consistently touted as a Canadian triumph: a commitment, in contrast to our neighbours to the south, to embrace the cultures of all of our citizens. The Department of Canadian Heritage recently smugly proclaimed that "[w]hat sets Canada apart from most other countries is how differences within the population have not only been accepted, but are today recognized as a source of strength."[39] However, Canadian multiculturalism has fallen short of its promise. At times the extent of Canadian commitment to multiculturalism seems to be a self-congratulatory willingness to sample ethnic cuisine and applaud the ceremonial dances of different cultural groups while changing nothing about the way Canadian society is structured.[40] This same critique can be applied to Kymlicka's conception of liberal multiculturalism, an impoverished vision whereby minority groups are **permitted** to "express their cultural particularity and pride without hampering their success in the economic and political institutions of the **dominant** society."[41] The implication of Kymlicka's vision is that such groups are outsiders who must integrate into the larger mainstream society. This simply is not sufficient to constitute **real** multiculturalism.

For multiculturalism to be effective, it must include institutional structures for cultural maintenance, **and** it must disrupt the social dynamics that currently leave the power to define societal norms (as reflected in institutions) solely in the hands of those who meet the universal, objective, white norm. According to Barbara J. Flagg:

> Even whites who do not harbor any conscious or unconscious belief in the superiority of white people participate in the maintenance of white supremacy whenever we impose white norms without acknowledging their whiteness. Any serious effort to dismantle white supremacy must include measures to dilute the effect of whites' dominant status, which carries within it the power to define as well as to decide.[42]

Thus, multiculturalism must reveal the racial and cultural bias existing in 'dominant' societal institutions, and demonstrate a willingness to reconceptualize Canadian culture, and reconstruct Canadian institutions so that they represent all Canadians. We might all benefit, for example, from the adoption of traditional First Nations' healing/sentencing circles in the place of imprisonment as a form of criminal disposition and conflict resolution for certain crimes, or from an understanding of the family law "best interests of the child" doctrine that

---

[39] Department of Canadian Hertiage, 2000, p. 1. *See also* Canadian Bar Association, 1999, p. 3 (finding that while "Canadians are sometimes smug about ... our multicultural heritage, ... we need to be honest about our past if we are to successfully eliminate the discrimination that is rooted in it"); Brown & Brown, 1996, pp. 48–49 (observing that "[m]any Canadians have clung to the myth that Canada is not really a racist country, [and that the] veracity of this myth is often supported by a self-serving distinction between Canada and the United States") as quoted in Aylward, 1999, p. 77.

[40] For example, Canadians attend and applaud the annual Caribana celebration of Toronto's West Indian community, admire the art of First Nations peoples at countless Canadian museums and galleries, and consume traditional Chinese cuisine in Chinatowns across the nation.

[41] Kymlicka, 1995, p. 31 (emphasis added).

[42] Flagg, 2000, p. 458.

acknowledges the value of communal child-rearing practices that are widespread outside of the realm of Anglo-Canadian law.[43]

However, it may not be enough to simply rebuild Canadian institutions. For some reason, and in spite of its official multiculturalism, Canada continues to be perceived as a white country. It is that perception that must also be subverted in order to achieve a real multicultural identity — a country in which a racialized existence, codified as non-white, is not automatically paired with an assumption of foreignness.

Conclusion — All Canadians Are White, and All "Ethnics" Are Immigrants

> All black people are "Jamaicans" or "from Africa." All South Asian people are "Pakis." East Asians are invariably "Chinese." First Nations people are drunks, or militant troublemakers. ... It is obvious to me that a Canadian is not a person of colour, nor an aboriginal person. A Canadian is white.
>
> Camille Hernandez Ramdwar[44]

Throughout its history Canada has been perceived, and **wanted to be perceived**, as a white country. A member of the Royal Commission charged with examining the 'Chinese phenomenon' on the West Coast of Canada in 1885[45] aptly summed up the dominant philosophy of the day concerning Canadian racial identity:

> It is a natural and well-founded desire of British subjects, of the white population of the Dominion, who come from either British or other European states and settle in this country, that their country should be spoken of abroad as being inhabited by a vigorous, energetic and white race of people.[46]

In light of the discriminatory history of Canadian immigration law and policy, it is apparent that the linking of Canadianness with whiteness was in no way a natural occurrence. Rather, a white Canadian identity has been deliberately constructed.[47] The predictable result is that rather than being equal participants in the Canadian polity, Canadians constructed as other (non-white) are merely "guest[s] in someone's home," who are "expected to ... accept the way

---

43 On the subject of circle sentencing, *see* Green, 1997. On the subject of the prevalence of communal child-rearing practices in the Black, Aboriginal, and immigrant communities, *see,* for example, Stack, 1975 (explaining that extended kinship networks in Black communities give children stability); McConnell, 1998, pp. 51–55 (describing the extended kin and non-kin system of child-rearing that exists within Aboriginal, Black, and Latina/Latino and Asian immigrant communities).

44 Hernandez-Ramdwar, 1994, pp. 2, 4.

45 Commission on Chinese Immigration, 1885.

46 *Hansard*, July 2, 1885, 3010, cited in Walker, 1997, p. 63.

47 *See,* for example, Dauvergne, 1997, pp. 323, 334. *See also* Haney Lopez, 1996, p. 117 (identifying the United States as "ideologically a White country not by accident, but by design at least in part affected through naturalization and immigration laws").

things are done ... [and] stay in their place."[48] Such expectations cannot realistically be the foundation for a truly inclusive, multicultural society.

Thus, the mere adoption of "official multiculturalism" by the very political system that orchestrated the racial composition of the country cannot bring about racial justice. But that is exactly what Will Kymlicka proposes. In this paper, by way of a challenge to Kymlicka's liberal multiculturalism, I have argued for a need not only to make more substantial changes to Canadian institutions such that all cultures will be on equal footing, but also to fundamentally reconceive of what it means to be Canadian. That is the challenge that faces our country in this new century, a challenge that, in my view, Kymlicka's vision is ill-equipped to meet.

References

Aylward, C.A. (1999). *Canadian critical race theory: Racism and the law.* Halifax: Fernwood Publishing.

Baines, M. (1994). Where are you from? A broken record. In C. Camper (Ed.), *Miscegenation Blues: Voices of mixed race women* (p. 151). Toronto: Sister Vision: Women of Colour Press.

Black, B. (1994). *B.C. Human Rights Review.* Report on Human Rights in British Columbia prepared for the Ministry Responsible for Multiculturalism and Human Rights, British Columbia.

Brown, R. & Brown, C. (1996). Comments: Reflections on Racism. In C.E. James (Ed.) *Perspectives on Racism in the Human Services Sector: A Case for Change.* (p. 48). Toronto: University of Toronto Press.

Came, B. (1995, November 13). Quebec City power plays; Bouchard may not get Parizeau's blessing. *Maclean's,* 108:46, p. 18.

Canadian Bar Association Working Group on Racial Equality in the Legal Profession. (1999). *The challenge of racial equality: Putting principles into practice.* Ottawa: CBA Communications.

Commission on Chinese Immigration. (1885). *Report of the Royal Commission on Chinese immigration* (Co-chairs J.A. Chapleau & John H. Gray).

Dauvergne, C. (1997). Beyond Justice: The Consequences of Liberalism for Immigration Law. Canadian Journal of Law & Jurisprudence, *10* 323.

Department of Canadian Heritage. (1999). *10th Annual Report on the Operation of the Canadian Multiculturalism Act, 1997-*1998. Ottawa: Minister of Public Works and Government Services.

Department of Canadian Heritage. (2000). *Annual report on the operation of the Canadian Multiculturalism Act: 1998–1999.* Ottawa: Minister of Public Works and Government Services.

Department of Canadian Heritage. Multiculturalism in Canada. Online: Canadian Studies Program website. Retrieved February 8, 2000 from: http://www.pch.gc.ca/csp-pec/english/about/multi/index.htm

---

[48] Saito, 1997, p. 309.

Flagg, B.J. (2000). 'Was blind but now I See': White race consciousness and the requirement of discriminatory intent. In J.F. Perea, et al., (Eds.). *Race and Races: Cases and Resources for a Diverse America.* (p. 458). St. Paul, MN: West Group.

Foster, C. (1986). *A place called heaven: The meaning of being black in Canada.* Toronto: HarperCollins.

Grant, J.N. (1990). *The immigration and settlement of the black refugees of the War of 1812 in Nova Scotia and New Brunswick.* Dartmouth, NS: Black Cultural Centre for Nova Scotia.

Green, R.G. (1997). Aboriginal Community Sentencing and Mediation: Within and Without the Circle. *25 Manitoba Law Journal,* 77.

Haney Lopez, I.F. (1996). *White by Law: The Legal Construction of Race.* New York: New York University Press.

Hernandez-Ramdwar, C. (1994). Ms. Edge Innate. In C. Camper (ed.) *Miscegenation Blues: Voices of Mixed Race Women.* (p. 2). Toronto: Sister Vision: Women of Colour Press.

Kulchyski, P. (Ed.). (1994). *Unjust relations: Aboriginal rights in Canadian courts.* Don Mills, ON: Oxford University Press.

Kymlicka, W. (1995). *Multicultural citizenship: A liberal theory of minority rights.* New York: Oxford University Press.

Mendes, E. (Ed.). (1995). *Racial discrimination: Law and practice.* Scarborough, ON: Carswell.

McConnell, J.E. (1998). Securing the care of children in diverse families: Building on the trends in guardianship reform. Yale Journal of Law & Feminism, *10* 29.

Parizeau blames loss on 'money,' 'ethnic vote.' (1995, October 21). *The Ottawa Citizen,* p. A5.

Saito, N.T. (1997). Alien and non-alien alike: Citizenship, 'foreignness' and racial hierarchy in American law. Oregon Law Review, *76* 261.

Stack, C.B. (1975). *All our kin: Strategies for survival in a black community.* Basic Books.

Trucios-Haynes, E. (1997). The legacy of racially restrictive immigration laws and policies and the construction of the American national Identity. Oregon Law Review, *76* 369.

Walker, J.W. St. G. (1992). *The black loyalists.* (2nd ed.). Toronto: University of Toronto Press.

Walker, J.W. St. G. (1997). *Race, rights and the law in the Supreme Court of Canada.* Toronto & Waterloo, ON: The Osgoode Society for Canadian Legal History & Wilfrid Laurier University Press.

Warwick, L. (1995, November 13). The 'Ethnic' Shock. *Maclean's,* 108:46, p. 20.

Winks, R. (1971). *The blacks in Canada: A history.* Montreal: McGill-Queen's University Press.

24

Social Cohesion and the Limits of Multiculturalism in Canada

Anver Saloojee
Department of Politics and School
of Public Administration
Ryerson University
Toronto

I would like to thank Dr. Charmaine Nelson and Professor Camille Nelson for their invaluable insights and commentary, which have strengthened this essay immeasurably. I would also like to thank the various reviewers whose constructive feedback has been greatly appreciated.

Introduction

Social identity is a complex phenomenon that can be understood at both national and subnational levels. In multicultural societies like Canada, this phenomenon is played out as a tension between a national identity and a specific group identity. The implicit sense in Canada is that holding on to and reproducing a specific group identity runs counter to and, in reality, detracts from a perceived non-race-based national identity. Individuals who identify too closely with subnational social groups — ethno-racial identities, for examples — will not easily identify with the nation state. Instead, in a multicultural society, too close an identification with a sub national social identity creates hyphenated nationals whose primary loyalty is either a subnational entity or a supranational identity. In reality, Canada's identity as a bilingual, binational country is rooted in its history of colonial conquest by both the French and the British empires. This national identity derives from the political and cultural hegemony of the two white racialized groups. It is intimately linked to the process of colonization that entailed the domination and subjugation of the First Peoples of this land. It also derives from the ability of the two white racialized groups to present themselves as non-raced and the norm to which other ethnic and racialized minority groups should acculturate. Thus, from a white-binational normative vantage point, the politics of cultural difference has made adherence to a national identity more problematic. From another vantage point, however, Canadian society has to transcend the racial exclusions inherent in its identity as a binational country and find new solutions to the redefined multicultural question. Simultaneously there has to be both recognition of, and the political will to deal with, the Aboriginal right to self-government. Such a right derives from original occupancy, not from the Constitution. The First Peoples of Canada are not multicultural minorities; they are descendants of the original inhabitants of the land. Their demands for self-determination and land rights and the resolution of treaty disputes go beyond the demands for the removal of barriers to equitable participation in society.

This essay will explore the extent to which an official state policy of multiculturalism (enshrined in the *Canadian Charter of Rights and Freedoms* as well as in legislation) has allowed for the proliferation of multiple identities and has detracted from the creation of national social cohesion. In addition, this essay will explore the extent to which multiculturalism in Canada has successfully grappled with the challenges of racism. Central to the latter is an analysis of how an official state policy of multiculturalism, in subsuming a race/rights discourse under its umbrella, has effectively depoliticized the challenges of racism in Canada. Such a policy has also been incapable of dealing with the challenges faced by the First Peoples of Canada.

From the viewpoint of the dominant culture, social cohesion entails individuals in society coming together on the basis of a common set of values. This requires that individuals from diverse backgrounds set aside their differences, and assimilate and acculturate. The processes of assimilation and acculturation would lead to social cohesion based on the values of the dominant culture. This form of social cohesion is rooted in conceptions of modernization and urbanization and liberal notions of individual rights and freedoms.

Social cohesion can also arise from differences and can be seen as the coming together of individuals who share a common class background, common language, religion, ethnicity, racial background, etc. Just as it is important to distinguish between an ethnic group and a racial group, it is important not to confuse racism with ethnocentrism. Racism is an ideology that seeks both to legitimate the inequality faced by racialized groups and to proclaim the superiority of the racial group that constitutes the status quo. Racism consists of a set of mechanisms that ensure socio-political domination over a racial group (or groups). And racism involves discriminatory practices that work to constantly exclude, marginalize and disadvantage the subordinate racialized groups. Ethnocentrism, on the other hand, involves the tendency on the part of individuals and groups to judge and evaluate others from the vantage point of their own set of norms, values and cultural traditions. Ethnocentrism leads to a hierarchy in which people of different cultures are ranked according to how much or how little of the dominant norms, values and cultural traditions they possess. In this sense, social cohesion can take multiple forms — for example, class affiliation, as distinct from ethnic and racialized identities. The two, or, for that matter, multiple forms of cohesion may intersect or they may diverge. These forms of social cohesion emphasize the politics of difference and challenge the homogenizing effect of modernization and urbanization. Social cohesion on the basis of identities engenders a politics of difference that focuses on the particular and the subjective and can run the risk of devolving into cultural relativism. Thus, Canada should embrace an inclusive vision that suggests common purpose and shared community can be achieved through intergroup solidarity.

Post-1970s global cities are the locus of political and economic power, and their pre-eminent position has turned them into the magnets that attract global migrants. These multicultural cities, like Toronto, now become the sites of struggle over issues of rights, citizenship, the allocation of resources and political representation. This is best exemplified in the struggle between the two conceptions of social cohesion articulated above. Ethnic and racial diversity and identity politics challenge the established order and cohesion. In a liberal democratic polity, these challenges, these competing notions of cohesion, need to be managed and require a measure of state intervention. One of the policy instruments used in Canada to mediate state/minority relations has been the policy of multiculturalism. This essay will focus on the extent to which the official state policy of multiculturalism depoliticized the issue of racism in Canada by having marginalized communities focus on their cultural differences and not on issues of systemic racial discrimination and exclusion in society.

The policy of multiculturalism in Canada, in its first iteration, stressed the value of preservation of cultural identity. Ethnic and linguistic minority groups were actively encouraged by the state to preserve and reproduce their cultural and linguistic differences. This found expression in the socio-spatial organization of a city like Toronto and a country like Canada. These expressions included the rise of ethnic enclaves within the city; the rise of ethno-specific commercial and residential space; the racialization of poverty; and competition for scarce resources, recreational space, and places of worship, etc. However, as ethnic, linguistic and racialized minority communities in Canada resisted pressures to assimilate, and as they encountered discrimination, exclusion and the anti-immigrant backlash, there emerged a new form of social cohesion. Social cohesion took on an expanded meaning. The politics of difference itself became outward looking and involved redefining difference, deconstructing it as "other", as marginal, and reconstructing it as the central feature of multicultural, multiracial Canada. In this way, the politics of difference began to confront the dominant discourse that posited ethnic and racialized minority groups as "other". This is the emancipatory, the positive meaning, of the politics of difference that springs from the second meaning of social cohesion. And this is the lasting contribution ethnic and racialized minority groups and communities have made to the politics of multiculturalism and anti-racism in Canada.

Demographics and the National Question

The development of social cohesion in Canada reflects the history of settler colonialism; as such, it is the product of the colonization of North America by the French and the British, with the latter establishing its political hegemony by the late 1700s. Subsequently the development of Canadian society, its governance, its bipolar national homogeneity and the resultant forms of Anglophone and Francophone social cohesion were all products of the particular form settler colonialism took in Canada. The modern state in Canada was born out of this history of colonialism and colonial settler violence. The various methods of subjugation of the First Peoples included the use of military force, the practice of genocide, the continuous practice of cultural genocide, the "Christianization and civilization" policies, land theft via the numerous treaties and the various iterations of assimilation and integration policies. It is singularly impossible to overestimate the devastating impact colonialism had on the First Peoples of Canada. From the point of initial contact until 1867, Native-White relations underwent a number of changes but, essentially, the rationale was always the same: colonize North America, subjugate the original inhabitants, and secure the land mass in the name of the British Crown. Over the centuries, the institutions of the state came to reflect British institutions, and white Canada's social cohesion derived from the domination and marginalization of the First Peoples and from racially exclusive immigration policies pursued in the nineteenth century and the first half of the twentieth century.[1]

---

1 For details on the demographic evolution and development of colonial and post-colonial Canadian society, the racially exclusive immigration policies, and the subjugation of the First Peoples, *see* Elliott & Fleras, 1990; Fleras & Elliott, 1992; Li, 1990; Ramcharan, 1982; Henry et al., 1995; Kalbach, 2000.

On the eve of Confederation (1867), the colonizers had neither successfully integrated Native people into the dominant society, nor had Native people been annihilated. In fact, the First Peoples collectively owned vast tracts of land west of Ontario that were central to British hegemony. In 1871, shortly after Confederation, 91 percent of the population was either of British (60 percent) or French (31 percent) origin. *The Indian Act* (1876) categorized the First Peoples into "status Indians" (those who fit the terms of the Act), "non-status Indians" (those who were Indian but did not fit the terms of the Act), "treaty Indians" (those whose bands had signed treaties with the government) and "non-treaty Indians" (those whose bands did not sign treaties with the government).[2] In 1881 "Indians" (not including Métis and Inuit) constituted 2.5 percent of the population of Canada. The colonizers for expedient economic and political reasons defined and legislated who was an Indian and who was not, thereby fragmenting and robbing many of the First Peoples of their birthright. This was consistent with the colonizers' approach of assimilation of the First Peoples, and was also a way for the government to legally and legislatively reduce the actual population size of the First Peoples. The policy of assimilation pursued under the Indian Act was a continuation of the earlier approach outlined in the 1857 *Act for the Gradual Civilization of Indian Tribes* and the 1859 *Civilization and Enfranchisement Act*. Through these two pieces of legislation the colonizers hoped to assimilate the First Peoples into white society. Over the decades the Indian Act was amended and new Indian Acts were passed (1911, 1927, 1951), but essentially, the paternalism and racism suffused in the Act remained intact.

In 1967, 230,902 individuals defined themselves as status Indians and, a few years later, the 1971 Census reported that 44.6 percent of the population claimed British ancestry, 28.7 percent claimed French ancestry, 23 percent claimed "other European" and 1.3 percent claimed Asian ancestry.[3] Between 1972 and the end of the twentieth century, the ethno-racial profile of Canada and its major cities changed drastically. By 1986, nearly 9.37 million out of 25 million (37.5 percent), the single largest component of the Canadian population, reported some non-British, non-French ethnic origins. Twenty-five percent claimed neither British nor French ancestry. On the other hand, 28.1 percent and 22.8 percent claimed British and French ancestry, respectively, and a further 4.0 percent claimed both British and French ancestry. The 1991 census showed that, nationwide, 31% of the population reported an ethnic background that did not include British or French origins — up from 25 percent in 1986.[4] Between 1961 and 1970, 75 percent of immigrants to Canada came from Europe, the United Kingdom and the United States. In the period 1991–1996, the percentage had declined to 21.8 percent — the remaining 78.2 percent came from Africa, Asia, the Caribbean and Central and South America. For the year 2000–2001, the figures were 20.49 percent and 79.51 percent, respectively.[5]

---

[2] Kalbach, 2000, p. 63.

[3] Ibid., p. 65.

[4] Ibid.

[5] Statistics Canada, 2002, http://www.statcan.ca/english/Pgdb/People/Population/demo25a.htm

While members of European ethnic minorities are still numerically dominant in the Canadian population, members of visible minority groups are becoming increasingly numerous. In the 1991 census, 1,002,675 people in Canada reported Aboriginal ancestry (3.7 percent of the population). In that census, 9.4 percent of the population identified themselves as members of a "visible minority". The 1996 census found that the total visible minority population in Canada was 3,197,480, or 11.2 percent of the population. These aggregate figures hide the more significant regional and municipal variations in racial and ethnic composition. In Canada, Ontario, is racially, most diverse province. Southern Ontario is more diverse than the rest of Ontario, and Metropolitan Toronto is considered one of the most racially and culturally diverse cities in the world. The Toronto census area is home to 1.338 million, or 42 percent, of the non-white minority population in Canada. Seventy percent of all visible minorities live in Toronto, Vancouver or Montreal — the three cities account for one-third of Canada's population.[6]

In addition, in 1998 the city of Toronto's Equity and Access Centre released a report titled "Diversity Our Strength, Access & Equity Our Goal," in which it concluded that by the 2001 census, members of racialized minority groups would likely make up 53 percent of the population of Toronto, up from 30 percent in 1991 and only 3 percent in 1960.[7] The study also noted that 48 percent of Toronto's population is foreign born (compared to 28 percent for New York), and these immigrants come from 169 countries and speak 100 different languages; 42 percent speak neither English nor French when they arrive.[8]

The 1990s were characterized by contradictory impulses in Canadian society. On the one hand there was recognition of the tremendous benefits continued immigration brought to Canada; on the other hand, a backlash developed against immigrants that was both explicitly and implicitly racist (for example, the Reform Party used coded language and campaigned against multiculturalism and called for tighter and more restrictive immigration policies). The anti-immigrant sentiment was also fuelled in part by the prolonged economic downturn Canada experienced from the late 1980s to the mid-1990s. These economic shifts unbridled and unleashed some disturbing passions, attitudes and prejudices against immigrants in general and racialized minority immigrants in particular.[9]

The contradictory impulses were also evident in relations between the state and First Nations communities. The policies of assimilation and integration had failed. In the late 1960s and early 1970s, Prime Minister Pierre Elliott Trudeau sought to terminate the "nation to nation" relationship with the First Peoples, and transfer authority to provincial governments. The federal government also sought to repeal the *Indian Act,* dismantle the Department of Indian and Northern Affairs, and divide Aboriginal assets on a *per capita* basis. These recommendations and many more were contained in the *White Paper* (1969), which

---

6   Statistics Canada, 2002, http://www.statcan.ca/english/Pgdb/People/Population/demo40f.htm

7   At this point it is not possible to verify this projection as the data from the 2001 Census has not been released.

8   City of Toronto, 1998.

9   Ibid.

also recommended the rescinding of all treaties and other federal obligations to the First Peoples. These recommendations, it was suggested by the federal government, were necessary in order to facilitate the assimilation and integration of First Peoples into the white community. Though the *White Paper* was eventually withdrawn, its lasting impact was to galvanize the Aboriginal community into collective political action. What began as a protest against the *White Paper* in 1970 has mushroomed into a very potent protest movement on the Canadian political landscape. In recent years protests have taken many different forms: negotiations on self-governing arrangements; the launching of court challenges to settle land-claims disputes and treaty violations; and armed standoffs, occupations and blockades.

At another level, the policies and priorities in Canadian society have also had to shift in response to the increasing ethnic and racial diversity of the population. The demographic changes of the 1970–2000 period brought issues of social cohesion and national unity to the fore. In the 1970s, the national question revolved around Québec's place in Confederation. By the beginning of the 1990s, the national question also included issues of social cohesion and the challenges of living, working and engaging in politics in a multicultural and multiracial environment.[10] The reports of the Abella Commission and the Special Parliamentary Committee on the Participation of Visible Minorities in Canada (1984) identified these shifts as a response to the demands for equity and social justice.[11] As Canadian society became increasingly multiracial, the demands for equity and participation by racialized minority communities increased. Thus, Canadian society has had to confront a massive paradigm shift and begin to articulate a vision of society that is capable of embracing both diversity and anti-racism.

Multiculturalism and Identity Formation: The Emergence of InterGroup Social Cohesion to Combat Discrimination and Exclusion

Identity formation and social cohesion of racialized minority and immigrant communities are a complex response to many factors. In no small measure, they are mediated by both the state and its multicultural practices, and they are mediated by the reality of discrimination and exclusion. This dual mediation is reflected in the two phases of multiculturalism in Canada. Through an official policy of multiculturalism, the state in Canada has attempted to significantly determine the nature of state/minority relations within a liberal tradition that promotes equality and encourages group social cohesion. In the first phase of multiculturalism in Canada (1971–1982), the state funded a range of initiatives for the preservation of language and culture as a means to encourage ethnic groups to maintain their distinctiveness. These initiatives were in contrast to the

---

[10] Lewycky, 1992; Henry et al., 1995.

[11] Abella, 1984; Canada, 1984.

approach of assimilation the federal government was taking in relation to the First Peoples as outlined in the *White Paper*. For members of ethno-racial communities, the social cohesion that resulted from the desire to preserve a group's distinctiveness was born of a genuine search to find a sense of belonging in a multicultural society. In this sense, multiculturalism was not seen in political terms; it was about the preservation of ethnic identities and was a reflexive response to the growing ethnic diversity of Canadian cities. In the second phase (1982 to the present), multiculturalism began to inform the discourse on national identity in new ways. In 1982, multiculturalism was accorded a protected place in the Canadian Constitution (section 27); and in 1988, the *Canadian Multiculturalism Act* was passed by the Parliament of Canada.[12]

The policies and programs of the Liberal government in the 1970s that tended to support integration of ethnic minorities into the mainstream proved ineffective in the 1980s. The pace of demographic change had accelerated beyond what the government had anticipated. Demographic patterns had shifted, and the emergence of a society that was both multicultural as well as multiracial was proving a challenge for the state. It was readily apparent that the old policy of multiculturalism was inadequate for dealing with the emerging challenges (notably, the demands by members of racialized communities for equity, participation, power sharing and representation). The first iteration of the discourse had reached its limit. It was becoming readily apparent to many groups that while they were developing internal social cohesion they were, on a broader level, consigned to the margins and excluded from the centres of decision making.

This recognition of exclusion and discrimination then prompted a reflexive, or what Manuel Castells elsewhere calls a "defensive", assertion of identity.[13] The assertion of an identity against discrimination and exclusion in turn creates a sense of social cohesion that is no longer rooted simply in the desire to hold on to that which is unique. Rather, social cohesion cuts across intergroup identity and intragroup solidarity to challenge the dominant discourse. Roger Giddens refers to this as "dialogic democracy" based on a mutual respect, a shared understanding of the effects of exclusion and marginalization and the emergence of solidarity: "Dialogic democracy ... concerns furthering of **cultural cosmopolitanism** and is a prime building block of that connection of autonomy and solidarity ... dialogic democracy encourages the **democratization of democracy** within the sphere of the liberal-democratic polity."[14] The growth of the multicultural and multiracial society, therefore, is producing the conditions for the emergence of a new sense of social cohesion, what David Held calls a "cosmopolitan democracy" that recognizes and respects differences and that argues for more than formal equality under the law.[15]

---

[12] Prime Minister Pierre Elliott Trudeau, in his statement in the House of Commons (October 7, 1971), referred to his government's 1971 policy as "A policy of multiculturalism in a bilingual framework". This essay will not deal with the first phase. For details and critiques of this phase *see* Brotz, 1980; Elliott & Fleras, 1990; Roberts & Clifton, 1990; Lewycky, 1992.

[13] Castells, 1997.

[14] Giddens, 1994, p. 112.

[15] Held, 1995, pp. 226–231.

Just as the federal government's policies of assimilation and integration of the First Peoples had to give way to a more concerted recognition of Aboriginal and treaty rights and a recognition of the inherent right of Aboriginal self-government, so too the policy of multiculturalism was found seriously wanting. The old policy of multiculturalism was simply incapable of responding to a set of issues that were now intensely political. In Canada, racialized and newcomer communities were shifting their focus from "song and dance" to an assessment of their rightful place in a democratic society that espoused the ideals of equality. Indeed, the highest law of the land, the Constitution, gave recognition to the value of multiculturalism. In 1987 the Parliamentary Standing Committee on Multiculturalism suggested that the 1971 policy was floundering and needed new direction.[16] The clear direction had to come in the form of a paradigm shift in relationships between the government and racialized and newcomer communities. The old paradigm that focused on the retention of cultural differences, on folklore, was outdated. The core issues that preoccupied racialized and newcomer minority communities now included issues of power, access, equity, participation, removal of discriminatory barriers, institutional accommodation, and anti-racism.[17]

The clear direction that the Parliamentary Standing Committee on Multiculturalism called for came in the form of the *Multiculturalism Act* of 1988. With the passage of the legislation, multiculturalism came to occupy a position of considerable significance in the debate on Canada's national identity. This position of importance was first openly acknowledged in the Canadian Constitution, where, in the *Charter of Rights and Freedoms,* multiculturalism was entrenched. According to Section 27 of the Charter, "This Charter shall be interpreted in a manner consistent with the preservation and enhancement of the multicultural heritage of Canadians." The continued politicization of multiculturalism with the passage of the *Multiculturalism Act* (1988) elevated multiculturalism from a celebration of diversity to the heart of Canada's nation-building project. The federal government sought to delicately balance a number of critical issues: namely, diversity and social cohesion, minority rights and majority rights, cultural identity and citizenship and cultural pluralism and equality.

In accordance with the legislation, the federal government developed a public policy on multiculturalism that committed it to three primary activities: first, recognizing and promoting an understanding that multiculturalism is a fundamental characteristic of Canadian society; second, eliminating the barriers to full and equitable participation by members of racialized and newcomer communities in all spheres of Canadian society; and third, ensuring that all individuals receive equal treatment and equal protection under the law, while at the same time respecting and valuing their diversity.

Multiculturalism had moved from a descriptive reality capturing demographic diversity to government programs, policies and practices. Ethnic and racial diversity was elevated to the level of national policy and was seen as a valued component of the evolving national identity of the 1990s. The appropria-

---

[16] Canada, 1987.

[17] Abella, 1984; Canada, 1984; Henry et al., 1995; Li, 1990.

tion of multiculturalism by the state was not without its limitations. The Conservative government of Brian Mulroney sought to "mainstream multiculturalism" by hosting a "Business and Multiculturalism" conference in Toronto in 1986. For Mulroney it was a sound business strategy and a rational policy response to the changing demographics of the labour market. Preservation of cultures was replaced by the mantra of the market.[18] Nonetheless, the fact that multiculturalism was accorded such a position of prominence in national policy in 1988 was an indication that the state could no longer ignore the growing demands arising from sectors of Canadian society that were previously excluded from a definition of Canada as a bilingual, bicultural and binational country. Diverse racialized and newcomer communities were demanding their rightful place in society. What had clearly emerged by the beginning of the 1990s was a debate about the future of Canada — could national unity be forged out of diversity?

At the heart of the debate about the so-called benefits of multiculturalism, however, remains a much larger debate about the value of multiculturalism: does it promote a healthy respect for diversity, or does it detract from the development of a Pan-Canadian identity? There is also an underlying fear that in promoting diversity, through for example employment equity policies, the state is caving in to minority demands. Will Kymlicka and Wayne Norman suggest that the argument about whether multiculturalism is fundamentally divisive because it detracts from democratic citizenship cannot be assessed in the abstract. Rather, it has to be assessed in very specific contexts. After compiling a list of minority groups and minority group claims, they argue that the fear that multiculturalism will promote fragmentation and hyphenation and erode social cohesion turns on four ideas: citizenship status, citizenship identity, citizenship activity and citizenship cohesion.[19] As to whether multiculturalism is corrosive or binding, Kymlicka and Norman are not definitive:

> In sum, whether we are concerned with citizenship status, virtue or cohesion, the relationship between minority rights and citizenship is more complicated than it might initially appear. We see legitimate worries about the potential impact on citizenship, but also countervailing arguments showing that some minority rights can actually enhance citizenship.[20]

Advocates of multiculturalism argue that minority rights are a natural extension of, and perfectly consistent with, liberal democratic rights and a concern for social justice. On the other hand, critics argue that the promotion of minority rights detracts from building "common citizenship" and erodes what Kymlicka and Norman call "democratic citizenship".[21] The preoccupation with "common citizenship" itself is quite problematic as the very essence of common citizenship in Canada privileged the status of English and French Canadians. Reginald Bibby, a critic of multiculturalism, argues that the policy has not led to increased tolerance; rather, it has led to increased fragmentation, hyphen-

---

[18] Lewycky, 1992.
[19] Kymlicka & Norman, 2000, p. 31.
[20] Ibid., p. 40.
[21] Ibid., p. 10.

ation and insularity. Multiculturalism, he notes, has resulted in the production of "individual mosaic fragments".[22] In a similar vein, Nathan Glazer argues that the politicization of ethnic and racial minority rights and of ethnicity gives undue prominence to ethnicity as a defining variable in public life, and is inherently divisive.[23] C. Ward talks of the salience of ethnic politics as acting "...like a corrosive on metal, eating away at the ties of connectedness that bind us together as a nation."[24] For these critics, the politicization of multicultural- ism with its promotion of minority rights can, at its worst, lead to civil strife and, at its best, weaken trust between and among citizens, not promoting the politics of solidarity. Kymlicka and Norman summarize the arguments of the critics as follows:

> A more moderate (and more plausible) version states that while minority rights may not lead to civil war, they will erode the ability of citizens to fulfil their responsibili- ties as democratic citizens — e.g., by weakening citizens' ability to communicate, trust, and feel solidarity across group differences. As such even if a particular minority rights policy is not itself unjust, examined in isolation, the trend towards, increased salience of ethnicity will erode the norms and practices of responsible citizenship, and so reduce the overall functioning of the state.[25]

It is not clear that a policy of protecting and promoting the equality rights of ethnic and racialized minority groups will erode the practices of responsible citizenship. What it will do is simultaneously erode the racialized conception of citizenship embedded in the notion of binationalism and build the case for a democratic pluralist conception of citizenship in Canada.

What the critics of multiculturalism, anti-racism and employment equity pol- icies also fail to appreciate is the significant power and privilege enjoyed by the white majority and denied others because of their race, disability or gender. Multiculturalism was not designed to dislodge the power and privilege of the white majority. M. Weinfeld refers to this flaw: "...the ideals behind the rheto- ric of multiculturalism have not been attained ... Canadian native people and other non-whites continue to be victimized, a fact reflected in economic inequality or in patterns of social exclusion, abuse, and degradation."[26] It is the pervasiveness of prejudice directed at members of racialially marginalized and newcomer minority groups and the widespread existence of discrimination that have contributed to the fragmentation, hyphenation and insularity in the urban environment.[27] It is exactly at the point when the disadvantaged and

---

[22] Bibby, 1990, pp. 14–15.

[23] Glazer, 1983, pp. 227–228.

[24] As cited in Kymlicka & Norman, 2000, p. 10.

[25] Kymlicka & Norman, 2000, p. 10.

[26] Weinfeld, 1981, p. 69.

[27] In the past two decades there has emerged an extensive body of data detailing the extent of socio-economic disadvantages faced by members of racially marginalized communities in Canada, in- cluding wage disparities, a split labour market, non-recognition of foreign credentials and racialized poverty. For details *see* Zureik & Hiscott, 1983; Henry & Ginsberg, 1985; Billingingsley & Musynzski, 1985; Canadian Civil Liberties, 1991; Hou & Balakrishnan, 1996; Frank, 1997; Li, 1998. Five recent reports have been highly illuminating: Ornstein, 2000; Kunz, Milan & Schetagne, 2000; Galabuzi, 2001; Jackson, 2001; Canadian Council on Social Development, 2002.

marginalized in society demand equality, representation, access and power sharing that there is a backlash that claims they are demanding too much and want
only their sectoral demands met.

The major contributing factor to what Bibby calls "mosaic madness" is not
the demands of racialized minority groups; rather, it is the existence of racism
and sexism that an official policy of multiculturalism has been singularly incapable of dealing with. Racialized and newcomer minority groups are the latest in
a long line of equity-seeking groups who are tapping into the broader liberal
commitment to equality and social justice. The greatest challenges posed by
diversity are to build on the traditions of equality espoused in liberalism and to
move from an official policy of multiculturalism to the incorporation of the ideals of anti-racism and anti-discrimination as core values exemplifying national
character.

The multicultural society is symbolic of the abject failure of attempting to
develop an urban social cohesion through a policy of assimilation. The two iterations of multiculturalism in Canada also point to the failure of state-sponsored
actions to deal with demographic diversity and the inability of the policy to
deal with systemic racial discrimination. The reality of multiculturalism, with its
multiple diverse, socially cohesive groups, suggests the failure of the so-called
modernization process to create a culture that transcends class and social division. Richard Day is even more critical: "I would suggest that integration within
multiculturalism in a bilingual framework is best seen as a creative reproduction
of the colonial method of strategic simulation of assimilation to the Other, and
not as an overcoming or break with this past."[28] The modern nation state, Day
notes, "simulated its unity and dissimulated its multiplicity". The post-modern
multicultural Canadian state, however, "dissimulates its unity and simulates a
multiplicity..[29]

The multicultural society is the site where the First Nations communities
and racially marginalized and newcomer communities contest the ideas of identity, citizenship and cohesion. They are struggling to have their identities recognized alongside the dominant culture's. Charles Taylor argues that the refusal
to recognize minority rights can be seen as a "form of repression", and he
points to the importance of the "links between recognition and identity."[30] The
struggle for recognition is inherently a political struggle against the dominant
discourse and against discrimination and oppression. It is the state and the
dominant discourse that are in the position of conferring "recognition" and,
thereby, affirming both their legitimacy and their positions of prominence. In
struggling to legitimate their identities, are racialized and newcomer minority
groups forsaking or eroding a common identity? For many racialized minority
groups, the process of being "othered" in society, the process of being considered a "minority", is problematic. For them, prejudice and discrimination are
major stumbling blocks to building a common identity. The current policy of

---

[28] Day, 2000, p. 197.

[29] Ibid., p. 205.

[30] Taylor, 1992, p. 50.

multiculturalism is one where "...the state does not recognize the value or equality of 'communities'; rather it merely recognizes their *'existence'*."[31]

Multiculturalism as recognition has not led to increased equality for members of ethnic and racialized minority communities. Multiculturalism as state policy does not even begin to address the critical issues facing the First Nations communities, as many of them continue to struggle against the detrimental impacts of settler colonialism and advance their inherent right to self-government. Multiculturalism has not overturned the pre-eminent position of the English and the French in Canadian society. Rather, it has preserved Canada's national and linguistic duality, and the "... Other Ethnic Groups [are] arranged in a complex ever changing hierarchy."[32] What is required is a more proactive policy that is anti-racist, accommodates the needs of the First Nations Peoples as well as the needs of racialized and newcomer minority communities, and creates conditions in which they can all develop their talents and capacities and become valued and respected as contributing members of society.

The struggle for legitimacy and "place claiming" by the First Peoples and by racialized and newcomer minority communities is the dawn of a new type of identity politics. Place and space reflect power relations extant in society. The struggle by the First Peoples and by racialized and newcomer communities for the redistribution of power and resources is not a class-specific struggle. The politics of difference, identity politics, is about an inclusive democracy where marginalized groups place issues of inclusivity, anti-racism, social justice and citizenship at the heart of the national question. There is no single public sphere, no single acceptable notion of citizenship, and no single notion of social cohesion. There are, instead, multiple "counterpublic" spheres in which marginalized groups develop their own sense of cohesion to contest oppression, discrimination and exclusion. According to Nancy Fraser:

> Historiography records that members of subordinated social groups — women, workers, people of colour, and gays and lesbians — have repeatedly found it advantageous to constitute alternative publics ... *subaltern counterpublics* in order to signal that there are parallel discursive arenas where members of subordinated social groups invent and circulate counter discourses to formulate oppositional interpretations of their identities, interests and needs.[33]

These counterpublics posit a different understanding of space, nation, citizenship and social cohesion. And in positing this different and alternate understanding, they are challenging the dominant discourse. They are also accentuating the politics of difference that puts issues of inequality and social justice at the heart of the national question, where they can then contest notions of rights and conceptions of citizenship. It is in housing, health care, education, employment, service delivery and in political and administrative representation that these issues are most hotly contested. And for the First Peoples, it is around claims of nationhood, sovereignty and land claims that these issues are most hotly contested.

---

[31] Day, 2000, p. 198.

[32] Ibid.

[33] Fraser, 1996, p. 123.

The exclusion and marginalization experienced and felt by the First Peoples and by many members of racially marginalized and newcomer communities in Canadian society have an effect on identity formation and social cohesion. The reality of multiculturalism is not translated into the day-to-day experiences of diverse communities. In its report titled "Diversity Our Strength, Access & Equity Our Goal," the city of Toronto's Equity and Access Centre recognized that though immigrants are the "economic engine" driving the global economy, not all immigrant groups are benefiting. The most disadvantaged groups are the First Nations peoples, Africans, Jamaicans, Tamils, Sri Lankans, Pakistanis, Bangladeshis, Vietnamese, Iranians, Latin Americans and Hispanics. The report concluded that there will be a "growing sense of frustration" among members of these communities if the situation of under-representation in decision making is not addressed, and if "...the incidents of hate activity and discriminatory practices and prejudicial attitudes that unfortunately continue to plague our city" are not effectively dealt with.[34] Discrimination, prejudice, exclusion and marginalization in an ostensibly multicultural, multiracial society form the context in which the search for identity and social cohesion is experienced. It is this reality that prompts Day to assert that there is "no Canada to reclaim from the past."[35] The Canada of the present has an umbilical cord linking it to the Canada of the past, with its history of violence against the First Peoples, the enslavement of people of African descent, institutional discrimination against racialized communities and political dominance and cultural hegemony by Anglophones.

The redefinition of social cohesion, however, as a response to discrimination, oppression and exclusion starkly poses the question of political risk. What this suggests is that the battle for civil and political rights has moved onto the terrain of civil and political equality. Why is the dominant culture so risk averse? Why is it reticent to settle all land claims and move more decisively to negotiate self-government arrangements for First Nations communities? Why is it resistant to the equality claims by racialized minority groups? Why is it not prepared to have its institutions, policies and practices held up to the litmus test of substantive equality, not just formal equality? In the realm of formal equality, laws, constitutions and human rights codes proclaim the equality of all citizens. In this realm, it is just that citizens should be equally entitled to certain rights typically associated with a democracy — the right to vote, to freedom of association, to freedom of religion, etc. In contrast with the realm of formal equality, there is the reality of inequality. Socio-economic inequality is a real and permanent feature of the landscape of a liberal democracy. In recent times the focus has been on how to deal with racialized poverty and the inequalities and disadvantages that result from racial discrimination.[36]

A public policy framework of equity is premised on a recognition that equality does not necessarily mean that all people are treated the same. Substantive, as opposed to formal, equality involves acknowledging and accommo-

---

[34] City of Toronto, 1998.

[35] Day, 2000, p. 223.

[36] Ornstein, 2000; Kunz et al., 2000; Canadian Council on Social Development, 1993.

dating differences and treating differences differently. Substantive equality involves equality of opportunity — creating conditions such that people, regardless of their race or ethnicity, can compete equally for the valued goods and services in society. This, as the discussion paper "A Theoretical Context for Employment Equity" produced by the Ministry of Citizenship (Government of Ontario) noted, is a reflection that people have a right to be free from discrimination in all walks of life.[37] Liberal theory is about formal equality related to fundamental freedoms to worship, to free association, to freedom of thought, etc. These freedoms are not absolute; they are circumscribed by reasonable limits (*Canadian Charter of Rights and Freedoms*, section 1). In the absence of absolute freedoms, the state has a role to play in advancing the overall well-being of its citizenry.

In the context of accommodating differences and promoting heterogeneous social cohesion, there is space for the state to intervene to ensure equal treatment (equality of opportunity). Within a liberal discourse, a societal commitment to equality of opportunity ensures that all members of society are provided with the opportunity to secure the valued goods and services free from discrimination. This is a shift from class inequalities to gender, racial or cultural inequalities that seriously erode equal citizenship, leading Anne Phillips to ask whether equal citizenship depends on all citizens being subject to the same civil codes or "does it depend on a wider diversity of institutional arrangements that can promote the collective goals of linguistic or cultural minorities..."?[38] Phillips suggests that same treatment is not the most desirable option to promote equality:

> When most countries are culturally, linguistically and ethnically diverse — when minorities and majorities "increasingly clash over such issues as language rights, regional autonomy, political representation, education, curriculum, land claims, immigration and naturalization policy, even national symbols" — the idea that equal citizenship involves assimilating minorities into whatever happens to be majority norms seems patently unfair. It should not be necessary for people to make themselves the same as the others in order to qualify for equal respect.[39]

In a multicultural society like Canada, this requires a fundamental movement from tolerating diverse cultures to recognizing and respecting them. And as the 1996 Royal Commission on Aboriginal Peoples noted, it also entails fundamentally restructuring relations with the First Nations communities to allow for Native self-government. Canadian multiculturalism, says Day, treats "emergent" identities as "competitive aberrations" to be assimilated, managed or, at best, recognized.[40] A politics of difference that addresses the reformulated national question must acknowledge a much broader sense of public purpose. In "affirming differences", in respecting differences, Canada can move from multiculturalism as state-centred management and state-sponsored hierarchy to a redefined social cohesion that challenges the dominant discourse of Canada as

---

[37] Ontario, 1989.

[38] Phillips, 1999, p. 27.

[39] Ibid., pp. 128–129.

[40] Day, 2000, p. 227.

a binational/bilingual country. Coalition politics comprising groups that represent the "counterpublics" is now producing that social cohesion. It is responding to the dynamics of diversity and systemic discrimination, and it is forging a vision of a multiracial, multiethnic polity at the national level.

Conclusion

The vision of a multiracial, multiethnic polity at the national level is one that "democratizes democracy". The democratization of democracy in Canada must also involve the full implementation of the inherent right of the First Nations to govern themselves. Self-government is seen by the First Peoples as the way out of their internal colonial status; it is their response to inequality and social injustice. It is their way of establishing their presence as equals and as self-governing entities within the Canadian Confederation. Seen in this light, self-government is a fight for justice and equality, the logical extension of democracy and democratic rule in Canada.

The socially cohesive counterpublics are demanding substantive equality, are moving away from essentialist politics, and are positing notions of "democratic citizenship". Roughly translated, this means that the institutions of government and the administration of government are being challenged to be more representative of diverse populations. Currently, the power and privilege of Anglo-Canadian elites and the pre-eminent position they occupy in Canadian society are being challenged. First Nations communities and other historically marginalized communities are asserting their rights and challenging the limits of multiculturalism. Multiculturalism contains within it the seeds of its own transformation. It must identify prejudice and discrimination and "Othering" as important sources of exclusion; it must assert that the Canada of the past should not be reclaimed, as it was built on violence and systematic exclusion; and it must affirm and value differences as central to a redefined social cohesion.

References

Abella, Rosalie. (1984). *Report on the Commission on Equality in Employment.* Ottawa: Supply and Services Canada.

Bibby, Reginald Wayne. (1990). *Mosaic madness: The poverty and potential of life in Canada.* Toronto: Stoddard.

Billingingsley, Brenda, & Musynzski, Leon. (1985). *No discrimination here?: Toronto employers and the multi-racial workforce.* Toronto: Urban Alliance on Race Relation.

Brotz, Howard. (1980). Multiculturalism in Canada: A muddle. *Canadian Public Policy, 6*(1), 41–46.

Canada. House of Commons. Special Parliamentary Committee on the Participation of Visible Minorities in Canada. (1984). *Equality Now!* Ottawa: Supply and Services Canada.

Canada. Standing Committee on Multiculturalism. (1987). *Multiculturalism: Building the Canadian Mosaic*. Ottawa: Supply and Services Canada.

Canadian Council on Social Development (CCSD). (2002). *Does a rising tide lift all boats?* Ottawa: CCSD.

Murray, M. (1991). "Agencies screen non-whites, group charges", *Toronto Star*, Jaunary 21, A8.

Castells, Manuel. (1997). *The power of identity*. Cambridge, MA: Blackwell Publishers.

City of Toronto. Task Force on Community Access and Equity (1998). *Diversity our strength, access & equity our goal*. Retrieved October 25, 2003, from the City of Toronto website: http://www.city.toronto.on.ca/accessandequity/exec_sum.htm

Day, Richard J.F. (2000). *Multiculturalism and the history of Canadian diversity*. Toronto: University of Toronto Press.

Elliott, Jean Leonard, & Fleras Augie. (1990). Immigration and the Canadian ethnic mosiac. In Peter S. Li (Ed.), *Race and ethnic relations in Canada*. Don Mills: Oxford University Press.

Fleras, Augie, & Elliott, Jean Leonard. (1992). *The challenge of diversity: Multiculturalism in Canada*. Scarborough, ON: Nelson Canada.

Fleras, A., & Elliott, J.L. (1999). *Unequal relations: An introduction to race, ethnic, and Aboriginal dynamics in Canada* (3rd ed.). Scarborough, ON: Prentice Hall Canada.

Frank, J. (1996). Indicators of social inequality in Canada: Women, Aboriginal people and visible minorities. In Alan Frizzell & Joh H. Pammett (Eds.), *Social inequality in Canada*. Ottawa: Carleton University Press.

Fraser, Nancy. (1996). "Rethinking the public sphere: A contribution to the critique of actually existing democracies" in Craig Calhoun (Ed.), *Habermas and the public sphere* (pp. 109–143). Cambridge MA: MIT Press.

Galabuzi, Grace-Edward. (2001). *Canada's creeping economic apartheid*. Toronto: Canadian Race Relations Foundation, CSJ Foundation for Research and Education.

Giddens, Anthony. (1994). *Beyond left and right: The future of radical politics*. Cambridge, UK: Polity Press.

Glazer, Nathan. (1983). *Ethnic dilemmas: 1964–1982*. Cambridge, MA: Harvard University Press.

Held, David. (1995). *Democracy and the global order: From the modern state to cosmopolitan governance*. Cambridge, UK: Polity Press.

Henry, Frances, et al. (1995). *The colour of democracy: Racism in Canadian society*. Toronto: Harcourt, Brace Canada.

Henry, Frances, & Ginsberg, Effie. (1985). *Who gets the work? A test of racial discrimination in employment*. Toronto: The Urban Alliance on Race Relations and the Social Planning Council of Metropolitan Toronto.

Hou, Feng, & T.R. Balakrishnan (1996). The integration of visible minorities in contemporary Canadian society. *Canadian Journal of Sociology, 21*(3), 307–326.

Jackson, Andrew. (2001). Poverty and racism. *Perception, 24*(4), 6–7.

Kalbach, W.E. (2000). Ethnic diversity: Canada's changing cultural mosiac. In Madeline A. Kalbach & Wareen E. Kalbach (Eds.), *Perspectives on ethnicity in Canada: A reader*. Toronto: Harcourt Canada Ltd.

Kunz, Jean Lock, Milan, Anne, & Schetagne, Sylvain. (2000). *Unequal access: A Canadian profile of racial differences in education, employment and income*. A report prepared for Canadian Race Relations Foundation by the Canadian Council on Social Development. Toronto: The Canadian Race Relations Foundation.

Kymlicka, Will, & Norman, Wayne. (2000). Citizenship in culturally diverse societies: Issues, contexts, concepts. In Will Kymlicka & Wayne Norman (Eds.), *Citizenship in diverse societies*. Oxford, UK: Oxford University Press.

Lewycky, Laverne M. (1992). Multiculturalism in the 1990s and into the 21st century: Beyond ideology, and utopia. In Vic Satzewich (Ed.), *Deconstructing a nation: Immigration, multiculturalism and racism in the '90s Canada* (pp. 359–401). Halifax: Fernwood Publishing.

Li, Peter S. (Ed.). (1990). *Race and ethnic relations in Canada*. Don Mills, ON: Oxford University Press.

Li, Peter S. (1998). The market value and social value of race. In Vic Satzewich (Ed.), *Racism and social inequality in Canada: Concepts, controversies and strategies of resistance* (pp. 115–130). Toronto, Thompson Educational Publishing, Inc.

Ontario. Ministry of Citizenship. (1989). *A theoretical context for employment equity*. Toronto: Queen's Printer.

Ornstein, Michael. (2000). *Ethno-racial inequality in Toronto: Analysis of the 1996 census*. Toronto: Access and Equity Unit, City of Toronto.

Phillips, Anne. (1999). *Which equalities matter?* Cambridge, UK: Polity Press.

Ramcharan, Subhas. (1982). *Racism: Non-whites in Canada*. Toronto: Butterworths.

Roberts, Lance W., & Clifton, Rodney A. (1990). Multiculturalism in Canada: A sociological perspective. In Peter S. Li (Ed.), *Race and ethnic relations in Canada* (pp. 120–147). Don Mills, ON: Oxford University Press.

Taylor, Charles. (1992). The politics of recognition. In A. Gutman (Ed.), *Multiculturalism and "The politics of recognition": An essay*. Princeton, NJ: Princeton University Press.

Weinfeld, M. (1981). Canada. In Robert G. Wirsing (Ed.), *Protection of ethnic minorities* (pp. 41–78). New York: Pergamon Press.

Zureik, Elia, & Hiscott, Robert. (1983). *The experience of visible minorities in the work world: The case of MBA graduates*. A report submitted to the Race Relations Division of the Ontario Human Rights Commission. Ontario: Ontario Human Rights Commission.

Bibliography

Abella, Rosalie Silberman. (1987, October). Employment equity: Implications for industrial relations. An address given at the annual fall industral relations seminar, Industrial Relations Centre, Queen's University, October 19–23.

Canada. Employment and Immigration Canada. (1989). *Immigration to Canada: Issues for discussion*. Ottawa: Employment and Immigration Canada, Public Affairs and the Immigration Policy Branch.

Canadian Council of Christians and Jews. (1993). *Attitudes towards race and ethnic relations*. Toronto: Canadian Council of Christians and Jews.

Castells, Manuel. (1978). *City, class and power*. London: Macmillan.

Castells, Manuel. (1996) *The rise of the network society*. Cambridge, MA: Blackwell.

Harvey, David. (1976). *Social justice and the city*. London: Edwin Arnold.

Harvey, David. (1989). *The condition of postmodernity: An enquiry into the origins of cultural change*. Oxford, UK: Blackwell.

Harvey, David. (1996). *Justice, nature and the geography of difference*. Oxford: Blackwell.

Holston, James. (1995). Spaces of insurgent citizenship. *Planning Theory (Special Issue)*, 35–52.

Sandercock, Leonie. (1998). *Towards cosmopolis: Planning for multicultural cities*. New York: John Wiley & Sons.

Saunders, Peter. (1981). *Social theory and the urban question*. London: Hutchinson.

25

Racializing Culture/ Culturalizing Race
Multicultural Racism in a Multicultural Canada

Augie Fleras
Sociology Department
University of Waterloo
Waterloo

I would like to thank the editors for their constructive comments on an earlier version of this essay.

Introduction: Marking Differences

Recourse to race appears to have lost what little discursive muscle it once flexed in Canada. Reference to race in the United States may secure a meta-discourse for diversity talk. In Canada, however, the principle of culturalism has pre-empted the race concept as a preferred explanatory framework. The foundational principles that govern Canada's constitutional order tend to deny the relevance of race as a basis for entitlement.[1] Canadians have rarely felt as comfortable as Americans with race talk, preferring instead to refract perceptions of alterity through the prism of ethnicity and culture.[2] Such a cultural commitment may help to explain a general antipathy towards explicitly race-based theories of racialized disadvantages or privileges. To be sure, an aversion to race as explanatory framework in Canada has not insulated minority women and men from marginalization and discrimination.[3] Nor has a race-aversive commitment heightened a national receptivity to diversity. If anything, Canadians appear increasingly ambivalent about diversity when putting principle into practice.[4] Nevertheless, a reliance on culture rather than race to explain, assess, and entitle has consolidated Canada's reputation as a model multicultural society.

The conflating of racism with culture instead of race may strike the reader as counterintuitive. But it is precisely this paradox that must be "theorized" in demonstrating how exclusionary discourses are increasingly constructed around the culture-blind commitments of an official multiculturalism. Put bluntly, Canada's official multiculturalism aspires to many things. Yet its animating logic has never wavered from a singular goal: namely, to construct an inclusive Canada of many ("multi") cultures by denying the salience of diversity in defining entitlements. According to this line of multiculturalism, a society of many cultures can exist, but only if peoples' differences do not preclude access to equality, participation, and citizenship. Nobody should be denied or excluded because of their differences; conversely, no one should be entitled to public rewards because of their ethnicity or race. This transformation of racial discourse into a culture-blind discursive framework not only corresponds with Canada's multicultural commitments; it also coincides with the universalistic principles of liberal pluralism. According to liberal pluralism, similarities are more important than differences. What we have in common as freewheeling and morally autonomous

---

[1] Consider, for example, the decision by Canada's Supreme Court to reverse an earlier lower court decision: Custody of a biracial child was reverted to his white mother rather than her lover, a black professional basketball player with the then Vancouver Grizzlies, on the grounds that race doesn't really matter. *See* Hill, 2001.

[2] Walker, 1997; Backhouse, 1999.

[3] Kunz et al., 2001.

[4] Henry et al., 2000.

individuals supersedes what divides or defines us because of group ethnicity —
at least for purposes of reward or recognition. Insofar as the ethnocentricity at
the heart of liberal pluralism is not conducive to "taking differences seriously"
— a profoundly disturbing turn in a deeply divided and multilayered Canada —
there is heuristic value in the seemingly oxymoronic expression "multicultural
racism".

This essay argues that Canada's official multiculturalism means well, yet is
blinkered by its good intentions. A commitment to a culture-blind multiculturalism contributes to cultural racism by engendering a distinct type of "subconscious" racism that excludes even as it includes. Two lines of reasoning are
pursued. First, the essay contends that contemporary racism in Canada is no
longer about race dominance, but entails a cultural ethnocentrism that hides
behind a veneer of multiculturalism to escape scrutiny and to justify its presence. Explanations of exclusion that once extolled race or biology are being dis-
lodged by those embracing the primacy of culture.[5] In racializing culture as a
marker of invidious distinction, the mainstream no longer defines itself as
racially superior but as culturally appropriate. Conversely, minorities are not
dismissed as racially inferior but as culturally incompatible. Three mutually distinct yet convergent forces may account for this cultural dynamic: (a) a multicultural fundamentalism that "miniaturizes" other cultures even when
celebrating diversity; (b) a pervasive Eurocentrism that normalizes
anglocentricity as the universally assumed norm for cultural coexistence; and
(c) a "subliminal" cultural racism that inadvertently exerts a hegemonic effect
without drawing attention. Ethnocentrism is used not only in terms of perceived
superiority, but also in the sense of defining something as acceptable because
of its normalcy. Such a "centrism" (including androcentrism and Eurocentrism)
reflects the almost automatic and routine tendency of people to interpret the
world from their point of view as necessary, normal, and natural, while assuming that others too are seeing the world in the same way, or would if they
could. It goes without saying that alternative interpretations are dismissed as
irrelevant or inferior.

Second, the essay turns its attention to explaining the (multi)culturality of
racism in Canada. Reference to multicultural racism goes beyond specifying a
distinctive racism in a multicultural society. Conveyed instead is a racism that is
implicit within the very logic of an official multiculturalism that purports to be
both culture blind and race neutral. A multicultural racism derives its legitimacy
from the logical consequences of a "monocultural" multiculturalism, with its
privileging of consensus over challenge, conformity over dissensus, containment
over empowerment, control over change, universality over particularity, and uniformity over diversity. Differences may be tolerated under such a mono-multiculturalism, but only if strings are attached. That is: (a) people can be
different, but everybody must be different in the same kind of way; (b) cultural
differences are tolerable, but they must not violate the laws of the land, challenge key values or institutions, or interfere with the rights of others; (c) ethnicity is acceptable, but is properly relegated to the private or personal lest it

---

5 Castles & Miller, 1998; de Fuente et al., 2001; Guimaraes, 2001.

foster messy public entanglements; and (d) diversity is permissible provided the centre controls what counts as difference and what differences count. Such a controlling dynamic is deemed to be exclusionary, at least in consequence if not necessarily by intent. A mono-multiculturalism is also racist by conveying the appearance of inclusiveness without compromising the distribution of power and privilege.

Multiculturalism in Canada: Securing the Mono in Multiculturalism

How do we account for the cultural racism implicit in a multiculturalism that is more in tune with the "mono" than the "multi"? The logic behind an official multiculturalism may have something to do with it. Multiculturalism arose in the politicized aftermath following publication of the Report of the Royal Commission on Bilingualism and Biculturalism in 1969. A policy of multiculturalism within a bilingual framework was subsequently tabled in 1971 when the Liberal government declared a new cultural policy for Canada. According to Prime Minister Pierre Elliott Trudeau:

> There cannot be one cultural policy for Canadians of British or French origins, another for the originals, and yet a third for all others. For although there are two official languages, there is no official culture. Nor does any cultural group take precedence over another.... We are free to be ourselves. But this cannot be left to chance.... It is the policy of this government to eliminate any such danger and to safeguard this freedom.

References to multiculturalism rarely meant what many believed. Instead of promoting cultural diversity, official multiculturalism attempted to rewrite the social contract by envisioning a diverse Canada in which personal racial or ethnic differences would not be used to deny, exclude, or exploit. Expressions such as the "equality of cultures" did not mean that all cultures were equal. Rather, the logic of an official multiculturalism conveyed the message that ·no one should be excluded from equal participation or denied democratic-citizenship rights because of cultural differences. Put bluntly, official multiculturalism was not about celebrating diversity, but primarily about neutralizing differences to remove disadvantage and ensure integration. These integrationist objectives of the 1971 Multiculturalism Policy were clearly articulated in the House of Commons:[6]

1. The government of Canada will support all of Canada's cultures and will seek to assist, resources permitting, the development of those cultural groups that have demonstrated a desire and effort to continue to develop, a capacity to grow and contribute to Canada, as well as a clear need for assistance.
2. The Government will assist members of all cultural groups to overcome cultural barriers to full participation in Canadian society.

---

[6] *House of Commons Debates* (Ottawa, 1971), p. 8581.

3. The Government will promote creative encounters and interchange among all Canadian cultural groups in the interests of national unity.

4. The Government will continue to assist immigrants to acquire at least one of Canada's official languages in order to become full participants in Canadian society.

In short, Canada's official multiculturalism is organized around a deceptively simple proposition. A society of many cultures can be constructed as long as cultural differences don't get in the way of living together. The passage of time has not compromised this commitment to inclusion through integration; only the means have shifted. A 1970s ethnicity multiculturalism appeared intent on breaking down prejudicial barriers by making all Canadians feel good about cultural diversity. A 1980s equity multiculturalism focused on improving inclusion by eliminating racialized meanings and inequities at institutional levels. And a 1990s civic multiculturalism continued to endorse the inclusivity principle through a shared civic identity.[7] The current version of multiculturalism remains focused around commonality by means of shared citizenship to enhance national unity. Clearly, then, a culture-blind multiculturalism revolves around a persistent theme: namely, a commitment to Canada-building by balancing national interests with minority concerns without forsaking the foundational principles of a monocultural constitutional order.

Endorsing the multicultural principle of integration regardless of difference was not without consequence. No one should underestimate the revolutionary potential of Canada's social experiment in breaking down the exclusionary barriers of cultural animosity. Nevertheless, the government's multiculturalism policy had no intention of taking differences seriously. Proposed instead was a de-politicized "pretend pluralism" that contrasted sharply with the critical multicultural discourses[8] at play in the United States.[9] The focus on "culture" in Canada's official multiculturalism was superficially narrow. Culture was not used in the holistic anthropological sense of meaningful lifeways, but more in the then conventional notion of the arts and aesthetics related to literature, drama, dance, and artistic expression. Nor did reference to culture imply the creation of self-sufficient communities. Proposed instead under an official multiculturalism was an individual right to identify with the cultural tradition of choice without paying a penalty in the process. The de-politicization of diversity could not be more artfully conveyed.

Such a multicultural commitment proved acceptable to many immigrants and minorities. But this pragmatic reading of multiculturalism did not bode well for those groups who sought social inclusion but without necessarily buying into cultural integration: especially so when Canada's immigration patterns shifted from European societies whose cultural differences embraced the foundational principles of Canada's constitutional order to those non-European sources whose fundamental cultural differences challenged the "Canadian way". It proved even less compatible for those national minorities and indigenous peo-

---

7 Fleras & Elliott, 2002.

8 Ibid.

9 Goldberg, 1993.

ples whose political agenda transcended a multicultural discourse.[10] In confusing inclusiveness with uniformity rather than diversity, the Trudeauian commitment to a "Just Society" sowed the seeds of a multicultural racism.[11]

Unmasking Racism

Every age has its hierarchy of crimes. This era is no exception, with racism near the pinnacle of crimes against humanity, judging by public reaction to racist transgressions.[12] Racism had its origins in race-based doctrines that justified inequality and exploitation on grounds of perceived inferiority, irrelevance, or danger. Race represents a socially defined construct rather than a reflection of biological reality. Human races do not exist except as artificial categories that are subject to racialized definitions and exclusions. Nor is there such a thing as race relations; more accurately, there are relations between groups that have been racialized by those with the power to impose and enforce such impositions.

Yet racism is not a uniform concept that reflects a singular experience or common reality. Racism as ideology ascribes a theory of inferiority that justifies and condones both exclusion and exploitation as well as expulsion or extermination. As practice it perpetuates inequality and privilege in ways inadvertent yet real. As dogma, it provides a theory of racialized hierarchy that defines as it denies. This vacuity in meaning complicates the defining process: To what extent is racism: (a) a thing, (b) a process, (c) a relationship, or (d) an attribute applied to something after the fact? Is it something that is done or not done; involving intent or consequences; embracing differences, or denying them as basis for equality or entitlement? Different dimensions of racism can also be discerned in terms of intent, awareness, magnitude and scope, intensity, and consequences. These variations permit the unmasking of diverse levels of racism, including (a) **interpersonal** (hateful and polite), (b) **institutional** (systematic and systemic), and (c) **ideological** (normative and subliminal).[13]

For our purposes, then, racism can be defined as *those ideas and ideals (ideology) that assert or imply the superiority of one social group over another because of perceived differences, both physical or cultural, together with the institutionalized power to put these beliefs into practice in a way that exploits or excludes the "other" because of who they are or what they do.*[14] This definition may appear convoluted. However, its comprehensiveness draws attention to the complexities of racism by: (a) encompassing both beliefs and practices, (b) focusing on the importance of institutionalized power, (c) emphasizing the structural embeddedness of racism within institutional frameworks and Eurocentric mindsets, and (d) conceding how unintended consequences have as much sting as deliberate intent. Two dimensions of racism prevail: racism as race, and rac-

---

[10] Kymlicka, 2001.

[11] Fleras, 2002, p. 63.

[12] Ibid.

[13] Fleras & Elliott, 2002.

[14] Fleras, 2001.

ism as culture. Other dimensions can be discerned as well, including: racism as structure, as power, as ideology, and as hate, but these are beyond the scope of this essay.[15]

Racism as Race

The biological dimension of racism is derived from the root, race, with its deterministic notion that biology is destiny. Racism as biology (or race) can be used in three ways. First, it entails a belief that behaviour is determined by genes or biology. These genetically wired racial differences are defined as fixed and unalterable. For example, assuming that blacks are natural-born athletes and the Japanese are naturally gifted scientists may be regarded as racist in conflating race with determinism. Second, racism refers to the use of race (or biology) as a basis for any kind of entitlement or exclusion. To "reward" or "entitle" visible minorities as an employment-equity target may be deemed just as racist (regardless of the intent or outcome) as excluding people of colour because of race. Third, racism as biology refers to the classic racial typologies of the nineteenth century. Racism transforms these perceived biological differences into an hierarchical ranking to justify the dominance of one group over another. Four core features comprise this theory of a raced hierarchy:

1. The human world can be partitioned into a set of fixed and discrete categories of population.
2. Each of these racial categories can be assigned a distinctive and inherited assemblage of social, cultural, and biological characteristics.
3. These attributes can be evaluated as good or bad, superior or inferior.
4. The resultant categories can be arranged in ascending/descending orders of importance.

Differential treatment of minority women and men is then justified on the grounds of innate and essentialized differences between races.[16]

Racism as Culture

The biological focus of racism has shifted in recent years to embrace assumptions about cultural superiority rather than pigment-focused inferiority.[17] Racism is no longer perceived as a universalist discourse of dominance over inferiorized "others", as once was the case when colonialism prevailed. The objective then was to destroy or exploit the "other" on the grounds of biological inferiority, or, alternatively, to incorporate the "other" forcibly into the colonizer's concept of progress.[18] The new rhetorics of exclusion go beyond assertions of racially endowed differences. Proposed instead is a new discursive framework based on the incommensurability of cultural differences as grounds for living together. Culturally different people can coexist, but only if their differences are

---

[15] Satzewich, 1998; Henry et al., 2000.
[16] Fleras & Elliott, 2002, pp. 32–34.
[17] Barker, 1981; Jayasurija, 1998.
[18] Solomos & Back, 1996.

ignored in the public domain of rewards or recognition. This racism without race transcends biological dominance or different physical endowments. Advocated instead is a belief in superiority and normalcy of the dominant culture discretely encoded around the language of citizenship, patriotism, and heritage.[19] This cultural racism is rooted in an ethnocentric dislike towards the "other" not because of who they **are** ("biology"), but because of what they **do** ("culture"). Dominant sectors are not defined as racially superior but as the cultural norm. Minorities, in turn, are dismissed as culturally incommensurate rather than racially inferior. Those who are too culturally different pose as much threat to the mainstream as racialized others because of incompatibilities that preclude belonging and acceptance.

This newer racism embraces a coded language that links social cohesion with national identity or a preferred culture.[20] Rhetorics of cultural exclusion are framed around the "apparent egalitarianism of culture talk" without posing a challenge to tacitly accepted racial hierarchies.[21] These exclusionary rhetorics often reflect a cultural fundamentalism. According to fundamentalist tenets, immutable cultural differences are deemed as innate and incompatible as those involving racial cleavages.[22] The incompatibility of cultures and identities suggests that people, by nature, prefer to live among their "own kind" rather than partake multiculturally.[23] Such a cultural fundamentalism is not without its racial underpinnings: Just as references to race and racial doctrines are culturally prescribed social constructions, so too are dialogues about cultural exclusion underpinned by race and racist imagery. This should come as no surprise: As noted by Joel Kahn in a 1989 issue of *Dialectical Anthropology,* the race concept and culture concept have much in common as totalizing systems of exclusion. Each constitutes a rigid explanatory framework for defining and assigning that is deterministic, reductionist, monocausal, and essentialist.

The language of cultural racism speaks of a new exclusionary rhetoric. This language is encoded around the inclusionary/exclusionary discourses of social cohesion and national unity, respect for the integrity and culture of the national community, and a linkage between culture and national identity. Culturalist discourses are introduced that combine biology with culture to diminish the "other" on the grounds they are too different to comply or integrate. Not unexpectedly, efforts to construct a viable society from multicultural arrangements are dismissed as unnatural and unstable. Such arrangements are also disparaged because of their potential to erode the homogeneity of the nation, endanger values of the mainstream, and unleash social discord because of misunderstandings.

The conclusion seems inescapable: Recourse to culturalist definitions of racism has proven as exclusionary as references to biological racism.[24] Cultural dif-

---

[19] Wieviorka, 1998; Powell, 2000.

[20] Henry et al., 2000.

[21] de la Cadena, 2001.

[22] Vasta & Castles, 1996.

[23] Stolcke, 1999.

[24] Ibid.

ferences are racialized by drawing on racial metaphors; conversely, racial differences are culturalized as socially anomalous. Targeted groups, such as Muslims, are vilified — and, more recently, "racially" profiled, in light of September 11 (2001) — because of their cultural values and religious practices. Each of these cultural prejudices intersects with a racialized non-whiteness to intensify interlocking patterns of exclusion.[25] The incommensurability of cultural differences resembles a kind of culturalizing of race because of a tendency towards ethnocentrism. Assigning an inherent inferiority to ethnicity ensures a radicalizing of culture. Culture, rather than biology, is manipulated to essential differences not unlike those rhetoric endorsed by biological determinism.

Subliminal Cultural Racism

If racism can prevail without race because of perceived cultural inferiority, two conclusions follow: First, exaggerating cultural differences may be racist when precluding full and equal participation; second, underplaying differences may be no less racist when cultural differences need to be taken seriously as a basis for living together. References to cultural racism can take different forms. In some cases, such as fundamentalist cultural racism, those who fall outside the perimeter of acceptability are openly criticized. In other cases, the dislike is couched in polite terms that exclude without the sting of bluntness ("Sorry, the apartment is already rented"). In still other cases, the reaction to cultural differences reflects an inherent ambiguity in sorting out competing value systems.[26] The principle of diversity may be endorsed at the conscious level, but there is a deep-seated reluctance to transform this principle into practice; preferred instead, the reassuring confines of the status quo. This conflict between opposing values is rarely conscious. What we have instead is an inner struggle between principle and practice whose "resolution" may have the effect of compromising minority interests.

Subliminal cultural racism is a racism that flourishes in the gap between inclusive principles and exclusionary practices. Subliminal racism is rooted in that class of persons who, in principle, abhor racism or discrimination yet harbour resentment in doing anything to eliminate this racism if cost or inconvenience are involved.[27] A subliminal racist may profess sympathy for the plight of disadvantaged others, but opposes measures whose implementation might entail sacrifices or violate cherished norms.[28] Criticism of minorities is couched in principled terms. Refugee claimants are condemned not in blunt racist terminology of too many from the wrong places, but by loftier appeals to fairness or national security. Their landed entry into Canada is criticized on procedural grounds (jumping the queue); alternatively, they are rebuked for taking advantage of Canada's generosity by exploiting refugee laws. Progressive goals may be upheld as a matter of principle, yet minority means for remedying these

---

[25] Modood & Werbner, 1997.

[26] Gaertner & Dovidio, 1986.

[27] Fleras & Elliott, 2002, pp. 73–74.

[28] Henry et al., 2000.

inequities may be discounted and discredited as a case of too much or too fast. The cumulative effect of such an unconscious cultural racism cannot be lightly discounted. A racialized status quo is reinforced because of an exclusionary consequence, however unintended this is.

At the heart of this subliminality is an unflinching ethnocentrism: ethnocentrism not in the sense of cultural superiority, but ethnocentrism as information processing that automatically and routinely interprets social reality from a fixed point of view as normal and necessary while dismissing other cultural realities as inappropriate or counterproductive.[29] Consider these instances of subliminal ethnocentrism. Employment equity for historically disadvantaged minorities may be theoretically acceptable yet, in practice, be disparaged as unfair, divisive, counterproductive, and at odds with society. Government initiatives to protect and promote diversity may be supported by the mainstream as long as they don't impose burdens over sharing power or cultural space. Minority cultural differences are acceptable unless they interfere with the rights of individuals, violate the law of the land, or undermine the dominant ideology or mainstream institutions. Immigrants are lauded as industrious contributors to society as long as they know "their place," mind their own business, and perform according to mainstream approval.

To sum up: talk is cheap when it comes to subliminal racism. Minority concerns and aspirations may be broadly endorsed, but principle and practice remain worlds apart. This dislike is camouflaged by "principled" opposition to government minority policies and minority initiatives that are deemed as "un-Canadian". Emergence of a subliminal racism should come as little surprise in a multicultural society that prefers its racism to be polite. As expressions of overt racism have become socially unacceptable, an alternative strategy is a display of righteous ethnocentrism towards racialized minorities. Criticism of minorities is rationalized on the grounds of mainstream values, national interests such as security or unity, on procedural grounds, or by appeals to a higher sense of fair play, equality, and justice. Aversive feelings towards others are not openly hostile or hateful. Dislike is coded in oblique and euphemistic ethnocentrisms that politely skirt the issue. Responses often involve discomfort or unease, which often leads to patterns of avoidance. Such indiscretions are neither less exclusionary nor less racist than a "red-necked" racism.

Culture-Blind Multiculturalism: Inclusion for Some, Exclusion for Others

Canadians and Americans are known to use the same words but speak a different language.[30] Nowhere is this pithy aphorism more evident than with multiculturalism, where repeated references to the cultural politics in Canada and the United States gloss over the discursive gap. The following polarized pairs provide conceptual bookends: "Mosaic" or "melting pot"? "Tossed salad" or

---

[29] Fleras, 2001.

[30] Fleras, 1998.

"kaleidoscope"? Society-building or minority empowerment? *E Pluribus Unum* [Out of many, one] or *E Unus pluribum* [Out of one, many]? The United States is normally defined as a melting pot. But the cultural wars in recent years have badly dented the cauldron, in effect exposing a lot of "pluribus" in the "unum". Conversely, Canada may claim to be a multicultural mosaic, but its "pluribus" appears more attuned toward the "unum". Reaction to official multiculturalism has varied: To one side are those who dismiss it as a "sheep in wolf's clothing"; to the other side are those who renounce it as a "wolf in sheep's clothing", with references to the "emperor has no clothes" in between.[31]

Canada's official multiculturalism is ultimately a social experiment in living together without differences. It envisages a culture-blind Canada in which many cultures coexist, but only by denying the relevance of diversity for purposes of inclusion or exclusion. There is much to commend in culture-blind multiculturalism that revolves around disadvantages, not differences; discrimination, not celebration; and "fitting in" rather than "opting out". But a different dynamic is required when deeply differenced minorities pursue the principle of inclusion without integration. The danger of a culture blind multiculturalism resides in its tendency to impose a monocultural uniformity because of a proclivity to "pretend pluralism". The superficiality of a pretend pluralism has had an excluding effect on those who prefer to live together differently by standing apart. Consider the deep diversity in a multi-layered Canada: Neither Aboriginal peoples nor the Québécois can possibly endorse an official multiculturalism that lumps together all diversities, both immigrant and indigenous, as well as the superficial and the deep. Since a culture-blind multiculturalism cannot speak of the language of deep diversity,[32] it has proven every bit as controlling as "old fashioned racism".

In short, the culture-blind superficiality of an official multiculturalism rejects diversity except in a symbolic and tokenistic manner. Diversity is relatively unimportant as a prerequisite of true equality since our commonalities as individuals trump any differences because of ethnic divisions. To be sure, national interests may be advanced by this refusal to take differences seriously. But such an agenda does so at the expense of those national minorities who seek inclusion without integration. A multicultural focus on "fitting in" has proven difficult for some, particularly for those whose differences are both a lifeblood and a political leverage. Moreover, in an era of identity politics and the politics of recognition, a monocultural multiculturalism inflicts a disservice on the human experience.[33] It is poignantly conveyed by an Aboriginal woman in her criticism of Canada's assimilationist agenda: "People are forced to suppress their identities, values, and intangible qualities that make them different, make them who they are, and make them human".[34]

---

[31] Fleras, 2002.

[32] Fish, 1997.

[33] Taylor, 1992.

[34] Dumont, 2001.

Augie Fleras

Multicultural Racism:
The Canadian Way

This essay is grounded in the following argument: Cultural racism has largely displaced race-based racism in Canada, in large part because of Canada's commitment to an official multiculturalism. A cultural racism involves a denial or exclusion not because of who people are (race), but because of how they fit (culture) into the broader picture of normalcy or acceptability. But the culture-blind multiculturalism is not as progressive as it appears. It not only endorses a pretend pluralism in an era of diversity but also embraces a monocultural multiculturalism that is racist in consequence. A multicultural racism rejects the salience of cultural differences as the basis for reward or recognition by those who want their cultures to be acknowledged as grounds for living together with differences. To be sure, culture-blind multiculturalism has de-legitimized racialized forms of racism. In their place, however, are more subliminal and acceptable faces of racism that, in de-politicizing cultural differences, may prove as exclusionary as old-fashioned racism.

Is there a Canadian "way" when it comes to multiculturally engaging diversity? Canada's official multiculturalism has been poorly theorised in terms of underlying logic. Official multiculturalism has rarely wavered from its staunch Canada-building commitments. Multiculturalism never set out to celebrate ethnic differences per se or to promote cultural diversity except in the most superficial manner. Nor was it concerned with fostering those cultural differences that would exclude Canadians from full and equal participation. And it most certainly never intended to endorse any creation of segregated ethnic communities with parallel power bases and special collective rights. Rather, multicultural policies and practices promoted the idea of Canada as a progressive and cohesive society that incorporates differences without compromising national interests. The focus implied the inclusion and integration of the historically disadvantaged through removal of prejudicial attitudes and structural barriers.

To achieve this goal of inclusion through integration, the de-politicization of cultural differences is actively pursued. Public institutions are transformed into relatively "neutral" spaces without openly favouring one group over another. Cultural differences are purged from the public domain in hopes of eliminating messy ethnic entanglements in the workplace or service delivery. To the extent that differences are tolerated, they are endorsed as a means to break down exclusion by establishing patterns of cultural exchange and sharing. Any commitment to taking differences seriously is compromised by a mono-multiculturalism that acknowledges diversity, but within strictly defined parameters. The permissible and tolerable range of diversity under this "we-know-what-is-best-for-you" mentality is, indeed, minuscule.

In other words, Canada's official multiculturalism is not about cultivating diversity — despite political assurances that differences are a strength rather than a liability.[35] Under the pretend pluralism of a culture-blind multiculturalism, differences are stripped of their context and history. Differences are not

---

[35] Dion, 2000, pp. 90–101.

celebrated under an official multiculturalism but are de-policed by "neutering" them of their potency to challenge, resist, and transform. The ethnicities of minority women and men are channelled ("de-politicized") into aesthetic pursuits in personal or private domains. The de-politicization of cultural differences also encourages the "morphing" of diversity into museum curiosities rather than living realities.[36] In that all diversity discourses and cultural heterogeneities are compressed into a single mono-multicultural paradigm that smooths and flattens while it homogenizes, the promise of a multiculturalism of many cultures is sharply circumscribed.[37]

Multiculturalism in Canada is predicated on the principle that people from many cultures can live together differently as long as these cultural differences aren't taken seriously. Two consequences follow from this approach to engaging diversity. First, official multiculturalism has reinforced the ongoing racialization of Canada by rejecting the legitimacy of diversity as a blueprint for living together.[38] The "pretend pluralism" of a monocultural multiculturalism is subliminally racist because such cultural neutrality denies and excludes those who want their cultural differences recognized in living together differently. Second, official multiculturalism is essentially a Canada-building exercise that seeks to de-politicize differences through institutional inclusion and removal of discriminatory barriers both social and cultural. The challenge rests in constructing a multicultural Canada that is safe **from** diversity, safe **for** diversity. In that Canada's multicultural discourses cannot cope with the challenge of making DIVERSITY safe **from** Canada as well as safe **for** Canada, a pattern of multicultural racism is established that is quintessentially part of the "Canadian way".

References

Backhouse, Constance. (1999). *Colour-coded: A legal history of racism in Canada, 1900–1950*. Toronto: University of Toronto Press.

Barker, M. (1981). *New racism*. London, Junction Books.

Brooks, Stephen. (1998). *Public policy in Canada*. Don Mills: ON: Oxford University Press.

Castles, Steven, & Miller, Mark. (1998). *The age of migration*. Oxford: Blackwell.

de Fuente, Alejandro, et al. (2001). The resurgence of racism in Cuba. *NACLA Report on the Americas, 34*(6), 29–34.

de la Cadena, Marisol. (2001). Reconstructing race: Racism, culture and Mestizaje in Latin American. *NACLA Report on the Americas, 34*(6), 16–23.

---

[36] Brooks, 1998.

[37] McRoberts, 2001.

[38] Thobani, 2000.

Dion, Stephane. (2000). Unity in diversity: The Canadian way. In Stephen E. Nancoo (Ed.), *21st century Canadian diversity* (pp. 90–101). Mississauga, ON: Canadian Scholars Press.

Dumont, Marilynn. (2001, September). Letter to the editor. *Windspeaker*, 5.

Fish, Stanley. (1997). Boutique multiculturalism, or why Liberals are incapable of thinking about hate speech. *Critical Inquiry, 23*(2), 378–395.

Fleras, Augie. (1998) The politics of posts and isms. *New Zealand Journal of Sociology, 13*(1), 62–96.

Fleras, Augie. (2001). *Constructions, conditions, and challenges. Social problems in Canada* (3rd ed.). Scarborough, ON: Prentice Hall.

Fleras, Augie. (2002). *Engaging diversity: Multiculturalism in Canada.* Toronto: Nelson.

Fleras, Augie, & Elliott, Jean Leonard. (2002). *Unequal relations. An introduction to race, ethnic, and Aboriginal dynamics in Canada* (4th ed.). Scarborough, ON: Prentice Hall.

Gaertner, S.L. & Dovidio, J.F. (Eds.). (1986). *Prejudice, discrimination, and racism.* New York, Academic Press.

Goldberg, David Theo. (1993). *Multiculturalism: A critical reader.* Oxford, UK: Blackwell.

Guimaraes, Antonio Sergio. (2001) Race, class and color: Behind Brazil's "racial democracy". *NACLA Report on the Americas, 34*(6), 38–39.

Henry, Frances, et al. (2000). *The colour of democracy. Racism in Canadian society* (2nd ed.). Toronto, ON: Harcourt Brace.

Hill, Lawrence. (2001). Black berry, sweet juice. *Black berry, sweet juice: On being black and white in canada.* Toronto, ON: HarperFlamingo.

Jayasurija, Laksiri. (1998), September/October. Old racism, new racism. *Australian Quarterly, September/October,* 4–5.

Kunz, Jean Lock, et al. (2001). *Unequal access. A Canadian profile of racial differences in education, employment, and income.* A Report prepared for the Canadian Race Relations Foundation by the Canadian Council for Social Development. Ottawa: Canadian Council for Social Development.

Kymlicka, Will. (2001). *Politics in the vernacular: Nationalism, multiculturalism and citizenship.* Don Mills: ON: Oxford University Press.

McRoberts, Kenneth. (2001). Canada and the multinational state. *Canadian Journal of Political Science, 34*(4), 683–713.

Modood, Taiq, & Werbner, Pnina. (Eds). (1997). *The politics of multiculturalism in the new Europe: Racism, identity, and community.* London, UK: Zed Books.

Powell, Rebecca. (2000). Overcoming cultural racism. The promise of multicultural education. *Multicultural Perspectives 2*(3), 8–14.

Satzewich, Vic. (1998). *Racism and social inequality in Canada: Concepts, controversies, and strategies of resistance.* Toronto: Thompson Educational Publishing.

Solomos, John, & Back, Les. (1996). *Racism and society.* London: Macmillan.

Stolcke, Verna. (1999). New rhetorics of exclusion in Europe. *International Social Science Journal, 125,* 29–42.

Taylor, Charles. (1992). The politics of recognition. In Amy Gutman (Ed.), *Multiculturalism and "the Politics of Recognition"* (pp. 25–74). Princeton, NJ: Princeton University Press.

Thobani, Sunera. (2000). Closing ranks. Racism and sexism in Canada's immigration policy. Race & Class, 42(1), 35–55.

Vasta, Ellie, & Castles, Stephen. (1996). *The teeth are smiling: The persistance of racism in a multicultural Australia*. Sydney: Allen & Unwin.

Walker, James. (1997). *"Race", rights, and the law in the Supreme Court of Canada*. Waterloo, ON: Wilfrid Laurier University Press.

Wieviorka, Michael. (1998) Is multiculturalism the solution? *Ethnic and Racial Studies, 21*(5), 881–910.

26

Re-articulating Multiculturalism
Transcending the Difference-Blind Liberal Approach

Jakeet Singh
Political Science Ph.D. Candidate
University of Toronto
Toronto

Special thanks to James Tully, Avigail Eisenberg, Warren Magnusson, Terence Morley, and the editors of this anthology for their helpful comments on earlier drafts of this essay.

In the past few decades, the concept of multiculturalism has become increasingly central to the identities of Canadians. This concept has also become very significant to the normative visions Canadians have for their society, providing a kind of model or strategy for achieving political inclusion and belonging in their political association. In this essay I will examine one pervasive way of thinking about the ideal of multiculturalism, which I will call the traditional or difference-blind liberal approach to multiculturalism. Using the philosophy of Ludwig Wittgenstein to critique this approach, I will argue that it has several flaws, including its racist manifestations within Canadian public discourse. I will then propose a different normative vision of multiculturalism based on the work of James Tully, which I believe transcends the various problems of the difference-blind liberal approach and provides a much better model for achieving political inclusion and belonging in Canadian society.

Multiculturalism in Canada

Multiculturalism is a concept that has quickly permeated Canadian public discourse. This concept has come to signify (1) a demographic fact about Canadian society, (2) a government policy, and (3) an ideology or normative vision for Canadian society.[1] While the demographic fact of multiculturalism is hardly controversial, the other two senses of the word have been the topic of much debate in recent years. Since the Government of Canada announced its first official policy of multiculturalism in 1971, many Canadians have expressed strong criticisms and concerns about it. These critics — most famously authors Neil Bissoondath and Richard Gwyn, as well as former MP John Nunziata — have argued "that official multiculturalism is divisive, that it ghettoizes visible minorities, fosters racial animosity, and detracts from national unity."[2] Will Kymlicka summarizes the critics' views as follows: "[Multicultural programs] are said to be undermining the historical tendency of immigrant groups to integrate, encouraging ethnic separatism, putting up 'cultural walls' around ethnic groups, and thereby eroding our ability to act collectively as citizens."[3]

Kymlicka's recent study of the effects of the multicultural policy on Canadian society since 1971, however, largely debunks many of these traditional criticisms. If the critics had been right, Kymlicka argues, then presumably naturalization rates in Canada should have declined since 1971, levels of political participation of cultural minorities should have decreased, the desire of

---

[1] Fleras & Elliott, 1996, p. 325.

[2] Dyck, 1996, p. 199.

[3] Kymlicka, 1998, p. 15.

immigrants to acquire an official language should have declined, levels of inter-marriage should have fallen, and residential concentration of cultural groups should have increased.[4] None of the above has actually proven to be true, how-ever, and, in several cases, opposite trends have been discerned.

To my mind, Kymlicka's findings point to the positive effects of the govern-ment policy of multiculturalism. By enacting an official policy and enshrining constitutional recognition of multiculturalism, the government has provided a level of recognition to cultural minorities that has proven to be beneficial in terms of engendering within many individuals and groups, a sense of ownership and attachment to political association.

However, in my view, the effects of the concept of multiculturalism on political inclusion and belonging in Canada cannot be assessed by examining the effects of the government policy alone; rather, significant effects on inclu-sion and belonging are also produced by the normative vision that we attach to this concept in our common discourse and, therefore, must also be considered. To this end, I would now like to examine what I believe to be the most com-mon of these normative visions of multiculturalism.

The Difference-Blind Liberal Approach

The notion of multiculturalism can be, and most often is, construed in a way that makes it simply an extension of a "difference-blind" liberal approach to political inclusion and belonging. This traditional liberal approach is chiefly con-cerned with achieving inclusion and belonging through neutrality or impartiality. A society is inclusive, by this view, if it maintains a neutral or impartial public sphere that favours no particular identity and, therefore, deals equally and fairly with all. Using Ronald Dworkin as his focus, Charles Taylor characterizes the difference-blind liberal view as follows:

> Dworkin makes a distinction between two kinds of moral commitment. We all have views about the ends of life, about what constitutes a good life, which we and others ought to strive for. But we also acknowledge a commitment to deal fairly and equally with each other, regardless of how we conceive our ends. We might call this latter commitment "procedural," while commitments concerning the ends of life are "sub-stantive." Dworkin claims that a liberal society is one that as a society adopts no par-ticular substantive view about the ends of life. The society is, rather, united around a strong procedural commitment to treat people with equal respect.[5]

In this picture, the "procedural" public sphere has no "substantive" commit-ments and is, therefore, neutral to diverse identities. Stated differently, "liberal theory tries to look at the problem of divining political rules from a standpoint which owes its allegiance to no particular interest — past, current, or prospec-tive."[6]

---

[4] Ibid., pp. 18–20.

[5] Taylor, 1994, p. 56.

[6] Kukathas, 1995, p. 233.

Because this liberal ideal has been central to Canadian society since long before the rise of the concept of multiculturalism, much of the discourse of multiculturalism has simply arisen as an extension of this liberal ideal. As such, this discourse, to a large extent, simply provides a new way of talking about an old liberal ideal. When multiculturalism is construed so as to simply fit into the traditional liberal model, the picture of the "multicultural" society becomes one in which "cultural" commitments are treated as substantive commitments and are, therefore, restricted to the private sphere. By this view, the procedural public sphere has no substantive commitments and is, therefore, culturally neutral. As Taylor points out, the assumption here is "that there are some universal, difference-blind principles" to which all cultures naturally conform,[7] and that serve as the basis for a public sphere that is blind and impartial to the various cultures that exist in the private realm. "In the end," as Chandran Kukathas says, "liberalism views cultural communities more like private associations."[8]

This liberal construal of multiculturalism captures much of the discourse of multiculturalism in Canada. When Prime Minister Pierre Elliott Trudeau introduced the first official policy of multiculturalism to the House of Commons in 1971, he stated that in Canada "there is no official culture. Nor does any cultural group take precedence over another.... We are free to be ourselves."[9] By this kind of view, if indeed there is "no official culture" in Canada but only an impartial procedure for dealing equally and fairly with the diverse cultures of Canadians, then, as is commonly asserted, all cultural groups are able to "keep their culture" in Canada. (Think of the popular Canadian rhetoric praising Canadian multiculturalism in relation to the American melting pot; the central idea here is that, while Americans compel cultural minority group assimilation into an overarching American culture, Canadians allow cultural minority groups to retain their cultural identities.) Because culture is relegated to the private sphere, cultural "communities" are free to adhere to cultural value systems and to practise cultural traditions. Indeed the prevalence of this idea that the public sphere is culturally neutral, and that Canada, therefore, has "no official culture" is illustrated by the popular assertion of (and about) Canadians who do not identify with a particular cultural group, that they have "no culture" at all. One recent culture minister in Québec made such an assertion when she claimed that "there is no real Ontario culture."[10]

Perhaps especially for those of us who are immigrants or the children of immigrants to Canada, however, the notion that cultural assimilation does not occur in Canada because (1) culture exists only in the private realm and (2) as a result, there is no public culture to assimilate such groups seems completely absurd. Indeed, our lived experience tells a very different story about Canada. Cleary this discourse has gone wrong, and in my view, the philosophy of Ludwig Wittgenstein provides useful tools for understanding how and why this is so.

---

[7] Taylor, 1994, p. 43.
[8] Kukathas, 1995, p. 236.
[9] Trudeau, quoted in Fleras & Elliott, 1996, p. 331.
[10] "Ontario has no culture", 2001.

A Wittgensteinian Critique

The philosophy of Ludwig Wittgenstein can help us to see the central problem with the liberal construal of multiculturalism by revealing the impossibility of a neutral public sphere. Wittgenstein can be viewed as belonging to a "contextualist" tradition that denies "the availability of a point of view that could be situated outside the practices and the institutions of a given culture and from where universal, 'context-independent' judgements could be made."[11] For Wittgenstein, each and every way of speaking and acting is part of a particular "language-game". Every language-game has a particular history and is practised by a particular (but not fixed) group of people. Furthermore, all of the symbols and meanings that construct the identities of, and orient the actions of, individuals arise from the language-games in which these individuals participate. In using the concept of the language-game, Wittgenstein wants to "bring into prominence the fact that the speaking of language is part of an activity, or of a form of life."[12] In other words, every way of speaking is tied up with particular ways of acting, and both are part of a particular identity, or what Wittgenstein calls "a form of life". A. C. Grayling summarizes Wittgenstein's use of this phrase as follows:

> [A form of life] is the underlying consensus of linguistic and nonlinguistic behaviour, assumptions, practices, traditions, and natural propensities which humans, as social beings, share with one another, and which is therefore presupposed in the language they use; language is woven into that pattern of human activity and character, and meaning is conferred on its expressions by the shared outlook and nature of its users. Thus a form of life consists in the community's concordance of natural and linguistic responses, which issue an agreement in definitions and judgements and therefore behaviour.... The form of life is the frame of reference we learn to work within when trained in the language of our community; learning that language is thus learning the outlook, assumptions, and practices with which that language is inseparably bound and from which its expressions get their meaning.[13]

For Wittgenstein, there are no "neutral" ways of speaking or acting; all ways of speaking and acting are part of certain identities, or forms of life — in a sense, they always **belong** to a particular group of people with a particular worldview in a particular place at a particular point in history. As such, difference-blind liberalism is only one language-game among many, and is not neutral in any sense.

Wittgenstein explains that "if language is to be a means of communication there must be agreement not only in definitions but also (strange as this may sound) in judgements."[14] Therefore, at base, every form of life consists of the agreements in judgements that are implicit in the distinctive "rules" or "grammar" of the language-game. As such, there is only so far a person can go in explaining and justifying his or her form of life to others: "If I have exhausted the justification I have reached bedrock, and my spade is turned. Then I am

---

[11] Mouffe, 2000, p. 63.

[12] Wittgenstein, 1958, p. 11.

[13] Grayling, 1996, p. 97.

[14] Wittgenstein, quoted in Mouffe, 2000, p. 68.

inclined to say: 'This is simply what I do'; What has to be accepted, the given is — so one could say — forms of life."[15] Eventually, for Wittgenstein, "Giving grounds ... comes to an end ... the end ... is our acting, which lies at the bottom of the language-game."[16]

What this Wittgensteinian perspective illuminates for us with respect to the liberal construal of multiculturalism is that there can be no set of procedures that is separate from a particular form of life and that is, therefore, neutral. Every set of procedures arises from, and further promotes, a particular language-game and a particular form of life. Chantal Mouffe articulates this Wittgensteinian insight as follows:

> It is because they are inscribed in shared forms of life and agreements in judgements that procedures can be accepted and followed.... The distinction between procedural and substantial cannot therefore be as clear as most liberal theorists would have it ... one cannot oppose, as so many liberals do, procedural and substantial justice without recognizing that procedural justice already presupposes acceptance of certain values.... Procedures always involve substantial ethical commitments.[17]

Liberal procedures are produced by, and serve to reproduce, liberal identities because they are based in, and serve to propagate, a particular liberal language-game. Clearly, these procedures are, therefore, not neutral. Just like any other form of life, there are substantive agreements in judgements that are implicit in this liberal language-game.

One central judgment that is implicit in the liberal form of life is the paramountcy of individual choice. The crucial sentiment here for liberals is that each of us has an individual way of being in the world and that, as such, each individual's choice should be respected unless it interferes with the choice of another. Indeed, it is this kind of substantive commitment that liberals often mistake as being impartial to different identities, without recognizing the assumptions and judgements implicit in such a commitment. As Kukathas explains:

> By insisting that the cultural community place a high value on individual choice, the larger society would in effect be saying that the minority culture must become much more liberal ... [the minority cultures] would surely object that to elevate individual choice and suggest the course of "liberalizing" their cultures "without destroying them" is to fail to take their culture seriously. If their culture is not already liberal, if it does not prize individuality or individual choice, then to talk of liberalization is inescapably to talk of undermining their culture.[18]

Clearly, a public sphere that is based in a liberal language-game and form of life is not neutral to different cultures or forms of life, but actually demands conformity to a liberal form of life. Indeed, "the supposedly neutral set of difference-blind principles ... is in fact a reflection of one hegemonic culture. As

---

[15] Wittgenstein, quoted in Grayling, 1996, p. 97.

[16] Wittgenstein, quoted in Grayling, 1996, p. 95.

[17] Mouffe, 2000, pp. 68–69.

[18] Kukathas, 1995, p. 243.

it turns out, then, only the minority or suppressed cultures are being forced to take alien form."[19]

There are a number of issues that this Wittgensteinian critique of difference-blind liberal multiculturalism allows us to raise — issues that are hidden by the language-game of difference-blind liberal multiculturalism — and a number of subsequent benefits that we gain through Wittgensteinian insights. First, by recognizing and understanding the cultural particularity of the public culture in Canada, we are able to see that the imposition of a supposedly difference-blind liberal identity onto all citizens is actually the imposition of the identity of the dominant culture.[20] As a result, we gain the ability to call into question the justice of this imposition. Second, we are in a better position to understand and explain why the promotion of a difference-blind liberal identity has largely failed to generate a sense of belonging in culturally diverse societies. The main reasons for this failure are: (a) such policies tend to incite resentment and resistance to the form of imposition and assimilation inherent in them[21] and (b) because the difference-blind identity is assumed to be something universal and neutral, insufficient attention is usually paid to the fact that social processes are needed in which citizens come to identify with the imposed citizen identity.

Third, Wittgenstein enables us to recognize the multiplicity of powerful forces of assimilation that are working on cultural minorities at all times. By showing us that identity is tied to the language-game and that identity is, therefore, both dialogical and intersubjective, Wittgenstein allows us to see that some of the most powerful forces of assimilation are the dominant language-games that each of us not only encounters but often gets pulled into through the media, the education system, the marketplace, the workplace, etc. This realization allows for an appreciation of the difficulties faced by immigrant groups in adjusting to life in Canada, as well as an appreciation of how difficult it is for cultural minority groups to resist assimilation and to maintain some form of their cultural identity within Canadian society (a hardship that is actively denied within the language-game of liberal multiculturalism). Fourth, by moving beyond the idea that cultures can be brought fully intact to Canada where they will remain undisturbed in the private sphere, we are able to move beyond the trivialization of culture that accompanies such an idea, in which cultures are reduced to the few tangible traits that **are** fairly easily transported, such as food, clothing, types of music and dance. Fifth, a Wittgensteinian critique allows us to transcend the aspect of difference-blind liberal multiculturalism that likens cultural identification to membership in a private association, which in turn gives rise to the view that culture cannot be what is common, but rather only what is out of the ordinary. This view is troubling in that it robs those Canadians who do not identify with a cultural minority group of their own particular sense of culture and history.

---

[19] Taylor, 1994, p. 43.

[20] Tully, 2002, p. 158.

[21] Ibid., p. 152.

Racism and the Difference-Blind Liberal Approach

The final benefit of the Wittgensteinian critique is that it provides us with tools to analyze the racism that arises within the difference-blind liberal construal of multiculturalism. It does so by providing a way of dealing with the symbols and meanings associated with race alongside the symbols and meanings associated with culture (not to mention gender, etc.). By this approach, all symbols and meanings arise within particular language-games and gain their meaning through the "rules" or "grammar" of these games. These games are intersecting, overlapping, and interacting, as every person participates in multiple games at once. As such, this approach is able to account for the multiplicity of meanings that comprise any particular identity.

In terms of race, we can see that the liberal language-game is also very much a white language-game. Not only has liberalism evolved within white societies, but it is intertwined with the normative identity of whiteness (in which the image of the tolerant, inclusive, open, liberal person is privileged). The language of liberalism is closely intertwined with white identities and is therefore more readily performed and lived by white people. As such, we can begin to see why the liberal construal of multiculturalism has racist manifestations. By disguising a white language-game as a neutral, public language-game, whiteness becomes politically endorsed and legitimized and takes on a privileged role as **the** public way of speaking and acting — **the** public form of life. While whiteness becomes associated with the public and universal, other forms of life become marginalized, as they are associated with the private and particular. By this logic, as the editors of this anthology point out in the introduction, "while white people **are** just people, everybody else is raced".

This racialization of cultural minority groups is furthered by the way in which the difference-blind liberal approach likens them to voluntary private associations. In doing so, this approach attributes a false degree of unity, coordination and commonality to these groups, perpetuating a racialized and homogenized image of them.

One illustration of the racist manifestations of the difference-blind liberal approach to multiculturalism arose in October 2000, in the preliminary stages of the Canadian federal election campaign. In the riding of Calgary North-East, the Canadian Alliance nomination campaign erupted in tension and controversy when the nomination of incumbent Alliance MP Art Hanger, a white man, was challenged by four candidates, all of whom were Sikh. With thousands of new memberships in the Alliance riding association having been purchased — many by Sikhs in that constituency — a great deal of speculation arose about bogus memberships, vote buying, and other forms of cheating, as many people, including Hanger himself, claimed that the Sikh community was conspiring to take over the Alliance riding association and the nomination. In one speech during this hostile nomination fight, Hanger stated:

> Now here's my response to my opponents: you will not hijack the democratic process that is set up here, and that we believe in. There are thousands of supporters of mine in this constituency committed to democratic principles and will [sic] not abuse these principles as tools of power or patronage. I am humbled by the groundswell of sup-

port I have received as people realized that democracy could be controlled by special interests. I thank everyone who put the democratic good ahead of special interests.[22]

After the speech, one Hanger supporter had this to say: "Well, they are [a special interest group].... See, they are all from the Sikh community, and from listening to their speeches, they have no valid reason to challenge Art's leadership. But yeah, they all represent the same Sikh community."[23]

We begin to get a sense here of the racism that is tied up with the difference-blind liberal approach to multiculturalism. Because the Sikh candidates in this nomination campaign were seen as being affiliated with a cultural minority group, they were viewed by many as members of a private, special interest group that would not, and could not, represent the interests of all constituents; as one Hanger supporter said, "None of those four yahoos can represent me in Parliament."[24] Meanwhile, because Hanger's whiteness allowed him to be viewed as simply "Canadian," without an affiliation to a cultural (minority) group, he was viewed as neutral — raceless — and as being the only candidate able to represent the public interest. This message was sent loud and clear to the Sikh candidates during one heated speech night in the campaign: when although the stage had been bare throughout each of their four speeches, Hanger's supporters symbolically unfurled a large Canadian flag behind him when his turn to speak arrived.[25]

Furthermore, ignoring the extensive diversity among Sikhs, many people assumed that, because all of Hanger's opponents were Sikh, they must all be "representatives" of the same private association or single "special interest" — the homogeneous Sikh "community". This community was treated as a monolithic group that, one would assume by the rhetoric, gathers together in a room every night to decide how to coordinate its views and actions. It was lost on Hanger and many of his supporters that if there truly were a conspiracy by the Sikh community to overthrow Hanger from power, surely the Sikhs would have chosen only one candidate to oppose him, behind whom the whole "community" could have thrown its political weight. Clearly, Hanger and many others in Calgary North-East did not see four separate candidates, each individually seeking to win the Alliance nomination. Instead, they saw four identical candidates whose common (racialized) religious affiliation apparently served to erase all other distinctions among them; their Sikh-ness was their sole defining feature.

This example illustrates the racist manifestations of the traditional liberal approach to multiculturalism. While liberal whiteness is identified with the public, and is disguised as neutral, raceless and universal, other forms of life are racialized and essentialized and are identified with particularity, special interest and the private. Furthermore, the example brings to light the liberal whiteness of public discourse in Canada, and the imperative placed on those wanting to participate in Canadian public life (broadly defined) to be able to perform this

---

[22] Shorten, 2000.

[23] Ibid.

[24] Ibid.

[25] Ibid.

liberal whiteness. If others should dare to speak and act publicly using a different language-game,

> Their identities are misrecognized or not recognized at all in the dominant norms of public recognition. Instead, an alien identity is imposed on them, without their say, through processes of subjectification, either assimilating them to the dominant identity or constructing them as marginal and expendable others.[26]

A Different Approach to Political Inclusion and Belonging

I want to suggest a different way of thinking about multiculturalism in Canada, one that transcends the insidious assimilation, racism, and ineffectiveness of the traditional liberal approach and offers an effective model for achieving political inclusion and belonging for diverse cultural identities in Canada. Rather than imagining multiculturalism to be the proper localization of "culture" within a public/private structure, we should think of multiculturalism as a kind of ongoing conversation among the diverse cultural identities within Canadian society. I take my bearings here from James Tully, a political theorist who is, incidentally, deeply influenced by the philosophy of Wittgenstein. Tully's approach to the issue of belonging in conditions of cultural diversity is

> the democratic approach of enabling citizens themselves to reimagine and create the appropriate sense of belonging to their culturally diverse association by means, and as a result, of their participation in the struggles over the political, legal, and constitutional recognition and accommodation of their identity-related differences and similarities over time.[27]

By this approach, citizens are not held together by anything that they share or upon which they all agree; rather, what holds them together "is nothing more, or less, than participation in the activities of public dialogue and negotiation themselves."[28]

This way of thinking about multiculturalism suggests that political inclusion and belonging are best generated by enabling citizens to participate in the perpetual shaping and reshaping of a shared public language-game. Citizens will participate in this ongoing conversation by presenting demands and responding to the demands of others regarding their shared association. Although they will sometimes succeed and sometimes fail in achieving their demands, citizens have reason to participate in this game because they feel that the negotiations are fair, and they know that because the game is always open to challenge and renegotiation, they will be able to influence it further over time.[29] Furthermore, these participants come to feel a sense of belonging in, and identification with, the political association because their identities "change in the course of the

---

[26] Tully, 2002, p. 161.

[27] Ibid., p. 153.

[28] Ibid., p. 156.

[29] Ibid., p. 171.

Jakeet Singh

discussions and negotiations"[30] and become intertwined with the shared, and continually renegotiated, language-game. Identity formation and change, Tully reminds us, are "intersubjective and dialogical".[31]

Because Tully's approach to multiculturalism does not seek to uniformly impose a fixed alien identity on a culturally diverse citizenry, but rather seeks the participation of diverse citizens in shaping and influencing their common association over time, it avoids (1) the injustice of such an imposition, (2) the racism of the difference-blind liberal approach, and (3) the incitement of resentment and resistance that renders the difference-blind liberal approach ineffective as a means for achieving political inclusion and belonging in culturally diverse societies. The participatory aspect of Tully's approach not only allows for diverse identities to influence the shared association but also provides the intersubjective and dialogical space — the space in which identities are transformed — that is necessary in order for citizens to develop a sense of identification as a member of the political association.

Conclusion

I began this project by examining one prevalent way of thinking about the ideal of multiculturalism in Canada. After sketching this particular construal of multiculturalism — which I called the traditional or difference-blind liberal approach — I used a Wittgensteinian critique to draw out a number of its flaws, including its racist manifestations. I then proposed a different and, in my view, superior way of thinking about multiculturalism, based on the work of James Tully.

While I do believe that the introduction of the concept of multiculturalism into Canadian public discourse is a valuable development, the degree of value of this development depends a great deal on the normative vision that underpins our use of this concept. If we simply adapt this concept to, and use it to reinforce, the traditional liberal approach to political inclusion and belonging, then it will, to a large extent, simply serve to perpetuate the racism and other drawbacks of this already ingrained language-game. However, if we interpret this concept in such a way that it serves to motivate us to bring our public language-game into contestation and negotiation by diverse cultural identities over time, then we will have gained something very valuable indeed.

References

Dyck, Rand. (1996). *Canadian politics: Critical approaches* (2nd ed.). Toronto: Nelson.

---

[30] Ibid., p. 174.

[31] Ibid., p. 155.

Fleras, Augie, & Elliott, Jean Leonard. (1996). *Unequal relations: An introduction to race, ethnic and Aboriginal dynamics in Canada* (2nd ed.). Scarborough: Prentice Hall.

Grayling, A.C. (1996). *Wittgenstein: A very short introduction*. Oxford: Oxford University Press.

Kukathas, Chandran. (1995). "Are there any cultural rights?" In Will Kymlicka (Ed.), *The rights of minority cultures* (pp. 228–256). Oxford: Oxford University Press.

Kymlicka, Will. (1998). *Finding our way: Rethinking ethnocultural relations in Canada*. Oxford: Oxford University Press.

Mouffe, Chantal. (2000). *The democratic paradox*. London, UK: Verso.

Ontario has no culture, Pequiste declares. (2001, March 9). *Globe and Mail*, ON

Shorten, Linda. (Producer). (2000, October 8). *Whose democracy is it anyway?* [Radio broadcast]. Toronto: CBC Radio.

Taylor, Charles. (1994). The politics of recognition. In Amy Gutmann (Ed.), *Multiculturalism* (pp. 25–73). Princeton: Princeton University Press.

Tully, James. (2002). Reimagining belonging in circumstances of cultural diversity: A citizen approach. In Ulf Hedetoft & Mette Hjort (Eds.), *The postnational self: Belonging and identity* (pp. 152–177). Minneapolis: University of Minnesota Press.

Wittgenstein, Ludwig. (1958). *Philosophical investigations* (G.E.M. Anscombe, Trans.). New York: Macmillan.

Questions for Discussion

1. Before you read the essays in this Part, consider what you knew of and thought about Canadian multiculturalism. After reading the essays, articulate how and why your perceptions may have changed.

2. Ash writes that many white Canadians have asked black Canadians, "What island are you from?" What does ancestral heritage have to do with national belonging? To what extent is whiteness the presumed racial identification of a Canadian? What other cultural or racial markers would disrupt this assumed belonging (i.e., accent, costume, etc.)?

3. Is it accurate to say that white Canadians, through promulgation of multiculturalism, decided to allow minorities to maintain some of their ethnic particularity? Offer examples to support your views by referring to information in this and previous parts. Is there something unsettling about a privileged race having the power to make such a decision?

4. Since multiculturalism has been deployed within a bilingual framework (English and French), how does multilingualism intersect with multiculturalism?

5. What does Saloojee mean by "social adhesion" and how is it applied?

6. Fleras explains that multiculturalism is "rivetted around the goal of ... a pan-Canadian identity to enhance national unity." Define "pan-Canadian". Articulate examples of this notion and argue its pros and cons.

7. According to Fleras, what is the potential for a racist agenda to be advanced through multiculturalism?

8. How is Fleras' definition of "subliminal cultural racism" relevant to "Part 1: Institutional Racism" of this anthology?

9. Arguably, while Ash, Saloojee and Fleras find fundamental problems with the concept of multiculturalism, Singh argues that it is a valuable development that could be further improved by challenging the normative vision that underpins it. Do you agree or disagree? Discuss.

10. Define, discuss and provide examples of two of Singh's key terms: "white language-game" and "liberal whiteness".

11. You have learned of Kymlicka's works through the explanations of four scholars. Using what you know of his work through Ash, Saloojee, Fleras, and Singh, and referring to his work directly, assess the legitimacy of Kymlicka's theories.

Biographies of Contributors

Melanie C.T. Ash obtained her LL.M. at the Columbia University School of Law in 2000, while working as an Associate in Law. She received a Social Sciences and Humanities Research Council of Canada Graduate Fellowship and a Law Society of British Columbia Graduate Scholarship. She is currently a litigation associate with Paul, Weiss, Rifkind, Wharton & Garrison LLP, New York, New York. She previously worked as an articling student and litigation associate with Arvay Finlay, Barristers, in Victoria, British Columbia. From September 1996 to September 1997 she was a law clerk to Madam Justice Beverley McLachlin, Supreme Court of Canada. She was a member of the National Executive of the Black Law Students' Association of Canada (1995–97). She is admitted to the Bars of British Columbia and New York.

Michele Byers competed her Ph.D. at the Ontario Institute for Studies in Education, University of Toronto, in 2000. Her thesis work was conducted in the areas of performance, media and youth, and was entitled *Buffy the Vampire Slayer: The Insurgence of Television as a Performance Text*. Shortly thereafter she began teaching at Saint Mary's University in Halifax, Nova Scotia. Most of her published work has been in the area of contemporary television and youth culture, including pieces on *My So-Called Life* (in *Signs*); images of women in higher education (in *Higher Education Perspectives*) *Beverly Hills, 90210* (in *Imagining the Academy*); *Buffy the Vampire Slayer* and third-wave feminism (in *Catching a Wave*), and youth, the body and television (in *Studies in Popular Culture*). Michele received funding from the Social Sciences and Humanities Research Council of Canada in 2001 to embark on a project of which her chapter will be the first published piece. The larger project will involve an in-depth exploration of the way television mediates and helps to produce Canadian identity through images of diversity in relation to the long-running and extremely popular *Degrassi* series. She is also at work on a number of other projects involving Canadian youth identity in relation to popular film and television, the *Canadian Idol* series, and the mediated production of Jewish girls and girlhoods in the media and popular culture.

Wendy Chan received her Ph.D. in Criminology at the University of Cambridge, England. She is an associate professor at the School of Criminology at Simon Fraser University in Burnaby, British Columbia. Her recent publications include *Women, Murder and Justice* (London: Palgrave Press, 2001); "From Race and Crime to Racialization and Criminalization" with Kiran Mirchandani (OISE, University of Toronto) in *Colours of Crime: Racialization and the Canadian Criminal Justice System,* which she edited with Kiran Mirchandani (Peterborough: Broadview Press, 2001); and "Gender, Risk and Crime" in the *British Journal of Criminology* (2002). Her recent conference papers include "Teaching and Researching about Processes of Racialization in the Canadian Criminal Justice System", presented at the Race and Gender Teaching Advocacy Group (RAGTAG) held at the University of British Columbia, Vancouver, May 2001; "On Categories and Crimes", co-presented with Kiran Mirchandani at the End Racism Activism (ERA21) Conference, Vancouver, November 2000; and "Psychiatrizing Legal Defences for Women: Is Madness the Only Way Out?" presented at the American Society of Criminology Annual Meeting, San Francisco, November 2000.

George Elliott Clarke was born in Windsor, Nova Scotia, in 1960 and is a seventh-generation "Africadian" of African-American and Mi'kmaq heritage. The E. J. Pratt Professor of Canadian Literature at the University of Toronto, he is also a revered poet, whose *Execution Poems* received the 2001 Governor-General's Award for Poetry. His major scholarly text is the pioneering *Odysseys Home: Mapping African-Canadian Literature* (2002).

Gina Cosentino is a doctoral candidate in the Political Science Department at the University of Toronto. Her major research interests include Indigenous politics in Canada and New Zealand; comparative federalism and constitutionalism; comparative social movements; women and politics; Charter/judicial politics; and contemporary theories of social justice, representation, and citizenship. She is currently a sessional instructor at the University of Toronto. Her dissertation is a comparative analysis of the participation and representation of Indigenous women's social movement organizations in Canada and New Zealand/Aotearoa in constitutional and treaty reform politics, 1975–2002.

Sarah de Leeuw is a doctoral student in the Geography Department at Queen's University. She received her M.A. at the University of Northern British Columbia in Interdisciplinary Studies, concentrating in Geography and English. She was the coordinator of the Terrace Women's Resource Centre in Northern British Columbia for three years and her poetry has appeared in a number of Canadian journals, including *Fiddlehead, The Pottersfield Portfolio, The Claremont Review,* and *Wascana.* Her fiction and non-fiction have appeared in the journal *The Inner Harbor Review* and in the anthology *The British Columbia Almanac.* Her first book is forthcoming in 2004 from NeWest Press in Alberta.

Karen Dubinsky is a professor in the History Department at Queen's University in Kingston, Ontario. She is the author of *The Second Greatest Disappointment: Honeymooning and Tourism at Niagara Falls* (Toronto: Between the Lines and New Brunswick, New Jersey: Rutgers University Press, 1999) and *Improper Advances: Rape and Heterosexual Conflict in Ontario, 1880–1929* (Chicago: University of Chicago Press, 1993), as well as numerous articles on the history of gender and sexuality. She is currently researching adoption controversies in three countries (Canada, Cuba, Guatemala) for a book entitled *Babies without Borders: A History of Interracial and International Adoption.*

Ryan Edwardson is a History Ph.D. candidate at Queen's University in Kingston, Ontario. His research interests include Canadian culture, nationalism, and national identity. His doctoral thesis explores the contested construction of a Canadian culture in the post-World War II period.

Augie Fleras completed his Ph.D. in Maori Studies and Social Anthropology in 1980 at the Victoria University of Wellington, New Zealand. He is currently an Associate Professor in the Sociology Department at the University of Waterloo, Waterloo, Ontario. He received a fellowship at the Macmillan Brown Centre for Pacific Studies, University of Canterbury, Christchurch, for research entitled "Re-constitutionalizing Maori-Crown Relations: The Waitangi Tribunal" and a research grant (with Jean Lock Kunz) for a project entitled "Multicultural Perspectives on Media-Minority Relations in Canada," Secretary of State for Canada. Recent publications include *Power, Persuasion, and Politics: Mass Media Communication in Canada* (Toronto: Nelson, 2003); *Unequal Relations: The Dynamics of Race, Ethnic, and Aboriginal Relations in Canada, 4/e* (Scarborough: Prentice Hall, 2002); *Media and Minorities in a Multicultural Canada* with Jean Lock Kunz (Toronto: Thomson Publishing, 2001); *Engaging Diversity: Multiculturalism in Canada* (Scarborough: Nelson, 2001); *The Politics of Indigeneity: Canada and New Zealand Perspectives* with Roger Maaka (Dunedin New Zealand: University of Otago Press, forthcoming in 2004).

Melanie Fogell received her Ph.D. from the University of Calgary in the Graduate Division of Educational Research. The title of her dissertation is "Broken Promises and Refigured Selves: Narrative and Jewish History". It is a hermeneutic, post-structural, narrative study concerning Jewish identity. It focuses on women and the connections between Israel and the Jewish Diaspora in Canada. Some of her previous research has explored the topic of Jewish women and intermarriage. She has been working as an instructor at the University of Calgary in the Faculty of Communication and Culture since September 1999. Most recently she has been teaching Women's Studies, "Contemporary Issues in Feminism" as well as "Heritage I — Western Civilization" in the faculty of Communication and Culture at the University of Calgary.

Lynda Hall, a 1998 Ph.D. graduate, teaches in the English Department at the University of Calgary. Her current research engages lesbian autobiographical writings, with a particular focus on writings by women of colour. She has published on the works of Audre Lorde, Gloria Anzaldúa, Chrystos, Carmelita Tropicana, and Jewelle Gomez. Her research has been published in *a/b: Autobiographical Studies*; *Ariel: A Review of International English Literature*; *Callaloo: A Journal of Afro-American and African Arts and Letters*; *Canadian Theatre Review; International Journal of Sexuality and Gender Studies; Journal of Dramatic Theory and Criticism; Journal of Gay, Lesbian, and Bisexual Identity; Journal of Lesbian Studies*; *Postmodern Culture*; and *Tessera*. She is the editor of *Lesbian Self-Writing: The Embodiment of Experience* (2000), which contains deliberations on the "process" of self-writing. Hall is the editor and a contributor to *Converging Terrains: Gender, Environment, Technology, and the Body* (2000). She is the editor of *Telling Moments: New Autobiographical Lesbian Short Stories* (2003), a collection of 24 short stories published by the University of Wisconsin Press.

Wendy L. Hoglund is a doctoral candidate in Life-span Developmental Psychology at the University of Victoria. Her Master's thesis examined the role of family, school, and classroom ecologies on changes in children's social competence and emotional and behavioural problems during first grade. Her doctoral research applies a strengths-based focus to examine how social-cognitive understanding of peers' perspectives in social interactions mediates the stress of peer victimization on academic, interpersonal, emotional, and behavioural outcomes in Aboriginal and non-Aboriginal children. She was awarded doctoral fellowships from the Social Sciences and Humanities Research Council of Canada, the Michael Smith Foundation for Health Research, and the BC Medical Services Foundation. She was also awarded fellowships to attend the Putting Children First Program in Child and Family Policy (2001) at Columbia University and the Institute on Youth Violence Prevention (2002) at the University of California Riverside. Her most recent publications include "Prediction and Prevention of Peer Victimization in Early Elementary School: Does Gender Matter?" with B. Leadbeater, M. Dhami, and E. Boone in *Girls and Aggression: Contributing Factors and Intervention Principles* (Eds.) M. M. Moretti, M. Jackson, and C. Odgers (New York: Kluwer Academic Publishers, 2004); "Changing Contexts? The Effects of a Primary Prevention Program on Classroom Levels of Peer Relational and Physical Victimization" with B. Leadbeater and Cpl. T. Woods in *Journal of Community Psychology, 31* (2003); "Pathways to Aboriginal Youths' School Outcomes: Socio-Cultural, Community, and Family Influences" with B. Leadbeater in *International Journal of Educational Policy, Research and Practice,* 3 (2002); and "Reducing Risks for Injury in Children and Adolescents: Using Community-University Collaborations to Translate Research into Policy and Practice" with E. Dickinson in *Advocate, 25* (2002).

Awad Ibrahim is assistant professor in the Educational Foundations and Inquiry Program, Bowling Green State University, Ohio. He is a doctoral graduate of the University of Toronto and teaches and publishes in the areas of anti-racism and critical multiculturalism, applied socio-linguistics, cultural studies, critical pedagogy and educational foundations. He is interested in film and popular music studies, especially hip-hop and rap. He has participated in many national and international conferences, such as AERA; TESOL; TESL Canada; Canadian Congress of the Social Sciences and Humanities; African Studies; American Sociological Association; AILA; Association Canadienne-française pour l'avancement des sciences (ACFAS); and Association of Black Sociologists. Among his recent publications are *Race-in-the-Gap: Imigrés, Identity, Identification, and the Politics and ESL Learning* (Contact, 2001); "Black-in-English: Towards a Symbolic Politics of Identification" in *Black Linguistics: Language, Society and Politics in Africa and the Americas* (Eds.) G. Smitherman, S. Makoni, and A. Ball (New York: Routledge, 2003); and "'Hey, Ain't I Black Too?' The Politics of Becoming Black" in *Rude: Contemporary Black Canadian Cultural Criticism* (Ed.) R. Walcott (Toronto: Insomniac Press, 2000). His current research is a longitudinal ethnographic project investigating the impact of Black popular culture, hip-hop/rap, on White youth.

Alice Ming Wai Jim is an art historian, curator and freelance art critic. For her M.A. at Concordia University, Jim examined the first exhibition in Canada to devote itself entirely to the work of Black women artists. In 2004, she completed a Ph.D. in art history at McGill University, focusing on media art, spatial culture and theories of representation in Hong Kong. Recent publications include contributions to the *Encyclopedia of Contemporary Chinese Culture* (forthcoming 2004), *HK LAB* (2002), and the *49th Venice Biennale China-Hong Kong Exhibition* catalogue (2001). In 2003 and 2001, respectively, she was co-editor of the special issue of the online magazine, chinese-art.com, on contemporary art in Hong Kong and Traversals, a book published in conjunction with Re-Considered Crossings: Representation Beyond Hybridity, an arts and cultural exchange between Hong Kong and Vienna. Jim's review articles have appeared in international contemporary art journals including *Flash Art, Parachute,* and *Art Asia Pacific.* Her "Urban Rhythms and Moving Images", the main essay for a book on the media art of Ellen Pau, and an essay contribution to the academic journal *positions: east asia cultures critique*'s first issue on contemporary Asian art, are forthcoming in 2004. In 2001, she was affiliated with the Centre of Asian Studies and the Centre for the Study of Globalization and Cultures at the University of Hong Kong. Jim is currently Curator of Contemporary Asian Art and Asian Canadian Art at the Vancouver International Centre for Contemporary Asian Art (Centre A) in Vancouver.

Colin McFarquhar obtained his Ph.D. in History from the University of Waterloo in 1998, specializing in the history of race relations in Canada. His dissertation was entitled "A Difference of Perspective: The Black Minority, White Majority, and Life in Ontario, 1870–1919". Since 1997 he has been a researcher in aboriginal issues for Leclair Historical Research in Toronto. He has also taught history courses at the University of Windsor and the University of Waterloo. His article entitled "A Difference of Perspective: Blacks, Whites, and Emancipation Day Celebrations in Ontario, 1865–1919" was published in the Autumn 2000 issue of *Ontario History*.

Josée Makropoulos is a doctoral candidate at the Department of Sociology and Equity Studies in Education at OISE/University of Toronto. She also teaches on a part-time basis for the Department of Sociology and the Faculty of Education at the University of Ottawa. Her research areas include French-minority and second-language education, multicultural diversity, and equity issues in the Canadian educational system.

Faizal R. Mirza received a M.A. from the University of Toronto in 1998 and a LL.B. from Osgoode Hall Law School in 2001. He was called to the Ontario Bar in 2002. His law firm, Brar, Mirza, Professional Corporation, practises criminal law and civil rights advocacy in Toronto. In addition to the work of his practice, he assists the African Canadian Legal Clinic (ACLC) to prepare cases related to systemic racism and criminal justice that are argued at the Ontario Court of Appeal and Supreme Court of Canada. He completed his articles of clerkship with the criminal defence firm Greenspan, Humphrey, Lavine (2001–02). He was a researcher for the Honourable Fred Kaufman Q.C. (Québec Court of Appeal, ret.) and Mark J. Sandler of the criminal defence firm Cooper, Sandler, West (2000–01). His principal research interests are criminal and human rights and constitutional law. He specializes in the study between racism, and criminal and constitutional law. He is also interested in the study of international law and the Muslim community in North America. He has volunteered for the Association in Defence of the Wrongly Convicted (AIDWC) and he participated in the Young Atlantic Generation Conference in the Hague, Netherlands. He is a recognized contributor to *Searching for Justice* a review of institutional abuse in Nova Scotia by the Honourable Fred Kaufman Q.C. and Mark J. Sandler (2002), and his article "Mandatory Minimum Prison Sentencing and Systemic Racism" was published in the *Osgoode Hall Law Journal 39,* (2001).

Johanna Mizgala received an M.A. in Art History from Concordia University in 1996. Since that time she has worked in the curatorial departments of photography and contemporary art at the National Gallery of Canada and as an independent curator. She has lectured extensively on contemporary and photo-based art and has taught workshops on writing art criticism. An arts advocate and regular contributor to contemporary art periodicals, her most recent publications include "Recognizance Mission: The Photographs of Lynne Cohen" for *CV Photo* (2002); "Ken Lum Works with Photography" for *para para* (2003); and the catalogue essay "Diary, Autobiography and Archives: Recollections from High Ground" for *Vera Greenwood: High Ground* (Ottawa: Ottawa Art Gallery, 2003). In 2001, she was appointed to the position of Curator — Exhibitions for the development of the Portrait Gallery of Canada, an initiative of the Library and Archives Canada.

Camille A. Nelson is a J.S.D. (doctoral) candidate at the Columbia University School of Law. She joined the Saint Louis University, School of Law faculty in the summer of 2000. Prior to joining the faculty of St. Louis University she was an Associate in Law at Columbia University School of Law teaching Legal Research and Writing and completing her Masters of Law. Prior to her time at Columbia University she was a litigation associate with McCarthy Tétrault Barristers and Solicitors in Toronto. Following law school she was head clerk to Canadian Supreme Court Justice Frank Iacobucci. Professor Nelson teaches criminal law, contracts law, critical race theory and legal profession. She lectures on issues of race, culture and the African Diaspora. She has written about the culture of elite firm practice, racism in the legal profession, the relevance of racial context to the Provocation defense, racism-related mental health issues, and Caribbean immigration, and she is concerned with the relevance of race to traditional legal doctrine. She is a member of the American Association of Law and Society, the Society of American Law Teachers, the American Bar Association, the Mound City Bar Association and the Foster Parents Plan of Canada.

Charmaine A. Nelson taught in the areas of Critical Theory, Post-Colonial Studies, Canadian Art, and Nineteenth-Century American and European Art as an assistant professor of Art History at the University of Western Ontario. She conceptualized critical and socially engaged courses that utilized local African-Canadian and First Nations cultural sites and histories. Her museum career is highlighted by the exhibition *Through An-Other's Eyes: White Canadian Artists — Black Female Subjects* (1998). Her publications include "White Marble, Black Bodies and the Fear of the Invisible Negro: Signifying Blackness in Mid-Nineteenth-century Neoclassical Sculpture" in *RACAR: Revue d'Art Canadienne/ Canadian Art Review,* (September 28, 2003) and the forthcoming "Edmonia Lewis' 'Death of Cleopatra': White Bodies, Black Fantasies and Racial Crisis in America" in Janice Helland and Deborah Cherry (Eds.), *Studio Space and Sociality: New Narratives of Nineteenth-century Women* (Aldershot, U.K: Ashgate, 2004). In 2003 she began her appointment in the Department of Art History and Communication Studies at McGill University, Montreal, Québec.

Sheila Petty is Professor of Media Studies at the University of Regina (Saskatchewan) and Adjunct Scientist (New Media) at TRLabs. She has written extensively on issues of cultural representation, identity and nation in African and African diasporic cinema. She has curated film and television series and exhibitions for galleries across Canada. She has a forthcoming book on African diasporic film and a monograph on the TV series, *Law & Order* with Wayne State University Press. Her current research focuses on interdisciplinary investigations of new media narrative strategies. In particular, she is exploring the intersection of film-based montage theory and computer-based aesthetics. Leader of an interdisciplinary research group and New Media Studio Laboratory spanning Computer Science, Engineering and Fine Arts, she is the recipient of the 2001 University of Regina Alumni Association Award for Excellence in Research and a University of Regina President's Scholar (2002–2004).

G. Bruce Retallack is a doctoral candidate in the University of Toronto History Department. His dissertation concerns the cultural history of editorial cartooning in Canada between 1840 and 1926, with particular emphasis on the ways the cartoonists have visually rendered women, racial minorities, and other marginalized groups as being both "other" and "lesser" than the dominant white male elites. His publications include the following: Article (Refereed): "Razors, Shaving and Gender Construction: An Inquiry into the Material Culture of Shaving" in *Material History Review/Revue d'Histoire de la Culture Matéielle, 49* (Spring 1999); Article (Refereed): "The Conformity of Dissent: Editorial Cartoons and the Visual Code of Representation in Canada, 1865–1929" in *Proceedings of the Seventh Annual History in the Making Conference: History and Media* (Montreal: Concordia University, 2002); Article (Refereed): "Paddy, the Priest and the Habitant: Inflecting the Irish Cartoon Stereotype in Canada" *Canadian Journal of Irish Studies* (Montreal: Concordia University, Fall 2003); Article (Solicited): "Editorial Cartoons" *Oxford Companion to Canadian History* (Toronto: University of Toronto Press, forthcoming 2004) 2 pages. His conference presentations include "The Life and Times of Jack Canuck and Miss Canada: A Canadian Family Romance" presented to "New Frontiers in Graduate History V", York University, 16 March 2001, and "Drawing the Line: Cartoon Representations of 'Racial' Minorities in Canada to 1914" presented to The 81st Annual Conference of the Canadian Historical Association, Toronto, 28 May 2002.

Anver Saloojee is a professor in the Department of Politics and School of Public Administration at Ryerson University of Toronto. In addition, he is Vice President of the Ryerson Faculty Association and an Executive member of the Canadian Association of University Teachers. He also Chairs the Equity Committee of the CAUT. Anver is a member of the Board of Directors at the Laidlaw Foundation. In 1997 he was appointed as a researcher to the National Commission on Special Needs in Education and Training, Government of South Africa. He has done extensive research in the areas of human rights, multiculturalism, anti-racism and both employment and education equity. Some of his most recent conference presentations include "Creating Inclusive Teaching and Learning Environments" at STLHE, St. John's, Newfoundland (2001); "Political Participation by Newcomer Communities: Case Study Toronto" at the 6th International Metropolis Conference, Rotterdam, Netherlands (November, 2001); and "Social Inclusion, Anti-Racism and Democratic Citizenship" presented at the Metropolis International Conference, Oslo, Norway (September, 2002). Anver's recent publications include "Employment Equity: The Limits of Liberalism" in *Restructuring & Resistence* (Ed.) Mike Burke *et al.* (Halifax: Fernwood, 2000), and "Social Inclusion, Anti-Racism and Democratic Citizenship" — published as part of the Laidlaw Foundation's series on Social Inclusion, January 2003.

Jakeet Singh is a Ph.D. candidate in Political Science at the University of Toronto. His current research interests include multicultural education, forms of modern subjectivity, and critiques of liberalism. He recently presented papers for conferences at the University of Wales, University of Victoria, and the Canadian Centre for Foreign Policy Development.

Anthony Stewart is an assistant professor of English literature at Dalhousie University in Halifax, Nova Scotia. He recently published *George Orwell, Doubleness, and the Value of Decency* (Routledge, 2003), in which he argues that Orwell's fiction demonstrates the importance of a doubled perspective (through which we see our own interests in relation to those of others) and how this doubleness, in turn, can lead to a capacity for decency (the willingness to treat others as befitting their status as human beings). Stewart has also recently completed "Vulgar Nationalism and Insulting Nicknames: George Orwell's Progressive Reflections on Race," an article to appear in *George Orwell into the Twenty-First Century* (forthcoming, from Paradigm Publishers). His next project examines how the fiction of Ralph Ellison, Hanif Kureishi, and Percival Everett critiques the commodification of otherness.

Joanne Tod is a Toronto artist and lecturer who has been exhibiting work for the past 20 years both nationally and internationally. Tod's work has been included in museum shows such as *Songs of Experience* (National Gallery of Canada), *Prospect 93* (Frankfurt, Germany), and the *Istanbul Biennial* (Turkey). In 1991, The Power Plant (Toronto) presented a 10-year survey exhibition of Tod's work, curated by Bruce Grenville. From an early interest in the issues of Pop Art and the process of representation, Tod developed a challenging critique of representation that examined the role of sexism, racism and patriarchy in the construction of feminine identity. These explorations led to paintings in which the natural perspective of the picture plane was disrupted in order to reflect, compositionally, the complexity of the subject. Tod currently teaches painting at the University of Toronto. She is represented in Canada by Greener Pastures Contemporary Art (Toronto) and Equinox Gallery (Vancouver). Her paintings are included in the collections of the National Gallery of Canada, the Art Gallery of Ontario, and the Musée d'Art Contemporain (Montréal). She is a member of the Advisory Board for Sotheby's Canada and also serves on the capital campaign committee for Interval House. Tod is now embarking on a sound/video project that will reflect her continuing interest in social critique.